PEARSON

Juan R. Abascal, Ph.D. • Laurel Brucato, Ph.D.
Patricia Stephenson, Ph.D. • Dominic Brucato, Ph.D.

Essential Elements for Effectiveness

Optimal Functioning Through Positive Psychology

Fifth Edition

Pearson Learning Solutions, 501 Boylston Street, Suite 900, Boston, MA 02116
A Pearson Education Company
www.pearsoned.com

Printed in the United States of America

2 3 4 5 6 7 8 9 10 V011 17 16 15 14 13 12

000200010271647670

MT

ISBN 10: 1-256-67511-3
ISBN 13: 978-1-256-67511-2

Contents

ABOUT THE AUTHORS

Juan R. Abascal, Ph.D., a graduate of Rutgers, the State University, and Kent State University, is a professor of psychology at Miami Dade College. He has been awarded an Endowed Teaching Chair and received the NISOD Excellence in Teaching Award. Dr. Abascal has also been honored with the Service Learning Professor of the Year Award. As a graduate of the Salzburg International Education Institute, he has been involved in the Global Education Initiative as well as the Earth Ethics Institute. He has also served the college as a department chairperson, Associate Dean, Academic Dean, and Associate Provost for Academic Affairs. A clinical psychologist by training, Dr. Abascal has conducted numerous personal effectiveness and stress mastery seminars and workshops with people from all walks of life, from the lay person to the professional health care provider. In conjunction with two of the other authors, he co-founded MindWorks, Int., Inc. a stress management center and comprehensive private practice of clinical psychology. In his clinical practice, Dr. Abascal specializes in helping individuals suffering from anxiety disorders and couples experiencing marital distress. He is committed to the principle that any individual willing to follow a step-by-step process can learn to function optimally and achieve joy in their lives.

Laurel Brucato, Ph.D., a graduate of the University of Illinois and Kent State University, is a clinical psychologist in private practice at MindWorks, Int., Inc., the Stress Management Center she co-founded in 1988. Dr. Brucato views herself as an eclectic positive psychologist who endeavors to help individuals develop and enhance their strengths to work toward optimal functioning, and to overcome their particular problems in living. In her clinical practice Dr. Brucato specializes in the treatment of anxiety and phobic disorders, obsessive compulsive disorders, depression, sexual dysfunctions, marital problems. She has also taught at Miami Dade College as an adjunct professor, as well as conducted numerous training workshops on stress mastery and assertiveness.

Patricia Stephenson, Ph.D., a graduate of the University of Florida and Florida State University, is a Professor Emeritus of psychology at Miami Dade College. Dr. Stephenson has been a counselor, director, and Associate Dean prior to returning to her first love—teaching. She is a two time recipient of an Endowed Teaching Award. She received a national award for contributions to staff and organizational development, and has served as a consultant to faculty groups writing curriculum, groups seeking conflict resolution, and training seminars for faculty staff and administration. As a health care professional, she is also an avid promoter of wellness lifestyles. She has presented numerous workshops for students, faculty, and health care practitioners on stress management, wellness, assertiveness and self-development. She is devoted to the teaching/learning process and helping individuals grow into their personal and professional promise.

Dominic Brucato, Ph.D., a graduate of the University of Notre Dame and Kent State University, is a clinical psychologist and psychology professor at Miami Dade College. He has been the recipient of an Endowed Teaching Chair and the Service Learning Professor of the Year Award. He is also a Core Council Member of the Earth Ethics Institute and is involved with the Global Education Initiative. Along with his wife, Dr. Laurel Brucato, and Dr. Abascal, he co-founded MindWorks, Int., Inc., a stress management center and psychology practice. Dr. Brucato divides his time between teaching and his clinical practice. He specializes in teaching courses aimed at helping students reach optimal functioning in their academic and personal lives. A dynamic speaker, Dr. Brucato has conducted numerous stress mastery and effectiveness workshops dedicated to helping people from all walks of life achieve their full potential.

Preface

TO THE INSTRUCTOR

In the fall semester of 1998 a new course was introduced at Miami Dade College, initially designated by the State Board of Education as PPE1005, and later reassigned as CLP1006, the Psychology of Personal Effectiveness. This course, along with a handful of others, was developed from information obtained from groups including college and university faculty, graduates of Miami Dade College, and potential employers in our community. They were asked to help identify the knowledge and skills that graduates need to be successful in the workplace and in upper level university settings. A mountain of interview and survey responses was collected, summarized, analyzed, and examined, which served as the basis for the competencies for this course. Many faculty and staff members at the college worked on the Educational Review Project, which resulted in this course being one of the new offerings to our students.

Around the time the course was being introduced, an expanded paradigm was emerging in the field of psychology with a focus on the study of excellence. Throughout psychology's history the primary emphasis had been on pathology and how to alleviate it. This movement, named Positive Psychology, argued that the study of optimal functioning also deserved attention. As a result, topics such as effectiveness, happiness, well-being, satisfaction, flow, constructive cognitions, optimism, and hope have become more mainstream. In the past ten years over 200 courses in Positive Psychology have sprouted in institutions of higher learning across the nation. Miami Dade College, in its role as a positive institution, was once again an early innovator and at the forefront in the field of psychology by establishing one of the first positive psychology courses.

CLP1006 can perhaps be best described as an applied positive psychology course. It differs from traditional university courses in that its focus is not primarily on educating students about theory and research, but rather on educating students in how to make use of this theory and research in their daily lives. As such, the goal of the course is not to have students who know a lot *about* optimal functioning, but students who have learned *how* to function optimally. This book was specifically designed to meet the objectives of this course. While it certainly addresses psychological theories and research, this is presented as the underpinning of the applied aspects rather than the central focus. In this manner, it also differs from most college textbooks as it does not present an exhaustive list of theoretical perspectives. The National Science Foundation has described the current trend in the teaching of the sciences as being "a mile wide and an inch deep." The argument typically espoused by proponents of this approach is that we must pass on all the knowledge in a field. However, although we may be attempting to cover all the material, evidence suggests that even if students learn it all, they are quickly forgetting it because they are not using it. In contrast, this book is organized around a limited number of principles, which are continually addressed and approached from various perspectives. We believe that when application is the goal, knowing a lot about a little is far more effective than knowing a little about a lot. Therefore, this book addresses a narrower number of critical topics in much greater depth.

We have consciously attempted to make this book conversational in nature rather than didactic. Our goal is to address the student directly through its pages, to literally encourage the reader to engage in a dialogue with the book. When appropriate we have incorporated material presented in our effectiveness seminars. We have also sought to frequently include humor and amusing anecdotes to help engage the reader, particularly given that the ability to find the humor in life is one of the characteristics of effective functioning.

We encourage you to require your students to actively involve themselves with the exercises, techniques and suggestions included in this book, and not just to read the book and regurgitate the information on tests. The value of this book is in the doing, not just in reading and memorizing facts.

STUDENTS WHO TAKE THIS COURSE ARE MORE LIKELY TO STAY IN SCHOOL.

At this point you might be wondering, "how effective is this course on effectiveness?" To help answer that question a statistical analysis was conducted to determine whether on not students who have taken this course are more likely to remain in school, that is, to be more successful academically in terms of retention. Although the course competencies for CLP1006 do not specifically include effectiveness in school, as that is contained in other courses offered at the College, it is reasonable to speculate that if students are, indeed, learning to increase their effectiveness, those behaviors would be manifested in their role as students.

In order to test this hypothesis, the fall to spring retention rate of a group of students who had taken CLP1006 in the fall semester was compared to a group of students who had not taken CLP1006. Seeking to minimize the effects of extraneous variables on the results, other courses, which students most frequently took in addition to CLP1006, were identified. Students who were enrolled in any or several of these courses (ENC1101, MAT1033, MAT0020, and SLS1535 for AA students and CGS1060 for AS students) made up the CLP group. The non-CLP group was made up of students who were enrolled in any or several of those courses without taking CLP1006.

The results of these comparisons revealed that for the two years studied, students in the CLP group were significantly more likely to return to school for the spring semester than students in the non-CLP group. In the 2003 school year, students who had taken CLP1006 were retained at a rate of 88.6% as compared to 84.2% for those who had not taken the course. Similarly, in the 2004 school year, the retention rate for students in the CLP course was 86.2% as compared to 80.4% for the non-CLP group. Significance tests of the difference between two proportions revealed the differences to be significant at the $p < .05$ level. Similar significant differences were evident when students were divided into AA or AS seeking, as evident by the table on the next page:

TABLE 1 CLP Group versus Non-CLP Group				
	CLP Group		Non-CLP Group	
Degree Type	Number	Retention	Number	Retention
Associate in Arts				
2003-1/2003-2	388	89.2%	4,289	84.3%
2004-1/2004-2	362	88.4%	3,927	81.4%
Associate in Science				
2003-1/2003-2	145	86.9%	979	83.5%
2004-1/2004-2	205	82.4%	889	75.8%
Degree Total				
2003-1/2003-2	533	88.6%	5,268	84.2%
2004-1/2004-2	567	86.25	4,816	80.4%

The data does support, then, that despite the fact that increasing student retention is not one of the explicit goals of the course, students taking CLP1006 are persisting with school more than their peers who have not taken the course. Perhaps, as hypothesized, students are choosing to apply their newly acquired knowledge and skills about effectiveness to their educational pursuits.

Preface

Hey you! Yes, you. We *are* talking to you. At least that's what we would really like to establish with you—a dialogue. Now you might ask yourself: "What do you mean . . . a dialogue? To dialogue takes two people; all I have is me and this book!" But that's not true. You have your classmates, your professor, your friends, your family, *and* this book. We sincerely hope that you take the principles and ideas contained within its pages and discuss them. Talk about them. Consider their validity. And most importantly, try them out in your own life.

You see, the material you encounter in this book will best serve you if you use it. We recognize that using it will likely require some changes on your part. And we all know that changing is not always easy. Dialogue about that too. With others for support, explore ways in which what you are learning can have an impact in your life. Expect it to happen, and you might be pleasantly surprised.

So, let's begin. To make the most out of this book, we suggest you take a moment to think about what motivated you to pick it up. Why are you reading it? Even if your initial response is that it was required for the course, think . . . is there something else you want to get, other than a good grade, from reading this book? If you were able to change something as a result of your experience with this book, what would that be? What would be different about you? How would you look, feel, and act differently? Take a moment now to think about these questions.

There is a story about a group of scientists who were walking along the countryside when they saw a field of fruit-bearing trees. A local inhabitant told them that the fruit was called "Mango" by the natives of this land. This kind of fruit was unknown to them and they wanted to learn all they could about it. Half of the scientists went into one side of the field and began measuring the mangoes' weight and their size. They noted the color and the shape and recorded their findings. These scientists now *knew about* mangoes. The other half of the scientists went into the field, each took down a mango from the tree and tasted it. These scientists *knew* mangoes.

Did you do what we suggested in the first paragraph? Did you take a moment to think about what you wanted to get from using this book? If you did, you are like the scientists who ate the mangoes. Continue tasting what we have to offer and we can promise you will notice a significant positive difference in your life. But if you didn't, your tendency might be to read this book much like the scientists who measured and weighed the mangoes. With that approach, this book might provide you with some interesting facts and general knowledge, but it is doubtful that it will create any significant changes in your life. The material discussed in this book will work for you only if you use it; only if you *do it*. Merely knowing about it is not enough. So if you have not considered the questions posed earlier, we invite you to go back and think about what you want to get, how you want to be different, and notice the results *after* you've tasted the mangoes. This way, you will not just know a lot *about* effectiveness when you are done. Instead, you will know how to *be* effective.

Acknowledgments

The authors would like to thank all of the faculty members who have used our book for their invaluable feedback and encouragement in the development of this edition. Your comments and your anecdotes about students have been inspiring. We would also like to acknowledge and thank the many students who have not merely read, but used this book in their lives and shared their experiences with us.

SECTION ONE

Personal Effectiveness

A Reality Check

Making Positive Choices

Experiencing Positive Emotions

Learning to Accept Yourself

Understanding Stress

Developing Wellness Skills

Creating a Meaningful Vision

Managing Yourself for Accomplishment

1

A Reality Check

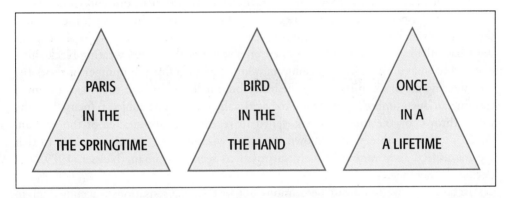

W̲hat do you think you just read within the three triangles above? Are you sure? Why don't you go back and read them again just to make sure and come back to this point. * Are you still seeing "Paris in the springtime", "Bird in the hand", and " Once in a lifetime"? After all, you certainly know how to read five little words. If you are so sure, would you be willing to bet your car on this? What about betting your next year's entire income? When we present this to our students in class, some of them are not willing to bet anything because they figure that something is up if the professor is setting the stakes so high and willing to wager at the same level. A small minority are not willing to bet because they recognize that it does not say what the majority of their classmates think it says. But the overwhelming majority of students are willing to bet their most prized possessions. Because after all, they can certainly trust what they see! They certainly *can* read three simple five word sentences. What about you? Did you see the double "the" and the double "a"? At what point did you see it? When you first read it, or when we invited you to reread it, or even after that? You know why? Because we really don't see what is there; *we see what we think is there.* And, believe it or not, this doesn't happen just with spiffy, little, five word, optical illusions like we presented above, this happens in every area of your life. Every time you face a situation, what you perceive is at least as much dependent upon your perspective as it is upon the external reality. Reality, as we see it, is a movie generated by our brains. Because we don't realize this, we are far too confident that the stuff appearing in the movie is actually "out there" in the world when, in fact, it is not.

To better understand how this is so, let's consider an important distinction within the field of psychology; the difference between *sensation* and *perception*. **Sensation** involves the process of receiving stimuli from our surroundings, such as light waves or sound waves. These then activate the receptors in our sensory organs, our eyes or ears in this case. Finally, through a process called transduction, the signals are translated into electrochemical impulses within our nervous system and brain. **Perception**, on the other hand, occurs when our brain interprets those electrochemical impulses and ascribes meaning to them. Perception, you see, is the process of attempting to understand the stimulation we receive. But the sheer amount of stimuli that impinges upon our senses is too much for us to capture it all. There are just too many things to hear and feel out there. In order to understand, before interpreting the stimuli, we must necessarily limit and organize it. Thus, not all the information available to our sensory organs ends up being perceived. Psychologists call this process of sensory analysis that begins at the entry level and works up as *bottom-up* processing.

A great example is **selective attention**, the fact that we focus our consciousness on only a partial aspect of all that we are capable of experiencing. In an experiment where the subjects watched a short, one-minute scene of three men wearing white shirts passing a basketball, which was superimposed on a scene of three men wearing black shirts engaged in the same activity; the subjects were asked to count the number of times the men wearing the black shirts passed the ball. About halfway through the video, a woman carrying an open umbrella slowly walked across the screen. The subjects, focused on the passes thrown by the men in black, failed to register the appearance of the woman. When they were subsequently shown the scene without their attention drawn to that specific aspect, they were extremely surprised to see the woman (Neisser, 1979, and Becklen & Servone, 1983).

In addition, we build our perceptions not just on the sensations traveling "up" to our brain, but also on our experiences and expectations coming down, more of a top-down approach. Not surprisingly, psychologists call this *top-down* processing. In a classic experiment, psychologists Bruner and Postman (1949) cleverly demonstrated the fact that what we see does not always correspond to what is really there. These researchers created a standard, North American deck of playing cards except that some of suit symbols were color reversed. For example, the nine of diamonds had black colored diamonds instead of red. These special cards were shuffled into an ordinary deck, and then were displayed one at a time to subjects who were asked to identify them as fast as possible. At first the cards were shown very briefly, too fast for accurate identification. Then the display time was gradually increased until all the cards could be identified. The interesting thing is that while all the cards were eventually identified with great confidence on behalf of the participants, none of the subjects noticed that there was anything peculiar about any of the cards! Subjects identified the red six of spades as either a six of spades or a six of hearts, but were not aware that anything was amiss. When the display times were lengthened even more, subjects hesitated and got confused, making comments such as, "this is a six of spades but there's something wrong," but still had difficulty determining what was out of the ordinary. Subjects were eventually able to identify the cards as being the wrong color only when display times were greatly lengthened.

This result illustrates **selective perception**, the fact that we see what we expect to see, and not necessarily what is there to see. Neuroscience sheds light on how this happens at a neuronal level. When we perceive something a whole *network of neurons* in our brain is activated, not just a single brain cell. This allows us to recognize something even if a cell is damaged. This is called **distributed processing** which enables our brains to be very efficient in processing information. Distributed processing also accounts for the fact that your brain can construct images even when no information is coming to your eyes, merely by firing a network. In fact, the brain structures used to imagine something are the same as those that process visual stimuli when you actually see it (Farah, 2000). That is one reason why it has been estimated that as much as 60% of vision is imagination.

The world that ends up being represented in our head, then, has been filtered by the stimuli we select to attend to, the way we organize that stimuli, as well as our expectations and past experiences. On top of that, our brains literally guess what we are seeing. To protect you from being inundated with information processing, your brain makes forecasts about what it is seeing, and changes these predictions only when it makes an error, a process called **predictive coding**. For example, did you know that for all humans there is an actual hole in the retina resulting in a blind spot? However, you don't actually see this black hole in your visual field, despite the hole in your retina! Your brain mentally fills in this void with its best guess of what should be there, much like how your cell phone tries to predict what you are texting. In our everyday life, sensation and perception blend into one continuous process and we are not aware of the distinction just described. The reality we perceive is none-the-less created by it.

THE CONCEPT OF FRAMES

How you view any event or situation in your life is greatly influenced by your expectations, your beliefs, your pre-conceived notions. This "way of seeing things" has been called by different terms that mean the same thing. Thomas Kuhn (1962) referred to it as a **paradigm**, in his landmark book, *The Structure of Scientific Revolutions*. Others have called it a perspective or a mind map or a **schema**. We prefer to call it a **frame**. Have you ever had an unframed print, painting, or photo which you later got framed? Can you remember when you first saw your picture with its new frame? Didn't it look clearer somehow, more in focus? It was finished now. Can you recall the sense of satisfaction you experienced when you put it on display and stood back? Each and every one of us is adept at developing **frames of reference** or paradigms to enable us to organize and understand our world, our perceptions, our experiences. In every situation in which you engage, you eventually put a frame of reference around it in order to understand it, to make sense out of it. Most of the time this happens instantly and you are not even aware of it.

So how do frames help us? When you are "confused" about something it takes longer to sort the experience into a frame of reference. Indeed, that is one definition of confusion, the inability to make sense of something or *place it within a frame*. Once we have developed a frame of reference it is ready to help us more quickly interpret our experience the next time we encounter it or a similar one. Our brains are hardwired, genetically programmed, to create frames of reference to organize our experiences. Without this inherent ability to construct frames the world would be a very perplexing and unpredictable place. We would have to figure out each experience again and again if we didn't have frames in place to help us make sense out of our world.

Experiences are made up of multiple perceptions, sensations and bits of data which we need to categorize. For instance, imagine this situation. You are home alone and have just crawled into bed and it is really late. It is very dark and quiet. As you are just about to fall asleep you suddenly hear something moving near your front door. Then you hear a scraping sort of tapping sound. You think, "Is someone trying to pick the front door lock? What should I do if they break in?" You feel confused, threatened, and fearful. Sensing danger, you wonder what you should do next …should you call the police? Cautiously you creep over near a front window and carefully and silently peek out. There he is! You see a huge possum on your front porch clumsily moving around. Instantaneously your frame changes, and at the same moment, your thoughts, feelings, and your behaviors shift as well. You no longer think you are in danger; you now feel relieved, beginning to relax. You yell and make a banging noise on the door which scares him off, and you head back to bed. Think how powerful your frames are in determining your thoughts, your emotions, and your behavior. The very moment your perspective of the situation changed, so too did your whole being!

You are fortunate that your brain is predisposed to develop frames of reference that were shaped by your learning history, including what you learned from your parents, your peers, in school, your place of worship, from the media and our culture. Some frames of reference remain in flux, but most become fixed. In fact, the more a frame of reference is used, and the more successful it is in helping you to derive meaning from your experiences, the more firmly your brain stores this frame. You tend to forget that it is only a paradigm, a frame, a habitual way of viewing things. The ability to recognize that you are operating within a frame, and shift that frame when appropriate, enhances your flexibility of thought and ability to solve problems. So how well can you do this? Try this problem now. **Connect the nine dots using only four straight lines and not lifting your pen off the paper.** By the way, use a pencil for we guarantee you will need to erase!

Figure 1.1 The Nine Dot Problem

Were you able to solve the problem? If you are like most people you will find that it takes you five lines to be able to connect all the dots without lifting your pencil or bending the lines. Is this problem impossible to solve? It is only if you stay within the parameters and limitations of your current frame. We suggest you try going outside the box. When you look at the nine dots, what do you see? If you had to give those dots a name, other than "nine dots", what would you call it? Most people would call it a square or a box. Change that frame. As long as you hold onto the paradigm that this is a square and act accordingly, you will be unable to solve the problem. Go ahead and try it again, this time allowing yourself to go beyond the square. Were you successful? If not, here's another hint. Can you see it as a sort of an arrow? Adopting this frame of reference might help. If all else fails, turn to the end of the chapter for the solution to the nine dot problem.

In another exercise designed to give you practice with shifting your frame of reference, look at the optical illusions presented below. These illustrations represent what psychologists refer to as **ambiguous figures**. In the real world, we are faced with ambiguous stimuli and sensations all the time. The recognition that your perceptions are not reality, but just your perceptions, can facilitate the development of flexibility of thought, improved problem solving, and ultimately your effectiveness as a human being.

Figure 1.2 Is the Book Looking Towards You . . . or Away from You?

Figure 1.3 Two Faces . . . or One?

Figure 1.4 Woman in Vanity . . . or Skull?
Hint: Move the book a bit farther away from you to see the skull or the woman looking at the mirror.

Figure 1.5 Man Playing Horn . . . or Woman Sillhouette?

Figure 1.6 A Face of a Native American . . . or an Eskimo?

Figure 1.7 A Rabbit . . . or A Duck?
Hint: The duck is looking to the left, the rabbit is looking to the right.

Figure 1.8 Old Woman . . . or Young Girl?
Hint: The old woman's nose is the young girl's nose and chin.

Figure 1.9 A Vase . . . or Two Faces?

PARADIGM SHIFTS AND THE HISTORY OF SCIENCE

Paradigms have also played a major role in the history of science. As Thomas Kuhn observed, most major scientific discoveries are preceded by a **paradigm shift**, a change in the overriding theoretical framework that governs a scientific discipline. Kuhn described in great detail how almost every significant breakthrough in the field of scientific endeavor is first a break with tradition, a break with old ways of thinking, a change of old paradigms. For example, in the field of astronomy a paradigm shift occurred after a long, hard fought struggle that spanned centuries until scientists finally accepted the fact that the earth revolved around the sun, instead of the earth being the center of the universe. Similarly, germ theory revolutionized medicine, but was initially resisted by those who found it incomprehensible that there could be infectious agents that could not be seen with the naked eye. Indeed, the reason we invented such tools as the microscope is that we believed in the possibility of extremely small, unseen creatures like germs.

In the *Structure of Scientific Revolutions* Kuhn observes that the history of scientific advancement is a result of paradigm shifts. What Kuhn refers to as "normal science" proceeds by building a foundation of research and data based upon proving and expanding existing theoretical paradigms. But invariably anomalous results begin to turn up, findings which cannot be understood or accounted for by the overriding paradigm. Often these anomalies are ignored or discounted. Scientists who reveal or publicize these seemingly bizarre results are dismissed, and often even discredited within their profession. New theories or paradigms which attempt to explain the anomalies by expanding or changing the existing paradigm are often treated as heresy. Inherent in this is a struggle between the old guard of a discipline (who believe they have the truth), and the mavericks who dare to challenge the accepted paradigm. It is no wonder that successful challenges to existing paradigms often come from outside the discipline, developed by individuals with a fresh perspective or different viewpoint. Eventually, the mass of anomalies builds to the point where the discipline must become open to a new paradigm in order to stay viable. Thus a scientific revolution occurs when the paradigm shifts. This may occur suddenly, but typically, given the resistance of the old guard, this is a more gradual process. Two or more paradigms may co-exist for a while with separate adherents, but eventually the paradigm with greater predictive value will win out. But Kuhn was primarily describing the process of change within the natural sciences. The process of change in the social sciences tends to be more incremental and appears to be more a process of gradual paradigm shift or paradigm expansion.

A good example of a gradual paradigm expansion exists within the field of psychology. Early in the 1900's Sigmund Freud posited his theory of psychosexual development. Initially this appeared to explain the development of mental disorders and it provided a framework for the treatment of emotional difficulties. It was the first global theory of how personality was formed and it described both normal and abnormal behavior. This new paradigm stimulated the development of a new treatment modality, that of talk therapy, and it provided avenues for new research. But then holes began to appear in the theory. Psychoanalytic theory was a cumbersome model for explaining many emotional problems and psychoanalysis as a treatment, often failed. Psychoanalytic theory had great explanatory value, but little if any, predictive value. Competing models were developed.

Learning theory explained behavior in terms of conditioning and reinforcement (i.e. rewards and punishment). These theorists were called Behaviorists since they believed that behavior was not a result of repressed psychosexual impulses, as Freud believed, but was driven by the consequences that followed the behavior. At around the same time, humanistic thought came into prominence. The humanists held man to be not quite as dark as Freud postulated, driven by sexual and aggressive impulses. Instead, they professed that humans are driven to continually improve themselves, to move towards self-actualization.

Each of these perspectives was a reflection and a natural outgrowth of the population studied. For example, Freud's patients were primarily neurotic females living in a highly repressive, Victorian society. Behavior theories stemmed primarily from laboratory research (often with animals) such as the pioneering work of Ivan Pavlov on classical conditioning, and B.F. Skinner on operant conditioning. Humanistic theories evolved from studying the best society had to offer as evidenced by Carl Rogers' research with college students, and Abraham Maslow's work with highly successful, self-actualized individuals. (In fact, Maslow initially studied gorillas, but they were the most dominant gorillas in the pack). With such varying experiences influencing their observations, no wonder such different paradigms emerged. For many years, perhaps even up until the present, these different frames coexisted which led to continual debate about what was truth in psychology. Currently, the majority of psychologists would agree that one of the best and well researched approaches for explaining and predicting human behavior is the Cognitive-Behavioral model. This is especially true when it comes to understanding psychopathology and abnormal behavior. Freud's original paradigm, while not completely discarded, has been greatly expanded and refined. So, to quote Kuhn:

> Examining the record of past research from the vantage of contemporary historiography, the historian of science may be tempted to exclaim that when paradigms change, the world changes with them. Led by a new paradigm, scientists adopt new instruments and look in new places. Even more important, during revolutions scientists see new and different things when looking with familiar instruments in places they have looked before. It is rather as if the professional community had been suddenly transported to another planet where familiar objects are seen in a different light and are joined by unfamiliar ones as well. Of course, nothing of quite that sort does occur: there is no geographical transplantation; outside the laboratory everyday affairs usually continue as before. Nevertheless, paradigm changes do cause scientists to see the world of their research-engagement differently. In so far as their only recourse to that world is through what they see and do, we may want to say that after a revolution scientists are responding to a different world. (p.111)

WELCOME TO POSITIVE PSYCHOLOGY

The paradigm governing psychology continues to shift and expand, most recently incorporating theory and research in the burgeoning field of **Positive Psychology** which is based upon the growing awareness that research and application in psychology has been incomplete, focusing primarily on understanding and fixing psychological problems. The ratio of journal articles about depression compared to happiness was approximately 100 to 1. There is a new emphasis on understanding and facilitating the healthy aspects of human functioning that make us effective in our lives due to the recognition that mental health is far more than the absence of mental illness. This expansion of the existing paradigm was named Positive Psychology in 1998 by Martin Seligman, the past president of the APA (American Psychological Association), who borrowed the term from an earlier work by Maslow in 1950.

As Martin Seligman (2002) tells it, the epiphany that led to Positive Psychology was set in motion by none other than his daughter Nikki when she was only five years old. According to Seligman, he used to be quite the "grouch." He was an overly serious guy who was very task oriented and had little time for idle chit-chat, even with his family. One day Seligman was working in his garden and little Nikki was helping him, but she was being playful in that wonderful way little children have, as she was laughing, dancing, and tossing weeds in the air. Seligman got irritated and yelled angrily at her. Little Nikki decided at that time to give her daddy some constructive criticism, so she walked up to him and said,

Daddy, do you remember before my fifth birthday? From when I was three until when I was five, I was a whiner. I whined every day. On my fifth birthday, I decided I wasn't going to whine any more. That was the hardest thing I've ever done. And if I can stop whining, you can stop being such a grouch. (p. 28)

At that moment Seligman had two life changing realizations. First of all, he realized what a curmudgeon he had become, and he vowed to change. But more importantly, he realized that raising his daughter, or any child for that matter, was not about correcting shortcomings, but about nurturing strengths. This was the ideological breakthrough that led to the development of Positive Psychology. Christopher Peterson (2006) talks about this watershed insight:

> Psychology as it existed had little to say about these remarkable strengths...In Nikki's case these strengths included a precocious will to improve herself and the ability to challenge her grumpy father to find that same will within himself...To describe anyone in terms of the weaknesses and shortcomings they do or do not have is to ignore half of the human condition- the good half, obviously, that makes life worth living. And yes the garden was eventually weeded, and yes, Seligman became less of a grouch. (p. 26)

Positive Psychology and Effectiveness

If Positive Psychology is concerned with the study of optimal human functioning, then what does this really mean? Optimal functioning is really just another way of talking about being an effective human being, of being effective and successful in your personal life, in your relationships and in your career. You could say that the guiding questions of the Positive Psychology movement are: (1) What is it that makes individuals emotionally healthy, happy and effective? (2) What combination of skills, attributes, attitudes, talents and behaviors leads to positive emotions, mental health, and effective functioning? So when thinking about effectiveness, it becomes impossible to separate this from all we can learn from the field of Positive Psychology as they have literally become one and the same. Positive Psychology also deals with many other fundamental questions about the meaning of life including such things as what is true happiness, whether virtue is its own reward, and what constitutes the good life, along with many other questions that will be addressed later in this text. The invaluable lessons from this domain are highly relevant to the study of what makes for an effective human being, as well as to the development of skills and attitudes necessary to function successfully in the world.

Positive Psychology is actually an umbrella term, the purpose of which was to bring together isolated lines of theory and research under one unified heading. These isolated topics were all avenues of psychological research and theory relating to what makes life worth living and how we enhance optimal human functioning. The seeds of Positive Psychology were sown well before 1998, in the Humanistic Psychology movement as conceptualized by Carl Rogers (1951) and Abraham Maslow (1970), in studies of giftedness (Winner, 2000), in conceptions of multiple intelligence (Gardner, 1983), in primary prevention programs based on wellness concepts, and in the human potential movement that was popular in the 1970's and 1980's.

Paradigm Evolution within Positive Psychology

The early conceptual underpinnings of Positive Psychology were built upon three main pillars:

1. The study of positive emotions and how to develop them more fully.
2. The study of character, of positive traits which include strengths, virtues, talents, and interests.
3. The study of positive institutions which facilitate character building.

By implication the three are connected although they certainly can function independently. However, positive institutions facilitate the development of positive traits which in turn help to promote positive experiences and emotions. However, Seligman (2011) in *Flourish,* has refined and updated his original theorizing. Initially, he proposed that the goal of positive psychology was to increase life satisfaction. Now he advises that the primary topic for positive psychology is **well-being** and the goal of positive psychology is to increase **flourishing** in your own life and on the planet. In order to do this, positive psychology must focus on measuring flourishing and determining what factors facilitate its development. "Flourishing" is his term for optimal human functioning. According to Seligman, well-being theory is composed of five elements summarized under the acronym PERMA. The five elements of PERMA are:

P Positive Emotions – a wide range of emotions from contentment to bliss
E Engagement – being totally absorbed in an endeavor
R Relationships – having positive, healthy relationships with significant others
M Meaning – having a sense of meaning and purpose in your life, often involving belonging to or serving something bigger than the self
A Accomplishment – your ability to achieve your goals

Each of these five elements has three distinct properties:

1. It contributes to well-being.
2. It is pursued for its own sake.
3. It can be defined and measured independently of the other elements.

In a similar vein, Huppert and So (2009) measured flourishing in over 43,000 adults across 23 European nations. As a result of their findings they defined flourishing as having the three core features of positive emotions, engagement and meaning along with at least three of six "additional features" which consist of: self esteem; optimism; resilience; vitality; self-determination; and positive relationships.

So the field of psychology has expanded to include the study of effectiveness and flourishing, but inevitably there is an old guard that resists this paradigm expansion by insinuating that it is not scientific enough. These critics of Positive Psychology have dismissed it as "Happiology," or the superficial study of happiness, when nothing could be further from the truth. While a study of positive emotions, including happiness, is part of the relevant topics we will cover, the real intent of Positive Psychology is to help you discover what it means to live a good, effective and meaningful life.

Paradigm Shifts in Everyday Life

You too may have a built in resistance to changing your own personal paradigms regarding your everyday beliefs. There is an "old guard" within each of us that wants to hang on to the old and familiar. And what compounds the problem is that most of what we perceive supports our original frame. Remember selective perception, the tendency to perceive that which we expect to be there? You see, when we frame something, we tend to see only that which lies within the frame. Phenomena outside of it, tend to be ignored or labeled anomalies. More often than not, we need to see things differently in order to discover the truth that it is so. Or as we often tell our students, if not the truth, then a whole new pack of lies to be considered until a new, more useful pack comes along. For example, as Mark Twain in his witty and clever manner noted,

> When I was a boy of fourteen, my father was so ignorant I could hardly stand to have the old man around. But when I got to be twenty-one, I was astonished at how much he had learned in seven years.

After a few moments of reflection, or after considering several examples, most people realize that they too experience these everyday shifts in perception. Sometimes they are trivial and sometimes they are profound. As noted earlier, you may have a good laugh after discovering that you are only the victim of an aggressive possum and not the target of a home invasion. Or you may find that your anger over a slow driver impeding your progress subsides when you finally pass her and realize that she is older than your grandmother. Most of us have had the experience of disliking someone, perhaps even intensely, at first meeting and then becoming very good friends later on when we got to know that person. First impressions are not always accurate. Our paradigms about people can change significantly as we get to know and better understand them. Sometimes the shifts are quite dramatic. On 9/11 many people went from frustration to immense gratitude when traffic problems prevented them from getting to their jobs at the World Trade Center or to their plane flights that were subsequently hijacked by terrorists. As the Dalai Lama said, "Sometimes not getting what you want is a wonderful stroke of luck."

Life will shift our perspectives without asking. What is worth asking is, how can we shift perspectives deliberately when we want our lives to be different? Effective individuals appreciate the observation of Einstein who noted that, "the significant problems we face today cannot be solved at the same level of thinking we were at when we created them." In order to solve them you are required to experience a paradigm shift, or a **reframe**. In his 1991 book, *The Seven Habits of Highly Effective People*, Steven Covey emphasizes that effective people are adept at questioning their frames and recognizing that "the way we see the problem is the problem." Thus, what we are after here is helping you build your skills at changing the way you think.

THE GLOBAL PERSPECTIVE—SPACESHIP EARTH (cont.)

Where do you live? Most of us learned our address and phone number at a very young age just in case we got lost. As we grew, we were introduced to the importance of geography and colored many maps as we learned the names and boundaries of states, cities, countries, and continents. Your family may have owned a globe where you could see the whole world turn on its axis. Just as we have discovered a truer notion of our place in the solar system, galaxy, and universe, we are realizing a truer picture of our own planet. When the astronauts began to embark on journeys orbiting our world, virtually all were struck by the vision of this beautiful blue planet as seen from space. There were no lines, no boundaries demarcating one country from the next. No latitude or longitude lines could be seen. The Atlantic Ocean did not have huge letters floating on it so that it could be clearly identified. In Buckminster Fuller's (1970) words, the astronauts had the profound realization that while they were traveling in a spaceship themselves, they had just left the spaceship that all of us are traveling on, Earth.

Effectiveness, however you define it, requires an inhabitable, sustainable world in which to be effective. All of us are traveling together on this *Spaceship Earth*. If the air is no longer fit to breathe, everyone's breathing will be affected. If the land can no longer support food production, everyone will eventually starve, some sooner than others. Modern humans have emerged in approximately the last 100,000 thousand years. For the vast majority of that time we functioned as hunter-gatherers. We took what we needed to sustain ourselves and moved on to let Earth naturally renew itself. Only 10,000 years ago we discovered agriculture and our population began its geometric expansion. Humankind unfortunately has been laboring under a very convincing yet false belief that we now call the *"fallacy of the commons."* For so long it seemed that we could fish, harvest trees, drill wells for water and oil without limit, and the planet was so large and abundant that there were no apparent consequences. Our best science now reveals that as untrue (Hartmann, 2004; Uhl, 2003). We are affecting the Earth, all of it. These changes that our choices are bringing about have no respect for borders.

James Lovelock (1979) in *Gaia: A New Look at Life* has proposed the Gaia hypothesis which posits that the Earth is not just the third rock from the sun with living organisms on it, but that Earth itself is alive and regulates itself to support the life on it. Humans and the choices they make are part of this process. How might your choices regarding the life you want to live be affected if your paradigm shifted and you saw the fate of yourself, your loved ones, and all of life inextricably linked as passengers on the same spaceship?

REFRAMING

There is an oft repeated story of a Chinese farmer that goes something like this...

> A farmer and his only son were busily plowing their fields when their horse broke free from its harness and ran off into the nearby hills. When their fellow villagers heard of their plight they began to commiserate, "Oh, what terrible luck! How unfortunate! What will you do?" To which the farmer responded, "Good luck, bad luck...who knows?" Several days later the farmer's horse returned with two other horses in tow. His fellow villagers were astonished as they exclaimed "What wonderful luck! You lose your only horse and end up with three!" To which the farmer responded, "Good luck, bad luck...who knows?" Several days later the farmer's son was attempting to break one of the horses so as to put it into service on his land. The son was thrown from the horse and broke his arm. All the villagers were united in their opinion that this was indeed bad luck. The farmer as usual responded, "Good luck, bad luck ... who knows?" The very next week the Imperial Army marched through their village conscripting all the able-bodied young men into the service. The farmer's son was spared due to his broken arm. The villagers were once again impressed with this man's extraordinary good luck and told him so. And he replied, "Good luck, bad luck....who knows?"

This story illustrates what we call **reframing**, the process of actively changing perspectives to create paradigm shifts. Because the farmer was able to see things differently (i.e. think about them differently than his fellow villagers) he was able to respond differently, and experience an emotional calmness and equanimity that evaded those around him. Reframing allows us to be creative, increase joy, reduce suffering, and solve problems. Ultimately, all the changes we will suggest that you make are changes in perspective supported by your actions. As with most things, this is easier said than done. However, be assured it is definitely easier on you to learn to do it than to not do it. The primary obstacle to making this change is habit. Imagine riding in a cart on a dirt road for years always going to the same destination. After a while you don't need to steer or choose a direction. The wheels have worn grooves that simply and automatically take you to the same place time after time. If you see a new direction that you would like to pursue, that cart will still more easily go in the direction of the old path. Going down a new path requires a deliberate effort to lift the cart out of the old path and onto the new. That old guard in you will want to keep things as they are. Within your brain something very similar happens where the equivalent of grooves are cut within the networks of frequently used neurons which access our paradigms. The first time you are presented with something, multiple neurons within the network might be involved. But by the sixth time, it has become much more efficient with most of the work accomplished by only a few neurons (Kalanit, Henson, and Martin, 2006). Yet this efficiency has a downside, as it creates limitations on our perceptions. Reframing requires a reconfiguration of the well-traveled network. This shift can be consciously initiated, but it requires deliberately engaging our frontal cortex by directing our attention and imagination in a different direction (Farah, 2000). Change takes time and effort. Sometimes it is relatively easy and sometimes it is challenging. It is almost always possible.

> *An adventure is only an inconvenience rightly considered.*
> *An inconvenience is only an adventure wrongly considered.*
> G.K. Chesterton

Consider these two differing viewpoints on the craft of acting. Actor Alec Baldwin was asking fellow actor Gene Wilder whether he preferred acting in the movies or acting on the stage in a theater. Wilder replied that he preferred movies because, "They [the audience] can't come and get you." Baldwin replied that he liked the theater better because when he saw the audience he thought, "Look! They all came to see me." These are obviously radically different ways to view the same situation and they result in totally different experiences all based on the reality they create.

Reframing in its most basic form is simply asking the question: "Is there another way of looking at this?" There always is. Please understand that this whole book is a suggestion to reframe. Shifting to various perspectives on your personal journey will maximize the possibility of a life well lived or at least a life that is lived in the most enjoyable possible way. Since we are at the beginning of this long journey together, we are going to suggest two general strategies for reframing. Bring these as you explore the world and your story unfolding before you.

The Importance of Humor

> An older gentleman approached his doctor with a problem. "Every morning at eight a.m. I have a regular bowel movement," he complained. His doctor was somewhat perplexed and responded, "That doesn't seem to be a problem to me. Most of my patients would be thrilled to have a regular bowel movement at eight a.m." The patient replied, "The problem is that I don't wake up and get out of bed until nine a.m.!"

Humor is the most familiar way in which reframing is used. We are led to believe a situation is one way and then suddenly we see it differently through an amusing lens. This contrast leads to the experience of laughter. Whenever you can bring humor to your perceptions, your emotions can shift and your effectiveness is potentially increased. Lefcourt (2005) summarized much of the research data on humor and noted clear evidence that it can moderate the effects of stress, lessen depression, enhance immune system functioning, reduce the use of pain killers, and "be a positive asset in the survival and recovery from illness." There is even research documenting that laughter is conducive to creative thinking for problem solving, as well as for changing frames of reference in general. In one study (Isen,1991) psychologists found that subjects who watched a highly amusing video were much better at solving a complex puzzle where the solution required creative thinking about combining or using familiar objects in unusual ways. Subjects who only watched a neutral video were more prone to lapse into **functional fixedness**, wherein they got locked into thinking about using objects only in the most conventional or familiar ways, therefore they had far more difficulty solving the puzzle. The researchers concluded that laughter was instrumental in promoting flexibility of thought; that it literally seems to help people to think more expansively and associate more easily, making connections that might otherwise go unnoticed. This strongly implies that one way to help someone think through a problem is to tell them a joke.

Often our most interesting and funny tales are our descriptions of harrowing or embarrassing moments from our past, told from the safety of the present moment. As we step outside of the experience and see ourselves in it, we see it differently and we can therefore feel differently. You need strategies for modifying your feelings and emotions so that you can choose an effective response. Being able to laugh at yourself is one of the best. This is a simple strategy for changing your point of view and provoking humor. Imagine that your life is being videotaped and consider what this difficult moment might look like to your viewers. One of the authors discovered this strategy accidentally while moving a very heavy sofa with several friends.

> The sofa was so awkward and heavy that everyone had to stop periodically to rest and readjust their grip. While we were doing this, I was intermittently warning all my friends to be careful not to set this large object on their feet. At that very moment I proceeded to lower the sofa onto my own foot! (And I realized that, indeed, it really was a very heavy sofa!) Just as my mouth was opening to ask for help, I mentally shifted to an outsider's view of my situation and started laughing hysterically. I had become Jerry Lewis or one of the Three Stooges, and I simply could not stop laughing long enough to speak. Luckily, my friends, also laughing now, realized I was pointing at my foot and removed the couch.

While we still recommend being careful with heavy objects, this incident demonstrates the power of shifting your point of view. The pain and upset would have been far more intense had our colleague not been caught up in the hilarity of the moment. Perhaps even more importantly being able to laugh at oneself not only keeps us humble but gives us an endless and always available source of amusement.

It is important to note the difference between the self-deprecating humor that we are referring to above and hostile humor which disparages others. Janes and Olson (2000) found that hostile humor is intimidating to people who merely observe it even though it was directed at someone else. These observers tend to become more sensitive to rejection and more afraid in general. The bottom line here is that the authors believe that hostile humor can lead to the social isolation of people who use it. So, while laughing at ourselves and with others can be a wonderful way to increase our sense of well-being and community, laughing at others is a far different matter. When we laugh at others, we risk, at the very least, incurring their anger or alienation. More than that, we risk becoming insensitive to the needs of others, and we fail to recognize our fundamental interdependence on other humans and forms of life. This brings us to the second important frame that we believe is fundamental on your journey to the good life, compassion.

Compassion: Opening Your Heart by Stepping into Their Shoes

One of the authors was educated largely in Catholic schools. To this day he considers it a mixed blessing because much of what he was taught, excessive guilt for instance, had to be overcome. However, one teaching from fourth grade always stuck with him. The phrase he was taught was, "There but for the grace of God go I." Whenever he saw someone in difficult circumstances, whether it was sadness, illness, disability, embarrassment, pain, or humiliation, he was urged to remember that under the right circumstances it could easily have been him. The message was to be grateful and be willing to help if you can. It could have been you. This, in essence, suggests a strategy for compassion. In humor we can step outside of ourselves and see ourselves. In compassion, we step into another's shoes and see through their eyes and feel what it is like to be them.

How often do we have conflict in our lives exactly because we failed to step into the other's shoes? There is a famous poem about six blind men in India who get into a heated argument about the nature of elephants. It seems that each of them approached the elephant at a different place and from a different angle, and each decided that he knew the true nature of the elephant. One decided it was like a wall because he had encountered the side of the animal. Another believed it was like a snake because he had grabbed the trunk. The others concluded that an elephant was really like a tree, a fan, a rope and a spear because they happened to approach from another angle. The poem concluded that they argued all night long about who was right and who was wrong. How much easier their evening would been had they only taken the time to step into one another's places and feel what the elephant felt like from a different point of approach. Next time you find yourself in conflict with a significant other ask yourself, "What part of the elephant am I grabbing?"

There is a beautiful story from the Talmudic teaching tradition that illustrates the wisdom of compassion. The story is called *The Sorrows Tree*. The Sorrows Tree is the place where all souls go after they die. They go to the tree to hang the burden of sorrows that they carried in that lifetime on a branch of the tree. The magic of the tree is that as you hang your sorrows up you get to see and feel the sorrows that all the other souls have left. You are then asked to choose a new batch of sorrows from the tree for the next lifetime that you will lead. Once each soul gets to really know what it was like to feel another's pain, they invariably seek out their old bundle of sorrows since they don't seem so terrible after all.

Now we are not suggesting that many among us have not suffered extraordinary, greater than average difficulties, but we are suggesting that if you only knew what it was *really* like to be inside someone else's skin, you would feel and act differently. We can also come to know the gifts that have been received by those who have overcome great sorrow. Some losses are so great that the individuals who endure them become almost fearless in their approach to the remainder of their lives. What else can truly harm them if they survived that?

Be willing to shift perspectives. Learn not to take yourself so seriously by stepping outside of yourself. Learn to take life seriously by stepping into another's shoes.

THE MAP IS NOT THE TERRITORY – NEUROPLASTICITY AND THE BRAIN

> *Reality is an illusion, albeit a very persistent one.*
> Albert Einstein

So we invite you to always view your perceptions as just that, your perceptions, nothing more, nothing less. Your perceptions are like maps you use to get around in your world. Remember that a map is not the territory (Bandler and Grinder, 1975). It is just one representation of a territory. And some maps are more useful than others, depending on the circumstances. If you want to drive from Atlanta to Washington, D.C., you will need a good road map. A topographical map of the southeastern United States will be useless. On the other hand, if you want to fly a jet plane from Atlanta to Washington D.C., a good road map will not help you, but a topographical map which helps you identify landmarks, will come in very handy. The same is true of your perceptions. Given that we each have a unique set of glasses which color our perceptions, it makes sense to wear the pair that will be most useful in a given situation. Be open to the possibility that the solution is found in a reframe. Actively seek reframes and you will find that the more you do, the easier it becomes to do so. This is the result of what has been called brain plasticity or **neuroplasticity**, the capacity of the brain to change its internal structure by reorganizing neural pathways based on new experiences.

It was once believed that as we aged, the brain's networks became fixed. In the past two decades, however, an enormous amount of research has revealed that the brain never stops changing and adjusting. For instance, London taxi drivers have a larger **hippocampus**, a structure in the brain responsible for memory and new learning, than London bus drivers (Maguire, Woollett, & Spiers, 2006). It is not a coincidence that, for the taxi drivers, this extra growth occurs in the region of the hippocampus specialized in acquiring and using complex spatial information in order to navigate efficiently. Taxi drivers have to navigate around London whereas bus drivers follow a limited set of routes.

The same example of brain-plasticity is also evident in the brains of bilinguals (Mechelli, Crinion, Noppeney, O'Doherty, 2004). People who speak two languages have a larger left inferior parietal cortex than those who only speak one language. It appears that learning a language facilitates these functional changes and then in turn, the changes facilitate the learning of the new language. Not surprisingly, once you have learned two languages, it becomes easier to learn three, four, or more. Another example of the malleability of the brain is the difference between musicians' brain as compared to non-musicians, (Gaser and Schlaug, 2003). The investigators compared professional musicians (who practice at least one hour per day) to amateur musicians and non-musicians. They found that gray matter (cortex) volume was highest in professional musicians, intermediate in amateur musicians, and lowest in non-musicians in several brain areas involved in playing music: motor regions, anterior superior parietal areas and inferior temporal areas.

Finally, Draganski and colleagues (2006) recently showed that extensive learning of abstract information can also trigger some plastic changes in the brain. They imaged the brains of German medical students three months before their medical exam and right after the exam and compared them to brains of students who were not studying for the exam at that time. Medical students' brains showed learning-induced changes in regions of the parietal cortex as well as in the posterior hippocampus. These regions of the brains are known to be involved in memory retrieval and learning (Michelon, 2008).

As we learn and revise our perceptions, we actually modify the internal structure of the **neurons** in our brain, particularly at the **synapses**, the spaces where one neuron communicates with another. We also increase the number of synapses between neurons, thereby increasing our ability to create new frames.

Do you know that exercising or stimulating your brain is highly recommended as part of a brain-healthy lifestyle! As neuroplasticity is becoming more apparent in cognitive science, an increasing amount of evidence has surfaced to validate the idea of "use it or lose it." When you exercise or stimulate your brain through new or merely unfamiliar activities, you can trigger changes in the brain, such as the increased connections between neurons described earlier. These changes contribute to an expansion in what psychologists call **brain reserve**. Research suggests that the more brain reserve, the more resistant the brain is to age or disease-related damages. A great example of this is what has been referred as The Nun Study, a longitudinal study of 678 Catholic sisters, 75 to 107 years of age, belonging to the School Sisters of Notre Dame. Callahan, McHorney, & Mulrow (2003) presented case studies of various nuns, some of whom were over 100 years old but evidenced no cognitive deterioration, and some who had dementia and clinically significant Alzheimer's disease. When examining convent archives, they discovered that those sisters who were more intellectually engaged and had more intellectual pursuits, i.e., those who used their brains more, appeared healthier and functioned better cognitively than sisters who had fewer intellectual pursuits. It was the latter sisters who were more likely to show clinical symptoms of Alzheimer's. So it appears that using your brain protects you against dementia. What was equally fascinating was that when postmortem neuropathologic evaluations were performed, they found that the brains of the healthy sisters actually exhibited the same or more of the plaques typical of Alzheimer's than those of the afflicted! So their intellectual endeavors did not prevent the Alzheimer's from developing, rather, it led to the build-up of more brain reserve so the disease did not affect these sisters!

The experimental evidence is by now compelling that learning a new skill produces structural changes in the brain. The new skill could be learning a new language, a musical instrument, human anatomy, a city map, or even a seemingly frivolous activity, such as juggling. Using a sophisticated whole-brain imaging technique to detect changes in gray matter, researchers demonstrated that mastering how to juggle led to a 3 to 4 percent increase in the size of gray matter, the processing portion of your brain tissue. Young adults were randomly assigned to either a juggling group who had three months to show that they could juggle three balls for at least 60 seconds, or a control group that continued with life as usual. Baseline MRIs revealed no significant difference between the two groups prior to the experiment. Only the jugglers evidenced the increase in gray matter after three months. Then, after not practicing for three months, repeat brain scans showed a decrease of 1 to 2 percent from the size they had attained when they were practicing juggling every day (Draganski & colleagues, 2004). A similar study, published in the *Journal of Neuroscience*, using individuals with an average age of sixty rather than young adults, demonstrated that older brains also have the flexibility to grow. Although the older adults did not learn to juggle as well as the younger adults, those that did learn showed similar increases in gray matter (Boyke & colleagues, 2008).

These increases are not limited to our gray matter. Even the white matter, the area of the brain where neuronal communication primarily occurs, shows an increase as a result of learning to juggle. A group of researchers from the University of Oxford, again using young adults, a matched control group, and pre/post measurements demonstrated that jugglers grew more white matter in the parietal lobe, an area involved in connecting what we see to how we move. No change was apparent in the brain of the non-jugglers. What is perhaps even more revealing is that the growth was evident in all the jugglers, irrespective of how well they could juggle (Scholz & colleagues, 2009). So it is apparent that it is the learning process itself that is important for brain development, not how well you perform. The brain, like a muscle, needs to be exercised, but it appears it also wants to be challenged to learn something new.

Thus, the ability to flex your brain is one avenue to creative thinking. What is creative thinking, if not the ability to look for innovative solutions to the problems at hand? Speaking of solutions, how successful were you in solving the problem presented to you earlier in the chapter? If you were stumped, let us close this chapter with the solution to the nine dot problem.

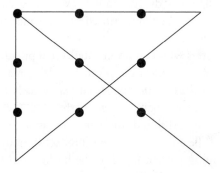

Figure 1.10 The Nine Dot Solution

Obviously, to solve this problem you had to go beyond the nine dots, beyond the originally preconceived square which you likely perceived. Your paradigm that this was a square led you to use the corner dots as the edges, which effectively inhibited you from solving this problem. Is this just another clever riddle? Or does it show us that we are predetermined to see things in a particular or familiar way, and what we see dictates how we interact with that reality (in this case how we attempt to solve the problem). Learning to think "out of the box" is one of the cornerstones of creativity, which in many ways is all about shifting your frame of reference.

POSITIVE PSYCHOLOGY EXERCISES:

1. Is there a situation where you are habitually stuck because you are totally unwilling to part with your point of view about it? We guarantee that if you think hard enough you will find that the answer to this question (for everyone) is typically yes. Can you think of a particular instance? Practice shifting your perspective on your issue using reframing. If you are at a loss for how to proceed, then experiment with reframing a past mistake or failure as a valuable learning experience. Think about how your life might have improved or been enriched today, either directly or indirectly, as a result of this experience. You may have to dig deep to adopt this perspective, or to see connections between past mistakes and current successes, but if you persist you will be rewarded.

2. In the same vein as the wise words of the Dalai Lama, there is an old quote, "When God closes a door, he opens a window." Think of a time when an important door closed for you. What windows opened?

KEY TERMS

Sensation	Perception	Selective Attention
Predictive Coding	Paradigm	Frames of Reference
Schema	Ambiguous Figures	Paradigm Shift
Positive Psychology	Selective Perception	Functional Fixedness
Reframing	Neuroplasticity	Hippocampus
Neurons	Synapse	Brain Reserve
Well-being	Flourishing	Distributed Processing

CHAPTER 1 QUESTIONS

True or False Questions (T or F)

1. _____ We always see exactly what is there.

2. _____ Sensation and Perception are the same.

3. _____ Frames of reference cause us to be confused.

4. _____ All frames of reference are constantly in flux.

5. _____ Our perceptions are greatly influenced by our expectations, beliefs, and pre-conceived notions.

6. _____ Effective individuals are flexible in their thinking.

7. _____ Traditional thinking is what stimulates scientific development.

8. _____ Paradigm shifts typically happen very easily.

9. _____ The field of psychology represents a good example of a more gradual paradigm expansion rather than a rapid paradigm shift.

10. _____ Positive Psychology explores the study of emotional health rather than illness.

11. _____ In the field of psychology, research studies on happiness outnumber studies on depression.

12. _____ Reframing involves significantly shifting the way you look at things or at a problem.

13. _____ Stimulating your brain with challenging mental activities can ward off symptoms of Alzheimer's disease later in life.

14. _____ As we age, the brain's networks become fixed.

15. _____ Reframing represents one way to exercise your brain.

Short-Answer Questions

1. Humans are adept at developing _____ to help us organize and understand our world.

2. _____ causes us to perceive what we expect to be there.

3. Major scientific discoveries are typically preceded by a _____.

4. _____ is a way of creating a paradigm shift on a small level in your personal life.

5. _____ _____ refers to the fact that we focus our consciousness only on a portion of all that we are capable of perceiving.

6. The emphasis on studying healthy aspects of human functioning, on effectiveness, and on mental health has been brought together under the heading of _____ _____.

7. Because of _____ our brains are capable of changing internally, of reorganizing neural pathways based on new experience.

8. The _____ is an area in the brain responsible for memory and new learning.

Essay Questions

1. How does sensation differ from perception?
2. What is a paradigm shift and how is this phenomenon important?
3. Why are paradigms (in science and in everyday life) so resistant to change?
4. Why is the 9 Dot Problem so hard to solve for many people?
5. How does the new paradigm of Positive Psychology differ from traditional psychology?
6. What is PERMA?
7. Describe the process of reframing and how it could prove useful in your life.
8. Describe several strategies for creating reframes.
9. What is neuroplasticity and why is it important?

2

Making Positive Choices

Have you ever wondered, at some time in your life, "Why am I the way that I am?" One of the authors recalls a question frequently asked of him at the start of his graduate career while in training to become a psychologist:

> 'What made you choose to become a psychologist?' people would ask me. My traditional retort was, 'because I'm screwed up and I want to figure myself out'. I guess that I was searching for the truth about myself. Along the way I discovered that I was not as screwed up as I feared I was, the *"I'm OK, You're OK"* school of thought as proposed in the book with the same title by Thomas Harris (1967). And later I concluded that maybe I was a bit screwed up, but that wasn't so bad, the "I'm not OK, You're not OK, and that's OK" school of thought proposed by Sheldon Kopp (1972), in his book *If You Meet the Buddha on the Road, Kill Him!* But most importantly I realized that there was no one truth, since the truth was dependent upon the frame of reference, or school of thought that I adopted. Early in my career, while enveloped in the Freudian mystique, I blamed my parents for my troubles and felt that I was the victim of an, at times, traumatic childhood. When studying Behavioral theories I concluded that I was the product of an unusual reinforcement and conditioning history. But the Humanists and the Cognitive- Behaviorists helped me realize I had some choices in the matter of who I was, and who I would ultimately become. I realized I was who I was, not because of what had happened to me, but because of the choices I had made in response to what had happened in my life. Lately, I have come to be intrigued by the positive psychologists who suggest that I am what I am by what I choose to focus on. I can entertain misery and wallow in it, or wonder what awaits me in the happiness and acceptance camp. In my life, I attempt to choose the latter.

DETERMINISM VS. FREE WILL

The history of science reveals that the various scientific disciplines developed, in part, in order to determine the causes of events. Meticulous observations and measurements led scientists to the conclusion that everything which occurs in nature has a cause. Theories of causation were postulated and then tested by scientific experimentation. This belief in cause and effect relationships has been termed **determinism**.

As psychology matured as a science, social scientists, in turn, began to posit that human behavior may also be the product of causal relationships, and therefore determined. That is, if nature encompasses all of humanity, then human behavior must also be the result of various determining factors. Determinists espouse the view that all human actions are caused by something, even if we are oblivious to these causative factors. Strict determinists go so far as to imply that free choice does not exist, that all our actions and decisions are the product of outside determining variables over which we have no control. At the other end of the spectrum we find the **Free Will** camp. According to this point of view humans can and do typically ignore so-called determining factors, such as genetics or environmental influences, and freely choose how and when to act.

Psychological theories of personality and behavior can be placed on a continuum between determinism, the belief that who we are is largely governed by outside forces, and free will, which obviously assumes that who we are is a result of the choices we make.

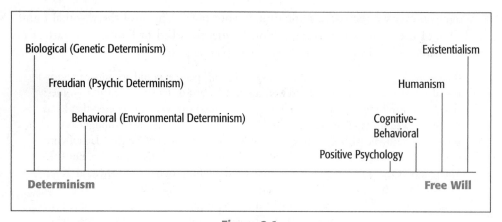

Figure 2.1

There are three main deterministic theories. The first of these are the biologically based theories which postulate that we are almost exclusively a product of our genetic heritage. Proponents of these theories claim that all of our behavior, both normal and abnormal, can be traced back to particular configurations of our genetic makeup. Support for these theories comes from the obvious fact that abilities, talents, and certain emotional and physical disorders clearly run in families. For example, it is evident that singing ability is passed down from generation to generation. Just look at the late, great reggae artist, Bob Marley, and his son Ziggy Marley, or Julio Iglesias and his son, Enrique Iglesias, or Nat King Cole and his daughter Natalie Cole, or Judy Garland and her daughter Liza Minnelli, or in acting ability where actor Michael Douglas followed in his father Kirk's footsteps. Or consider athletics where sons often follow in their father's footsteps like quarterbacks Eli and Payton Manning and their quarterback father Archie Manning, or baseball superstar Ken Griffey, Jr. and his father Ken Griffey, Sr. As another example, let's take the rather severe emotional disorder known as **schizophrenia**. Individuals suffering from this malady have difficulty differentiating traditional reality from their own internal fantasies or fears. Schizophrenic individuals are prone to **"psychotic episodes"** where they lose contact with reality, and suffer from **hallucinations** (seeing or hearing things that aren't really there), and/or **delusional thinking** (believing in ideas that are not reality based, like those involving fears of persecution). Research clearly shows a strong genetic component to this disorder (Mirsky & Quinn, 1988). The **concordance rate** (the probability that two individuals display the same trait or characteristic) of schizophrenia is much higher for identical twins (who have the same genetic makeup) than for fraternal twins (whose genetic makeup is the same as any sibling), or siblings in general. All of these, however, were much higher than for non related individuals raised in the same environment (Gottesmann, 1991; Cannon et. al, 1998). So theories of genetic determinism espouse a view of reality that "my grandparents did it to me. I am who I am because of my genes (and we don't mean the kind you wear on your body)."

A second set of deterministic theories are those of psychic determinism which postulate that you are who you are because of how you were raised. The most famous of these is Freud's (1924) **Psychoanalytic Theory**. Proponents of this theory believe that your personality is determined by your early experiences, and that by the time you reach six years old, it is pretty well set. So such things as the tenure of your toilet training or your mother's style of feeding you have a profound influence on your later development. This theory says "my parents did it to me. I am who I am because of the way they brought me up."

The third set of deterministic theories, known as **Behaviorism**, postulates that we are a product of our conditioning and learning histories, and of our current reinforcement schedules. There is a wealth of data that the aforementioned factors greatly influence the behavior of both animals and humans. In order to insure that psychology was accepted as a "science," Behavioral theorists argued that the only unit worthy of study was overt, observable behavior. According to theorists such as B.F. Skinner (1953), and Ivan Pavlov (1927), it is our overall environment that shapes our personality and behavior. Thus, you became a good student because you were rewarded for academic achievement. Or you learned how to be fearful because you copied the behavior of significant others who modeled being afraid. These theories say, "my environment (parents, teachers, bosses, coaches, siblings, peers, etc.) did it to me. I am who I am because of the pressures they exerted and the rewards they provided."

But are these theories based on reality? Is this really all there is to human behavior? Are we just essentially victims of our genes, our upbringing, and our environment? The proponents of the Free Will theories would argue that these deterministic paradigms only tell a part of the story. They are accurate maps of a portion of the territory, but fail to include a key component of the human existence. The fact is, we believe that while you are certainly influenced by all of these factors, human beings are ultimately free to choose. Perhaps the earliest of these theories is based on the European philosophy of **Existentialism**, as popularized by John Paul Sarte and Albert Camus. These philosophical theories, when translated into psychological thought, basically posited that although, undoubtedly, life throws waves at you that are outside of your control, how you ride those waves is up to you. You could choose to be drowned by the rising waters, or you could learn to tread water, or you could master surfing.

Here in America this view was developed further by the **Humanists**, such as Abraham Maslow (1970) and Carl Rogers (1959). They too hypothesized that our personalities and our behavior were not so much a product of our conditioning and our conditions, but of the choices we made in response to those. They were much more optimistic than the existentialists by promoting a belief that if anything occurred naturally, it was human beings striving towards self-actualization, towards becoming all that we can be. These humanistic theories developed partly in reaction to the strictly deterministic Freudian view which dominated psychology and psychotherapy practice at the time. **Cognitive-Behaviorists**, such as Albert Ellis, Aaron Beck, and Martin Seligman pointed out that, when studying humans, we should not focus solely on the study of overt behavior, as the strict Behaviorists would have it, but must take into account "covert behavior," our thoughts, the internal self talk that preceded the behaviors. The strict Behaviorist model is an S - R (stimulus - response) model. Simply stated this cause and effect model holds that all behavior is controlled by the stimulus which precedes it. For example, you walk into your house and your spouse or parent screams at you (the stimulus)for being late, and as a consequence of this you get angry and yell back (the response). This model was based on research with animals, which appear to be more stimulus bound. But for humans a more descriptive model is that of S - O - R (stimulus - organism - response). A stimulus impinges upon you, but before you respond, you have a thought about that stimulus, you imbue it with meaning. It is *that thought* that leads to your particular response. To go back to our earlier example, after you've been screamed at, if your first thought is, "how dare you?" or "that jerk, she/he is always picking on me," you are likely to respond in kind. However, if your first thought is "he/she must have been really worried about me," you are much more likely to respond with an apology. You see, it was not the screaming that led to your response, but what you said to yourself about the screaming. It is here, between the stimulus and the response that choice resides. To quote Steven Covey (1991), "Between stimulus and response humans have the greatest freedom, the freedom to choose that response." The difficulty lies in the fact that our thoughts tend to be automatic and rather telegraphic, and we are generally not aware of them. But more on this later in this chapter.

Human history is replete with examples of individuals who, when faced with extraordinarily difficult situations, stimuli which would overwhelm most of us, exercised this freedom to choose their responses. Take, for example, the story of Ruben "Hurricane" Carter, as described in his 1974 book *The Sixteenth Round*, and popularized in the 1999 movie "The Hurricane." Carter, a successful boxer, was falsely imprisoned for nineteen years for a triple murder he did not commit. He refused to allow prison to rule his life. He opted to wear pajamas rather than prison garb. He chose to sleep by day and be awake all night to avoid the normal prison routine. This was not just an act of blind opposition; rather, he used his time to educate and transform himself. He read extensively and spent years working on the manuscript that later became his autobiographical work. His book inspired others to work on his behalf, eventually leading to his release. His goal while in prison, besides, of course, to get released, was not to be bound by the routines and prescriptions of prison life, but to make his own world within the prison walls. Those of you who have seen the movie "Life is Beautiful," which won the 1998 Academy Award for best foreign film, will recognize it as a perfect example of our freedom to choose our actions even when faced with intolerable circumstances. Those of you who haven't seen it, we strongly recommend that you *choose* to do so. Lest you think that this is just a romanticized version of a possible response to the tragedy which was the Holocaust, we recommend reading Victor Frankl's (1959) autobiographical account of his time in a concentration camp, as described in his book *Man's Search for Meaning*.

If we take an objective look at the body of knowledge and data amassed in psychology over the last hundred years, the inescapable conclusion is that human behavior can best be understood as lying somewhere in the middle of the free will vs. determinism continuum. There is conclusive research evidence that certain emotional disorders (such as schizophrenia and bipolar disorder) have a strong genetic component, in the same way that inherited predispositions towards diabetes or heart disease run in some families. Likewise, we cannot ignore the overwhelming evidence that we are strongly affected by environmental factors ranging from our past experiences, our learning history (including what we have learned through operant and classical conditioning as well as observational learning), to our current situation. Could it be that our belief in free will is just a fantasy? Do we harbor an illusion of free choice because at any given moment we are bombarded with so many determining variables that we are unable to perceive them or sort them out? Most psychologists have come to the conclusion that human behavior is affected by a combination of determining forces along with each individual's inherent ability to choose, to set and pursue goals, and to decide to change the path set by determining factors. Not all humans rise to this challenge, however, but the capability to do so exists nonetheless. This mixed viewpoint has come to be known as *soft determinism*.

Where does positive psychology fit on this continuum, you may wonder? Positive psychology is not just one theoretical framework or orientation but an umbrella orientation that subsumes aspects of many theories that pertain to human flourishing. So in this regard it incorporates much of Humanistic psychology, aspects of the Cognitive-Behavioral approach, even aspects of the Psychoanalytic/Psychodynamic models (see attachment theory in Chapter 11), as well as recognizing the genetic/biological link involved in both positive emotions and our signature strengths (which we will elucidate in the next two chapters). But while positive psychology acknowledges the role of genetics, it puts its focus on what we can do about our situation, placing it more squarely on the free will end of the continuum. Research in neuroplasticity, as presented in Chapter 1, shows that when you change your choices and thereby your behaviors, you can change your genetic expression. Even more surprising, when you change your own genes, your future generations profit from the choices you make today.

PROACTIVITY

This freedom of choice, referred to in the current literature as **"proactivity,"** is an important paradigm guiding the behavior of effective individuals. We have found that a good way to begin to understand the nature of proactivity is to consider your first responses to the word *responsibility*. What first comes to mind when you hear this word? If you are like most of our students you think of things such as paying your bills, doing your homework, picking up the kids, cleaning the house, cooking dinner, washing your clothes or your car, and so on. These are things you feel you should be doing. The image that frequently comes to mind is that of a large ball and chain attached to your ankle, which drags you down and limits your freedom. But, proactivity involves placing a different frame around the concept of responsibility, as aptly described by Covey (1991) in his seminal book, *The Seven Habits of Highly Effective People*:

> While the word proactivity is now fairly common in management literature, it is a word you won't find in most dictionaries. It is more than merely taking initiative. It

means that as human beings, we are responsible for our own lives. Our behavior is a function of our decisions, not our conditions. We can subordinate feelings to values. We have the initiative and the responsibility to make things happen. Look at the word responsibility—'response - ability'—the ability to choose your response. Highly proactive people recognize that responsibility. They do not blame circumstances, conditions, or conditioning for their behavior. Their behavior is a product of their own conscious choice, based on values, rather than a product of their conditions based on feelings. (pgs. 70-71)

Locus of Control

The concept of proactivity has also been previously referred to, by psychologist Julian Rotter (1966), as an internal locus of control. **Locus of control** is on a continuum ranging from external to internal. Individuals with an **external locus of control** see themselves as victims, buffeted and abused by external events over which they have no control. Individuals with an **internal locus of control** believe that they are responsible for the ultimate outcomes in their life. They do not wait for fate to lead them in a direction, rather they endeavor to take active control over their own life. For Covey, an internal locus of control is "proactivity," while an external locus of control is "reactivity." Reactive persons are at the mercy of forces beyond their control. Have you ever heard someone say, "It's raining outside, how can I be happy?" or, "It's Monday so I don't have any energy." For these people their mood or their energy level is determined by the weather or the day of the week. Proactive people, while certainly influenced by their environment, recognize that they are response-able to choose their responses to these conditions. If you are curious to see where you fall on the continuum of locus of control, we suggest you take the time to fill out the following inventory.

Student Locus of Control Inventory

Check Yes if you agree with a statement; check No if you do not agree.

YES	NO	
____	____	1. If I can do the work, I can get a good grade in any course no matter how good or bad the instructor may be.
____	____	2. If the teacher isn't a good speaker or doesn't keep me interested, I probably won't do well in the class.
____	____	3. I believe that I have the power to control what happens to me.
____	____	4. I believe that I have very little control over what happens to me.
____	____	5. When I make a mistake, it's usually my fault.
____	____	6. When I make a mistake, it's usually because someone didn't make clear to me what I was supposed to do.
____	____	7. My grades are the result of how much studying I do.
____	____	8. My grades don't seem to be affected by the amount of studying that I do.

Student Locus of Control Inventory (cont.)

____ ____ 9. I can adapt easily to a change of plans or events.

____ ____ 10. Adapting to change has always been difficult for me. I like things to be as predictable and orderly as possible.

____ ____ 11. When I fail a test, it's either because I didn't study or I didn't understand the material.

____ ____ 12. When I fail a test, it's either because the test was unfair or the instructor did not cover the material sufficiently.

____ ____ 13. I usually don't need anyone to push me or make me study.

____ ____ 14. I can't seem to make myself study.

____ ____ 15. I am a self-motivated person.

____ ____ 16. I need someone to motivate me.

If you checked "yes" to mostly odd-numbered statements, then you tend towards having an internal locus of control. We congratulate you! The rest of this chapter will help you refine and polish skills to make you an even more proactive individual. On the other hand, if you found yourself endorsing more even-numbered statements, then we suggest you consider the possibility that your locus of control is more external. If effectiveness is your goal, then we strongly recommend that you take the ideas and strategies presented in the rest of this chapter and incorporate them into your behavior. Remember, it is not enough to know about mangoes, you must be willing to taste them.

Students with an internal locus of control recognize the connection between the effort they put forth and the grades they receive. These students tend to be self-motivated and optimistic. They believe in themselves and that they can do whatever they set out to accomplish. They welcome challenges and are not afraid of change. If a student with an internal locus of control fails a test, he does not blame the teacher or the test questions. He takes responsibility for the failure, and attempts to determine what action is needed to avoid this in the future. When these students make mistakes, they endeavor to figure out what they did wrong or what they did not understand. These students don't believe that their grades are a function of luck or fate. When things go wrong, they look to see what they can do to put things right.

Students who have an external locus of control cannot see a connection between the effort they put forth in a course and the grades they receive. If they do poorly on a test or in a course, these students may focus their blame on the teacher, in their belief that the tests were too hard or the grading standards too stiff. These students tend to be pessimists who need someone to motivate them and give them a push to succeed. They believe that many of the things they want in life are out of reach or that other people are holding them back. They may be afraid of change and prefer to follow familiar routines. When they make mistakes, they blame others for being unfair or for not giving them the right information. They see themselves as victims in the drama that is their lives. When something goes wrong, they may feel there is nothing they can do about it. They forget that the way they see the problem is the problem.

Research in Positive Psychology has helped to illuminate the connection between effectiveness and locus of control. Studies (Myers, 2004; Burger, 2004) demonstrate that individuals with an internal locus of control are more likely to do the following:

- Succeed academically
- Cope better with stress
- Experience higher levels of job satisfaction
- Be happier with their lives
- Work more diligently towards long term goals
- Are more independent
- Deal more directly with marital problems
- Are more persuasive
- Successfully stop smoking
- Wear seat belts
- Use birth control (rather than depend on fate or luck for protection)

In general, people with an internal locus of control take charge in many areas of their lives and accept responsibility for the outcomes of their actions (Larson & Buss, 2002). In addition, internally oriented individuals are more disposed towards working for social and political change or causes (Levenson, 1981). In sharp contrast, those with an external locus of control are more likely to suffer from anxiety and/or depression. They tend to avoid challenges and give up when faced with obstacles or setbacks.

Three Ways to Increase Proactivity

Perhaps we have convinced you that being proactive is a skill you want to spend some time cultivating. You might be asking, "OK, but how do I go about doing that?" We have found that a useful method for increasing proactivity involves focusing on three key areas: (1) your thoughts; (2) your language; and (3) your actions. We believe that all things are created three times. First, when you think about it; second, by how you speak about it, and lastly by when you take some action to make it happen. You will find that we deal with this last aspect of the process in more depth in Chapter 7. Creating the reality of becoming a proactive individual involves a sustained focus on all three areas.

Focusing on Your Thoughts

Reactive individuals tend to be worriers. If a worrier were conscious of the direction of his or her thoughts, he or she would discover that the focus is mostly on the bad things that could possibly happen. We are not suggesting that you should not plan for the possibility of negative eventualities, but to spend most of your time doing this is clearly counterproductive. This is particularly the case if you consider that *fully 80% of what we worry about never happens!* Yet the effects on our emotional and physical health, as well as our productivity, are similar to what might have occurred if the feared event had actually happened. This topic will be dealt with in more detail in Chapters 5 and 6. Are you a worrier? Proactive people make a conscious effort to give more time for considering what might go right and how to make it go right. In other words, they are more likely to be considered optimists.

Focusing on Your Language

Have you ever heard yourself saying things like, "he made me angry," or "I couldn't make it to class, I was just too tired to get up on time?" If you have said things like this, and who among us has not, realize that you are speaking reactively. You were giving your freedom to choose away and giving someone else control of your emotions, in the first example, or letting circumstances (i.e. apparent fatigue) determine what you could or could not do, in the second example. Proactive individuals realize that they are ultimately in control of their feelings and emotions, and speak in a way that creates and reinforces this reality. So instead of, "he made me so mad," they might say, "I am angry about what so and so did." We hope the difference between these two is clear. When you say, "I am angry about what he did," *you* are in control of your response. Please don't think that this is merely semantics. Our language is one of civilized man's prominent ways of defining reality. How we speak has a profound impact on how we view the world.

Focusing on Your Actions

Increasing proactivity in this area simply requires adopting two habits: (1) making promises and keeping them; and (2) setting small goals and working to achieve them. Proactive individuals are keenly aware of the power of their word. Unfortunately, the authors have noticed that many people fail to grasp or heed this important concept. So people say things like, "I'll call you," after running into someone they haven't seen in a while, when, even at the time, they know they are highly unlikely to follow through. Or many students promise themselves that they will study for that test in plenty of time, only to, at best, end up cramming desperately at the last minute. Such behavior has the unfortunate consequence, not just that others stop believing in what you say, but more importantly, that you stop believing in yourself. We recognize that it might not be possible to keep your promises 100% of the time. You can, however, own up to it. Be willing to acknowledge the lapse and seek ways of amending it.

Most people can't wait to be successful so they can do just what they feel like doing. It is this thought, however, that can interfere with ever achieving success in the first place. The bottom line is that *effective people do the things that ineffective people don't feel like doing*. They don't feel like doing those things either, necessarily, but they want to do them out of the strength of their purpose. We strongly believe that there is a big difference between wanting and feeling. Feeling is merely a momentary desire ("I don't feel like getting out of bed"), wanting encompasses not just the present but the future consequences of the present behavior. A proactive individual acknowledges his present feeling ("I feel tired"), but decides to want to get out of bed because he wants the results of this action, like doing well in class, or keeping his promise. Now at this point you might be thinking, "This is all well and good, but it is easier said than done." You are absolutely right. As is often remarked, "Talk is cheap." But to quote an old mentor of ours, Norman Brenner, "To be effective you must be willing to do what is necessary." Perhaps even more proactively stated, "You want to be willing to do what is necessary." So what about you? What do you choose?

SELF-EFFICACY

In the Positive Psychology literature this whole notion of proactivity and locus of control is approached somewhat differently or more broadly, with what is termed **"self-efficacy,"** a perception of perceived of competence. This is one of the most heavily researched areas in positive psychology and it is an outgrowth of Albert Bandura's Social Cognitive theory. So what is self-efficacy and how does it differ, if at all, from proactivity and locus of control? Bandura (1997) defined self-efficacy as "your belief in your capability to produce a desired effect by your own actions." In a similar vein, Maddux (2005) characterized self-efficacy as "what I believe I can do with my skills under certain conditions." The bottom line is that self efficacy is all about believing that you can accomplish what you want, if you do what is necessary in order to reach a desired goal, after you first examine what is required of you in order to reach that goal. In a sense, self-efficacy represents a marriage between an internal locus of control, that is, the belief that you can control your destiny, and proactive behavior defined as making the appropriate choices and taking the necessary action steps for success. Self efficacy in many ways appears to be a dimension of effectiveness with both a cognitive component (locus of control) and a behavioral component (proactivity).

Snyder and Lopez (2007) explain that the self-efficacy model flows from Bandura's Social Cognitive theory where humans learn by modeling or copying other humans; therefore self-efficacy is a learned pattern of thinking and behaving rather than a genetically determined pattern. That is, we actively shape our lives rather than passively react to our environment (Bandura, 1986). That's the good news. You have a choice to think and behave in ways that are self-efficacious.

There are three main components to Social Cognitive theory: (1) humans can create powerful symbolic cognitive models of their experiences; (2) humans can then compare their own actions to that of their symbolic models and make course corrections if necessary; and (3) there is an interaction between those cognitive models and the environment which further shapes our personalities. In simpler terms, we can watch how someone acts in order to successfully achieve a goal, and make a mental map (i.e. model) of that and learn from it. We can then choose to copy such successful behaviors based on our mental map (i.e. modeling) which then causes interactions between our cognitions, behaviors and the environment further shaping our behavior and our personalities. These "interactions" typically revolve around whether our efforts worked out or not. If not, we continue to modify our behavior until we obtain some success or reach the desired goal.

To obtain a measure of your own level of self-efficacy, fill out the inventory on the next page developed by Fibel and Hale (1978) which assesses your expectancy of success.

The Practical Impact of Self Efficacy

Research in self-efficacy has varied depending on whether researchers measured self-efficacy in specific situations, an approach favored by Bandura, or whether they looked at a more overall (global) measure. There are a variety of questionnaires that measure self-efficacy, some from a global standpoint and others from a much more situation specific context. Snyder and Lopez (2007) summarized Bandura's (1997) research with situation

The Expectancy for Success Scale—A Measure of Self-Efficacy

Indicate the degree to which each item applies to you by circling the appropriate number, according to this key.

1 = highly improbable
2 = improbable
3 = equally improbable and probable, not sure

4 = probable
5 = highly probable

IN THE FUTURE I EXPECT THAT I WILL:

1. Find that people don't seem to understand what I'm trying to say   1 2 3 4 5
2. Be discouraged about my ability to gain the respect of others   1 2 3 4 5
3. Be a good parent   1 2 3 4 5
4. Be unable to accomplish my goals   1 2 3 4 5
5. Find my efforts to change situations I don't like are ineffective   1 2 3 4 5
6. Not be very good at learning new skills   1 2 3 4 5
7. Carry through my responsibilities successfully   1 2 3 4 5
8. Have a stressful marital relationship   1 2 3 4 5
9. Deal poorly with emergency situations   1 2 3 4 5
10. Discover that the good in life outweighs the bad   1 2 3 4 5
11. Handle unexpected problems successfully   1 2 3 4 5
12. Get the promotions I deserve   1 2 3 4 5
13. Succeed in the projects I undertake   1 2 3 4 5
14. Not make any significant contributions to society   1 2 3 4 5
15. Discover that my life is not getting much better   1 2 3 4 5
16. Be listened to when I speak   1 2 3 4 5
17. Discover that my plans don't work out too well   1 2 3 4 5
18. Find that no matter how hard I try, things just don't turn out the way I would like   1 2 3 4 5
19. Handle myself well in whatever situation I'm in   1 2 3 4 5
20. Be successful in my endeavors in the long run   1 2 3 4 5
21. Be very successful working out my personal life   1 2 3 4 5
22. Experience many failures in my life   1 2 3 4 5
23. Make a good first impression on people I meet for the first time   1 2 3 4 5
24. Attain the career goals I have set for myself   1 2 3 4 5
25. Be able to solve my own problems   1 2 3 4 5
26. Succeed at most things I try   1 2 3 4 5
27. Have difficulty dealing with my superiors   1 2 3 4 5
28. Have problems working with others   1 2 3 4 5
29. Be a good judge of what it takes to get ahead   1 2 3 4 5
30. Achieve recognition in my profession   1 2 3 4 5

Scoring: In order to calculate your total score for this inventory, first reverse the scores for the following items: 1, 2, 4, 6, 7, 8, 14, 15, 17, 18, 24, 27, and 28. That is, change a 1 to 5, a 2 to a 4, leave a 3 alone, change a 4 to a 2 and 5 to a 1. Then add up all of the scores.

The range of total scores can vary from 30 to 150. The higher your score, the greater your expectancy for success in the future, and according to Bandura's social learning and self-efficacy theory, the more motivated you will be to apply yourself in facing difficult challenges in your life. The researchers who developed this inventory (Fibel & Hale, 1978) administered this test to undergraduate students taking psychology courses and found that women's scores ranged from 65 to 143 and men's scored ranged from 81 to 138. The average score for each gender was 112 (112.32 for women and 112.15 for men).

specific measures of self-efficacy. They concluded that high levels of self-efficacy are associated with:

1. better academic performance
2. lower anxiety
3. higher pain tolerance
4. following diet and exercise regimens
5. more political participation
6. good dental hygiene
7. sticking with smoking cessation programs

Bandura pointed out that high levels of self-efficacy play a protective role in helping individuals cope with psychological problems. By virtue of what he termed enablement factors, people make choices to structure their environments in ways that increase the likelihood of positive outcomes. It is reasonable to assert that this would apply more to a global level of self-efficacy. Research supporting this comes from Maddux (1995) who demonstrated that self-efficacy is associated with successful coping with a variety of psychological problems, and DiClemente, Fairhurst and Piotrowski (1995) who found that it was an important variable in overcoming eating disorders.

Self-efficacy also plays an important role in maintaining physical health as individuals with high levels are far more likely to engage in healthy behaviors, to eliminate unhealthy ones, and to live a healthy lifestyle in terms of diet, exercise, avoidance of tobacco products, etc. Furthermore, high self-efficacy enables such individuals to maintain this lifestyle over time. This may be due to the same enablement factors which offer a protective role with psychological problems, but in this case operating within the realm of physical health. Ultimately it comes down to making wise choices and believing you have the power to control the outcomes in your life. Many of the methods utilized for helping people adopt healthier lifestyles often focus on building self-efficacy in order to accomplish this. Increasing self-efficacy does appear to improve physical health, whether the focus is on resistance to infection (O'Leary and Brown, 1995), levels of neurotransmitters in the brain that affect mood, or endorphin levels for decreasing pain (Bandura, 1977).

How to Increase Your Self-Efficacy

Bandura (1997) explained that self-efficacy develops when individuals have opportunities to:

* Experience success in similar situations and call upon those positive memories.
* Watch others who have succeeded and copy them (modeling).
* Imagine or visualize behaving effectively to reach a desired goal.
* Be reassured or persuaded by others who are trusted or have special expertise.
* Pair positive emotions with arousal to heighten their sense of competence.

Therefore, it follows that if you want to enhance your personal level of self-efficacy, it would be useful to practice the following suggestions…

- ❧ Recall in vivid detail success experiences you have had. Remember the steps you took to get there and the behaviors that led to those positive outcomes.

- ❧ Observe other people who you know who are effective and successful in various situations. Pay exquisite attention to how they behave; watch what they do that works in detail and try to make a mental map or cognitive model of their behaviors. Anyone is fair game to watch including friends, relatives, teachers, mentors, co-workers, even people you read about or see on TV. But be careful with the latter; and make sure you are watching a realistic model. Don't pick a superhero or a glamorous movie star to model yourself after because you will be setting yourself up to follow an unrealistic standard.

- ❧ Imagine yourself stepping into the picture, performing those same behaviors effectively and reaching your desired goal.

- ❧ Accept reassurance, praise and advice from those you trust or who have knowledge/expertise you do not possess. This will enhance your expectations for success.

- ❧ Maintain your sense of humor and learn to relax (See Chapter 6). This will create comfortable physiological sensations and a calm demeanor which will then help to boost your level of confidence in your abilities.

DEALING WITH IRRATIONAL SELF-TALK

To make the process of becoming proactive a doable enterprise, we thought it would be helpful for you to learn some specific strategies for modifying the way you think and the way you talk in a more proactive direction. A powerful way humans undermine their effectiveness is by doing what Albert Ellis (1975) called **catastrophizing**, when you give yourself messages that a situation is too awful or overwhelming to bear or that the worst is about to happen. These messages, also termed **self-talk** by Ellis or **automatic thoughts** by Aaron Beck (1970), refer to the running commentary that goes on in your head during the course of the day. Most of it is mundane and benign, but problems will arise when your perceptions are influenced by automatic thoughts reflecting irrational beliefs. Many studies have documented the link between irrational beliefs and anxiety (Bonner & Rich, 1991). These typically fall into two general categories: (1) beliefs that the world, someone, or something should be different; and (2) beliefs that your perceptions reflect reality rather than your subjective impressions of reality. Many times these irrational beliefs operate on a subconscious level, yet guide your emotional reactions nonetheless.

Self-talk tends to be circular in nature. Figure 2.2 illustrates this cycle. It begins with events in the environment, events that have no valence until you are there to interpret them or ascribe meaning to them. Next, we have your sensory impressions of the event (your perceptions and sensory input). This is followed by your cognitions and interpretations of your perception of events (your self-talk about the event). This may include irrational ideas or self statements. The next step is the reaction of your emotional and physical system, not so much to the events themselves, but to your interpretations (self-talk) about the events. These physical/emotional reactions then feed back into your self-talk. For example, if you are feeling disappointed or depressed because of how you have interpreted an event, this sadness will then further influence your self-talk, predisposing you to further negative cognitions. And the cycle goes on. Negative thoughts create unhappiness, and depression stimulates further pessimistic thinking.

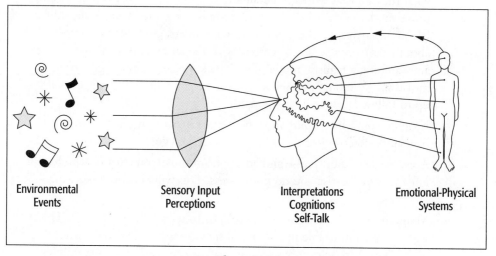

Environmental	Sensory Input	Interpretations	Emotional-Physical
Events	Perceptions	Cognitions	Systems
		Self-Talk	

Figure 2.2

At the root of all irrational thinking is the assumption that things are done to you, rather than recognizing that events happen in the world. Going back to the S-O-R model presented earlier: you experience those events (**S**); engage in self-talk about those events (**O**); and then experience an emotion (**R**) resulting from your self-talk. **S** does not cause **R**, rather it is **O** that causes **R**. If your self-talk is irrational and unrealistic, you will create negative emotions. The two common forms of irrational self-talk are: (1) statements that catastrophize; and (2) statements that revolve around absolutes. Catastrophic thinking involves expecting the worst and/or giving nightmarish interpretations of your experience (i.e. being a worrier). Thus, a momentary chest pain becomes a heart attack, your boss's bad mood means you are going to get fired, if you do poorly on a test you assume that you will fail the course. The emotions that follow such expectations are very unpleasant, but you are responding to your own description of the world. Irrational self statements involving absolutes typically include words such as "should, must, ought, always and never." Here you assume that if things are not a certain way, or if you do not conform to some standard, it is disastrous. Any deviation from that particular value or standard must be bad.

Cognitive Restructuring

A potent strategy for refuting irrational beliefs and changing your self-talk involves the use of **cognitive restructuring techniques**. The first step in this process is to attempt to identify the irrational belief that is underlying your reaction. Once you have uncovered this belief you may immediately notice the absurdity of it. Common irrational beliefs include:

1. Everyone needs to like you. It is awful if someone dislikes you.
2. You must be competent and perfect in all that you undertake.
3. Mistakes are sure proof that you are a failure.
4. You should never hurt anyone or refuse a request/favor.
5. It is horrible if things don't turn out the way you want.
6. You are helpless and have no control over your feelings or experiences.
7. You will be rejected if you don't go to great lengths to please others.
8. There is a perfect love and a perfect relationship.
9. You shouldn't have to feel pain. Life should always be fair.
10. Your worth as a human being depends on how much you achieve and produce.

The next step is to examine and challenge the irrational belief with your rational mind. Notice how so many of the irrational beliefs above revolve around a "should," or a "must," or the idea that it is catastrophic if something doesn't turn out in a particular way. Challenging irrationalities can be facilitated by asking yourself the following questions:

1. Is there any reason to think that this belief is true?
2. Is there evidence that this belief might not be true?
3. If I reject this belief, what is the worst that could happen to me?
4. If I reject this belief, what good things might happen as a result?

The third step is to substitute a new, rational belief in place of the old, irrational idea. Initially this may seem artificial, a bit phony. But replacing the negative thoughts that led to painful emotional responses with more positive and rational alternatives is a good start, even if you don't completely believe it at first. In time you will start to believe your rational thoughts, particularly after you experience improvements in your situation reflecting the change in you. The changes in your thinking patterns will become natural and comfortable after a while. As you practice reappraising your thoughts in this fashion, your brain is also establishing new habits. It has been shown in a recent fMRI study that successful cognitive restructuring is reducing activity in the amygdala, which is responsible for triggering your fear responses. Simultaneously, activity is increasing in the left frontal cortex, the area from which our thought processes originate (Ochsner et al, 2002). The area of your brain that thinks is literally calming the area of your brain that reacts in the interest of your survival. Thus, with practice, it will get easier and easier to reframe reality, and to view things from a more positive viewpoint. Cognitive restructuring does not imply that you should repress your thoughts. It is a process of acknowledging those thoughts and feelings that are reactive in nature, then examining/challenging them, and finally replacing them with more rational thoughts when appropriate. For example, the rational statements below can be substituted for each of the irrational thoughts above. These are not the only options. We invite you to create your own rational alternatives if the choices below do not fit for you. Notice that these rational statements utilize elements of reframing. Oftentimes, the process of thinking rationally involves the process of reframing, of learning to view a situation from a different, more rational, perspective.

1. It is impossible to be well liked by everyone. No one achieves that. It certainly isn't the end of the world if _____ (insert the name of the person or persons in question) doesn't like me. And, who knows, next month the situation could be totally different.

2. It is impossible to be good at everything. Besides, if I did succeed at being extremely competent in everything I did, many people would no doubt resent me.

3. Everyone makes mistakes. Mistakes can be learning experiences that lead to eventual success. "Failure" is just another word, not an enduring part of my character.

4. _____ will surely survive if I don't do things his/her way.

5. It is unfortunate if things don't turn out the way I would like, but it is hardly the end of the world and I can handle it. By this time next year I will no doubt be completely indifferent to this whole situation.

6. I *always* have a choice over how I respond to situations.

7. If I don't go out of my way to please someone there is a chance I might get rejected, but it certainly is not guaranteed. And, if I need to go to great lengths to please someone in order for that person to like me, then that individual is not someone that I care to have as a friend. I want to be liked and appreciated for who I am, not for what I can do for someone.

8. There are no perfect relationships. I will focus on making this a healthy, honest, enjoyable relationship and learn to accept the inevitable disappointments and imperfections that come up in all relationships.

9. Life isn't always fair. Feeling pain is part of being human. If I had never experienced sadness or despair I would not know what it means to be happy and content.

10. My worth as a human being is much more dependent on my capacity to be fully alive, feeling everything it means to be human, the good with the bad. My worth depends more on how I am in relation to the people who are important to me.

David Goodman (1974), in his book *Emotional Well-Being through Rational Behavior Training*, offers six rules or guidelines for rational thinking. You may find these rules to be quite useful for guiding you to think rationally and challenge your irrational beliefs.

1. **It does not do anything to me.**
   That is, the situation does not make you anxious or afraid. The things you say to yourself are what produce the negative emotions you may feel at any given moment. In the same vein, no one can make you feel anything. How you feel is always your choice. Other people may provide provocation, but ultimately, you always choose how you feel in response.

2. **Everything is exactly the way it should be.**
   The conditions for things or people to be otherwise do not exist. To say things should be different is tantamount to believing in magic. Things are the way they are because of a long series of causal events. To say things should be different is to throw out causality.

3. **All humans are fallible creatures.**
   This is an inescapable truth. If you have not set reasonable quotas of failure for yourself and others, you increase the prospects for your disappointment and unhappiness.

4. **It takes two to have a conflict.**
   Before pointing your finger in blame, consider the 30% rule. Any party to a conflict is contributing at least 30% of the fuel to keep an argument going.

5. **The original cause is lost in antiquity.**
   It is a waste of your time to try to discover who did what first. It is often impossible to find the original cause of chronic painful emotions, as such dilemmas are usually extremely complicated, and often the product of multiple interactions. The best strategy is to make decisions to change your behavior now.

6. **We feel the way we think.**
   To again quote Covey, "The way you see the problem is the problem." And what you say to yourself determines your feelings.

Correlation ≠ Causation

Irrational thinking takes other forms as well. In our attempts to make sense of our world we often make a common error in thinking by assuming that if things occur together or are associated in some way, that one must therefore cause the other. In statistical terms, when two variables tend to be reliably associated with one another, this is called a **correlation**. The greater the degree of association, the higher the correlation will be. When a correlation is present, it could be that one variable does cause or influence the other (such as in the relationship between height and weight), but this is not necessarily the case. It may be that some other factor or variable is actually influencing or causing the correlation. For example, let's take the common characterization of the bespectacled intellectual (i.e. the high IQ kid with the thick glasses). There is a reason for this stereotype. A correlation does exist between myopia (nearsightedness) and intelligence, as individuals with higher IQ's are more likely to be nearsighted. But what does this mean? Is it that being myopic somehow magically makes you smart? Or does having a high IQ somehow harm your vision (maybe from reading too many books!)? We are sure you would agree that both of these positions are totally absurd. Rather, this correlation is the byproduct of other genetic variables which are beyond the scope of this book to discuss.

Some of the studies and research cited throughout this text are correlational in nature. We advise you to be very wary of inferring any causation from the results of correlational research. Disclaimers to this nature will pop up periodically in reference to these correlational studies. It is only through controlled experimentation that we can get valid information about causation.

When combating irrational thinking, remember that just because two things occur together, that alone does not offer proof that one has caused the other. A prime example of the folly of inferring causation from correlation was found in the field of psychology. For decades it was widely thought that childhood schizophrenia was caused by the "schizophrenogenic mother," a parent who was cold, aloof and gave a child inconsistent and confusing messages. Although a correlation does exist between parenting styles and the incidence of schizophrenia, we now know that this disorder is primarily a function of a genetic, biochemical disturbance in the brain, and is not caused by cold parents. It is actually more likely that the so-called schizophrenogenic parenting style could have been in reaction to, rather than the cause of raising an emotionally troubled child.

It is also relevant at this point to alert you to be aware of the very human tendency to perceive a correlation or relationship between things that really does not exist. We call this an illusory or **spurious correlation**. If we believe there is a relationship between variables, we will likely (and unconsciously) use selective perception to detect and recall only those circumstances which confirm our belief. This is one way stereotypes and racial prejudices get ingrained. All of us fall prey to perceiving spurious correlations and using selective perception to reinforce these mistaken notions. Being aware of this tendency can help you combat this form of irrational thinking. Remind yourself that incidents that superficially appear to confirm your beliefs could just be nothing other than random coincidences.

KEYS TO EFFECTIVENESS: THE POWER OF POSITIVE THINKING

Effective individuals develop the habit of perceiving and interpreting potential problems in ways that give their life meaning and a sense of control. That is, they look for reasons to be happy and satisfied with life, imperfect as it is. They have become adept at turning lemons into lemonade and finding the proverbial silver lining in the cloud. Therefore, effective individuals are optimists and are typically more satisfied with life in general. In other words, they are happier. But it is a far cry from recommending that you adopt an optimistic outlook, or develop an internal locus of control, or follow Bobby McFerrin's advice to "Don't worry, be happy," to actually achieving all this. Martin Seligman, who spearheaded the field of positive psychology, contributed three groundbreaking books, *Learned Optimism* (1991), *Authentic Happiness* (2002), and *Flourish* (2011) where he offers valuable lessons for developing an optimistic life outlook and leading an effective, satisfying life.

OPTIMISM

Given that effective individuals are optimists, we recommend that you consciously choose to adopt optimistic perceptions. Why? Because that particular map of the world will be the most useful for helping you achieve your goals. Optimists are not necessarily unrealistic, or unwilling to accept or face negative circumstances, rather they choose to focus on what is right, rather than bemoaning all that is wrong. It is a matter of focus. They look for evidence that life is good and that they are doing all right. When misfortune strikes, as it does in everyone's life at some point, optimists recover more quickly

THE GLOBAL PERSPECTIVE–ACHIEVING GLOBAL CITIZENSHIP

What does it mean to be a **global citizen**? Consider the concept of citizenship. For many immigrants, citizenship evokes reminders of what they are not. Of the rights and privileges, along with the responsibilities, they wish to attain. It reminds them of separateness. Since we are all human beings existing on this planet, global citizenship is the reality for all of us. Rather than separateness, it is the recognition of our interconnectedness. It is the acknowledgement that, in this no longer so large sandbox we call Earth, our actions on one corner of the box invariably affects the other three corners. A global citizen "places emphasis on individual choice, in a collective setting, for the greater good." Reckmeyer, William J., *Developing Global Citizenship–Leadership for the 21st Century* (2005).

It is important, however, not to confuse interconnectedness with homogeneity. A global paradigm does not imply working towards making us all the same. On the contrary, it acknowledges our individuality and autonomy and celebrates our diversity. The power of our cultural, religious, ethnic, gender, racial, you-name-it, diversity is that it provides a rich and valuable pool of differing paradigms. As you learned last chapter, changes in perspective account for most of the greatest discoveries of our scientific era. What better to promote paradigm-shifting than numerous paradigms from which to choose and an attitude that says let's look for solutions that benefit all?

Going back to Reckmeyer's definition, global citizens value individual choice. They value what Positive Psychology describes as autonomy, not in the sense of being selfish or detached, but instead being able to be conscious of their freedom to choose. In other words, global citizens are proactive. They are aware that their life is a product of their decisions, not their conditions. And global citizens also understand that the freedom to choose must be exercised in a context, which acknowledges their obligations to others as well as to themselves. It is our greatest gift that we want to be connected with others as much as we want to be free (Deci, 1995; Ryan & Deci, 2000).

Global citizenship, then, is caring about the common good as well as our own and making choices that reflect that concern. It is about being aware of our interconnections. But it is also about choosing to be aware of our disconnections. Did you know that in 1900, the top 25% of the population enjoyed 7 times as many resources as the bottom 25%? By the year 2000, the bottom 25% had improved their lot tenfold. That is, one hundred years later, they are 10 times better than they were. However, the top 25% improved their fortune by more than 100 times, as evidenced by the following table:

Year	1900	2000
Top 25% of population	7	730
Bottom 25% of population	1	10

So the disparity between the haves and have-nots has grown. Where it used to be 7 to 1, it is now 73 to 1. And whereas in 1900 the have-nots were certainly aware that the haves were much better off, they did not have the evidence presented daily in their living rooms by television, nor heavily marketed by the media and its advertisers as something to covet.

Ultimately, however, global citizenship is about taking action. About making choices that reflect the reality that is our interconnection. It doesn't start by changing the world, but by changing ourselves. The choice is ours. How mindful are you of conserving resources such as water and energy? How well informed are you about international affairs? How tolerant are you of others' perspectives? How well do you listen? How open are you to considering other views, even when you initially disagree? What behaviors could you change that would bring you closer to global citizenship?

because they find lessons in adversity that continue to give their life meaning. But it is also essential that you differentiate between **"flexible" or "realistic" optimism** (Seligman, 1990; Schneider, 2001), and wishful thinking. Flexible optimists are people who are filled with hope but who keep their eyes open. They distinguish between what they can and cannot control and focus on the former. Optimists work on acceptance of that which is uncontrollable, while pessimists are far more likely to engage in denial about unfortunate circumstances (Carver & Scheier, 1999). Optimists simply refuse to let go of their positive expectations. Just as irrational or negative self-statements can create depression, anxiety, or other negative emotions, positive or optimistic self-statements can create and reinforce effectiveness and happiness.

In Seligman's theory of learned optimism, an optimist answers the question, "why did that bad thing happen to me?" with attributions that are *external, variable* and *specific*, unlike the pessimist who views negative events as being a product of *internal, stable* and *global* actions on his or her part. So it is an **explanatory style**, a perspective one has in dealing with the world. In simpler terms, an optimist would explain a bad event as: (1) taking into account the role of other people and the environments as causal agents (an external attribution); (2) less likely to happen again (variable) and; (3) representing just one area of life or performance and not others (a specific domain).

We encourage you to test your own level of optimism by completing the following survey developed by Scheier, Carver & Bridges (1994).

Life Orientation Test (LOT): How Optimistic Are You?

Use the following scale to respond to each question.
0 = strongly disagree   1 = disagree   2 = neutral   3 = agree   4 = strongly agree

_____1. In uncertain times, I usually expect the best.

_____2. If something can go wrong for me, it will.

_____3. I am always optimistic about my future.

_____4. I hardly ever expect things to go my way.

_____5. I rarely count on good things happening to me.

_____6. Overall, I expect more good things to happen to me than bad things.

_____ **TOTAL SCORE**

To determine your score, reverse the numbers you placed in answer to statements 2, 4 and 5 by changing 0 to 4, 1 to 3, 3 to 1 and 4 to 0, with 2 remaining at 2. Leave the remaining numbers in front of the rest of the statements unchanged. Then add up all of the updated numbers in front of all items to compute your total score. The score range is from 0 to 24 and the higher your score the more optimistic your outlook. The average score is between 14 and 15. Scores above 15 reflect higher levels of optimism.

THE BENEFITS OF AN OPTIMISTIC LIFE OUTLOOK

Research indicates that your level of optimism vs. pessimism is a powerful determining factor in your physical and emotional health. Indeed, a review of the research on happiness has consistently identified four traits manifested by happy people: (1) optimism; (2) good self esteem; (3) an internal locus of control; and (4) extroversion (Myers and Diener, 1995). Given that these were correlational studies, it is unclear whether these four personality dimensions lead to happiness or the reverse, but in any event, it is surely safe to conclude that these characteristics help to maintain happiness. The same group of researchers who developed the previous survey found that high LOT scores were highly correlated with a sense of self mastery and self esteem, and negatively correlated with depression and anxiety. Pessimism has been associated with high stress levels, depression, psychosomatic problems, higher levels of physical illness, and even premature death (Peterson, Seligman and colleagues, 1998). Likewise, where a person falls on the optimism-pessimism continuum is related to health in the future and how quickly that individual will recover from serious illness (Scheier & Carver, 1993). Optimistic new mothers are less likely to experience post partum depression (Carver & Gaines, 1987). Optimistic individuals are better able to weather major surgery, independent of the severity of their condition. This relationship has been demonstrated with heart bypass surgery (Fitzgerald, Tenner, Affleck & Pransky, 1993), and breast cancer surgery (Carver and colleagues., 1993) where LOT scores predicted both short and long term post surgical, emotional resilience.

Research with other measures of optimism other than the LOT questionnaire have yielded similar results and broader findings as well, indicating that those with optimistic explanatory styles as opposed to pessimistic explanatory styles displayed the following...

- More effective coping with life stressors (Nolen-Hoeksema, 2000)
- For men, greater overall health decades later predicted by optimism scores in college (Peterson, Seligman & Valliant, 1988)
- More productivity at work (Seligman & Schulman, 1986)
- Greater physical health (Peterson, 2000)
- Better outcomes for cardiovascular disease based on a meta-analysis of 83 studies (Rasmussen, Scheier, & Greenhouse, 2009)
- Lower vulnerability to depression (Abramson, Alloy & colleagues, 2000)
- More satisfaction in interpersonal relationships (Fincham, 2000)
- Superior athletic performance (Seligman, Nolen-Hoeksema, Thornton & Thornton, 1990)
- Stronger academic performance (Peterson & Barrett, 1987; Seligman 1998b)

Referring to the last point about stronger academic success, you might also be surprised to learn that optimism is actually a better predictor of college academic success than standard measures such as SAT scores or high school GPA's! That was exactly what researchers at the University of Pennsylvania found when they measured the optimism levels of 500 incoming college freshmen, and then compared that to their later college grades. A strikingly similar result was obtained at the University of Kansas when freshman were administered measures of their level of "hope" (a major factor in optimism). Again, hope was a better predictor of freshman grades than the usual standard measures. These researchers concluded that the student's emotional attitudes were the critical factor in academic success. Aspinwall & Taylor (1992) found that optimistic college students handled the challenges of college more successfully and reported less stress, depression, and loneliness than pessimistic students.

Impact of Optimism on History

Psychologist Chris Peterson, along with Marty Seligman and other researchers devised an intriguing method for determining whether an individual is an optimist or a pessimist by analyzing recorded comments or writing samples, based on language usage. This method can be used, after the fact, to analyze the explanatory style of historical figures and then compare it with outcomes years later, to see whether optimists really do tend to succeed more than pessimists. This approach, the Content Analysis of Verbal Explanations (or CAVE approach), has been utilized in many studies to demonstrate the power of positive thinking. Seligman, an avid baseball fan, decided to use his CAVE method to predict the outcome of the 1986 baseball season based on statements made by players and managers of all the major league baseball teams in 1985. In an enormous undertaking, he and others analyzed all of the recorded comments printed in all the hometown newspapers sports pages. In particular, they compared two evenly matched teams (regarding talent and potential for the 1986 season), the N.Y. Mets and the St. Louis Cardinals. From the CAVE analysis, it was determined that the Mets were by far the more optimistic team in 1985, especially compared to the Cardinals. In 1986 the Mets went on to win the World Series while the Cardinals finished below .500. The 1985 CAVE rating for the other major league teams, based on their optimism scores, also predicted how they finished in the standings in 1986. Seligman was so impressed with these results that he found it difficult to believe, so he redid the study in 1986 to predict for the 1987 season and got similarly impressive results. The more optimistic the team based on CAVE analysis of players and managers comments, the better they performed the following season.

Optimism appears to affect another type of competition as well, in the political arena. The professed optimism of candidates for political office often has a profound impact on their electability. A research project headed by Harold Zullow (Zullow, Oettingen, Peterson & Seligman, 1988) explored whether the optimism displayed by a presidential candidate in his acceptance speech at the nominating convention would influence the election outcome. That is, would the more optimistic candidates be more likely to win? The results indicated that in presidential elections from 1900 through 1984 the more optimistic candidate won 18 out of the 22 elections! After 1984 that relationship began to break down. Why? The campaigns found out about this finding regarding optimism and began go all out to exceed each other in appearing to be optimistic. To quote Peterson (2006)...

> Our attempts to distinguish presidential candidates based on their professed optimism has since been a total failure (e.g. Peterson & Lee, 2000). Each loudly proclaims himself to be an optimist and certainly more of an optimist than his opponent. Each says the sorts of things in speeches that end up being scored by us as hopeful. Again, I wonder if the results of our earlier study had anything to do with this new way of campaigning. Regardless the conclusion follows that, all things being equal, U.S. voters prefer an optimist over a pessimist as their leader, a conclusion consistent with the results of many other studies of every-day people leading their lives (Peterson, Maier & Seligman, 1993, p.110)

Optimism and Effectiveness

Why do optimism and hope improve effectiveness? And just how does this work, you may be wondering? First of all, when you believe that something is possible, you are more likely to take action. Optimism provides motivation. Secondly, optimism spurs perseverance in the face of obstacles; optimists are more likely to carry on because of their belief in eventual success. Seligman explains that pessimists tend to view problems as permanent (lasting forever), global (affecting everything), and internal (a result of personal incompetence or faults). This particular framework leads to feelings of helplessness, so why even bother to do anything. This refers back to his pioneering work on **learned helplessness** (Maier & Seligman, 1976; Peterson, Maier & Seligman, 1993) which is defined as the belief that nothing you can do will alter your circumstances or an outcome, therefore you totally give up. On the other hand, optimists are more likely to view their troubles as temporary, specific (applying only to one area of life), and external (due to factors other than personal incompetence). *In other words, pessimism is paralyzing while optimism is energizing.* So it comes as no surprise that optimism is associated with greater success and effectiveness whether you are a college student, an insurance salesman (Seligman & Schulman, 1986), or in any other endeavor.

There is a whole school of metaphysical thought that presumes that you create your own reality with your thoughts. If this is indeed true, then by adopting an optimistic world view you are maximizing your chances for success, happiness, and getting what you want. What have you got to lose by trying? Some of you may answer, "If I expect a positive outcome and it does not happen, then I will be disappointed." You would be a subscriber to the "don't expect anything and you will never be disappointed" philosophy of life. But if you are really honest with yourself, you will admit that even if you truly expect nothing, there's still a small part of you that hopes, and if what you hope for fails to materialize, you still end up disappointed. The problem with expecting nothing is that you might not do what is necessary to get what you want in life. There is an old saying, "If you want your ship to come in, you must go to the dock." The problem with being a pessimist is that you might not bother to go to the dock. Optimists go to the dock and find ways to enjoy their time there whether their ship comes in or not.

Some may argue that it is a lot easier to be an optimist if you are one of those people who just happen to be lucky. Well, believe it or not, whether or not you are "lucky" or "unlucky" may have more to do with whether you are an optimist or a pessimist than on random chance. Professor Richard Wiseman claims he can tell whether you are lucky or unlucky merely by handing you a newspaper and asking you to count how many photographs are in the paper! Some people finish this task in a few seconds, while others take several minutes. The difference has nothing to do with counting speed. Rather, the secret lies on the second page of the newspaper where Wiseman inserted a not so hidden message in **HUGE** one inch block letters. The message is:

STOP COUNTING – THERE ARE 43 PHOTOGRAPHS
IN THIS NEWSPAPER

Surprisingly, many people are so caught up in counting photos that they miss the headline completely – they simply fail to notice it. The headline is not a trick as there really are exactly 43 pictures in the paper. Wiseman teaches that those who notice the announcement on page two right away and stop counting tend to be "lucky" individuals who are open to random opportunities and seize them. Those who don't spot the message are more likely to be unlucky individuals who may miss out on good fortune just because they fail to see opportunities on their horizons. This brings us back to our discussion of selective attention in the first chapter. People who are more laid back and cope well with stress (who tend to have an internal locus of control) are typically more open to life's possibilities-like giant newspaper headlines unexpectedly giving you the right answer. On the other hand, unlucky people are more uptight and tend to be closed off, sometimes to potentially useful information.

To test yourself take a quick look at this domain name sometimes used by stress researchers: www.opportunityisnowhere.com. What do you see? Many people see a discouraging message that opportunity is nowhere. But other individuals see the opposite message – opportunity is now here! Lucky people perceive more of the world around them so they are more likely to see the hidden words – they are able to step out of selective attention to get a more holistic view of their environment. Wiseman (2003) writes in his book, *The Luck Factor*, "It is not that they expect to find certain opportunities, but rather that they notice them when they come across them."

Wiseman's study of lucky people led him to conclude that some people really do have all the luck, but it is a byproduct of their mindset. Lucky individuals appear to have four characteristics in common.

1. A heightened awareness of the world around them - they notice and seize upon openings that others simply miss.

2. An optimistic outlook- perseverance in the face of obstacles or failure due to a belief that things will eventually work out if you hang in there.

3. A willingness to listen to their intuition – trusting their gut feelings.

4. The special ability to turn bad luck into good fortune. This plays a vital role in survival situations. Wiseman recounted the work of Siebert (1996) who investigated what he called the "survivor personality," that is, individuals who managed to survive natural disasters or other calamities (e.g. plane crashes) where many others perished. Siebert believes that life's best survivors not only cope well, they often turn potential disasters into lucky developments.

How to Become an Optimist

Seligman offers a variety of suggestions for channeling your thinking in an optimistic direction. Many of the cognitive techniques for doing this are similar and/or identical to the cognitive restructuring methods for defusing irrational thinking. This is not surprising because in many instances pessimism is just one form of irrational thinking. Optimism is not about being unjustifiably positive about the world, but rather about learning to challenge negative thinking. Learning to think optimistically involves learning to dispute pessimistic thoughts. Seligman recommends the following four strategies for defusing negativity.

1. Look for evidence
The most convincing way of combating a negative belief is to show that it does not fit the facts, that it is clearly incorrect. Since pessimism is usually either an overreaction or dead wrong, the facts will typically be on the side of a more optimistic viewpoint. This does not mean that we are recommending that you naively repeat positive affirmations to yourself in the hope they will somehow change your life. Most educated people are too scientifically minded or skeptical to blindly believe a positive affirmation without some confirmation that it could be true. *Just repeating positive thoughts to yourself is not a guarantee of success or happiness. Rather, it is how you deal with your negativity that deter-*

mines whether optimism or pessimism will rule. In general, negative beliefs that accompany or follow adversity are almost always untrue.

Seligman offers a very useful tip for disputing pessimistic thoughts. He suggests that you challenge your negative thoughts by treating them as if they were uttered by another person whose mission in life was to undermine you, make you miserable, or push you to give up on your goals. You already, no doubt, have developed skills for arguing with others whose ideas, opinions, or accusations about you are unfounded. But chances are that you not as adept at challenging the accusations that you launch at yourself. Just because it is you putting yourself down, does not make it true. Your negative self-statements can be just as off base as those of a jealous rival. For example, let's say you fail an important exam. Common negative thoughts include assuming you are stupid, or that you can't cut it in college, or that you are destined to flunk out so why try at all. This is another example of catastrophizing, of picking the worst possible alternative from all the possibilities. One of the most effective techniques is to look for evidence pointing to the distortions in your disastrous explanation of events or catastrophic expectations of what will occur. Evidence to the contrary might include the fact that you got a B on a test last week; that failing one test does not necessarily mean that you will fail every test or flunk out in general. Our professors in graduate school continually reminded us to *never generalize from one piece of data.* You could also remind yourself that even smart people can have a bad day and do poorly at times.

2. Generate other alternatives

Most things that happen in life have multiple causes rather than just one cause. Most things that will happen in your life are a product of interactions among many factors. It is useful to keep this truism in mind. Pessimists make a habit of latching onto one cause and one cause only, and typically it is the worst of all the possible causes. They usually pick the cause that it is the most *permanent, pervasive* and *personal.* Challenging this typically has reality on its side. To effectively challenge your negative thoughts look for all the possible alternatives. What else could have caused the situation? What else could happen as a result? Focus on what is *changeable,* what is *specific* and what is *nonpersonal.* Returning to our failed exam example, you could focus on the fact that you didn't study hard enough (a condition that is changeable), that the exam was unusually hard (a specific instance that may not repeat in the future), and that the rest of the students also fared poorly (a nonpersonal explanation for your poor grade). You may have to work hard to generate alternatives, and you may not be thoroughly convinced they are accurate. But the process of searching for alternatives (reframing) trains you to think differently, and oftentimes you will come up with an alternative that makes a lot more sense than your worst case scenario. But you have to look for the alternatives to get to that place. Latching onto the worst possible alternative and stopping there is a sure fire recipe for undermining your effectiveness.

3. Realistically assess the implications

What do you do if the facts are not on your side, if your negative belief turns out to be true? In that case you need to use a technique called decatastrophizing. Ask yourself what the implications are if your belief is true. Generate a variety of alternatives. Challenge the most negative alternatives by asking yourself just how likely those implications really are. For example, let's say that you haven't just failed an exam, but that you are actually in danger of flunking out of college altogether. What does this mean? Is it a catastrophe which guarantees that you will never get a good job, that you will be a failure in life? The answer, of course, is no. Having a college degree certainly helps, but with the right attitude and willingness to do what is necessary, anyone can succeed, even without a college degree. This is not to say that flunking out is a good thing, but it is also *not the end of the world*. Other people have gone on to success without making it through college. For example, look at Bill Gates of MicroSoft fame! Even if you flunk out of college, this does not preclude you from coming back at a later time and being successful. And, in addition, you need to remind yourself that flunking out is not a foregone conclusion. You have some choice in the matter depending on how seriously you take your studies from this point forward.

4. Evaluate usefulness

Occasionally there are situations where the consequences of holding a belief are potentially more problematic than the belief itself, true or not. You need to evaluate whether the belief is potentially dangerous. For example, if you truly believe you are stupid, even if you are not a rocket scientist, the damage to your self-esteem could be heavy. There are other instances when the best strategy is to distract yourself from a belief rather than taking time to challenge it. This is the case when negative thoughts interfere with your performance. Engaging in negative thinking or the evaluation of such is not useful in a situation where you need to perform now. Distracting yourself and focusing on the task at hand is the most useful response.

Other Tips for Becoming Optimistic

When faced with adversity optimists typically follow the steps outlined below:

- Face the problem squarely. Pessimists tend to avoid dealing with problems because of their negative expectations.

- Develop a plan. Optimists create specific plans to deal with situations.

- Accept the reality of the situation. Contrary to popular belief, optimists are realists. It is just that they expect (and thus are more likely to get) positive results or the eventual resolution of the situation. It is this hopeful belief that allows optimists to persevere.

- Learn to grow from adversity. Optimists make the best of a bad situation and are cognizant of the personal growth they can experience as a result. Pessimists cannot see the value in adversity and typically quit trying because they only expect negative results. The section on Stress Hardiness characteristics in Chapter 6 explores this in more detail.

The Limits of Optimism

At this point you may be wondering whether optimism has limits, or whether a person can be overly optimistic to an unrealistic degree? Of course the answer is yes. An unbounded optimism not tied to reality can and will have costs and could be dangerous. For example, Weinstein (1989) reflected on how people often underestimate their personal risk for illness, accidents or mishaps, sometimes carrying an unrealistic aura of

THE GLOBAL PERSPECTIVE—Growing Inequality

Earlier you learned about the growing gap between the haves and have-nots in our world. But that growing inequality is not solely apparent when comparing so called third-world countries with those of the industrialized West. It is happening right here in America. Following the Great Recession of 2008-2009 many American families were worse off than they were just thirty years ago. Jobs were lost, home values plummeted, and savings, including those meant for retirement, got depleted for many middle class Americans. Yet even given the Great Recession, the US Economy is much larger that it was in 1980. But if the average American is not better off, who is? It appears that the increase in wealth has been enjoyed primarily by the very rich. The latest data reveals that by 2007 the top 1% of earners in America received 23% of the nation's total income. By comparison, in 1980 they enjoyed only 8% of the total. That means that in less than 30 years the gap between the 1% and the rest of the 99% has tripled in size! (Wilkinson & Picket, 2010) It is this growing inequality that has spurred movements such as Occupy Wall Street.

A similar trend is evident when comparing CEOs of major American corporations with their average workers. During the 1950s and 1960s, the top administrators in major American companies earned about 25 to 30 times the salary of a typical worker. By 1980, the difference had increased to 40. Just a decade later it had swollen to 100. By 2007, just before the Great Recession, the gap had bulged so that the CEOs were making about 350 times what the typical worker earned. To make the comparison a bit more vivid, in the 1950's if a typical worker made, say, $20,000 a year, his top boss was making $500,000. By 2007, if that typical worker was earning the same $20,000, his chief was bringing in 7 million dollars.

But is this growing gap inherently negative? It appears that at least in our perception of fairness it is. Research has evidenced that people would rather take a cut in pay as long as everyone else was taking a similar cut, than get a raise in pay if others were getting an even higher raise. Imagine you received a totally unexpected inheritance of one million dollars. You are really surprised as you were not aware your parents had amassed that much savings. You call your sister to discuss this, mentioning how surprised you are that your parents left you that much money and she excitedly responds, "Yes, I was blown away, ten million dollars!" How would you feel? What would you think?

What about society in general? Does the growing inequality lead to negative consequences? In their book, *The Spirit Level*, Richard Wilkinson and Kate Pickett present persuasive evidence that income inequalities are at the core of a wide range of health and social problems in society. They affect the level of trust among members, the percentage of mental illness, life expectancy and infant mortality, obesity, children's educational performance, teenage births, homicides, imprisonment rates, and social mobility.

Let's consider social mobility as an example. In the United States having the right parents increases your chances of ending up middle to upper middle class by a factor of three to four. In countries where the gap has not ballooned as it has here, including Canada, Australia, the Nordic nations and even Germany and France, the ability to climb up the economic ladder is much more favorable. While 42% of American men with fathers in the bottom fifth of the earning curve remain there, only 25% of Danes and Swedes do and only 30% of Britons do. Isabel Hawkins, co-director of the Brookings Institution's Center on Children and Families described it aptly when she said, "When the rungs on the ladder are further apart, it's harder to climb up them" (2009). Based on the data they present, Wilkinson and Pickett show that greater equality benefits not just the poor, but all occupational levels.

> Having come to the end of what higher material living standards can offer us, we are the first generation to have to find other ways of improving the real quality of life. The evidence shows that reducing inequality is the best way of improving the quality of the social environment, and so the real quality of life, for all of us … this includes the better-off.

What do you think?

invulnerability. When asked to estimate their risk for such mishaps, most individuals rate themselves as below average in risk for most maladies in comparison to their peers. This, "it won't happen to me" mindset is very pervasive and sometimes leads people to neglect their health, postpone eliminating bad habits (such as quitting smoking), or to overlook safety precautions that make accidents more likely. Just about every one of us has fallen prey to this false sense of safety at some point. Yes, even you! Unrelenting optimism that avoids caution and conservation of resources can prevent you from contingency planning or coping adequately with setbacks. Peterson and Park (1998) found that although optimists are more likely to achieve positive outcomes as a result of their positive expectations, they are also likely to underestimate the likelihood of future bad events (Peterson and deAvila, 1995). There are lessons to be drawn here. For example, just because you believe in yourself and your ability to get a good job and earn a good living doesn't mean you should spend every penny in your savings, if you are fortunate enough to have money saved at this time.

Even when optimism is reality based, you still should be careful not to let optimism blind you into over-confidence to the point where you do not plan adequately for success. Believing you will succeed in college will help you immensely to reach your goal, but that does not mean that you do not need to study. Belief in your ability alone will not get the job done. That is where self-efficacy comes in. A great recent example of this is in the 2008 Democratic presidential primary race where Hillary Clinton's intensely optimistic belief that she would win the Democratic nomination handily prevented her campaign team from developing a workable campaign plan. As a result they were outmaneuvered, outsmarted and out-campaigned by a very prepared Barack Obama. By the time Hillary realized she needed to shift her strategy, it was too late as she was too far behind in the all important delegate count. Although Hillary had ample reason to be optimistic, as she was the clear front runner touted by the press as the "inevitable nominee," it was still unrealistic for her to expect to coast to victory without a plan. Since perhaps Senator Clinton did not seriously entertain the thought of losing, she and her team never prepared any contingency plans and were caught unprepared. *The moral of this story is that optimism without self-efficacy is a recipe for ineffectiveness.*

Is It Possible to Be High on Both Optimism and Pessimism?

Optimism is not simply the absence of pessimism. Optimism and pessimism are typically thought to be mutually exclusive, but surprisingly there is ample evidence that they are not! Some individuals expect both good and bad outcomes to be plentiful. Other people compartmentalize and are very optimistic in some situations and very pessimistic in other circumstances. This ability to be simultaneously optimistic and pessimistic is often observed in Eastern cultures and in Asian Americans, and is addressed in the following sections. Realistic optimists recognize that bad outcomes are possible and at times probable, even though they expect to weather the difficult circumstances, and survive and thrive, nonetheless. So it is not that realistic optimists expect that nothing bad will ever befall them; they just believe that they have the wherewithal to cope with life's vicissitudes and surmount obstacles.

Defensive Pessimism

If we consider the cautionary tale of how Hillary Clinton lost the 2008 Democratic nomination battle, this is where the strategy of **defensive pessimism** comes into play. In most cases an optimism outlook will maximize your chances for success. However, it turns out that things are a bit more complicated than that. For certain types of people in certain situations, a strategic type of pessimism may actually prove to be more effective! Defensive pessimism can be defined as a strategy that anticipates a negative outcome and then takes steps to avoid that outcome. This is based on the work of psychologist Julie Norem (2001) and presented in her fascinating book, *The Positive Power of Negative Thinking: Using Defensive Pessimism to Harness Anxiety and Perform at Your Peak.* The most intriguing thing about her work is that she has demonstrated through a series of controlled experiments that defensive pessimists are just as successful as what she terms strategic optimists, but both groups do worse if their normal strategies for effective performance are disrupted. That is, if you interfere with a defensive pessimist's ability to perform last minute worrying and over preparation to counteract such ruminations, then her performance will suffer as a result. By the same token, if you prevent an optimist from spending her last moments relaxing before an anxiety provoking task, then her performance will also diminish.

Norem's signature contribution was to distinguish between defensive pessimism and **dispositional pessimism**, as well as to articulate the role of anxiety in this process. Defensive pessimists are those who are anxious about outcomes in their future. They tend to plan to diminish the anxiety generated by all their *"what if"* questions and worries. Many times their over preparation comes in very handy which tends to reinforce it. On the other hand, dispositional pessimists are negative thinkers in general, based on their thoughts about the past, and they are the subjects of most negative thinking studies. With regard to the role of anxiety, Norem took into consideration the fact that people tend to vary widely in their baseline anxiety levels, as well as their susceptibility to spikes or reactivity in their anxiety levels.

According to Norem's research, she estimates that approximately 25-30% of Americans consistently utilize defensive pessimism as a coping mechanism, while 30% consistently use strategic optimism. The other 40-45% vacillate, making use of both. Nationality and culture also influence which predominates. In America, optimism is favored as a cultural ideal while in Asia defensive pessimism is more the norm and the ideal.

Her research (Norem & Cantor, 1986) demonstrated that for anxious individuals who routinely used defensive pessimism, disrupting this pattern or instilling more positive expectations actually hindered their performance. The bottom line is that for those people, worrying and preparing (even to point of over preparation) constitutes a more effective approach in terms of later performance. In one study, the defensive pessimists' typically low expectations for success on a test were artificially manipulated by giving them false feedback to lead them to believe they would score really well. Norem hypothesized that the group led to have higher expectations would become complacent and abandon their typical success strategies. True to her predictions, the group with inflated expectations performed worse than a defensive pessimist group whose expectations had not been modified.

In another experiment, defensive pessimists and optimists engaged in a dart throwing activity and were divided into three groups. Group 1 engaged in a coping imagery exercise where they imagined something going wrong (impaling someone with a dart) and how to prevent this mishap. Group 2 visualized themselves throwing darts perfectly (mastery) and Group 3 did a relaxation exercise. True to form, the defensive pessimists performed best after engaging in coping imagery and performed worst after relaxing. The reverse was true for the optimists who performed best after relaxing (their preferred strategy) and worst after visualizing the worst case scenarios and how to fix them.

In yet another exploration of how worry helps or hinders defensive pessimists, Norem devised an experiment where she provoked anxiety in subjects prior to a performance task, but prevented them from engaging in their usual coping strategy of worrying and preparing by distracting them with busywork. The outcome was that those who were distracted from worrying performed significantly worse than those who were allowed to engage in defensive pessimistic mechanisms.

"Worries, Norem concluded, are exactly what defensive pessimists need on their minds. Trusting in their abilities by setting high expectations or distracting themselves by 'thinking good thoughts' or staying busy can hinder their performance" (Stewart, 2002). Although defensive pessimists report higher anxiety levels prior to performance situations than optimists because of their worries, afterwards they report equally successful outcomes as their optimistic peers. So it seems that the road to success or effective performance is just different for those with higher anxiety levels. The question arises as to what would happen if defensive pessimists learned other methods for lowering anxiety (such as the methods explicated in Chapter 6), but that is a question open for future research.

Norem's work, while superficially contradicting many of the findings and claims of positive psychology, can be reconciled within the positive psychology framework. Defensive pessimism certainly fits within positive psychology because it can lead to better performance and personal growth (Paul, 2011). Norem herself argues that defensive pessimists have been inappropriately associated with other negative thinkers. Because defensive pessimists report high anxiety levels and appear to be pessimistic on the surface, they tend to be lumped in with dispositional pessimists, those who have an overall pessimistic explanatory style in general. Defensive pessimists typically are not dispositional pessimists, according to Norem. She claims that when anxiety is statistically factored out of the pessimism studies, the defensive pessimists turn out to be no more pessimistic than the strategic optimists.

Thus defensive pessimism is an effective coping mechanism for individuals who tend to be of moderate to high anxiety. It is a strategy that is not recommended for individuals who are not prone to anxiety. But we can begin to see here where realistic or strategic optimism, self efficacy (which contains an optimism component) and defensive pessimism lie on a continuum of sorts. Which alternative to pick depends on your personality makeup, anxiety level, and the reality of the situation that you may face. But in any event, Norem's work helps to bring a broader dimension to this discussion.

The Ehrenreich Error

Despite the plethora of scientific evidence for the beneficial effects of optimism on physical health, emotional well-being, performance and even luck, not all scientists are enamored of the value of an optimistic paradigm. One notable critic, Barbara Ehrenreich (2009), argues that what is needed is not optimism but realism, and she goes on to assert that optimism can be down right harmful. For example, she blames the "tyranny of positive thinking" and the nation's "reckless optimism" for the poor decisions leading up to the war in Iraq and the economic crash. For the latter, the unwise choices made by lenders and individuals were due to unrealistically rosy expectations that housing prices would never plummet. She asserts that individuals with serious illnesses (Ehrenreich herself is a breast cancer survivor) need to accept the reality of their illness. She complains that optimism just sugar coats the situation and promotes denial. However, when drawing those conclusions she cherry-picked the research literature on optimism, citing only those studies where an optimistic outlook was not helpful.

In what he refers to as the *"Ehrenreich error,"* Seligman (2011) demolishes her argument by pointing out that she confuses optimism that does not influence reality with optimism that can influence reality. To understand this point we must momentarily digress to distinguish between two types of reality. **Nonreflexive reality** is not influenced by the thoughts, expectations, desires or wishes of humans. For example, our weather on a given day is an independent reality. If a hurricane is coming your way, your expectations will not influence the path of the storm, and if it is forecast to come in your direction you are well advised to heed reality, prepare or evacuate if necessary. **Reflexive reality**, on the other hand, is influenced by and sometimes even directly determined by our beliefs, perceptions and expectations. Self fulfilling prophecies are a great example of this. For instance, if you want to ask your boss for a raise, if you truly believe that you deserve it and can make a strong case, your chances of success are much greater than if you think it is a long shot. Your demeanor in asking for the raise, based on your expectations, will affect your outcome. To quote Seligman:

> ...In the case of whether there will be a total eclipse of the sun viewable from Philadelphia next year, my hopes have no influence. However, in the case of future price of stocks, investors' optimism and pessimism strongly influence the market. Enhrenreich ... ignores the enormous number of reflexive realities in which what a person thinks and feels goes on to influence the future. The science of positive psychology is entirely about such reflexive realities. (pg. 235-236)

Ehrenreich assumes that all reality is nonreflexive, therefore optimism is useless at best and delusional at worst. Flexible or realistic optimism takes into account that our outlook does not affect every aspect of reality and in some cases the best approach is cold eyed realism without denial. However, how one chooses to deal with the aftermath of any nonreflexive situation (like the weather, or injuries sustained from an accident, or a cancer diagnosis) ultimately becomes a reflexive reality where optimism is proven to facilitate coping, healing and success.

Balancing Optimism and Pessimism

Annie Paul (2011) reports that as positive psychology matures, it is moving away from a one-size fits-all optimism. The key is to use optimism and pessimism strategically to match your mind-set to the demands of the situation. If you are job hunting, for example, it will behoove you to be as optimistic as possible, as that will definitely increase the likelihood you will be hired (Kaniel, Massey, & Robinson, 2010). Nevertheless, be wary of overconfidence when you have been successful before and have a realistic expectation of a repeat performance. Utilizing defensive pessimism in this situation, that is, imagining what could go wrong and developing contingency plans, could help you avoid potential pitfalls. Paul reminds us that those who excel in using defensive pessimism are often very dynamic, successful individuals. In the same vein, in some situations (when bad news is likely to be delivered) bracing yourself for a potential negative outcome (i.e. expecting the worse) can have the positive psychological effect of helping you cope better because you are not blindsided. Even Seligman, while still advocating optimism, warns us to link positive thinking with reality testing, to rigorously check the results of our efforts to prevent overly positive expectations from leading us astray.

Cross-Cultural Considerations

Non-Western cultures may not necessarily share the same perspectives or explanatory styles (such as optimism) or express them in the same way as in the United States. And we must be careful about over generalizing results based on research with subjects, often overwhelmingly from a Caucasian American background, which may not generalize to other cultures beyond our shores or even to other cultures or subcultures within our country.

For example, there has been research comparing optimism in Western and Eastern cultures. Lee and Seligman (1997) found that Asian Americans and Caucasian Americans had similar levels of optimism but mainland Chinese students studying here were less optimistic. Chang (1996a) found that Asian American were not less optimistic but were more pessimistic, but their higher levels of pessimism were also associated with greater levels of problem solving. This appears to be a function of what Norem refers to as defensive pessimism. So according to Chang (2001a), "what works for Asians relative to Caucasian Americans simply might be different, not necessarily more effective." We cannot assume that Western based measures and theories will always translate or apply to Eastern cultures.

POSITIVE PSYCHOLOGY EXERCISES:

1. The next time you find yourself feeling anxious or depressed, look deeper into yourself, and determine whether there are any irrational thoughts fueling your feelings. Look at the list of irrational thoughts and check whether any of your unconscious cognitions are a close match. If so, follow the three step cognitive restructuring technique to counteract those irrational messages.

2. Identify that area of your life about which you are most pessimistic. Experiment with the techniques presented for thinking optimistically and notice how you are able to shift your perceptions or expectations in a more optimistic direction.

3. Think of a situation where it would behoove you to adopt a mindset of defensive pessimism in order to cope in the most effective fashion.

KEY TERMS

Determinism	Self–Talk	Optimism
Free Will	Cognitive Restructuring	Pessimism
Psychoanalytic Theory	Catastrophizing	Behaviorism
Correlation	Hallucinations	Existentialism
Spurious Correlation	Humanism	Schizophrenia
Cognitive-Behaviorism	Psychotic Episode	Delusional Thinking

Concordance Rates External Locus of Control Internal Locus of Control
Proactivity Self-Efficacy Dispositional Pessimism
Global Citizen Defensive Pessimism Reflexive reality
Explanatory Style Locus of Control Non-reflexive reality
Learned Helplessness

CHAPTER 2 QUESTIONS

Short-Answer Questions

1. The _____ theory of personality claims that you are who you are because of your upbringing.
2. The _____ theory of personality claims that you are who you are because of your learning history.
3. The existentialists epitomize the concept of _____.
4. Effective individuals are typically _____.
5. Students who take responsibility for their performance on a test have an _____ locus of control.
6. Students who blame the teacher if they do poorly in a course have an _____ locus of control.
7. Individuals who are not proactive (i.e. reactive) tend to have an _____ locus of control.
8. When you combine locus of control and proactivity you get _____-_____.
9. Social Cognitive theory asserts that humans learn by _____ other humans.
10. The two common forms of irrational self-talk are statements that _____ and statements that involve _____.
11. ____% of what we worry about never happens.
12. Proactive individuals typically have an _____ outlook.
13. A reliable relationship between variables is termed a _____.
14. Levels of _____ are a better predictor of college academic success than SAT scores or high school GPA's.
15. Defensive pessimists need to _____ and _____ in order to perform at their best.
16. History shows that the most _____ political candidates typically win elections.
17. The Ehrenreich error confuses _____reality with _____reality.

Essay Questions

1. What is the main difference between Determinism and Free Will?
2. Which theory of human behavior is the most deterministic and why?
3. What drives mankind according to the Humanistic theorists?
4. Differentiate the Cognitive-Behaviorists from the strict Behaviorists.
5. What are the characteristics of a proactive student?
6. What are the three areas that you need to focus on in order to increase your proactivity?
7. According to Bandura, what steps would you follow in order to increase your level of self-efficacy?
8. Describe the three steps of cognitive restructuring.
9. Explain whether causation can be inferred from correlation.
10. How does optimism differ from repeating positive affirmations to yourself?
11. Explain how pessimism is incompatible with proactivity.
12. What is the difference between flexible/realistic optimism and wishful thinking?
13. Describe the difference between how pessimists and optimists perceive and interpret reality.
14. Describe your favorite strategy for promoting an optimistic outlook.
15. How does defensive pessimism differ from dispositional pessimism?
16. What is the difference between nonreflexive and reflexive reality as related to the effects of optimism?

3

Experiencing Positive Emotions

When it comes to flourishing as a human being, what often takes center stage is our ability to feel **positive emotions**. In particular, to be able to know what it is to be happy and to experience an enduring sense of well-being. For many of us, this is a dream, a goal that is never quite fulfilled, or a peak moment that is short lived, evanescent, or gone with the wind. One of the core elements of flourishing is the study of positive emotions (the P in PERMA) and how to develop them more fully. This mission purports not only to understand how and why individuals experience the range of positive emotions, but also to enable positive psychologists to guide individuals like you to maximize your ability to find and develop happiness, and all the other positive emotions available to you in your life. Although the right to the "pursuit of happiness" is guaranteed to all Americans by the Declaration of Independence, the scientific study of such had been meager until the advent of positive psychology.

If we consider the lessons of the previous two chapters as we embark upon an exploration of positive emotions, it raises many interesting questions. Do positive attitudes such as optimism generate positive emotions? Or do positive emotions generate positive attitudes? Or is it a little bit of both? Are some people naturally happier than others? Are some people born smiling with a perpetually sunny disposition, while others are born with a more melancholic bent? And if this is so, is there anything we can do to offset or affect this in a positive direction? Is your level of happiness related to how satisfied you will be with your life later on? Is your level of happiness related to how effective you will be in your personal life, in your relationships, or in your career? These are complex questions, but research and data in positive psychology are beginning to provide us with some intriguing and helpful answers.

For example, were you aware that there are two very different kinds of smiles? One type of smile is referred to as a "**Duchenne smile**" (named after its discoverer, Guillame Duchenne), which is a full face smile where not only your mouth turns up, but the corners of your eyes crinkle, as well. That is, you smile with your eyes as well as with your mouth. It is that kind of authentic, from the heart smile that is hard to fake. It can often be infectious, coming across as warm, friendly, and inviting to others. The other smile, with the mouth only, does not involve the eyes. It is often perceived as an insincere, polite, or half-hearted smile. Researchers Lee Anne Harker and Dacher Keltner (2001) analyzed 114 female high school yearbook photos from 1958 and 1960 and rated these photos on the degree to which the subjects displayed a Duchenne smile on a scale of one to ten. These particular women were chosen because they had already been subjects in a long term longitudinal study of life events (Helson, 1967); therefore mounds of data had been previously collected on them including marital status, marital satisfaction and over-all happiness levels. The extent to which the women displayed the Duchenne smile in their high school photos strongly predicted their marital and life satisfaction decades later. Interestingly, their level of physical attractiveness was not related to how satisfied they were later on, either in their marriages or in their lives, nor was it related to the extent of their Duchenne ratings (Argyle, 2001). Was there something about how those with that special smile viewed the world that enabled them to maintain a sense of well-being? Were those with Duchenne smiles just so pleasant to be around that they drew positive people and events toward themselves, like magnets? When writing this section one of the authors had an interesting realization…

Courtesy of Alex Wong/Getty Images.

I'm one of those political junkies who like to watch all of those MSNBC news shows with the talking heads pontificating endlessly about politics. My favorite "pundit" who often appears on these programs is a Washington Post columnist named Eugene Robinson. Mr. Robinson is an erudite, humorous, interesting fellow whose views I typically agree with, but the same could be said for many of the pundits who regularly appear. Yet for some reason that I never understood before, I always got very excited and felt really good whenever he would appear on the TV screen, but not for any of the others. I always felt "happy" to see his face, and I actually looked forward to seeing him. It wasn't until I was writing this piece that I figured out my fascination with Eugene – he has the most incredible Duchenne smile I have ever seen. Just seeing his smile brightens my mood. His happy face is contagious.

THE ROLE OF POSITIVE EMOTIONS

Why address the importance of happiness in a book about effectiveness? Barbara Fredrickson's (1998) theory about the function of positive emotions sheds light on this. In a nutshell, Fredrickson posits that positive emotions serve an indispensable evolutionary purpose. Fredrickson put forth the *broaden and build theoretical framework* to explain the wide ranging, beneficial effects of positive emotions on humankind. Fredrickson points out that while negative emotions serve the important purpose of alerting us to danger, positive emotions let us know when we are safe. Positive emotions let us know when the coast is clear to engage in activities geared for the future. Therefore, we are free to "**broaden and build**" upon our existing skills, because we don't need to focus on fighting for survival in the present moment. Thus the evolutionary reward for positive emotions is in the future, pushing our adaptation in ways that enhance our abilities and our knowledge.

Fredrickson has helped to validate her theories with a variety of research studies which flesh out aspects of her theoretical perspective. For example, Fredrickson and

Branigan (2005) exposed college student subjects to short film clips designed to induce different emotional states such as anger, anxiety or opposite emotions such as amusement or contentment. The subjects were then given a visual processing task requiring them to match visual stimuli. These same subjects could choose between a higher order, global (big picture) strategy or a lower order (small details) strategy to approach the task. The subjects who spent time watching a video that elicited positive feelings were significantly more likely to utilize the global, big picture approach to problem solving. This is typical of Fredrickson's experimental findings, which demonstrate that positive emotions lead to broader attention, greater working memory, enhanced verbal fluency and increased open-mindedness, all of which facilitate problem solving, learning and adaptability; therefore, positively influencing effectiveness.

Fredrickson (2000) also experimentally demonstrated that joyful emotions led to expanded concepts of what people would be willing to do at a given moment in time, eliciting a "broadening" of their behavioral repertoires. Negative emotions had the opposite effect, effectively shutting down ideas and actions, and therefore constricting what individuals were willing to do. Joy also makes it more likely that we will behave in positive or caring ways towards others and build good relationships. From an evolutionary standpoint, joy was also very important because it induced playfulness (Frijda, 1994). Play has always been adaptive in the acquisition of resources and the development of skill sets, especially for youngsters.

Fredrickson also expanded her theory to encompass what she termed an **undoing** component. She proposed that positive emotions can literally function as an antidote to undo the physiological effects of negative emotions. This was demonstrated in two studies (Fredrickson, Mancuso, Branigan & Tugade, 2000 and Tugade & Fredrickson, 2004). In these experiments subjects were given an anxiety provoking task (told to hurriedly prepare a speech that they would later have to present and be rated upon) while hooked up to a variety of psychophysiological monitors to measure their arousal levels. Then each subject was shown one of four different videos. Two of the films elicited positive emotions, one film invoked sadness, and the last one was neutral. The undoing hypothesis was supported as the subjects who watched either of the positive videos produced significantly more rapid reductions in arousal (i.e. faster cardiovascular recovery) back to a normal state than those who watched the neutral video or the sad video. Clearly, the positive emotional state created by the videos offset or undid the anxiety created by the difficult task.

Fredrickson's work is especially important because of its relevance beyond the research lab or the theories taught in a classroom. These results match what we all know from common sense or can observe about what works well for coping in real life stressful situations. We all know how keeping your sense of humor and maintaining an optimistic outlook, even in the face of difficulty, are invaluable. Or to quote Christopher Peterson (2006), "I also suspect that broaden and build theory strikes a special chord among those of us who were told during school or maybe yesterday at work not to have so much fun."

Given the potential for positive emotions to undo the damage from negative emotional states, Fredrickson and Losada (2005) further theorized that optimal mental health or flourishing is associated with positive emotions. They even came up with an equation they say reflects and predicts human flourishing based on extensive data collected on undergraduate participants who provided mental health data for research purposes. The research team determined that there is a ratio of approximately 2.9 to 1 positive to negative emotions as the "magic ratio" which predicts human flourishing. And this certainly makes sense. When happy, our intellectual, physical, and social resources expand, and can build reserves to draw upon in times of stress. Interpersonal relationships are more likely to flourish in a positive emotional climate, improving the likelihood of propagation, and therefore the survival of our species. Happy people are more empathic and helpful to others which can also promote survival. Unlike negative emotions which tend to constrict our thinking, positive emotions promote flexibility, tolerance, creativity and openness to new perspectives. A variety of experiments on functional fixedness, as described in Chapter 1, validated that people are more creative and quicker when solving problems after a positive emotional state has been established. Estrada, Isen and Young (1997) also provided evidence that positive emotions can help boost decision making skills by maximizing openness to problem solving options. This was demonstrated in a well known study with physicians who were divided into two groups. One group of doctors received a gift which contained a bag of candy while the other group of doctors did not receive a gift. Although the doctors were not permitted to eat the candy, the gift recipients displayed superior reasoning and decision making compared to the doctors who didn't receive any candy. The candy group did not jump to conclusions and were more cautious, even though they arrived at correct diagnoses sooner. Theoretically, the positive feelings engendered from receiving the gift, even though it had not been consumed, enabled those physicians to function more skillfully on that day. These results suggest you should bring a candy bar with you at your next doctor appointment to maximize the care you receive! All kidding aside, when in a good mood we typically think clearer and use better judgment. Thus positive emotion has survival value and also clearly facilitates our effectiveness. This text will offer you many paths toward a more effective life, as obviously there are many avenues to becoming all that you can be. Learning to maximize your positive emotions is an enjoyable and essential road that you do not want to miss. To quote Seligman (2002):

> ...positive psychology takes seriously the bright hope that if you find yourself stuck in the parking lot of life, with few and only ephemeral pleasures, with minimal gratifications, and without meaning, there is a road out. This road takes you through the countryside of pleasure and gratification, up into the high country of strength and virtue, and finally to the peaks of lasting fulfillment, meaning and purpose. (p. xii)

Positive emotions contribute not only to the propagation of our species, but to longevity as well. A long term study of the happiness and longevity of nuns (who all live a very similar lifestyle in terms of living circumstances, diet, medical care, and social support) showed that the best predictor of health and long life was the amount of positive emotions expressed in their writings over the years. A full 90% of the most cheerful nuns lived to be at least age 85, while only 34% of the least cheerful sisters made it into old age (Danner, Snowdon & Friesen, 2001). The researchers painstakingly ruled out all other factors in accounting for this remarkable result. Even more remarkable was the fact that the happiest nuns outlived the least happy by an average of ten years! To put that into context, consider the fact that non-smokers outlive smokers an average of seven years, a considerable difference of time but still three years less than the effect of happiness. Does this mean that happiness is a more potent variable in longevity than abstinence from tobacco products?

> "So, what can you tell from a personal statement? If you focus on the happiness expressed, you can tell whether someone will have a long life… We can suspect that these effects were not wrought by magic but rather by their mundane day-to-day activities, with the happy women slowly building good lives one smile and one word at a time….I will conclude that happiness is not just a feeling in the moment but an important influence on the future." (Peterson, 2006, p. 77)

Another study (Abel & Kruger, 2010) found a relationship between the Duchenne smile and longevity. The researchers examined old issues of the Baseball Register, analyzing photos of 230 players. They found that on average, the guys with big smiles lived 4.9 years longer than the players with partial smiles, and a full 7 years longer than the men with serious facial expressions.

Positive emotions and emotional style are related to many aspects of health including susceptibility to the common cold (Cohen, 2003). These researchers discovered that those who scored low on positive emotional style were three times more likely to catch a cold than those who scored high after the subjects were administered a shot of rhinovirus.

Happiness pays other major physical and emotional dividends as well. When compared to unhappy people, happy individuals are more productive at work and have higher incomes, are more tolerant, creative, decisive, persistent, empathic, have more friends and better marriages (Seligman, 2002).

HOW SHOULD WE DEFINE HAPPINESS?

Okay, it is clear that happiness is good. You are healthier, live longer and are more productive, among other things. But what exactly is happiness? Seligman takes great pains to distinguish the study of what he terms "authentic happiness" from **hedonism** – the pursuit of momentary pleasures. The most useful definition, one that is agreed upon by positive psychologists, neuroscientists, and even Buddhist monks is more akin to satisfaction or contentment rather than happiness in the form of jumping for joy or floating on cloud nine. It contains depth and deliberation. It encompasses living a meaningful life, utilizing your skills and talents, and involves taking the time to live your life with purpose. It is maximized when you feel part of a community. It is enhanced when you are able to confront irritations and crises with grace. It involves a willingness to learn, stretch and grow, which can sometimes cause temporary discomfort. It is far more than temporary exhilaration or even sensual pleasure, although such feelings often accompany living each day to its fullest.

As you embark on your personal journey to maximize positive emotions, take a few moments to fill out the Authentic Happiness Inventory on the next few pages, adapted from a questionnaire developed by Christopher Peterson, to help you determine your current level of happiness.

Authentic Happiness Inventory

Please read each group of statements carefully. Then pick the one statement in each group that best describes the way you have been feeling this past week, including today. Be sure to read all of the statements in each group before making your choice. Circle the one that best applies.

A. 1. I feel that I am extraordinarily successful.
2. As I look back on my life, all I see are victories.
3. I feel like I have succeeded more than most people.
4. I do not feel like a winner.
5. I feel like a failure.

B. 1. I am usually in an unbelievably great mood.
2. I am usually in a great mood.
3. I am usually in a good mood.
4. I am usually in a neutral mood.
5. I am usually in a bad mood.

C. 1. When working, I am totally oblivious to outside events.
2. When working, I rarely notice what is going on around me.
3. When working, I attend more to my work than what is going on around me.
4. When working, I attend as much to what is going on around me as to my work.
5. When working, I attend more to what is going on around me than to my work.

D. 1. I have a very clear idea about the purpose or meaning of my life.
2. I have a pretty good idea about the purpose or meaning of my life.
3. I have a hint about my purpose in life.
4. I do not know the purpose or meaning of my life.
5. My life does not have any purpose or meaning.

E. 1. I always get what I want.
2. I usually get what I want.
3. Somewhat more often than not, I get what I want.
4. Sometimes I get what I want sometimes not.
5. I rarely get what I want.

F. 1. My life is filled with joy.
2. I have much more joy than sorrow in my life.
3. I have more joy than sorrow in my life.
4. I have neither sorrow nor joy in my life.
5. I have sorrow in my life.

G. 1. Most of the time I feel fascinated by what I am doing.
2. Most of the time I feel quite interested in what I am doing.
3. Most of the time I feel interested in what I am doing.
4. Most of the time I feel neither bored nor interested in what I am doing.
5. Most of the time I feel bored.

H. 1. By objective standards, I do amazingly well.
2. By objective standards, I do quite well.
3. By objective standards, I do rather well.
4 By objective standards, I do neither well nor poorly.
5. By objective standards, I do poorly.

I. 1. I am extraordinarily proud of myself.
2. I am very proud of myself.
3. I am proud of myself.
4. I am not ashamed of myself.
5. I am ashamed of myself.

J. 1. My existence has a lasting, large and positive impact on the world.
2. My existence makes the world a better place.
3. My existence has a small but positive effect on the world.
4. My existence neither helps not hurts the world.
5. In the grand scheme of things, my existence may hurt the world.

K. 1. I do really well at whatever I am doing.
2. I do well at most things I am doing.
3. I do well at some things I am doing.
4. I do okay at most things I am doing.
5. I do not do most things very well.

L. 1. I have so much enthusiasm that I feel I can do most anything.
2. I feel enthusiastic doing almost everything.
3. I have a good amount of enthusiasm.
4. My enthusiasm level is neither high nor low.
5. I have little or no enthusiasm.

M. 1. I truly love my work.
2. I really love my work.
3. For the most part, I like my work.
4. I feel neutral about my work.
5. I do not like my work (paid or unpaid)

N.
1. I feel extraordinarily optimistic about the future.
2. I feel quite optimistic about the future.
3. I am somewhat optimistic about my future.
4. I am neither optimistic nor pessimistic about the future.
5. I am pessimistic about the future.

O.
1. I have accomplished a great deal more in my life than most people.
2. I have accomplished more in life than most people.
3. I have accomplished somewhat more in life than most people.
4. I have accomplished no more in life than most people.
5. I have accomplished little in life.

P.
1. I feel close to everyone in the world.
2. I feel close to most people, even if I do not know them well.
3. I feel close to friends and family members.
4. I feel neither close to nor cut off from other people.
5. I feel cut off from other people.

Q.
1. Time passes so quickly during all of the things that I do that I don't notice it.
2. Time passes quickly during all of the things that I do.
3. Time passes quickly during most of the things that I do.
4. Time passes quickly during some things that I do, and slowly for other things.
5. Time passes slowly during most of the things that I do.

R.
1. I could not be any happier with myself.
2. I am happy with myself.
3. I am neither happy nor unhappy with myself.
4. I am neutral.
5. I am unhappy with myself.

S.
1. My skills are always challenged by the situations I encounter.
2. My skills are often challenged by the situations I encounter.
3. My skills are sometimes challenged by the situations I encounter.
4. My skills are occasionally challenged by the situations I encounter.
5. My skills are never challenged by the situations I encounter.

T.
1. I spend practically every moment every day doing things that are important.
2. I spend most of my time every day doing things that are important.
3. I spend some of my time every day doing things that are important.
4. I spend a lot of time doing things are neither important nor unimportant.
5. I spend all of my time doing things that are unimportant.

U.
1. If I were keeping score in life, I would be far ahead.
2. If I were keeping score in life, I would be ahead.
3. If I were keeping score in life, I would be somewhat ahead.
4. If I were keeping score in life, I would be about even.
5. If I were keeping score in life, I would be behind.

V.
1. My life is filled with pleasure.
2. I experience much more pleasure than pain.
3. I experience more pleasure than pain.
4. I experience pain and pleasure in equal amounts.
5. I experience more pain than pleasure.

W.
1. I like my daily routine so much that I almost never take breaks from it.
2. I like my daily routine so much that I rarely take breaks from it.
3. I like my daily routine but I take breaks.
4. I feel neutral about my daily routine.
5. I do not enjoy my daily routine.

X.
1. My life is a wonderful one.
2. My life is a very good one.
3. My life is a good one.
4. My life is an OK one.
5. My life is a bad one.

Results:

Add up the numbers associated with each of your circled answers. Once you have tabulated this total then divide the total score by 24 to get your Happiness Score.

Scores between 3.0 and 2.5 indicate moderate happiness and contentment.

If you scored under 2.5 you are generally happy and often very happy.

If you scored under 2.0 you are extremely happy. (If your score is between 1.0 and 1.5 you may not have been realistic in your assessment – everyone has some issues in life.)

Scores between 3.0 and 4.0 indicate that you have some dissatisfaction in your life.

If you scored above 4.0 you are not happy with your life and may be depressed.

MISCONCEPTONS ABOUT WHAT LEADS TO HAPPINESS

However, many misconceptions about what leads to happiness are unfortunately ingrained in our culture. Before we help you embark on your personal journey to greater happiness, fulfillment, and effectiveness, it will be useful to spend some time correcting the mistaken notions most of us hold about what will really make us happy. For example, were you aware that…

- Wealth, and all the possessions it can buy, has a surprisingly low correlation with levels of happiness. Believe it or not, the wealthy are only slightly happier than the poor! While pay raises can temporarily boost job satisfaction, average salaries do not correlate with happiness. In the U.S., those who are extremely poor tend to be unhappy, but once people have the basic necessities, more money does not buy nor build happiness. One study, cited in *The Week* (Dec. 5th, 2008) found that the happiness benefits of money peaked at the modest income of $20,000! Even the super rich, such as multi-millionaires, are only slightly happier than the typical middle class American. This people have the basic necessities, more money does not buy nor build happiness. One brings to mind a bumper sticker one author recently saw which opined, "He who dies with the most toys is still dead."

- There appears to be no reliable correlation between physical attractiveness, despite any advantages that beauty may provide, and happiness.

- Physical health also does not reliably predict happiness.

- IQ and educational level are not reliably correlated with happiness.

Take a moment and consider statistics showing that, according to survey research, people in the U.S. are no happier than their counterparts were 50 years ago. This is true despite the fact that, by all objective measures, life has improved for most Americans in terms of standard of living and health over the last half century. Even the poor have much more material goods than their counterparts of 50 years ago, although they still may be quite poor relative to others. We have far more abundant material goods that provide safety and comfort, life expectancy is longer, information is much more readily available, transportation is more easily accessible, and literacy rates are higher. Yet despite all this, our self-reported happiness levels have not kept pace with the increase in health, wealth and education. This phenomenon has been called the **progress paradox** by George Easterbrook (2003).

Surveys have shown that most people would actually be happier making less money, but on one condition: that everyone else made even less (Solnick and Hemenway, 1998). In fact, most people prefer that scenario to one in which their income rises but everyone else's income increases more. In other words, it's not how much we have that counts; it's how much we have compared to the Jones'! This could explain why people in more egalitarian societies generally report higher levels of life satisfaction. Scandinavian countries with large social safety nets consistently score the highest on the happiness scales. Inhabitants of Costa Rica, a relatively poor Central American country compared to the U.S., also post very high happiness scores compared to our country. The Costa Rican national motto, "*Pura Vida*" or "living well" may offer a clue to the attitudes of the typical Costa Rican.

The Hedonic Treadmill

Why is it that riches, beauty, health, or education (or any combination of such) do not reliably lead to lasting happiness? There are two main explanatory factors for this, one lying in genetics and the other in adaptation, the latter of which has been referred to as the "**hedonic treadmill.**" The first factor, your genetic makeup, reflects the fact that to a certain extent your level of positive emotion is genetically inherited. That is, each of us has a personal, genetically determined setpoint for happiness to which we tend to revert after the passage of time. Consider the fact that studies of major lottery winners reveal that although these lucky individuals may at first experience elation, followed by several months of increased happiness, after a year or so they were no happier than a matched control group, similar in all ways but minus a lottery windfall (Brickman, Coates & Janoff-Bulman, 1978). In that study, 22 lottery winners, each of whom received a minimum of $ 50,000 with some netting over one million during that year, were asked to rate their past, present and future happiness, as well as the pleasure they derived from everyday activities. Believe it or not, the lottery winners were only a wee bit happier than the non-winners in terms of present and future happiness, and they actually found less pleasure in everyday activities than the controls. But the reverse is true as well. Individuals who become paralyzed as a result of spinal cord injuries are typically emotionally traumatized at first (some to the point of becoming suicidal), but after a few years of adjustment their happiness levels are only slightly lower than those who are able-bodied. The same research group (Brickman, Coates, & Janoff-Bulman, 1978) interviewed 29 individuals who had become paralyzed the preceding year due to accidents and compared their happiness levels to the lottery winners. Although their present happiness was lower, as would be expected, their expected future happiness and pleasure in everyday activities was actually higher than the lottery winners! However, although there is strong evidence that happiness levels are partially set by your genetic inheritance, **do not make the mistake of assuming that you are stuck**. Again, happiness setpoints are only partially determined by your genetic inheritance, and as such there is a wide variety of things you can do to affect your happiness levels, as will be outlined in this and later chapters.

The second factor accounting for the failure of money, beauty, health, or a high IQ to generate long term happiness is the fact that we tend to inevitably adapt to fortunate circumstances and take these for granted. Brickman and Campbell (1971) first introduced this concept of the hedonic treadmill where we continually adapt to improving circumstances to inevitably return to a point of relative neutrality. Due to the hedonic treadmill our expectations tend to rise as our bank accounts grow, our houses and cars get more expensive and luxurious, and our wardrobe bulges out of our closet. So we tend to need something more or better to recreate the thrill. Likewise, the more we accomplish, the more we expect of ourselves. The more we accumulate, or accomplish, or the more attractive we become, we tend to compare ourselves with those who have more, are more successful, or more attractive, so we still feel incomplete. We keep running on the treadmill and getting nowhere. The more money we have, the more beautiful we become, the more we strive because what was exciting before is now commonplace. If this treadmill did not exist, individuals with more good things going for them would be happier than those who are less well off, yet this is just not the case. Possessions and accomplishments appear to only raise happiness levels in the short term. But adaptation also works to help us recover from loss and disappointments as well.

So why does this adaptation occur? Why can't our honeymoon with our beloved last forever? Why does our excitement about the new job, or promotion, or award evaporate? Why does the fascination with the new car, or house, or _____ (you fill in the blank) wear off? One potential reason for this adaptation response has much to do with the survival of the human species. Pleasure can be very distracting, as preoccupying as pain, especially if very intense. The fact that pleasurable experiences tend to be brief and diminish over time allows us to get back to the rest of our life and not be diverted (Barkow, 1997), which clearly has survival value. Think of what happens to drug addicts if they spend all of their time pursuing their next fix. Or for a healthier example, remember the last time you fell head over heels in love (in the beginning). For many of us, falling in love makes it hard to concentrate, to eat, to sleep, or to work, as all we want to do is think about our beloved, to be with that person, or talk on the phone to that person, or tell our friends all about that person. Not much of a productive nature gets done in the early stages of being in love. (And this is all well and good – everyone needs to know the joy of this in their lives at least once.) Once you calm down a bit you can begin to accomplish what you need to do in your life, but if you stayed madly in love all the time you might never finish anything.

It also appears that people often make mistakes in their predictions regarding how long their future positive emotions will endure, that is, they tend to overestimate how long pleasurable feelings will last. In a series of studies, Gilbert, Wilson and colleagues (1998, 2000, & 2001) examined the expectations and emotional reactions of people before and after significant life events of both a positive and negative nature. The events included romantic break-ups, getting a desired job, being fired from a job, receiving tenure in teaching positions, or failing to get tenure. The results from these studies clearly showed that while people correctly predicted that favorable outcomes would boost their happiness levels, they consistently overestimated how long the improvement would last. The same was true for negative outcomes. The subjects correctly predicted that they would be depressed and/or disappointed by that setback, but they consistently overestimated the length of their emotional reaction. So the hedonic treadmill can certainly work in our favor to help us recover from difficult times, often quicker than we anticipate. Most people are more resilient than they realize. When depressed, whatever the reason or source, it is often useful to remind yourself that, "this too shall pass."

The other good news is that adaptation does not permanently damage our ability to enjoy a given pleasure. We can come back for more later on as long as a sufficient amount of time has passed to allow adaptation to subside. The notion of what is a sufficient time period will vary widely depending on the person, the pleasurable stimulus and the context of the situation. But as a rule, it is wise to spread out your pleasures over time to maximize the satisfaction each produces, whereas cramming them all together leads to adaptation and under appreciation. Think about children who are overindulged and get every new toy on the market in a short time frame. They are often easily bored and play with each toy a few times before tossing it aside in pursuit of the next.

The Role of Genetics

In *Authentic Happiness* Seligman introduces an equation to guide you on your journey to happiness:

$$H = S + C + V$$

H refers to your enduring level of happiness, not momentary blips of happiness or pleasure, but your overall happiness level over time. **S** refers to your genetic setpoint which partially accounts for your baseline happiness level. Research has indicated that approximately 50% of most personality traits are genetically determined, but that means that we have much more control over the remaining 50%. **C** reflects the circumstances of your life, some of which you can control and some you can not. **V** represents your internal mind-set, those all important cognitive, emotional and behavioral factors over which you have voluntary control. One goal of positive psychology is on altering the **V** (voluntary) factors to maximize life satisfaction, which has profound implications for your ability to be effective. According to the research of Lyubomirsky, Sheldon and Schkade (2005), the S (genetic) factor accounts for 50% of your happiness level, the C factor only 10%, and the all important V factor (your internal mind-set) accounts for 40% in their happiness model. In an even more specific breakdown of the genetic determinants of emotional states, Tellegen and his colleagues (1988) estimated that 40% of positive emotionality and 55% of negative emotionality (i.e. such as vulnerability to depression) are genetically based.

Meehl (1975) was one of the first to suggest the possibility that happy people were just born with more of what he called *cerebral joy juice*. He referred to the ability to experience positive emotions as an individual's **hedonic capacity**, and he theorized that it represented individual differences between people which were influenced by genetics as well as environment and learning histories. He further hypothesized that hedonic capacity was linked to the personality trait of **extraversion**, being outgoing and comfortable around other people. Research has supported much of Meehl's theorizing about hedonic capacity which is now referred to in the positive psychology literature as **positive affectivity**. Watson (2000) confirmed that positive affectivity is more common among extraverts, whether male or female. Those who are high in positive affectivity are more socially active, have more friends and belong to more social organizations. They are more likely to be married and to be satisfied with their marriages, and to be happy with their jobs as well. People high in positive affectivity are also very likely to be low in neuroticism, meaning that they have fewer neurotic (anxiety based) symptoms. But since these are correlational results, we do not know what causes what. Does positive affectivity lead to personal, marital, and occupational satisfaction, or is it the other way around? The results of the Duchenne smile study suggest that the positive affectivity may help produce or create the conditions for later life satisfaction in a variety of areas. It can be said that an extraverted, non-neurotic has a bit of head start in achieving happiness. Individuals who are religious or very spiritual also score high on positive affectivity (Clark & Watson, 1999). Here again, we don't know whether positive affectivity leads one to religion, or whether the sense of meaning, comfort and community that religious affiliation provides boosts positive affect. Argyle (1987) stressed the community aspect of religion as being the important linchpin here, as religious individuals rate themselves as being less lonely as compared to the nonreligious.

Twin studies do support the heritability of positive affectivity (Finkel & McCrue, 1997 along with the aforementioned work of Tellegen and his colleagues). But heritable does not mean fixed or unchangeable. Depression is even more heritable than positive affectivity and that is readily changed through psychotherapy and/or ameliorated with psychotropic medications. According to David Watson (2005), one of the world leading authorities on positive affectivity, "The genetic and biological data should not induce a fatalistic resignation; we are still free to increase our positive affectivity."

HOW TO BOOST YOUR HAPPINESS—THE "V" FACTOR

Seligman recommends that you pay much more attention to the role of the V factors in your life rather than spending all your time trying to improve your life circumstances. In terms of the effects of the C factor—the external circumstances of your life—upon your level of happiness, Kasser & Ryan (1993.1996) studied whether the American dream—riches, fame and beauty—really fosters happiness. They found that striving for this actually led to lower vitality, lower fulfillment of potential, and physical distress. In stark contrast, the pursuit of self-acceptance, friendship, and being helpful to others was linked with greater psychological well-being. Thus, Seligman makes the following recommendations based on what situations are related to happiness and which are not. Remember that these relationships are correlational in nature and may or may not reflect causality. To maximize your chances of happiness you should:

◈ Get married (strongly correlated with happiness)

◈ Develop a varied social network (strongly correlated with happiness)

◈ Involve yourself in religion or find meaning through spiritual belief or practice (moderately correlated with happiness)

Seligman further recommends that you do not bother to do the following if you hope to increase your happiness level:

◈ Make more money. The more materialistic you become, typically the less happy you become.

◈ Stay healthy. Surprisingly, it is how you view your health rather than your objective health that affects happiness levels.

◈ Get more education. Although certainly a worthy pursuit, it is not related to happiness levels.

◈ Attempt to change your race (no correlation with happiness).

◈ Move to a warmer or sunnier climate (no correlation to happiness).

We offer the following chart to summarize the myriad findings regarding what does and what does not correlate with happiness and life satisfaction and to what extent.

TABLE 3.1 Positive Correlations with Happiness and Life Satisfaction

No Correlation	Moderate Correlation	High Correlation
Age	being married	optimism
Gender	number of friends	gratitude
Education	physical health	being employed
Income level	agreeableness	good self-esteem
Social class	religiosity	high frequency of sexual intercourse
Intelligence	level of leisure activity	extraversion
Ethnicity	internal locus of control	happily married
Physical attractiveness	conscientiousness	many good friends
Having children	open-mindedness	low neuroticism

Seligman divides positive emotions into three temporal categories depending on whether they relate to the past, the present, or the future. Positive future oriented emotions include optimism, hope, and trust. Pleasure, joy, ecstasy, enthusiasm, and calmness reflect positive emotions in the here and now. Past oriented positive emotions range from satisfaction, pride, contentment and serenity. It is very possible to experience positive emotions in one time dimension, but not the others as these emotions are related but not all encompassing. Some of your present emotions are instantaneous and not dependant on thought. You don't have to think to experience the pleasure of chocolate melting in your mouth. You don't need to interpret anything to enjoy the feeling of a good massage on tense, sore muscles. But your emotions about the past and the future are totally reliant on your thoughts, your interpretations, and your habitual frames. And here we can put the lessons from Chapter 1 on reframing, and in Chapter 2 on cognitive restructuring and optimism to work for us. Developing and enhancing your positive emotions about the future is the best place to start, because those can also affect your present feelings, and potentially can help you interpret your past in the most favorable light.

How to Brighten Your Expectations for Your Future—Flexible Optimism and Hope

In Chapter 2 we discussed the importance of optimism to effectiveness and provided specific steps for enhancing an optimistic outlook. Here we want to remind you that optimism is a necessary ingredient in happiness. Research in cognitive psychology has shown that just as negative self statements can create depression, anxiety, or other negative emotions, positive or optimistic self-statements can create and reinforce effectiveness and happiness. Many studies have demonstrated that levels of optimism vs. pessimism are a powerful determining factor in our physical and emotional health. Indeed, a review of the research on happiness has consistently identified optimism as one of the four traits manifested by happy people (Myers and Diener, 1995). In addition, pessimism is often linked to depression in a wide variety of studies.

Optimism refers to beliefs regarding the future, regarding the probability of negative vs. positive outcomes and regarding one's ability to cope in the event of a negative outcome. Optimists believe they are likely to experience positive outcomes and success, and, in the event of a negative outcome, they will be able to cope. Because of this optimists are more likely to persevere in the face of obstacles due to their belief in eventual success. And that is why *optimism is energizing, while pessimism is paralyzing.* If you believe you are going to fail, it is so much easier to give up. But if you believe you will win, or succeed, or eventually prevail, then you find the strength to keep on going no matter how difficult the challenge.

Is there experimental evidence that boosting optimism levels will lead to increased happiness? There have been few direct experimental interventions in this regard, but in one notable study with children, Seligman, Revich, Jaycox, and Gillham (1995) identified elementary school children who were at risk for depression and exposed them to optimism training. Using cognitive restructuring techniques and social problem solving training, the kids were taught to look on the bright side of things. Following the training period, the children exposed to optimism training were significantly less depressed than the control group of kids who did not receive any training, and this effect was even more pronounced at a two year follow-up of the progress of the children.

Finding Happiness in Your Past—Maximizing Satisfaction and Contentment

Your feelings about your past are determined by the nature of your memories, which are heavily colored by your interpretations of past events. Since you can't change your past, you are left with finding ways to influence these interpretations to generate satisfaction and a sense of meaning. There are three main methods of moving your feelings about your past towards greater contentment and satisfaction. The first involves letting go of the paradigm that your past, particularly your childhood, solely determines your future. Are you stuck believing that you are a prisoner of your upbringing, or forever a helpless victim of your past traumas, hurts, or disappointments? The deterministic branches of psychology which ruled the discipline in the mid 1900's promoted extensive research to establish evidence of the destructive effects of bad childhood events (i.e. parental death, abuse, divorce). But upon reviewing a wealth of research, Seligman and others have concluded that the influence of childhood trauma on adult personality is negligible, despite strong expectations to the contrary on the part of so many researchers. So there you have it. Again, the choice is yours. You have choice over whether you allow a troubled past to define you or to strengthen you.

The second and third strategies for improving happiness about the past involve making a proactive effort to engage in both gratitude and forgiveness. Gratitude works to enhance your appreciation of your past and present, while forgiveness gives you the power to let go of bitterness, while potentially allowing you to rewrite the meaning of your personal history in the process.

So cultivate what we call an **attitude of gratitude**. This is far more than counting your blessings, although that is a part of it. Adopting an attitude of gratitude involves noticing, appreciating, and being thankful for the people, events, and even the small benefits of your life. Highly grateful people operate from the framework where everything they have, all that they have experienced, past and present, is a gift. The French novelist Colette was quoted on her deathbed as saying, *"What a wonderful life I've had. I only wish I'd realized it sooner."* Gratitude improves your satisfaction with life because it revivifies your good memories and colors how you interpret them. On top of this, those who are grateful are less at risk for negative emotions such as depression, anxiety, or envy. They are more empathic, forgiving, and helpful to others. Emmons & McCullough (2003) assigned two groups to keep a daily journal. One group kept a journal of all they were grateful for, past and present. The other group kept a journal of hassles and ongoing neutral life events. It is no surprise that happiness levels soared for the former group. Sarah Ban Breathnach (1995), in her book *Simple Abundance* suggests that you keep such a gratitude journal and record at least five things daily about which you are grateful. These entries need not be major accomplishments or gifts, just simple pleasures that you may often take for granted. For example, one of the authors worked as an intern on a spinal cord injury ward for a year. The most important thing that he drew from that experience was a constant appreciation for having an intact body and being able to walk, something that we regularly take for granted. We recommend that, whenever you feel particularly mistreated by life, consider the ramifications of losing one of your senses, or the function of some part of your body. Remember the last time you were ill, or had a toothache, or headache, and appreciate just how wonderful normal is.

Researchers have recently identified a very healthy neuropsychological pattern that is associated with gratitude. McCraty (2002) and McCraty & Atkinson, (2003) reported a synchronization of alpha brain wave activity (associated with relaxation and positive emotions) and heartbeats after experimental manipulation of appreciation levels in their subjects. McCraty concluded that the gratitude related human response of appreciation appeared to have a coherent psychophysiological pattern.

Seligman, Steen, Park & Peterson (2005) asked students in their positive psychology classes to write gratitude letters and found that the senders of those letters felt significantly happier for several weeks afterward. It would be interesting to know what the effect was on the recipients of the letters.

Positive Psychology Exercise #1 The Letter of Gratitude

Following the model utilized by Seligman and his colleagues in the experiment mentioned above, we encourage you to think about all of the people in your life who have been helpful to you, kind to you, who have been there for you in one way or another to whom you have never expressed your gratitude in a meaningful way. This could be a friend, relative, parent, teacher, employer, member of the clergy, neighbor, teammate, coach, co-worker, fellow student, etc. It could be anyone. Write a letter of gratitude to that valued person and describe in concrete terms why you are so grateful to him or her. If it is at all possible, deliver the letter in person and allow that individual to read the letter in your presence. If this is not possible, send it by fax, regular mail or e-mail, and then call the person afterwards by phone. While doing all of it by e-mail might be tempting, a follow-up phone call is preferable to keep it on a more personal level. Following through with this assignment will give you, and most likely the recipient of your letter, a real lift in spirit and mood, even if only temporarily. To make these results last, send a new gratitude letter out every few months to someone whose efforts you truly appreciate.

Positive Psychology Exercise #2 Three Good Things

A variation on the gratitude journal involves writing down three things that went well at the end of each day. Why three things instead of five or ten? According to the research of Seligman and his colleagues, who varied both the number of good things to be listed and the timing of when to do it, the combination of listing three things at the end of the day (as opposed to the morning) was optimal for boosting happiness levels. To further enhance the benefits you can obtain from this exercise, answer a simple question after each entry of a positive event. The question is, "why did this happen?"

The next strategy has to do with being able to forgive. **Forgiveness** allows you to let go of the energy attached to bad memories without necessarily forgetting what happened. Trying to forget about something is rarely a useful strategy. Sometimes, the more we try to forget, the more we just remember. For example, give this a try. For the next few seconds, whatever you do – *do not think about **Pink Elephants**!* Chances are that this did not work. Why? Because in order to not think about pink elephants, you must first conjure up a rosy colored pachyderm, and then try to erase this image. This is a task of elephantine proportions. The fact is that every time we command ourselves to *just forget about it*, the more we remind ourselves. Thus the only viable strategy left is to forgive, which leaves your memories intact (preserving whatever important life lessons you have gleaned), but allows for the hurt and bitterness to dissipate. You can choose to forgive, whatever the circumstances, because ultimately forgiveness is not for others, it is for you. It frees up your energy and allows you to move on and increase your sense of life satisfaction. A far more comprehensive discussion of forgiveness, along with suggested steps to achieving it, will come at the end of Chapter 9 in the section entitled *The Nature of Anger.*

There are other considerations regarding whether we view our past with positive feelings and that relates to factors influencing the nature of memory. Realize that when we think about pleasant memories from the past, our recollections of pleasure are not necessarily accurate, faithful, blow by blow accounts or summaries of what happened. Rather our memories are influenced by the intensity of the experience, as well as how it ended, a formula referred to as **peak-end theory** by psychologist Daniel Kahneman (1999). Studies have corroborated peak end theory which states that evaluations of past experiences reflect an average of the highs and lows, along with an assessment of how it was just before it ended. Another factor often overlooked is how long the experience lasted. Kahneman called this phenomenon **duration neglect** and this also affects how we interpret the positive or negative impact of experiences in our past. The practical lesson here is that it is useful to build in high points and good finales or finishes, if possible, with respect to your experiences so that you will be more likely to remember things in a favorable light. This is a way to insure that your remembrances of things past will be more positive. This could be a strategy to use, for example, when planning for a vacation. Remember to plan in at least one high note and end with a big adventure so your recollection of your past trip will be maximized as a positive memory.

Finding Happiness in the Present Moment—Pleasures and Gratifications

Happiness in the here and now differs from happiness about your past or future. Present moment happiness falls into two separate categories: (1) the pleasures; and (2) the gratifications. Pleasures are temporary and typically involve enjoyable sensory sensations and minimal, if any, thoughts. This is the territory of joy and thrills, emotions and feelings such as orgasm, ecstasy, comfort, bliss, merriment and excitement. Pleasures are wonderful, part of the spice of life, but they habituate quickly (remember the hedonic treadmill), and, as such, are almost always short-lived. Gratifications, on the other hand, represent activities that we find very fulfilling, that we tend to lose ourselves within, that absorb us fully. Gratifications can be anything from hobbies, reading a great book, painting, sculpting, building, fixing, creating, writing, singing, playing a musical instrument, gardening, collecting, anything that enjoyably fills our attention. When we engage in activities we find gratifying we often lose track of time, our skills are up to challenges we face, and we tap into our strengths. This relates to **engagement**, the E in PERMA. Gratifications are more long lasting than pleasures because they are far more resistant to habituation, while often leading to self improvement due to the exercise of our strengths.

While we all enjoy indulging in our own personal pleasures, focusing our lives on the pursuit of continual pleasure is very unlikely to bring about lasting happiness. When we repeatedly encounter the same pleasure producing stimulus over and over, it elicits less pleasure in us over time and often quicker than we realize. This is adaptation. Because of the hedonic treadmill, you will never be satisfied for long, and will need something more to capture the thrill and escape boredom. When this becomes obsessive, addiction is born. Addictions can be to substances that bring momentary pleasure such as alcohol, drugs, food, or chocolate, or behaviors like compulsive gambling, shopping, or sexual addictions. To counteract this we recommend that you consider spacing your pleasures out over time as the best way to enhance them. Try to find the optimal interval between pleasures that prevents habituation from occurring. For example, if you ride that awesome roller coaster five times every day for a month, it will soon get quite dull. But riding that same coaster one to two times a year will remain a great thrill. Or, eating that creamy chocolate sundae can be a great sensual treat, but if you eat three a day for a few days, you will get to the point where you won't even taste it anymore (not to mention the bloat). Adding the element of surprise is another approach that helps ward off habituation. Work to put a little unpredictability into your sensory pleasures.

Seligman (2002) laments how the rat race of modern life combined with our future-mindedness keeps us from appreciating the present moment. Bryant and Veroff recommend **savoring** as a way of maximizing pleasure in the present. They define savoring as the awareness of pleasure that comes from paying deliberate conscious attention to your experience of pleasure. Bryant (2003) found that those who routinely savor, who anticipate positive events and relish them in the moment, are happier and more satisfied with life. Bryant and Veroff distinguish between four kinds of savoring:

1. **Basking** (openly receiving praise and/or congratulations)
2. **Thanksgiving** (being thankful for your blessings)
3. **Marveling** (being filled with awe at the wonder of the moment)
4. **Luxuriating** (indulging your senses)

Other savoring strategies include:

1. **Sharing**—Talking about it with others
2. **Memory Building**—make mental pictures or even take a physical souvenir of the experience, if possible, to help you reminisce
3. **Self-Congratulation**—remind yourself of a job well done. Congratulate yourself
4. **Sharpen your perception**—Narrow your focus to certain aspects of an experience and block others out
5. **Absorption**—allow yourself to get totally immersed in the pleasure of the moment and shut out other stimuli

Practicing **mindfulness** is one key avenue for savoring pleasure. Mindfulness can allow you to see the present moment as new, a practice of shifting perspective to see things in a fresh light. This is best achieved through the practice of mindfulness meditation which allows you to slow down your mind, and be open and attentive to the present moment. A detailed discussion of mindfulness meditation and guide to the practice of such is included in Chapter 6.

What we are really trying to convey here is that the royal road to happiness is through the gratifications. The "pleasures" are about enjoyable sensory stimulation and emotional experience. The "gratifications" are much more about discovering and using your own strengths and virtues, and becoming totally absorbed in the process. This absorption, this stoppage of time, is called **flow** (Csikszentmihalyi, 1990), a very important concept that we will explore in greater depth in Chapter 14 in reference to the role of flow in your occupational life. Flow is such an important concept in positive psychology because it represents a person working at full capacity. The aftermath of the flow experience is typically invigorating, although joy is not typically felt during the experience which is often non-emotional. Flow is most likely to occur when there is an optimal balance between a person's skills and the degree of challenge (Moneta & Csikszentmihalyi, 1996). Gratifications produce flow, but pleasures typically do not. While experiencing pleasure you are typically caught up in the good feelings. While engaging in gratifying activities you will often be unaware of feeling – you can literally get out of your head for awhile. And it is precisely this escape aspect, this absorption in something else, that allows the best in you to blossom, ultimately resulting in a far deeper level of happiness over time than the momentary pleasures. Pleasures typically come easy, while gratifications, which involve the effort of using your skills and virtues to meet challenges, offer a deeper, more enduring level of satisfaction.

Be careful to distinguish between activities that truly lead to flow and those that create "junk flow" or "faux flow" such as video games or watching TV shows. Those activities have some aspects of flow as they can be quite interesting and absorbing, but they are not overly challenging and do not typically lead to feelings of satisfaction. In this regard, consider the conclusion of 34 years of survey data on how people spend their time, collected from more than 45,000 participants (Robinson and Martin, 2008), where unhappy individuals were found to watch 30% more TV than people who reported being happy. Individuals who described themselves as very happy tended to spend more time in social activities, attending religious services, and reading the newspaper. In contrast, those who described themselves as unhappy tended to spend their free time watching television. Since this was correlational research we cannot make the assumption that watching TV causes unhappiness; rather, it is just as plausible that individuals who are unhappy are unmotivated to go out, and therefore opt for the comfortable fix of TV viewing. Watching TV is easy in that you don't have to go anywhere, get dressed, spend money, expend energy or interact with anyone. But while TV might be entertaining for the moment, it is unlikely to provide the kind of fulfillment or gratification that could shift depression to happiness.

Seligman bemoans the fact that our modern culture often encourages preoccupation with momentary pleasures, while neglecting the gratifications. That is, we try to take shortcuts to happiness by pursuing pleasure, based on the inaccurate assumption that pleasures are what happiness is all about. He warns that the reliance on pleasure at the expense of the gratifications is more likely to lead to depression than joy. Therefore, if you ask the question, "How can I be happy?" you must make the distinction between pleasures and gratifications or risk being seduced by pleasures alone. Seligman makes a point to distinguish between the good life (steeped in gratifications) as opposed to the pleasant life (full of pleasures), and clearly he recommends you pursue the good life. Ultimately, finding a balance between pleasures and gratifications is essential to happiness in the present.

One of the most robust findings in positive psychology is that a deeper sense of satisfaction and happiness in the long run comes from being actively concerned for the welfare of others, rather than from the pursuit of hedonistic pleasures. We will be dealing with this subject in more depth when we discuss altruism in Chapter 11, but Seligman devised another exercise to help you discover this distinction for yourself.

Positive Psychology Exercise # 3 Fun vs. Philanthropy

Make a list of all of the things you like to do, that you consider to be fun, and that are within your ability and budget to easily arrange to do. Then make a list of the things you could personally do to be helpful to others. This could involve volunteer work at a local hospital, offering to mow your neighbor's lawn or baby sitting for free, helping a young family member with homework, assisting at an animal shelter, or anything else you can come up with that would be of service in your community, or for your friends, family and neighbors. Next week pick one fun thing and one helpful activity from your lists and engage in both. Flip a coin to determine which to do first. Spend an equal amount of time on both pursuits. Afterward write a brief reaction paper summarizing your thoughts and feelings about each activity and how it affected you. Pay attention to anything you have learned.

In summary, according to Seligman you can maximize your positive emotions in all the temporal domains by rejecting the limiting deterministic paradigm, embracing optimism and hope, adopting an attitude of gratitude, learning to forgive, practicing savoring and mindfulness to enhance your enjoyment of the present moment, and creating balance between engaging in pursuits of sensory pleasure and doing that which provides gratification.

THE GLOBAL PERSPECTIVE–Gross National Happiness GNH

After his tiny Buddhist nation was criticized for slow economic growth, the King of Bhutan proposed the concept of Gross National Happiness, the GNH, in 1972 to help identify more appropriate indicators to truly measure the quality of life within nations and organizations. This is based on the radically different paradigm that conventional development concepts such as the GNP (Gross National Product) or Per Capita Income do not really adequately reflect the general well-being of the inhabitants of a nation. While conventional developments models stress economic growth as the ultimate objective, the concept of GNH is based on the premise that optimal development within a country occurs when the material, spiritual and positive emotional development occur side by side and reinforce each other. The GNH measure is based on the concept that indices of emotional well-being are more relevant than objective measures like consumption. The government of Bhutan is devoted to pursuing a policy with four pillars: equitable and sustainable economic growth; environmental conservation; cultural preservation; and good government. Med Yones, president of the International Institute of Management, created the first global GNH survey in 2006, incorporating the following seven metrics: (1) economic wellness; (2) environmental wellness; (3) physical wellness; (4) mental wellness; (5) workplace wellness; (6) social wellness; and (7) political wellness. In a recent study using a GNH measure (White, 2007), Bhutan raked 8th out of 178 countries in subjective well-being even though it is not an economically advanced nation.

In other studies of happiness across the globe, political science professor Ronald Inglehart at the University of Michigan published a paper in *Perspectives in Psychological Science* (July, 2008) in which he refuted the long held assumption that happiness across societies worldwide has remained constant. His research indicated that significant changes in happiness levels have occurred for societies as well as for individuals. The study was based on an analysis of polls conducted by the World Values Survey from 1981 through 2007 covering 88 countries containing 90% of the earth's population. This particular survey measured happiness and overall life satisfaction. Martin Seligman referred to this study as the best he has seen on happiness within the last five years.

The results of this study demonstrated that in the 52 countries that completed all surveys over the 17 year period, 86% of those countries (45 nations in all) experienced a rise in average happiness levels within the population. Happiness levels declined in six countries and stayed constant within one. Even the British are showing interest in happiness research. British Prime Minister Gordon Brown, encouraged by fellow Labor Party member and renowned happiness scholar Richard Layard, has shown interest in using happiness studies to advance "well being" in the U.K., as reported in *The Week* (Dec. 5th, 2008).

THE GLOBAL PERSPECTIVE–Gross National Happiness GNH (cont.)

According to Inglehart, the most likely variables accounting for the increase in happiness levels are improved economic development, democratization, and increased social tolerance. Economic development results in a significant improvement in subjective well-being, particularly for poorer third world nations. But for less impoverished nations, democratization and social tolerance are more salient contributing factors. Why? Democracy allows individuals greater freedom and more choice which helps produce an environment conducive to happiness. "Support for gender equality and tolerance of people who are different from oneself are also strongly linked, not just because tolerant people are happier, but because living in a tolerant society enhances everyone's freedom," (Inglehart, 2008).

What Do Other Experts Recommend for Boosting Your Happiness?

Many books have been written on the subject of enhancing or boosting happiness. There is considerable overlap in terms of the recommendations put forth by many of the better known and respected authorities, psychologists, and philosophers in the field. So you may notice some redundancy in the suggestions put forth by various experts, but that speaks to the fact that these recommendations have been shown, both experimentally and in practice, to help people improve their mood when depressed, discover happiness, and even find their bliss. One expert in the field, David Myers, put forth the following suggestions in his 1993 best selling book, *The Pursuit of Happiness*...

1. **Fake it till you make it.** Act as if you were happy. Sometimes you can actually act yourself into a new and better frame of mind. Going through the motions can trigger more positive emotions. We will discuss this phenomenon further in Chapter 6 from a different perspective.

2. Understand that success, wealth or possessions do not lead to enduring happiness. **Remember the hedonic treadmill.**

3. **Seek work and leisure activities that engage and make use of your skills.** This refers to the importance of gratifications and flow experiences to enduring happiness.

4. **Build close relationships** and give them priority in your life.

5. **Engage in regular exercise** which has been shown to help boost mood and decrease anxiety (Learn more about this in Chapter 6).

6. Learn to be in control of your time. **Don't let time control you.** Learn to set limits and not over commit yourself (More on this in Chapter 8).

7. **Get an adequate amount of sleep.** Sleep deprivation is a silent cause of depression. Sleep researchers warn that many of us are sleep deprived (Dement & Vaughan, 1999). Getting an optimal amount of sleep is essential to maintaining your positive emotional equilibrium.

8. **Get in touch with your spirituality.**

9. Focus beyond yourself. Helping others helps you to feel good. This is also called the **Do good, feel good effect.** (read more about this in the altruism section in Chapter 11).

10. **Keep a gratitude journal.**

Martin Bolt (2004), in a review of the positive psychology literature on the pursuit of happiness, offers the following summary tips for finding your happiness and maintaining it.

- ❖ Don't confuse being well-off with well-being.
- ❖ Make wise comparisons
- ❖ Keep a gratitude journal
- ❖ Discover your flow
- ❖ Finish what you start and wholly experience it along the way
- ❖ Strive for excellence but not perfection
- ❖ Find a hobby
- ❖ Cultivate family ties and friendships
- ❖ Know your neighbors
- ❖ Volunteer
- ❖ Practice spirituality

Peterson (2006) conceptualizes four possible routes to happiness and opines that individuals need at least one route, with some routes working better than others to achieve happiness. The four routes he outlines are:

1. hedonism
2. eudemonia
3. engagement
4. victory

Although Peterson does not deny that hedonism, the pursuit of maximal pleasure and minimal pain, is relevant to life satisfaction, he strongly cautions us that hedonism contributes far less to long term happiness than eudemonia. What is **eudemonia**? This is a complex concept, going all the way back to the writings of Aristotle, which refers to being true to your inner self. According to the eudemonic view, happiness is about identifying your own signature strengths and virtues (which we explore in detail in the next chapter) and then living your life in accordance with those. This is very much in line with Maslow's (1970) concept of self-actualization, or Carl Rogers (1951) vision of the fully functioning person, or Ryff and Singer's (1996) ideal of psychological well-being. Peterson implores his readers to favor eudemonic pursuits over hedonistic ones stating that

> Some of our own recent research suggests that eudemonia can trump pleasure as a predictor of life satisfaction (Huta, Park, Peterson & Seligman, 2005; Peterson, Park & Seligman, 2005b). Using different samples and different methods, we found that those who pursue eudemonic goals and activities are more satisfied than those who pursue pleasure. This finding is robust, occurring across Canada, and other nations. He who dies with the most toys may or may not win, but he will not do so as happily as he who dies after a life of helping others. (p. 79)

It is also very important to note that happiness and well-being are not always synonymous. True psychological well being occurs when you have both happiness and a sense of meaning and purpose in your life (the eudemonic life), fulfilling the M in PERMA. Or put more simply: **Well-being = Happiness + Meaning.**

The third route, engagement, subsumes the E in PERMA including activities that Seligman would call gratifications, particularly those that involve flow. The last route, the victory route, has to do with competition. Some people thrive on the pursuit of victory, whether in sports, games, business, the battlefield, or in love. While we can debate the merits of this, for some individuals engaging in competitive activities provides enormous pleasure and a sense of meaning and purpose in life. For some this fourth route also exemplifies accomplishment, the A in PERMA, for winning is one aspect of achievement.

After several years of teaching positive psychology classes and noticing the powerful effects of prescribed happiness boosting exercises on the satisfaction and mood of their students, several researchers (including Seligman and Peterson) decided to do a controlled study of the effects of such exercises. In the experimental design (Seligman, Steen, Park & Peterson, 2005) participants were required to engage in five separate happiness boosting exercises, each of which took one week to complete. Two of the exercises will be familiar to you as they were discussed in detail earlier in this chapter. The five exercises were as follows:

1. **Gratitude Visit.** Write and deliver a letter of gratitude.
2. **Three Good Things.** Keep a special journal where every day for one week jot down three things that went well that day and describe them in detail.
3. **You at Your Best.** Write a story about an event that brought out the best in you. Review this story every day for a week.
4. **Identifying Signature Strengths** (explained in next chapter)
5. **Using Signature Strengths in a Novel Way.** Once you have identified your personal strengths, figure out unique ways to utilize them during the following week.

The subjects were recruited from the internet and were given pre and post measures of happiness and depression in order to determine whether the exercises had any effect (short term and long term) on their mood and life satisfaction. To control for placebo effects (i.e. the possible mood elevating effect of being a participant in a research study), they created a placebo control condition, as well. Placebo group subjects, also recruited online, were given a series of writing exercises regarding early childhood memories over a five week period, a plausible task for a psychology experiment. All subjects were randomly assigned to either the placebo control group or the experimental group who had to complete the happiness exercises. Follow ups were completed at one month and six month intervals to check the happiness levels of the participants at those times.

The results were clear and unequivocal. First of all, the placebo subjects did report increased happiness and decreased depression, but this effect was very short lived and was not present at the follow-ups. Placebo effects like this are quite common in studies of the effectiveness of techniques, treatments and/or medications, which is why placebo controls are included in the first place; that is, to discriminate real treatment effects from pure placebo effects. The biggest overall boost in happiness resulted from the Gratitude Visit, but this effect evaporated after one month. Long term effects for increased happiness, present at the six month follow-up, were found for the Three Good Things exercise and for Using Signature Strengths in Novel Ways. The subjects who got the greatest benefit in terms of improved happiness were those who continued to practice the techniques beyond the required time periods. The lesson here is that for these techniques to have a lasting effect they must become part of the fabric of your life. But isn't that true about so many things in life? In order for healthy habits that promote well-being to work, whether it involves eating right or exercising, or taking care of your emotional health, you need to follow through. Seligman and his colleagues reported that 60% of the subjects in their study continued to practice the Three Good Things exercise six months later. Of the subjects who were married, some made it a routine in the marriage to share their list with their partner at the end of each day. Going to sleep happy with your partner will certainly increase the likelihood that both of you will wake up happy!

Positive Psychology Exercise # 4 Have a Good Day

This exercise challenges you to systematically figure out what makes a good day for you, a day that would elicit positive emotions (in terms of variables you have control over), and then, based on patterns you discern, to build a structure to increase the number of those good days. Many people have never really considered what makes for a good day in terms of the concrete measurable events of what you did and didn't do in a particular day which helped to make it a good day. What are those variables, over which you typically exert a lot of control, that you can choose to include in your life to increase the frequency of good days? There are some things you just can't control. You can't control the weather on a given day, or the behavior of others, or the ups and downs of the stock market or other myriad external factors which may affect you. You do, however, have control over your own behavior and your reactions to those external events. So keep track in detail of what you do during the day, each day, for one month. At the end of each day rate on a 1 to 10 scale how good that day was for you, with a rating of 1 representing awful and a 10 representing one of the best days of your life with gradations in between. Ratings of 7–8 would be good days. A 9 would be a great day. Average days would be in the 5–6 range. After a month of listing your daily activities in detail and compiling your ratings, look at the pattern of what you were doing on your good days. Were you more productive on the good days? Were you more social? Were you more likely to exercise? How much sleep did you get? Trends and patterns will emerge that you may not have been aware of before. Having a good day is often about a lot more than finding a $20 bill in the street, or getting an A on a paper in class, or a raise at work, although any of those fortuitous events are certainly mood boosters. For example, when this author did this exercise it was abundantly clear that my best days were when I was very productive at work, but also found time to connect with family and/or friends to balance my hard work; when I spent at least 40 minutes exercising; and when I cooked a nice meal for my family, but found someone else to do the dishes! Good days also tended to end with watching a particular late night TV comedy show that spoofed politics and allowed me to go to sleep with a smile on my face.

More on *Fake it til you make it*

Referring back to David Myers first suggestion to *fake it til you make it*, and following in the footsteps of the Have a Good Day exercise mentioned above; it would be useful to mention the results of yet another study which looked at the results of asking people to "act as if" they felt better. Fordyce (1977, 1983) published a series of studies wherein he evaluated a program designed to boost levels of happiness. The program was based on the hypothesis that levels of subjective well-being could be increased if people could learn to imitate the traits and behaviors of happy people, such as keeping busy, being well organized, spending more time socializing (acting like extraverts), maintaining an optimistic outlook and developing a healthy personality. Fordyce found that this program produced increases in happiness for the group that acted happy, compared with a placebo control group, as well as compared with participants in conditions receiving only partial information. In a follow up 9 to 25 months after the study, Fordyce discovered that there were lasting effects as those who learned how to act happy remained much happier than either of the control conditions.

Happiness—A Cause or Effect of the Good Life?

We began this chapter with a series of questions as to whether happiness is a cause or an effect of a variety of positive life outcomes. To summarize the research findings, clearly happy individuals are more likely to experience success in many domains of life including:

- Marriage
- Employment
- Income
- Work performance
- Friendships
- Psychological health

Lybormirsky, King & Diener (2005) tackled this chicken or egg problem by conducting a thorough review of two different kinds of happiness studies: (1) longitudinal studies that looked at what variables were correlated with happiness over time; and (2) experiments that manipulated positive moods to see what caused what. They concluded that happiness is not just a byproduct of living the good life, but also one of its causes. So, as we expected, happiness is both a cause and an effect! For a specific example, happy people are more likely to find and attract a mate. They are typically more outgoing, more optimistic about their prospects for relationships, and more fun to be around. Happy people tend to make a better adjustment to marriage, thus they are more likely to experience marital satisfaction. Then being in a happy marriage leads to greater happiness. It is like a positive cycle where positive emotions beget positive outcomes which beget happiness. The key is to break into the cycle at some point, using any and all of the strategies outlined in last two chapters, if your life circumstances or your genetics have not predisposed you in a cheerful direction.

Could Happiness Be Contagious?

A fascinating study was published online in a British Medical Journal (Christakis and Fowler, 2008) which reported that happiness appears to be contagious, that it spreads among friends, relatives and next-door neighbors like the flu! This study demonstrated that emotions have ripple effects throughout social networks of people, even to the point of affecting people who do not know each other.

Christakis and Fowler conducted a longitudinal study of 4700 subjects followed over a span of 20 years. They found that individuals who were happy or who eventually became happy increased the chances that someone they knew would be happy. Furthermore, this power of happiness spanned yet another degree of separation, boosting the happiness of those in the social circle of that happy person known by the original subject!

According to researcher Nicholas Christakis, a medical sociologist at Harvard, "You would think that your emotional state would depend on your choices and actions and experiences. But it also depends on the choices and actions and experiences of other people, including people to whom you are not directly connected. Happiness is contagious." The even better news is that the researchers found that this effect can linger for as much as a year, and while unhappiness can also rub off, it appears to be far less infectious than happiness.

Although previous research has documented the common experience that one person can lift the spirits of another who is in a bad mood, or, for example, seeing someone laugh often triggers giggles in others, this study is the first to demonstrate happiness spreading across groups, a *social networking effect*, for extended time periods. The researchers reported that when one person in the network became happy, the chances that friends, relatives, a spouse, or next-door neighbors became happy increased anywhere between 8% to 34%. These results do not hold for neighbors down the block beyond those who live next door. This effect persisted through three degrees of separation (e.g. friends of friends), although it grew progressively weaker with each degree of separation, dropping from 15%, to 10%, to 6% before completely disappearing. These findings provide stunning new evidence of the power of social networks. This research was conducted by the same team that did the social network study demonstrating that obesity was contagious.

New Trends in Positive Psychology

Like all branches of psychology, positive psychology has continued to evolve. Martin Seligman (2011) has once again spearheaded a shift away from his previous emphasis on attaining authentic happiness and life satisfaction, to a focus on flourishing and its five core elements (PERMA). His original theory postulated that happiness could be subdivided into three different elements: (1) positive emotions; (2) engagement (gratifications and flow); and (3) meaning and purpose. Over time Seligman realized that there were three basic inadequacies in this model. First and foremost, he recognized that happiness is often disproportionally tied to ones' mood of the moment. For example, Veenhoven (2006) demonstrated that subjects' mood colored their questionnaire responses to a large extent. He found that up to 70% of self reports of life satisfaction are heavily determined by mood at the time of assessment, while only 30% of the respondents reported life satisfaction reflected their subjective judgments of the quality of their lives in general.

Secondly, in a nod to the critics of positive psychology as "Happiology," Seligman recognized that undue emphasis was put on the attainment of positive emotions, with not enough focus on developing engagement and meaning. This is further complicated by the fact that your happiness level is often partially constrained by your genetically determined level of positive affectivity. Seligman himself bemoans the fact that he is relatively low on cerebral joy juice and therefore, he puts more emphasis on engagement and meaning for his personal well-being and life satisfaction.

Lastly, Seligman came to appreciate that his focus on the triumvirate of positive emotions, engagement and meaning was too limited. He recognized that for truly well rounded flourishing, you also need positive relationships as well as a sense of accomplishment. Adding these dimensions rounds out the concept of well-being and gives each of us many worthwhile options of where to put our energies in our own personal journey toward flourishing.

A Final Note: Pain Is Ultimately Part of Happiness

Just as we could not acknowledge beauty if we had no conception of ugly, nor could we recognize light if we did not experience dark; we cannot truly appreciate happiness unless we have known sadness. It is because of these contrasts that we become aware of our deepest feelings. Real life can be full of disappointments, loss, and inconveniences. Therefore, in any rich and meaningful life there will be a full range of emotions. We can learn from what hurts us, that is, pain often has inherent gifts which help us to grow. This is a phenomenon known as **Post Traumatic Growth**. We can learn to appreciate life more. We can develop coping skills. Ultimately it is about learning to flourish in spite of pain, emotional or otherwise.

Ultimately, crossing the finish line is not as rewarding as the anticipation of achieving your goal or the pursuit of such. Recognize that often, it is your actions within the journey toward your goals that leads to happiness, rather than the goals themselves. The hedonic treadmill eventually takes it toll on all goals, but not on the journey towards the goal. Easy hedonic pleasures rarely offer the lasting pleasure that mastering a new skill or creating something from scratch will.

Events in our life are almost never as bad or as good as we expect them to be. In general, humans are rotten at predicting our future feelings accurately, especially if our predictions are based on our past memories. Our memory is a very unreliable recording device, to a great extent because the passage of time skews our perceptions of happiness in many ways, either magnifying or minimizing it. The truism, *"this too shall pass"* holds many lessons for developing positive emotions. That is, when things are good, appreciate them to their fullest because they will not last forever. Conversely, when times are bad you can console yourself with the fact that they too will pass.

Lastly, it is nice to know that learning how to increase your level of positive emotions may have a delightful side effect – you may inadvertently boost the mood of loved ones and others around you, in subtle and indirect ways. Smile and the world smiles with you, especially when you flash a Duchenne smile, a beacon of contagion for joy.

KEY TERMS

Positive Emotions	Hedonic Treadmill	Attitude of Gratitude
Duchenne Smile	Hedonic Capacity	Forgiveness
Broaden and Build	Extraversion	Peak-End Theory
Undoing	Positive Affectivity	Duration Neglect
Hedonism	Savoring	Flow
Progress Paradox	Mindfulness	Eudemonia
Post Traumatic Growth	Engagement	

CHAPTER 3 QUESTIONS

True or False Questions (T or F)

1. ____ Individuals who exhibit a Duchenne smile tend to be rather melancholy.

2. ____ Positive emotions have served the evolutionary purpose of signaling safety.

3. ____ Positive emotions are distracting thus tending to limit our effectiveness.

4. ____ Positive emotions can serve as an antidote for stress.

5. ____ Abstinence from smoking is more important to longevity than happiness.

6. ____ The best way to increase your level of happiness is to make more money.

7. ____ People who are rich, famous, or beautiful are naturally happier than others.

8. ____ Your genetic heritage plays a role in your level of positive emotions.

9. ____ 100% of your happiness level is due to your genetic heritage.

10. ____ The hedonic treadmill helps us recover from loss or disappointment.

11. ____ People typically underestimate how long positive feelings will last.

12. ____ An optimistic outlook is an essential ingredient to happiness.

13. ____ Spacing out your pleasures over time will help enhance your enjoyment of them.

14. _____ Hedonists practice flow on a regular basis.

15. _____ People who are happy watch more TV than people who are unhappy.

16. _____ Attitude change follows behavior change. That is, fake it 'til you make it.

17. _____ Regular exercise has no relationship to happiness levels.

18. _____ Well being = Happiness + Meaning

19. _____ Happiness is both a cause and an effect of positive life outcomes.

20. _____ A strong social network is more important to happiness than financial wealth.

21. _____ Individuals living a eudemonic life tend to be alienated from their true selves.

22. _____ Unhappiness is contagious like the flu, but happiness is not contagious.

23. _____ Displaying a Duchenne smile is associated with the risk of premature death.

Short-Answer Questions

1. The _____ and _____ theory explains the wide ranging beneficial effects of positive emotions on humankind.

2. Positive affectivity tends to be related to levels of _____ and _____.

3. A study of longevity in nuns demonstrated that the best predictor of health and long life was the amount of _____ _____ expressed in their writings.

4. Riches and beauty do not lead to happiness in the long run because of the _____ _____.

5. Improving happiness about your past involves cultivating an attitude of _____ and practicing _____.

6. _____ are more long lasting than _____ because they are more resistant to habituation and allow us to utilize and build upon our strengths.

7. _____and _____ are ways to maximize pleasure in the present.

8. _____ is the awareness of pleasure that comes from paying deliberate conscious attention to your present experience.

9. _____ is most likely to occur when there is an optimal balance between a person's skills and degree of challenge.

10. Living a _____ life involves being happy and having a sense of meaning and purpose in your life.

Essay Questions

1. Why is it that wealth and beauty do not lead to happiness in the long run?

2. How can you prevent your pleasures from becoming addictive?

3. Of all the happiness boosting techniques and strategies mentioned in this chapter, which three were most relevant for you?

4. What is the role of genetics in happiness?

5. Describe broaden and build theory and its relevance to human evolution and everyday coping with stress.

6. Does happiness cause positive life outcomes or is happiness the result of fortuitous circumstances?

7. What role does optimism play in happiness?

8. Why does Seligman encourage us to focus on gratifications over pleasures in the pursuit of enduring happiness?

9. What produces flow for you?

10. What are the five elements essential for flourishing?

4

Learning to Accept Yourself

How is **self-esteem** relevant to effectiveness? At least in the Western World, studies suggest that effective individuals have learned to value themselves, to have what psychologists refer to as "healthy" or "positive" self-esteem or self-regard. There are numerous examples evidencing that in our part of the world, people with "low" or "negative" self-esteem have a significantly greater chance of feeling dissatisfied with their life, and suffering from poor mental and physical health, along with troubled relationships and school failure (Antonucci & Jackson, 1983; Dawes, 1994; Diener, 1984; Leary, 1983; Taylor & Brown 1988). Those with low self-esteem are at an increased risk of developing eating disorders, depression, and committing suicide (Emler, 2001). Additionally, studies have demonstrated that self-esteem is positively correlated with values and behaviors such as self-direction, achievement, and personal competence (Feather, 1991). But what is this thing we call self-esteem?

THE CONCEPT OF SELF-ESTEEM

Historically, self-esteem has referred to the relationship you have with yourself, the degree to which you regard yourself in a positive or negative light. It is a measure of how much you value yourself and feel useful and necessary in the world. It is different from your **self-concept** which is your paradigm about yourself and is reflected in how you might describe yourself. In contrast, your self-esteem refers to how you judge and evaluate yourself based on this paradigm. J. D. Brown (2007) defined self-esteem as the feelings of affection you have for yourself, further describing positive self-esteem as a general fondness or love for oneself. Those people with healthy self-esteem maintain a basic sense of self-acceptance even when they feel bad due to failure or rejection. They seem to possess an internal safety net that helps them keep disappointments in perspective. Seligman (1995) believes that self-esteem is a measure of how well you are doing in life. Commonly, self-esteem seems to refer to your global evaluation of yourself, and according to Carl Rogers (1959), it results from the discrepancy between your **ideal self** (the person you feel you should be) and your **real self** (the person you feel you actually are).

More recently, however, self-esteem has been defined as a socially constructed emotion, not much different than fear, anger, or joy (Hewitt, 2005). As such, the researchers argue that self-esteem can vary according to the person's mood at the time, and that it is difficult to envision self-esteem as a stable characteristic over time.

Nonetheless, while most psychologists would agree that there is certainly a broad measure of self-esteem, that is, the degree to which you like yourself in general, the fact is that self-esteem also fluctuates depending on how you regard yourself in specific areas. For example, you might have healthy self-esteem and confidence in yourself as an athlete, but low self-esteem as a scholar. Studies have identified several key areas, which help determine self-esteem, including physical appearance, scholastic ability, work performance, popularity and social skills, and athletic ability (Fleming & Courtney, 1984). The importance that you place on each of these areas will determine the weight they carry in influencing your global sense of self-esteem. For example, if you overemphasize the importance of physical appearance and you believe that you are unattractive, your self-esteem will clearly be negatively affected.

Why is having positive self-regard so important to your effectiveness? Because in our culture when you have faith in yourself, it enhances your ability to do your best, which in turn improves your performance and further reinforces your good feelings about yourself. Baumeister (1996), in his review of the research on self-esteem, concluded that people with healthy self-esteem are generally happier and tend to show perseverance in the face of failure. They don't let apparent obstacles or failed attempts dissuade them from their goals. As aptly described by Brehm (1998),

> When your self esteem is strong, mountains become molehills. A positive self-regard attracts others; when you are happier with yourself, you are happier with life and a pleasure to be with. A healthy self-esteem is essential to clear communication. When you value yourself, you value your thoughts and feelings and can express them more clearly to others. A positive self-esteem allows you to give more of yourself and enjoy other people. Best of all, a positive self-regard gives you freedom, the freedom to try new things, to make the most of opportunities, to be the best you can be, and get the most out of life. (p. 277)

On the other hand, low self esteem is a circular, self-defeating process where your negative feelings about yourself result in negative attitudes in general. These negative attitudes then become a driving force in your negative behaviors. Such negative behaviors then promote negative feelings, and so on. Thus, the person with low self-esteem becomes a psychological prisoner of his or her own poor self-image. The Neo-Freudian theorist, Alfred Adler (1928), described individuals with chronically low self-esteem as having an **"inferiority complex"**. Figure 4.1 illustrates both the positive cycle described above by Brehm and the contrasting negative vicious cycle.

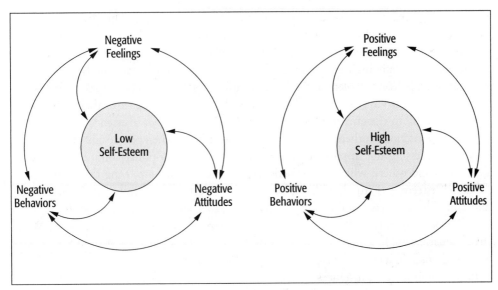

Figure 4.1

Lastly, having healthy self-esteem greatly facilitates your ability to cope with stress (Aspinwall & Taylor, 1992). When you have positive self-regard it is much easier to be an optimist, to view life's difficulties as opportunities for growth and self-discovery rather than as problems.

A word of caution here: Don't make the mistake of confusing positive self-esteem with being conceited or self-centered. Some people are afraid to hold themselves in positive regard because they fear it will make them seem stuck-up. Keep in mind; people who are conceited or stuck up are often braggarts. If you truly have healthy self-esteem you will not need to broadcast it. There is an old saying which sums this up perfectly, "when you have arrived, you don't need to shout." That is, people with healthy self-esteem don't need to boast about themselves or their achievements. They can recognize their strengths and accept compliments *and* criticisms. It is likely that those who feel the need to brag are actually trying to compensate for low self-esteem.

Thus, self-esteem is, indeed, correlated with effectiveness in our culture. Yet don't make the mistake of assuming that having positive self-esteem necessarily leads to effectiveness. Remember the difference between correlation and causation we mentioned earlier. Various investigators have demonstrated that there are times when a positive evaluation of the self is counterproductive. For example, a study investigating the relationship between self-perceptions that are positively biased and aggression found that the two were positively correlated. The investigators found when studying children in third, fourth, and fifth grades that the higher their self appraisal, the more the children's peers felt they were both overtly and relationally aggressive (David & Kristner, 2006).

Similarly, there are people who exhibit inordinately high self-esteem. They have an unrealistic self-appraisal termed the "superiority complex," which is equally problematic. Oftentimes these individuals have antisocial personalities or characteristics, or are overly narcissistic (i.e. extremely self-centered). These people tend to see themselves as above or superior to others and act out of that belief. For example, many (but not all) psychopathic individuals have extremely high self-esteem based on a grandiose, inflated self-image. This distortion of self-image leads sociopaths to harbor unrealistic expectations of what the world owes them, and can contribute to disordered, selfish, and even cruel behavior. Studies support the fact that people with an overly high evaluation of themselves might be a threat to others as they are more likely to be racist, violent and criminal (Emler, 2001). These people see themselves as separate from their environment and have little regard for the impact of their behavior on others. They fail to recognize our interconnectedness, the fact that in essence, we are neither superior nor inferior to others. As Hewitt (2005) described, "when people talk of self-esteem, they are expressing the importance of the affective link [emotional connection] between themselves and others; when they experience self-esteem, they are living this connection." "True self-esteem and true humility arise out of that realization" (Tolle, 2005). Self-esteem and humility may seem contradictory, but in truth, they are one and the same.

Unrealistically high self-esteem inhibits effectiveness. In fact, at times, an elevated positive evaluation might lead to feelings of entitlement, the belief that you deserve things, such as a good grade in a class, the latest clothing fashion, or a particularly hot car, regardless of your actions or the circumstances. This sense of entitlement is often accompanied by a belief that if you try your hardest, you should always be rewarded. These individuals seem to confuse the fact that trying to do something is not the same as doing it, and that often in life you can either have success or the excuses for not having achieved it, but not both.

Positive Self-Esteem Not Necessarily a Universal Experience

So, while in our culture, successful individuals tend to have a positive self-concept, having healthy self-esteem is not necessarily indicative of being a successful individual. But is the desire for positive self-esteem a universal experience? Do successful people typically experience positive self-esteem everywhere on the globe? You might have noticed that as we spoke about the importance of self-esteem as it relates to effectiveness, we kept qualifying it with "in our culture." There is some evidence that the motivation to have positive self-regard is not necessarily a cross-cultural reality. For example, Asian cultures do not seem to relate feeling good about the self with effectiveness (Heine, Lehman, Markus, & Kitayama, 1999).

In contrast, there is evidence that self-critical and self-improving orientations might be more related to being successful among Japanese and other Asian cultures. Some researchers have theorized that this difference between Western and Asian cultures is grounded on the fact that while Western cultures, and particularly North America, tend to stress the importance of the individual, Asian cultures are more focused on the importance of the collective. Thus, how one feels about the self is just not as important as how others feel about you. "Japanese tend to be motivated to gain the esteem of others rather than dwell on their own self-evaluations (Kuwayama, 1992, Spence, 1985)." Not surprisingly, while it is clear that in our culture there is a tendency to seek to enhance our self-esteem, for the Japanese their goal is to enhance their sense of belongingness (Heine, Lehman, Markus, & Kitayama, 1999).

Perhaps, as social psychologists Romin Tafarodi and William Swann suggest, a universal concept of self-esteem should include two factors: 1) self-liking, which they describe as a sense of social worth and 2) self-competence, a sense of personal efficacy (Tafarodi & Swann, Jr., 1995). When so defined, it again becomes evident that in collectivist societies such as the Chinese, the development of self-liking or social worth is emphasized much more strongly than the development of self-competency or personal efficacy. The inverse is true in individualistic societies such as the United States. Therefore, perhaps rather than talking about high self-esteem, we should focus on healthy or optimal self-esteem.

The Question of Self-Worth

So self-esteem is based on your appraisal of your **self-worth**. But, what is your self-worth based on? When we ask this of students in our classes, they typically respond with answers such as their achievements, caring for others, physical appearance, intellectual attributes, financial success, and even the extent of their material possessions (i.e., whether they drive a "hot car" or have fashionable clothes). Jennifer Crocker and Connie Wolfe (2001) examined possible sources of self-esteem, calling these "contingencies" of self-worth – the areas of life in which people believe that success means they are worthwhile and failure means they are worthless. These investigators identified seven possible domains in which people may invest their self-esteem. They labeled these: (1) family support; (2) competition; (3) appearance; (4) God's love; (5) academic competence; (6) virtue; and (7) others' approval. This is, by no means, an exhaustive list. The list merely reflects some of the more common domains that people identify as important to their self-esteem. We are sure you can think of other factors that might be important in determining the way we feel about ourselves.

Crocker and Wolfe (2001) argue that major problems such as depression, drug abuse, and aggression may be linked not so much to our general level of self-esteem, but rather to the source of our self-esteem. In a study of 600 college freshmen (Crocker, Luhtanen, & Bouvrette, 2001), self-esteem based on appearance was linked to more hours per week grooming, shopping, and partying. Self-esteem rooted in God's love positively correlated to spending more time in religious activities, such as praying and going to church or synagogue, and less time partying. Self-esteem based on academic competence was associated with greater success in gaining admission to graduate school. Not surprisingly, research upholds that if we base our self-esteem on physical appearance, our susceptibility to eating disorders increases. By the same token, people whose self-esteem is based on approval by others are especially susceptible to anger and hostility when others challenge them.

People who are unable to feel good about themselves on the basis of one source may shift to another. Out of frustration, they may even reject one source altogether and this rejection may lead to less than effective lives. For instance, the high dropout rate among African-American college students may be the consequence of rejecting academic performance as a source of self-worth after numerous frustrating attempts to succeed in an environment that assumes they are academically inferior (Steele, 1997).

Research suggests that having multiple sources or contingencies of self-worth is more effective than only having one or just a few. People with various sources of self-worth are less likely to be overwhelmed by negative life events affecting one of the sources. If feeling inadequate in one area of life, they can shift their attention to other important areas where things are going well.

Yet perhaps most effective, is to have self-esteem that is "non-contingent." Our students are often startled by our suggestion that *your self-worth is based on nothing*. It is a given. It is your birthright. Ideally, your self-esteem should be based on recognition of your inherent sense of worth as a human being independent of your achievements and attributes. You are worthy because you are a unique individual with your own special potentials. Research consistently suggests that contingent self-esteem is too often accompanied by anxiety, hostility, defensiveness, and the risk of depression. Edward Deci and Richard Ryan (1995) compared contingent self-esteem with what they labeled "true" or non-contingent self-esteem. The latter, they claimed is more stable and securely based in a solid sense of self. People with such non-contingent self-esteem are pleased when they succeed and disappointed when they fail, but their sense of self-worth is not at risk in the process. They have learned that it is not that "you can do it," but that "it's all right if you can't do it; it doesn't mean you are a bad person" (Brown, 1998). Too often we define our self-worth based on our performance or accomplishments. While your achievements are an integral part of who you are, and will undoubtedly contribute to your self-esteem, you will be doing yourself a great disservice if you define your worth solely on the basis of this dimension. You are worthy because you are human. It helps to believe that you are basically good, kind, caring, and worthy of being loved despite your faults or temporary failings. This is, of course, only a frame, but a very useful one, one that will lead to healthy self-esteem and greatly enhance your effectiveness as a human being. To quote the well-known author and motivational speaker Tony Robbins (1986), "I used to have to achieve to feel happy, now I happily achieve."

If you are curious about your level of self-esteem, we invite you to complete this questionnaire. Be honest and answer the questions to reflect how you really feel about yourself.

SELF-ESTEEM SELF-ASSESSMENT

Answer the following questions by assigning each one the appropriate number from the following scale:

1 = strongly agree   2 = agree   3 = disagree   4 = strongly disagree

_____ 1. I feel that I am a person of worth, at least on an equal basis with others.

_____ 2. I feel that I have a number of good qualities.

_____ 3. All in all, I am inclined to feel I am a failure.

_____ 4. I am able to do things as well as most other people.

_____ 5. I feel I do not have much to be proud of.

_____ 6. I take a positive attitude toward myself.

_____ 7. On the whole, I am satisfied with myself.

_____ 8. I wish I could have more respect for myself.

_____ 9. I certainly feel useless at times.

_____ 10. At times I think I am no good at all.

_____ TOTAL SCORE **(Read directions below before adding)**

Scoring: **On questions 3, 5, 8, 9, and 10 convert your numbered answers as follows: Change 1 to 4; change 4 to 1; change 2 to 3; change 3 to 2. Now total your responses. The lower your score the higher your self-esteem.**

        10–15 **Healthy Self-Esteem**
        16–20 **Good Self-Esteem**
        21–30 **Moderately Low Self-Esteem**
        31–40 **Very Poor Self-Esteem**

So how did you do? Where do you lie on the continuum of negative to positive self-esteem? Now that you have an added measure of your level of perceived self worth, let's look at the characteristics of individuals with healthy vs. low self-esteem listed in Table 4.1.

TABLE 4.1 Characteristics of People with Healthy and Low Self-Esteem

Healthy Self-Esteem	Low Self-Esteem
• Believe that they are worthwhile and valuable.	• Believe that their worth is based on their accomplishments or the opinions of others.
• Sees demanding goals as a challenge.	• Is highly critical of self and others.
• Recognizes the strengths and achievements of self and others.	• More likely to be prejudiced.
• Acknowledges their personal power without being manipulative.	• Doubt their personal power.
• Takes responsibility for their own actions without blaming or making excuses.	• Likely to be hero worshipers.
• Able to take risks. Is not afraid of failure.	• Resistant to change.
• Do not view failure or rejection as a reflection upon their self-worth.	• Fearful of taking risks that may lead to failure.
• Accepts compliments.	• View failure or rejection as evidence of their lack of self-worth.
• Accepts and values constructive criticism.	• Discounts praise from others.
• Generous with their praise for others.	• Show an inability to accept constructive criticism.
• Is able to give themselves positive self messages.	• Give self negative internal messages.
• Do not feel the need to continually prove themselves.	• Tend to be highly competitive.
• Is able to communicate their needs and wants effectively.	• Feel a need to win to prove themselves.
• Is able to develop satisfying interpersonal relationships.	• May resort to workaholism to prove their worth.
• Recognizes the value of all experiences.	• Have difficulty communicating their needs.
• Is capable of working well as a team member.	• Are likely to remain in unsatisfying relationships.
• Have trust in themselves.	• Tend to value appearances over substance.
• Seeks balance in their life.	• Inability to make decisions and take action without clearly defined rules.
• See the value in continued personal growth and self exploration.	• Doubt themselves.
• Surround themselves with people who validate them.	• Lack balance in their lives.
• Are seldom controlled by guilt.	• Are threatened by personal growth experiences.
• Are optimistic about themselves, others and the world.	• Often attract people who denigrate them.
• Value the power of their word.	• Are guilt ridden.
• Are proactive.	• Are pessimistic about themselves, others and the world.
• Accept all of their feelings as natural, human and a part of life.	• Typically don't live up to their word.
• Are good losers.	• Are reactive.
• Are not afraid to be different or take an unpopular stand.	• Consider negative emotions as further proof of their lack of worth.
	• Are poor losers.
	• Resort to fadism to be included in the "in crowd."

The Pathological Critic

How is it that we sabotage our self-esteem? Each of us has an inner voice, which evaluates and judges our actions and ourselves. The nature of this inner voice reflects the quality of your relationship with yourself. Psychologist Eugene Sagan coined the term **"pathological critic"** to describe what he saw as a negative inner voice that attacks and judges you. Although it is true that for most people their inner voice tends to be critical, this is clearly not necessary or particularly effective. Perhaps a more appropriate metaphor would be that of a misguided critic or coach. The intention behind this inner coach's behavior and communications is always positive, i.e. it is always trying to help you do or not do that which it believes is best for you. However, the way that it goes about this frequently accomplishes just the opposite of what it is trying to do. Our goal is not to help you get rid of this coach altogether, but to train it in using methods which are more aligned with assisting you to improve your self-esteem, to value yourself more positively.

To illustrate this point, we ask that you entertain the notion that change or growth in the human being occurs in a similar fashion as that of the task of toilet training a child. Initially, the child does not even recognize that she is not to relieve herself in her clothes. After some training, she knows what is expected, but cannot translate this into appropriate anticipatory behaviors. Thus she can only report to us once she has already messed her clothes. Later on she can recognize it as it is happening, and thus can change her behavior midstream (pun intended). After a while she can anticipate the need to defecate or urinate and can go and do it in the toilet. Now, we know that toilet training occurs quickest and most effectively if we acknowledge and reinforce (reward) the child every step of the way, for indeed this is clearly a process of step by step learning. If we want to make toilet training difficult and lengthy, then we need to criticize and demean the child for the mistakes she makes. The same holds true for how we deal with ourselves. If we criticize and demean ourselves, we get stuck repeating the same behavior or mistakes over and over again, and as an added bonus we lower our self-esteem. But if we approach ourselves as we would someone we respect, admire and love, then we find we feel better about ourselves and can notice changes in ways which promote our growth.

THE ROOTS OF SELF-ESTEEM

Self-esteem has its roots both in genetics and in learning (i.e. environmental effects). Studies of identical twins reared apart, as well as studies comparing the personalities of adopted children with their biological and adoptive parents clearly reveal that our adult personalities are influenced by our genetic makeup (Lykken, and colleagues, 1992; Plomin and others, 1994; Bergemen and others, 1993). Identical twins reared apart are more like each other in such traits as shyness, well-being, intelligence, anger, neuroticism, and depression (traits which would influence our self-esteem), than fraternal twins reared together. Similarly, adopted children are more similar as adults to their biological parents than to their adoptive parents, with regards to these traits. Thus, there is little doubt that your genetic makeup does contribute to your level of self-esteem. Remember that people with healthy self-esteem retain an innate sense of self-acceptance even when saddened by rejection or failure. Those with low self-esteem lack this internal safety net. When they fail at something or experience rejection, they plummet much lower. And they tend to perceive rejection and failure even when it does not exist. Jonathon D. Brown, one of social psychology's most frequently cited authors, believes that we all have a basic level of self-esteem that is set during our childhood interactions with parents. He believes the solid safety net of basic self-esteem grows out of a secure attachment to a parent (Brown, 2007). As you will see in more detail in Chapter 11 when we discuss attachment theory, it might be that a corrective relationship wherein you are loved and valued for more than your accomplishments or characteristics is the best way of achieving an optimal level of self-esteem.

By the same token, your interactions with those around you are also a major contributing factor to how you evaluate yourself. Many people and events in your life combine to shape your self-esteem from the moment of your birth. Infants can sense whether people respond to them with acceptance and love, contempt, or indifference, which helps lay the early groundwork for self-esteem (Pelham & Swann, 1989). Your self-esteem is influenced by your parents, siblings, relatives, schoolteachers, peers, bosses, co-workers, etc. Although many of these individuals may no longer be involved in your life, what you learned from them may still wield a dramatic impact on your self-perceptions. The foundation for self-esteem appears to be laid very early in life, and it is believed that some children have poor self-esteem even prior to starting school.

Parental Influences

For most of us, our parents are the most significant influence in shaping our self-esteem, particularly early in life. In most cases, they were our major source of love, security and need fulfillment. If you were fortunate enough to have been raised by parents who cherished you and treated you as a valued human being, worthy of love, you will probably enjoy positive self-esteem in your later life. However, if your parents were too preoccupied with their own troubles, or with work, to give you the attention and love you deserved, the development of healthy self-esteem, while not impossible, would certainly be more difficult.

Many theorists have speculated on how parental behavior influences the self-esteem of children. Carl Rogers (1951) observed that children develop positive self-esteem when parents show them **unconditional positive regard**, which refers to their acceptance of them as having intrinsic merit regardless of their behavior at the moment. Unconditional positive regard involves a consistent expression of love and esteem for the child as a person. When parents show children **conditional positive regard**, that is, they judge the child's value and deliver their love based on the acceptability of the child's behavior, children develop **conditions of worth**, meaning that they only think they are worthwhile or lovable if they behave in certain ways or meet certain standards. Karen Horney (1956) suggested that parents often unknowingly diminish their children's self esteem by being erratic, domineering, overprotective, demanding, critical, overindulgent, partial to other siblings, or indifferent. Harry Stack Sullivan (1953) noted that when children are treated badly they can develop what he described as **the malevolent attitude**—the belief that one is surrounded by enemies. As a result of this attitude the child comes to view him or herself as someone who is detestable and will always be treated poorly, and moreover, who does not deserve to be treated well.

Returning to our coach metaphor, it is safe to say that for most of you, your original coaches did the best they could and most likely had your best intentions in mind, however, their coaching styles may not have always been healthy. If your coach was overly critical, that took a toll on your self-esteem. Perhaps even more crucial, many of your coaches may have failed to differentiate between you and your behavior when correcting or disciplining you. Have you ever heard, "You are a bad boy," or "You are so lazy," or "How stupid could you possibly be?" These statements are directed at the self and teach you to evaluate yourself neg-atively. Had your coaches been able to differentiate between you and your behavior, they may have made comments like, "I don't like it when you act that way," or "That behavior is unacceptable," or "I get angry when you do..." In addition, your level of self-esteem is also a byproduct of how you saw your coaches treat themselves, that is, what they modeled for you. If your coach was overly self-critical you may have learned to adopt this particular style. The bottom line is that how you treat yourself, or more specifically, how you coach your-self, typically resembles how you were coached.

Parenting Styles

At this point you may be wondering what kind of parenting is likely to maximize the oppor-tunities for the healthy development of self-esteem in the child. To answer this we first need to consider what have been termed parenting styles. Diana Baumrind (1991) identified three basic parenting styles that impact on child development: (1) **authoritarian parenting**; (2) **authoritative parenting**; and (3) laissez-faire (permissive) parenting. Other theorists (Maccoby and Martin, 1983) further differentiated permissive parenting into two sub-groups: (1) **permissive-indifferent** and (2) **permissive-indulgent**. Authoritarian parents have a restrictive, punitive style of parenting focusing on following rules and assuming that the child is incompetent. Permissive-indifferent parents are uninvolved in their child's life. They are not particularly harsh or punitive, but basically treat the child as if he/she is not particularly important. Permissive-indulgent parents are very involved in the child's life and often very loving, but they fail to set limits or provide meaningful controls over the child's behavior. They may be very indulgent without requiring the child to earn any of the rewards, thus the child may end up quite spoiled. Authoritative parents are warm and nur-turing while at the same time setting meaningful limits and controls for the child. These parents are very involved in the lives of their children.

It may seem rather obvious to you that the authoritative parenting style should be the most effective for fostering self-esteem in the child. You are correct if you have made this assumption, and it useful to know that research backs this up, as well, according to Bolt (2004). The classic research of Coopersmith (1967, 1975) demonstrated this by studying the self-esteem patterns of fifth and sixth grade boys. The boys with healthy self-esteem typ-ically came from homes where their parents were strict, but not harsh. Their parents were affectionate, accepting, very involved in their son's activities, and used consistent, reasonable discipline for enforcing clear cut limits. Boys with low self-esteem came from families where the parents were in some ways more permissive, but were quite harsh when discipline was enforced. These parents were far less involved in their son's lives, often oblivious to misbe-havior until it reached a critical point where the parents might overreact. The parents of the boys with positive self-esteem were more demanding of their sons in terms of achievement and meeting standards, but their involvement in their son's lives communicated a deep car-ing and value for the child. Coopersmith also found that once self-esteem was established it remained relatively consistent across the school years.

But is this always the case? You may be interested to know that other researchers have found that some children develop healthy self-esteem even though they were raised in very dysfunctional environments. For example, Emmy Werner (cited in Hamburg, 1994) con-ducted a longitudinal study of 700 children from dysfunctional homes, where parenting styles were far from ideal. Some of the children in this study had positive self-esteem despite inadequate parental influences. These resilient children all appeared to have four character-istics in common: (1) they took an active approach to problem solving, believing they could find solutions; (2) they found positive ways of reframing their experiences, even the bad ones; (3) they were adept at getting positive attention from others; and (4) they were opti-mists. How did this happen? We are not certain from the research, but somehow these chil-dren had learned to be more proactive, perhaps on their own, or perhaps out of their proclivity to attract positive people into their lives (i.e. teachers, coaches, etc.) to serve as mentors, and perhaps some were genetically predisposed to higher levels of self esteem.

Let us also make clear that when we talk about the different parenting styles, we are oversimplifying a very dynamic and complex relationship. No parents are always authorita-tive or always authoritarian or always permissive. Their behavior towards their children varies depending on a multitude of factors including level of stress, difficulties at work, and hours of sleep. Since parenting is not one way, but an interaction, the parents' behaviors are also influenced by the behavior of their children. A particular behavior pattern, which might have produced the desired results with one child, might result in quite different and often surprising reactions from a sibling. Each child is different, and as such, parents must, by necessity, behave differently with each child.

Other Important Influences

Obviously, parents are not the only agents who influence self-esteem. Teachers can often have a deep impact on the development of a child's self-esteem, particularly in the early years. A highly critical teacher can certainly inflict damage on a child's self image, especially if it involves being ridiculed in front of the class. On the other hand, a good teacher, one who encourages and praises a child's progress, can help repair the faltering self-esteem of a child who is very unsure of her abilities. Certainly peer influences are paramount as well. The agony of being rejected by peers, ostracized on the playground in elementary school, left out of the cliques in middle school, not being invited to parties, or picked for sports teams in P. E. class, can each take a heavy toll.

But the development of our self-esteem is not only dependent upon what we have learned from others or how others treated us. It is also a byproduct of what we learn from experiencing life independently. Failure experiences can certainly undermine self-image, whether this occurs in childhood or in adulthood. Given that our level of self-esteem repre-sents an ongoing process, events in adulthood can either enhance or detract from our per-ceived level of self-worth. So if you enjoy success at work and/or in your relationships, you will likely experience enhanced self-esteem. If you are losing jobs or failing to gain advance-ment at work, or you are suffering disappointments in love, you may experience diminished self-esteem.

HOW TO BOOST YOUR SELF-ESTEEM

If your self-esteem is a measure of how you evaluate yourself, then let's return for a moment to two previously mentioned concepts which are central to your level of self-esteem, that of your real self and your ideal self. Your real self, your evaluation of yourself regarding various characteristics and attributes is, for most people, regularly compared to your ideal self, the desired state of being which you seek to achieve. Many people hold their ideal self to be something they *should* be and then feel disappointed with themselves when they fail to reach this goal. What many people forget is that the ideal self is just that, an IDEAL. It serves as a guiding light in your continual process of growth rather than a grade you need to achieve. The person with healthy self-esteem realizes that their real self is in an everlasting process of change, moving towards their ideal self but never reaching it. This is what Carl Rogers described as "The Process of Becoming."

The first step in learning to improve your self-esteem is to realize that your current level of self-esteem is, ultimately, your choice. This is, of course, not to say that the myriad of past and present influences on your level of self-esteem, both positive and negative, as well as your genetic makeup, did not influence how you feel about yourself. Your genes and your experiences *influenced* your self-image, but they do not determine it. You can choose to work towards developing a satisfying level of self-esteem. The task of enhancing and then maintaining positive self-esteem is a life long process of personal growth in which we all proceed slowly, step by step. This is made challenging by the fact that the world is often a far less than ideal place to live. Disappointments occur, things change, and events will not always go your way. You will inevitably make mistakes, and you will not succeed at everything you attempt. Your self-esteem can be a casualty in this process unless you have learned how to nurture yourself. What follows are strategies and guidelines for building a nurturing relationship with yourself that will allow you to truly appreciate who you are, in bad times as well as good times.

Uncovering Irrational Beliefs

To begin, we suggest you examine your paradigm regarding the qualities you believe a person worthy of optimal self esteem must possess. Could some of your beliefs be based on unrealistic expectations or irrational thoughts? As described in Chapter 2, it is important that you take a look at any irrational thoughts which may be influencing the frame by which you evaluate yourself. Albert Ellis and others have described how irrational beliefs affect the way we feel about ourselves. Irrational beliefs, which impact on self-esteem, typically take the form of what we should and should not do and be. These *shoulds* are generated by parental, cultural, and peer expectations, as well as by your need to feel loved, to belong, and to feel safe and good about yourself. What gives theses shoulds their power is your belief that they represent the truth. This is the *tyranny of the shoulds:* the absolute nature of beliefs, this unbending sense of right and wrong. If you don't live up your shoulds, you then judge yourself to be a bad, unworthy person and your self-esteem goes out the window.

The following is a list of some of the most common irrational beliefs people hold about themselves. Look through this list carefully. If a statement fits you, even occasionally, place an X in the space next to it. This exercise will help you identify your irrational beliefs and give you insight about thoughts, which stand in the way of your self-esteem.

COMMON PATHOLOGICAL SHOULDS QUESTIONNAIRE

1. ____ I should be the epitome of generosity and unselfishness.
2. ____ I should be the perfect lover, friend, parent, teacher, student, spouse, and so on.
3. ____ I should be able to endure any hardship with equanimity.
4. ____ I should be able to find a quick solution to every problem.

5. ____ I should never feel hurt. I should always feel happy and serene.

6. ____ I should be completely competent.

7. ____ I should know, understand, and foresee everything.

8. ____ I should never feel certain emotions such as anger or jealousy.

9. ____ I should love my children equally.

10. ____ I should never make mistakes.

11. ____ My emotions should be constant—once I feel love, I should always feel the same.

12. ____ I should be totally self-reliant.

13. ____ I should never be tired or sick.

14. ____ I should never be afraid.

15. ____ I should always be busy; to relax is to waste my time and my life.

16. ____ I should have achievements that bring me status, wealth, or power.

17. ____ I should always put others first; it is better that I feel pain than cause anyone else to feel pain.

18. ____ I should be unfailingly kind.

19. ____ I should never feel sexually attracted to _____.

20. ____ I should care for everyone who cares for me.

21. ____ I should make enough money so that my family can afford _____.

22. ____ I should be able to protect my children from all pain.

23. ____ I should not take time just for my own pleasure.

24. ____ I should be more like other people.

Overcoming the Tyranny of the Shoulds

How many of the above items did you endorse? Even if only a few, recognize that the pathological critic feeds and thrives on these shoulds. What image comes to mind when you hear statements such as, "You should be successful," "You should always be considerate of others," or "You should never get angry?" For most people the image that comes up is that of a parent or authority figure pointing their finger and scolding them, telling them what they should or should not do, or think, or feel. To increase your self esteem, we encourage you to *stop shoulding on yourself.* You have the right to question any and all of these shoulds. When you recognize that your behavior is being guided by "a should," ask yourself, "Should according to whom?" Are these your choices, or are you merely parroting some often heard messages that you have gotten from others? If the latter is so, realize that you are being reactive, literally giving away your power to that internalized authority figure. You would be proactive if you can say with certainty that these are values that you truly want for yourself, and *you* decide to set them as the standards by which you live. The irrational beliefs, which undermine your self-esteem, the *tyranny of the shoulds,* are a subset of the irrational beliefs discussed in Chapter 2. Remember that many of us were taught unrealistic beliefs such as those above. That is why we have such terrible feelings when someone does not like us or when we fail. In spite of their commonness, though, these beliefs are irrational. They are based on the premise that our self-worth is solely determined by the approval of others and by continual striving for perfection. We urge you to challenge the frames by which you are judging yourself, using the techniques of cognitive restructuring discussed earlier.

According to Ellis and Harper (1961), the negative self-statements used by the pathological critic, which are generated by these irrational beliefs, must be replaced by positive self-statements. Following the four step framework for challenging irrational beliefs presented earlier in Chapter 2, question your shoulds. You will find that by replacing these with more rational self statements, your self-esteem will steadily climb. For example:

> It is definitely nice to have people like and approve of me, but even without that, I can still accept and love myself.

> Doing things well is satisfying, but it is human to err.

> It is healthy for me to relax at times. It is important to recharge my batteries.

> Not all problems lend themselves to quick solutions.

> It is part of the human experience to occasionally feel emotions such as anger, sadness, jealousy and hurt.

One of the most salient differences between individuals with positive self-esteem vs. individuals with low self-esteem is in the nature and content of their self-talk. People with healthy self-esteem do not continually barrage themselves with negative messages or observations about themselves. This does not mean that they are unaware of their faults or that they discount constructive criticism, but rather that they tend to give positive, self-affirming messages to themselves. For example, a person with positive self-esteem who is required to give a speech but nervous about the upcoming performance would prepare himself by recalling other successful public speaking experiences, and by reassuring himself that he knows the material. A person with low self-esteem in the exact same situation would likely remember only uncomfortable public speaking experiences, and tell himself that he was going to do poorly, or make a fool of himself.

Research has shown that people with low self-esteem can successfully change irrational negative beliefs about themselves. Individuals with low self-esteem tend to attribute their failures to internal causes (weaknesses and shortcomings), reflecting doubts about their self-worth. However, when these individuals succeed they tend to attribute their success to external sources such as luck. Brockner and Guare (1983) hypothesized that by inducing people with low self-esteem to ascribe their failures to possible external causes (factors beyond their control), and their successes to internal causes (ability and effort), self-esteem could be modified. In addition, they theorized that people with low self-esteem could be encouraged to try harder, thereby maximizing their chances for success, which could further elevate their self-esteem. Does this sound familiar? It harkens back to the lessons on developing an optimistic outlook.

In their study, college students were divided into two groups based on low and positive self esteem. All students were then given an insoluble task so that each student experienced failure. Following this initial failure experience each student was given a task that was solvable. Prior to the second task, some subjects in both groups were told that their previous failure stemmed from external causes (e.g. the task could not be solved). Other subjects in both groups were led to believe that their previous failure was due mostly to internal causes.

And the remaining subjects in both groups were given no information regarding possible causes of the initial failure. The results indicated that students with low self-esteem were able to accept that failure may be due to external causes. But more importantly, the students with low self-esteem who were led to believe that the initial failure was not their fault, performed the best of any group on the second task! So a positive cycle had been set in motion. Now, this does not imply that it is wise to teach people with low self-esteem to always attribute all failures to external causes; that certainly would not be proactive. But the process of challenging irrational, perfectionist beliefs can assist individuals with low self-esteem to evaluate themselves more realistically and fairly.

Eliminating Cognitive Distortions

Irrational beliefs are also fueled by **cognitive distortions**, which refer to the tendency to look for verification to support your existing opinion of yourself. In other words, via selective perception we tend to pay attention to that which supports what we already believe about ourselves. Epstein (1992) pointed out that individuals with low self-esteem are prone to look for evidence of where they fall short, rather than appreciating their achievements. If your self-esteem is low and you are focusing only on where you come up short, return to the guidelines for facilitating optimism covered in Chapter 2. Using the method of looking for alternative evidence, challenge your cognitive distortions. If you look for contrary evidence, it is quite likely that you will find it.

Alternative Ways of Framing Mistakes

> *"I have not failed 10,000 times,*
> *I have successfully found 10,000 ways that will not work."*
>
> Thomas Edison

Most people think of a mistake as something they did wrong. But this is simply not the case. A more appropriate definition is that a mistake is any behavior, which you do or fail to do which later, as you reflect about it, you wish you had not done or had done differently. The key word here is LATER. At the time you behaved or did not behave in a particular fashion, you did the best that you possibly could. All decisions are made on the basis of insufficient information, for none of us has the power to foretell the future. "Mistake" is a label which you apply later on, when you wish you had done something else based on 20/20 hindsight. The issue here is awareness. At the time you did or did not do something, you were functioning with a certain degree of awareness. By the time you labeled something a mistake, you had more information and were more aware of the consequences. Within that awareness you always behave in a way that you believe will best meet your needs. If you want not to repeat the same mistakes, we suggest you focus on expanding your awareness, that is, gathering more data before acting, or learning to anticipate the consequences of actions, rather than just resolving to never make the same mistake again. Unless you expand your awareness, it is almost guaranteed that you will repeat the same mistakes. In addition, the more you berate yourself for having made them, the greater the probability that you will make them again.

Thus a mistake becomes a mistake only after some time has passed. The length of time is not important. What is important is that at the time you did it, you did the best you could. It makes no sense to criticize yourself about it. Thinking about mistakes in this fashion allows you to see them in a different light or to reframe them. To further this new perspective, consider that a strong case can be made that mistakes serve as invaluable teachers. They provide you with information about what works and what does not work. When you were a toddler learning how to walk, you needed to fall in order to learn your balance. Had you been afraid of making mistakes, you would still be crawling! This is true for everything in your life. Mistakes are an absolutely necessary part of the learning process. Rather than fearing them you need to welcome them. It might help to think that the more mistakes you make, the more you are learning. Ultimately, there is no such thing as mistakes, only feedback. If you set perfectionistic standards for yourself, you rob yourself of the ability to accept yourself as a fallible but worthwhile human being.

Another way to view mistakes is to think of them as warnings. If you get a poor grade on a test, that could be a warning that you need to study more or change your study habits. It is only when you think that you need to be perfect that mistakes become an indictment rather than a warning.

Yet another way to throw a different frame around mistakes is by realizing that if you are going to behave in a spontaneous fashion, you will most certainly make some mistakes. Without the willingness to make mistakes, you can only act in totally predetermined ways in familiar situations. How boring! You would also kill your self-expression, since to say what you feel or what you think does not always have predictable results, i.e. you risk making a mistake. If you don't allow yourself to say the wrong thing, then you are never free enough to say the right thing.

In his book *Building Self-Esteem*, Glenn Schiraldi (1993) recommends utilizing a particular technique for maintaining your self-esteem in the face of mistakes. This technique is called "Nevertheless," which helps you to acknowledge your mistakes while simultaneously affirming your basic self-worth. People with low self-esteem typically are likely to engage in "because...therefore" thinking, reflected in such statements as, "because of _____, therefore I am no good." You can replace this with "even though _____, nevertheless." So for example, instead of saying, "because I did poorly on this test, therefore I am stupid," you could say, "even though I did poorly on this test, nevertheless I am capable of doing much better if I study harder."

We hope by now you may be beginning to see mistakes in a different light, perhaps as friends rather than enemies. Some people believe that all mistakes are to be avoided, that intelligent, competent people somehow don't make them. That is nonsense. A much wiser position is to allow for a quota for mistakes, for without them you would not be human.

Love Your Inner Child

Speaking metaphorically, of course, we all carry within ourselves a child, the child we used to be. Our perceptions of how others treated us as children are later reflected in how we treat this child within, also referred to as the **"inner child."** If you are critical with yourself, or at best try to be logical and rational with the inner child all the time, it will inevitably fail to have the desired effect since, like most children, your inner child does not respond to logic and rationality. Have you ever tried convincing a four or five year old that there is no monster in the closet? What works to reassure an insecure child are communications indicating that she is safe, protected, loved and that, she will certainly survive. Part of maintaining your self-esteem is having this compassionate relationship with your inner child.

THE GLOBAL PERSPECTIVE–The Power of Service

One of the most encouraging developments on college campuses throughout the United States has been the explosion of **service-learning**. The American Association of Community Colleges defines service-learning as "the combination of community service and classroom instruction, with a focus on critical, reflective thinking as well as personal and civic responsibility." But use of service learning as a teaching strategy is not limited to our nation. Some countries such as Nigeria, China, Ghana, Canada, France, and Germany have well-established national service programs similar to the federal AmeriCorps programs in the U.S. (Gottlieb and Robinson, 2002). A growing body of research makes evident the power of service learning in teaching students to be more involved citizens. Studies out of UCLA revealed that participating in service learning while in college significantly improved students' civic responsibility, academic development, and overall life skill development (Astin and Sax 1998; Astin and colleagues, 2000). Other studies support the fact that students who partake of service-learning through their classes subsequently demonstrate greater citizenship, social responsibility, cooperation, and leadership (Andersen, 1998; Putnam, 2000). Similarly, another research project showed that students who performed community service were more aware of the need to become involved in the policy process, felt a greater connection to the community, and were better able to view situations from other's perspectives (Eyler, Giles, and Braxton, 1997).

For many of the students, the experience was a powerful one as reported by Gottlieb and Robinson (2002):

> *"My idea of citizenship and civil society has changed as a result of my [service learning] experience. I now feel like it is my duty to give back to the community by becoming an involved citizen. Because of this wonderful experience, I now see the positive effects service learning has on society."*

(Service learning student at Miami Dade College).

Research in Positive Psychology has clearly demonstrated the link between service and positive self-esteem. The "***feel good/do good effect***" is in fact now a well-established psychological principle. People who feel good about themselves are more helpful. But the reverse is also true, what we may call the "***do good/feel good effect***." People who help others feel better about themselves. In fact, they feel better, in general. A survey of over 1700 women who frequently participated in pro-social activities, reported that they experienced a "high" while helping and a sense of "calm" following the experience (Batson, 1991). It seems it is true that it is better to give than to receive. Indeed, giving support and assistance is a better predictor of longevity than receiving it (Brown and colleagues, 2003). Individuals who engage in service to others are half as likely to die within a specified time period, than those who receive help from others, when other variables related to mortality, such as age, gender, smoking and drinking were factored out. It seems that focusing beyond the self allows us to expand our view of ourselves to include our interconnectedness. When we become genuinely invested in others or in a task larger than ourselves, we find more meaning and evaluate ourselves more positively. As Mother Theresa counseled "nothing makes you happier than when you really reach out in mercy to someone who is badly hurt" (Myers, 1992).

ENHANCING YOUR SELF ESTEEM: THE POSITIVE PSYCHOLOGY APPROACH

Earlier in the chapter we mentioned how a measure of self-esteem that is relevant worldwide might need to include two factors: (1) your perception of how other members of your community appraise you; and (2) your own sense of personal efficacy and worth. Positive psychology suggests an approach to enhancing self-esteem, which encompasses both of these factors. This involves the study of **character**—the development of **virtues** and their corresponding **signature strengths**.

Consideration of the role of character in human development was virtually ignored once Behaviorism became the dominant paradigm in psychology in the second half of the twentieth century. The indirect study of character was relegated to one corner of scientific psychology – the study of personality. The direct study of character was abandoned because of the bias that science should only describe behavior, rather than recommend certain behaviors, and also because character was viewed as a value-laden construct tied to Victorian morality and therefore non-scientific and unworthy of study.

Positive psychology resurrected the study of character by enlisting a distinguished panel of mental health professionals to create a system designed to be the opposite of the DSM–IV (Diagnostic and Statistical Manual of Mental Disorders–Fourth Revision, which classifies and describes mental illnesses) to catalogue the components of mental health. They began this process by setting three criteria for strengths, which are as follows:

- They are valued in almost every culture.

- They are valued in their own right, not just a means to other ends.

- They are malleable, changeable by choice and exercise of will.

After surveying writings spanning over 3000 years covering virtually every major religious, philosophical and cultural tradition, they discovered that all endorsed and agreed upon these six core virtues which encompass good character.

- **WISDOM AND KNOWLEDGE**
- **COURAGE**
- **LOVE AND HUMANITY**
- **JUSTICE**
- **TEMPERANCE**
- **SPIRITUALITY AND TRANSCENDENCE**

These broad areas comprising the six core virtues can be further subdivided into what Seligman refers to as "signature strengths," which are traits and behaviors that you can develop by exercising proactive choice. These strengths are not the same as talents. Talents are typically inborn (such as musical or artistic abilities, athletic virtuosity). You can choose to develop your talent or capitalize on it, but it is innate, a genetic gift of sorts that you may or may not cultivate with practice, training or dedication. In other words, you either have a talent or you do not. You can learn to play a musical instrument competently, but you can't learn to be a talented musician. On the other hand, strengths based on virtue can be built, even from scratch, with enough dedication, persistence, practice or access to good teaching if you choose to do so. You cannot waste nor squander a strength as you can with talent. This is because the development of signature strengths is based upon decisions, the choice as to whether to acquire it in the first place, where and how to utilize it, and whether to keep developing it. Signature strengths also have the following hallmarks:

- A sense that this represents the real you, the core of who you are (eudemonia).

- A feeling of excitement while displaying it, particularly at first.

- A rapid learning curve as the strength is displayed, especially in the beginning.

* A strong desire to find new ways to demonstrate it.
* A feeling of empowerment, as if it would be hard to stop you from practicing it.
* A sense of invigoration rather than exhaustion while using the strength.
* The pursuit and creation of projects that provide opportunities to use the strength.
* Experiencing positive emotions while using it.
* At times having flow experiences when exercising the strength.

Before we talk in more depth about these signature strengths, it is important to clarify the link between the development of character and self-esteem. When you develop good character, which is manifested through developing and using your strengths, it can have a significant, real world positive effect upon your self-esteem. For example, if you find a wallet with ID that is loaded with cash and you return it with all funds untouched to its rightful owner, or you alert a store cashier that you were given too much change and return the balance, you deserve to feel pride that you did the right thing. You know that despite any inner temptations to pocket the money, you put forth the effort to behave honestly. If you are fair to yourself, you will feel good about you. When you behave honestly, kindly, wisely, fairly, prudently, which are all matters of choice; you provide a plethora of opportunities to feel good about yourself and enhance your self-evaluation. Learning to challenge negative self-statements and silence the pathological critic can help you stave off self-imposed assaults on your self-esteem, but developing your character is also guaranteed to directly improve your estimation of yourself.

A strength is more than a solitary act (of kindness for example); it is a **trait** which can be defined as a psychological characteristic exemplified by consistent behaviors across time, place and situations. Strengths are valued in their own right and typically produce good consequences or outcomes. But strengths are displayed for their own sake (i.e. because it is the integral way to behave), whatever the outcome. Strengths represent what every parent wishes for in their newborn children. When you display a signature strength, no one is diminished and everyone has the capacity to be inspired or elevated. When you engage in your signature strengths you can feel pride, satisfaction, joy, harmony, fulfillment, etc, and your self esteem benefits as a result. Seligman (2002) identifies twenty-four signature strengths, which make up the six core virtues.

THE CORE VIRTUES AND CORRESPONDING SIGNATURE STRENGTHS

Wisdom and Knowledge

1. CURIOSITY
This incorporates your hunger for new experiences and your openness to and flexibility about matters that do not necessarily fit your pre-conceived notions about the world. You are tolerant of uncertainty and ambiguity. In other words, you make the choice to be open to exploring new and unfamiliar paradigms.

2. LOVE OF LEARNING

You value knowledge and learning for its own sake, whether in school or on your own. You are open to the opportunities to learn even in mundane situations and you go out of your way to educate yourself, to read, visit museums, travel, and explore.

3. JUDGMENT/CRITICAL THINKING/OPEN MINDEDNESS

This embodies the choice to examine things from all sides, to resist jumping to conclusions based on preconceived notions, looking at all the data and relying on solid evidence from which to draw conclusions and make decisions. You are open to changing your mind. Critical thinking involves choosing to use objectivity and rationality to process information, rather than falling prey to selective attention and only focusing on facts that confirm your old paradigm. You choose to avoid black and white thinking and open yourself to the gray areas.

4. CREATIVITY

This strength is not at all limited to the fine arts. It encompasses your willingness to think out of the box, to use your ingenuity, originality, common sense and street smarts. You are open to finding unconventional ways or methods of doing something or approaching a problem.

5. EMOTIONAL INTELLIGENCE - EQ

This important and broad concept involves your knowledge of yourself and others and takes into account how well you deal with people. In Chapter 9 we explore this construct in depth and delve into methods for enhancing your EQ.

6. PERSPECTIVE

The authors agree with Seligman's conclusion that perspective is the "most mature strength in this category, the closest to wisdom itself." To have perspective, you must have the life experience and emotional distance to be able to deduce and see the higher level meaning and purpose in things. Typically this takes many years to achieve, although we all know people who are wise beyond their years (the proverbial "old souls"), because they have a perspective that belies their youth. When you have perspective, others will often seek your advice and help because your way of looking at the world is useful, beneficial, reassuring, and makes sense. When you have perspective, you are an expert in understanding life.

Courage

7. BRAVERY AND VALOR

You choose to face your fears squarely, despite being scared. You do not run away from threats, pain, difficulties, or challenges. This includes having the guts to take controversial or unpopular positions (either intellectually or emotionally) that may expose you to ridicule, yet you stand firm in your beliefs. The concept of valor has broadened from physical or battlefield courage to moral and psychological courage. Nelson Mandela and Rosa Parks exemplify moral courage. Psychological courage refers to the optimistic stance needed to face serious illness, natural disaster, or catastrophic loss.

8. PERSEVERANCE AND INDUSTRIOUSNESS

Effective individuals finish what they start. This persistence is not about obsessively pursuing unrealistic goals or being perfectionistic, but diligently following through and doing what is necessary, even if inconvenient or unpleasant. It involves flexibility and taking pride in your work.

9. HONESTY/INTEGRITY/GENUINENESS

The cornerstone of what we mean by integrity involves being honest, telling the truth even if it is not in your best interest to do so. Yet it is more than simply telling the truth. It is also about presenting yourself in an authentic and genuine fashion, about being open and sincere in words, deeds, and commitments. It is about making the choice to keep your word and live by your principles – to walk the talk.

Humanity and Love

10. KINDNESS AND GENEROSITY

You choose to treat people well and live by the Golden Rule. You are generous in spirit as well as materially in that you are willing to give of yourself and your time to help others, do favors, be a true friend, or a listening ear. You enjoy doing good deeds for others even if you hardly know them. We are reminded of ordinary people who snuck into New Orleans to help rescue the Hurricane Katrina survivors. Three college students from Duke University drove non-stop from North Carolina to New Orleans with the intention of helping total strangers in any way they could. When denied entry to the city of New Orleans, they stole press passes to sneak in and they personally drove two carloads of stranded disaster victims to the Houston Astrodome shelter. True kindness and generosity requires an acknowledgement of the worth of the other person and is fueled by empathy and compassion. Just as with the other strengths, anyone can choose to be kind, compassionate, and generous. That gift of yourself to others ultimately comes back to you by bolstering how you regard yourself.

11. LOVING AND ALLOWING YOURSELF TO BE LOVED

The capacity to love and receive love may represent the ultimate fulfillment in life and relates to our purpose on the planet. This is choosing to open yourself up to intimacy beyond what is traditionally considered romance.

Justice

12. CITIZENSHIP/DUTY/TEAMWORK/LOYALTY

This cluster of strengths is often manifested in civic activities and reflects how you relate to groups such as your family, community, country, and the globe. It is about making a commitment to being a responsible, loyal, team player, doing your share of the work and contributing to the success of the whole. It is also about thinking of yourself as a global citizen and how you can contribute to the health of our planet. But this does not imply blind obedience or deference to authority. Sometimes being a good citizen or team member means that you must challenge or resist authority that is harmful or not in the best humane interests of the group.

13. FAIRNESS AND EQUITY

You choose to set aside your personal feelings or biases to make the most impartial and even handed decisions or judgments possible. You choose to use overriding moral principles of fairness to guide you in your dealings with others, whether family, friends or strangers. To do this you must choose to look at what is fair for all involved. It also involves looking for win-win solutions whenever possible (refer to Chapter 9 for an in depth discussion of Win-Win).

14. LEADERSHIP

While it is certainly true that some people are born leaders, leadership skills can be learned (refer to Chapter 12). Effective leaders have learned how to organize others, resolve conflicts and facilitate harmony, motivate others to get things done, and set a good example. Effective leaders are fair and impartial. A good leader learns lessons from history in general, and the history of the group in particular. A good leader takes responsibility for his or her mistakes as well as the errors of the group, exemplifying former President Harry S. Truman's famous motto, "The buck stops here."

Temperance

15. SELF CONTROL

You develop the ability to hold back on your needs, wants, desires and impulses until the appropriate time. That is, you know how to wait, or how to defer gratification (for more on this see Chapter 8). Positive psychologist Roy Baumeister (2007) believes that self-control is the most important of the signature strengths.

16. CAUTION AND DISCRETION

You choose to think before you speak or act to minimize doing or saying something you may later regret. When possible you proceed carefully and get as much information as you can before choosing a course of action. You choose to make the effort to take a far sighted view in matters of importance. You can recognize when the pursuit of short term rewards will sabotage long term goals and you decide to resist immediate gratification.

17. HUMILITY AND MODESTY

You can choose to be proud of yourself, yet humble, allowing your accomplishments to speak for themselves or your good character to be readily apparent. You do not put yourself above others or act in a condescending way. You choose to behave in an unpretentious fashion.

Transcendence

18. APPRECIATION OF BEAUTY AND EXCELLENCE

You bring a sense of awe and wonder to the table as you relish the beauty, skill and excellence in all facets of life, whether in nature, art, science, everyday matters, or the first words or steps of your own child. Not only do you stop to smell the roses, you take the time to admire their color, design, and relationship to the landscape.

19. GRATITUDE

As elucidated in the previous chapter, you choose to adopt an "attitude of gratitude." You choose not to take things for granted and you take the time to give thanks.

20. OPTIMISM AND HOPE

Given our emphasis on this in Chapter 2, we won't belabor the point except to remind you that you have a choice whether to be hopeful and optimistic. Choosing to do so enhances your overall effectiveness, can improve your interpersonal relationships, and ultimately helps boost your self-esteem because you believe in yourself and your ability to create positive outcomes.

21. SPIRITUALITY

You have made the effort to adopt a strong, coherent guiding set of beliefs about the meaning and purpose of life and your role in the universe. You know where you fit in within the larger scheme of things. Your spiritual beliefs and values guide your actions and provide comfort for you. Your spirituality may be based on the organized religious beliefs and traditions in which you were raised or chose to adopt, or it may come from more secular sources. What is important is that you have a philosophy of life that is meaningful for you and provides a sense of purpose. See Chapter 7 for a more in depth discussion of the role of spirituality in effectiveness.

22. FORGIVENESS AND MERCY

You have learned how to forgive and give others a second chance. You choose to allow mercy, not revenge, guide you down the oftentimes rocky road to forgiveness. Refer to the end of Chapter 9 for guidance on how to be more forgiving in your own life.

23. HUMOR AND PLAYFULNESS

You love to laugh and make others laugh. You choose to see the absurdity and silliness around you and revel in it. You choose not to take yourself so seriously and know how to kick back and have fun. Refer back to Chapter 1 for tips on how to enhance a humorous world view.

24. ENTHUSIASM/ZEST/PASSION

You are full of life and embody "joie de vivre" (zest for life). When you do something of import to you, you throw yourself into it wholeheartedly and, as such, your enthusiasm can rub off on others. You give yourself permission to feel things intensely. You risk giving up detachment for a chance at deeper fulfillment and enjoyment of life.

Identifying Your Signature Strengths

Which of these signature strengths do you already possess? Which would you like to develop? Fill out the following inventory, adapted from one developed by Seligman (2011), to help you identify your own signature strengths. We suggest that after identifying your strengths, you use these to help enhance those which are in need of improvement.

Signature Strengths Inventory

Respond to the following descriptive statements using the scale below. Circle your answers.

5 = Very much like me   4 = Like me   3 = Neutral   2 = Unlike me   1 = Very much unlike me

a.) I am always curious about the world.	5 4 3 2 1
b.) I rarely get bored.	5 4 3 2 1

1. Total these two to get your **Curiosity Score** _____

a.) I am thrilled when I learn something new.	5 4 3 2 1
b.) I often go out of my way to visit museums.	5 4 3 2 1

2. Total these two to get your Love of **Learning Score** _____

a.) When the topic calls for it, I can be a highly rational thinker.	5 4 3 2 1
b.) I rarely tend to make snap judgments.	5 4 3 2 1

3. Total these two to get your **Judgment Score** _____

a.) I like to think of new ways to do things.	5 4 3 2 1
b.) I am more imaginative than most of my friends.	5 4 3 2 1

4. Total these two to get your **Ingenuity Score** _____

a.) No matter what the social situation, I am able to fit in.	5 4 3 2 1
b.) I am very good at sensing what other people are feeling.	5 4 3 2 1

5. Total these two to get your **Social Intelligence Score** _____

a.) I am always able to look at things and see the big picture.	5 4 3 2 1
b.) Others often come to me for advice.	5 4 3 2 1

6. Total these two to get your **Perspective Score** _____

a.) I have taken frequent stands in the face of strong opposition.	5 4 3 2 1
b.) Pain and disappointment rarely get the better of me.	5 4 3 2 1

7. Total these two to get your **Valor Score** _____

a.) I always finish what I start.	5 4 3 2 1
b.) I rarely get sidetracked when I work.	5 4 3 2 1

8. Total these two to get your **Perseverance Score** _____

a.) I always keep my promises.	5 4 3 2 1
b.) My friends tell me I'm down to earth.	5 4 3 2 1

9. Total these two to get your **Integrity Score** _____

a.) I have voluntarily helped a neighbor in the last month.	5 4 3 2 1
b.) I get as excited about good fortune of others as I do about my own.	5 4 3 2 1

10. Total these two to get your **Kindness Score** _____

a.) There are people who care as much about my feelings and well-being as their own.	5 4 3 2 1
b.) I have no trouble accepting love from others.	5 4 3 2 1

11. Total these two to get your **Being Loved Score** _____

a.) I work at my best when I am part of a group.	5 4 3 2 1
b.) I am willing to sacrifice my self-interest for the benefit of groups I am in.	5 4 3 2 1

12. Total these two to get your **Citizenship Score** _____

a.) I treat all people equally, regardless of who they might be.   5 4 3 2 1
b.) If I don't like someone, I am still able to treat him or her fairly.   5 4 3 2 1

13. Total these two to get your **Fairness Score** _____

a.) I can always get people to do things together without nagging them.   5 4 3 2 1
b.) I am very good at planning group activities   5 4 3 2 1

14. Total these two to get your **Leadership Score** _____

a.) I control my emotions.   5 4 3 2 1
b.) I am typically able to stay on a diet.   5 4 3 2 1

15. Total these two to get your **Self-Control Score** _____

a.) I avoid activities that are physically dangerous.   5 4 3 2 1
b.) I rarely make poor choices in friendships and relationships.   5 4 3 2 1

16. Total these two to get your **Prudence Score** _____

a.) I change the subject when people pay me compliments.   5 4 3 2 1
b.) I very rarely brag about my accomplishments.   5 4 3 2 1

17. Total these two to get your **Humility Score** _____

a.) I always say thank you, even for little things.   5 4 3 2 1
b.) I often stop and count my blessings.   5 4 3 2 1

18. Total these two to get your **Gratitude Score** _____

a.) In the last month I have been thrilled by excellence in the arts, sports, science or math.   5 4 3 2 1
b.) I have created something of beauty in the last year.   5 4 3 2 1

19. Total these two to get your **Appreciation of Beauty Score** _____

a.) I always look on the bright side.   5 4 3 2 1
b.) I typically have a well-thought-out plan for what I want to do.   5 4 3 2 1

20. Total these two to get your **Optimism Score** _____

a.) My life has a strong purpose.   5 4 3 2 1
b.) I have a calling in life.   5 4 3 2 1

21. Total these two to get your **Spirituality Score** _____

a.) I always let bygones be bygones.   5 4 3 2 1
b.) I never try to get even.   5 4 3 2 1

22. Total these two to get your **Forgiveness Score** _____

a.) I always mix work and play as much as possible.   5 4 3 2 1
b.) I often say funny things.   5 4 3 2 1

23. Total these two to get your **Humor Score** _____

a.) I throw myself into everything I do.   5 4 3 2 1
b.) I rarely mope around.   5 4 3 2 1

24. Total these two to get your **Zest Score** _____

Record your scores on the following page.

Scoring

Wisdom and Knowledge
1. Curiosity _____
2. Love of Learning _____
3. Judgment _____
4. Ingenuity _____
5. Social Intelligence _____
6. Perspective _____

Courage
7. Valor _____
8. Perseverance _____
9. Integrity _____

Humanity and Love
10. Kindness _____
11. Zest _____

Justice
12. Citizenship _____
13. Fairness _____
14. Leadership _____

Temperance
15. Self-Control _____
16. Prudence _____
17. Humility _____

Transcendence
18. Gratitude _____
19. Appreciation of Beauty ___
20. Optimism/Hope _____
21. Spirituality _____
22. Forgiveness _____
23. Humor _____
24. Zest _____

Typically you will have five or fewer scores of nine or ten and these represent your highest strengths, according to your self-report observations of yourself. You will also have several scores in the four to six range and these represent your weaknesses. It may be interesting to have a significant other fill out this inventory about you, to get a sense of whether your perception of your strengths matches that of others.

Developing Your Signature Strengths More Fully

Remember that, in most cases, developing the traits or characteristics comprising signature strengths just involves a conscious choice or decision to do so, even if it may be hard, inconvenient or awkward at first. Unlike talents, there is no genetic basis for character. There are no genes or chromosomes for kindness, or honesty, or open-mindedness. *Rather these are behaviors that you have direct control over. As your signature strengths build and expand, so too will your self-esteem. You will learn to respect and value yourself more deeply, as will others around you, because you have character.* That is invaluable. Here are some suggestions for how to develop your strengths offered by Lynn Johnson (2008). Remember that the more energy and emphasis you put into practicing his suggestions, the more dramatic the effect will be in your life.

1. **Curiosity and Interest in the World**
   a. Ask questions of people.
   b. Discover new places.
   c. Explore the stacks in a library; browse widely, or pick an interesting looking book each day and spend twenty minutes skimming it.
   d. Eat something new that you never otherwise would have tried.
   e. Go to a meeting or hear a speaker.

2. Love of Learning
   a. Discover one new place in town everyday.
   b. Read a newspaper other than your usual.
   c. Ask a question of someone you admire.
   d. Go to an online search engine like *Ask.com* and ask a question and explore sites you never otherwise would have discovered.
   e. Read a book about something you've always found intriguing but never found the time to learn more about.

3. Judgment, Critical Thinking and Open-Mindedness
   a. Go to a multi-cultural group or event.
   b. Play devil's advocate and discuss an issue from the side opposite to your personal views.
   c. Take a colleague out to lunch who is different from you in some way.
   d. Go to a different church or religious event or political gathering.
   e. Every day pick something you believe strongly, and think about how you might be wrong. Ask yourself how you would know if you were wrong.

4. Creativity, Ingenuity and Originality
   a. Keep a journal. Work on a picture or poem.
   b. Submit a piece to a literary magazine or newspaper.
   c. Decorate a room in your home or your workspace.
   d. Pick one object in your room and devise a use for it rather than its intended one.
   e. Find a new word everyday (perhaps at *dictionary.com*) and use it creatively.

5. Emotional/Social Intelligence
   a. Meet one new person each day by approaching them.
   b. Go into a social situation where you would normally feel uncomfortable and try to fit in.
   c. Whenever you talk with someone, try to figure out what his or her motives and concerns are.
   d. Encounter someone who is all by himself and, by being friendly, include that person in your group.

6. Perspective (Wisdom)
   a. Get a quote a day online.
   b. Give advice to an upset friend.
   c. Think of the wisest person you know. Try to live each day as that person would live.
   d. Look up prominent people in history and learn their views on important issues of their day, and/or find a significant quotation that they said.

7. Valor
   a. Speak up in groups or volunteer to speak publicly (if you don't normally).
   b. Go against peer pressure or social norms.
   c. Stand up for someone even if you disagree with him/her.
   d. Ask someone to spend time with you.

    e. Introduce yourself to a stranger.

    f. Speak up for an unpopular idea (if you believe in it).

8. Industry, Diligence, and Perseverance

    a. Finish work ahead of time.

    b. Notice your thoughts about stopping a task, and ignore them. Focus on the task at hand.

    c. At work, resist daydreaming and distractions.

    d. Plan ahead – use a calendar for appointments and meetings.

    e. Set a high goal (i.e. for exercise or studying) and stick to it.

    f. When you wake up in the morning, make a list of things that you want to get done that day that could be put off until the next day. Make sure to get them done that day.

9. Honesty, Authenticity, and Genuineness

    a. Refrain from telling small white lies to friends (including insincere compliments). If you do tell one, admit it and apologize right away.

    b. Monitor yourself and make a list of every time you tell a lie, even if it is a small one. Try to make your daily list shorter every day.

    c. At the end of each day, identify something you did that was attempting to impress people, or put on a show. Resolve not to do it again.

10. Zest, Enthusiasm, and Energy

    a. Go out of your way to become more involved in an organization to which you already belong.

    b. Take up a greater interest in other's work, i.e. volunteer to help them in a project.

    c. While eating or drinking something, concentrate on the taste and sensations. Try to really savor and appreciate every aspect of that food or drink.

    d. Get a good night's sleep and eat a good breakfast, to give yourself more energy during the day.

    e. Do something physically vigorous in the morning (e.g., jogging, push-ups). Note carefully how you feel ten minutes later, an hour later.

11. Kindness and Generosity

    a. Leave a huge tip for a small check.

    b. Do a random act of kindness every day (a simple small favor). Make it anonymous if possible.

    c. Ask a friend how their day was and actually listen to the answer before telling them about your own day.

    d. Send an e-card to a different friend each day.

    e. Pay the whole tab when you are out with friends.

12. Capacity to Love and Be Loved

    a. Tell spouse/boyfriend/girlfriend/sibling/parent that you love them.

    b. Send a loved one a card or e-card to say that you were thinking about him/her.

    c. Give loved ones a big hug and a kiss.

    d. Show great enthusiasm when a friend achieves something.

    e. Write a nice note where someone you love will find it sometime during the day.

13. Citizenship and Teamwork

    a. Volunteer at a school.

    b. Take on added responsibility within an organization in which you are already a part.

    c. Pick up litter that you see on the ground.

    d. Pick up litter in your neighborhood.

    e. Organize a neighborhood dinner.

    f. Organize a volunteer group in you neighborhood.

14. Fairness, Equity, and Justice

    a. Allow someone to speak their peace while keeping an open mind by not passing judgment.

    b. Stay impartial in an argument between friends despite your beliefs (be the mediator).

    c. Notice when you treat someone based on a stereotype or pre-conception; resolve not to do it again.

15. Leadership

    a. Organize something special for your friends one evening.

    b. Organize a study group, book club, or a volunteer group in your neighborhood.

16. Modesty

    a. Don't talk about yourself at all for a full day.

    b. Dress and act modestly, so as to not attract attention to yourself.

    c. Find a way in which someone you know is better than you. Compliment him or her about it.

17. Self Control and Self-Regulation

    a. Set aside a designated amount of time and work on a work project in a quiet, private place.

    b. Exercise four days a week (if you don't already do so).

    c. Clean or organize your living space. Every day, make sure that you pick up whatever mess you made during the day.

    d. Leave something uneaten on your plate that you usually regret eating afterwards.

    e. When something upsets you, attempt to block it out of your mind and instead focus on the good things in your life.

    f. Make a resolution to not gossip. Stop yourself whenever you find yourself doing it.

18. Caution, Prudence, and Discretion

    a. During a conversation, think twice before saying anything. Weigh the probable effect of your words on others.

    b. Before you decide to do something important, reflect on it for a moment and consider if you want to live with its consequences.

19. **Forgiveness and Mercy**
    a. Think of someone that you found very hard to forgive. Try to see the situation from their perspective.
    b. Actively seek to forgive others.
    c. When someone does something you don't understand, try to imagine his or her intentions for their actions.

20. **Appreciation of Beauty and Excellence**
    a. Go to a museum and pick out a piece of artwork or a display that has aesthetic value and touches you because of its beauty.
    b. Write down your thoughts about a piece of art, or something beautiful that you see.
    c. Take a walk with a friend and comment on something pretty that you see.
    d. Keep a journal and every night record something you saw during the day that struck you as extremely beautiful or skillful.

21. **Gratitude**
    a. Keep a journal and each night make a list of three things you are grateful for in life.
    b. Every day thank someone for something that you might otherwise take for granted (e.g., thanking the janitor who cleans your office).
    c. Keep a record of the number of times you say "thank you" in a day. Try to double the times within the first week.
    d. Send someone a "thank you" e-greeting.

22. **Hope, Optimism, and Future-Mindedness**
    a. Keep a journal and every night, record a decision you made that day that will impact your life in the long run.
    b. When you are in a bad situation, turn it around to see the bright side to it.
    c. Notice your negative thoughts. Counter them with positive thoughts.
    d. Reaffirm to yourself that you can and will succeed at whatever you decide.

23. **Spirituality and Sense of Purpose and Faith**
    a. For a few minutes a day, relax and think about the purpose of life and how you fit in it.
    b. Explore different religions. You can do this by going to a library, looking on the Internet, or asking your friends about their religions.
    c. Spend time each day in meditation or prayer.
    d. Invest in a book of affirmations or optimistic quotes. Read a few every day.

24. **Humor and Playfulness**
    a. Every day, make someone smile or laugh.
    b. Learn a joke and tell it to your friends.
    c. Watch a funny movie or TV show.
    d. Read the comics.
    e. Learn a magic trick and perform it for your friends.

OTHER POSITIVE PSYCHOLOGY SELF EXERCISES:

1. **Deliberately Making Mistakes:** While this exercise may not seem logical, following through with it will prove to be invaluable in terms of building your self-esteem. What we want you to do is to experientially give yourself permission to make mistakes. The most effective way of achieving this is for you to go out and deliberately make a mistake. We want you to think of a relatively harmless, innocuous mistake you can make, preferably one that is humorous, and to plan it out and set a date to do it. It could be something as silly and mundane as wearing two different color sucks or putting your make-up on wrong. But be creative and let your child play. By the way, did you catch our mistake above?

2. **Looking at Yourself Through the Eyes of Someone Who Loves You:** Think of someone who you believe really loves and values you for who you are. Imagine that person standing in front of you as vividly as you can. Look at them looking at you with that expression which lets you know how much they appreciate you. Now imagine in your mind's eye that you can look at yourself through their eyes. Seeing, perhaps for the first time, what someone who loves you sees as they look at you. Watching and listening closely to your own gestures, words, looks, as perceived by someone who loves you. Can you recognize qualities and attributes which were perhaps viewed as faults by your own eyes? Allow yourself to perceive what it is about you that this person cherishes. Now describe yourself to yourself as you know this person would, highlighting your endearing qualities and traits, using the positive adjectives you know this person would use.

3. **Using Signature Strengths in Novel Ways:** Set aside a time to use one of your strengths in a new or creative way. For example, if appreciation of beauty is one of your strengths, you could deliberately take a different route home from work that passes through an attractive area, even if it takes you longer to get home.

KEY TERMS

Self-Esteem	Conditions of Worth	Character
Ideal Self	Malevolent Attitude	Virtues
Real Self	Authoritarian Parenting	Signature Strengths
Self-Worth	Authoritative Parenting	Inferiority Complex
Self-Concept	Permissive-Indulgent Parenting	Service Learning
Pathological Critic	Permissive-Indifferent Parenting	Traits
Unconditional Positive Regard	Conditional Positive Regard	Cognitive Distortions

CHAPTER 4 QUESTIONS

True or False Questions (T or F)

1. _____ Unfortunately, once your self-esteem is set it cannot be changed.

2. _____ Low self-esteem creates a negative vicious cycle.

3. _____ People with healthy self-esteem are always conceited.

4. _____ People with healthy self-esteem are afraid to take risks.

5. _____ People with low self-esteem are prone to resort to faddism in order to be accepted and included by others.

6. _____ Healthy self-esteem leads to proactivity and vice versa.

7. _____ People with low self-esteem give themselves negative internal messages.

8. _____ People with healthy self-esteem cannot accept constructive criticism.

9. _____ People with low self-esteem are often very competitive.

10. _____ Your self-esteem is purely a function of your genetic heritage.

11. _____ Children can develop healthy self-esteem even if raised in very dysfunctional environments.

12. ____   Non-contingent self-esteem is more stable and based on a solid sense of self.

13. ____   Self-esteem can be influenced by irrational beliefs.

14. ____   You should ignore your inner child so it will finally grow up.

15. ____   One of the biggest differences between people with healthy vs. low self-esteem is in how they talk to themselves.

16. ____   Character is inborn and cannot be developed.

Short-Answer Questions

1. Your self esteem is influenced by the discrepancy between your _____ and your _____.

2. The negative inner voice that attacks and judges you had been termed the _____.

3. Carl Rogers observed that children develop positive self-esteem when parents show them _____. When parents treat children with _____, the children develop _____, whereby they think they are only lovable if they meet certain standards.

4. Harry Stack Sullivan noted that when children are treated badly they can develop the _____, where they believe they are surrounded by enemies.

5. Research and observations indicate that the _____ parenting style has the healthiest impact on the self-esteem of children.

6. You can challenge your *shoulds* using _____ techniques.

7. Looking for evidence to support your existing view of yourself can result in _____.

8. _____ _____ are traits and behaviors you can develop by exercising proactive choice.

Essay Questions

1. How does self-esteem differ from self-concept?

2. What should self-worth be based upon?

3. Describe the characteristics of the parenting style which is most conducive to fostering positive self-esteem in the child.

4. How does the *tyranny of the shoulds* impact upon self-esteem?

5. What do the authors suggest you do to avoid repeating the same mistakes over and over?

6. Why is it that mistakes are not bad?

7. How can improving your character by developing your signature strengths contribute to raising your self-esteem?

5

Understanding Stress

Effective individuals have learned how to become *masters* over stress. Mastering stress is an essential element in maintaining a healthy lifestyle which is fundamental to wellness. The study of factors that contribute to high level wellness comprises an important aspect of positive psychology. This chapter and the next will prepare you to master the stress in your life by first giving you a thorough understanding of how stress affects you, and then teaching you a variety of strategies and techniques for modifying your thinking and your physiology in ways that will allow you to develop resistance to, and mastery over stress. The following chapter will also explore the concept of wellness in a more comprehensive fashion.

Stress Mastery vs. Stress Management

You may notice that we refer to the concept of **Stress Mastery** in this chapter rather than using the more common name: Stress Management. This is not just a semantic difference. We really see a difference between the ability to achieve mastery over stress versus the ability to merely manage your stress. See, the key is not just *surviving* stress, but *thriving* from stress. Stress management is suggestive of one more "thing" to do. As if you didn't have enough things to do already! Stress mastery is more a part of the fabric of your life. It is not *work*, it is a *craft*. It is a way of taking the raw material of the stresses of life and creating a reality in which you can live. With the passage of time, your craft improves. It does not take time away from your schedule. It actually adds time to your life. Often people see stress management as having to do specific exercises in order to lower stress. But stress mastery is really about cultivating wisdom. It is not mechanical or rote. It is becoming increasingly aware of your situations and, perhaps even more so, of your reaction to these situations. The truth is that life is not always a calm sea of tranquility. Life throws waves at you, and these waves do not appear to be of your choosing. You do have a choice, though, on how you ride these waves. Do you choose to surf them gracefully, making use of the opportunities presented or do you choose to go under, feeling as if you can't breathe and might drown at any moment. Stress mastery is organic. It changes and it is flexible while always remaining consistent with certain core skills and habits.

Stress Management	vs.	Stress Mastery
One more "thing" to do		Part of the fabric of your life
Work		Craft
Takes time		Adds time
Do exercises		Cultivate wisdom
Mechanical		Increase awareness

The core skills and strategies presented in this chapter and the next form the foundation on which stress mastery is based. They are absolutely necessary if you are to be able to cope gracefully with the demands placed on you by life. To acquire them will require an initial investment of time and focus. We promise that you will ultimately gain time as a result of the increased energy and improved concentration you will experience. As you learn to master your stress, other priorities in your life will become clearer. You might find that you are not only climbing the ladder of success, but that you know for sure that the ladder is against the right wall. As a result, the quality of your time will improve.

THE DEFINITION OF STRESS

What is stress? When we ask students, employees, and employers this question, they typically respond that it is tension, nervousness, headaches, having deadlines to meet, etc. Basically what we hear is a list outlining the effects of stress, or specific causes of stress. The official definition of stress is that *stress is anything that requires an adaptive response on the part of the organism.* But, what does that mean? It means that anything that requires you to respond, to make a change or an adjustment is stressful. So, when people say they want to get rid of stress, the reality is that this is impossible. That is not to say that you cannot reduce the amount of change or responsibilities you have in your life. Indeed, this is at times recommended as a way of minimizing your stress level. But we want you to understand that, even if you went and hid out on a mountaintop in order to escape the rat race, you would probably eventually get bored and boredom itself is stressful. See, the fact is, *stress is an inescapable part of modern life.*

That is not necessarily as bad as it may sound. One of the best-known experts on stress, a Canadian scientist by the name of Hans Selye, was quoted as saying that "stress is the spice of life." Just as spice can make your food tasteful and come alive, stress can give your life meaning and excitement. This depends, of course, on the amount and type of spice you use. We all know that the wrong spice, or too much spice can make you sick to your stomach. Selye (1956) differentiates between these two types of stress, referring to positive stress as "**Eustress**" and negative stress as "**Distress.**" So stress is not all bad. We all need an optimal level of change and stress in our life to keep things interesting. And that level varies from person to person.

Given the pejorative connotations given to stress, it is easy to forget that an appropriate level of stress in your life is often helpful. Stress can help motivate you to perform and meet the challenges you will face. The physiological and psychological aspects of the arousal produced by stress can be useful, and unless you are routinely overloaded and aroused, stress may not necessarily harm you (Kobasa, 1982). It may surprise you to find out that you need an optimal level of stress and arousal in order to perform at your best. This fact was established many years ago by pioneering psychologists Yerkes and Dodson (1908) who demonstrated that performance on a given task improves as physiological arousal increases until some optimal point, after which performance declines as arousal continues to climb. This optimal level of arousal varies with the type of task. The more complex the task for an individual, the less arousal can be tolerated before performance suffers. In layman's terms, when you are totally cool, calm and collected in a performance situation, you may not have the required motivation or edge necessary to perform at your best. If, on the other hand, you are panic-stricken or you are a nervous wreck, your high arousal level will interfere with your performance. *Many tasks are best performed with moderate levels of arousal.* This relationship is known as the Yerkes-Dodson Law. This is useful to remember next time you have to speak before a class, or group, or are in any type of performance situation. There is a misconception that you should be "super cool". This is not necessarily true, for you will actually perform better if you are moderately aroused, that is, stressed. What does this have to do with stress mastery? If you are under aroused you will experience the stress of boredom. If you are over aroused you will experience anxiety. If you can find your optimal level, where you are stimulated and performing at your best, you can experience satisfaction and master stress. This is best illustrated in the following graph which demonstrates peak performance under conditions of moderate arousal.

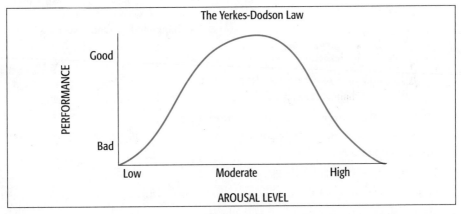

Figure 5.1

STRESS AND ILLNESS

Do you believe that stress can make you sick? If you are like most people, you would answer with a resounding, "YES!" When we ask people this question in our classes all believe that stress can affect their emotional well-being, and the majority realize that it can lead to physical illness. Unless you have been living off planet for the last few years, you have had some exposure to the fact that stress can and does have deleterious effects. However, had we asked this question just forty-five to fifty years ago to people in general, or even to a group of health professionals, the majority would probably have denied the relationship between stress and our health. Then we were just emerging from the era of infectious diseases where we believed that illnesses were caused by exposure to germs and bacteria, and that the way to keep healthy was to create vaccines and medicines to combat these external agents. At that time, to have considered the notion that stress could lead to illness would have been *avant garde* thinking.

Then, Thomas Holmes, M.D., a professor at the University of Washington School of Medicine, began doing research on the effect of changes on our physical and emotional well being. Remember that change is stressful because it requires an adaptive response on our part. Together with Richard Rahe, Holmes developed a questionnaire measuring life changes and set out to study whether there was a relationship between the number, seriousness, and pervasiveness of changes, and our frequency of illness (Holmes & Rahe, 1967). Using army personnel, because they were a captive audience and their progress could be followed easily, they demonstrated that the questionnaire could help them predict with remarkable accuracy those soldiers who would get ill within the next two years and those who would remain healthy. We suggest that you complete and score the Holmes-Rahe Life Readjustment Scale to determine your own level of stress as measured by this inventory.

LIFE READJUSTMENT SCALE Part A

Instructions: Think back on each possible life event listed below, and decide if it happened to you within the last year. If the event did happen, check the box next to it.

	Check here if event happened to you.	Mean Value (Use for scoring later)
1. A lot more or a lot less trouble with your boss.	_____	_____
2. A major change in sleeping habits (sleeping a lot more or less, or change of sleep habits).	_____	_____
3. A major change in eating habits (a lot more or a lot less food intake, or very different meal hours or surroundings).	_____	_____
4. A revision of personal habits (dress, manners, associations, etc.).	_____	_____
5. Major change in your social activities (clubs, dancing, movies, visiting, etc.).	_____	_____
6. A major change in your usual type and/or amount of recreation.	_____	_____
7. A major change in church activities (a lot more or less than usual).	_____	_____
8. A major change in number of family get-togethers.	_____	_____
9. A major change in financial state (for better or for worse).	_____	_____
10. In-law troubles.	_____	_____

11. A major change in the number of arguments
    with your spouse.
    _____   _____

12. Sexual difficulties.
    _____   _____

LIFE READJUSTMENT SCALE Part B

Instructions: In the space provided, indicate the number of times that each applicable event happened to you within the last two years.

	Number of times	×	Mean Value	Your Score
13. Major personal injury or illness.	___		___	___
14. Death of close family member (not spouse).	___		___	___
15. Death of a spouse.	___		___	___
16. Death of a close friend.	___		___	___
17. Gaining a new family member (through birth, adoption, oldster moving in, etc.).	___		___	___
18. Major change in the health or behavior of a family member.	___		___	___
19. Change in residence.	___		___	___
20. Detention in jail or other institution.	___		___	___
21. Minor violations of the law (traffic tickets, jaywalking, disturbing the peace, etc.).	___		___	___
22. Major business readjustment (merger, reorganization, bankruptcy, etc.).	___		___	___
23. Marriage.	___		___	___
24. Divorce.	___		___	___
25. Marital separation from spouse.	___		___	___
26. Outstanding personal achievement.	___		___	___
27. Son or daughter leaving home (marriage, attending college, etc.).	___		___	___
28. Retirement from work.	___		___	___
29. Major change in working hours or conditions.	___		___	___
30. Major change in responsibilities at work (promotion, demotion, lateral transfer).	___		___	___
31. Being fired from work.	___		___	___
32. Major change in living conditions (building a new home, remodeling, deterioration of home or neighborhood).	___		___	___
33. Wife beginning or ceasing work outside the home.	___		___	___
34. Taking on a mortgage greater than $25,000 (purchasing a home, business, etc.).	___		___	___

35. Taking on a mortgage or loan of less than $25,000 (making a large purchase).   ___   ___ ___

36. Foreclosure on a mortgage or loan.   ___   ___ ___

37. Vacation.   ___   ___ ___

38. Changing to a new school.   ___   ___ ___

39. Changing to a different line of work.   ___   ___ ___

40. Beginning or ceasing formal schooling.   ___   ___ ___

41. Marital reconciliation with mate.   ___   ___ ___

42. Pregnancy.   ___   ___ ___

YOUR TOTAL SCORE   ___   ___ ___

Scoring

The "Mean values" for each life event are listed below. Write in the mean values for those events that happened to you. For items in Part B, multiply the mean value by the number of times an event happened, and enter the result in "Your Score." Add up the mean values in Part A and scores in Part B to get your total score.

Life Event	Mean Value	Life Event	Mean Value
1	23	22	39
2	16	23	50
3	15	24	73
4	24	25	65
5	19	26	28
6	18	27	29
7	19	28	45
8	15	29	20
9	38	30	29
10	29	31	47
11	35	32	25
12	39	33	26
13	53	34	31
14	63	35	17
15	100	36	30
16	37	37	13
17	39	38	20
18	44	39	36
19	20	40	26
20	63	41	45
21	11	42	40

Interpreting Your Results

The more change you have, the more likely you are to get sick. Of those people with a score of over 300 for the past year, almost 80% get sick in the near future; with a score of 200 to 299, about 50% get sick in the near future; and with a score of 150–199, only about 30% get sick. A score of less than 150 indicates that you have a low chance of getting ill. So, the higher your score, the harder you should work to stay well. Stress can be cumulative. Events from two years ago may still affect you now. If you think this applies to you, repeat this test for the events of the preceding year and compare your scores.

While this questionnaire succeeds in establishing the relationship between life changes and illness, it fails to take into account individual differences in our abilities to cope with the changes and demands of our lives. We will address this point in greater detail in the next chapter.

NEGATIVE EFFECTS OF STRESS

So what are the negative effects of stress? What can happen when stress overloads your coping resources, when your skills are inadequate to deal with the demands placed on you by circumstances? *Stress negatively affects your physical, psychological and occupational functioning in a variety of ways.*

Physical Consequences

The relationship between stress and your health is not simple or straightforward. Stress will not automatically cause you to become physically ill. The impact of stress on your health is mediated by a variety of personality variables, as well as your genetic makeup and environment. But physically, it is clear that when you are under prolonged stress your immune system can be weakened, creating vulnerability to illness and bodily system breakdown. Chronic high levels of stress hormones, known as **glucocorticoids**, are known to weaken immune functioning (Brehm, 1998), leading to an increased susceptibility to diseases, including cancer and heart disease. Glucocorticoids are adrenal secretions associated with the primitive survival circuitry of the brain/body. They quickly turn cells into energy to mobilize the body to deal with danger, much like a desperate person might burn the furniture to keep from freezing in a frigid night. Cells of the hippocampus, the area in charge of memory and meaning, and those of the cardiovascular system are most vulnerable to the destructive effects of glucocorticoids. A recent meta-analysis (an analysis of multiple studies including over 18,900 subjects within 293 independent experiments) conducted by Segerstrom and Miller (2004) provided powerful confirmation of the fact that stress alters immunity. The major findings of this study were three fold: (1) short term stress actually "revs up" the immune system in an adaptive way to prepare individuals to cope with injury or infection; (2) chronic or long term stress causes excessive wear and tear leading to eventual systemic break down; and (3) the immune systems of individuals who are older or already sick are more prone to stress related damage. Furthermore, as illustrated by the list below, stress can create a wide assortment of psychosomatic problems in which the weakest link in your system of organs, muscles and glands is affected. For some individuals the heart is affected, for others the stomach or the pancreas; thus, some develop heart disease, others ulcers or diabetes.

- Approximately 75-90% of all visits to doctor's offices are for stress related disorders.
- In 2007, the American Psychological Association (APA) conducted a "Stress in America" survey with a sample of 1,848 adults. According to the survey results, 77% of Americans reported stress related physical

symptoms, with 51% enduring fatigue, 44% suffering from headaches, 34% reporting upset stomachs, 30% experiencing muscular tension, and 23% noting stress induced changes in appetite.

❦ There is an increased risk of cardiovascular diseases, such as heart disease and stroke when individuals report high levels of job stress (Brydon, Magid, & Steptoe, 2006). This is further supported in a Swedish study of 7000 men (Rosengren and colleagues, 1990) where men who reported the highest levels of stress were 50% more likely to have a heart attack in the next eight years than men who were less stressed. They were also 80% more likely to have a stroke.

❦ Most heart attacks occur around 9:00 a.m. on Monday mornings (Elliot, 2001).

❦ Hypertension (high blood pressure), a stress related disorder, afflicts at least 35.7 million people in the U.S. (National Ambulatory Medical Care Survey, 2006) with some estimates going as high as 80 million. The stress hormone **cortisol**, unleashed by the adrenal glands in times of stress, is linked to increases in free fatty acids in the bloodstream, which contribute to the buildup of plaque in the lining of blood vessels and the subsequent narrowing of these pathways. These processes combine to produce hypertension, atherosclerosis and coronary heart disease.

❦ Cholesterol levels in the bloodstream rise during periods of stress (Mattiasson, Lindgarde, Nilsson, & Theorell, 1990).

❦ According to *The Crohn's Disease and Ulcerative Colitis Fact Book* (1983), chronic diarrhea (irritable bowel syndrome) may have a causal relationship to emotional factors and stress. This is not the case for inflammatory bowel disease.

❦ Ulcers, spastic colon and similar gastro-intestinal disorders are the direct result of elevated acidity brought on by the release of cortisol. These disorders are classified as **psychophysiological disorders**, illnesses that are triggered and exacerbated by stress. With any of these disorders the most severe symptoms often do not manifest until after the stressor has diminished or ended. Ulcers are a good example of this. Sapolsky (1994) noted that the stomach is more vulnerable to ulceration after a long period of stress is over.

❦ About 18% of women and 6% of men are stricken with migraine headaches. Estimates of the frequency of tension headaches in the American population vary from 30 to 80%. Stress is one of the many factors that trigger headaches of all types (Elkind, 2004).

❦ It has been estimated that 70 million visits a year to doctor's offices are due to pain complaints (Koch, 1986). Estimates of the number of adult Americans suffering from chronic pain are as high as one-fifth of the population (Joranson & Leitman, 1994). Negative emotions and stress can aggravate pain and cause acute pain to develop into chronic pain. The stress hormone ACTH can impede **endorphin** production. Endorphins are our body's natural painkillers. Inability to produce endorphins leads to increased pain and discomfort.

- Recent research indicates that stress even plays a significant role in the development of osteoporosis in women due to increased levels of stress hormones (Kumano, 2005).

- Psychological factors such as stress are clearly implicated as a factor in what is known as nocturnal **bruxism**, or teeth grinding at night (Carvalho, Cury, & Garcia, 2008).

- Periods of elevated stress are "linked to the onset and worsening of rheumatoid arthritis" (Nakazawa, 2008). The hormone prolactin, released by the pituitary gland in response to stress, triggers joint swelling.

- A study by Deinzer and colleagues (2000) revealed that during college exam week students possess lower levels of salivary immunoglobulin, a defense against respiratory infections. This suppression of immune response was observed to last up to two weeks after the stressful period ended. In addition, student's acne worsens during times of high stress (Chiu, Chon, & Kimball, 2003).

- A study showed that people ranking high on a test of perceived stress were more likely to develop colds when intentionally infected with a virus (Cohen, Tyrell, & Smith, 1991). These same authors repeated this study in 1993 and replicated these findings.

- Most dentists report an association between stress and gum disease, known as gingivitis (Brehm, 1998).

Psychological Consequences

It is not surprising that stress is also a key factor in the development of emotional difficulties and behavioral problems. Can you remember a time when you felt there were too many demands placed on you? What was that like for you? Did it affect your ability to relax and enjoy life? Stress clearly influences our psychological well-being in a host of different ways as elucidated below:

- Stress is a major factor in the development of anxiety, phobias, panic attacks, depression, post traumatic stress disorder, obsessions, compulsions and all major psychiatric disorders. The 2007 APA Stress in America survey found that 73% of the participants reported experiencing psychological symptoms related to stress. Forty five percent of the subjects reported anxiety, 50% had issues with anger or irritability, 35% had depressive symptoms, and 48% had problems with insomnia.

- According to the World Health Organization (WHO), depression, often a stress-related disorder, is the number one cause of disability worldwide. The most current statistics from WHO estimate at least 120 million people world-wide suffering from depression.

- It has been demonstrated that stress alters serotonin pathways. Imbalances in serotonin levels have been linked to depression and in some cases aggression. According to the APA, approximately 19 million American adults are afflicted with depression.

- The National Institute of Mental Health (NIMH) reports that 19 million American adults have anxiety disorders, including approximately 2.4 million manifesting panic disorder.

- According to the National Institute on Alcohol Abuse and Alcoholism, an estimated 14 million Americans are alcoholic. Relief of stress and anxiety is one of the primary motives for the use and abuse of alcohol. Repeated use for that purpose is viewed as an important factor in the development of habituation and addiction. Millions more use and/or abuse drugs, both illegal and prescription medications, to cope with stress. The 2007 APA survey found that 39% of the participants admitted to drinking and 19% to smoking cigarettes far more regularly during periods of high stress.

- Fifty-five percent of all marriages end in divorce. According to the APA survey, stress causes more than half of Americans (54%) to fight with people close to them. Twenty-five percent of survey participants reported that they became alienated from a friend or family member because of stress, and 8% cited stress as a major factor in a divorce or separation. Experts report that stress is a major contributing factor to relationship conflicts and the rising incidence of divorce. For example, in one longitudinal study (Kiecolt-Glaser and colleagues, 2002) couples who divorced after 10 years of marriage displayed 34% higher levels of stress hormones at the *beginning* of the study than those whose marriages remained intact.

Consequences in the Workplace

At times of stress, how well can you concentrate on the task at hand? Do you find thoughts, preoccupations, and fears interfering with your ability to function? The ability to concentrate is significantly affected by stress. It is no wonder that an inability to cope with life stressors leads to lowered productivity and an increased frequency of mistakes on the job. In addition, you are more likely to miss work due to both emotional and physical illness. As the following list demonstrates, this leads to major financial losses for business, industry and employees.

- The American Institute of Stress (AIS) reports that, according to the 2000 Attitudes in the American Workplace VI Gallup Poll, 80% of American workers feel stressed on the job and half of those admit they need help managing their stress. AIS notes a smaller 2002 Gallup job stress survey which found 31% of workers feeling extremely stressed out by their jobs, along with a 2000 Integra Survey of job stress which reveals 65% of workers reporting workplace stress, and 25% of those respondents even admitted to crying on the job due to stress! AIS further discloses that 25% of Americans consider their jobs to be the number one stressor in their lives, while the 2007 APA survey found that money and work were the leading causes of stress for 75% of Americans.

❦ People are more accident prone during periods of stress (Williams & colleagues, 1993). According to AIS statistics, 60-80% of accidents on the job are stress related. Industrial accidents account for 2 million disabling injuries per year, more than 15,000 deaths, and 3 billion dollars annually in lost productivity. Peterson (1984) reviewed research studies linking stress to work related accidents and concluded that high stress levels are an important risk factor. Raymond & Moser (1995) implicated stress as a major risk factor in aviation accidents associated with pilot error. Murphy (1987) hypothesized a *stress-accident model* whereby stress symptoms such as anxiety have a detrimental effect on workers capabilities, such as attention and reaction time, which leads to increased accident risk. That is, transient unsafe behaviors due to stress create disorganization and lead to more mistakes and accidents.

❦ As reported by AIS, according to a survey of 800,000 workers in over 300 companies, the number of employees calling in sick because of stress tripled from 1996 to 2000. An estimated 1 million workers are absent every day due to stress. Unanticipated absenteeism is estimated to cost American companies over $600 per worker/year with the price tag for large companies exceeding millions annually! AIS also cites a three year study concluded in 1997 which determined that 60% of employee absences could be traced to psychological problems stemming directly from job stress.

❦ According to AIS, the Integra Survey (2000) indicated that 19% of respondents had quit a previous position due to the demands of an overly stressful job.

❦ According to Keita & Hurrell (1994), Workers Compensation claims for psychological disorders are at unprecedented levels causing reduced productivity and increased absenteeism due to workplace stress. They cite data from the Northwestern National Life Ins. Co. survey noting that 13% of their claims involved stress related disorders, a marked increase over time. The researchers also referred to a national survey showing that 72% of workers surveyed reported frequent stress related physical or mental symptoms. More and more insurance companies have been plagued by a nationwide epidemic of sick, disabled and wealthy professionals, especially doctors, but also accountants, architects, insurance agents and lawyers filing claims for disability due to stress related disorders.

❦ Stress is eroding the bottom line for business. According to AIS statistics, job stress is estimated to cost U.S. business over $300 billion annually as a result of accidents, absenteeism, employee turnover, diminished productivity, workers comp, insurance, medical and legal costs.

THE PHYSIOLOGY OF STRESS

There is more than sufficient data demonstrating that stress can lead to physical, emotional and behavioral maladjustments. But how does this happen? How is it that changes in our lives lead to ill health? The answer lies in a physiological mechanism known as the **"Fight or Flight response."** The fight or flight response is a survival mechanism present in humans and most animals which prepares us to deal with physical danger. When faced with threat, two almond shaped structures in our brain called the amygdalae, which play a primary role in the processing and memory of emotional reactions, are activated. They send messages to the HPA axis (hypothalamus-pituitary-adrenal axis), which forms the circuitry responsible for connecting the brain and the body. Imagine our ancestors, cavemen and cavewomen, exploring their terrain, perhaps even enjoying the wonders of their prehistoric environment, when suddenly out of the corner of their eyes they spot a saber-toothed tiger, licking his lips in anticipation of a tasty human morsel. The fight or flight reaction would kick in preparing their bodies to either fight or flee from the tiger. It would do this through a series of instantaneous physiological and psychological changes which prepare us to take immediate physical action in the face of danger. These changes and their resulting physical signs are outlined in the following Tables.

In short, fight or flight shows a picture of autonomic hyperactivity. If we return to the example with the cave dwellers, the Caveperson's body and mind would be on "red alert" in order to deal with the impending danger. This activation would not go on for long, however. If the tiger had his way and caveperson ended up serving as a meal, he would definitely be relaxed as the deceased tend to show no autonomic activity. If, on the other hand, our friend was lucky enough to escape and tell the story to his friends back in the cave, his physiology would return to a state of **homeostasis** or balance. After a slight period of recovery, caveperson would be no worse for the wear. Visually, this may be represented as follows:

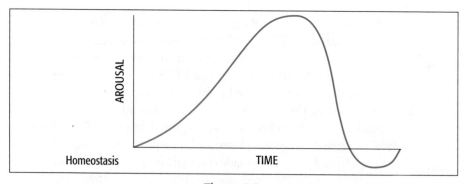

Figure 5.2

It also appears that men and women often respond differently to stress. Women's blood pressure goes up less than men's in reaction to stress, possibly related to the fact that in men the size of the amygdala is typically twice that of women, but women tend to react to a wider range of stressors than men. Women feel stress more often because they take a more holistic view of everyday life (Taylor, 2000).

TABLE 5.1 Signs of Fight or Flight

❖ Racing thoughts	❖ Attention span narrows
❖ Rapid pulse	❖ Pounding heart
❖ Gritting of teeth	❖ Muscular tension
❖ Can't sit still	❖ Jaw clenching
❖ Tremors	❖ Stomach tightens
❖ Rapid, shallow breathing	❖ Perspiration increases
❖ Serious, concerned expression	❖ Field of vision narrows
❖ Numbness	❖ Cold, clammy hands
❖ Impulsive behavior	❖ Gripping emotions
❖ Inability to concentrate	❖ Dry mouth

TABLE 5.2 Physiology of the "Fight or Flight" Response

❖ The breathing rate becomes more intense and rapid, increasing the oxygen supply in the blood.

❖ Breathing becomes more shallow, switching from diaphragmatic to thoracic respiration, again shifting the oxygen/carbon dioxide balance.

❖ Muscles tense in preparation for strenuous action.

❖ Heart rate speeds up insuring sufficient blood supply to needed areas, especially to the brain for optimized control over conscious functions as well as to major muscles to prepare the individual for action.

❖ Peripheral blood vessels constrict in order to send the bulk of the blood supply and the oxygen it carries to needed areas. Blood clotting mechanisms are also activated to protect against injury. This prevents excess bleeding should the person be cut in a struggle.

❖ The increased heart rate and constriction of peripheral blood vessels cause blood pressure to soar.

❖ Digestion ceases, so blood may be diverted to muscles and brain.

❖ Stored sugar and fats pour into the blood stream to provide fuel for quick energy.

❖ The adrenal gland is activated releasing adrenalin into the system, along with the hormone norepinephrine.

❖ Triggered by the pituitary gland, the endocrine system steps up hormone production.

❖ All senses are heightened. Pupils dilate making vision more sensitive. Hearing becomes more acute.

❖ Electrical resistivity (perspiration/galvanic action) and skin temperature change.

❖ Perspiration increases and saliva decreases.

❖ The urethra and anal sphincter muscles (controlling bowel and bladder function) initially loosen, in order to evacuate waste if necessary, but then constrict to prevent waste elimination when running or fighting. So when people say, "I was so scared that I peed in my pants," there is a physiological mechanism underlying this humiliating phenomenon.

The Downside of the Fight/Flight Reaction

This mechanism is clearly an adaptive response to the presence of physical danger. The problem is that the response is triggered not only by actual physical danger, but by perceived danger. The tigers that chase modern man and woman are not of flesh and blood. They are things like deadlines, unpaid bills, confrontations with others, overload from homework or final exams, rush hour traffic, demands from bosses, professors, children, or spouses. All these and many more trigger the fight or flight response in the person of today. But it gets worse, for not only are the tigers the actual events, but also those events remembered and anticipated by us. So not only does the act of asking the boss for a raise lead to increased autonomic activity, but also our anticipation of our meeting, along with the recollection of the event, particularly if we didn't obtain the desired results. The predicament lies in the fact that the fight or flight reaction prepares us to either fight or run away and neither of these responses is particularly useful nor adaptive for dealing with most of the stresses we face in our modern world. To further aggravate the situation, caveperson's stresses had a distinct beginning and a definite ending, whereas the tigers we face today seem to be much more ongoing. No sooner have we begun to recover from fight-flight activation when another event, real or imagined, triggers the response. Thus, we never really have the chance to fully recover and return to homeostatic balance before we are faced with the onslaught of new or old stressors recurring in our environment. This can be expressed visually as follows:

Figure 5.3

Day after day we are faced with a continuous barrage of stressors. We get some relief at night when we sleep, but even in our sleep we might dream about our stressors, again triggering the fight-flight response, and the next day we awaken with our physiology just a bit above homeostasis, to begin the whole cycle over again. After years of this pattern we forget what relaxation really feels like, as we habituate to a state of autonomic arousal. This state feels relaxed in comparison to full blown fight-flight activation, but in reality it is higher than true homeostasis, which we need to maintain health. This is illustrated in the graph on the next page:

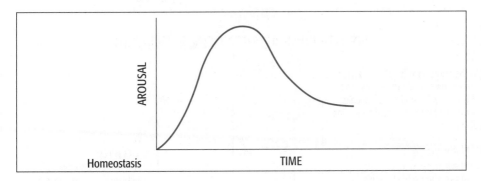

Figure 5.4

Thus a person under chronic stress is like a car with its idle set too high. Imagine for a moment a car whose engine is idling just a little too fast. What would happen to it? For one thing, it would use more gas, just as we tend to spend more energy for diminishing returns when we are under stress. In addition, the engine will wear out prematurely as it similarly appears to happen to our bodies. The stress researcher Hans Selye, mentioned earlier, described this phenomenon as a three stage process which he named the **General Adaptation Syndrome (GAS)**. The first stage of GAS, called the *Alarm Reaction*, is basically the fight or flight response. If the stressor continues, as is typical of modern day tigers, we enter into the *Stage of Resistance* where our bodies habituate to the specific stressors. Overt signs of the fight or flight reaction would disappear or go underground, but subtle signs persist, like our neural and glandular systems remaining hyperactive, leaving us over stimulated and vigilant. The last phase, known as the *Stage of Exhaustion*, occurs when stressors are prolonged despite our best attempts at coping. Just as we have to rest, so must our glandular system rest in order to regain balance. Without rest it wears down and eventually out, resistance deteriorates, and stress related symptoms resurface. Clearly, if there is no relief, even death is possible (Selye, 1982). See Figure 5.5.

Stress Sensitization

To make matters even worse, before the Stage of Exhaustion overtakes us, recent research indicates that we can become sensitized, or acutely sensitive, to stress. That is, we may respond to stress as we do an allergy. Once that happens, even ordinary stress can trigger a torrent of chemical reactions in both our brain and body that besiege us from within, making stress the psychological equivalent of ragweed (Carpi, 1996). Even though at some level we realize that what we are facing are normal, daily hassles, our brain is signaling our body to overreact. We may not think we are getting worked up over running late for an appointment, but our brain is responding as though it were a life or death situation. Years of research has demonstrated that people become sensitized to stress and this sensitization actually alters physical patterns in the brain. We may produce too many excitatory chemicals or too few calming ones; either way we are responding inappropriately. According to Carpi:

STRESS
THE GENERAL ADAPTATION SYNDROME

In the short term it's vital, but over time it turns destructive. Research shows how chronic stress breaks down the body and makes way for disease.

1. IMMEDIATE
In response to a perceived threat, the body channels resources for strength and speed.

Brain: Stress protectively dulls the body's sense of pain. Thinking and memory improve.

Eyes: Pupils dilate for better vision.

Lungs: Take in more oxygen.

Liver: Sugar stored as glycogen is converted to glucose for energy.

Heart: The bloodstream brings extra oxygen and glucose – fuel for power. Heart rate and blood pressure rise.

Adrenal Glands: The medulla secretes fight-or-flight hormone Epinephrine (adrenalin).

Spleen: Extra red blood cells flow out, allowing the blood to carry more oxygen to the muscles.

Intestines: Digestion halts, allowing the body to dedicate energy to the muscles.

Hair: Body hairs become erect. Puffed-up hair makes animals look bigger and more dangerous.

Muscles: Tense to prepare to fight or flee.

2. DELAYED
A few minutes after the fight-or-flight response, the body makes changes to stabilize and replenish itself.

Brain: The hippocampus, a center of memory/learning, gets activated to process the stress.

Immune System: Infection fighting is diminished, perhaps increasing available energy.

Liver: Fat-stored energy is converted into usable fuel.

Adrenal Glands: The cortex secretes cortisol, which regulates metabolism and immunity. Over time, though, this can be toxic.

3. CHRONIC
If activated too often, the response may harm the immune system, heart, and brain.

Brain: Cortisol becomes toxic to the brain cells, potentially damaging cognitive ability. Fatigue, anger and depression increase.

Immune System: Repeated suppression of disease-fighting cells ultimately weakens infection resistence.

Intestines: Decreases in blood flow leave mucous lining vulnerable to ulcers.

Circulatory System: Elevated blood pressure and heart rate damage elasticity of blood vessels.

Figure 5.5

The revelation that stress itself alters our ability to cope with stress has produced yet another remarkable finding. Sensitization to stress may occur before we are old enough to prevent it ourselves. ...studies suggest that animals ranging from rodents to monkeys to humans may experience still undetermined developmental periods during which exposure to extreme stress is more damaging than in later years. 'For example, we have known that losing a parent when you are young is much harder to handle than if your parent dies when you are an adult', says Jean King, Ph.D. of the University of Massachusetts Medical School. What we now believe is that a stress of that magnitude occurring in childhood may rewire your brain's circuitry, throwing the system off kilter, leaving you less able to handle normal, everyday stress. (Psychology Today, Jan./Feb. 1996 p. 12)

So clearly, stress does not just grab us for a time and then release us. It changes us by altering our bodies and our brains.

WHAT IS POSSIBLE?

But enough of this doom and gloom scenario! Are we totally at the mercy of our past and current stressors? Is there nothing we can do? Research in positive psychology and an overwhelming amount of anecdotal evidence supports the idea that, just as we have the potential to slowly destroy ourselves, that our mind/body system can also create miraculous beneficial results. What is possible can sometimes border on the unbelievable.

For example, you may have heard the story of Norman Cousins (1981), who wrote about his remarkable recovery from a supposedly incurable and very painful connective tissue disease that leads to spinal deterioration and paralysis, in his best selling book *Anatomy of an Illness*. Cousins was a distinguished author and editor of the *Saturday Review* who, in the mid 1960's developed a very painful, degenerative, connective tissue disease called ankylosing spondylitis. He became partially paralyzed and was given only months to live. He refused to buy into the gloomy predictions of his physicians, who gave him a 1 in 500 chance of recovery, so he designed a regimen of self healing based largely on using humor as a stress reducer. He checked out of the hospital, moved into a hotel room, took very large does of vitamin C, and as part of his regimen he spent several hours daily watching slapstick comedies. Initially he reported that ten minutes of belly laughter had a powerful anesthetic effect, allowing him to sleep at least two hours without painkillers. Laughter also reduced his inflammation, probably by stimulating the release of endorphins. Slowly he regained the use of his limbs and his condition steadily improved over several months. Gradually he resumed his busy life, and ultimately, much to the surprise of his physicians, he went into a complete remission. He returned to his full time work as the editor of the magazine, and wrote the book to tell the story of his recuperation. Clearly the power of optimism in promoting healing was at work in this case.

Fifteen years after his bout with the collagen disease, he suffered a near fatal heart attack. Just as before, he followed a similar regimen for healing himself and gradually improved. He chronicled this recovery in his book *The Healing Heart* (1983). Cousins died in 1990 at the age of 75. He lived many years longer than his doctors had predicted, surviving 10 years after his first heart attack, 16 years after being diagnosed with heart disease, and 26 years after his bout with collagen disease.

THE GLOBAL PERSPECTIVE–Coping with Stress Around the World

One of the advantages of living in a global society is the availability of choices from around the world. We enjoy a wide array of food, music, dance, film, sports, and literature that have their beginnings in other places. Since stress itself is a universal human experience, it behooves us to consider how other cultures successfully deal with the problem.

For instance, consider this approach to reducing stress and increasing well being that began in India and is already making inroads into the United States and all over the world. In 1995 Dr. Madan Kataria from Mumbai, India began the practice of laughter yoga. In this practice people gather in groups and simply begin to pretend laughing. In short order the whole group will begin to genuinely laugh and this is carried on for 15 to 20 minutes. Participants feel that their breathing patterns shift to a slower, deeper movement associated with relaxation. They also feel a reduction in stress and an improved sense of humor. An increased resistance to illness is also reported.

Humans have known for a long time that positive emotions seem to promote good health. For instance, in the Bible it is said that a merry heart is like a medicine. But, is there scientific evidence to support these anecdotal claims about laughter? Indeed there is.

❧ Laughter was shown to reduce cortisol levels and increase the production of lymphocytes essentially improving the functioning of the immune system (Berk et. al., 1988).

❧ The body's first line of defense against respiratory infections is a substance called salivary immunoglobulin A (IgA). Dillon, Minchoff and Baker (1985) found that IgA concentration increased significantly after exposure to a funny video.

❧ In a study conducted at Indiana State University, laughter led to a significant increase in natural killer cells as compared to control subjects (Bennet, et. al., 2003). Natural killer cells are a special type of white blood cell with the task of attacking cancer cells and microbes that invade the body.

Stress is also impacted by our lifestyle. The island of Okinawa in Japan is home to an exceptional number of very healthy centenarians (people at least 100 years old). The Okinawa Centenarian Study began in 1976 in an attempt to understand the reasons why so many live for so long with outstanding health. Genetics definitely seems to play a role but when Okinawans move to other countries and abandon their traditional lifestyle, their mortality rate increases. The investigators have also isolated other lifestyle variables that they believe contribute to the exceptional well being of these people. For instance, they note that successful aging seems enhanced by the following factors.

❧ Diet and dietary practices are important. Okinowans eat fewer calories in general due to a cultural practice known as hara hachi bu (eating to a point of 80% fullness). Their diet itself is high in vegetables and fruits, good fats, fiber, and soy proteins and grains which contain high concentrations of estrogenic compounds. These foods tend to confer protection from heart disease and stroke as well as leading to much lower rates of cancer of the breast, prostate, ovaries, and colon.

❧ Their lifestyle includes regular exercise all through their lifespan and avoidance of smoking which in conjunction with their diet also protects their hearts, their bones, and lowers stress levels.

❧ They seem to possess an optimistic and easy going approach to life.

❧ There are also strong social support systems in place. Individuals are involved in their communities and generally have deep spiritual practices.

Thus it is clear that our global family has much to offer that can reduce your stress, improve your health and the quality of your life. What else might you learn by keeping your global antenna tuned to lessons from other lands?

The Power of Belief

Or what about the amazing story reported by Ernest Rossi (1986), in his book *The Psychobiology of Mind-Body Healing?* Dr. Rossi recounted the story of Mr. Wright, as told by his personal physician, Dr. Phillip West, over 30 years ago. Mr. Wright suffered from advanced malignancy of the lymph nodes known as lymphosarcoma. His condition was terminal and he had deteriorated to the point where his physician thought death was imminent. He had tumors the size of oranges in his neck, groin, chest, and abdomen. His spleen and liver were grossly enlarged. Copious amounts of fluid were drawn from his chest on a daily basis. He was bedridden and having severe difficulty breathing. All standard cancer treatments of that time, including radiation, had proved useless. Although his doctors had given up hope for his recovery, Mr. Wright maintained an optimistic attitude, for since the onset of his illness he held fast to a belief that a miracle drug would come along to save the day. This expectation was fulfilled when newspapers reported that a newly developed drug, Krebiozen, showed significant promise in the treatment of cancer. This hope was further heightened when he learned that the hospital where he was staying would be included in a research project studying the effectiveness of this new drug. Even though he did not fit the criteria for inclusion in the study, because of the advanced nature of his condition, he begged his doctors to include him in the treatment protocol. Against their better judgment his doctors included him in the study, fully expecting he would die within the week, thus freeing up a supply of Krebiozen for another patient. His response to the drug was nothing short of miraculous! Within several days he went from death's door to walking around the ward, joking with nurses. His tumors were half of their original size. After ten days of Krebiozen treatment, he was discharged from the hospital with his cancer in complete remission. In the meantime, early results of the study indicated that this miracle drug appeared to be ineffective in the treatment of cancer. Unfortunately, Mr. Wright became aware of these initial reports of the lack of effectiveness of the drug, and within a short period of time he completely relapsed.

Clearly, it wasn't the Krebiozen that was responsible for his improvement, but the power of his belief. In order to test this out, his doctors decided to see if they could recreate the previous results. They deliberately lied to him and told him not to believe the discouraging results he had read in the newspapers. They further informed him that Krebiozen was highly effective, and that his relapse occurred because his last doses had deteriorated on the shelf. They further added that he would be receiving double strength dosages from a fresh shipment of the drug which should restore him to health. They then, with great fanfare, proceeded to inject him with saline solution, nothing but a placebo. What do you think happened? Again he made a remarkable recovery, even quicker than the first time. He was discharged from the hospital and remained in complete remission for two months, until reports appeared in the press that Krebiozen had proven to be totally worthless in the treatment of cancer. Mr. Wright quickly relapsed and was readmitted to the hospital, dying two days later.

What can be learned from this? You could conclude that the lesson here is that Mr. Wright should have stopped reading the newspaper! But obviously what is evident, and rather amazing, is that it was the power of Mr. Wright's belief that affected his physiology. Doctors would dismiss this as a dramatic example of the **Placebo Effect**. We often hear our colleagues in the health profession refer to similar, if less dramatic, results with their own cases as "just a placebo." To us, the fact that IT'S JUST A PLACEBO! opens up a whole new range of possibilities. Rather than an area to be dismissed, we consider this to be a phenomenon to explore fully. The consensus in the field is that 30% of the effectiveness of any treatment, including drugs, can be accounted for by placebo effects. One highly respected researcher in the area of stress reduction and mind/body connection, Herbert Benson (1997), believes the placebo effect is responsible for 80% of the success of all treatments!

THE MIND-BODY CONNECTION

So clearly, just as we have the capacity to do ourselves tremendous harm through our reactions to stress, so too do we have the ability to create dramatic positive outcomes in our lives. The first step is acknowledging this possibility. Our mind and body are not as separate as was once thought. In fact, they are profoundly interconnected and interdependent. As a result of this shift from the old paradigm where mind and body were thought to operate separately, a whole new branch of psychology, called **psychoneuroimmunology** or PNI, has developed over the last thirty years. PNI is the study of the relationship between stress, our immune system and health outcomes in order to uncover the workings of the mind-body connection, and discover how to use these mechanisms to fight illness, ranging from AIDS to the common cold.

One facet of PNI research is focused on proving the mind-body connection by establishing a direct physiological link between the body's immune system and the brain. This is based on a theory (Maier and Watkins, 1998) which hypothesizes that the immune system functions as a messenger which signals the brain of injury or impending illness by releasing cytokine proteins which travel to the nervous system and the brain. In response, the brain then releases its own cytokines to prompt the nervous system to discharge a cascade of responses, such as fever and fatigue, which assist the body's healing mechanisms by lowering activity level and thus conserving energy. These researchers question whether depression in humans may have developed as a survival mechanism for saving energy during times of illness.

PNI researchers, Margaret Kemeny and her colleagues (2000), at UCLA are exploring a theory which challenges and expands upon Selye's well accepted G.A.S. model of the stress response. Kemeny and her associates propose that there are actually two potential stress reactions: (1) the classic fight/flight reaction Selye describes; and (2) a withdrawal response where people cut back to conserve energy (by, for example, getting depressed rather than anxious). Kemeny's team is also studying the cognitive aspects of these two reactions. They have found that people respond differently to the same stressful events depending on the meaning given to the stressor. That is, the interpretation given to the stressor helps determine whether a person withdraws or becomes agitated. Our bodies respond not so much to our environment, but to our interpretations of our environment. By now this should be starting to sound very familiar to you, as it once again reflects that the way you view the problem often is the problem. This aspect will be dealt with in much greater detail in the next chapter which focuses on wellness and stress mastery.

A related theory about alternative stress reactions (Taylor, 2000) posits that women will often respond with "tend and befriend" behaviors rather than fight/flight reactions. That is, when under stress females will often initiate nurturing behaviors to protect their children and their loved ones, as well as themselves. That is, women often respond to stressful situations by protecting themselves and their young through nurturing behaviors and cleaning up their environment, the "tending" part of the model, and forming alliances with the larger social group, particularly other women, the "befriend" part of the model. Men, in contrast, when stressed tend to respond more with a typical fight/flight pattern, opting to either isolate/withdraw (go out to the garage and work on the car) or fight. For women, talking about stressful issues typically reduces stress levels, while for men, at least initially, withdrawal is needed to lower arousal levels before communication is desired. Taylor and her colleagues presented evidence from human and animal studies that demonstrated that when under stress, females prefer being with others, while males prefer being alone. "It is one of the most robust gender differences in adult human behavior," notes Taylor.

Does this mean that women do not respond to stress with the fight/flight response? Not necessarily. The fight/flight response seems to be present in women under acute stress. The tend and befriend response then seems to kick in with females, but not typically with males. Female animals may need to protect their young in stressful situations when fleeing too soon would expose their young to danger. Taylor's research suggests that hormones play a role in these differences. Males under stress produce androgens such as testosterone, in addition to stress hormones like cortisol. Females, on the other hand, produce oxytocin which creates a feeling of relaxation, thereby lowering fear and decreasing some aspects of fight/flight arousal. Oxytocin is also a chemical which promotes social bonding.

Your Immune System Can Learn!

Experiments with animals have demonstrated that the immune system is capable of learning by association, or classical conditioning. In one study (Ader & Cohen, 1975), rats were given sweetened water, the equivalent of rat Coca-Cola, which contained a drug which suppressed immune functioning, and not surprisingly, they began to get sick at an abnormally high rate. After a hiatus when no sweetened water was available, it was reintroduced but without the drug. Guess what? The rats started getting ill again, as the flavor of the water created a conditioned response that once again inhibited their immune functioning even though the immunosuppressant drug was absent. In another rodent experiment (Ader & Cohen, 1982), mice were bred to be genetically vulnerable to an autoimmune disease, where an overactive immune system literally attacks the body's own tissues. They were then fed a flavored solution which included an immunosuppressant drug, and as a result, it delayed the onset of the disease because their immune systems were suppressed. The researchers then continued giving the mice the flavored solution minus the drug, and the mice continued to resist the disease. Once again the immune system had learned to inhibit itself by association to a taste. In yet another rodent study (Shmeck, 1985), mice were repeatedly exposed to the smell of camphor while simultaneously receiving an injection which enhanced "natural killer" (NK) cells. NK cells, a type of white blood cell, are vitally important to immune functioning because they kill germs. Later on, when these mice were exposed to the smell of camphor without the injection, their NK activity increased once again.

This, of course, raises the intriguing question of whether we can modify our immune systems by what we learn. The answer appears to be an enthusiastic yes. An exhaustive review of all the PNI research is beyond the scope of this text, however, consider the following two unpublished studies cited by Rossi (1986). Barbara Peavey (1982) investigated the effects of a relaxation training program on the immune functioning of her subjects. In particular, she looked at the neutrophil counts for these subjects. Neutrophils are blood cells that comprise approximately two-thirds of our body's white blood cells, a significant aspect of our immune system. Anything that boosts neutrophils amplifies resistance to illness. Although the subject's neutrophil counts did not increase, these cells were found to function significantly more effectively following the relaxation training. Schneider, Smith, & Witcher (1984) carried out an even more creative study designed to facilitate neutrophil activity using subjects' imagery to boost immune functioning. Students were given information about how white blood cells functioned, and then shown microscopic slides of actual neutrophils, pictures which they could then incorporate into their imagery training. They were then trained in relaxation and imagery techniques. The subjects practiced imagining modifying their neutrophils levels and also drew pictures to accompany their imagery. After six sessions it was found that subjects could reliably and significantly increase or decrease the number of circulating neutrophils in their bloodstream. So when it comes to our own bodies, there really is such a thing as mind over matter in some instances.

More Research Evidence for the Mind-Body Connection

The Harvard Mental Health Letter (April, 2002) reviewed a variety of PNI studies which demonstrated a link between stress levels and vulnerability to illness on the human level. For example, researchers have demonstrated that NK cells decreased in medical students preparing for exams, but those students who were calmer and had slower heart rates exhibited less immune suppression. Similarly, another study showed that unhappily married women had lower numbers of certain immune cells than happily married women. Individuals caring for relatives with Alzheimer's disease, which is a very stressful task, have also been shown to have higher than average cortisol levels and lower levels of antibody response to influenza vaccines. In a 1991 English study, the stress levels of 420 subjects were evaluated immediately following an administration of nose drops containing a cold virus. These subjects were then quarantined for nine days, and those reporting the highest levels of stress were more likely to catch the cold. In a similar study in the late 1990's (Cohen and colleagues,1998) at the University of Pittsburgh, 276 healthy adults were given cold virus nose drops. Those under the most stress manifested the most severe cold symptoms, but mainly when their stress levels were affected by serious problems such as troubled marriages or unemployment. In another study, 1900 subjects were monitored for one year and were required to keep a diary of life events and their emotional reactions. Periodically, they were examined for bacteria in throat cultures and antibodies to viruses in their blood. The results showed that stressful events were four times more likely to precede rather than follow incidents of illness.

With regard to healing from injuries, one study found that biopsy wounds healed more slowly in women who were under high levels of emotional stress. In another experiment, students' wounds healed slower if inflicted just before an examination rather than just before vacation. Slow healing has also been reported in people caring for relatives with Alzheimer's disease.

Social stress appears to be even more damaging than physical stress for animals as well as humans. Our poor friends the rodents were once again tortured in the next study where one group of mice were put into a cage with highly aggressive mice. Another group of mice were kept in tiny cages without food or water for long periods of time. Then both groups were exposed to a bacterial toxin. The mice who were socially stressed were twice as likely to die as the mice who were just physically stressed.

For humans, isolation often inhibits immune functioning. Some studies have reported lower NK cell activity in separated and divorced men compared to married men. Medical students who are lonely have been found to have lower NK activity than non-lonely med students. In a year long study of people caring for spouses with Alzheimer's, decreases in immune functioning were greatest in those who had the weakest social networks and the least outside help. In general, good social support is strongly correlated with stronger immune functioning in the elderly, even after factoring out variables such as emotional health, health habits, and stress levels. In the University of Pittsburgh study mentioned previously, social support was correlated with resistance to the cold virus, that is, those with the weakest social networks were four times more susceptible to the cold that those with the strongest ties.

There have even been a few studies of the effects of traumatic stress on our immune functioning. According to one report, four months after Hurricane Andrew, Miami residents in the most heavily damaged neighborhoods demonstrated reduced activity in four out of five immune indicators. Similar results were found in a study after the Los Angeles earthquake. Weakened immune functioning has been reported among women who are victims of physical abuse. Another article suggested that men with a history of Post Traumatic Stress Disorder (PTSD), even though recovered, showed weakened immune functioning which may indicate a long lasting suppression of their immune systems.

The Harvard Mental Health Letter (April, 2002), which summarized these findings, concluded that...

> Animal experiments suggest that the nervous system responds differently to acute and chronic stress. The acute stress reaction is often a healthy response to a challenge. But chronic stress may cause the feedback controls to fail, turning the emergency response into a condition that persists when it no longer has any use. Stress hormones and sympathetic activity remain at a high level, suppressing immune function and possibly promoting illness. The immune system of people who are under chronic stress may also respond abnormally to acute stress. (p.5)

The Healing Power of the Mind

What really matters is whether our minds can influence our immune system to prevent or lower the risk of illness or injury, and also promote healing. At this point you may have several questions such as, "How can I cope better with stress?" Or you may want to ask, "How can I get the mind-body connection to work for me?" We now know enough of the necessary steps to harness this power. What remains is to learn and then practice these steps. If you follow the techniques and suggestions outlined in the next chapter and also in chapter 7, in the section on using visualization techniques to promote healing, we promise you will reap significant benefits. But let us caution you that knowing the steps is not enough, it is only in the doing that solutions are found. The following chapter on wellness will enumerate specific techniques for mastering stress and staying healthy.

WELLNESS SELF EXERCISE:

Be aware of the relationship between stress and the fight or flight response in your own life. Next time you are feeling anxious or shaky, note what is triggering this reaction. Is it actual danger or more likely just perceived danger? Conversely, the next time you are faced with a stressor, pay attention to how your body reacts. Awareness of increased arousal or fight/flight activation is the first step in learning to calm you, which is addressed in the next chapter.

KEY TERMS

Stress Mastery	Fight/Flight Response	Stress
Homeostasis	Eustress	Stress Sensitization
Distress	General Adaption Syndrome (GAS)	Glucocorticoids
Placebo Effect	Endorphins	Psychoneuroimmunology
Cortisol	Psychophysiological Disorders	Bruxism

CHAPTER 5 QUESTIONS

True or False Questions (T or F)

1. _____ A commitment to mastering stress will add time to your schedule.

2. _____ It is definitely possible to escape all the stressors in your life.

3. _____ We need an optimal level of stress in our lives to keep things interesting.

4. _____ There is no clear cut relationship between stress and health.

5. _____ The more changes in your life, the less likely you are to get sick.

6. _____ The fight or flight response can be triggered not just by actual physical danger, but by any perceived danger or stressor.

7. _____ The fight or flight response is a natural mechanism which prepares us to either fight or flee.

8. _____ Death is possible if there is no relief from the Stage of Exhaustion of the General Adaptation Syndrome.

9. _____ Despite popular myths, the mind and the body function separately.

10. _____ The mind/body connection is capable of facilitating healing.

11. ____   Psychoneuroimmunlogy is the study of the relationship between neurosis and neurological damage.

12. ____   Divorced men are less likely to get sick than married men.

Short-Answer Questions

1. _____ is anything that requires an adaptive response on the part of the organism.
2. Many tasks are best performed with _____ levels of arousal.
3. Stress negatively affects your _____, _____, and _____ functioning in a variety of ways.
4. _____% of all visits to doctors offices are for stress related disorders.
5. The _____ response is a survival mechanism present in humans and most animals which prepares us to deal with physical danger.
6. When _____ sets in it is possible to respond to stress as you would to an allergen.
7. When people report feeling better after being given a sugar pill and told it is a painkiller, this is an example of the _____ _____.
8. A theory about alternative stress reactions posits that women will often respond with _____ and _____ behaviors rather than fight/flight reactions.

Essay Questions

1. Distinguish between eustress and distress.
2. Explain the Yerkes-Dodson Law and its implications in performance situations.
3. Describe the physiological changes that occur during the fight or flight response.
4. Discuss the General Adaptation Syndrome (GAS).
5. What is stress sensitization?
6. How do women respond differently to stress than men?
7. What conclusions can be drawn from research in psychoneuroimmunology?

6

Developing Wellness Skills

WHAT IS WELLNESS?

Wellness as a term was introduced decades ago when a forward thinking physician began writing about well-being as an integration of the mind, body and spirit and encompassing many components of human functioning (Davis, 1961). Today **wellness** as a term has caught on, but to many it is associated primarily with physical fitness. We see "Wellness Centers" in communities and on campuses that are actually gyms with exercise equipment and machines. This reinforces the connection between wellness and exercise rather than suggesting a more comprehensive meaning of the term. The wellness concept we are referring to in this text is indeed more multi-dimensional.

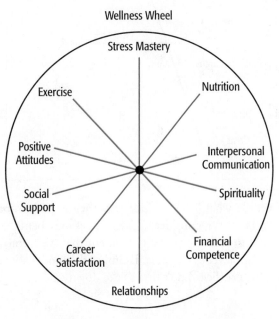

Wellness Wheel

149

As the literature and practice of wellness has expanded over the decades, numerous models have emerged that illustrate the components of well-being. Drawing from many of the various schemas, we have included those elements most prominent in other models into our own wellness wheel.

Ideas regarding the development of *Positive Attitudes* were covered in Chapter 3. This current chapter will build further understanding of *Stress Mastery* and offer specific strategies for stress reduction through relaxation and meditation practices. **Exercise** is examined here as it relates to minimizing stress as well as other benefits that being active engenders. The importance of **Nutrition** and its significance for wellness is reviewed. Pointers for attaining **Financial Competence** are also offered. Finally, the power of **Social Support** to sustain and enrich our sense of well-being is also addressed. The remaining components of our wellness wheel are addressed in other chapters to follow. So, welcome to the world of wellness. Further skill building through the concepts presented here will propel you onward in your quest for excellence.

Wellness, or the state of being well, is a lot more than just feeling that you are not ill. By the same token, mental health is not the same as an absence of mental illness. Mental health reflects the presence of PERMA: of having positive emotions; a sense of meaning and purpose in life; good relationships; accomplishment; and engagement, all the elements of flourishing. John Travis (1981), a physician, has developed a model of progression that amply illustrates the path to wellness.

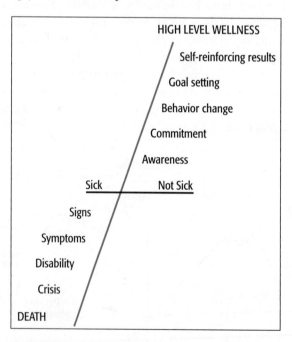

If you asked most people what "wellness" means, they would probably answer that it means you're not sick. However, considering wellness as only being "not sick" is too limiting. Most of us would probably say at this moment that we are not sick, yet we could be a long way from a high level of wellness. Examine the model above depicting the differences in being sick or not sick. Look first at the downward progression of being sick.

It starts with signs and symptoms, the origin or cause of which can be physical, cognitive or emotional. For example, you could experience physical changes such as fatigue, a headache, or shortness of breath on exertion. Cognitively, you could be confused, unable to focus your thoughts, have difficulty remembering, unable to organize ideas or derive solutions. Emotionally, you could be overly anxious, frightened, sad, or engulfed in anger. Any of these signs and symptoms reflects that something is not right, and you may say to yourself, "There's a problem here."

If you don't recognize the problem, or don't do something to reverse the symptoms, you will probably slip further downward to serious dysfunction, even to the point of being disabled. For example, physically your fatigue could reflect a severe lack of red blood cells and you could become very anemic, completely without energy, unable to ambulate. Cognitively, you may not be able to keep up with projects, or assignments. Emotionally you may not be able to maintain normal relationships or may exhibit behavior that is negative or destructive to yourself and others. You may not need a wheelchair, need someone else to think for you, nor be in a straight jacket, however, you are still disabled from functioning productively and may spend time in bed, sleeping, resting, and not able to meet daily tasks like attending work or classes. If you do nothing to reverse being disabled, you may plunge further to acute illness, reaching a crisis state where the status of your survival is critical. And yet again, if something is not done to reverse the crisis it means that you can sink to the lowest point in the paradigm...death. So we note that there are stages or steps to being "sick." Most of us have been through some of these stages so we are quite familiar with this process; however, we may be less informed regarding the progression of being "not sick."

When you look at the higher end of the continuum, progressing up the "not sick" side, you see that there are also stages on the wellness side of the continuum, beginning with **awareness**. To move up the ladder toward a higher state of wellness, the first step is recognizing your current state. Being aware is the starting point. As someone once said, "You can't fix something, if you don't know it's broken." For example, let's suppose you find that because you have gained weight, your clothes no longer fit which has led to pummeling yourself with self-deprecating thoughts. Being so unhappy, what do you do? You comfort yourself with chocolate cake. In this situation, you are not sick, but you are not that well either. However, if you become aware of your physical condition, negative thoughts, and destructive behavior, you have taken the first step toward a higher level of wellness.

Now you have the opportunity to make positive choices to take better care of yourself. Choosing to change your body composition, restructuring your thinking to positive self talk, and modifying how you reward yourself will result in *commitment*. This makes you want to continue in proactive behavior that leads to a healthier you. Actually taking the steps to develop and follow a meaningful weight loss program is what we mean by self-efficacy.

As you can see in this model, the road to wellness involves specific stages from awareness, to commitment, to *behavior change*. The next step is to set specific goals, such as changing your nutrition and exercise patterns. Achieving these goals brings you the desired positive behavior. These results become a natural *reinforcer* to continue the newly acquired behavior. Now that your clothes are a size smaller and fit great, you are more optimistic, and you feel terrific about yourself, the "new you" solidifies your continuing positive behavior. This is the way we move from awareness to a *high level of wellness*. May your journey up the line bring you to a heightened state of well-being!

MASTERING STRESS THROUGH THE MAGIC IN BREATHING

Mastering stress on the path to high level wellness is a life long process. If you choose to incorporate the concepts and techniques presented in this chapter into the daily fabric of your life, your capacity to cope with and thrive from stress will flourish. Clearly, to deal with stress effectively, you must pay attention to both your body and your mind. Deepak Chopra (1993) in *Ageless Body, Timeless Mind* summarizes research which showed that meditators tended to age slower than non-meditators, a rather dramatic finding. During meditation one focuses on quieting both the body and the mind through the act of fixing on a single thought, image, or visualization.

Truth be told, the distinction between body and mind is really an artificial one, as we discussed in the previous chapter. We now know that body and mind are really one, an intricately interrelated system where thoughts give rise to our physical reactions and, in turn, our physical reactions trigger our various thoughts. But for the purpose of training, of learning how to begin moving toward stress mastery, it is useful to talk about addressing your body first. It is very difficult to change the way you think if your body is simultaneously sending messages of danger. Addressing the body is best accomplished by learning **active relaxation**.

Most people confuse inactivity with relaxation. You might say, "I do relax. I go home and sit down in front of the TV, watch my favorite programs, and let the stress of the day melt away." But the fact is that when subjects' level of stress, as indicated by physiological arousal, is measured while watching TV, negligible, if any decrease is evident. You see, **passive relaxation** such as this is not nearly as effective in reducing stress. What is needed is relaxation aimed at reducing the fight/flight response and thereby restoring balance or homeostasis. Active relaxation involves becoming aware of your body and your physiological reactions so that you may consciously reduce your level of arousal.

Diaphragmatic Breathing

Any journey which you undertake begins with a first step. The key to any practice of active relaxation is to relearn proper breathing patterns. Breathing slowly, deeply, and regularly is the easiest and most accessible relaxation technique (Loehr & Migdow, 1986). Most of the time, you are no doubt oblivious to your breathing patterns. Let's first begin by discovering where you are now. Sit with your back supported, your feet flat on the floor and your eyes closed. Put one hand on your chest, and the other on your diaphragm, the muscle right above your stomach, as you focus on your breathing. Notice the pattern and rhythm of your breath as you breathe in and out. Then, take a few deep breaths, noticing as you breathe in and out which hand moves more. Does the hand on your chest move up and down, with the shoulders rising and falling, as you breathe? Or is it the hand on your abdomen that does most of the movement? Take a few moments to do that now.

So what happened? Which hand moved more as you breathed deeply? We notice in our classes and workshops that for the majority of students and participants, it is the hand on the chest that evidences more movement. If you have ever seen a baby breathing while she is at rest or asleep, you may have noticed that it is the stomach that moves up and down, while the baby's chest remains relatively still and quiet. This is called **diaphragmatic breathing** and it is a natural antidote to stress. Diaphragmatic breathing involves deep, slow, rhythmic breaths.

Pay attention to what happens to your breathing the next time you feel stressed. You may notice that your breathing became quicker, more shallow and irregular. Some people even hold their breath or begin to hyperventilate when under significant stress. What happens to many adults is that after years of frequently activating the fight/flight response, the fast, shallow, upper chest breathing characteristic of this physiological reaction becomes a habit. This breathing is ineffectual, disrupting the proper balance of carbon dioxide and oxygen in your blood stream and thereby creating a continual, if not full blown, over-activation response. There is an optimal balance of oxygen and carbon dioxide that needs to be maintained in your bloodstream for you to remain calm. When you breathe in air, your blood cells receive oxygen and release carbon dioxide (CO_2). CO_2 is a waste product that is carried back through your body and exhaled. **Hyperventilation**, a rapid, shallow type of over breathing, reduces the level of carbon dioxide and calcium in the blood. This causes the blood vessels in the brain to constrict, leading to physical symptoms including dizziness, numbness, headache and/or muscle tension, even tremors. These symptoms can be frightening and tend to cause considerable psychological distress along with increased panic and anxiety. That is why hyperventilation is so counterproductive. The more quickly you breathe, the worse you feel.

Practicing Diaphragmatic Breathing

Retraining yourself is, in most cases, a rather simple procedure. What is required is just about five minutes a day of conscious focusing on your breathing. You can do this by practicing the following technique, once a day, for three weeks. Three weeks are generally required to bring tone to the diaphragm muscle. We have discovered that a few minutes prior to going to sleep is a good time to practice for many people. Others prefer to take five minutes when they return home from either work or school. It is important for you to discover which time is best for you.

Find a quiet place where you are unlikely to be disturbed. Recline and put one hand on your diaphragm and one hand on your chest. Focus on allowing the hand on your diaphragm to rise as you breathe in, as if your stomach were a balloon filling with air. Then watch it go back down as you breathe out and the balloon deflates. Notice the rhythm of the rising and falling of your abdomen as you inhale and exhale. Focus on the particular feelings and sensations you experience in your diaphragm as the breath comes all the way into your lungs and then completely empties from your lungs. Do this for about five minutes, gently focusing your attention on your breath.

If you find yourself having difficulty initially lifting your abdomen as you breathe, try imagining that you are putting on a tight pair of jeans, when they come out fresh from the drier. You would let all the air out of your lungs first, as if you wanted to touch your spine with your bellybutton, then slowly inflate the balloon as you let the air come all the way into your lungs.

Yet another technique that has proven successful for many people is to use a heavy book placed on top of your stomach as you practice your breathing exercises. You could watch the rising and falling of the book as you breathe in and out. This method has the added advantage of providing a weight against which the diaphragm is rising and falling, thereby conditioning the muscle much quicker. Most people find that with just a little attention and practice they can return to that slow, diaphragmatic breathing they knew as a child.

We cannot emphasize enough how important this first step is. Without shifting your breath to a calm, relaxed, diaphragmatic pattern, it will be very difficult to start your journey on the path towards stress mastery. The type of breathing you employ is the key to unlocking the magic. We know it sounds simple, but it is nonetheless true.

Take, as an example, people suffering from panic attacks, a disorder in which intense anxiety (often accompanied by hyperventilation) is experienced at various times, often causing the individual to withdraw and increasingly restrict their activities in the hope of preventing the attacks. In the extreme, these individuals develop a condition known as "agoraphobia" where they become house bound as a way of coping with the fear of the attacks reoccurring. Developing appropriate diaphragmatic breathing patterns has been identified as essential in learning to overcome the panic.

Focusing on your breathing helps keep you in the present moment. Your worries, anxieties and stress occur when you focus on either the past, (i.e. mistakes you have made or things you wish would have happened differently), or you focus on the future, (i.e. worrying about what is going to happen and how you will be able to survive). But the past has already happened: there is little you can do to alter that except change your attitude or perception about what occurred. And the future is yet to come. You can only affect it by working in the present, the here and now. Breathing helps you exist in the now in a way which increases your effectiveness.

Most spiritual traditions recognize the importance of the breath. It is often considered our direct link to God or a Higher Power. The word "inspiration" has a double meaning, being used both to describe breathing as well as being infused with spirit and motivation. Alterations in breathing can create dramatic effects on our consciousness. Holotropic breathing, an alteration in breathing in which controlled hyperventilation is employed, for example, has been shown to create dramatic shifts in consciousness in the practitioners, akin, if somewhat less intense, than those experienced when using hallucinogens. So breathing is clearly a powerful tool; one that can create numerous changes in our bodies, and in our experience of ourselves and our world.

Once you can breathe comfortably using your diaphragm as you think consciously about it, it becomes important to be able to generalize that response to your daily life. One easy way to do this is to set up a number of reminders in your everyday environment. For example, do you know those sticky colored dots that are often used in offices to color code charts? You could take a few of these (3-5) and place them in different places around your home and work environment. We suggest that you resist the temptation to place these dots on the foreheads of people who are a source of stress to you. However, feel free to use your imagination. Each time you see a dot, stop for a second, take one or two breaths using your diaphragm, and then go on with your activity. Or, you could set a reminder alarm on your cell phone. This will allow you, with minimal effort, to remind yourself to breathe this way at different times during the day. In just a short time you will be pleasantly surprised, as you focus on your breathing, to discover that you are automatically breathing deep, diaphragmatic breaths.

Another way to insure that you generalize the correct breathing response to a variety of situations is by using a higher order classical conditioning principle. This principle states that when a new behavior is paired, and thus eventually associated, with a behavior which is frequently emitted, the new behavior becomes conditioned. This means that you will learn how to breathe correctly faster and better if you do it at the same time that you are doing things which you do frequently, like answering the phone, going to the bathroom, or stopping at red lights.

Another obvious way, and indeed, the first building block, is to remember to breathe from your abdomen whenever you feel yourself becoming stressed. This will help interrupt the automatic cognitive and behavioral strategies you may be using now, which merely lead to an escalation of the stress response. Remembering to breathe in these situations allows you a pause which opens up the possibility of thinking or behaving differently, thereby using stress rather than being used by it.

We should caution you, however, that it is not wise to use only situations when you are feeling stressed as reminders to practice your breathing. You will clearly find it more difficult initially to successfully focus on appropriate breathing at these times. Until you have learned and feel comfortable with abdominal breathing, you need to practice in situations which are less demanding and in which the fight/flight response is not fully activated.

You need only do the most basic breathing awareness exercises to achieve a much more relaxed state of body and mind. As long as your breathing is becoming slower, quieter, and deeper you are moving in the right direction. Quite frankly, the hardest part is remembering to remember to be aware of your breathing and then to practice. But the fact remains that wherever you are, you still have to breathe, so you might as well practice doing it properly in a manner that will help keep you calm yet alert.

Cultivating Awareness

By now you have become more aware of your breathing. You can notice just how you are breathing. Are you using your diaphragm or your chest? Are you breathing deeply and slowly, with a comfortable rhythm? Or is your breath fast and chaotic? In any situation, if you notice you are engaged in unhealthy, stress producing breathing, this awareness allows you the opportunity to shift the pattern to a more appropriate one.

Can you do this? If you can't, we strongly urge you to continue your practice. Without the ability to breathe appropriately, it will be difficult for you to master stress. If you can, we congratulate you! You have taken the first, and most fundamental step towards stress mastery. It is important that you now remember to do this throughout your day, in a variety of settings; that you think about it at work, and at home; that you notice your breathing as you are going to sleep, and shortly after you wake up. It is essential that you remember to remember to notice your breathing. The more you do this, the more you are cultivating awareness. You are replacing your automatic behavior with conscious behavior.

THE VALUE OF SELF AWARENESS

You see, all human beings have the ability to be aware, not just of our breathing, but of a multitude of things that make up who we are. Let us demonstrate what we mean. Imagine, in your mind's eye, that a part of you can float out of your body, floating up to a particular corner of the room, so that you can see yourself, from that perspective, sitting over there reading this book. What would it be like to do this, what would it feel like? How would you describe the particular sensations that the "you" who is sitting there is experiencing right now? Focus in on a particular part of your body and become aware of your experience there. Perhaps you can be aware of pressure, or temperature, or perhaps some other sensation. It's not important what the specific sensation is, just your ability to notice it. How about your overall mood? How would you characterize that? What can you say about your thoughts? Are you thinking about what you are reading right now, and yet perhaps at the same time wondering what's the point of all this? As you answer these questions, make sure you get back into your body. We certainly wouldn't want you to remain floating around the room somewhere while you continued reading this chapter.

The Witnessing Stance

By doing what you just did, answering the questions we just asked, you have demonstrated your ability for **self awareness**. All human beings share the ability to be aware of ourselves. The fact that we can do this; that we can stand apart from our feelings and our thoughts suggests that we can have some control over them. Ram Dass (1990), formerly known as Richard Alpert, a Harvard psychologist who studied extensively in India and is renowned for integrating both Eastern and Western techniques, describes our ability to stand apart from ourselves, to view ourselves from the outside, as assuming the **witnessing stance**. Whenever you are involved in the many experiences that make up your life, you have the choice to be a *witness* to your own life. This shift in perspective provides you with the possibility that you can change the particular situation. The fact is (as we addressed in Chapter 2), that you cannot always change situations (i.e. external stressors or events) you are faced with, but you can always change your reaction towards the stressor. Assuming the witnessing stance allows you to do this. Remember that, as we mentioned earlier, what inappropriately triggers your fight/flight response and therefore your stress, is not actual physical danger. Not many of you have guns pointed at your head, at least not on a daily basis. What triggers your stress response is your perception of danger. And whether you perceive something as dangerous or not depends on the meaning you give the particular situation. Fortunately or unfortunately, human beings are the kind of beings that give meaning to everything. And what we say, especially to ourselves, about a situation or event determines our attitude towards it. Assuming an observer perspective allows you to get a glimpse of the meaning you are ascribing and therefore provides you an opportunity to change your attitude.

Psychologists also have other labels to describe the processes involved in becoming self aware. The term **metacognition** refers to becoming aware of your thought processes, and **metamood** to becoming aware of your emotions. The process of assuming the witnessing stance allows you to step back from your experience, to go "meta," where you hover somewhere above the main flow, aware of what is happening rather than being immersed and therefore lost in it, which facilitates getting a better perspective. This refers to the difference between being furious and having the thought, "I'm feeling anger." But this subtle shift in mental activity is the first step in gaining some control. Becoming aware of your underlying thoughts and emotions is essential to developing emotional self control. Certainly, there is a big gap between being aware of a feeling and being able to change it, but the two often go hand in hand. That is, if you recognize that you are in a rotten mood, typically you will want to get out of it. Self awareness appears to have a greater impact on intense negative feelings. The recognition of what it is you are feeling gives that slight bit of distance that sets in motion an awareness of alternatives, such as the option to attempt to let go of the feeling.

Attitude is Everything!

Research has revealed that the attitude you have at the beginning of a task determines the outcome of that task more than any other single factor (Seligman, 1991). For example, if you believe you will be able to succeed at a particular undertaking (if you are optimistic), and you approach the endeavor with a sense of excitement and joyful expectation, your chances of achieving success are much higher than if you face the task with dread and apprehension. Self-fulfilling prophecies can be positive or negative, depending on your expectations. So your attitude is more important than any other possible factor, both external and internal. This is clearly true when it comes to stress and whether we thrive from it or are buried by it.

Remember Thomas Holmes and his research showing that there was a relationship between the number, severity, and pervasiveness of life changes and our physical and emotional health? We mentioned that this series of studies did not take into account individual differences in abilities to cope with the changes and demands. This research only focused on the effects of external events or stressors. A psychologist by the name of Suzanne Kobasa (1979) decided to focus her research interests on individual differences in coping skills. What makes some people capable of handling enormous amounts of change and demands without suffering the devastating physical and emotional consequences predicted by the Holmes research? Kobasa studied individuals whose lives seemed so filled with stressors that, according to Holmes, they should have been growing massive tumors on the sides of their heads. Yet, these folks were successful in their endeavors and seemed to be suffering no apparent negative consequences from their demanding lifestyle.

STRESS HARDINESS ATTITUDES

Kobasa discovered three attitudes which these people all shared and which appeared to make them resistant to the negative effects of stress. She called these three attitudes, the **Stress Hardiness** attitudes because individuals who possess them appear to be "stress hardy," i.e. capable of dealing effectively with stressors. These three attitudes are **control**, **commitment**, and **challenge**. These attitudes are also referred to as the *three Cs of stress hardiness* (Kobasa, 1979).

Control

Let's take a look at the first, the attitude of **control**. Stress hardy individuals believe that they are in control of their lives, rather than stressors having control over them. They recognize that they have resources and options that allow them to influence events in their lives. Although stress hardy individuals recognize that they may not always have direct control over the actual onset or occurrence of an event, they certainly have control over their own response to the stressor. And this is not only true of humans, but also true of such higher life forms as rats. For example (Weiss, 1971), let's say you placed two rats in cages capable of delivering an electroshock to their unsuspecting paws. (Psychologists do, indeed, do this and other perhaps less kindly things to these animals. That is why our standing as a profession is rather low in the rat community!) Using what is known in experimental psychology as a "yoked research design," both rats are then shocked simultaneously at various intervals. One rat has a lever available in its cage which if pressed will discontinue the shock. The second rat has no such escape opportunity. When the first rat presses the lever, it stops the shock for both rats. This assures both rats are exposed to the same level and intensity of the shock, but only the first rat has control over discontinuing the stressful event. Can you guess what happens? The first rat, the one with control, is minimally, if at all affected by the series of shocks. The second "helpless" rat, on the other hand, suffers negatively, developing multiple psychosomatic symptoms such as ulcers.

These differences in stress response are maintained even when the escape lever is removed and replaced merely by a light which precedes the shock. In this design, the first rat had no means of escape, but was warned that a shock was imminent. Although the rat could do no more than dance around the cage, the effects of the stressor were somehow reduced perhaps because the rat knew it was going to be dancing around and was therefore, more prepared to do so. Thus, our sense of control is also affected by the extent to which we can anticipate and prepare for the onset of stressors and change. Involvement in exercise is a perfect example of this. We know that physical exercise is stressful. Yet it is stress over which we have control because we typically can choose when to begin and when to end our exercise routine. Stress researchers conclude that it is this sense of control which is at least partially responsible for the beneficial effects of repeated exercise (Brehm, 1998).

So, stress hardy individuals refuse to see themselves as victims, buffeted and abused by external occurrences over which they have no control. Persons exhibiting this attitude see themselves as active players in their own lives. They possess what was discussed in Chapter 2 as an *internal locus of control*; for such individuals believe that they are responsible for the ultimate outcomes in their life. They do not wait for fate to lead them in directions, rather they endeavor to take active control over their own life. This is the same attitude described by Covey as *proactivity*.

Commitment

The second attitude characteristic of stress hardy individuals that was identified by Kobasa involves **commitment**. It is not merely the persistence in following through with a goal, it is an attitude which expresses a real *joie de vivre*, a zest for life. Commitment involves believing that what you do is of value and importance. Individuals exhibiting this attitude seem to possess an almost romantic relationship to their own life and the pursuits which they choose. When they wake up in the morning they don't start their day with, "Oh God, I wonder what could go wrong today? What horrible ambush can life have planned for me?" Instead they wake up expectant of the possible surprises and wonderful experiences that the day has in store for them. They have an optimistic outlook. Stressors are viewed as potentially interesting and meaningful. Commitment is the opposite of alienation and is characterized by involvement.

It is not surprising that research has linked how one answers two simple questions with the likelihood of developing heart disease. The two questions are: *Are you happy?* And, *do you like your job?* If you answer yes to both of these, your chances of developing heart disease are much lower. Clearly the reverse is true when the answer is no. We are not implying here that overall life/job dissatisfaction causes heart disease. Obviously there are many other factors operating in the development of cardiovascular problems. But your attitude towards your life is one important contributing factor. What is your attitude when you first open your eyes in the morning? We suggest you begin with the before mentioned *attitude of gratitude*. One that says, "thank-you. I'm glad I'm alive. I wonder what adventures and experiences this day has for me." You see, happiness is not a condition, but a decision. You can choose to focus on all that can make you miserable. If you do, you will get results fitting this attitude. Or you can choose to count your blessings, to be thankful for all you have, and all you still have coming. To quote the great comedienne Gilda Radner shortly before her untimely death, "Happiness is not about getting what you want, but about appreciating what you have."

Challenge

The third and final attitude discovered by Kobasa to be typical of stress hardy individuals is that of **challenge**. This attitude can perhaps be best explained by considering the concept of *crisis*. The Chinese write this word using two characters as illustrated below:

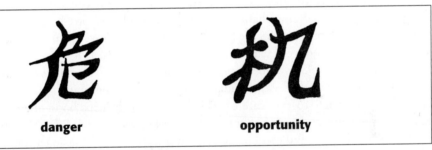

danger   opportunity

The first character is the symbol for danger; the second is the symbol for opportunity. Think about that, what a wonderful way to describe a crisis. Not a catastrophe, or a problem, but a *dangerous opportunity*. Individuals exhibiting the attitude of challenge focus not so much on the danger aspect of the crisis, but on the opportunities available as a result. Every crisis, no matter what, has inherent opportunities. Those who cope well look for these opportunities and capitalize on them. Those who cope poorly get paralyzed by the inherent danger. To quote Don Juan, from Castañeda's *The Teachings of Don Juan* (1998):

> The basic difference between a warrior and an ordinary man is that a warrior sees everything as a challenge. While an ordinary man sees everything as either a blessing or a curse.

Or to quote another colorful literary character, Zorba, from the movie *Zorba the Greek*.

> Life is trouble, only death is not. To be alive is to undo your belt and go looking for trouble.

Hardiness and Stress Resistance

Take a moment and fill out the Stress Hardiness Inventory below. Research has documented an association between high hardiness scores and lower rates of physical illness among white collar male executives and women in various occupations (Rhodewalt & Zone, 1989), blue collar workers (Manning, Williams, & Wolfe, 1988), college students (Roth and colleagues., 1989), and adolescents (Sheppard & Kashani, 1991). Hardiness is also associated with psychological health. Stress hardy individuals report lower anxiety levels, less depression, greater job satisfaction and lower levels of tension at work. In other studies hardy subjects were shown to have stronger physical tolerance for stress. When exposed to a stressor they have a lower increase in diastolic blood pressure (Contrada, 1989) and a smaller increase in heart rate (Lawler & Schmied, 1987).

One interesting study (Allred & Smith, 1989) demonstrated that male college students who scored low on hardiness experienced high levels of tension before the onset of a stressor (i.e. as they waited and anticipated), while those scoring high on hardiness measures displayed higher arousal only during exposure to the stressor. It appeared that the hardy subjects got aroused only when they needed an adrenalin surge to confront the stressor more effectively, while the others spent valuable energy worrying. Hardy individuals do get physiologically aroused but at the right time and to the right level.

Strong resistance to stress is associated with optimism, and clearly the ability to think positively is a defining characteristic of the stress hardy. Stress resistant people are more likely to use problem-focused coping measures, positive thinking, and support-seeking strategies when faced with stress (Cohen & Edwards, 1989; Holt, Fine & Tollefson,1987; Nowack, 1989). Those scoring low on measures of hardiness tend to respond passively to stress, whether with avoidance or maladaptive behaviors. Hardy individuals are much more likely to take care of their health, which helps boost their stress resistance. A strong sense of personal control over one's life is associated with better health habits, such as exercise and good nutrition, lower likelihood of abusing alcohol, drugs or nicotine, or of aggressive acting out when under stress.

STRESS HARDINESS SELF-ASSESSMENT INVENTORY

Use this scale to indicate how much you agree or disagree with the statements below:

0 = **Strongly disagree**   1 = **Mildly disagree**
2 = **Mildly agree**   3 = **Strongly agree**

_____ **A.** Trying my best at work and school makes a difference.

_____ **B.** Trusting to fate is sometimes all I can do in a relationship.

_____ **C.** I often wake up eager to start on the day's projects.

_____ **D.** Thinking of myself as a free person leads to great frustration and difficulty.

_____ **E.** I would be willing to sacrifice financial security in my work if something really challenging came along.

_____ **F.** It bothers me when I have to deviate from the routine or schedule I've set for myself.

_____ **G.** An average citizen can have an impact on politics.

_____ **H.** Without the right breaks, it is hard to be successful in my field.

_____ **I.** I know why I am doing what I'm doing at work or school.

_____ **J.** Getting close to people puts me at risk of being obligated to them.

_____ **K.** Encountering new situations is an important priority in my life.

_____ **L.** I really don't mind when I have nothing to do.

To get your scores for control, commitment and challenge, write the number of your answer, from 0 to 3, above the letter of each question. Then add and subtract as shown below. Then add up the column of scores for control, commitment and challenge.

(A + G = _____) − (B + H = _____) = _____ **Control**

(C + I = _____) − (D + J = _____) = _____ **Commitment**

(E + K = _____) − (F + L = _____) = _____ **Challenge**

_____ **Total Hardiness Score**

Score	Interpretation
10–18	**Hardy personality**
0–9	**Moderate hardiness**
Below 0	**Low hardiness**

The Three Cs in Action

The authors had an opportunity to witness, firsthand, how stress hardiness attitudes affected the ability of literally thousands of people to cope with a monumental crisis. Being based in Miami, Florida, we, along with thousands of other people, back in 1992 experienced Hurricane Andrew, one of the strongest and most destructive storms ever to ravage the mainland U.S.A, prior to Hurricane Katrina. The scale of property destruction and disruption of normal life for months afterward was extensive. Just about everyone in the hurricane zone (including the authors) suffered severe damage to their homes, businesses, cars, and personal property. Rebuilding took years and normal routines were totally disrupted for at least six months for most. As psychologists we paid close attention to how individuals coped with the aftermath of the storm and we found that three distinct styles emerged: (1) The Whiners—individuals who spent months bemoaning their plight and all the inconveniences, hassles, and property losses they suffered; (2) The Stiff Upper Lip Crowd—individuals who were very upset but focused on cleaning up, rebuilding, and didn't spend an inordinate amount of time complaining, but internally they focused primarily on how awful it all was; (3) The Adventurers—individuals who did not deny the reality of the damage but who focused on how interesting, how exciting, what an adventure it all was. These people relished rebuilding their homes with insurance money. They delighted in the sense of camaraderie and community that developed between neighbors who found themselves in the same boat, who previously had barely spoken to one another. Needless to say, the latter group experienced far fewer emotional disturbances and physical illnesses than the other two groups. They believed that they could *control* their destiny, even in the face of incredible ruin. They were *committed* to making the rebuilding process as joyful as possible. And they viewed the crisis as a *challenge* and opportunity to recreate their living situation and make new friends.

For them, the hurricane became an epic, fascinating story to share with friends rather than merely a tragic event.

Clearly, you should be able to perceive the wisdom in Covey's oft quoted phrase, "The way you see the problem is the problem." Ultimately, whether something is stressful or not depends on the way you look at the situation. Remember, it is not the world out there that makes you a victim, it is your perception of the circumstances and events which lead you to be either defeated by stress or to survive and thrive from the challenges and opportunities presented to you. You may not have control over all that happens to you, but you certainly always have control over the meaning you give to the events in your life. There is an old saying, "When God closes a door, he opens a window." Remember this as you face apparent hardships in your life. Always look for the windows; we guarantee that they will be there, no matter what the circumstances.

Problem-Focused vs. Emotion-Focused Coping Strategies

Other factors influence how individuals choose to cope with stress as well. Richard Lazarus (1966, 1991) emphasized the role of how an individual *appraises* a stressful situation in determining both the impact of the stressor, and in the choice of the appropriate method of coping. Coping strategies can be partitioned into two broad categories where **Problem-focused coping** refers to attempts to deal with the stressor head-on to remove or defuse its effects, and **Emotion-focused coping** is a more indirect method, where attempts are made to moderate one's own emotional response to the stressor. For example, a broken down car would call for problem-focused coping (i.e. get the car repaired a.s.a.p.) while a broken heart would require emotion-focused coping. Lazarus pointed out that there is no one preferred strategy of coping as different stressors or stressful events demand different coping styles. The effective individual appraises events in ways that allow for the choice of the most appropriate coping strategy given the particular stressor. Emotion-focused coping strategies for dealing with stress include relaxation techniques such as diaphragmatic breathing, progressive relaxation and meditation along with cognitive restructuring methods.

The Biology of Stress Hardiness

What is actually happening on a physiological level to promote health in individuals who display the 3 C's? Let us begin this discussion by focusing on the effects of hardiness on cardiovascular disease (CVD). We know that optimism, an essential component of hardiness, is strongly associated with cardiovascular health and mortality rate. In one longitudinal study with over 97,000 women (Tindle & colleagues, 2009), optimists had 30% fewer coronary deaths than pessimists. This brings up the question of whether the real culprit was depression since dysthymia is correlated with pessimism. However, not all pessimists are depressed. Indeed, this study controlled for levels of depression as well as other risk factors and found that optimism was the crucial factor. In yet another study, 120 men who suffered one heart attack were studied over 8 ½ years, and within that time frame half of them had died of a second heart attack. The usual risk factors such as blood pressure, cholesterol levels, or amount of damage from the first attack were not predictive of who would die of a second heart attack. The only reliable predictor turned out to be levels of optimism vs. pessimism. Fifteen of the sixteen most pessimistic patients died, but only five of the sixteen most optimistic men lost their lives to a second coronary event (Buchanan & Seligman, 1995). Optimism was also shown to be strongly associated with fewer deaths from all causes, including CVD, in a large Dutch study (Giltay & colleagues, 2004).

One potential biological explanation for the protective effects of optimism on cardiovascular functioning has to do with the repercussions of stress on our bodies. Due to their mindset, pessimists tend to give up which increases their stress levels. The opposite typically occurs for optimists who cope better and report lower stress levels. Ongoing or episodic stress triggers the production of the stress hormone cortisol along with other circulatory responses (such as higher blood pressure and heart rate) that can weaken the lining of blood vessels or worsen existing damage. This is part of what causes atherosclerosis, the hardening of the arteries and plaque deposits in the vessel walls. Another factor in CVD is inflammation. Stress is known to elicit higher production of neurotransmitters known as catecholamines along with cortisol. Both of these can provoke the inflammatory processes which exacerbate atherosclerosis. Yet another CVD risk factor is the possibility of forming blood clots which could get lodged in an arterial wall and lead to a heart attack or stroke. Women who score low in feelings of mastery (the sense of control over the environment) were shown to have higher degrees of calcification (plaque buildup) in their aortas, the major artery of the heart (Matthews & colleagues, 2006). The mechanism for this may relate to the production of fibrinogen, a substance produced by the liver, which promotes clotting. Excess fibrinogen makes the blood thicker which can lead to the formation of blood clots within the circulatory system. Research (Steptoe, Wardle, & Marnot, 2005) has shown that those who display higher levels of positive emotions produce less fibrinogen when under stress than those with low levels of positive emotions.

Optimists are much less vulnerable to all types of disease, in general. What mechanisms enable optimists, who are likely to be more stress hardy, to stay healthy? Due to the fact that optimists believe they have control over their health, that their actions matter, they are more likely to make healthy lifestyle choices. They are also more likely to follow medical advice because they expect it will make a difference. For example, after the early warnings about the dangers of cigarette smoking, it was the optimists who were more likely to quit (Vaillant, 2003). Pessimists revert to learned helplessness, making poor lifestyle choices because they do not believe they have any control over their health.

Optimism appears to facilitate immune functioning, thereby improving resistance to illness. In one study (Kamen-Siegel, Rodin, Seligman & Dwyer, 1991) the blood drawn from optimists contained significantly more infection fighting cells (T lymphocytes) than for pessimists. In the previous chapter we mentioned a series of studies demonstrating that subjects exposed to a cold virus were more likely to become ill if they were under stress. In a later series of studies by some of the same researchers (Cohen & colleagues, 2003; 2006) the relationship between positive emotions and susceptibility to cold and flu viruses was analyzed. They found that subjects displaying high levels of positive emotions developed fewer colds and were less likely to catch the flu. The biological mechanism for this appears to be the production of the protein interleukin 6, which causes inflammation. Inflammation is the culprit that leads to a host of bodily dysfunctions including susceptibility to illness. The greater the subjects' level of positive emotion, the lower their interleukin 6 production and, therefore, the less the inflammation (Doyle, Gentile & Cohen, 2006).

Based on all of this data, Seligman (2011) asserted that "optimism is robustly associated with cardiovascular heath and pessimism with cardiovascular risk." In addition, he concluded that positive emotions protect us by boosting immune functioning, while negative emotions increase our risk of getting sick. In summarizing the literature he concludes that "well-being is associated with less risk for death from all causes." The one exception where this cannot be stated conclusively is with regard to cancer. While optimism may lower cancer risk, the research results supporting this are inconsistent.

THE GLOBAL PERSPECTIVE–The Effects of Ikigai on CVD

The lower rate of CVD in Japan has often been linked to a healthier diet rich in seafood and vegetables. But another factor appears to be at work, relating to a cultural trait combining optimism with a strong sense of meaning and purpose in life (the M in PERMA). This is the Japanese concept of **ikigai** which can be translated as "something to live for." Three Japanese studies all point to high ikigai levels being associated with lowered cardiovascular risk. In one study (Sone & colleagues, 2008) the death rate from CVD for individuals with very low ikigai was 160% higher than for individuals with high ikigai!

Can Hardiness Be Taught? The Penn Resiliency Program

Martin Seligman and his research team put together a training program for children through young adults geared to develop the skills for resilience. **Resilience** is his term for what we have described as stress hardiness. The major goal of the Penn Resiliency Program (PRP) is to increase the ability of students to cope with common daily problems or stressors. There have been over 3,000 participants in the PRP ranging in ages from 8 to 22. Over the last two decades more than twenty separate studies have evaluated the effectiveness of this program. Seligman (2011) claims that it is "the most widely researched depression prevention program in the world." PRP develops participants' coping abilities by teaching realistic optimism, assertiveness, relaxation techniques, and decision making, among other skills. The widely diverse subject population is representative of multiple racial, ethnic and socioeconomic backgrounds, as well as urban and rural settings in the U.S., Europe, China and Australia.

A meta-analysis of all of the PRP studies revealed that the training significantly reduced or prevented symptoms of depression compared to the control groups, and these results endured for at least two years afterward (Brunwasser & Gillham, 2008). The meta-analysis also demonstrated that PRP significantly increased optimism and well-being levels while reducing hopelessness, the precipitant of learned helplessness. PRP reduces and prevents severe levels of depression (Gillham, Reivich, Jacox, & Seligman, 1995) and anxiety (Gillham, Hamilton, Freres, Patton & Gallup, 2006). In addition, conduct problems were reduced (Cutuli, Chaplin, Gillham, Reivich & Seligman, 2006). Lastly, students who went through PRP were healthier; they got sick less often while exercising more and eating better than the controls (Seligman, 2011). These results were consistent for children of all racial and ethnic backgrounds (Brunwasser & Gillham, 2008). Clearly PRP succeeded in building stress hardiness skills for the participants.

Buchanan, Gardenswartz & Seligman (1999) took PRP one step further by singling out and training college freshman identified as at high risk for depression based on their highly pessimistic explanatory style as assessed by questionnaire responses. These pessimistic freshmen were randomly assigned either into a no intervention control group or an eight week "stress management seminar" which consisted of the PRP. The results were identical to that obtained with the children and adolescents. The group that received the training was significantly more optimistic and physically healthier than the controls. They got sick less often and had better health habits.

Acquiring Body Wisdom: The Warrior Stance

If you have been applying what you have learned thus far, your breathing will be becoming slower, deeper, and quieter. Your awareness will be keener as you notice that you can observe and stand apart from your attitudes and emotions. It is from this very place that all systems of personal change and development begin. Now that you have gotten your feet wet, it is time to dive a little deeper and focus your new tools more intently on both body and mind.

This section will focus on acquiring what we call **body wisdom**. Usually we think of wisdom as having an awful lot to do with the things we say and think. For many it is a measure of how many facts they know or how intelligent they are. Body wisdom, however, is not about how thoughts affect your body but about how your body affects your thoughts. We maintain that the body is intelligent, wise if you will, and that this wisdom can be tapped to improve your health, well-being, and performance.

Midway through graduate school one of the authors made a personal discovery which has guided his work as a therapist, trainer, and student ever since. The story illustrates the central premise of this concept.

> It was the most difficult emotional period I had ever experienced in my life. I was a novice psychotherapist facing the pressures of a new job, a new relationship, physical illness, and the most difficult examinations of my academic life. My symptoms were classic: difficulty eating and sleeping, obsessive thoughts, a lack of energy and feelings of hopelessness. Since I had never experienced anything like this before, I had no clear idea how to get better. The difficulties lingered for months, even after many of the problems had been resolved. It certainly didn't make sense to me that it just kept going on and on. It was as if my emotional life was going downhill and all I could do was watch. I was alternately frightened, sad, and bewildered by my inability to feel the way I used to feel, joyful and engaged in life. Finally, one afternoon as I sat alone in my office, particularly exasperated, I asked myself the key question. How did I act when I felt better? I was, as they say, sick and tired of being sick and tired. Thinking alone had not really changed anything for me. I knew I used to be different and I began to focus on **acting** that way again. Quite literally I decided to change my posture, the speed of my walk, the tilt of my head, the expression on my face. I walked out of my office **in character**, whistling a happier tune in my head, and asked the first person I saw how **he** was feeling. I played this part the remainder of the day and I noticed that I felt better. I decided to continue playing the role for a while longer and soon forgot that I was playing the role. I simply began to be the way I was with one important difference: I now knew there was a way out of the darkness. I knew I would never be quite that lost again. This was the beginning of a series of physical and mental practices that have served me very well over the years. My body led me out of the wilderness the way a horse carries an injured rider back to the stable.

Shakespeare once wrote "If you lack the virtue, act the virtue." Today we say "Fake it, til you make it." What we are suggesting is that there is a stressed stance as well. If you act stressed, holding your body in the manner characteristic of the fight or flight response, you will feel stressed, even if there is no particular reason to be stressed. Luckily, there is an antidote for this and that is to discover what we call the **warrior's stance**.

At first blush the notion of a warrior's stance leading to a more peaceful, less stressed existence may seem like an oxymoron. Why not a monk's stance or a gardener's stance? However, since life, business, and relationships are often presented in terms of struggles, battles, conflicts, and competitions, we might find it useful to examine this metaphor more carefully. Contrary to popular belief, successful warriors are ultimately peaceful individuals whose primary battles are fought internally. They display a relaxed and balanced posture. This enables them to have exceptional reaction times and full freedom of movement. This capacity for relaxed balance also begets a fluidity of response that allows them to pull an opponent who pushes them or push one who pulls. It is a capacity to literally flow around obstacles. Anyone who has gone white water rafting has been given the wise counsel to let the river carry you to a safe place when you have been thrown from the boat. To resist overpowering force is to risk being thrown into the rocks. A warrior knows that it is best to stay relaxed and alert and float feet first so you can be aware of genuine routes of escape.

A warrior cultivates fearlessness. This does not mean recklessness. It simply speaks to the survival value of being able to notice the body's response to a threat and, by the force of the regular practice of a discipline, still maintain the ability to choose a course of action. This grace under fire is often the difference between life and death in survival situations. Fear is a process that necessitates that we step out of the moment and contemplate the past or future. An intense focus in the here and now is the best way to keep fear at bay. The easiest way to maintain this focus is to cultivate the breathing and relaxed posture of the warrior. A warrior does not seek out or create conflict. Their preference is to walk away. But once engaged in battle, they are fully committed to their chosen course of action.

This is truly a critical piece of information for individuals who have attempted to change their lives by changing the content of their thoughts through endless affirmations. In our experience, "nice thoughts" have very little impact on someone's long term well being if their body is wracked with tension and stress related hormones. You must actively change your physiology if you hope to contend successfully with stress. Consider a parallel from the study of communication. The best estimates that we have suggest that only 7% of the meaning of any communication is actually in the words themselves. The remaining 93% of the meaning is communicated by our body language and the tone and tempo of our speech (Mehrabian, 1971). In a similar vein, if we wish to communicate to ourselves the value of a more relaxed stance, we will need more than words. We need to speak to our bodies in a way that they will understand.

However, in the realm of relationships, the behavior that most of us are in need of cultivating is listening. This is no less true of our relationship with our body. The disorders that are brought on by chronic, excessive muscle tension begin as mere brief episodes of tension. We may grit our teeth in anger and still maintain some residual tension even after the cause of our anger is gone. Over time this can develop into bruxism, the grinding and gnashing of the teeth while sleeping. We may tighten our neck and shoulder muscles in response to fear or anxiety and again retain excess tension even after the threat has disappeared. This is how tension headaches begin. Why exactly does this occur?

You might say that in each of the cases above someone failed to listen to his or her body. Now the body's usual response is to continue communicating in its language of rising tension. Ultimately when we are stricken with a stress related illness, the body is now screaming, "Why didn't you listen when I was whispering?" This is the primary aphorism of this chapter: **IF YOU LISTEN TO YOUR BODY WHEN IT WHISPERS, YOU WON'T HAVE TO LISTEN TO IT SCREAM.**

Once again we return to the issue of awareness. To listen to the whispers of tension we must be aware of what it means to be truly relaxed. In point of fact, most people simply do not know what it means to be relaxed. We have seen many clients claim that they are relaxed only to be shown otherwise when they are monitored by biofeedback equipment. As noted earlier, breathing is the starting point of your relaxation practice. But to go deeper into relaxation requires an additional practice and we would like to introduce that to you next.

PROGRESSIVE MUSCLE RELAXATION

In the 1929 the book *Progressive Relaxation* by Edmund Jacobson, a Chicago physician, was published. He theorized that physical tension leads to mental tension which further exacerbates physical tension. Therefore, learning to relax your body should promote mental relaxation and lowered stress levels. This technique has been used very effectively to treat a wide variety of stress related disorders (Seaward, 1997). The theory of its use is simple, that is, if you induce a feeling of deep relaxation in your body you simply cannot be feeling stressed. As your body experiences a return to homeostasis, your body's natural inclination towards healing and health is activated and enabled.

While we will present a formal protocol which you can follow to implement **Progressive Relaxation**, it is most important that you understand the principles and guidelines that will allow you to succeed as long as you commit to regular practice for several weeks. The reward for this short term commitment is that you will be able to reduce the time needed to reach a relaxed state from 25 minutes down to 5 to 7 minutes. Before you begin you may find the following guidelines to be helpful for your practice:

- Prepare a convenient time and place, and practice regularly. Remove distractions.

- Set up a regular practice schedule. Several times weekly is recommended until you have mastered the technique. You can then use it on an as needed basis.

- Be comfortable. Wear loose fitting clothing. Recline on your bed, sofa or in a cozy recliner chair. Some people place a rolled towel under their knees and lower back to maintain a comfortable spinal alignment.

- Avoid falling asleep, unless you are using this procedure to facilitate sleep.

- Don't try too hard. Paradoxically, if you try too hard to relax it will only increase your level of tension.

- Allow yourself to "let go." Sometimes people fear letting go, for it is equated with losing control. The only thing you have to lose here is unhealthy muscle tension. Learning to relax increases your control, but first you have to let go and allow this to happen.

⬧ If you find your mind wandering, gently bring your focus back to your breathing and to this technique without scolding yourself or passing judgment.

⬧ Finish your relaxation practice by coming back slowly. At the end of your practice session, slowly bring your attention back to your surroundings, gently stretch your muscles, and open closed eyes. If you are lying down, roll over slowly onto your side, pause, and then sit up. When your muscles are deeply relaxed you do not want to contract them suddenly. Coming back slowly allows your relaxed state to linger for hours.

One goal of this procedure is to help you become aware of the difference between feelings of muscle contraction vs. muscle relaxation. Begin by taking a few moments to scan your body for tension and to focus your attention on any physical sensations. The basic method in Progressive Relaxation is to first carefully tense a particular muscle or group of muscles. This is to further develop your *awareness* of that part of your body, specifically when that part is tense. It is important that you contract the muscle only to a low level of tension. Be particularly careful not to over tense any muscle or muscle group where you are prone to experience muscle spasms. Contracting a muscle as hard as you can only leaves you more tense and does not cultivate relaxation. Tense each muscle group for up to 5 to 7 seconds, and then release the muscle and focus your awareness on how the muscles feel as they relax for the next 20 to 30 seconds. Allow yourself to focus on any sensations of warmth and heaviness. As you continue from muscle to muscle, slowly but surely the sensation of warmth and heaviness begins to spread throughout your body. It can help to talk to yourself during this process with self instructions such as the following:

> Clench your right hand into a fist. Tighten your fist and study the tension as you do so. Become aware of the tension and discomfort in your hand and forearm as you tense. Now let go of the tension and let your hand go limp. Pay careful attention to the feelings of relaxation spreading in your hand as the tension drains away. Notice the difference between the comfortable sensations of relaxation in your hand now, compared to the uncomfortable feelings of tension. Let go more and more, letting the muscles in your hand and forearm grow more and more deeply and fully relaxed.

	TABLE 6.1 Progressive Relaxation Sequence	
1.	HANDS AND FOREARMS	Clench fists—left then right; bend hands backward at wrist, left and then right
2.	BICEPS	Flex by bending elbows and bringing hands up to your shoulders
3.	TRICEPS	Straighten arms and push down against the chair or floor.
4.	FOREHEAD	Wrinkle forehead
5.	EYES	Squeeze tightly shut
6.	JAW	Press teeth together then let jaw drop
7.	TONGUE	Press into roof of mouth
8.	LIPS	Press together
9.	HEAD AND NECK	Push head back; bend head forward—touch chin to chest
10.	SHOULDERS	Shrug and try to touch ears

TABLE 6.1 Progressive Relaxation Sequence (cont.)		
11.	CHEST	Take three deep breaths–hold each several seconds
12.	BACK	Arch
13.	ABDOMEN	Suck stomach in; make it hard as if it was going to be hit
14.	THIGHS	Tense thigh muscles–stretch legs out
15.	ANKLES AND CALVES	Point toes toward face; point toes downward

After you have gotten familiar with this sequence of movements, there are a number of techniques for coordinating your breathing, language, and imagination to creatively deepen and enrich your experience.

- Experiment with coordinating your breathing with the tensing and relaxing of each muscle group. Inhale and briefly hold your breath as you tense the muscle group. Exhale as you let go. Be aware of the sounds of the breath as you relax as well as the feelings of relaxation. Over time the hissing of the slow release of breath will become associated with relaxation and speed up the process of letting go.

- Some people prefer to visualize their breath as light that carries warmth and relaxation to their muscles. In this scenario, as you tense a muscle and inhale you are pulling light to the muscle group. As you exhale you expel darkness and tension from the muscles. Gradually you build an image of your body filled with light. If another set of colors feels better to you feel free to experiment. For instance, some people like to use the color blue to symbolize relaxation and red to indicate tension. Once you have reached a relaxed state you can really embrace your relaxation experience by imagining a scene that is pleasant to you, such as lying on a beach or walking in the woods.

- There is also a time honored method known as **Autogenic Training** in which one literally talks oneself into relaxation. This is done by repeating certain phrases over and over while focusing your attention on a particular muscle group. For instance, if after going through a Progressive Relaxation exercise, you still feel residual tension in a body part, then you would repeat to yourself, "My (name the part, i.e. arm, hands, thighs) feel warm and heavy." Or you could say to yourself, "My (arms) feel loose and relaxed." In fact, this method of systematically repeating relaxing phrases over and over again can be used on its own to induce relaxation. It can, however, be terminally boring, so be certain to tailor your program to your needs and interests. Create a routine that interests you and you will increase the likelihood of following through and mastering this skill.

One main goal of Progressive Relaxation training is to help you achieve **differential relaxation** throughout your day. Accomplishing this means that you are able to contract only those muscles which are necessary to accomplish the task at hand, while keeping all other muscles relaxed (McGuigan, 1984). For example, there is no need to clench your jaw, stiffen your shoulders, or squeeze the steering wheel while driving. But your arm and leg muscles will certainly need to contract in order to operate a car.

Barbara Brehm (1998) extols the virtues of relaxation techniques such as progressive muscle relaxation for people who she characterizes as "hot reactors." These are individuals who startle easily, who get stressed out easily, and who tend to over react physically to stress. Such relaxation techniques are essential for people with stress-related psychophysiological disorders or illnesses. Many people report that daily relaxation practice is an effective antidote for stress related illness (Matheny and colleagues, 1986). Muscle relaxation techniques are being prescribed by physicians and psychologists for the treatment of stress-related disorders such as headaches (Sorbi &Tellegen, 1986), heart disease (Ornish, 1990), gastrointestinal problems and insomnia (Hellman and colleagues, 1990), muscular pain due to muscle tension (Kabat-Zinn, 1990), and anxiety disorders (Sachs, 1991). The technique is also useful for helping individuals cope with academic stress (Rajendran & Kaliappan, 1990) and workplace stress (Stanton, 1991). Progressive muscle relaxation has been used successfully with all types of people of all ages to lower baseline tension and stress levels (Brehm, 1998).

MEDITATION

One of the most powerful and efficient methods for reducing stress is to include regular meditative practice in your life. At Herbert Benson's Mind/Body Medical Institute participants experience the "relaxation response" by repeating a word or sound that can be anything from reciting a Hail Mary to chanting "Ommm," silently while exhaling. Benson reports that such meditative practice leads to a calm state of mind, slower breathing, and lower blood pressure. Richard Davidson at the University of Wisconsin's Center for Mindfulness demonstrated that regular meditative practice positively affects our brain (Davidson, R. & Kabat-Zinn, 2003). Davidson took brain images of 25 participants, all of whom worked at a biotech firm, who meditated 6 days a week for 8 weeks straight. The results showed increased activation in a part of the brain associated with decreased arousal and increased positive emotion, along with suppression of another part of the brain, the amygdale, which is the fear and anxiety center of our brain.

There is no shortage of reading material regarding the value of meditative practice (Goleman, 1977; Kabat-Zinn, 1990; Ram Dass, 1990). Nor is there any lack of scientific research demonstrating that the practice of **meditation** indeed works to reduce and relieve pain (Kabat-Zinn, 1990), to lower blood pressure and the advance of atherosclerosis (Benson, 1984; Ornish, 1992) and to facilitate healing in general. Deep relaxation, euphoria, and heightened awareness can also be byproducts of meditative practice (Wallace & Benson, 1972; Kabat-Zinn, 1994; Alexander and colleagues., 1993). People who regularly meditate report less stress, anxiety, depression, and hostility than non-meditators. However, while meditation has these many benefits, they are ultimately not the point of the practice. All meditation methods are like roads leading to Rome. There are lots of ways to get there. In this case Rome is the ability to maintain a focused awareness in the present moment. It is to be in each and every moment without being preoccupied with thoughts of the past or the future. It is to realize that you are much more than you think you are. That realization depends upon recognizing that you are more than your thoughts. Meditative practice is designed to break you out of your habitual patterns of perceiving and thinking about the world and who you are. While practical results abound in terms of improved concentration, relaxation, health, and awareness, it is ultimately a spiritual journey of discovery. *Every* religious tradition has some practice within it which can be considered meditative.

Attitudes for Mindfulness Meditation

Before we embark on a discussion of technique it is important to consider the attitudes that you want to bring to whatever practice you begin. In his book *Full Catastrophe Living*, Jon Kabat-Zinn (1990) suggests cultivating the following attitudes as part of the practice of meditation, particularly the practice of mindfulness.

1. Non-Judging

As you begin a meditative practice you can be sure you will immediately discover that you are making judgments about every aspect of your experience: "This is good." "This is bad." "Who cares about that?" These judgments create feelings and often stress. When you notice this kind of thinking arising, remind yourself to suspend judgment and just notice whatever comes up including the tendency to judge.

2. Patience

Suffice it to say that things emerge in their own time. You cannot make a butterfly emerge from its cocoon sooner than necessary without damaging the butterfly. You can generally recognize impatience when you decide that there is something missing in this moment, a kind of judgment. All these practices take time and you make progress by accepting each moment of practice as being just where you need to be for now, simply because it is now.

3. Beginners Mind

To quote Kabat-Zinn, "We tend to take the ordinary for granted and fail to grasp the extraordinariness of the ordinary." To see things with the wonder of a child seeing things for the first time is to practice **beginners mind**. So often we don't really see, hear, or feel what is here, but instead react to our memories of similar moments, but not this moment. How many times have you walked in a familiar place and suddenly seen something that you never noticed before and realized it had *always* been there? That is all too typical of our perceptions. We often see those closest to us as we remember them and not as they are now. Experiment with this. Look at someone familiar to you and see them as they are now. Look at how they may have changed.

4. Trust

This is a most crucial point. Just as there is no shortage of texts about meditation, there is no shortage of teachers and gurus either, and not all necessarily have your well-being or best interests at the top of their agenda. Ultimately you must learn to trust your own internal guidance and intuition. Everyone makes mistakes along the way. The best teachers will strive to help you develop this trust in *yourself*. You are not here to imitate others and follow their orders and ideas about who you should be. You are here to become more fully yourself.

5. Non-Striving

This is very similar to a recommendation for a "passive attitude" that Herbert Benson (1976) makes in his landmark text *The Relaxation Response*. Most everybody begins meditation because they want something. The promise of meditation is that you will get something, but not if you try too hard. You simply need to do the technique and not worry whether it is working. If you notice that you are unable to let go of a preoccupation with certain thoughts, simply notice this instead of striving to rid yourself of these thoughts, and then return to your technique.

6. Acceptance

Kabat-Zinn again summarizes this attitude beautifully. Although he does not talk directly about effectiveness per se, the relevance of adopting this attitude to the cultivation of personal effectiveness should be obvious.

> Acceptance does not mean that you have to like everything or that you have to take a passive attitude toward everything and abandon your principles and values. It does not mean that you are satisfied with things as they are or that you are resigned to tolerating things as they 'have to be.' It does not mean that you should stop trying to break free of your own self-destructive habits or to give up on your desire to change and grow, or that you should tolerate injustice, for instance, or avoid getting involved in changing the world around you because it is the way it is and therefore hopeless. Acceptance as we are speaking of it simply means that you have come around to a willingness to see things as they are. This attitude sets the stage for acting appropriately in your life, no matter what is happening. You are much more likely to know what to do and have the inner conviction to act when you have a clear picture of what is actually happening than when your vision is clouded by your mind's self-serving judgments and desires or its fears and prejudices. (p. 38-39)

7. Letting Go

If you know how to fall asleep, you know how to let go. If you have ever had insomnia you also know how difficult letting go can sometimes be. You cannot will yourself to fall asleep. Paradoxically, sleep comes when you let go and stop trying to fall asleep. Letting go means that it is important not to try to hold on to any aspect of our experience but simply to notice it and let it go. When we want to hold on to certain thoughts, this can tell us a lot about what may be causing difficulty in our lives. There are things to discover in the practice of meditation that go beyond the power of words to say. No one of us is ultimately any better or worse or less capable of discovering the beauty of their existence. However, you do need to practice something to move you down the road toward Rome. What follows is a discussion of basic techniques to get you started.

The Practice of Meditation

Meditation can be divided into techniques which emphasize focused concentration on a word, phrase, sound, image, physical movement or posture, or on techniques which emphasize the cultivation of mindfulness or awareness in each present moment.

Focused Concentration

To begin the practice it is best to find a quiet place and to sit in a comfortable position with an erect spine. You could do this practice lying down or in a recliner but very often the tendency is to then fall asleep and not cultivate concentration and awareness. So for that reason, we recommend that you do your practice in an upright sitting position. You next need to choose a mental device, i.e. something upon which to focus your concentration. Some people choose to focus on their breath, the sound and feel of the process of the breath moving in and out of their body. Some focus on the word *in* as they breathe in and *out* as they breathe out. Other people simply choose a word or phrase to focus on such as *relax* or *peace*. Still others choose a sound with resonance which is referred to as a **mantra**. A common example of a mantra is the sound "Ommmm" which is repeated over and over again in the mind. An important point to note here is that there is data that suggests that focal points which have some spiritual significance or deep meaning for the meditator have led to more clinical improvement and more disciplined practice (Benson, 1984).

Once you have chosen your focal point, simply sit and bring your attention to it. To use breathing as an example, you would bring your attention to the in and out movement of the breath and, if you like, repeat in your mind the word *in* on the inhalation and *out* on the exhalation. That is basically it in terms of technique. What you will initially and over time experience may vary considerably. One thing is certain: You will find your mind wandering everywhere and that is fine. When this occurs, notice that you are thinking and label it as thinking. Then return to the in and out of your breathing. Do not try to stop thinking because that is just doing more thinking. Notice your thoughts and let them go. You may want to think of your thoughts as bubbles rising before your eyes. Let them float by and return to noticing your breath. With continued practice and cultivation of the proper attitudes you will begin to notice the differences in your life.

If you were to practice chanting, or **Tai Chi** (a moving meditation) or **Qi Gong** (a focus on the movement of energy) or any other discipline, the challenge and ultimate results tend to be quite similar. All roads lead to increased awareness and that is to be treasured above and beyond any specific path. These paths take you toward awareness by way of concentration. That is, as you gain the ability to concentrate you are able to stay more aware and involved in the moment, and you are less distracted by the meanderings of your thoughts.

Mindfulness

Mindfulness is the cultivation of awareness by practicing awareness. Virtually any activity whether eating, walking, lovemaking, driving, bathing, etc. can become the vehicle for your practice. You can even consider the breathing meditation above as a kind of mindfulness practice. Attention brought to the breath over time generally results in slower, quieter, deeper breathing, i.e. relaxation.

Perhaps mindfully eating is the best place to get a feel for how unaware we are and how practicing mindfulness can increase awareness and lead to very practical results. How many times have you sat down to a meal and ate without truly tasting more than the first bite or two? Do you eat while reading or watching TV? Do you eat when you are not really feeling hungry? No, this is not a chapter on dieting, but a lack of mindfulness of all of the processes involved in eating can certainly lead to gaining weight. Try this mindfulness experiment when you have some quiet, uninterrupted time to enjoy a meal.

Positive Psychology Self Exercise: Mindfulness Meditation

Set your plate down and simply look at your food. Attend to the colors, shapes, and textures. Notice the aromas or perhaps steam rising up from the dish. Also at this moment attend to your own body. Is your mouth salivating? What is your tongue doing? Is your stomach growling? Do you find it difficult to be patient while doing this exercise? What are your thoughts like? Does this seem pointless to you? Do you wonder if you are doing this correctly?

As you prepare to take your first bite notice your intention to pick up your utensil. Feel your arm, hand, and fingers move to grasp the fork or spoon. Feel the utensil in your hand. Are you breathing or holding your breath? Feel the additional weight of the food on your fork. Notice your arm rising, your mouth opening. Now taste the food. Notice the actual action of chewing and the change in taste as the food moves around your mouth. Be aware of the impulse to swallow. Keep chewing. Swallow. Feel the food go down your esophagus. Perhaps feel one bite heavier. Set your silverware down with full awareness. Are you breathing? Begin again.

> What did you become aware of in this process?
>
> How satisfying can a single bite of food be?
>
> Do you think you would eat more or less if you ate mindfully?
>
> Did the food really taste good? Did you taste something different from what you expected?
>
> How might your experience change if you were blind or had a head cold?

This same intensity can be brought to observing any process including your own thinking. To bring this discussion full circle, there is incredible value in observing your thoughts because that is how you create the world of your experience. As we said at the very beginning of this text, you create your reality. Meditation allows you to see how you have been doing it. If you take the responsibility and make the commitment to practice, you can reshape your life. If you are creating your reality with your thoughts, words, and images, why not be proactive and deliberately choose to create a reality by consciously employing thoughts, words and images that promote your effectiveness.

The Importance of Stretching Your Muscles

As noted earlier, an intrinsic part of the fight/flight response is muscle tension. When muscles tighten they also shorten. One way to reverse the fight/flight response is to lengthen your muscles. This is accomplished quite simply by stretching the muscles. Our goal here is not to provide a comprehensive manual on stretching exercises, but we would like to mention some guidelines for stretching intuitively.

Intuitive Stretching

As you cultivate body awareness and relaxation you will notice an urge to stretch your body in various ways. Many people notice that yawning is accompanied by an almost instinctual urge to lean back and extend one's arms. We are very aware of the need to stretch after sitting in a car or at a desk for a prolonged period of time. Anyone who has dogs or cats can watch them stretch when they awaken or when they anticipate they will go for a walk. The point we are making is that while we would suggest it is a good idea to read a manual on stretching or to take a yoga class to learn a specific routine, your body is actually a very good guide to this procedure if you will pay attention to it. After all, someone figured this stuff out without referring to a textbook. Nor has anyone found the family dog curled up in front of the fireplace with an autographed copy of *The Autobiography of a Yogi*. This information is inside of you. These are guidelines for intuitive stretching:

* Set up a comfortable environment for your practice. This might include soft music.

* It is always easier to stretch muscles when they are warm. Thus, some light exercise like walking until you begin to break a sweat is recommended. Another alternative would be to stretch after or while in a hot shower.

* Stretch on a firm padded surface such as an exercise mat.

* Pay attention to what you are doing. It should not hurt when you stretch. Pain is a sure signal that you are doing something with too much intensity or in a direction that your body was not meant to accommodate. Progress in stretching will come rapidly, within weeks, but it is accomplished in small, incremental steps. Stretch and move your body until you feel a solid pull on the muscles and maintain that position as long as you feel comfortable. Return to your original position slowly.

* Move slowly, and do not bounce into any stretch.

* Do not hold your breath while stretching, but keep your breath flowing. Breathe in through your nose and exhale slowly through your mouth. Visualize or sense your breath carrying oxygen to the areas being stretched. See and sense them loosening.

* Rest for a short time after each stretch.

* At the end of your stretching period take time to cool down and relax. An excellent time to do a breathing meditation or Progressive Relaxation is following stretching.

* While it is optimal to do a set stretch routine on a daily basis, do not limit your stretching to only one time or place. There are many moments throughout the day, at your desk, stopped in your car, etc, where you can relieve the stress and tension in certain muscle groups with a quick stretch.

* The muscles that support the head and neck are also intensely involved in the fight/flight response as primates (including humans) tend to pull their shoulders up to protect their necks, and appear bigger when threatened. Over time chronic tension in these muscles leads to tension headaches. Pay particular attention to these muscles in your stretching routine.

The ancient tradition of yoga also offers many stress mastery and wellness benefits (Patel, 1984). Many relaxation techniques are ultimately outgrowths of yoga practice. **Hatha yoga** is a branch of yoga that emphasizes physical postures and stretches that incorporate breath control and focused, meditative concentration. Although stress mastery is one enormous benefit of yoga practice, its primary purpose is to enable the practitioner to attain spiritual enlightenment. Proper practice of Hatha yoga typically requires coaching and guidance. Most communities offer yoga classes.

Massage

Let us not ignore the healing power of touch as a powerful stress reducer. A wonderfully enjoyable way of reducing physical tension, lowering your stress level, and getting deeply relaxed is to treat yourself to a massage. As reported in an article in Newsweek magazine in June, 1999, Tiffany Field, director of the University of Miami's Touch Research Institute, exposed 60 schoolchildren who had been traumatized by Hurricane Andrew to half hour massages twice a week for one month. The levels of the stress hormone cortisol, an important indicator of stress, decreased significantly for the kids who received the massages compared with a control group who only watched a relaxing video. Overall, the stress levels for the control group did not change at all. If you cannot afford to get professional massage, offer to swap a good massage with a friend, family member, or significant other. You can then give the gift of relaxation as well as receive it.

STAYING HEALTHY

Given the mind-body connection, it naturally follows that what is good for your body will be good for your mind and vice versa. Another important aspect of mastering your stress involves adopting a healthy lifestyle. A new branch of psychology called health psychology was developed in the 1970's to study the psychological factors that cause or contribute to illness and to promote behaviors that foster wellness. In particular, there is a focus on **psychosomatic illness**, where a physical disorder is affected (or in some cases even caused) by stress and/or emotional/psychological factors.

An unhealthy lifestyle, characterized by lack of exercise, poor diet, cigarette smoking, and alcohol or drug abuse will definitely impact your stress and wellness levels, and eventually even your mortality. One study (Powell, Spain, Christenson & Mollenkamp, 1986) found at least half of premature deaths in the U.S. were a direct result of such unhealthy behaviors. The 1979 U.S. Surgeon General's report reached this same conclusion and went on to state that seven of the ten leading causes of death in the U.S. (such as from heart attacks, stroke, etc.) could be significantly reduced by adopting the following six lifestyle modifications:

- **improving diet**
- **quitting smoking**
- **getting regular physical exercise**
- **eliminating substance abuse**
- **practicing stress reduction techniques**
- **properly following medication regimens (especially for hypertension)**

Breslow (1983) found that when people adopted these healthy lifestyle behaviors, mortality rates declined significantly over a nine year period. In addition, this study showed that older people derived an even greater benefit from adoption of healthy behaviors than younger individuals, and the effect of lifestyle in general appeared more crucial to the health of males as compared to females.

The Importance of Exercise

By far, one of the simplest and most effective methods of mastering stress to enhance wellness is to engage in regular exercise. Your body immediately reacts to stress by gearing up to respond physically to a stressor. Given that the original evolutionary purpose for the "fight or flight response" was to enable humans to fight or to flee physical danger, it follows that the natural outlet for built up physiological arousal is some type of vigorous physical activity or exertion. Exercise releases pent up muscular tension, allowing your body to return to equilibrium.

Throughout most of human history our ancestors got plenty of exercise while taking care of basic living tasks such as searching or hunting for food, walking from one place to another, chopping wood for fires, etc. In current times, the advent of modern conveniences such as the automobile, elevator, supermarket, or washing machine, have greatly reduced the need for physical activity in order to accomplish basic tasks. It has gotten to the point where we don't even have to move to change the channel on the TV, thanks to the ever present remote control! Consequently, if you don't make a point of exercising you are probably leading a sedentary lifestyle, unless you are involved in a job or profession involving physical labor or physically exerting activities. But the vast majority of us have sedentary occupations, sitting behind a desk, barely flexing our arm muscles to push papers. The majority of college students are trained for, and hold sedentary jobs after graduation. Leisure activities often involve sedentary pursuits as well. Thus, even though the tempo of modern life and the rate of change is accelerating (further adding to our stress), our activity levels are falling. And this comes at a time when our need for regular exercise to bolster coping resources and wellness is increasing.

A comprehensive exercise program to improve your well being has three major types of exercise: (1) **aerobic exercise** that conditions your cardiovascular system; (2) **strength training** that builds, strengthens and maintains muscle capacity and balance; and (3) **flexibility exercises** that maintain healthy joints, good posture, body alignment and the capacity to move the body in its potential for full range of motion. Aerobic conditioning for your heart and vascular system is achieved by continuous exercise. This is not stop-and-go movement like tennis, baseball, and other such activity, but rather activity that maintains *continuous* exertion on your heart without stopping for 20 or 30 minutes in a session. Such activities as uninterrupted brisk walking, running, jogging, swimming, and bicycling will build your aerobic capacity and enhance cardiovascular fitness. You should be able to talk while completing these exercises and not be out of breath. A study at the Cooper Center for Research examined three groups: Low, Moderate, and High Fitness to compare the rate of deaths in each group. The low group included basically unfit, sedentary persons who did not exercise, the moderately fit group exercised 150 minutes a week, and the highly fit group included extreme exercisers who spent many hours a week in cardiovascular training. At the conclusion of the study, the results indicated that the number of deaths in the moderate exercise group was 50% less than in the low fitness group. The participants in the moderate group *walked* on a treadmill for 150 minutes a week, in other words, 30 minutes a day/5 days a week, something most of us could do easily on a treadmill or in our neighborhood. The high fitness group had slightly fewer deaths than either the low or moderate groups. However, the dramatic finding in this study was that there were half as many deaths in the moderate exercise group as in the sedentary low fitness group. The lesson here is that you don't have to run a marathon to be fit! Moderate regular exercise can prolong your life. Dr. Church (2006), the physician who conducted this study, says his three favorite exercises are: (1) walking; (2) walking; and (3) walking! If you are starting an exercise regimen, it is important to get a doctor's approval before beginning.

Other Benefits of Exercise

Is there proof that exercise improves our wellness by helping us to cope with stress? Research clearly indicates that exercise is an effective stress reducer. Indeed, many studies have found that one of the most reliable differences between individuals with high vs. low levels of stress resistance was exercise and activity level (Brown, 1991; Kobasa, Maddi, & Puccetti, 1982; Roth & Holmes, 1987, just to name a few). In one study, McGilley and Holmes (1989), found that individuals who exercised regularly had lower cardiovascular and subjective responses to psychological stress than individuals who were not physically fit. Studies have also been done linking regular aerobic exercise to reductions in depression (McCann and Holmes, 1984), anxiety (Long, 1984) and improvements in self-esteem (Sonstroem, 1984). And remember, as discussed previously, the amount and intensity of exercise necessary to produce stress mastery and other wellness effects, need not be overly extensive.

Regular exercise, even of only moderate intensity, literally provides a dress rehearsal for dealing with stress (Brehm, 1998). Why is this the case? Because the way your body responds to exercise is very similar to the way your body reacts to stress. During exercise your heart rate increases, blood pressure rises, respiration quickens, stress hormones are released, and muscles tense to perform the activity. Does this sound familiar? Therefore, engaging in regular exercise gives your body practice in experiencing stress, allowing you to develop more strength and stamina to cope.

It appears that the stress reducing effects of exercise are both short and long term. Many people find a single exercise session to be an excellent way of releasing tension. Proponents of regular exercise, who exercise at least three times weekly, typically report lowered levels of tension overall, even on days when they are less active (Holmes & Roth, 1988). So clearly, exercise has powerful positive effects on both our psychological and physical well being. These are some of the most notable benefits that are possible from engaging in regular exercise:

THE CUMULATIVE BENEFITS OF REGULAR EXERCISE

- **Improved sense of well-being, decreases in depression.**
- **Lowered anxiety and muscular tension.**
- **Greater ability to handle domestic and job-related stress.**

- **Increased endorphin production.**
- **Decreased production of stress hormones such as adrenalin and cortisol.**
- **Improvements in concentration and productivity.**
- **Quicker recovery from acute stress.**
- **Decreased fatigue; more energy and stamina.**
- **Reduction in blood pressure and resting heart rate.**
- **Improved cardiopulmonary functioning. Lower risk of heart disease.**
- **More restful sleep.**
- **Fewer physical complaints in general. Boosts in immune functioning.**
- **Better self-image and more self-confidence.**
- **A more attractive physique.**

There is also evidence that fitness can help compensate for obesity (Lee, Sui & Blair, 2009) in terms of mortality rates. Researchers compared the death rates for all causes between both fit and unfit obese individuals with that of normal weight individuals who were fit and unfit. Factors such as age, smoking and pre-existing health conditions were kept constant between the groups. The death rate for fit but overweight individuals was significantly below that of unfit persons. The results indicated that those who were fat but fit had almost half the risk of death as the fat and unfit. Meanwhile, individuals who were obese but fit were only slightly more at risk for death that those who were thin and fit (Sui & colleagues, 2007). The stark conclusion appears to be that your fitness level is much more important than what you weigh. Ultimately, inactivity is the biggest problem. If you are fit, even if overweight or moderately obese, your risk of mortality is much lower. If you are unfit, your risk of death is much higher whether you are thin or not. To enhance your fitness level, consider the suggestion in the following exercise.

Positive Psychology Exercise: 10,000 daily steps

The 2008 Surgeon General's report made clear cut recommendations emphasizing that adults need to take 10,000 steps daily to maintain fitness. If you average below 5,000 steps daily, you are in that dangerous couch potato zone that puts you at undue risk for death. One way to check whether you are sufficiently active, that is, getting in an average of 10,000 daily steps, would be to utilize a pedometer. Many cellular phones have a pedometer app. This allows you to check your activity level and take corrective action if you are too sedentary. For example, you could choose to take a walk after dinner if you are well below the recommended step goal on any given day.

The Role of Proper Nutrition

The average American diet is a direct reflection of our lifestyle—everyone is busy, in a rush, looking for the fastest, easiest, cheapest way to procure food. Cooking at home has given way to eating out. Not only have we lost nutrition, but we no longer have the family connections of dinner conversations. This results in a pattern that includes skipped breakfast and "drive through" meals or visits to the vending machines for daily food choices. The outcome of this pattern is an epidemic of obesity, diabetes, malnutrition, and diminished wellness. This in turn leads to increased stress and diminished stress resistance which further complicates the cycle.

The old adage, "You are what you eat," is more true than you might imagine. Why is this? Because how well or how poorly you eat has a direct relationship to your level of wellness including your ability to handle stress. Your body needs 40 to 60 nutrients to stay healthy. When you are under stress your need for all nutrients increases, especially for B vitamins (which help combat stress) and calcium. Calcium is especially important because it counteracts the lactic acid buildup created by muscular tension. If your diet is deficient in milk and leafy vegetables your ability to reduce high levels of lactic acid related to stress would be impaired along with your bones and other systems. This would leave you feeling more fatigued, anxious and irritable than if your diet was more balanced. You also need to realize that certain foods provide the biochemical building blocks for the neurotransmitters (brain chemicals) that affect mood and behavior, and consequently your ability to handle stress and interact positively in relationships. For example, your body synthesizes the neurotransmitter **serotonin** from the amino acid tryptophan which is found in certain high carbohydrate foods such as bread, potatoes and pasta. Healthy levels of serotonin help you to stay relaxed, sleep well and have less sensitivity to pain. That is why we tend to crave carbohydrate rich foods when we are in a bad mood in order to get a temporary lift. And it is also important to know that protein rich foods tend to improve concentration and alertness, particularly if you have them for breakfast. Missing breakfast altogether can deprive your brain of essential nutrients needed for effective functioning throughout your day. You can learn to make changes in your diet that will help you to cope more effectively, increase your productivity, and heighten your wellness level by heeding the following seven steps to good nutrition.

1. **Eat a Variety of Foods** including low fat proteins, fruits and vegetables and other healthy carbohydrates, as well as healthy fats such as monounsaturated fatty acids.

2. **Eat More Whole Foods**—foods that are in their natural state, i.e. not with coatings removed, color changed, nor additives or preservatives included.

3. **Drink Caffeine in moderation** (no more than 1 or 2 cups) or not at all.

4. **Drink Alcohol in moderation** (no more than 1 drink/day for women, 2 drinks/day for men) or not at all.

5. **Take Vitamin and Mineral Supplements** remembering that these do not absorb as well as getting vitamins and minerals from food eaten.

6. **Eat Small, Frequent, Calm Meals.**

7. **Maintain a Healthy Weight—Body Mass Index or BMI = (weight in pounds/height in inches^2) × 703. Values between 18.5 − 24.5 are within the healthy weight range.**

THE GLOBAL PERSPECTIVE—Sustainable Food Choices

Do our eating habits not only harm ourselves, but the earth? In this country, dieticians have designed and publicized the U.S.D.A.'s (U.S. Department of Agriculture) food pyramid which urges eating mostly grains, cereal, rice and pasta, then fruits and vegetables, with small amounts of meat and dairy products, and using fats, oils and sweets sparingly. Unfortunately, most of us ignore the food pyramid or turn it upside down, eating mostly sweets, fat, oils, meat and few, if any, vegetables and fruits.

However, when we look at the eating styles of cultures around the world there are many valuable lessons to be learned:

- In Asian cultures where rice is a staple complimented with vegetables and very small portions of meat or fish, breast cancer and obesity are rare.

- In the Mediterranean region, people had the lowest incidence of chronic diseases and the highest life expectancy, as discovered by the WHO (World Health Organization) in the 1960's. The eating habits of these people included daily amounts of bread, whole grain, rice, pasta, and potatoes; then fruits, vegetables, beans and nuts; then olive oil, cheese and yogurt. Only weekly were fish, poultry, eggs and sweets eaten. Meat was consumed only once a month (Ozner, 2005).

- In African cultures with high vegetable, high fiber diets, it was found that colon cancer (a major killer in the U.S.) was virtually non-existent (Reuben, 1981).

Decades ago, Frances MooreLappe (1991), suggested eating lower on the food chain. In other words, instead of eating the cattle who consumed the grain and vegetation, why not just eat the grains and vegetables which are healthier for us than the large quantities of meat that Americans consume?

It seems clear then, that eating less meat and following the food pyramid guidelines would result in better health for humans. However, we must also consider whether poor food choices lead to unintended consequences, not only in terms of our own health, but taking into consideration what will also threaten the well being of humanity by poisoning the environment, depleting drinkable water supplies, and accelerating global warming. Consider the following facts cited on www.earthsave.org.

- As noted earlier, the aquifers which supply drinkable water are being rapidly depleted. The main drain on these aquifers is the irrigation of crops that are used to feed cattle. Not only could 10 people be fed with the grain used to produce meat for one person, but it takes at least 2500 gallons of water to produce a pound of beef!

- Livestock waste is a primary source of water pollution. Natural processes to disperse sewage are overwhelmed by the enormous quantities of waste produced by the factory farming of animals. For example, consider that the drinking water of 65% California's population is threatened by pollution from dairy cow manure!

- Cattle also pass gas, lots of gas! Cattle are actually the source of 1/5th of the world's methane, which is 21 times more powerful than CO_2 in the acceleration global warming.

- Huge tracts of rainforest are destroyed every year to create grazing land for more cattle. Rainforests are not only a great source of biodiversity but also reabsorb carbon dioxide from the atmosphere. Many scientists believe this is a critical facet of long term control of global warming.

- In order to minimize the disease caused by the crowded conditions of factory farming, the animals are fed huge quantities of antibiotics. Due to this overuse of antibiotics, we now have disease organisms that are resistant to virtually all antibiotics and, therefore, extremely hazardous to human health.

THE GLOBAL PERSPECTIVE–Sustainable Food Choices (cont.)

❖ Last, but not least, modern agriculture has grown extremely dependent upon pesticide use. These pesticides accumulate in the animals that eat the grains that are treated with these chemicals. Thus, the higher you eat on the food chain (meaning the more meat you eat), the greater your exposure to these toxic chemicals. As you may have guessed, these toxins also end up polluting the ground water through the animal waste and by being absorbed in the soil during application. These chemicals are implicated as possible causes of Parkinson's disease and suspected as causes of cancer and other disorders. This is one of many reasons for the movement towards growing food organically without pesticides.

After considering all this you may be wondering, *"How can I make a difference in my own health and the sustainability of my environment?"* It seems that something as simple as what you choose to eat today has enormous consequences not only for your health and well being but for the health and well being of everyone else and the earth itself. Eating for good health means investing more time, more thought, and (to eat naturally) perhaps a bit more money. Again you are faced with choices, the results of which have consequences for sustaining your life and that of your planet.

Enhancing Financial Competence

The next area on our wellness wheel relates to your ability to manage your finances. An extensive primer on financial management is beyond the scope of this text, but we will offer you the most salient pointers. It is important to have thoughts, feelings and behaviors regarding money that are positive for your well-being. How we treat our money is a statement about how we value ourselves. There is a connection between *net worth* and *self worth*. Although most of us have never had a course in personal finance, it is important that we take control of our financial destiny. To be financially competent means you have knowledge and skills in the areas that follow (Orman, 2007, 2010).

Checking and Savings Accounts

❖ Know how to develop and follow a budget, use your bank statements, balance your checkbook and find free checking.

❖ Have a savings account, make monthly payments into it for your financial security, and know how to find the best interest rate.

❖ Build a savings account that alone would cover your living expenses for at least eight months as your financial safety net.

Credit Cards and Credit Scores

❖ Have only a few credit cards and check your statement carefully every month.

❖ Be aware of fees and avoid extra fees and high interest rates.

❖ Pay your total statement balance off each month. If you are only paying the minimum, it may takes months, or years, to pay it off.

❖ Understand what a credit score is and what events can change it. Obtain and review your score every year.

❖ Remember that a credit card *used* is money *borrowed*.

Growing Your Money—Investing for Later

❈ Invest your money to guard it from losing buying power through inflation. **Inflation** is the rise of the costs or goods and services that, over time, erodes the value of your funds.

❈ Go on-line and search *inflation* or *inflation rate* to find numerous calculators that estimate changed values due to inflation.

❈ Do not rely on Social Security as your sole financial support in your later years. To estimate your benefits, go to *www.socialsecurity.gov/planners/calculators.htm*.

❈ Additionally, you must contribute to a personal retirement fund such as an IRA or 401K.

Protecting Yourself and Your Assets—Legal Documents and Insurance

❈ Have a revocable living trust that has an incapacity clause and owner-ship of your assets; also have a will.

❈ Purchase protection for you and your family through life, health, home, personal property, and other appropriate insurance.

To learn more about the details of implementing the actions discussed here, seek more detailed information on personal finance. Go to *mappingyourfuture.org* and download the free "12-Step Guide to Financial Success" (2009). Be sure to also use College materials and programs available to you for furthering your financial competence.

Social Support and Wellness

Remember Kobasa's three C's of Stress Hardiness? Her colleague Salvatore Maddi posited that there is actually a fourth C, that of **connection** (Maddi and Kobasa, 1984). Having meaningful connections to others has often proven to be the crucial factor for individuals who bounce back from and resist stress. Creating and maintaining a supportive, caring social network goes a long way to enhancing your level of stress hardiness. Being in a committed relationship, having close family ties, friendships, and other avenues for social support, such as involvement in religious or spiritual activities, community based clubs or interest groups, or volunteer work, has been shown to contribute significantly to health and happiness (Seligman, 2002). Cacioppo & colleagues (2002) found that those who are lonely are far less healthy than those who are sociable.

Perhaps the most striking example of the salutary effect of social support on health was documented by Bruhn and Wolf (1979, 1993), based on their epidemiological research in the small town of Roseta, Pennsylvania. Roseta is a city populated almost exclusively with descendants of Italian immigrants who came to the U.S. in the late 1800's from a town of the same name in Italy. Inhabitants of Roseta enjoy an extremely low rate of heart disease, virtually half that of the U. S., in general, or of surrounding towns or counties in Pennsylvania. The researchers systematically ruled out diet, exercise and genetics as contributing factors in the health of Roseta's population. Their diet was not overly healthful, in fact, many had abandoned their healthy Mediterranean cooking style (olive oil based), and ate too much fat. They did not exercise any more than people in nearby towns with similar topographies. Close relatives from the same gene pool who had moved away from Roseta began to develop cardiovascular disease at the same rate as non- residents, which ruled out genetics. The researchers realized that what made Roseta special was the incredible level of social support and connection that existed in the town, the close friendships and kinship, multigenerational family units, extensive civic organizations for a small town, and neighbors helping and supporting one another. This provided a layer of protection that appeared to insulate the inhabitants from many of the detrimental effects of stress. Not only was their rate of cardiovascular disease much lower, there were no suicides reported, no substance abuse, and very little crime uncovered by the researchers.

Not all of us are lucky enough to live in a supportive community like Roseta. For many individuals, loneliness is synonymous with stress and perhaps a lack of healthy relationships. Consider the following facts regarding the connection between social support and wellness.

- In general, people who are in stable relationships and have a strong social network are typically happier (Seligman, 2002).

- Married men tend to live longer than single men (Seligman, 2002).

- Cancer patients who join positively oriented support groups are more likely to go into remission and typically live longer.

- Those who are lonely are more at risk for heart disease. Dean Ornish (2005), the cardiologist who pioneered the well known, state-of-the-art lifestyle regimen for those with cardiovascular disease, described three studies to illustrate this point. In the first, individuals who felt high levels of love and support in their lives had significantly less coronary artery blockages. In the second, researchers from Case Western Reserve University studied 10,000 married men and found that those who felt loved by their wives had less angina (chest pain). In the last study, from Duke University, individuals with heart disease who were single and lacked confidants were three times as likely to have died after five years.

High stress levels have long been identified as one of the major factors in the development of cardiovascular disease. The availability of a strong social support network appears to have a powerful impact on our ability to cope with stress (Grambling & Auerback, 1998). Numerous studies have linked strong social support networks to superior ability to cope with stress and higher levels of wellness (Andrew, Tennant, Hewson, & Schonell, 1979; Auerback, Mastelli, & Mercuri, 1983; Gore, 1978). But again, perception plays a key role in whether such support will offer protection from stress. It is the recognition of the availability of the support, rather than the actual amount of it, that is more closely related to stress mastery (Cohen & Will, 1985; Sarason, Sarason & Pierce, 1990). That is, if you dismiss the support available to you from family or friends, it will not have a beneficial effect.

Dr. Ornish's program focuses on a low fat diet and exercise, but he places equal emphasis on stress reduction though social support groups, yoga and meditation to help prevent further heart attacks. The following quote from Ornish, in *Newsweek magazine* (10/03/05) makes an eloquent case for the importance of relationships, social support, and altruism to our wellness.

Medicine today focuses primarily on drugs and surgery, genes and germs, microbes and molecules. Yet love and intimacy are at the root of what makes us sick and what makes us well. If a new medication had the same impact, failure to prescribe it would be malpractice. Connections with other people affect not only the quality of our lives but also our survival. Study after study finds that people who feel lonely are many times more likely to get cardiovascular disease than those who have a strong sense of connection and community. I'm not aware of any other factor in medicine—…—that has a greater impact on our quality of life, incidence of illness, and premature death…

…Instead of viewing the time we spend with friends and family as luxuries, we can see that these relationships are among the most powerful determinants of our well-being and survival. We are hard-wired to help each other. Science is documenting the healing values of love, intimacy, community, compassion, forgiveness, altruism and service-values that are part of almost all spiritual traditions as well as many secular ones. (p.56)

SUMMARY

In this chapter we have outlined how to achieve high level wellness including in depth discussions of dimensions of wellness such as stress mastery, exercise, nutrition, and social support. A special emphasis has been placed on stress mastery because stress is such a pervasive and powerful force in our culture. In planning to achieve a high level of wellness, it is important to select one dimension at a time on which to focus your efforts. Review the wellness wheel at the beginning of the chapter and choose one area on which to focus. Pick the one that you think might be the easiest to begin your journey of self improvement. When you have made good progress on that dimension, move on to another. Mastering one area of wellness is motivating---and it inspires you to continue on to other new behavior patterns that will bring you to a high level of wellness. Go forth…keep progressing upward…and be well!

WELLNESS EXERCISES:

1. The next time you are feeling stressed or anxious, or anticipate that this will be the case, take the time to focus on your breathing. It is likely that you will note more rapid, shallow respiration. Take several deep, slow, diaphragmatic breaths to center yourself, and notice the difference this makes. As suggested earlier in the chapter, practice this relaxed breathing pattern at non-stressful times to insure mastery of the technique for when you really need it.

2. If you are feeling tense, or are suffering from a tension headache, neck or shoulder soreness or stiffness, or have back pain, take the time to practice Progressive Relaxation exercises. Relieving the tension in various muscle groups will go a long way towards improving how you feel. Remember, pain can be reduced up to 40% just by relaxation alone! In fact, much of the effectiveness of painkillers comes from the fact that these medications relax you. Better yet, make practice of Progressive Relaxation exercises part of your regular routine and you will find that the frequency and severity of stress related aches and pains will decrease sharply. That is, you can prevent your body from cramping up in the first place.

KEY TERMS

Wellness	Stress Hardiness	Beginner's Mind
Exercise	Control	Mantra
Nutrition	Commitment	Tai Chi
Social Support	Challenge	Qi Gong
Awareness	Problem-Focused Coping	Mindfulness
Active Relaxation	Emotion-Focused Coping	Hatha Yoga
Passive Relaxation	Body Wisdom	Psychosomatic Illness
Diaphragmatic Breathing	Warrior's Stance	Aerobic Exercise
Self Awareness	Progressive Relaxation	Strength Training
Witnessing Stance	Autogenic Training	Flexibility Exercises
Metacognition	Differential Relaxation	Serotonin
Metamood	Meditation	Connection
Hyperventilation	Financial Competence	Resilience
Inflation		

CHAPTER 6 QUESTIONS

True or False Questions (T or F)

1. _____ Wellness means the same thing as being physically fit.

2. _____ Wellness is a lot more than just not feeling ill.

3. _____ Passive relaxation, such as watching TV, is not nearly as effective for reducing stress as practicing active relaxation techniques.

4. _____ When under stress most people breathe slowly, deeply and rhythmically.

5. _____ Rapid, shallow breathing reduces the level of CO_2 in your bloodstream which increases feelings of anxiety.

6. _____ Stress hardy individuals have an internal locus of control.

7. _____ Stress hardy individuals focus on the problems inherent in adversity rather than wasting their time attending to opportunities.

8. _____ Stress hardy individuals tend to be pessimistic so that they can be ready to deal with potential problems.

9. _____ Meditative practice requires relinquishing mindfulness.

10. ____ When meditating it is important to try as hard as you can to achieve a meditative state.

11. ____ Mindfulness is the cultivation of awareness by practicing awareness.

12. ____ Tai Chi and Qi Gong are Eastern methods for improving your sexual performance.

13. ____ Your body will let you know which muscles need to be stretched.

14. ____ Exercise is a potent stress management technique because it can provide a dress rehearsal for dealing with stress.

15. ____ The foods you consume have no bearing on your stress level or your ability to cope with stress.

16. ____ An exercise program is complete if you have cardiovascular fitness and stretching as your components.

17. ____ The residents of Roseta, Pa. had very low rates of heart disease because of good genetics, healthy diets and lots of exercise.

Short-Answer Questions

1. High level _____ is about achieving a state of physical and emotional health based on living a healthy lifestyle.

2. _____ relaxation techniques are aimed at decreasing fight or flight arousal and restoring balance or homeostasis.

3. _____ breathing is a natural antidote to stress.

4. Adopting the _____ stance makes it easier to be objective about a situation and therefore helps you to choose the most effective response.

5. Stress hardy individuals possess attitudes of _____, _____, and _____.

6. If you are feeling stressed out and overwhelmed by your full schedule of classes and work, dropping a class to lighten your load would be an example of _____ -_____ coping.

7. If you were having problems sleeping due to stress, practicing progressive muscle relaxation at bedtime to help you fall asleep would be an example of _____ -_____ coping.

8. _____ Relaxation Exercises are an effective method for reducing and/or eliminating muscular tension.

9. _____ is the type of breathing that triggers or accompanies panic attacks.

10. _____ _____ is an ancient form of stretching that reduces stress and can lead to spiritual enlightenment.

11. Proper _____ and getting plenty of regular _____ are vital not only for staying healthy but for stress management.

12. _____ _____ conditions the cardiovascular system.

13. The neurotransmitter _____, which helps keep us calm, is synthesized from amino acids found in certain carbohydrates.

14. Having a good network of _____ _____ in place is vital to wellness.

Essay Questions

1. What is the difference between passive relaxation and active relaxation methods?

2. How does diaphragmatic breathing differ from everyday breathing, anxious breathing, and hyperventilation?

3. What is the benefit of adopting the witnessing stance?

4. Describe the stress hardiness attitudes and how they contribute to stress resilience.

5. How does body wisdom differ from the typical conception of wisdom?

6. How can acting as if you feel better before you actually do feel better promote positive changes?

7. Describe the warrior's stance.

8. What is Progressive Muscle Relaxation and how does it work?

9. Summarize the attitudes necessary for successful practice of mindfulness meditation.

10. What is the purpose of a focal point for meditative practice?

11. What is the value in stretching your body, either by following a prescribed routine or following your intuitions?

12. Give some examples of the relationship between nutrition and the ability to cope with stress.

13. Explain why exercise can be an effective stress reducer.

14. Discuss the four C's of stress hardiness.

15. Describe a person who is functioning at a high level of wellness.

16. List the steps one goes through to reach a high level of wellness.

7

Creating a Meaningful Vision

Each path is only one of a million paths. Therefore, you must always keep in mind that a path is only a path. If you feel that you must not follow it, you must not follow it under any circumstances. Any path is only a path. There is no affront to yourself or others in dropping it if that is what your heart tells you to do. But your decision to keep on the path or to leave it must be free of fear or ambition. I warn you! Look at every path closely and deliberately. Try it as many times as you think necessary. Then ask yourself, and yourself alone, one question...It is this...Does this path have a heart? All paths are the same. They lead nowhere. They are paths going through the brush or into the brush. Does this path have a heart is the only question. If it does, then the path is good. If it doesn't, it is of no use. Both paths lead nowhere, but one has a heart and the other doesn't. One makes for a joyful journey; as long as you follow it you will be one with it. The other will make you curse your life. One makes you strong, the other weakens you. (p. 82)

Carlos Castañeda, *The Teachings of Don Juan* (1998)

In the 1970's a song with a somewhat obvious but very true lyric was published. Joe Jackson wrote, "You'll never get what you want til you know what you want." One of the hallmarks of effective people is that they have a very clear sense of where they are going and how they intend to get there. When we say that effective people know "how" they are getting to their destination, it does not always mean that they know ahead of time what each specific step of their journey will entail. It is a cliché to say that our plans seldom work out as we intend them. But, one thing does seem to be a constant among them and that is that effective people have a deep awareness of their values which guide their choices at each step. It can be said that they are on a mission based on a vision that emanates from their heart. As Joseph Campbell recommended, they are following their bliss. Unless you are one of those rare individuals who seem to have always known what you want, you will need to do what has been done from ancient times. You will need to go on a vision quest. But before we discuss the specifics of establishing the path of our lives' endeavors, how can we not consider questions regarding the ultimate meaning and purpose of life.

THE BIG PICTURE

Have you ever felt helped by unseen hands?

Do you ever feel sorry for the man who has no invisible means of support?

Bill Moyers' questions to Joseph Campbell

To discuss a spiritual perspective in a book about personal effectiveness may impress some as painfully obvious, and others as patently unscientific and unnecessary. After all, we, the authors are scientists and as such are obligated to attempt to cite evidence to substantiate our point of view. Traditionally, spiritual matters have been outside the realm of the scientific and relegated to the corridors of faith and speculation, or, at worst, merely the superstitions of those with an unsophisticated grasp of probability theory, placebo effects, and psychopathology. Yet the vast majority of people on our planet hold to some kind of belief system which affects their day to day quality of life. These beliefs, unscientific or not, can be sources of great pain, guilt, feelings of inadequacy, hopelessness, confusion, and fear. But they can also be the source of love, compassion, joy, vitality and a peace that surpasses understanding. A complete treatise on this subject is well beyond the scope of this text, but to leave it unaddressed is to abandon our charge of presenting you with a wide buffet of ideas regarding the process of becoming an "effective individual."

But what if you are scientifically minded? Then you are in great company because many of the leading scientific minds of our time and the past century realize that, in fact, the most advanced representations and speculations about the nature of reality do not preclude the possibility of a spiritual reality. Furthermore, they do not suggest a reality which is capricious and unlawful. They simply suggest that our most sophisticated attempts at measurement, in the scientific sense, have led us to the realization that consciousness, the activities of our minds, directly affects the "reality" around us. For example, when scientists study the nature of light they find that it literally behaves as either a wave or a particle, presenting a different appearance when projected on a surface. The really strange thing is that the way in which light behaves appears to depend on what the scientists decide to measure! That is, it depends on their decisions or thoughts. While much of modern Western psychology has been based on extrapolations of work with animals to create models for human experience and treatments for problems, there is no shortage of theories regarding the interface between psychology and spirituality. These various models are grouped under the rubric of what has come to be known as **Transpersonal Psychology** which explores this overlap between the realms of psychology and spirituality. That is, these models speak to the belief that humans are much more than a bag of skin and bones with a very sophisticated computer animating the machinery. Carl Jung's most important work began after he broke with Freud over Freud's unwillingness to see humans as anything more than advanced, complicated animals driven by sex, aggression, and pleasure seeking. Jung took a larger view of humankind and explored the possibilities of spiritual experience with concepts like the **collective unconscious**, a storehouse of experience to which all of us are connected, and **synchronicity** which refers to meaningful coincidences and also implies that events in our lives are connected in a way that is beyond our material measuring devices.

Currently, theoreticians like Stanislov Grof (1985, 1988), Ken Wilbur (1979), and Charles Tart (1986) are actively pursuing ideas like the reality of the soul, reincarnation, and the whole realm of paranormal phenomenon. The domain of the paranormal includes extra sensory perception, as manifested by such phenomena as clairvoyance, telepathy, precognition (knowing the future), and telekinesis. There is even an Association for Transpersonal Psychology which was founded in 1972 and a publication called *Journal of Transpersonal Psychology* which addresses these issues as well. Both the American Psychological Association and the British Psychological Society explore these issues within their various divisions. As we proceed through the remainder of this chapter we will cite references, when appropriate, to current theoretical models which bridge what appears to be the gap between the spiritual and the scientific.

> "We do not know what anything is. The summarization of our existence is Mystery, absolute, unqualified confrontation with what we cannot know. And no matter how sophisticated we become by experience, this will always be true of us." (p. 89)

Da Free John, *Easy Death* (1983)

We began this book with a tale of tasting mangoes. Our simple premise being that it is one thing to know about mangoes intellectually and quite another to truly taste a mango, savor the experience, and be fully alive in that moment. After all, when we cut through all of the words and rationalizations about mastery and optimal functioning, what we are after is a sense that we are really alive and living an existence that is meaningful to us. Some might refer to this as a spiritual quest. This chapter, too, is full of words and ideas and questions, but if you do not taste them, chew on them, and mull them over then you will have missed the point. Words, while they are wonderful tools, always reduce experience. They aren't the experiences themselves. Joseph Campbell (1988) once related in a lecture that the best things in life cannot be told because they are beyond thought. The next best things are misunderstood, and the next best are those things about which we talk. Consider the words written here as only fingers pointing at the moon. As the ancient expression goes, "focus too much on the fingers and you miss the heavenly splendor above." If you get caught up in the rightness or wrongness of these words you will fall into the trap of being right that we will discuss in Chapter 9, and miss the opportunity to choose happiness. Paraphrasing the words of the mystic Rumi, out there beyond ideas of right doing and wrong doing there is a field. We would like to meet you there. We'll bring the mangoes.

As you consider the goals that you want to pursue in your life, you must come to terms with what we believe are fundamental human concerns that we all must confront if we are to truly become masters of living our lives joyfully and effectively. Something that is fundamentally stressful to humans is the experience of having an inadequate map for a territory that they are exploring. Unfortunately or fortunately, depending on your perspective, life lived well will present you with the unexpected and you will be scrambling to find directions and maps to guide you. We would like to humbly offer some landmarks that we hope will help you find your way, or at least help you learn to enjoy being lost. Remember, maps are never the territory that they represent. You do not eat the menu when you go to a restaurant. We hope these maps are useful. Some may even be true!

This chapter is also about how you face the inevitable choices and decisions that you must make throughout the course of your life. If you avoid making these choices, ultimately they will be made for you. If you want to maximize your effectiveness by enhancing your sense of control, you need to again consider the maps on which you base your decisions. You must determine what is important to you, or your life will not be your own and surely your effectiveness will be undermined.

What follows are simply guideposts, ideas worth considering. When you find yourself struggling to get your bearings, attempting to make some sense out of life and your place in it, remember these things.

Life Is a Mystery.

For one of the authors, who was educated largely in Catholic schools, a very frustrating memory of childhood was being told that the answer to his inquiries about God and life was "It's a mystery." Now, he appreciates the essential truth of that assertion. No matter how many books we read, how much knowledge we acquire, or experiments we conduct, there will always remain that which is elusive, mysterious. Consider building a fire on a moonless night deep in the woods. The larger the fire the more trees we illuminate. However, the amount of darkness that we become aware of expands in direct relationship to the areas of light. Of this you can be sure, nobody knows what's really going on here. Life is ultimately a mystery that won't ever be solved no matter how big you build your bonfires. But, you can develop a relationship with life. That relationship begins by humbly acknowledging the depth of the mystery and then setting out to seek answers anyway.

When we suggest building a relationship with the mystery (or God, Goddess, the Fates, or whatever you choose to name it), we mean this literally. In the privacy of your own mind begin to have a conversation with the source of the mystery. Say the things you've always wanted to say. Ask the questions you've always wanted to ask. Now, like most conversations, the real key to success is *listening*. To listen means quietly focusing your attention so as not to be drawn into the meandering of your own mind. It means to be open to signs and synchronicities (meaningful coincidences). Answers may appear in many forms. For example, while standing in a line, you may meet a stranger who just happens to say something particularly meaningful to you at that moment. Unexpected feelings of contentment or joy may flow through you without warning. And, it is possible to hear "the still small voice" that is spoken of within metaphysical literature. Meditation is one key skill in quieting the mind. Some suggested readings in this area would be:

The Search for the Beloved	By Jean Houston Ph.D. (1987)
Journey of Awakening	By Ram Dass (1990)
The Meditative Mind	By Daniel Goleman (1988)

Therefore, Life Is Uncertain.

Things change. Get used to it. Be thankful for it. This is the one thing you can be certain of, that things will change. This is true not only in the world of work, but in all aspects of your life. You may ask yourself, "will my life ever calm down, become stable and predictable? Will I ever get caught up?" The answer is yes and then things will change. When things are going bad, things will change. When things are going good, things are going to change. Peace seems to lie in realizing and accepting this fact. It is about reassuring yourself that *when times are bad, that this too shall pass.* Repeating that phrase to yourself is one of the most effective stress reducers. Thus, you can be grateful for the changes you know will carry you out of difficult times and be appreciative for the good times, because all good things will ultimately change or come to an end.

Everything Is Connected.

One of the most profound illusions of our being is the essential solidity of the objects around us. Science, particularly physics, assures us that in spite of appearances, things are more empty space than solid matter. What appears to be solid is really a vibrating group of particles, most of which have no mass. These particles seem to be influenced by the people who try to study them. These particles also retain a relationship with one another over astronomical distances! Furthermore, all beings constantly exchange particles with one another. Chaos theorists (Gleick, 1987) have demonstrated that profound changes can be induced by minor perturbations in a system, meaning something as minor as a butterfly flapping its wings in one part of the world can lead to a powerful storm somewhere else. The science of ecology demonstrates that change in one part of a system necessarily provokes change across the system. Remember the notion of Spaceship Earth that was discussed in Chapter 1. As global citizens, it is as if we are all swimming in the same pool. You cannot have a "no peeing section" in one part of a swimming pool. We are ultimately not separate from anything. Therefore be careful and consider the actions you take on every level including your thoughts. Whatever you do, you do it to yourself. Do not burn your own house down. This is the fundamental truth that underlies the various versions of the Golden Rule. It makes sense to treat others how you would like to be treated. After all, they are you!

You can reinforce this belief by reading about cutting edge discoveries in science. Paradigms for understanding the mystical/spiritual view of life are becoming more and more accepted and are supported by experimental data. Some reading to whet your appetite includes:

The Holographic Universe	By Michael Talbot (1991)
Recovering the Soul	By Larry Dossey M.D. (1989)
A New Science of Life	By Rupert Sheldrake (1981)
The Conscious Universe	By Dean Radin (1997)

Life Is Trouble.

To again quote Zorba the Greek, "Life is trouble. Only death is not. To be alive is to undo your belt and go looking for trouble." Now before you seek out a barroom brawl, let us suggest that it is the attitude that is important here. Life very often involves dealing with problems. We have a choice. We can whine about them or we can deal with them. We have tried whining. Sometimes, even very dedicated whining! It doesn't help. We recommend taking the challenge, jumping into the fray and solving problems. Trouble simply cannot be avoided. Those, who have tried to elude it, report that it comes looking for you.

These musings about the reality of a spiritual domain lead us to ask questions about our lives. The questions you ask go a long way towards shaping the possible answers you will find. Questions like, "What should I do with my life?" have an inherent appeal to look outside of yourself for answers, for validation, for reassurances that you are doing the right thing. Yet all wisdom traditions suggest that it is knowing and trusting yourself, that is looking inside yourself, that leads to the best and most fulfilling answers.

The Sufi mystic Rumi once said, "Start a large, foolish project, like Noah. It makes absolutely no difference what people think of you." If you don't take the time to seek answers, if you don't make the effort to really get to know yourself and what really moves your heart, you risk living somebody else's life. Yes, life is difficult, full of choices, seemingly unfair at times. But life is also beautiful, effortless, and involving when you do the things you love, the things that come easily to you. When you find ways to serve others while doing what you love, success is virtually inevitable. Keeping the big picture in mind, let's move on now to seeking a vision that will inspire you and then composing a mission statement to keep you focused on your vision.

THE GLOBAL PERSPECTIVE—A Global Vision

In this chapter you set about to establish a personal vision to guide your day to day choices. What this implies, however, is that there will be a viable world in which your vision can occur. Thom Hartmann (1998) in *The Last Hours of Ancient Sunlight* summarizes a most convincing case that we are utilizing vital resources and affecting the climate in such a way that Earth will be fundamentally altered. For example he notes the following:

- Three-quarters of the world's fisheries have been fished to or beyond their sustainable limits and the oceans have lost over 90% of large predatory fish.

- We are in the midst of a mass extinction of plant and animal species not seen since the time of the dinosaurs. The normal rate of loss of species is approximately 250 species every thousand years. Because of the effects of human development, we are losing anywhere from 17,000 to 100,000 species a year!

- Due to radically ascending damage claims from increasingly erratic and powerful storms, the insurance industry called for a decrease in carbon dioxide emissions. Many scientists warn that global warming is affected by human activity, and the possible consequences might be another ice age.

- "The human need for fresh water will outstrip the entire planet's replenishable supply by 2025—even before we run out of oil."

THE GLOBAL PERSPECTIVE—A Global Vision (cont.)

These changes will not destroy Earth and all of its life. But, the human population may be radically reduced or, in the worst case scenario, go the way of the dinosaurs. These conditions are brought about by our current vision of our place on Earth that is based upon questionable assumptions like these cited by Christopher Uhl (2004) in *Developing Ecological Consciousness*.

- ❧ Humans are separate from nature.
- ❧ Our resource supplies are inexhaustible.
- ❧ Humans are only motivated by self interest.
- ❧ Economic growth is more important than environmental protection.

What we might ask ourselves at this point is what vision does Earth have for itself? What vision will provide an environment where humans can continue to exist? Since humans have been gifted with the ability to envision a future, what is our responsibility to life? Is there a way to arrive at a global vision that can find general agreement amongst people?

It is easy to feel overwhelmed at the scale of problems on a global level. After all, what can one person do? However, feeling helpless and small is not a very useful state of mind. Perhaps remembering that we are also a part of the incredible web of interconnections that constitutes life can serve us better. Here is a notion currently being explored that may provide an antidote to feeling small. Rupert Sheldrake (1981) in his book *A New Science of Life* explores the notion of **morphic resonance**. In a nutshell, it implies that all matter and living things are connected and affected by fields that influence not only their structure but also their behaviors. It has been observed, for instance, in a particular species of monkey that when a new behavior has emerged and been adopted by a certain number of monkeys, then all the monkeys acquire this behavior. This occurs even when they have been isolated on another island from the monkeys who originally expressed the new behavior. Thus, there seems to be an interconnection that cannot be explained by traditional science. Sheldrake suggests that these fields function at every level of organization of matter, plants, animals, and societies. The implication for our purposes is that when enough people begin to believe something new, then that idea or possibility becomes a new reality for all people. No one knows what that tipping point may be, but each person who develops his or her consciousness as a global citizen is helping to move all humanity towards that consciousness.

How might we develop a global vision that inspires us to move toward it? As we discussed in this chapter, the larger goals are reached by taking smaller steps first. Local goals compatible with a global vision are a way to begin this process. A method for establishing positive goals is known as **Appreciative Inquiry** (Hammond, 1998). The focus of this technique is to consider what is right about a situation and ask how more of it can be created. In other words, when you look around, what is wonderful about the world in which you live? How can we bring more of those things into being? This stands in stark contrast to our usual tendency to begin by noticing all the things that are wrong. Some examples of possible questions to help a global vision emerge could be:

- ❧ Where has peace broken out between previously warring peoples? What brought this about?
- ❧ Where is the air most fit to breathe? How can that be duplicated?
- ❧ What cities are easiest to live in with low rates of poverty and crime? What happened there?
- ❧ South Africa has gone from apartheid to radically improved racial relations? How was this accomplished?
- ❧ Europe was previously besieged by world wars but has now formed the European Union. How did they do this?

For those of you interested in viewing a comprehensive vision of a possible future, we recommend that you read *The Earth Charter*, "a declaration of fundamental principles for building a just, sustainable, and peaceful global society in the 21st century." You can view this document at *www.earthcharter.org*.

THE VISION QUEST

Dream lofty dreams, and as you dream, so shall you become.

Your vision is the promise of what you shall one day be.

James Allen

A **vision quest** can be thought of as a search for or recognition of an aspect of your destiny. Not only does it include a strong sense of a place that you are moving toward, but also an awareness of allies that will help you along the path of your journey. In archaic times shamans, the spiritual guides and healers of their cultures, would direct individuals to undertake ordeals, oftentimes involving strenuous, food deprived quests after objects or animals. Sometimes these vision quests involved the ingestion of psychedelic substances which can produce an ordeal in their own right. Dreams were also interpreted to assist the seeker in discovering what they really want. The object of all these techniques was to help an individual transcend the limitations of their everyday perceptions, and thus the limits that may have been placed on their own possibilities. Even today, many people report that it was in moments of extraordinary stress and upheaval, often life threatening, that what they wanted from life became crystal clear and ever after directed their actions.

Now before you close this book out of concern that we are going to recommend that you bungee jump out of a helicopter to determine your heart's desire, relax. There are alternatives available. The good news is that you need to spend more time with your dreams and fantasies. Take quiet time to remember times that have made you smile, warmed your heart, filled you with compassion, excited you, put you at peace. While you are feeling any of these feelings, follow the flight of your thoughts. Your heart is a compass that will point to your path. In this respect it can be said that the successful life requires constant questioning and attending to how you answer those questions, moment to moment, and day to day until you die and get the answers to the ultimate questions. Here are some questions to live with and by. Put them on your mirror or in your notebook, and check them regularly. They can begin to focus you on what is really important to you.

WHO AM I?

WHAT DO I LOVE TO DO?

WHAT IS MY PURPOSE?

HOW CAN I HELP? (Instead of, "What's in it for me?")

WHAT IS LIFE? (A dance, banquet, seasons, game, comedy, etc.)

HAVE I LAUGHED TODAY?

WHAT IS SUCCESS FOR ME?

IS THERE ANOTHER WAY OF LOOKING AT THIS? (Of course there is!)

IS THIS THE DAY I'M GOING TO DIE?

AM I LEADING THE LIFE I WANT TO LIVE?

AM I THE PERSON I WANT TO BE?

DO I KEEP MY WORD? (Especially to myself)

HOW WOULD THE PERSON I'D LIKE TO BE DO THE THINGS I'M ABOUT TO DO?

It has been said that at the end of our lives we will be concerned with the answers to only two questions:

WAS I LOVED?

DID I LOVE WELL?

Your vision quest can also begin with a *wishing quest*, something you've been playing with since childhood. We all know the stories of three wishes conferred upon some fortunate soul by an enchanted being. We also know that these stories usually end with those so-called fortunate souls making some very bad choices. Subtly, we can be discouraged from the wishing process because we fear that we are not worth it (due to low self esteem), or that we will just screw it up, or that we will be disappointed if our wishes don't come true. Nonetheless, this is where it begins and we recommend that you start by engaging in a process we call **wishstorming**.

Positive Psychology Self Exercise: Wishstorming

Wishstorming is basically brainstorming about what you would wish for if you had an unlimited supply of wishes. In fact, you *do* have an unlimited supply of wishes. There are no wish police out there making certain that you don't exceed the wish limit. As in brainstorming, you want to let your imagination run free and unrestrained. However, be aware that there will be effort involved in overcoming habits established in our brains and genetics. Because the brain likes to categorize things, it gets comfortable seeing things as it has always seen them. This can put limits on the range of our imaginations since the same brain areas are used for perception and mental imagery (Kosslyn & colleagues, 1995). As a species we are also constrained by a tendency to conform to the larger groups' perceptions. The amygdala of the brain responds as if threatened when individuals risk saying that they see things differently than the majority. When people conform, the activity in the amygdala begins to decrease. Most people would rather conform and restrict their imaginations to how things have always been seen (Berns and colleagues, 2005). Since it is your imagination, give yourself permission to really let go, but be as *specific* as possible when wishing and write your wishes down on paper. In other words, don't just wish for a car. Wish for a specific make, model, and color. Don't just wish for a relationship. Wish for someone with specific qualities. Wish for as many things as you can imagine, one hundred or more. Do this now and you will have taken the best first step towards freeing your imagination and establishing your mission.

A Consultation with the Grim Reaper

"No one on their death bed wishes they had spent more time at the office."

Anonymous

"The question is not whether we will die, but how we will live?"

Joan Borysenko

Wishing is like stretching in that you begin to become more comfortable with your desires. Common sense suggests that you can't go after all your desires simultaneously. And a closer look at your wish list will certainly suggest that some wishes are more of a priority to you than others. One of the ways to begin to narrow and clarify a vision is to make the possibility of your death part of the equation. You began this process in the previous section on the importance of questions. You can also do this in fantasy without risking life and limb. After all, it is true that not one of us is promised any more life beyond this moment.

Leo Buscaglia (1982) suggested that you can begin this process by answering the following question: What would you do if you had six days to live? What activities would you seek to do? Where would you like to visit? Who would you like to see? What would you want to say to them? How would your answers change if you had six months to live rather than six days?

Steven Covey (1991) suggests a slightly different strategy for using the specter of your own death to clarify your goals and values. He recommends an exercise wherein you attend your own funeral, and listen to several individuals eulogize you. These individuals should come from different areas of your life experience. For example, you might listen to a friend speak about you. Alternatively, you could listen to a family member, a wife or husband, a boss, a professor, or a child of yours even if it is yet to be born. Done properly this exercise will help you discover what things are really important to you. We are rather certain that you will realize that you must take into account the importance of relationships in the pursuit of your goals. Success in the presence of failed relationships can hardly be called success at all.

Ground Hog Day

By now you may be thinking, "I've had enough already of this death stuff." Is there another way to approach the process? We maintain that there is always another way to look at things. Another strategy is what we call Ground Hog Day, named after the movie of the same name. In this film the main character is faced with the dilemma of living the same day over and over again. Initially this is a frightening situation for him, but soon he realizes that he is virtually immortal. He can do whatever he wants each day with no fear of death. In the beginning he indulges himself in all manner of pleasures. However, in time he becomes bored with a purely hedonistic life (remember the hedonic treadmill!) and becomes depressed to the point of wanting to commit suicide. He cannot though, because he cannot die. Thus, he is forced to look deeper inside himself to find that which he really loves to do. Ultimately, the only thing which brings him satisfaction is to help others, and to master various skills, such as playing the piano, sculpture, and French Literature, which bring him joy. He has discovered a truly eudemonic life, a life not merely filled with pleasantries but filled with meaning.

Use your imagination and put yourself in a similar scenario. What would you do with eternity? What warms your heart and excites you? What can you do that leads you to become so absorbed in it that you lose track of time? What would be a part of a perfect day for you? So often we can let the outside world dominate our choices of what to do. We end up doing what we "ought" to do or "should" do. No one else can tell you what you love to do. It is a most personal and crucial decision because life already has enough difficulties even when you are doing what you love to do. When you are doing something that doesn't really reflect your heart's desire, life can become downright miserable.

YOUR MISSION, SHOULD YOU CHOOSE TO ACCEPT IT

A country sets down its fundamental principles in its constitution. When there are questions about how the country should respond to ongoing concerns in the pursuit of its goals, the people turn to this document and seek guidance. A mission statement is similar, akin to your own personal constitution which can function as the basis for making major life decisions as well as everyday decisions. It is a statement of your largest goals based upon your largest beliefs about the mystery of life that we discussed above. What kind of person do you want to be? What do you value? How important are your family, friends, career, etc? It reflects your uniqueness as a person. Your mission statement can help you exercise your self-efficacy as you choose short and long term goals.

It is important that your personal mission statement takes into consideration all of the major roles you play in your life. This could include your role as a son or daughter, husband or wife, as a parent, or as a family member. It would include your roles in your job or career, and your role as a student, whether you are in school full or part time. It should also include your role in any other pursuit or hobby that takes a reasonable amount of your time and/or interest (i.e. golfer, sculptor, skier, runner, boat owner, guitar player, gardener, etc.). Make sure your mission statement addresses each of the major roles you play. Be aware that many people feel torn between various roles which can seem in constant conflict and/or competition for their limited time and attention. This conflict is most often pronounced between work and family roles. Finding your balance is not always easy and goes to the heart of effectiveness. Composing your mission statement with all your vital roles in mind, and then committing to live by it, can assist you in finding that balance.

One strategy for composing a mission statement is to use the 100th birthday technique which helps you adopt a useful perspective on long range accomplishments. Imagine that you have made it to your 100th birthday and you are still alive, and well, and lucid. A newspaper reporter comes to interview you to write the story of your life and asks you to name your most important contributions in terms of accomplishments and roles you have played. How would you answer? Would you want to say that you were a good parent or loving wife/husband, that you made a million dollars, that you wrote a best-seller, climbed Mt. Everest, invented a new household appliance, became a CEO, achieved a black belt, mastered gourmet cooking, broke par when golfing, ran a marathon, wrote and sang a hit song, operated your own successful business, or? Of course, the list is endless, limited only by your interests and imagination. But be realistic. Do not set goals you cannot possibly achieve.

GETTING CLARITY: THE GOAL OF THE GOAL

By now you should have a list of goals that excite you. But before you can proceed taking action toward the goals, you must take another action first. You must examine the goals themselves. In *Heart of the Mind*, Connie Rae and Steven Andreas (1989) recommend a number of steps that will assist you in thinking about your goals in a way that can increase the likelihood of your meeting them. But before we detail these steps, it is worth considering another critical question raised by the Andreas'. They suggest that many people choose unrealistic goals, goals that are really impossible to achieve. For example, people might want to live lives free of mistakes or want to be loved by everyone. Their recommendation is to seek out the "goal of the goal" by asking this important question: "What will this goal get for me?" This question enables you to dig deeper into what it is that you really want. Many people have the goal of becoming rich and famous. Yet a moment's glance at tabloid T.V. or the history of the rich and famous shows that this is not a group of very happy people. The more basic issue is: "What do you hope to get by being rich and famous?" If the goal of the goal is to feel worthwhile or loved, then clearly there are other ways to achieve this without pursuing fabulous wealth and fame.

If you are pursuing a specific career, say medicine, because you believe it will secure money and respect, but you really hate studying science, then it would be wise to consider many other options that offer money and respect. You don't have to narrow the doorway to one specific career path. By seeking the goal behind the goal you broaden the number of options available to you for getting what you want. Thus, it is worth examining your goals carefully to make sure you really want them. Oftentimes what we really want is much more basic and involves feelings of safety, security and self-worth.

Six Steps for Securing Your Goals

Assuming now that you know what you really want, we can move onto the steps the Andreas' recommend for securing your goal.

STEP 1: *The goal must be stated in positive terms and in a way that you can achieve it yourself regardless of the behavior of others.*

Rather than saying, "I no longer want to be lonely and overweight," it would be better to say, "I would like to have a healthier lifestyle and spend more time with friends." This way of thinking motivates you instead of reminding you of the aspects of yourself you dislike. It is also critical to set goals that do not depend upon others. For example, if your goal is, "I want my girlfriend to be more affectionate," you have set a goal over which you have only indirect control. This is when it is appropriate to ask what is the goal of the goal. What would getting more affection from her do for you? Would it help you feel confident or more secure? You would probably benefit more from working directly on feelings of self-confidence that would allow you to ask for what you want and move on if it is not forthcoming.

STEP 2: *Make certain you know how you will know that you have reached your goal.*

There are a couple of things to note here. One is that you don't generally achieve your goals in one step. It will take time, and it is good to have small benchmarks along the way that let you know that what you are doing is working. For instance, you may want an A grade in a course you are taking (perhaps even this course). In that case it makes sense to keep track of your grades on all tests and projects along the way. This is realistic evidence that lets you know if you are on the path to success. Sometimes people rely on evidence that does not give them useful feedback. For example, you are not necessarily an effective parent because your children tell you that you are doing a great job. Nor are you an effective employee on the rise in your career because you feel good at the end of the workday. Perhaps you feel great because you spend your time at work catching up on your sleep! Performance evaluations are a better measuring rod. Therefore, take the time to ask how you would know if you are reaching your goals. Then take the time to feel satisfaction at each step along the way.

STEP 3: *Describe your goals as specifically as you can.*

This will be particularly important when we discuss the actual processes of moving towards your goals. Where, when, and with whom you want to reach your goals are critical questions that will help you clarify your goals. If one of your goals is to feel more passion and excitement about your life, do you want to feel that all the time, at every moment? Is passion and excitement what you want to feel at a funeral, or while having lunch with your grandmother? Do you want to feel passion and excitement during a proctological exam? As you prepare to reach your goals, ask yourself what will be the sights, sounds, and feelings that will accompany reaching your goal. For example, "When I hear my professor assign a large term project, I will feel challenged and confident that I can do what is necessary to get the grade I want."

STEP 4: *Are your goals compatible with each other?*

Most of us have more than one goal we want to reach. This step simply asks that you make sure you find a way to reach both goals or once again return to evaluating what you really want. For example, since the women's rights movement many women were faced with the dilemma of balancing career and motherhood. Now, having a career and being a mother are not incompatible goals, but it requires very clear thought about how they are to be balanced or sequenced in order to support reaching both goals.

STEP 5: *Assess what you already have and what you are going to need in order to reach your goals.*

In other words, what are your skills, your assets? If you want to be a stand-up comedian, you may already possess a wonderful sense of humor and a quick mind. You may need a lot of confidence building, public speaking skills and practice, an ability to withstand criticism so as to grow a thick skin and continue to improve, or even some training regarding how to formulate an act. This kind of thinking allows you to direct your energy in the appropriate directions.

STEP 6: *Make a plan.*

A journey of a thousand miles begins with a single step. It is often useful to work backwards from the place where you want to be to the place where you are now in order to determine your very next step. For example, if you've decided upon a career as an attorney, the step just before entering practice is passing the bar exam. The step before that is completing law school. The step prior to that is getting into law school which requires taking and scoring well on the law boards (LSAT). And of course you need to have a bachelors degree before the law boards results are significant. Obviously we can take this process all the way back to toilet training, as most attorneys do not practice in diapers either. However, the point is that there is a next reasonable step to take and you need to take that step. Working backwards from your goal lays out a path for you to follow.

Positive Psychology Self Exercise: Compose Your Personal Mission Statement

Really give it some thought based upon all the guidelines for thinking it through. You will find that the time and effort you put into this will be well spent.

VISUALIZATION

As an infant, before you learned to speak, you were able to think, but this rudimentary thinking took the form of images rather than words or phrases, which you had not yet mastered. That is why, for most people, our earliest memories from childhood tend to be fragmented images rather than conversations or events. Indeed, mental imagery is perhaps the most basic way that your mind represents and stores information. And imagery is the primary medium by which your **unconscious mind** operates. Freud (1924) in his psychodynamic theory, developed the concept of the unconscious mind to describe that part of the mind containing aspects of our functioning of which we are totally unaware. Freud believed that the mind is like an iceberg which is mostly hidden underwater. He saw our conscious mind as being the part of the iceberg that is above the waterline. But below the surface is the much larger unconscious region containing thoughts, wishes, feelings and memories of which we are largely unaware, but which influence our feelings and behaviors nevertheless. When asleep, as you detach from your conscious mind and waking verbal thought, your unconscious mind emerges and dream images abound. The imagery of the unconscious mind is not confined to just mental pictures; it can represent impressions from any of your senses, i.e. remembered sounds, feelings, aromas, tastes, etc.

Visualization is a time honored method of deliberately using imagery, visual and otherwise, to alter your feelings, your behavior, and even your physiology. Because of the dominance of imagery in the functioning of your unconscious mind, which has a powerful effect upon your motivation, visualization practice can have a profound effect on your emotions or behavior, over and beyond your conscious efforts to change. Early in the twentieth century, the French pharmacist, Emil Coue (1922), wrote that the power of the imagination exceeds that of the conscious will. That is, you may or may not be able to will the achievement of a specific goal, but repeatedly visualizing attaining that goal greatly increases the probability of success. Mastery of the art and practice of visualization will help propel you down the road to effectiveness.

Covey (1991) also speaks to the importance of this as he exhorts us to "begin with the end in mind." With this he is talking both about the importance of setting goals *and* then being able to visualize the achievement of those goals as necessary prerequisites to effectiveness.

Applications to Sports Performance

In a now classic study (Richardson, 1969), three groups of boys were tested on their ability to make free throws on a basketball court. After the initial assessment they were instructed to spend the next two weeks in one of three ways. One group practiced shooting free throws. Another group did nothing with a basketball for two weeks. The third group was instructed to mentally rehearse shooting the basketball, to visualize themselves shooting and making free throws. All the groups were then retested. The group that did nothing showed no change in their free throw proficiency. The group that actually practiced with the ball improved 24%. The group that only visualized improved 23%! This is only one of many demonstrations of the power of human beings to achieve extraordinary results by controlling the content of their thoughts.

In a comprehensive treatise called *Peak Performance*, Charles Garfield (1984) documents extensive research done with world class athletes in Russia and the United States. He states unequivocally that almost all world class performers are visualizers. In fact, in the realm of the world class athlete, he cites a study done in the then Soviet Union where they compared different training regimens among their athletes. Some athletes spent almost 100% of their time in physical training for their event. Others spent between 25%, 50%, and 75% of their time in mental training and rehearsal, i.e. visualization for their event. The results showed that performance results improved as the amount of time devoted to mental practice increased. Garfield also points out that "peak performers are highly motivated by a deep and personal sense of mission which is distinctly different from the highly specific and measurable goals each person may set."

In yet another fascinating demonstration of the power of imagery and belief, Talbot (1991) cites a study done at Hebrew University in Israel. In this study several groups of soldiers were sent on a march of 25 miles. Each group of soldiers, however, was given different information as to the actual distance they had marched or had yet to march. When stress hormone levels were measured in each group, the levels reflected how far the soldiers thought they had marched, not the actual distance. In other words, their bodies responded to their *imagined* stress, not the reality of the extent of their exertion!

There is little doubt that visualization or imagery works. How, when, where, and under what circumstances it works is being actively studied. Morris and colleagues (2005) summarize the current state of affairs in their text, *Imagery in Sport*.

> Until a thorough understanding of imagery emerges, systematic research programs that examine one aspect of it in a variety of ways are needed....In particular, we propose that substantial evidence indicates that imagery works in a range of sport contexts. Imagery can enhance learning, performance, confidence, and motivation, reduce stress and anxiety, and facilitate recovery from injury, among other benefits. We need more research on how imagery works, because by understanding the mechanisms we will be able to predict and control its use, even in untested circumstances. (pg. 11)

Applications for Healing

Cancer researcher O. Carl Simonton (1975), in *Getting Well Again*, reports increased longevity in cancer patients who practice relaxation and visualize their diseases remitting. This process literally involves creating vivid mental images of the disease process, a tumor for instance, and then deliberately imagining that the image is changing. For example, you might imagine a tumor as a black octopus with tentacles reaching into various body parts. You then imagine that your chemotherapy or radiation treatment is acting as a weapon, shrinking the octopus, damaging its arms, changing or fading its color to white, and causing it to eventually disappear. While this treatment approach is still controversial, it is becoming a widely used technique in fighting cancer.

Simonton is far from alone in his faith in the power of belief that is reflected in how one "sees" things. Both Jeanne Achtenberg (1985) and Bernie Siegel (1986) in their respective texts, *Imagery in Healing,* and *Love, Medicine and Miracles*, cite many examples that indicate that our beliefs affect our physical health for better or worse. When you believe you will survive and thrive, your probability of doing so increases. If you believe your disease is a death sentence, then unfortunately that becomes true with increasing frequency as well. In fact, Achtenberg achieved a 95% rate of accuracy in predicting who would survive their illness and who would die simply by a careful analysis of patient's drawings of themselves, their cancers, their immune systems, and their treatment.

Anees Shiekh (2005) summarizes the current state of the research on the uses of imagery in healing in *Healing Images: The Role of Imagination in Health*. He points out that imagery has been demonstrated to create measurable physiological changes in heart rate, blood pressure, blood flow, sexual response, body chemistry, various ocular effects, electrodermal activity, muscle tension and the immune system. And this is only a partial list! He notes further that the effectiveness of procedures such as biofeedback and hypnosis is clearly related to the capacity of those being treated to become absorbed in imagery. His conclusions are remarkably similar to the findings in the area of sport. Imagery practices work, but much more research is needed to determine which techniques under various circumstances are most effective for different disorders. Exactly how imagery assists the body to heal is the focus of much current theory and research.

The placebo effect, as discussed in Chapter 5, also stands as powerful proof of the role of belief and how we see things in the creation of our reality. In fact, in the realm of metaphysical and spiritual practice it is understood that the eyes are more than simply receptive organs. The root word of eye actually translates as "fountain." That is, the eyes send energy out and thus are involved in creation itself. Pick up virtually any revered text of wisdom teachings and you will find references and specific instructions for controlling and shaping your thoughts and images to manifest the life you desire. This is best summed up by Michael Talbot (1991) in his book *The Holographic Universe*.

> Paramahansa Yogananda advised people to visualize the future they desired for themselves and charge it with the "energy of concentration." As he put it, "Proper visualization by the exercise of concentration and will power enables us to materialize thoughts, not only as dreams or visions in the mental realm, but also as experiences in the material realm."
>
> Indeed, such ideas can be found in a wide range of disparate sources. "We are what we think," said the Buddha. "All that we are arises with our thoughts. With our thoughts we make the world. As a man acts, so does he become. As a man's desire is, so is his destiny," states the Hindu pre-Christian Brihadaranyaka Upanishad. "All things in the world of Nature are not controlled by Fate for the soul has a principle of its own," said the fourth-century Greek philosopher Iamblichus. "Ask and it will be given you . . . If ye have faith, nothing shall be impossible unto you," states the Bible. And, "The destiny of a person is connected with those things he himself creates and does," wrote Rabbi Steinsaltz in the kabbalistic *Thirteen Petaled Rose*. (p. 222)

Possible Explanations for How Visualization Works

How does visualization work? One explanation seems to be based on principles first outlined by Albert Bandura (1977) in his Social Cognitive Learning theory. While this theory has many elements, it relies on thoughts, beliefs, and a principle known as modeling to explain why you behave as you do and how you acquire behaviors and skills. The principle of **modeling** describes the ability of humans to learn how to do something simply by observing others. This is also referred to in the literature as **observational learning**. It works whether the models are live or on a TV screen. It also apparently works when the models are in your imagination. *And* it also works well when the model is a new, improved, and more successful you that is created in your imagination.

Modeling or observational learning may be partially explained by the presence of mirror neurons in the brain (Ramachandran, 2000). Whenever we observe someone performing an action, the same neurons required to perform that action being observed are being triggered in the observer as well. The neurons firing in the observer are called mirror neurons. It is as if we are hard wired to learn by watching others.

Other speculations as to why visualization works (Morris, Spittle, and Watt, 2005) include that it increases feelings of self-confidence and self-efficacy. It may well work by raising arousal levels to their best level for optimal performance as suggested by the Yerkes Dodson curve relating arousal and performance. Some suggest that visualization enhances motivation. Others believe that visualization practice sends electrical impulses to the actual muscles that are used in the execution of the imagined activity thereby providing a virtual rehearsal of the actions one is imagining. Truth be told, it is probably a combination of all of these, and there is research data to support each explanation.

The Process of Visualization

Now that a case has been made for the power of **visualization**, it remains for us to specify how to actually use this capacity in a way that works to your advantage. What follows is a discussion of critical principles in understanding and using this process.

1. Begin by Mastering Voluntary Relaxation Skills.

This is an absolutely critical element in the use of visualization. Your body is a reflection of your mental state. If you are tense, anxious, fearful, or lack confidence, this is reflected in your musculature. Thus you may verbalize positive thoughts and even conjure up positive images. But if your body is presenting a competing picture of negativity then you are sending mixed messages to yourself and your results will be mixed at best. When you relax completely prior to your visualization practice, you are creating on a blank sheet of paper. There are no competing images to interfere with the process of your learning. You might also think of this process as familiar to recording music in a studio. Recording studios are deliberately soundproofed so that only the music played in the studio is recorded, not the sound of traffic or conversation in the hallway. Relaxation is the moral equivalent of silence in your body, and allows for a clearer recording of the behaviors, skills, and attitudes you wish to acquire.

The techniques discussed in Chapter 6 will allow you to master the act of relaxation. Pay special attention to the discussion of basic meditation technique which is another pathway to relaxation and the quieting of competing thoughts.

2. Garbage in, Garbage out.

Your consciousness is an equal opportunity employer. It really doesn't care if what you visualize is good or bad for you. It just produces results. In this case, what you see is what you get. Consider this analogy. You can think of visualization as being to your mind what food is to your body. Positive images are the equivalent of health food and negative images are like feeding yourself junk food. If you recall, earlier we stated the necessity of stating your goals positively. This is to avoid the pitfall of visualizing and manifesting what you don't want. For example, one of the authors discovered this principle in a rather embarrassing fashion...

> I was waiting at the first tee of the golf course with my father and some of his friends. The first tee is the one place on a golf course where you are being observed by many people. My concern, my absolute preoccupation, was that I did not want to embarrass myself by hitting a terrible shot in front of my father and all of these people. To that end I began saying to myself, "just don't shank the ball," a particularly bad shot. I kept thinking this over and over again until it was my turn to hit. In short order, I stepped up to the ball and shanked it! I got exactly what I didn't want because I had rehearsed it so thoroughly.

3. Visualization Is much more than Images.

You don't necessarily see things when you visualize. This is a crucial point because many people are not aware of the visual aspect of their thoughts. If you ask them to visualize something they panic because they believe that they should be seeing a mental television set with crisp, clear images. For those of you that can do this, that is wonderful. For those of you that cannot, there is no need to worry because *all* of your senses are involved in the visualization process. It is sufficient to have a *sense* of what it would be like if your imagined future or outcome was occurring. In other words, as long as you *know* what your image would look like if you could see, or hear, or feel it; that is good enough for the purposes of creation. In an ideal scenario the outcome that you imagine should be developed as vividly as possible. You should see, hear, and feel your future in as much detail as possible. For instance, if you want to be more assertive in your communications, it would be best not only to hear the words in the appropriate speed and tone of voice, but also to see yourself acting in an assertive fashion. You could also see the people you are speaking to responding appropriately and receptively to your communication. And lastly, you should feel what it would be like to communicate in this way.

Positive Psychology Self Exercise: Enhancing Your Visualizations

If you have difficulty with making visual images and would like to learn to enhance your ability, try this simple exercise. Just close your eyes and allow yourself to recall your bedroom, or a pleasant experience, either recent or from childhood, or what you ate at your last meal, in as much detail as possible. Pay special attention to the colors, shapes and lighting, as well as any tastes, smells, textures, temperatures, sounds, physical sensations and feelings you experienced. If you are not a strong visualizer that likely means that you tend to store your memories in another **representational system**. We use representational systems to encode information in our brain. There are five primary representational systems relating to each of the five senses: **auditory** (our hearing represented in sounds, words and language); **visual** (our vision represented in mental pictures); **kinesthetic** (our sense of touch represented by feelings and physical sensations); **gustatory** (taste); and **olfactory** (smells). Each person has a dominant representational system, a sense that they favor for encoding and remembering information. Although the visual system is typically dominant, many individuals prefer another representational system for storing memories. If this is the case for you, remember any experience by tuning into whatever sense is most dominant for you, and then imagine any visual images associated with these other sensory images. So, for example, if you are remembering your bedroom, first recall the sensation of lying in your comfortable bed and feeling the softness and warmth of your comforter or bedspread while listening to music or talking on your cell phone. Now connect that with actually seeing what that comforter or bedspread looks like. What color is it? Does it have a pattern? What color are the walls in your room or the floor? Where is your dresser, or your desk? What can you see when you look out of your window? Basically, you can use memories from one sense to bridge into memories from any other sense. Doing this enables you to make your visualizations more vivid by giving them the depth of multiple sensory representations.

4. Use Participant and Observer Imagery.

This brings us to another subtle but critical distinction in the visualization process, participant and observer imagery. Consider for a moment that all of the movie special effects you have ever witnessed originated first in someone's imagination, therefore, these are available to you as well. Special effects have different effects on you as you watch them. For example, most likely you have experienced simulation rides (such as those at Disney World or other amusement parks) and their powerful impact on your physiology. You can actually feel as if you are on a roller coaster or an airplane if the ride presents you with the sights and sounds you would experience if you were actually on the plane or coaster. This is what is referred to as participant imagery - you feel as if you are actually participating in the experience. Observer imagery occurs when you see a roller coaster or airplane "out there" or in the distance. The difference in your experience is that you may have feelings about the airplane or coaster but you don't feel as if you are on it, directly experiencing it. It is the difference between watching a mental image of yourself riding the coaster (a third person experience) vs. imagining yourself actually riding it (a first person experience). Depending upon the results that you want you need to use these two variations appropriately.

Participant imagery involves actually practicing the result you want in your mind. This is how world class athletes prepare for their events without leaving their rooms. You feel what it is like to be doing what it is you want to be doing. Your muscles are actually experiencing the same electrical impulses that they would during the actual activity. In other words, there really is no difference to your brain between real and imagined. Observer imagery has a different effect. In this context it tends to be more motivating. As you see yourself behaving, looking, and sounding as you would like, you tend to be positively motivated to expend the energy to do what is necessary to achieve the result. Using observer imagery can also be helpful when imagining yourself doing something which is frightening or anxiety provoking for you. Since you are viewing yourself at a distance when using observer imagery, it can give you more emotional distance, and as a result help allay anxiety. You can then shift to participant imagery once you feel comfortable with your observer images.

5. *The Recommended Sequence for the Process of Visualization Would Be as Follows:*

   a. Decide on your goal, the actions and attitudes you wish to adopt.

   b. Think of a model who can do what you want to do.

   c. Get into a comfortable position.

   d. If possible, make sure that your environment is relatively quiet and free from distractions.

   e. Use a relaxation technique to establish a receptive mental state.

   f. Begin to imagine or sense your model doing the desired goal or behaviors.

   g. Study what the model does, how does he or she look, sound, move, until you can vividly "sense" him or her in your imagination.

   h. Substitute yourself for the model. That is, see yourself doing the desired goal and allow yourself to feel motivated.

   i. Step into the image and see, hear, and feel what you would feel if you were doing the desired goal.

   j. Practice this for 15 minutes daily. For faster results practice 2-3 times daily.

6. *Let Go and Be Patient.*

This part is a little trickier. Visualization is effective. You do it all the time effortlessly. When you begin to deliberately direct it, it is often difficult to maintain that effortless quality. After all, you want something and have been taught that you need to try your hardest to get those things you want. Unfortunately, trying hard can be counterproductive because it is associated with tension which interferes with the visualization process. Also, there is a tendency when embarking on this process to worry whether or not it will work. You may remember other things you wished for and never got. You may find yourself looking for results each day and feeling frustrated that your progress isn't more obvious. All we can say is to continue to practice, relax, and let go. All of the other worry and concern leads to visualizing all of the things you don't want. If you are having difficulty with this, review the lessons from Chapter 2 on maintaining an optimistic perspective. Visualization is similar to gardening. You plant seeds of positive thought through imagery and pluck out the weeds of negative thoughts by refusing to invest your energy in contemplating all the things that can go wrong. When you plant a seed, you don't dig it out of the ground every day to check its progress. Now we are not suggesting that you never plan for the possibility of things not going your way (i.e. engage in defensive pessimism if that style suits you better). Life will definitely surprise you. But, when you are exercising the power of visualization it is important to keep your eye on the prize. Obviously, what is required is a mind able to maintain a focus on the present moment. This is also a skill that can be learned and is the primary benefit of the practice of meditation.

A Final Note

A story is told of a good and holy man named Saul who had lived a life of love and service to his family and community. Saul began to pray regularly at temple with a particular request of God. After praising and thanking God, Saul reminded God of all of his good works and finished with the statement, "I don't think it's too much too ask that I should win the lottery." This routine went on for several months but Saul failed to win the lottery. Still he persisted until one day a booming voice from behind the altar said, "Saul, do me a favor. Buy a ticket!" Visualization seems like a miraculous process but it requires effort and it ultimately requires that you take action. You may visualize yourself getting an A in a college course but you will have to register, buy the book, go to class, and study. You may visualize a perfected athletic technique but you will still have to practice on the field of play. The Universe is wondrous and mysterious. So, by all means, expect miracles, but remember to do your part.

KEY TERMS

Vision Quest	Representational Systems	Collective Unconscious
Wishstorming	Auditory	Synchronicity
Visualization	Visual	Morphic Resonance
Unconscious Mind	Kinesthetic	Transpersonal Psychology
Modeling	Gustatory	
Observational Learning	Olfactory	

CHAPTER 7 QUESTIONS

True or False Questions (T or F)

1. _____ State your goals in negative terms so you won't be disappointed later on if you don't achieve them.

2. _____ When goal-setting it helps to be as specific as possible.

3. _____ Athletes who practice their sport with mental rehearsal (visualization) typically find it to be a waste of time.

4. _____ Visualization promotes healing.

5. _____ For world class athletes in the U.S. and Russia performance improvement directly corresponded to the percentage of time spent in mental rehearsal.

6. _____ Sacred texts warn you to avoid visualization practices.

7. _____ Humans often learn how to do things by observational learning or modeling.

8. _____ Relaxation is irrelevant to the visualization process.

9. _____ Negative visualizations are more powerful than positive visualizations.

10. _____ One thing you can be certain of is that things will change.

11. _____ Change in one part of a system provokes change across the system.

12. _____ You are separate from your environment.

13. _____ You create your reality with your thoughts, your words, and your mental images.

14. _____ Effective people consistently look outside of themselves for reassurance that they are doing the right thing.

15. _____ Your effectiveness will be undermined if you allow yourself to be fully in the present moment.

Essay Questions

1. What is Transpersonal Psychology?
2. What is the purpose of examining the goal of your goal?
3. Describe the steps for securing your goals.
4. What is the relationship of modeling to the effects of visualization practice?
5. How does relaxation facilitate the process of visualization and its effects?
6. What is the relationship of visualization practice to effectiveness?
7. Distinguish between participant and observer imagery.
8. What is Appreciative Inquiry?

8

Managing Yourself for Accomplishment

When we think about "effective" people what typically comes to mind are individuals who are accomplished and productive, who not only do most things competently, but who do them in a timely manner. Effective people respect deadlines and usually finish tasks on time, sometimes with time to spare. But effectiveness is much more than just producing a lot of work. The quest for optimal functioning requires organization as well as creativity. Effective people are typically well organized, and have learned to juggle multiple responsibilities, projects, and tasks while still making time for relaxation, enjoyment and personal relationships. Success in our current world usually requires an ability to see the big picture followed by a sustained focus on the critical details for getting it done. What enables effective individuals to develop and maintain competence and maximize their chances for success is that they are adept at culling out what is important, and then they use their time wisely.

MANAGING YOURSELF IN TIME

Indeed, the ability to use time wisely is typically a hallmark of effective individuals. Please notice we are not talking about time management, but rather about managing "yourself in time." We often hear people talk about needing to "make more time," as if we all didn't get just 24 hours in a day. The key is to manage yourself and the decisions you make regarding how to use the resource that is time. But, you need to be wary of the common tendency to confuse efficiency with effectiveness. While effective individuals are typically well organized and they may be efficient, an over emphasis on efficiency will actually diminish your effectiveness, but more on this later.

Have you ever spent a day, at work or at home, where you were busy almost non-stop, but by the day's end you felt as though you had accomplished nothing? Perhaps this was because you put your focus on tasks, concerns, projects or undertakings that were really not very important. You may have spent your day doing busywork, trivial jobs that were easy, or tasks requested by others, but which were of low relevance to your own agenda. Perhaps you felt you had accomplished little because nothing was finished, or because you were immersed in multiple tasks in a disorganized fashion, flitting back and forth and never really making any headway on any. Every one of us has had at least one day like this, but if you find yourself fitting this pattern on a regular basis, it is time to look at how you manage yourself in time and experiment with more effective strategies. Even if you are adept at utilizing time, you many find at least a few tips or tools in this chapter that will refine or add to your skills.

The Eight Strategies for Success

If you follow these central strategies for everyday success, you will increase your productivity, your effectiveness, and as a side benefit, you will lower your stress level.

1. *Focus First on High Priority Items.*

Think in terms of the Pareto principle, a concept from economics, which is also called the 80/20 rule. The Pareto principle teaches that 80% of the benefit comes from doing 20% of the work. Figure out the most important and beneficial 20%, and make that your priority to tackle first. Completing the important 20% often expedites or simplifies completion of the remaining 80% of the work.

How do you determine what is or should be a high priority? How do you know what is really important? This is not always that obvious. Tasks, jobs, or things you have to do are rarely either important or unimportant. Importance lies on a continuum ranging from low to high. Covey (1991) recommends that you determine importance based on how closely an activity is tied to your life goals and desired results as defined by your personal mission statement explained in the previous chapter. Time management expert, Dru Scott, (1980) advises completing "marginal matters," the hundreds of relatively trivial but time consuming tasks (i.e., washing dishes, looking through email, running errands, or updating your files), last. Many people try to get these little tasks out of the way first to make time to focus on the important stuff. But too often these small, marginal tasks end up consuming your whole day, and before you know it, nothing of lasting value is accomplished. Give these tasks the lowest priority. That does not mean that you ignore them. After all, these tasks do have their place in the scheme of things. Just do them last when possible.

2. *Group Related Tasks and Do Them Together.*

It is common sense that when you group similar jobs together you can accomplish them faster than if you did each one separately. For example, if you have three errands to run, it is certainly more efficient to do all at once rather than take the time to drive your car three different times.

3. *Get Organized.*

Lack of organization contributes to ineffectiveness. When you approach your work in a disorganized fashion tasks generally take longer to accomplish, and the finished product often is not as good. Experiment with the following tips for improving your organization.

a. Things To Do Lists

Making a list of Things to Do on a daily or weekly basis is an excellent way of getting yourself organized, and helping to remember small items or tasks that are easily forgotten. Post your list in a prominent place (like the bathroom mirror or the refrigerator door) where you will be likely to see it often, or keep it in your phone to refer to regularly. Scratching finished items off your list becomes quite rewarding, leading to a sense of relief and accomplishment each time an item is crossed off.

b. Create a Realistic Schedule

Things to Do lists are very useful, but they have their limits. In particular, avoid getting caught in the trap of spending all your time accomplishing marginal items and scratching those off your list, while ignoring important, more difficult and time consuming tasks. Without some sort of schedule, you can create stress by wasting time, working inefficiently, and missing opportunities because you didn't plan ahead. But over scheduling yourself is stressful as well. There is an art to creating a workable daily, weekly and monthly schedule. Start by compiling a list of all you want and need to accomplish over a certain time period, say a month. Begin your daily schedule by arranging time for any scheduled appointments or meetings. Next, block out chunks of at least an hour for high priority projects that require sustained work over time. The earlier in the day you can get to these, the better. Then build in time for other required tasks. Complete your schedule with the routine, quick or easy, marginal tasks that need to be completed that day. Make your schedule flexible. Build in time for interruptions, unexpected events, problem solving, and travel time, as well as for breaks and relaxation. If you can't finish everything, and this may occur often, postpone the lowest priority items. Following a schedule will not guarantee that you always get everything done that day, but if you have made progress on your high priority goals you will feel more in control. Engaging in this type of planning may seem time consuming at first, but it will increase your time in the long run.

c. Get Rid of Unnecessary Papers

Is your desk at work or at home piled high with stacks of papers waiting for your attention, be it unopened junk mail, bills to pay, magazines, or forms to fill out? Do you feel overwhelmed just looking at the paper piles? If so, follow these guidelines. Handle each piece of paper only once, if possible. Each time you handle a piece of paper do something to move it along (i.e. pay that bill, toss out junk mail, file that important paper, fill out that form). Most importantly, when in doubt, THROW IT OUT. If you don't, it is likely to just sit there on your desk, collecting dust and adding to your pile. Once you have made sufficient headway on clearing the pile, keep your desk cleared of everything except the highest priority items.

4. *Break It into Doable Chunks.*

Many tasks, particularly if complicated or time consuming, can appear overwhelming, leading to avoidance, delays, or disorganization. We can't emphasize enough how helpful it can be to break big jobs into workable steps. Taking time to initially subdivide the project into steps, then listing and ordering those steps, will save you time later on.

It will help you proceed more smoothly, and often with less frustration. Approaching the task in an organized fashion minimizes chances of forgetting an important step, allowing you to feel a sense of task accomplishment as each step is completed. Remember, a skyscraper may look huge, but it was built one brick at a time.

5. Develop and Use Timetables.

We humans are much more likely to begin and to complete something when we have committed to a deadline. Deadlines bring home the reality that we have to get moving. If you do not have a deadline from an external source such as a boss or a teacher, set your own target date or time for completion. After breaking the task or assignment into doable chunks, estimate how much time each chunk will reasonably take to finish. Then give each chunk its' own target date or time for completion. Doing this gives you an opportunity to plan accordingly to leave yourself ample time for task completion. This will help you avoid the stress of last minute rushes, or settling for slip-shod work if you run out of time.

For example, if you are a student facing a big assignment, such as a term paper that is due in two weeks, you could chunk the job in a format such as the following:

1.) Get relevant articles and books from the library	2 hours
2.) Do Internet search	2 hours
3.) Read through sources and pick out relevant information	4 hours
4.) Organize report into 3 sections.	1 hour
5.) Write introductory paragraph	1/2 hour
6.) Write section one.	2 hours
7.) Write section two.	2 hours
8.) Write section three.	1 hour
9.) Proofread report.	1 hour

You would next assign each chunk to a date and time of day to work on it within your school or work schedule. You have nine chunks to be divided over fourteen days. The four hour preparatory chunk (reading through source material) could be subdivided into two, two hour chunks scheduled for consecutive days for continuity. This schedule takes a large intimidating job and makes it doable.

6. Focus on One Thing at a Time.

It often helps if you focus on one task at a time. People with problems managing themselves in time often flit from one project to another, or try to do several things simultaneously. The end result is often delays, mistakes and disorganization which wastes rather than saves time. Uninterrupted concentration on a task, when possible, produces a better product in less time. Arrange your work space to minimize distractions. This does not mean you can only do one thing at a time. It is certainly possible to type your term paper while your clothes spin in the dryer. The key here is *not to try to do two or more things that require concentration or focus at the same time.*

7. *Finish It Fully.*

Effective individuals finish what they start. This involves utilizing the signature strengths of perseverance and industriousness discussed previously. No matter how much work you may do in the course of a day, if you don't finish anything, you may end up feeling frustrated and your effectiveness is diluted. You will be far better off with three finished projects as opposed to six half finished jobs. Finishing will boost your personal satisfaction and motivation, lower your stress level, and enhance your ability to concentrate because you have fewer tasks with which to be concerned. That is, you only have three tasks to finish rather than six. Finishing tasks on a regular basis has a large impact on how others view you as well, whether you are perceived as effective, dependable, successful. Starting many tasks or projects and leaving them unfinished wastes time and energy, contributes to disorganization, and also makes mistakes or careless errors more likely. Although attempting to focus on one task at a time sets the stage for task completion, we certainly realize that in the real world this is not always possible. At work phones ring, colleagues interrupt you with pressing concerns, meetings must be attended, or equipment breaks down. But when possible we recommend that you opt for task completion, rather than switching to another task that is not pressing or vitally important.

8. *Do It When You Think of It.*

Oftentimes it is just the sheer volume of tasks which makes you want to delay. By doing the task immediately, if possible, you can avoid the inefficiency involved in relocating the necessary materials which saves time and effort. You also prevent yourself from forgetting to handle it.

COMMON TIME-WASTERS AND EFFECTIVE ANTIDOTES

There are always a myriad of potential time wasting or time consuming influences, both internal and external, which can interfere with accomplishment. Which of the following obstacles apply to you? Consider how you might put these suggestions to good use to creatively turn potential time wasters into opportunities for getting something done.

Information Overload Sabotaging Decision-Making

Your ability to make decisions can be significantly slowed or stymied altogether by **information overload**. Do you feel that you always have to do exhaustive research in order to make the best decisions? Do you then find that because of the plethora of available information, that the more data you acquire, the more confused you become? The science of decision making has demonstrated that too much information can literally paralyze you, or lead to poor choices on your part. Research has shown that many decisions benefit from letting the issue percolate. Opening yourself to a steady stream of new information interferes with that process. Why? Incoming information presents you with choices. Do you attend to it, ignore it, reply to it? Decision science shows us that there is a tipping point; when you have too many choices or too much information, you are apt to postpone a decision or make an unwise choice. Although many people desire to accumulate more information to assist with decision making, past a certain point this actually becomes "debilitating" according to Sheena Iyengar (2010) in her book *The Art of Choosing*.

The more data you have to juggle, the harder the decision, particularly when information is complex and/or the stakes are high. The reason for this has to do with the capacity of our brain's working memory, which can typically hold an average of seven items at one time. Therein lays the beauty of seven digit phone numbers. Anything beyond seven items represents an overload and is much harder to remember in its entirety. According to JoAnne Cantor (2009) in her book *Conquer Cyber Overload*, when overloaded our brain struggles to figure out what to discard, which inhibits decision making.

Research reveals the important finding that some of our best decisions are made through unconscious processes rather than just rational analysis. It can be harder to reach a decision if you expose yourself to a constant barrage of new data because you are not giving your unconscious, intuitive mind the time to make the connections that lead to a wise judgment. Taking a break allows your brain to subconsciously integrate new information into existing knowledge to guide you. How can you prevent yourself from the effects of information overload?

1. Recognize that you need to set a limit on how much data you gather to avoid exceeding your tipping point. Focus on gathering data for the one to three criteria that you determine to be most important for your decision. The next section in this chapter will assist you in setting priorities.

2. Deliberately take breaks to allow your unconscious mind to process and consolidate the information.

3. Don't be afraid to make snap judgments regarding inconsequential, everyday matters. If nothing of any significance is riding on your decision, then just pick because either way it will not matter very much. Whether you pick chocolate or vanilla ice cream does not really matter.

4. Deal with tasks like emails and text messages (part of the ongoing barrage of information) in batches rather than piece meal all day long.

5. Lastly, when you start to feel overloaded, take that as a cue to stop searching because you probably have more than enough data from which to reach your decision.

Worrying

Do you spend a lot of time worrying about all you have to do or would like to do, rather than doing it? Rumination can be a major time waster for it is neither a productive nor rewarding use of your time. But trying not to worry is destined to fail. Telling yourself not to worry is the equivalent of commanding yourself, "Don't think about pink elephants." What happens? Of course, the first thing you think of is a pink elephant! The key is not to try to stop worrying, but rather to schedule it, to literally set up a time devoted exclusively to worry at a time that is convenient for you, that does not interfere with your work. Effective individuals worry just like everyone else; they just limit the distraction of non productive worry by scheduling it. To this end, try the following exercise.

Positive Psychology Self Exercise: The Worry Appointment

If daily worrying is an issue for you, set up a daily fifteen minute period to worry to your heart's content. Avoid scheduling your worry time right before or at bedtime because this could disturb the winding down for sleep. If you do not worry on a daily basis but have difficulty letting go of worries when you do ruminate, schedule a weekly half hour worry appointment. Scheduling such worry times helps put your mind to rest. If worries, fears, or obsessive concerns pop up in your mind, remind yourself that you will definitely consider this concern later at your worry time. Sometimes we worry because we fear that we will forget to do or handle something unless we remind ourselves with worries. The value of scheduling worry time is that it makes it much easier to let go of those worries because you know you will get to them later. This frees you to focus on your work. Many people find that once they begin their worry time, some concerns have already evaporated and others can be dismissed quickly. You may end up finishing your worrying even before your time is up.

Attempting to Do Things Perfectly

Don't try to do things perfectly, just focus on doing them well. Striving for perfection typically leads to fear of failure, procrastination, or difficulty finishing due to delays until it is "perfect." Effective individuals strive for excellence—not perfection. In most cases an 80% job is all that is necessary to accomplish the task appropriately. Does that inter-office memo really have to be perfect every time? Is it really the end of the world if there is some dust on top of the TV? There are some rare tasks that are worth doing as close to perfect as you can. Determine what those are, and typically they should relate closely to your high priorities. Abandoning the need for perfection on unimportant tasks will save you valuable time and energy. Invest that time and energy saved on what is really important.

Working Against Your Body Rhythms

Sometimes we slow ourselves down or lower our effectiveness by failing to heed the rhythms of our bodies. If you are a morning person, have you ever tried to finish an important report late at night to meet a deadline? Remember how hard it was to stay awake and focused? If you are a night owl, can you recall how difficult it can be to try to effectively plan your day at the crack of dawn? Pay attention to your body rhythms. Schedule difficult, challenging tasks for the times when you are most alert and energetic. If you are a morning person, do the difficult, energy consuming tasks early in the day. If you are a night person, save the challenging projects for the evening. Save the easy, routine tasks for times when your energy is at low ebb, which is mid-afternoon for many people.

Failing to Recharge Your Batteries

Effective individuals work hard, play hard and know when to relax. Rest and relaxation are essential to keeping your energy level up so you can be productive. Working until you burn out will only slow you down and limit your effectiveness. Take short breaks to refresh and revitalize, particularly if you notice your concentration faltering. Sometimes engaging in a **power nap**, shutting your eyes for five to ten minutes and reclining in your chair, is all you need to perk up. Or take a five minute walk around your workplace and step outside for some fresh air. Likewise, all work and no play is a sure way to maximize stress. Make time for relaxing activities and fun. Don't be afraid to occasionally take a day off to recharge and revitalize yourself. We refer to this as a "mental health day," taking a day off so as to prevent yourself from getting sick while increasing your energy for work.

Feeling that You Are Responsible for Everything

Is your motto, "If you want it done right, then do it yourself?" If so, you may often find yourself bogged down by insignificant tasks that you could easily delegate. Delegating tasks to others at work or at home is an investment that could really pay large dividends of time later on. What if others don't do those tasks perfectly or as well as you can? If there are no major consequences, then don't sweat it. Give them feedback to help them improve and put your focus on the important aspects of your own work. Remember, *perfection for the sake of perfection is a total waste of time.*

If you are in a situation where you have no one to whom you can reasonably delegate any of your tasks, consider that effective individuals can say "No" to low priority items or requests from others which distract from completing work that is really important. Remember that spreading yourself too thin detracts from your effectiveness.

Getting Stuck Waiting

One of the most notorious wastes of time is getting stuck waiting. Whether waiting at the doctor's office, a checkout line, or stuck in traffic, these common, insidious little delays add up. They rob you of time that could be better spent accomplishing something or better enjoyed in a relaxing or pleasurable pursuit. Have you ever wished to find an extra hour in your day? Using waiting time constructively or finding ways to reduce it can help you find that magical "25th hour" in your day.

Sometimes it is possible to reduce or eliminate waiting time. For example, you could call ahead to your physician's office before a scheduled appointment to check whether the doctor is on time, or, as is usually the case, behind schedule and then adjust the time you leave accordingly. Or you could choose to purchase groceries when the supermarket is not crowded.

Waiting may be a fact of life but wasting time while stuck waiting is not. If you anticipate that you will need to wait, come prepared. Small chunks of time often offer great opportunities to complete quick, routine tasks. For example, while waiting at the dentist's office, use that fifteen or twenty minutes to pay bills, read your mail, send that text or answer that phone call. If you are at work and are waiting on someone else, switch to other tasks, rather than watching the clock in frustration. When waiting at the offices of others, bring portable work with you that you could do while waiting. Laptops and cellular phones are the perfect tools for this situation.

Many people who habitually come prepared to make constructive use of waiting time often end up appreciating those extra minutes, that extra hour or two. One of the authors found ways to utilize waiting time at her daughter's monthly orthodontist visits. Every month she would come prepared and use this time to balance her checkbook, and catch up on reading. She came to look forward to those quiet times to catch up. Remember, found time is like found money. The time you save in one venue will free you to spend more time enjoying yourself, or to earn your living.

URGENCY VS. IMPORTANCE IN TIME MANAGEMENT

At the beginning of this chapter we made a point to distinguish between managing your time and managing yourself in time. Time is our most precious commodity and none of us really knows how much we have. Yet we do know it is a limited amount. How we spend out time should take into account what we truly want. As Covey, Merrill, and Merrill describe in *First Things First* (1994) you need to ask, "Am I doing the right things?" before "Am I doing things right?"

Covey approaches time management from a whole different perspective than traditional systems. He recommends that you organize your schedule around priorities rather than prioritize your schedule. After the first step of composing your personal mission statement, you can use that as your guide in determining not only your current priorities, but in deciding what is really important to your life and the level of importance. Covey recommends that you divide your work tasks and projects into four categories (or quadrants) as illustrated next:

Quadrant I Urgent and Important	Quadrant II Non-Urgent but Important
Crises	Proactive activities
Pressing problems	Long-range planning
Projects with deadlines	Networking
Some meetings	Relationship building
Some preparations	Prevention/Maintenance

Quadrant III Urgent but Not Important	Quadrant IV Neither Urgent nor Important
Interruptions	Busywork, trivia
Some phone calls	Some phone calls
Some meetings	Some mail/junk mail
Some reports/some mail	Pleasant activities
Many pressing matters	

The two aspects that define any activity are its urgency and its importance. Things which are urgent, such as a ringing phone, demand to be attended to immediately, or at least very soon. Urgent matters are often popular or important to others, but they may or may not be important for you. Covey further recommends that you define importance based on how closely an activity is tied to your goals and desired results, as well as to your personal mission statement in life. Urgent activities call for a quick reaction. Tasks that are important, but not urgent, typically require more initiative and proactivity. If you have not defined your goals and therefore are unclear as to what is important to you, it is very easy to be swallowed up by urgency. That is why it is so important to develop your mission statement and attempt to live by it.

Quadrant I tasks, both urgent and important, typically take the form of crises or problems which require immediate attention. Although we all have some Q I activities in our work lives, many people are consumed with Q I work and are beset with problems all day long. While the demands of any quadrant could potentially be stressful, clearly it is Q I activities that contain the greatest potential for raising your stress level. It is not surprising that individuals mired in Q I activities are more prone to burnout. And the more time spent in Q I, the more it appears to expand because you are not taking the time to be proactive and prevent future problems. When overly immersed in Q I work, the tendency is to escape to the more mindless, easy Quadrant IV activities. While that might provide a temporary breather, it does little to set the stage for a meaningful decrease in Q I and its inherent stress.

When people spend a lot of time in Quadrant III activities, urgent but not important, it is usually because they assume these tasks are really important and lie in Q I. This is based on being influenced by the expectations of others, because the matter is urgent or important for them. That does not necessarily mean that it need be urgent or important for you unless it fits with your goals. Quadrant IV activities are often pleasant and offer an opportunity to take a break. Be wary of spending the majority of your time in Q III or Q IV for that leads to irresponsibility. Successful, effective people minimize time spent in Q III or Q IV, saving that for mini-breaks, because, urgent or not, they are not important.

The key to effective personal/time management is to maximize time spent on Q II activities which are important but not urgent. This involves work which is proactive and preventative such as long term planning, networking and building business relationships, establishing a business plan and your personal mission statement, preventative maintenance and preparation, along with maintaining your health and personal relationships. These are all things we want to do, and know we should do, but tend to put off because they are not deadline driven. But it is only by engaging in Q II activities that you can shrink the stressful Q I, by preventing crises and problems in the first place, thereby increasing your effectiveness. This is all about exercising the signature strength of caution and discretion by thinking ahead, deferring gratification and engaging in long term planning for your future.

Initially, the only way to spend more time on Q II activities is to subtract time from Q III and IV. Increasing your emphasis on Q II requires that you practice proactivity, that you make it a priority to attend to important tasks that relate to your life goals, even if these tasks are not deadline driven or urgent. Obviously you cannot ignore Q I, but it will begin to diminish once you increase your Q II proactivity. In order to lessen time spent in Q III and IV you have to learn to say, "No" to some activities, even if important or urgent to others, or to delegate. This may require that you strengthen your assertive skills which we will address in Chapter 10.

A ringing phone is a typical example of a Q III situation. It urgently demands that you interrupt your work to answer and respond, but often the calls are only important to the caller. The perfect example of this is telephone solicitation. This author has lost count of how many times my work has been interrupted by someone trying to sell me something they think I desperately need, be it a new long distance phone service, a new credit card, or computer supplies. These sales people are fast talking and know every trick in the book to keep you on the phone. I am amazed by how many of my colleagues patiently sit through sales pitches and then list all the reasons why they are not interested. Meanwhile, five to ten minutes was wasted. Our method for handing such calls is short and sweet. We nicely and diplomatically state, "Sorry, we don't accept telephone solicitation," and then hang up immediately without waiting for a response. Over the years we have probably saved days worth of valuable time by ducking such time wasters.

The focus here is on determining what is really important to you, on what you want to accomplish and what type of person you want to be. This helps to address the large gap that many people perceive between they way they spend their time and what is really important to them. Too often we fall into the trap of focusing on our "schedule," which can lead to perceiving other people and relationships as interruptions or barriers to efficiency. Keeping to the schedule becomes paramount rather than assessing how much of the schedule is really worth keeping. No matter how hard you try it is impossible, not to mention unwise and unfulfilling, to be efficient with people. You can be efficient with things, with writing reports, housecleaning, bookkeeping, or errands, but being in relationship with other people is not about cutting corners, delegating intimacy to others, or setting limits on conversation. If your spouse is feeling lonely and needs to spend some quality time with you, scheduling a ten minute appointment to fit him or her into your schedule isn't the way to proceed. If your child is very upset because the family pet was hit by a car, you wouldn't delegate the job of comforting her solely to your babysitter. The advantage of this system is that it focuses more on results and on your relationships.

THE GLOBAL PERSPECTIVE—The Time Is Now

The lessons gleaned from Covey's time management quadrants are especially relevant when we consider the best approach to many global problems. That is, the only way to prevent many QI crises is by focusing on QII long term planning and prevention. Are humans utilizing the resources of the planet in a way that is not sustainable? By this we mean, are we are meeting our present needs for food, water, energy, and various manufactured goods in such a way that future generations will be unable to meet their needs?

On a planetary scale, humans now exceed the earth's carrying capacity. We are drawing down natural stocks of water in Earth's aquifers, soil in Earth's agricultural lands, timber resources in Earth's forests, and fish in Earth's oceans. We are also exceeding the "capacity" of Earth's atmosphere to absorb our wastes as evidenced by ozone thinning, acid precipitation, and climate change. Slowly but surely these overdrawn natural capital accounts will come due:
Developing Ecological Consciousness by Christopher Uhl pg. 147

Most of these changes are not readily visible to the untrained or inexperienced eye. In this country we still have ready access to drinkable water and energy. But, in many places in the world hours a day are spent just gathering wood and water to survive another day. Thus, what might seem to us to be long term considerations that are important but not urgent are in reality important and urgent elsewhere. Since we are so interconnected, the crisis affecting the poorest among us really will affect all of us eventually. In Jared Diamond's (2005) book, *Collapse*, he notes that the difference between civilizations that failed and those that weathered environmental crises was the ability to realize the causes of the crisis and then take proactive action.

So, it appears that we cannot continue on as we have been or we risk everything, not necessarily for ourselves but for our children and our grandchildren. But we cannot live only in a crisis mode. Thus we are brought to a further consideration of time and values. How will we use the time we have and to what end to reduce crises with which we have to cope? While we worry about whether or not there is a viable future for humans on the planet, could it be that our preoccupation with progress and acquiring wealth and possessions has taken us away from the most important time – NOW. Might we need new priorities? However, it is our inability to stop and engage our senses in the present moment that prevents us from remembering what is most important in life. Until we can come to some agreement as human beings about what our priorities are, we cannot enact a coherent plan.

Taking time to slow down, to meditate, contemplate, and appreciate is how we can discover our personal priorities. Talking to people from other countries and cultures and cultivating an understanding of what they value is the beginning of finding a common ground and purpose. A global citizen values establishing a dialogue with others. These are all activities that are extremely important, but not necessarily urgent. However, the failure to do them will no doubt make them important and urgent activities.

There is no lack of individuals who feel that the only way humans will change their ways is when they face a severe crisis. Perhaps, they are right. What do you believe? When you take the time to be silent and fully immerse yourself in this moment, what do you want for yourself and your children?

PROCRASTINATION

Earlier in this chapter we discussed a variety of influences that contribute to mismanaging yourself in time. But this book would be incomplete if we did not address what, for many people, is one of the most notorious enemies of optimal functioning and accomplishment: **procrastination**. "Never do today what you can put off until tomorrow," is the motto of the procrastinator. We all procrastinate at least some of the time, to one degree or another. It becomes a major problem in your work, academic, or personal life when important tasks or responsibilities are left undone or are completed in a slipshod manner because inadequate time was left to complete the task properly. Gura (2008) estimated that 15 to 20 % of American adults routinely put off activities that would be better accomplished as soon as possible. Steel (2007) conducted a meta-analysis which indicated that a whopping 80 to 95% of college students, whose lifestyles often mix packed academic schedules with frat party distractions and/or part time work obligations, are plagued with procrastination issues.

Whether putting off starting a term paper until tomorrow because it creates anxiety, or delaying a simple task like cleaning up your room because it is boring, procrastination provides a convenient escape from anticipated unpleasantness. Procrastination lowers anxiety in the short run due to the relief you feel from task avoidance. But it greatly increases your stress in the long run as tasks pile up or time runs short. Meanwhile, you are sabotaging your effectiveness the longer you delay. Diane Tice and Roy Baumeister (1997) examined procrastination among college students and found that those who delayed seemed to benefit in the short run from their laissez-faire or casual attitude, but this advantage was very short-lived. These researchers found that procrastinators had higher levels of stress, poorer physical health, and lower academic achievement. When it came to the quality of specific academic assignments, procrastinators typically spent a lot less time and produced inferior work. In addition, procrastination often carries other penalties as well, in terms of finances, career advancement and in relationships. According to Gura (2008):

> Experts estimate that 40% of people have experienced a financial loss because of procrastination, in some cases severe. In 2002 Americans overpaid $473 million in taxes as a result of rushing and consequent errors. And American's dearth of retirement savings can be attributed, in part, to people putting off putting away cash...In 2006 psychologist Fuschia Sirois...reported in a study of 254 adults that procrastinators had higher stress levels and more acute health problems than did individuals who completed jobs in a timely manner. (Scientific American Mind p.28-29)

Is procrastination a problem for you? Take a moment to complete the following scale to see how you compare to other undergraduate students.

The Procrastination Scale

For each statement, use this scale to indicate whether or not this is characteristic of you.

1 = That's not me for sure   2 = That's not my tendency   3 = That's my tendency   4 = That's me for sure

—— 1. I needlessly delay finishing jobs, even when they are important.

—— 2. I postpone starting on things I don't like to do.

—— 3. When I have a deadline, I wait until the last minute.

—— 4. I delay making tough decisions.

—— 5. I keep putting off improving my work habits.

—— 6. I manage to find an excuse for not doing something.

—— 7. I put the necessary time into even boring tasks, like studying.

—— 8. I am an incurable time waster.

—— 9. I am a time waster now, and I can't seem to do anything about it.

—— 10. When something is too tough to tackle, I believe in postponing it.

—— 11. I promise myself I'll do something and then I drag my feet.

—— 12. Whenever I make a plan of action, I follow it.

—— 13. Even though I hate myself if I don't get started, it doesn't get me going.

—— 14. I always finish important jobs with time to spare.

—— 15. I get stuck in neutral even though I know how important it is to get started.

—— 16. Putting something off until tomorrow is not the way I do it.

To obtain you total score, first reverse your responses for items 7, 12, 14, and 16 (where 4 = 1, 3 = 2, 2 = 3, 1 = 4). Then add up the numbers for all 16 items. Scores range from a low of 16 to a high of 64, with higher scores reflecting a greater tendency to procrastinate. The average score for college undergraduates is approximately 40, at the midpoint of the scale. How does your score compare?

Why Do We Procrastinate?

Tice and Baumeister (1997) remind us that procrastination, like other self-defeating behaviors, is fueled by short term benefits with many long term costs. The main and most direct cause for procrastination is **low frustration tolerance** (Ellis & Knaus, 1977). You need to accept the fact that in order to receive future rewards you often need to undertake present discomfort. In essence, you need to be able to **defer gratification**. *Just so you don't underestimate the profound impact of being able to defer gratification, consider the results of this landmark study.* Researchers Walter Mischel and Phillip K. Peake (1990) offered four year olds at a preschool at Stanford University a simple choice. They could receive and eat one marshmallow at the start of class, or, if they waited until the end of class, they could get two marshmallows. A longitudinal study of these children years later, once they had graduated high school, revealed that those who opted to wait for two marshmallows were far more successful and effective in their lives, in general, than those who had grabbed for one marshmallow now. The implications of these results were discussed at length by Daniel Goleman in his 1995 book *Emotional Intelligence*, where he stated:

The emotional and social difference between the grab-the–marshmallow preschoolers and their gratification delaying peers was dramatic. Those who had resisted temptation at four were now, as adolescents, more socially competent, personally effective, self-assertive and better able to cope with the frustrations of life. They were less likely to go to pieces, freeze or regress under stress, or become rattled and disorganized when pressured; they embraced challenges and pursued them instead of giving up even in the face of difficulties; they were self-reliant and confident, trustworthy and dependable; and they took initiative and plunged into projects. And, more than a decade later, they were still able to delay gratification in pursuit of their goals (p. 81).

Thus, one of the key building blocks of effectiveness is the ability to wait for your rewards, to delay gratification. In the positive psychology literature the ability to defer gratification is referred to as **self control**. Various studies of self control, such as the marshmallow research, underscore the importance of this for academic and job success. Tangney and Baumeister (2000) found that individuals measuring high in self control were more successful, especially with college academic achievement. Indeed, underachievement in college is often tied to procrastination.

Low frustration tolerance is based on the irrational notion that present pain or discomfort is "too hard to bear." This belief that you cannot stand present pain for future gain invites and practically commands you to continue your delay tactics. This can be a very debilitating cycle. Again, everything hinges upon what you tell yourself about the "onerous task." In order to overcome a tendency to procrastinate you need to begin by learning to identify your irrational thoughts (Ellis & Knaus, 1977), and then replace them with thoughts that promote productivity. If your frustration tolerance is adequate, you will take the temporary discomfort in stride and conclude that, indeed, the task may be aversive, boring or anxiety provoking, but, "So what!" Where was it decreed that you have to like everything you do? After all, the task will not go on forever, particularly if you start now. If you tell yourself that it may be unpleasant, but so are many things that you easily survive, it will help you to persevere. If you remind yourself that there actually may be aspects to the task that will even intrigue you or benefit you, it can give you the wherewithal to get started.

For example, if you are avoiding beginning and/or completing a certain project at work or school, it is likely that you are thinking (on either a conscious or unconscious level) one or more of the following irrational and ridiculous thoughts: (1) that you will be totally miserable the whole time you are working on this task; (2) that you cannot possibly bear the torture of this duty; (3) that it is entirely unfair and sadistic for your boss or professor to foist such a terrible assignment upon you; (4) that you cannot possibly enjoy any part of this project; (5) that you are destined to fail horribly at this task; or (6) that if you rebel you will get a hero's acclaim down the road. In place of these self sabotaging statements you can choose to substitute the following: (1) that you can choose not to be miserable; (2) that you certainly won't die from working on this task so of course you can stand it (no doubt you have endured much worse); (3) your bosses goal is not to ruin your life but to make the business succeed; (4) perhaps some aspect of the work will prove reasonably interesting; (5) there is no guarantee you will fail, and it is not the end of the world if you don't succeed in everything; and (6) the one you hurt the most by delaying is yourself.

Many people believe that if they wait until they feel more like doing the avoided task, then they will be able to finally get moving. But actually, it is the reverse that is more often true and certainly more effective. That is, if you wait around for your feelings to change, you could wait forever. But if you change your behavior, your feelings will change to match your new actions. This follows the tenet *attitude change follows behavior change*. When you behave differently you will tend to feel different as emotions tend to shift to fall in line with your actions. Therefore, acting in a timely, efficient and productive manner, even when you don't feel like it, will actually create the motivation to continue working and may even, in some cases, lead to increased task enjoyment. At the least you can enjoy the fact that you have completed the task and it no longer hangs over you.

Some people delay because of a misguided belief that they work best under pressure, that they love or perhaps even need the rush of a last minute deadline to get started. Some even believe that it is only through procrastination that one can finally get enough adrenaline pumping to have a true "flow experience." If you are someone who believes that you do your best work under pressure, then we hate to burst your bubble, but there is quite a bit of evidence to the contrary. According to Lee (2005), as cited in Gura (2008), procrastination does not facilitate flow. Lee surveyed 262 students and found that procrastinators tended to have less, not more, flow experiences.

Six Steps to Overcoming Procrastination

1. The Bits and Pieces Approach

One of the best antidotes to procrastination is to break tasks or projects down into doable chunks. Are you prone to letting tasks pile up until you feel overwhelmed and/or indecisive as to where to begin or how to prioritize the task? You might feel as though you need to accomplish an entire task once you get started, and this can become an overwhelming undertaking. Giving yourself permission to do just one small piece can get you started, and provide the necessary momentum for completion of the whole project over time. By using the bits and pieces approach you can whittle down unfinished tasks and finish parts of projects, and eventually the entire project. Once you start a small part of a task and get into the swing of it, you might discover that you feel like finishing the whole thing, especially if it goes faster or smoother than you had anticipated. Or you can use your energy to switch over to another avoided task which may prove to be easier once you have built up positive momentum from the former, especially if the tasks are related.

Peter Gollwitzer (1999) encourages procrastinators to create what he terms implementation plans, which involve approaching complicated tasks by converting doable chunks into short term goals. Gollwitzer recommends using an implementation plan to get started because such a plan tells you when, where and how to start by linking a specific situation to a specific response, such as, "When situation x arises, I will perform response y." Gollwitzer and Veronica Brandstatter (1997) asked college students to identify two projects they hoped to complete during their holiday break, an easy one and a complicated one. With regard to the difficult projects, two thirds of those who formulated implementation plans had finished their projects. Almost all of those who did not make plans did not finish their projects. The presence of a plan for the easy projects was not related to task completion. Thus, such plans are especially useful for difficult or complicated tasks, especially if you tend to procrastinate. Owens and colleagues (2008), as cited in Gura (2008), demonstrated that procrastinators at Hofstra University who formed implementations plans were eight times more likely to follow through than subjects who had not formed such a plan.

2. Getting Organized

Lack of organization contributes to procrastination for when you approach your work in a disorganized fashion tasks feel more overwhelming and generally take longer to accomplish. Follow the suggestions from earlier in the chapter regarding:

a. *Things to do Lists.*

b. *Create a realistic schedule.* Smart scheduling can also thwart procrastination. Dan Ariely (2008) in his book *Predictably Irrational* recounted an instance where, when teaching at MIT he asked students in an education class to set their own deadlines for three papers due that semester. Ariely set penalties for papers turned in after the self imposed deadlines. Despite the penalties, 70% of the students chose to set their deadlines spaced out over the semester rather than clustering all the due dates at the end. In other words, they chose not to procrastinate. Those who chose to space out the deadlines performed better in the class, on average, than the students who left all their work for the end of the semester. According to Ariely, by imposing the staggered deadlines those students became better performers.

c. *Do it when you think of it.*

d. *Modify your work environment.*
Your work environment can be conducive to getting down to business or it can promote procrastination depending on how you arrange your work space. Remove as many distractions as possible from your work sphere. Take an hour to clean up your desk or work space. Throw out all unnecessary papers or paraphernalia.

e. *Block off escape routes.*
Put your cell phone on silent, close your door, turn off the TV, pull down your window shades. Arrange your work station so you have all the materials you need to get started. That way you avoid getting up, and possibly getting distracted, to get various items.

3. The Five Minute Method

You can use this technique to start a wave of positive momentum. Pick that task or project that you have been delaying starting and then agree to start and work on it for just five minutes. At the end of this time period you can stop or you can ask yourself whether you are willing to invest another five minutes. Do this as a non-demand procedure and follow your sincere inclinations. You do not have to work beyond the first interval, but if you are like most people, once you have gotten past the first five minutes you will probably find that you can easily continue, as getting started is often the hardest part. So you can work for another five minutes, and perhaps another, and before long you are working steadily. Many people find that once they get started it is far less onerous or aversive than anticipated. Once a significant amount has been done the drive for completion kicks in as you desire to get the task finished and behind you. Likewise, when you begin or complete one task it is often easier to switch over to other long post-poned activities (particularly if related to the first task), due to the build up of positive momentum.

Timothy Pychyl (2000) advises procrastinators to "just get started." He explains that the anticipation of the task typically is far worse than the actual task itself. To demonstrate this fact, he gave 45 students pagers and checked in with his subjects 40 times over the course of five days to inquire about their moods and how often they were putting off a task that had a deadline associated with it. He found that when his sub-jects actually got down to doing the task that they had been avoiding, their perceptions of the task changed significantly. Frequently they reported that they actually enjoyed working on the task.

4. Don't Wait for Inspiration

> *Genius is 1% inspiration and 99% perspiration.*
>
> Thomas Edison

People who procrastinate when faced with a creative endeavor often delay in order to wait for that moment of "inspiration" to overtake them before they begin. Instead of putting off your project, use probability theory to help you begin. When you begin a project, with or without any particular inspiration, you stand a good chance of perhaps stumbling into a streak of spontaneous brilliance and producing extremely good work. Or at the very least, you greatly increase your chances of getting some very good ideas for that task or future projects. The more you produce the greater the probability that some of it will be very good.

But what if your work or creation fails to live up to your high standards? It is per-fectly okay if some of what you turn out is not very good. Do you really think that every canvas turned out by Picasso was ready to hang in the Louvre? And do you honestly believe that Mozart never wrote a sour note, or that your favorite author doesn't have a wastebasket filled with crumpled, rejected pages? As consumers or admirers of artwork or books we see only the finished products which usually have been refined countless times. Successful artists, musicians, and writers thrive by giving themselves permission to make mistakes and produce a certain amount of garbage in the process of doing good work. Ericsson & Ward (2007) make the case that high expertise is not a function of genius, but rather it flows from the amount of time and energy spent in deliberate prac-tice. The fact of the matter is that most geniuses throughout history worked extraordi-narily hard (Dweck, 1999). In many cases genius is as much made as born. Famous geniuses such as Einstein, Darwin, and Tolstoy were not considered to be exceptional children. Even musical geniuses, while obviously gifted with talent, typically put in thousands of hours of practice while they were very young. Scientists who research cre-ativity have developed the *ten year rule*, that is, no truly great creative contributions come without at least a decade of intense effort. For example, Mozart is well known for having composed symphonies as a child, but his early works were not noteworthy or particularly original, as compared to his later compositions which were an outgrowth of all of his hard work. Along these same lines, Gladwell (2008) in his book *Outliers* insists that in order to achieve true mastery in a discipline, one has to put in *at least 10,000 hours of practice*. According to Gladwell, it takes the brain that long to assimilate all that it needs to learn in order to achieve true mastery, whatever your level of talent. If you want to achieve world class status, whether you are playing a musical instrument, training for the Olympics or any sport, playing chess, writing, or anything else, you have to put in your 10,000 hours which often ends up taking about 10 years (the ten year rule). If we refer back to the research on neuroplasticity this makes perfect sense. Your brain evolves and changes depending on how you habitually use it. Individuals who practice regularly really do change their brains in the long run!

Playing the probabilities also gives you the opportunity to hone your skills through experience from practice. If your work requires creative projects or writing, or if you are an artist, musician or writer who is not currently inspired, forcing yourself to work at the very least will improve your level of craftsmanship. So when inspiration does come you will be far better prepared to perform.

5. Reward Yourself

All human behavior is motivated by reward or by the expectation of reward in the future. A reward is anything that feels good, be it money, praise, awards, a new car, a vacation, or a back rub. Humans can often sustain unrewarded behaviors for long periods of time as long as there is some hope for reward down the line. Procrastination persists because it is reinforced by the immediate reward of relief from task avoidance. Tasks that you dread and delay may often have rewards associated with them, but typically they are in the future or you need to wade through discomfort first to get those rewards. Even though procrastination carries with it many long term punishments, including lowering your effectiveness and increasing your stress level, the short term rewards motivate you to keep delaying. To counterbalance the rewarding aspects of procrastination, it is important to find ways to make the "dreaded task" also rewarding in the short run. Peruse these suggestions for ways to reinforce yourself and see which ones appeal to you. Try them out the next time you put something off.

One way to build in rewards for getting it done is to utilize the **Premack Principle**, postulated by David Premack (1959). The principle states that if two behaviors differ in their likelihood of occurrence, the less likely behavior can be reinforced by using the more likely behavior as a reward. In layman's terms, this strategy capitalizes on the fact that any enjoyable activity can be used as a reward or incentive for working on a task you tend to put off. Here you give yourself permission to engage in rewarding activities contingent upon doing the tasks you tend to put off. For example, you could schedule a massage for yourself after finally completing that report.

6. Viewing Mistakes as Feedback

Perhaps you procrastinate for fear of making a mistake or doing something poorly. However, it is quite irrational to think that leaving yourself even less time to complete something will make you less likely to make mistakes. And where is it written that it is catastrophic or even necessarily bad to make a mistake? Mistakes are feedback, nothing more and nothing less. Both forms of feedback, correct and incorrect, are equally vital for the learning process. Without both we learn more slowly.

Research reveals a strong link between procrastination and perfectionism (Flett, Blankstein, Hewitt & Koledin, 1992). Perfectionism goes hand in hand with fear of failure. If you maintain a perfectionistic attitude you will be more prone to stall until you can do it right, or you avoid because you fear that you can never do it right. So what if you do it and part of it is wrong? Is the world going to come to an end? If you delay, that is the equivalent of doing it wrong anyhow. At least, if you go ahead and complete it, you stand a chance of getting part or all of it right. We have no quarrel with striving for excellence, but that is not the same as holding out for perfection.

You cannot achieve excellence without making mistakes along the way or risking making other errors. In short, making mistakes is an essential part of improving yourself. What is necessary is to adopt a healthy attitude about being in error. It means learning to laugh at yourself, and not take yourself so seriously all the time. Oftentimes, what endears you to others are memories of those times when you made a funny mistake. We recognize that not all mistakes are funny, but the vast majority of errors are harmless and ultimately can be humorous or neutral if reframed to the proper perspective. Think about the life stories of great men and women. Almost invariably they are stories of failures that were converted into learning experiences which then led to success. For example, were you aware that Abraham Lincoln lost eight elections, failed in business, went bankrupt and suffered a nervous breakdown before he was elected president? There was a guy who didn't let failure get in the way of his success. His numerous failures built his character and made for a fascinating life story.

ACCOMPLISHMENT

Overcoming procrastination removes a big obstacle to **accomplishment**, one of the five essential elements of flourishing. A sense of accomplishment is a necessary component of well-being. Attainment of success is often pursued by individuals for its own sake.

In our culture there is a tendency to confuse accomplishment with talent, with high IQ, or athletic ability, or artistic or musical gifts. Talent is helpful for success, but not necessary. Skill is essential for success, but skill can be developed without talent. Beyond sheer intelligence and talent, character plays a major role. If one is long on smarts or talent, but short on signature strengths denoting character, then accomplishment is much harder to realize or sustain. Most people know someone gifted with high intelligence or great talent who squandered it because of a lack of character. Studying character and signature strengths, central to positive psychology, provides a roadmap for enhancing the ability to achieve.

In the early years of psychology, character was at the forefront, however, in the twentieth century this changed to a focus on environmental variables that shape behavior. An emphasis on the environmental causes of low achievement placed minimal weight on the role of individual responsibility. Psychology centered on pathology and weakness and tended to attribute poor achievement to external factors such as parenting or poverty. Alternatively, accomplished individuals from all walks of life were given personal credit for their achievements rather than ascribing their success solely to the effects of a fortuitous environment. The end result of this, what Seligman refers to as "psychology-as-usual," was a psychology of victims where individuals are driven primarily by the effects of their past. According to Seligman (2011):

> Positive psychology's take on all this is very different from psychology-as-usual: sometimes people are indeed victims…, but often people are responsible for their actions, and their untoward choices stem from their character…This has direct

implications for how to intervene: in positive psychology the world can be bettered not only by undoing malignant circumstances (I do not remotely advocate giving up on reform) but also by identifying and shaping character, both bad and good…That we are drawn by the future rather than just driven by the past is extremely important and directly contrary to the heritage of social science and the history of psychology. It is, nevertheless, a basic and implicit premise of positive psychology (pp. 105-106).

The invaluable role of character in achievement can be expressed by the following equation:

$$\textbf{Achievement = Skill} \times \textbf{Effort}$$

Assuming that opportunities for accomplishment are kept constant, achievement can be represented as the multiplicative product of skill (defined as intelligence and/or talent) and effort. Therefore, a high level of effort can compensate for a low level of skill and vice versa, but if either is zero then achievement will be nil. That is, no matter how skilled you are in any area, if you put in no effort you will accomplish nothing. If your skill level is high, greater effort will reap even greater rewards. This applies whether we are talking about academics, sports, your job, the arts, playing computer games or chess, or any area where you care to achieve. Sustained effort, it turns out, is all about character.

The Role of Fast and Slow Thinking in Accomplishment

One component of skill often involves some form of intelligence, whether we are talking about verbal, mechanical or athletic intelligence. IQ levels and speed are highly correlated as, in general, the smarter you are, the faster your mind works. Any complex cognitive task has fast, automatic components and slower voluntary deliberations which require far more effort and mental energy. A great deal of what we call "skill" relates to how much you have on automatic, which determines how quickly you can complete the basic steps of a task. This is what Kahneman (2011) refers to as **fast thinking**. The more material you have on automatic the more you "know" about a task. What differentiates a world class surgeon, or chess player, or golfer from you is how much is on automatic. Experts in a field often appear to have great intuitions because they have so much on automatic that they appear to know certain things instantly. The more material stored on automatic, the more one readily knows about a task.

Having a lot of skill (a lot on automatic) frees up extra time. What you do with this extra time has direct implications for your level of achievement. The non-automatic features of a task typically require what Kahneman refers to as **slow thinking**. Slow thinking activates the **executive functions** of the brain which include planning, judgment, focusing and screening out distractions, recalling, using and integrating new information, organizing, and inhibiting thoughts and actions. The more time spent in slow thinking, typically the better your performance. Engaging in executive functions requires the ability to control impulsivity. Remember the results of the marshmallow study? The children who chose two marshmallows later used the executive functions of their brain to defer gratification. It is not surprising that these children were more successful later in life than their more impulsive counterparts.

Another factor in your level of skill is your rate of learning, or how quickly you can assimilate new information into your automatic processes. You can compensate for a slow learning rate by putting in more effort, which usually means spending more time. The more information you can transfer to automatic, the greater your skill level because the extra time available for the slow thinking aspects of the task allows you to refine your performance, thereby enhancing your achievement level. The best way to put information on automatic is to practice. Never underestimate the value of practice in achievement.

Ultimately, to maximize your ability to achieve you have to utilize self-discipline and exercise self-control. If you already possess these signature strengths then you are poised to achieve. This is where putting in your 10,000 hours is vital if you want to achieve mastery (Ericsson & Ward, 2007). This applies whether in your job, playing the violin, or perfecting your jump shot. It takes self-discipline and self-control to put in those 10,000 hours. Baumeister (2006, 2007) considers self-control to be by far the most important of all the virtues. If self-discipline and self-control are not your strengths, consider implementing the exercises in Chapter 4 to further develop these areas.

The Power of Grit

If you have a very high level of self-discipline, characterized by both high persistence and an extraordinary passion to complete a goal, you may display what is referred to as **GRIT**. Self- discipline underlies achievement, but grittiness often underlies extraordinary accomplishment. This level of exceptional achievement is rare. Grit is a never give up form of

---

The GRIT Scale

Respond to the following statements using the following scale.

1= Not like me at all   2 = Not much like me   3 = Somewhat like me
4 = Mostly like me   5 = Very much like me

—— 1. New ideas and projects sometimes distract me from old ones.

—— 2. Setbacks do not discourage me.

—— 3. I have been obsessed with a certain idea or project for a short time but later lost interest.

—— 4. I am a hard worker.

—— 5. I often set a goal but later choose to pursue a different one.

—— 6. I have difficulty maintaining my focus on projects that take more than a few months to complete.

—— 7. I finish whatever I begin.

—— 8. I am diligent.

____ **SCORE**

Scoring: 1. Add your score on statements 2, 4, 7 and 8.
2. Add items 1, 3, 5 and 6 and subtract that total from 24.
3. Add the two steps together and divide by 8.

Understanding your results:
Low Grit: Below 3.03 for males; below 3.13 for females
Medium Grit: Between 3.04 and 3.74 for males; between 3.26 and 3.78 for females
High Grit: Above 3.75 for males; above 3.79 for females
Superior Grit: Above 4.21 for males; above 4.25 for females

self-discipline where very high effort is the byproduct of the signature strength of extreme persistence. It follows that the more grit you display, the greater your effort (i.e. the time and energy spent on a task), and all that effort multiplies your progress towards your goal. To determine your personal level of grit, fill out the inventory on the previous page.

The Four Elements of Achievement

There are four basic elements of achievement that can be derived from our achievement equation. The first three deal with skill.

1. **Fast Thinking** – your performance affected by all that is on automatic. This is directly increased with practice which shifts information into automatic, leading to increased skill and knowledge.

2. **Slow Thinking** – the executive functions. The more time spent here allows you to refine your skills which typically leads to better outcomes.

3. **Rate of learning** – how quickly you can assimilate new information into automatic.

4. **Effort** – the time and energy spent on a task. This is determined by the level of self-control and self discipline you bring to the table.

Therefore, the simple secret to success is effort. The more time you put in, the more information goes on automatic, which frees you up to do the non-automatic aspects that enhance performance. You may not have control over how much natural ability you bring to a task, but how much effort you put in is always up to you. Making the choice to put in maximal effort involves utilizing and refining your self-control. If you expend really extraordinary effort, you can even achieve grittiness.

THE EFFECTIVE STUDENT

The fact that you are reading this book and/or taking this course indicates that you are a student, if not in school per se, than at least a student of your own life, interested in learning how to function more effectively. Whether you are a full time or a part time student, whether you are fresh from high school or returning to college after years in the workplace, it pays to master the techniques and strategies that can enable you to achieve academic success. The ability to manage your time wisely and stay on task will serve you well in this context. A comprehensive review or an in–depth exploration of the myriad ways to develop and improve your study habits is certainly beyond the scope of this text, but in the pages that follow we will offer you a sampling of tips that we have found to be the most crucial for promoting academic effectiveness. These tips fall into three broad categories: (1) improving your memory; (2) mastering a good study method; and (3) learning test taking strategies including overcoming test anxiety and developing test taking sophistication.

Improving Memory Retention

While there are many gimmicks and so-called herbal panaceas for supercharging your memory, the fact remains that you first have to learn something, and often learn it well, before you can expect to remember it. There are no magic substitutes or reliable short cuts for the memory enhancement steps outlined below, but if you follow these strategies we guarantee significant improvement in your retention skills.

1. **Pay attention.** If you are not paying adequate attention, information will never be properly encoded and thus never transferred into either your short term or long term memory. This is why popular sleep learning products rarely work, such as tapes to learn a foreign language while you sleep. It's likely you can remember a time when you went to class but were so distracted or preoccupied with other matters that you were clueless as to what was presented. Just showing up is not enough.

2. **Learn the material very well.** Contrary to popular belief, over learning aids in retention.

3. **Organize the material.** Create an organizational structure that makes sense to you. One way to do this is to rewrite your lecture notes in outline form while it is still relatively fresh in your mind, or outline a chapter in your textbook. To the extent that you can make information meaningful to you by relating it to other concepts or experiences with which you are familiar, it will be much easier to remember. This occurs because it promotes the kinds of associations which facilitate memory retrieval.

4. **Use rehearsal.** Brain pathways that ultimately establish long-term memories are created through the repetition of the material you are attempting to learn. Review of material works best within ninety minutes of its initial presentation. Quite literally, new connections beginning to sprout from neurons in your brain begin to retract if not stimulated within this short time period. (Medina, 2008). The more you rehearse information you are learning, the stronger your ability to retrieve and recall it. But this does not mean that you should just reread the same material over and over again, rather, what is more effective is to paraphrase the information by putting it in your own words, or even better, attempting to explain it to another person by making a connection to an event in your own life. This is known as **elaborative rehearsal** which has been shown to really facilitate memory (Gardiner & colleagues, 1994).

5. **Minimize rote memorization.** The rote method, where you attempt to just memorize information without any organization, has only limited utility. As stated above, we tend to remember that which is meaningful to us, so rote memorization is only helpful if and when you create a meaningful structure and attempt to commit that to memory.

6. **Write it down.** Taking notes or writing about material you are attempting to learn, particularly if you paraphrase, is a powerful tool for transferring information into long term memory. This is also important for remembering day to day, practical information as discussed earlier in this chapter. That is why Things to Do lists, reminder lists, and appointment calendars are so helpful. Among researchers in the field of memory enhancement, these are the most frequently used memory aids.

7. **Use memory aids when appropriate.** These techniques, called **mnemonics**, are very helpful, particularly for remembering strings or lists of information. These systems work by making material more meaningful by adding a structure, such as making it into a song or rhyme, or linking it with other entrenched memories like the letters of the alphabet.

8. **Reduce interference and distractions.** One of the biggest factors causing you to forget is the role of interference. Competing information, both related and unrelated, that you have learned before and after you study, can interfere with memory retrieval. When new learning interferes with previous learning, this is termed **retroactive interference**. When old learning inhibits retention of new material, this is called **proactive interference**. Smart timing of studying can minimize interference factors. For example, studying just prior to going to sleep helps to prevent interference. Also, be careful not to study similar topics within the same study interval. Confusion between topics can lead to retroactive and/or proactive interference. By the same token, limit distractions while studying, such as a TV or radio in the background, because this can also create interference and disrupt later recall. Save watching TV or listening to music for your study breaks, or for a reward for staying on task for a specified work period. There can be some individual variability, however, as some people concentrate better with some background noise or music.

9. **Sleep on it.** As mentioned above, going to sleep immediately after studying minimizes interference with new learning because you are limiting your mental activity after studying. There is also evidence that sleep allows for the consolidation of newly learned material.

10. **Distribute learning sessions.** Avoid cramming by spreading your study periods over spaced time intervals. Data indicates that two or three shorter study periods interspersed with breaks are usually more effective than one long, unbroken, exhausting study session. When studying more than one subject, be sure to take breaks between subjects so as to reduce the potential for interference effects. To further inhibit interference, make sure you engage in activities unrelated to your studying during your breaks. Kick back and have some fun! But if you must study several subjects in one day, try to vary the topics as much as possible, again to decrease the potential for interference.

11. **Exercise.** Research appears to indicate that physical exercise facilitates memory in humans as well as animals (Samorajski, Delaney, Durham, Ordy, Johnson & Dunlop, 1988). The reasons for this are still unclear, but researchers believe that increased levels of oxygen and brain nutrients stimulated by exercise are responsible for the boost in memory acuity.

12. **Test yourself.** Periodically obtain self feedback about what you have and have not retained by testing yourself. There are numerous ways to do this including end of chapter questions, practice exams, listing the

important points you have learned from memory, and crosschecking this with your notes. Keep in mind that, just because you felt that you understood the material presented in class or in your textbook, this does not guarantee that you will remember it the next day without practicing the steps outlined above.

13. **Be aware of the influence of learning contexts.** It helps with information retrieval if you can learn the material in a situation similar to the one requiring recall of that same information. This applies to the physical environment in which you are learning such as the room, the seating arrangement, or the lighting, as well as to your emotional state. In other words, if you study in the library, and it is very similar to your classroom, then it is easier to remember. And did you know that interference can be reduced just by studying two different subjects in two different rooms (Higbee, 1988)?

An Effective Study Method – The SQ3R

In the introduction to this book we mentioned a particular study strategy that we recommend for approaching this textbook. Actually, we advocate that you use this method for studying in general. To reiterate, many educators laud a study system known by the acronym of the **SQ3R** (Robinson, 1970). If you use this technique for studying any textbook or course, you will find that it will greatly enhance your understanding and retention of course material. The SQ3R method consists of the following:

- ❧ **Survey:** Before beginning the book thoroughly survey the Table of Contents to get the big picture of what is covered. Then before reading each chapter, look over the chapter headings, tables and graphs to get an overview of the information covered in that particular section.

- ❧ **Question:** Before reading each chapter in full, briefly skim it and jot down any questions that occur to you about the material.

- ❧ **Read:** Carefully read the chapter and find answers to the questions that you previously asked while skimming the chapter.

- ❧ **Recite:** Paraphrase what you have learned. To reiterate, putting material into your own words greatly enhances your ability to understand and retain information. One helpful hint for doing this is to explain the material to yourself as if you were attempting to explain it to a friend or younger sibling.

- ❧ **Review:** After each chapter, go over the material carefully including answering the end of chapter questions and making sure you know the definitions to all key terms.

The Art of Taking Tests

In your role as a student you are inevitably faced with the onerous task of taking tests, often multiple exams in each course you take. Unlike in high school, in college your test scores may determine most, if not all, of your grade in many classes. One of the most frequent student complaints centers around an inability to do well on tests despite adequate preparation. Meanwhile, other students breeze through tests, getting high grades with minimal preparation. Is this just a function of the *survival of the smartest*? No, not at all. Psychologists have long recognized that certain students possess a set of skills, along with an emotional equilibrium, that contributes to passing and doing well on tests. Of course, adequate preparation lays the solid foundation, but test taking skills can confer an added edge. These test taking skills fall into two main categories.

Mastering Test Anxiety

Recall from Chapter 5 when we talked about the Yerkes-Dodson law, the fact that you are more likely to perform well when you are moderately aroused. In test taking terms this means that having some anxiety before an exam is actually a good thing, because it heightens your mental alertness and acuity. But very high anxiety levels can interfere with performance, particularly on difficult tasks such as a hard or confusing exam (for many people this means math!). Have your ever failed or done poorly on a test for which you thought that you were well prepared? Have you ever been so anxious about a test that you totally blanked out, unable to think straight or recall information you knew well just hours before? If you suspect that test anxiety is a problem for you, fill out the following brief self test to check this out.

Measuring Test Anxiety

Read the following statements and rate how they apply to you, using the following scale.

0 = Never   1= Sometimes   2 = Often   3 = Always

_____1. I do not feel that I study properly for tests.

_____2. I typically begin to feel nervous several days before a test.

_____3. My nervousness increases on the day of the test.

_____4. I believe that I will do poorly on tests.

_____5. If I do not know an answer, I begin to panic.

_____6. I get confused when taking rests.

_____7. Even if I have prepared adequately, I feel unsure of my answers.

_____8. I forget information that I have studied.

_____9. While I'm taking a test, I tell myself that I do not know the answers.

_____ **Your Score**

Interpretation:
A score of 12 or higher indicates you suffer from test anxiety. The higher your score beyond 12, the more debilitating your test anxiety will be. If all or even most of these statements frequently apply to you, pay particular attention to and follow the guidelines in the next section.

If your test anxiety level is high, there are a variety of techniques that can enable you to reduce your anxiety prior to an during test taking. *Remember, the goal here is not to be completely cool, calm and collected, but to get your anxiety down to that moderate, manageable level which will enhance your performance.*

Practice Active Relaxation – To help yourself unwind, do Progressive Muscle Relaxation just prior to your exam. You needn't even go through the whole sequence if you are pressed for time or in a setting not conducive to the technique. Just focus on tensing and relaxing the muscles in your shoulders, neck and head. Engage in diaphragmatic breathing at least six to ten times prior to the test and use it during the test if you need to calm yourself. Review the guidelines for progressive muscle relaxation and breathing for relaxation.

Use Cognitive Restructuring – Following the instructions for cognitive restructuring, identify your irrational thoughts and fears regarding the test. Challenge your assumptions about failure and humiliation. Substitute rational, reassuring messages reminding yourself of past test taking successes, and about how well prepared you will be (based on heeding the study tips in the last few pages, of course!).

Visualize Success – Using the teachings on visualization as your guide, first vividly imagine yourself in a relaxing scene. Pick a scene that you typically associate with calmness and tranquility, and put yourself there in your mind's eye. Once you are feeling mellow, then fantasize that you are about to start the test. Imagine yourself remaining tranquil, reading each exam question thoroughly and calmly, recognizing that you do know the right answer and then envisaging yourself getting fully absorbed with putting down your answers. Allow yourself to recall previous times of test taking success. Clearly remember those scenes and that sense of flowing with the exam. Visualizations of this type will boost your self confidence and help you to relax during the test. Remember that being able to vividly imagine a realistic scene makes it far more likely that you can realize that goal.

Testwiseness

Developing **testwiseness**, which is also called test sophistication, involves learning strategies for guessing that can help increase the likelihood of picking the right answer, particularly on multiple choice exams. Many studies have demonstrated that these methods can be learned, and that utilizing them improves test performance (McClain, 1987). McClain's work also revealed that high test scorers as a rule carefully read and consider each test question and answer alternative, and that A students often try to come up with the correct answer prior to reading the answer alternatives. But being testwise is much more than just using tricks to improve guesswork. It involves:

- ❀ Using your time during exams wisely
- ❀ Mastering strategies to minimize your errors
- ❀ Applying deductive reasoning by proceeding from the general to the specific
- ❀ Recognizing clues inherent in the tests which point to the right answers

We must stress, however, that *learning these strategies is not a substitute for studying.* Don't fool yourself into thinking you can go into a test totally unprepared, armed only with this system, and walk out with a good grade. These strategies can enhance your performance, to elevate a C performance to a B, or a B to an A, but no amount of cleverness in test taking can replace studying and learning the subject matter.

Testwiseness involves recognizing that many multiple choice tests have built in flaws within the questions that can help you determine or deduce the right answer, or at the very least, help you eliminate certain alternatives. The common flaws are as follows:

1. Information in earlier or later questions can reveal the right answer. If you are stumped, skip a question for the time being because information that turns up in later questions may hold the key or clues to the correct answer.

2. Alternatives that are highly implausible or improbable are likely to be incorrect and should be rejected. Options that contain flippant or overly judgmental words or phrases often fall into this category.

3. If two answers are equivalent or basically the same then neither can be correct, and both can be eliminated. On the flip side, if two answers are contradictory, then one is likely to be the correct option.

4. Correct answers are likely to be more detailed, longer and specific. When in doubt, pick the most detailed option.

5. Beware of all-inclusive words. Incorrect answers are far more likely to include words such as always, never, every time, everyone, etc.

6. Look for the greatest similarity in terminology between the question and the answers. The answer most similar to the question is more likely to be correct.

7. Be aware of grammatical inconsistencies between questions and answers like changes in verb tense, or singular to plural nouns. Exclude answers which contain such inconsistencies, and pick the options which match grammatically.

8. When questions have answer alternatives that include dates or numbers that are ordered, avoid picking the first or the last. The correct answer is usually somewhere in the middle rather than at the extremes.

9. If you have no idea as to the right answer, and there are no hidden clues anywhere in the question, select option C. For some reason, exam writers seem to slightly favor the third position (option C) for the correct answer.

10. Don't be afraid to change your answer. A myth has been perpetrated that your first guess has the greatest chance of being right. This is not necessarily the case. Several studies have demonstrated that regarding answer changes during tests, wrong to right changes outnumber right to wrong changes (Benjamin, Cavell & Shallenberger, 1987).

Conclusion

Ultimately, managing yourself wisely for accomplishment is about making choices for your life. No one is born a wizard at managing themselves. Competent individuals recognize that a fundamental aspect of effectiveness involves being well organized, focused on important goals, productive, and punctual. But accomplishing this often does not come naturally; it requires some effort and choice. To achieve this end you need not be perfect. It is not the end of the world if you occasionally waste your time; sometimes you need to just kick back and do nothing. And you are not an abject failure if you are not the epitome of organization at every moment in time. Effective individuals are adept at balancing, at knowing when to be organized, productive, and efficient, and when to rest and have fun. There are other areas of life where effective people are faced with important choices, most notably in the area of relationships. The next few chapters focus on how to facilitate satisfying interpersonal relationships.

POSITIVE PSYCHOLOGY SELF-EXERCISES:

1. Pick two or three of the myriad suggestions for managing yourself in time that appeal the most to you, or are the most relevant for your particular situation. Make a commitment to experiment with using them for a two week period. Pay careful attention to the effects in your life.

2. If you have never experimented with using the SQ3R study method, try using it to prepare for next upcoming exam and evaluate whether it was useful for you.

KEY TERMS

Pareto Principle (80/20 Rule)	Retroactive Interference	Fast Thinking
Premack Principle	Proactive Interference	Slow Thinking
Procrastination	SQ3R	Grit
Low Frustration Toleration	Defer Gratification	Information Overload
Power Nap	Test Anxiety	Elaborative Rehearsal
Self Control	Mnemonics	Testwiseness
Accomplishment		

CHAPTER 8 QUESTIONS

True or False Questions (T or F)

1. _____ Effectiveness is only about being efficient.

2. _____ Effective individuals focus on getting trivial busywork finished first in order to have time to focus on important tasks.

3. ____ Tasks which other people think are important should always be designated as your high priority items.

4. ____ Making Things To Do Lists is a total waste of time.

5. ____ Effective people tend to be disorganized because that contributes to their creativity.

6. ____ Breaking a large project into doable chunks or steps is an excellent strategy to avoid feeling overwhelmed.

7. ____ Effective people spread their focus and do multiple important tasks simultaneously.

8. ____ Effective individuals always strive for perfection.

9. ____ It helps to schedule tasks to correspond to your personal body rhythms.

10. ____ Unfortunately, it is impossible to make productive use of time you spend waiting.

11. ____ Effective people spend most of their time dealing with tasks that are urgent but not important.

12. ____ Attitude change follows behavior change.

13. ____ Memory enhancement strategies work well even if you are not paying attention.

14. ____ Long, unbroken study sessions are superior for learning and retention over study periods interspersed with short breaks.

15. ____ Sleeping after studying helps consolidate the material you have reviewed.

16. ____ Paraphrasing your study notes only contributes to interference with memory.

17. ____ In order to do well on a test you need to be completely calm and relaxed.

18. ____ On multiple choice tests, correct answers tend to be longer, more detailed and specific.

Short-Answer Questions

1. Covey recommends ordering your work tasks based on _____ and _____.
2. Setting a limit on _____ facilitates decision-making.
3. In order to maximize time spent in Q II activities you must be _____.
4. The main cause of procrastination is _____.
5. The executive functions of the brain are activated when you engage in _____.
6. _____ combines high persistence with extraordinary effort and passion for an objective.
7. When new learning interferes with old learning this is referred to as _____.
8. _____ refers to approaching test questions in a way that facilitates picking the correct answer.

Essay Questions

1. Define the 80/20 rule.
2. Describe two common time wasters and how to counteract them.
3. What is a power nap?
4. What kinds of irrational beliefs contribute to procrastination?
5. Describe the Five Minute Method for combating procrastination.
6. Which of the six techniques described for overcoming procrastination would you use if you found yourself delaying unnecessarily on something?
7. What signature strengths contribute to accomplishment and why?
8. Describe the five steps of the SQ3R method.
9. What are some methods you can use to decrease debilitating test anxiety?
10. Explain the role of interference factors in disrupting retention of learned material.
11. Why does organizing study material make it easier to learn and remember?

SECTION TWO

Interpersonal Effectiveness

Developing Your Emotional Intelligence

Building Effective Communication Skills

Establishing Positive Relationships

9

Developing Your
Emotional Intelligence

This textbook has spent a lot of time talking about effectiveness and optimal functioning. But what do we really mean by this? To define it as success in school, or in a career, or in terms of income level, is of course, far too narrow a definition to be meaningful. In general, effectiveness refers to competency in skills for living in your personal life, in your relationships, and in your chosen occupation, hence the overall organization of this book to address those three broad areas. This book has been designed to foster the development of building blocks for optimal functioning. Acquisition of various skills build in a cumulative fashion which will become evident as you read further.

THE CONCEPT OF EMOTIONAL INTELLIGENCE

In his groundbreaking 1995 book, *Emotional Intelligence*, psychologist Daniel Goleman summarizes a body of theory and research emphasizing the fundamental role of **emotional intelligence** in effectiveness and life success. Goleman reminds us that high intelligence (as measured by IQ tests, SAT tests, G.P.A.'s. etc.) is a very poor predictor of who will succeed and/or be effective in life. In fact, Goleman refers to the **EQ**, or the emotional quotient as the counterpart to the IQ. So the good news here is that you don't need to be a rocket scientist to be an effective human being. But why is it that, among individuals with relatively equal potential in terms of levels of intelligence, education and opportunity, only certain ones excel while others flounder? For example, a longitudinal study (Valliant, 1977) was conducted with a sample of Harvard graduates from the 1940's, following them over several decades of life. Back in the 1940's there was much greater variability in admission testing scores for Harvard enrollees than exists today. Those with the highest SAT scores actually tended to be less successful than their lower scoring counterparts with regard to career success, income and even more importantly, in their interpersonal lives, as measured by marital satisfaction and quality of social life. In a similar vein, an ongoing study of valedictorians and salutatorians graduating from high schools in Illinois in 1981, as reported in the Chicago Tribune on May 29th 1992, revealed that while this group continued to achieve academically in college, they did not necessarily excel later on in their careers. Ten years after high school graduation, only 25% of this group had risen to the higher levels of their chosen professions. Another study (Felsman & Valliant, 1987), conducted with hundreds of boys who grew up in a slum in Massachusetts, many of whom had low IQ's, found that IQ level was not a good predictor of employment stability. The researchers concluded that other factors such as frustration tolerance, ability to control emotions, and to get along well with others were far more important.

Goleman concludes that IQ contributes at most about 20% to the factors leading to success in life. The other 80% is due to other factors. Goleman makes the convincing case that many of these other characteristics comprise that set of attitudes, skills and behaviors that we have come to know as emotional intelligence. So what exactly is this "emotional intelligence?" It includes such skills as being able to motivate yourself and persevere in the face of frustration, to delay gratification, to control your emotions and impulses, that is, think before you act, to empathize with others and to think positively. Psychologists are discovering that EQ is just as important, if not more powerful than IQ in contributing to your effectiveness. And while IQ is a relatively stable attribute, your EQ can be modified and improved far more readily.

Gardner (1983) was one of the first to attack the notion of an overall IQ, preferring to break intelligence into a wide spectrum of intellectual abilities. Initially he posited seven types of intelligence, with the first two representing the traditional academically based abilities of verbal and mathematical aptitude. Along with this he described spatial intelligence (relating to artistic abilities), kinesthetic intelligence (related to athletic ability), musical intelligence, and two levels of emotional intelligence characterized by leadership skills and people skills. Later Gardner subdivided emotional intelligence into four components: (1) leadership skills; (2) the ability to make friends and nurture relationships; (3) the ability to resolve conflicts and (4) emotional perceptiveness. He emphasized the role of what he termed intrapersonal intelligence, that is, knowing and understanding yourself and your emotional reactions, and interpersonal intelligence, the ability to read and understand other people along with how to work cooperatively with them. Goleman takes this one step further and divides emotional intelligence into five domains. Notice the similarity between these and what you have learned so far in this text. The five domains are as follows:

1. **Self Awareness**—the ability to know your own emotions. This involves being able to adopt the witnessing stance so as to master self understanding and insight into your own needs and feelings. Knowing and understanding your feelings gives you more information for wise decision making.

2. **Managing your emotions**—the ability to master stress, control anger, overcome depression and anxiety all contribute to skills in being resilient so as to bounce back from life's inevitable setbacks. The lessons gleaned from Chapters 1 through 6 are relevant here, along with the section on managing anger in the later part of this chapter.

3. **Self-motivation**—the ability to persevere, to delay gratification and wait for your rewards (i.e. remember the marshmallow study!), and to stay focused and on task is essential in most life endeavors, particularly those that involve long term goals. Recall how to manage yourself in time, in particular the section on overcoming procrastination is very applicable here.

4. **Perceptiveness**—the ability to perceive and correctly identify the emotions of others along with skill at recognizing the impact of your behavior on others. The cornerstone of this is the ability to empathize with others, to literally be able to put yourself in the shoes of another person. This chapter and the next will help you acquire and sharpen these important skills.

5. **Handling relationships**—skill in relating to others and managing their emotions. It involves listening skills, conversational skills, being able to resolve conflicts, and knowing how to be appropriately assertive. It also subsumes the ability to establish rapport with others along with leadership skills. The next few chapters will develop and hone your abilities in these areas.

Take a moment to complete the following **Multifactor Emotional Intelligence Scale** (Salovey, Mayer and Carusok 2002) to get a rough estimate of your own EQ level. When the researchers used this scale in studies they found that higher EQ levels were linked to…

- Higher levels of prosocial behavior and lower aggression levels in both college and high school students
- Lower substance abuse in adolescents
- More effective leadership skills in the workplace
- More effective performance in handling consumer complaints in the workplace
- Greater levels of optimism
- Lower levels of depression
- Lower levels of impulsiveness
- Higher first year academic achievement (but unrelated to SAT or ACT scores, reiterating the findings mentioned earlier in this section).

Measure Your EQ: The MultiFactor Emotional Intelligence Scale

Indicate the extent to which each item applies to you using the following scale

**1 = strongly disagree   2 = disagree   3 = neither agree nor disagree
4 = agree   5 = strongly agree**

1. _____ I know when to speak about my personal problems to others.
2. _____ When I am faced with obstacles, I remember times I faced similar obstacles and overcame them.
3. _____ I expect that I will do well on most things I try.
4. _____ Other people find it easy to confide in me.
5. _____ I find it hard to understand the nonverbal messages of other people.
6. _____ Some of the major events of my life have led me to reevaluate what is important and not important.
7. _____ When my mood changes, I see new possibilities.
8. _____ Emotions are some of the things that make my life worth living.
9. _____ I am aware of my emotions as I experience them.
10. _____ I expect good things to happen.
11 _____ I like to share my emotions with others.
12. _____ When I experience a positive emotion, I know how to make it last.
13. _____ I arrange events others enjoy.
14. _____ I seek out activities that make me happy.
15. _____ I am aware of the nonverbal messages I send to others.
16. _____ I present myself in a way that makes a good impression on others.
17. _____ When I am in a positive mood, solving problems is easy for me.
18. _____ By looking at their facial expressions, I recognize the emotions people are experiencing.
19. _____ I know why my emotions change.
20. _____ When I am in a positive mood, I am able to come up with new ideas.
21. _____ I have control over my emotions.
22. _____ I easily recognize my emotions as I experience them.
23. _____ I motivate myself by imagining a good outcome to tasks I take on.
24. _____ I compliment others when they have done something well.
25. _____ I am aware of the nonverbal messages other people send.
26. _____ When another person tells me about an important event in his or her life, I almost feel as though I have experienced this event myself.
27. _____ When I feel a change in emotions, I tend to come up with new ideas.
28. _____ When I am faced with a challenge, I give up because I believe I will fail.
29. _____ I know what other people are feeling just by looking at them.
30. _____ I help other people feel better when they are down.
31. _____ I use good moods to help myself keep trying in the face of obstacles.
32. _____ I can tell how people are feeling by listening to the tone of their voice.
33. _____ It is difficult for me to understand why people feel the way they do.

To compute your total EQ score, first reverse the numbers that you have placed in response to items 5, 28, and 33 (1= 5, 2 = 4, 3 = 3, 4 = 2, 5 = 1), and then total the numbers in front of all 33 items. Total scores range from 33 to 165 with higher scores suggesting greater EQ. The mean score for males is 125 and 131 for females as reported by the developers of this scale, therefore scores above the mean are indicative of above average emotional intelligence.

EFFECTIVENESS IN RELATIONSHIPS

When you were a child, you were dependent on your parents for all your basic needs. You needed them to feed you, look after your safety, educate you, and generally make sure that you survived. You even needed them to wipe your behind! As you grew and matured you became increasingly less dependent on others for meeting your basic needs, but you still remained dependent financially and emotionally. The United States has traditionally been described as a highly individualistic society where independence is highly valued. If you are like most Americans, your goal is to become independent. Indeed, independence has been glorified by our culture and by the media. History books pay homage to the rugged individualists who helped tame and expand our country from coast to coast. These were individuals who depended primarily on themselves and the land for their survival. Popular culture lionizes heroes who personify the qualities of independence and courage. The current drive to own a car (no pun intended) is partly an outgrowth of this need for independence, the ability to rely on yourself to get where you want to go.

From Independence to Interdependence

In the previous chapters we have explored what we believe to be the essential elements of personal effectiveness. If you practice these and incorporate them into your life you will find yourself becoming a truly independent person, someone who recognizes that his life is his own responsibility, who sets a direction for his life and then can make things happen. But truly effective people realize that independence, while certainly a worthy goal, is not the end of the road. You see, we really are not islands onto ourselves. Personal effectiveness is not enough. To be genuinely effective, you have to learn to become interdependent. **Interdependence** is the relationship that ensues when two or more independent individuals decide to come together to achieve a common goal. They recognize that by working together they can achieve much more than the mere sum of their individual accomplishments. This has been referred to in the literature as **synergy**. Healthy marriages are characterized by interdependence, resulting from two spouses working as a team to satisfy mutual interests, such as paying the bills, raising the children, or cleaning the house. In fact, interdependent relationships, whether in a marriage, a business partnership, or a friendship are typified by mutual respect and a workable division of labor.

Unfortunately, many individuals in our society go from being dependent to being **co-dependent**. Co-dependent individuals depend on each other because deep inside they feel they could not survive on their own. Rather than give support to each other's growth, they seek to create situations which assure them that they will not be left alone. That is, they seek to make the other person dependent on them, just as they are dependent on the other person. The classic example is that of an alcoholic husband and his co-dependent wife. Although she professes that she wants her husband to stop drinking, she dutifully buys his six packs so that he won't be angry at her. While co-dependency can masquerade as interdependence, the difference lies in that true interdependence can only be achieved after you have successfully become independent. Figure 9.1 visually represents the continuum from dependence to interdependence with co-dependence as an offshoot which bypasses independence.

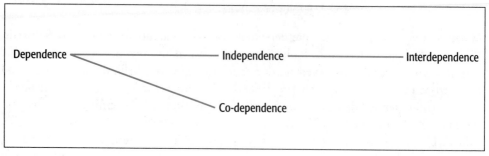

Figure 9.1

While we are saying that the road to interdependence, that is, interpersonal effectiveness, goes through independence, we are not implying that you must be perfectly independent. Becoming independent and interdependent is an ongoing, life-long process. This is not a static goal that you achieve, but rather one which you continually move towards.

THE WIN-WIN FRAME

Just as personal effectiveness required adopting a frame of proactivity, interpersonal effectiveness begins by embracing the paradigm of win-win. To be interdependent, and therefore interpersonally effective, you must set out looking for **win-win outcomes**. According to Adler and Towne (1993), when you approach an interaction within the framework of win-win...

> the goal is to find a solution that satisfies the needs of everyone involved. Not only do the parties avoid trying to win at the other's expense, but they also believe that by working together it is possible to find a solution that goes beyond a mere compromise and allows everyone to reach their goals. (p. 395)

This might be obvious, but we are here to tell you that it is easier said than done. We often introduce this concept to our students by engaging in a simple demonstration. We ask for two volunteers to come up in front of the class and arm wrestle with each other. The rules are that each time one participant pins the other, he receives a dollar as a reward. We tell them that they have one minute to get as many pins as possible. What would you do if you were one of those students? What typically happens is that the two struggle against one another, trying with all their might to pin the other whom they perceive as their opponent. As a result, very few pins are recorded and very little money is earned. If they approached the task with a win-win outlook, they would quickly realize that the way to maximize earnings is to offer no resistance, and merely take turns quickly pinning one another. With this frame of mind they could conceivably pin each other as often as once per second and each walk away with a bulging wallet.

Win-Lose or Lose-Win Outcomes

The model that has been ingrained in almost all of us is one of competition, not cooperation, leading to **win-lose outcomes** where (hopefully) you win and they lose, or

lose-win outcomes where you lose and the other person wins. Think about it. Sports are based on win-lose. Card games and board games are also based on win-lose. Similarly our educational system is based on a win-lose paradigm where students are compared to each other, with some coming out on top with A's and B's, and others winding up on the bottom with D's and F's. Admissions to most universities, and access to scholarships and grants are dependent on how you stack up against your fellow students on various measures. So it is not surprising that we hang a frame of win-lose when approaching most situations, even when such a frame does not yield the most effective results. We often fail to realize that other frameworks even exist.

If you are playing tennis, or chess, basketball, or any other competitive event, we recommend that you still put your focus on beating your opponent. After all, it would get really boring to shoot hoops if you would you let each other score without playing defense. However, we strongly recommend extreme caution in trying to win in the arena of interpersonal relationships, whether at home or at work. If someone asked you who was winning at your marriage or at your relationship, we hope you would recognize the absurdity of this question. Yet most often, spouses with troubled marriages enter marital counseling with the hope that the psychotherapist will choose their side and explain to their partner how wrong they are. You see, they are hoping the psychologist will declare them the winner and their partner the loser. Perhaps this helps to explain why over fifty percent of marriages end up in divorce. It is explained rather early on in the process of marital therapy, that in interdependent relationships if you are both not winning, you both end up losing in the long run.

Lose-Lose Outcomes

A **lose-lose** outlook is one which assumes that none of the participants can get what they want and neither side is satisfied with the outcome. It's hard to imagine how anyone could deliberately go for a lose-lose outcome, yet this is a fairly common way of failing to resolve conflict. Since both parties have their focus solely on winning, they fail to realize that as a result of their struggle they often both end up losers. Perfect examples of this on the global scene are the many wars which have been waged throughout history. On an interpersonal level most of us have witnessed battles of pride where both parties dig in their heels and end up losing in order to save face.

Other Possible Outcomes

Covey, who teaches us to "Think Win-Win" in his popular *Seven Habits* book (1991), also lists two other possible outcomes. One alternative is to go for **Win** without concern for whether the other party loses or wins. Here the outcome for the other party is irrelevant. You don't necessarily want to defeat the other person, your only concern is whether your needs get met. Another possibility is what Covey refers to as **Win-Win or No Deal**. Here the parties agree that if they cannot find a solution that is mutually beneficial then there is no deal. The parties walk away agreeing to disagree. This is more common in the context of a business deal where parties negotiate and discover that a mutually beneficial arrangement is not possible so they agree not to enter into the deal. This is a far better outcome than if the parties entered into a business relationship, deal, or contract which later turned out poorly, and led to disillusionment and conflict.

Win-Win Outcomes

Good relationships embody the ability to compromise, to find ways that allow each party to get some of what they need. Great relationships embody the ability to synergize. That is, they find ways for both parties to collaborate and create means that allow for the needs of each to be met. In other words, they find a way for everyone to win. As Covey has said, "this requires courage and consideration." Courage helps us stand up for what we need. Consideration allows us to honor the fact that others feel their needs as deeply as we feel ours. Consider this story for a moment...

> Two young girls are fighting over a single remaining orange. Both simply insist that they need it. In a win-lose relationship one of the children will end up with the orange, and one will end up with nothing but bad feelings and a desire to win the next time. In a good relationship they will cut the orange in half and share it. They will compromise and this is better than one of them losing. Neither, however, is completely satisfied. In a great relationship they speak to one another about why they want the orange. As it turns out, one of them needs the peel for a recipe and the other simply wants some orange juice. Both can have everything they want because they had the courage to speak up for themselves and the consideration to listen.

It is also important to note that the value of win-win solutions is deeply ingrained in our evolutionary history and brain structure. All primates seem to have an inherent negative reaction to what they perceive as unfair treatment. When capuchin monkeys are subjected to witnessing another monkey get a treat while they get none, their interest in continuing to interact with the researchers plummets (Brosnan and de Waal, 2003). Humans are no different. When subjected to unfair conditions while playing a game, an area of the brain, the anterior insula, increases in activation. This part of the brain also reacts when we taste something disgusting and the more active it is the less we are interested in cooperation. We seem to have a deep attraction to fairness and win-win solutions that probably can be traced to how vital cooperation was and is to our survival (Sanfey & colleagues, 2003).

Barriers to Win-Win

It is obvious that win-win resolutions to conflict are superior to win-lose and lose-lose solutions. Why is it then that win-win outcomes are rare? There are three basic obstacles to win-win solutions with the first being that often people are oblivious to the possibility of a win-win solution. As mentioned beforehand in the arm wrestling example, we are all socialized to be competitive and to mistakenly define winning as defeating our opponent.

A bigger barrier that prevents many people from seeking win-win solutions is anger or resentment. Disagreements and conflicts are often emotional affairs where people get so caught up in their emotions, in their need to be right, to win, or come out on top, that they reflexively resort to a combative approach without stopping to consider other alternatives. The latter part of this chapter deals with handling anger. Learning to work through negative emotions constructively will help put you in the frame of mind necessary to think clearly and be open to win-win possibilities.

Lastly, win-win outcomes are unusual because they require the cooperation of the other person as well. No matter how creative and open you are to generating a win-win outcome, it can be difficult to do so if the other person's primary agenda is to defeat you. In this case the challenge is to persuade the other to see how a spirit of cooperation is in his or her best interests as well as yours.

THE GLOBAL PERSPECTIVE—Reducing the Gap—A Global Win-Win

At the Seattle Special Olympics, nine contestants, all physically or mentally disabled, assembled at the starting line for the 100-yard dash. At the gun, they all started out, not exactly in a dash, but with a relish to run the race to the finish and win. All, that is, except one little boy who stumbled on the asphalt, tumbled over a couple of times, and began to cry. The other eight heard the boy's agonizing lament and despite their desire to cross the finish line first, slowed down and looked back. Then, to the surprise of most of the spectators, they all turned around and returned. Every one of them rushed to lend aid to their competitor. One girl with Down's syndrome bent down and kissed him and said, "This will make it better." Then all nine linked arms and walked together to the finish line. Not a soul in the stadium remained sitting as the sound of awe and appreciation erupted. The cheering and clapping went on for several minutes. Why did the crowd react with such emotion? Because these young people that we call "retarded" were showing their deep understanding of the reality of life. What matters in this life is more than winning for us. What matters in this life is helping others win, even if it means slowing down and changing our course.

In Chapter 2, you learned that the disparity between the haves and the have-nots has grown to a staggering 73 to 1 ratio. In fact, a more accurate description of the economic reality of the world today would be to divide it into the haves, have-nots, and have-lots. Truth be told, the poverty rate on our planet remains untamed. A recent United Nations report revealed that about 40 percent of the world's people struggle to survive on less than two dollars a day! That means 2.5 billion people in a world housing about 6 billion people must make due with less than what we typically pay daily for watching cable television. At the 2005 United Nations general meeting, Sri Lankan President Chandrika Kumaratunga said "it is unconscionable" to let 6 million children die from malnutrition before their fifth birthdays and to have more than 50 percent of Africa's people suffer from diseases caused by contaminated drinking water. At the same meeting of world leaders, Peruvian President Alejandro Toledo warned, "poverty and exclusion conspire against peace, security, and democracy."

"I am what I am because of what we all are," an old South African proverb wisely reminds us. As you learned in this chapter, the paradigm of interpersonal effectiveness is "win-win." As global citizens, we must extend this paradigm beyond our family, community, or nation, to include our whole human family. What would win-win look like on a global scale? From an economic perspective, most experts agree that it would mean reducing the gap between the have-lots and have-nots. Thomas P. M. Barnett (2003) in his book, *The Pentagon's New Map – War and Peace in the Twenty-First Century*, argues that to ensure domestic security the new paradigm for defense of the United States must include bridging the divide between what he describes as the Functional Core nations and the Non-Integrating Gap nations - namely, the Caribbean Rim, Africa, the Balkans, The Caucasus, Central Asia, the Middle East, Southwest Asia, and much of Southeast Asia.

Yet for this to truly be win-win, the bridge between the Core and the Gap must not be built at the expense of the environment, for to do so would be to enter into a win-lose with our children and grandchildren. The world's snowcaps are changing drastically. Greenhouse gases are increasing. Our rainforests are being depleted. The River of Grass, our Everglades, is drying up. We cannot develop the Gap without regard to dwindling resources and increasing pollution. Instead, we must practice what the World Commission on Environment and Development described as **Sustainable Development**. Sustainable Development is development that meets the needs of the present without compromising the ability of future generations to meet their own needs (World Commission on Environment and Development, 1987, p.43). Sustainable Development makes sense not just environmentally, but economically as well. As a prime example, consider the country of Haiti, where a shortsighted vision led to the depletion of their forests and natural resources and a population that is mired in poverty and squalor. We cannot afford to indulge in what has been called the "fallacy of the commons." Countries cannot make use of our shared resources, our "commons," such as our oceans, our energy sources, our very air, as if they were unending. As global citizens we must be good stewards of our planet.

Mental Sets Essential for Win-Win

Effective individuals operate from a model of looking for win-win solutions to disagreements or conflicts, whenever possible. As stated before, not all situations lend themselves to win-win outcomes, but in the arena of interpersonal relationships, most conflicts can be approached from a standpoint of cooperation. There are three mental sets that you will need to incorporate into your way of thinking that are prerequisites to generating win-win options and win-win solutions.

Making Deposits into the Emotional Bank Account

In order for win-win to be possible, both parties need to trust one another. But how do you build trust? Covey (1991) coined the concept of an **emotional bank account** which we hold with each other just by virtue of being in a relationship. We continually make withdrawals from and deposits into this bank account. The amount of trust experienced in a relationship is directly proportional to the balance in this account. Consider a romantic relationship. When you first meet the person, you make numerous deposits into the emotional bank account. You are attentive, complementary, you listen because you really want to get to know the other person. You call them often, spend time with them, and maybe exchange gifts. Perhaps you might even put the object of your desire up on a pedestal. But as so often happens after the novelty wears off, you begin to take the other person for granted. You stop making as many deliberate deposits. There is a tendency to assume that the balance will stay static. After all, you have made many deposits. You forget that you make withdrawals just because you have different needs or because you may, at times, act in an insensitive fashion. As time passes, all the little withdrawals add up, and you no longer have funds in the account. That is when the relationship gets into trouble.

Our ongoing relationships, like marriage, parenthood, or business partnerships, require frequent, ongoing deposits. Old deposits evaporate if you don't replenish them. If you run into an old friend that you haven't seen for years, it is often possible to pick-up right where you left off because your earlier deposits are still there and there have been no withdrawals. But with people that you interact with regularly, more frequent investment is necessary. Remember, you are likely oblivious to some of your withdrawals. In fact, recent research in positive psychology indicates that for relationships to thrive, a ratio of at least 3 to 1 positive to negative interactions must exist (Gottman, 1994). Covey recommends six types of deposits that help build the fund in your emotional bank account with another:

- **Understand the Individual**—In order to make deposits, you must first know what the other considers a deposit. You can only do this by learning to really listen to learn about a person's needs or interests. Remember that what may be a deposit for you, may be meaningless, or even a withdrawal for someone else.

- **Attend to the Little Things**—Oftentimes it is the little things that count the most. Small insensitive things that you do or forget to do, add up to be large withdrawals. On the other hand, those small niceties or favors that you do for another are often the purest proof that you care. In fact, frequent small deposits typically lead to larger balances than the occasional huge deposit. In relationships, the little things are the big things.

- ❧ **Keep Your Commitments**—Remember the power of your word. Keeping your promises constitutes a major deposit and is an essential element of trust. Breaking your promises, particularly if this happens regularly, constitutes a major withdrawal.

- ❧ **Clarify Your Expectations**—You can create many problems and potential withdrawals by assuming that your expectations are self-evident and understood by the other person. *Keep in mind, other people are not mind readers.* It is a major deposit to make your expectations explicit and clear right from the beginning.

- ❧ **Show Personal Integrity**—Integrity embodies many things, all of which are essential for trust to develop. Integrity is more than just being honest or keeping your word. It is also about being loyal and fair. One of the best ways you can show that you are loyal and fair is by acting this way towards those who are *not* present. If you are two-faced and criticize or gossip about others behind their back, those present can't help but wonder if you will do the same to them.

- ❧ **Apologize Sincerely When You Make a Withdrawal**—Those with integrity admit when they have been wrong and apologize from the heart. It takes courage and healthy self-esteem to do this. Yet a genuine apology is a major deposit into any relationship.

Giving up Being Right

When relating to others, one of the strongest barriers to cooperation is our incredibly strong need to be right. It seems that human beings are the kind of beings who just need to be right. And this seems to be the case only with humans. Think about it, animals clearly do not display this tendency. For example, if a stray dog was used to frequenting a certain restaurant to feast on leftovers and steak bones in the garbage, and then suddenly the restaurant discontinued the practice of having easily accessible leftovers, the dog would no doubt return several times to check it out, but he would then roam elsewhere in search of a good meal. Doggy is able to forget about being right. He just switches his behavior to something else that works. Animals don't care about being right; they just want to be happy. People, on the other hand, are a different story. If a group of people was used to eating a certain favored dish in a restaurant and it was taken off the menu, they would first complain bitterly. If the restaurant did not capitulate, they then might form a committee to investigate the problem further. They might decide to picket the restaurant or call for a boycott. Perhaps they would even sue the restaurant for denying them their constitutional right to their favorite meal. But all the time they were being right they would be hungry!

Interpersonally effective individuals realize that always needing to be right does not lead to satisfying relationships. Instead they operate from the premise that they would rather be happy than right. We suggest that when involved in interpersonal struggles, you ask yourself the question: Would I rather be right or happy? You see, being happy often requires giving up the need to be right. Please understand that giving up being right does not necessarily imply you are wrong. It just means that you switch your focus from winning the argument or disagreement to accepting that there are probably valid aspects of each viewpoint. Remember the lessons from Chapter 1? There is no substitute for your willingness to experiment with different pairs of glasses and notice what happens when you do. In other words, there is no right way to see things. Of all the possible ways of looking at the world, the one most guaranteed to impede your effectiveness and create conflict is the one that insists that your way of seeing things is the right way.

Giving up trying to always be right is a really hard thing to do. Why? We all love being right. Right? We've been taught since our youngest days to do the "right thing" according to the authority figures that surround us. We are rewarded for it. We feel good about ourselves for doing it. We try to figure out what the right thing is because we want to succeed, to win. Our culture worships winning. We remember the winners and display their names prominently in our stadiums, magazines and commercials. Winners generally make a lot of money. The losers don't get the endorsements, the high praise. When you win you typically feel good about yourself. Losing often hurts. And losing can be stressful and threatening to your self esteem. The key is to remember that in the long run, in interpersonal relations, if all parties involved do not win, then you all lose.

THE GLOBAL PERSPECTIVE—The Elephant in the Room

What if what unites us is more than we realize, and what divides us is less than we fear?
Let's Talk America

There is a famous poem about six blind men in India who get into a heated argument about the nature of elephants. It seems that each of them approached the elephant at a different place and from a different angle, and each decided that he knew the true nature of the elephant. One decided it was like a wall because he had encountered the side of the animal. Another believed it was like a snake because he had grabbed the trunk. The others concluded that an elephant was really like a tree, a fan, a rope and a spear because they happened to approach from another angle. The poem concluded that they argued all night long about who was right and who was wrong. This poem is really a short hand summary of politics and competing cultures. Everyone is prone to believing that their point of view is *the truth, the right way*. We tend to seek out others who agree with us and read and listen to sources of information that assure us that we are right and the others are wrong. Via selective perception, we are more prone to notice facts or data that support our beliefs, while we ignore or are oblivious to that which may contradict our views. We don't stop there either. We often make the other evil, stupid, corrupt, sinister, unholy and/or dangerous. We assume we know what they are really like and what they really want, and therefore real communication is unnecessary. After all, we already know *the truth*.

This polarized way of thinking is dangerous. It has conflict built into it and ignores some obvious facts of our existence on Earth. Fact one: No one knows or can even speak to the full depth of the mystery of our existence. Fact two: We all come from the same beginnings, and all aspects of life on this planet are interconnected and interdependent. Fact three: We don't perceive the absolute truth but instead view the world through frames that we have assimilated through immersion in our families and culture.

Here is the bottom line. We must move beyond seeing one another in rigid categories. Labeling each other as liberal/conservative, pro choice/pro life, right/left, infidel/faithful, American/anti-American, and then pretending to listen to one another when we have really already decided what the other is about and wants will not solve the problems that we face. We must communicate especially with those we think are so different from us. The next time you are in a conflict with someone, ask yourself, "Which part of the elephant am I grabbing?" When we take the time to really look through each other's eyes, we get a clearer picture of the world on which we all must ride.

Stepping into the Shoes of the Other

But practically speaking, how do you give up the need to be right, to win in your personal relationships? When we are trying to be right, by definition we see the other as wrong in their point of view, in their way of thinking. In order to go for a win-win solution to a problem it helps to be able to step into the other person's shoes and experience the world through their eyes. To accomplish this we suggest that you use the skills of visualization and imagination that we have discussed earlier. Start the process by doing your relaxing breathing, and then begin to allow a sense of the other to form in your mind. See that person in detail. Notice the facial expressions. Pay attention to the language communicated through the body, the nonverbal communications. Hear not only the words spoken by the person, but the tone, tempo and volume of their speech. Speculate about what that individual might be feeling. As you do this, imagine that you can step into his body and look out of his eyes. Hear yourself saying the words and thinking the thoughts that person might be thinking until you can feel what he is feeling. Do this until you can feel his sense of being right. Then step back into your own body and notice if you feel any differences. Could he possibly feel as strongly as you do? Is it possible that his position has merit as well? Remember, the idea is not necessarily to give up your position and adopt his, though that might happen. The idea is to move yourself to a place where you can work towards both of you meeting your needs, where both of you can win. Allowing yourself to feel, think and experience the other person's viewpoint is a powerful way of facilitating the process of win-win.

When Not to Try for Win-Win

Given that not every situation will lend itself to a win-win outcome, despite your best intentions, how do you know beforehand whether to approach a conflict from a win-win standpoint? Adler and Towne (1993) offer some guidelines to help you tailor your approach. They recommend that you:

1. Consider giving in to the other person and accepting a lose-win outcome when...
   * you discover that you are in the wrong.
   * the issue is very important to other person and of minimal importance to you.
   * other people need to learn a valuable lesson by making a mistake.
   * the long term cost of winning outweighs the short term gains of such.

2. Consider a compromise when...
   * sufficient time does not exist to forge a win-win solution.
   * the issue is not important enough to spend time in further negotiation.
   * the other person is definitely not open to a win-win outcome.

3. Consider competing and going for a win-lose outcome when...

   ❧ the issue is very important to you, the other person is certain to take advantage of you if you approach the situation in a noncompetitive fashion, and you are really not concerned with establishing a long term relationship.

4. Consider cooperation and trying for a win-win outcome when...

   ❧ the issue is too vital to settle for a compromise.

   ❧ a long term relationship between you and the other is at stake or in jeopardy.

   ❧ the other person is willing to cooperate.

Conflict Resolution

When conflicts or disagreements erupt between friends, lovers, spouse or relatives, typically the problem is approached in an informal fashion. Ideally, all parties discuss their positions and needs, possible options and solutions are discussed, and eventually a consensus is forged. Giving up being right and a willingness to step into the shoes of the other allow you to create a climate for effective problem solving, as well as the possibility of a win-win outcome. We recommend that all parties agree to a time and place for a discussion to resolve the matter, preferably when everyone is relatively calm.

When conflict or disagreement exists between people who do not have emotional bonds with each other, the steps to effecting what has come to be called in the literature as "conflict resolution" tend to become more formalized. The rules for resolving conflicts in formalized settings such as in business, or the workplace, or in mediation situations such as a divorce are covered in Chapter 14.

EMPATHY

In the previous sections we expounded upon the importance of looking for win-win solutions for resolving conflicts. We explained that in order to do this it was often helpful, and sometimes even vital to step into the shoes of the other. It is this that enables us to have **empathy**. According to Martin Bolt (2004) in *Pursuing Human Strengths*:

> ...philosophers and psychologists have claimed that empathy is the bedrock of human morality...but compassion is more than a rule. In many respects, it is the most natural thing in the world. Most of us come hard wired for empathy. Newborns cry in response to the sound of another infant's cry. In hospital nurseries, one newborn's distress can evoke a chorus of crying. Rudimentary forms of compassion and helping-for example, offering a toy to a distraught sibling-can be observed in children before their second birthday. (pgs. 57-58)

The term empathy was first used by psychologist Edward Bradford Titchener back in 1909 in reference to the tendency of observers to project themselves inside the scene of a painting. Modern conceptions of this term refer to our ability to imagine how the world looks through the eyes of another. As we see what they see, we can also begin to feel what they feel. Our heart begins to resonate with the heart of the other and we feel the emotional impact of the other person's experience. Batson and his colleagues (2005) define empathy as "an other oriented emotional response elicited by and congruent with the perceived welfare of someone else." Empathy is closely linked to compassion, a term derived from the Latin *cum passio* which means "to suffer alongside the other."

Science has recently discovered the existence of **mirror neurons** in our brains which seem to explain, in part, our capacity for empathy and our ability to learn through observation. Mirror neurons may provide the neurological basis for the empathic response. These neurons have the ability to fire in the exact pattern that they would have to fire in order to execute the behavior that is being observed. In other words, as you watch a friend juggle, eat soup, or scratch his ear, the same areas in your brain that would juggle, eat, or scratch are also stimulated. Rizzolatti and Craighero (2004) recounted how mirror neurons were first discovered in animals. But they have now been directly observed in humans (Ramachandran, 2000). We appear to be literally hardwired to be empathic. When former President Bill Clinton said, "I feel your pain," he was not just playing politics. He was speaking to a deep truth about humanity's interconnectedness. We all have the ability and are even compelled by our biology to be empathic. To differing degrees, we all, unless we have a lack of these neurons, feel each other's pain; but we also feel all the other emotions as well. It has even been speculated that a deficiency in the network of mirror neurons may underlie some disorders such as autism, which is, in part, characterized by an inability to emotionally connect with others (Oberman and colleagues, 2006).

It has been empirically demonstrated that stepping into the shoes of the other leads to empathy. Stotland (1969) conducted a study where subjects watched a patient undergo what they were led to believe was a painful medical procedure. One group of observers was instructed to imagine how the patient felt during the painful treatment. The other group of observers was instructed to merely watch the patient's movements. Not surprisingly, the group instructed to step into the patient's shoes manifested greater psychophysiological arousal and reported stronger empathic feelings than the other group.

To get a sense of your own level of empathy fill out the following Empathy Self Assessment, designed by Mark Davis (1980).

Empathy Self-Assessment

For each item, indicate the degree to which the statement is self–descriptive using the following scale.

0	1	2	3	4
Does not Describe me well				**Describes me very well**

_____ 1. Before criticizing somebody, I try to imagine how I would feel if I were in their place.

_____ 2. If I'm sure I'm right about something, I don't waste much time listening to other people's arguments.

_____ 3. I try to understand my friends better by imagining how things look from their perspective.

_____ 4. I believe there are two sides to every question and try to look at them both.

_____ 5. I sometimes find it difficult to see things from the "other guy's" point of view.

_____ 6. I try to look at everybody's side of a disagreement before I make a decision.

_____ 7. When I'm upset with someone, I usually try to put myself in his or her shoes for a while.

_____ 8. When I see someone being taken advantage of, I feel kind of protective toward him or her.

_____ 9. When I see someone being treated unfairly, I sometimes don't feel very much pity for him or her.

_____ 10. I often have tender, concerned feelings for people less fortunate than I am.

Empathy Self-Assessment (cont.)

____11. I would describe myself as a pretty soft-hearted person.

____12. Sometimes I don't feel very sorry for other people when they are having problems.

____13. Other people's misfortunes do not usually disturb me a great deal.

____14. I am often quite touched by things that I see happen.

____Total Score

Items 1 through 14 assess one's ability to step outside the self and assume another's perspective. In scoring your responses, first reverse the number before statements 2, 5, 9, 12 and 13 (i.e. 0 = 4, 1 = 3, 2 = 2, 3 = 1, 4 = 0). Then add the numbers in front of all items to obtain a total score. Average scores are 28 to 30; higher scores indicate a greater capacity for being empathic towards others, for being able to shift your perspective.

Benefits of Empathy

If you have the ability to empathize with others, it brings with it a vast array of potential benefits to you as an individual, as well as to those in relationship with you, or who come within your sphere of influence. Since empathy enables you to have more compassion for others, you will be less likely to be totally self absorbed, which frees you to be more responsive or helpful to others. This, in turn, gives you increased opportunities to live your life with a greater sense of meaning and purpose. Batson, Ahmed, Lishner & Tsang (2005) reviewed over 25 studies and concluded that empathy clearly leads to the altruistic motivation to be helpful. Thus, when you are empathic you will be more likely to be responsive to the people in your life and they will theoretically benefit. For example, Schroeder, Penner, Dovidio, & Piliavan (1995) reported on a series of studies which demonstrated a strong relationship between scores on the Empathy Self Assessment and prosocial action, whether it involved volunteering at the Special Olympics or responding to an unexpected request for help. Unger and Thumuluri (1997) found that among 400 adults with heavy involvement in charitable organizations, all were high scorers on empathic measures.

When we see other people in distress, particularly strangers, this often makes us feel uncomfortable and we may want to try to avoid this by finding a way out of the situation. But having empathy for the affected party can lead to a response of helping rather than leaving the scene. For example, Batson and colleagues (1981) conducted a study where they had subjects watch a young woman called "Elaine" receive what appeared to be a series of painful electric shocks. They then instilled empathy in some of the subjects by informing them about how similar they were to Elaine in many ways. Elaine then told the subjects a story about a childhood accident that made her exceptionally sensitive to the pain of electric shocks. At that point the researchers gave all subjects the option of taking Elaine's place and receiving the rest of the shocks that she was due to receive. Some of the subjects were told that they could leave at that time (i.e. escape was possible), while others had to stay and watch Elaine's next shock session. Those who felt empathy for Elaine chose to take her place whether they could have escaped or not. Those without empathic concern for her were far more likely to choose to leave and avoid the discomfort of watching Elaine in pain.

The ability to empathize with others and to convert this into being helpful has been linked to happiness, as was discussed in Chapter 3. Rimland (1982) noted that people devoted primarily to making themselves happy, who we might deem as rather selfish, tend to be far less happy than those who are committed to making others happy.

The Global Perspective in Chapter 4 titled the Power of Service discussed what has come to be called the *do good, feel good effect*, referring to how psychological and physical well-being are enhanced as a result of helping others due to empathy-induced altruism. In that same section we also cited a study which indicated that compassion, empathy, and helping others appear to contribute to longevity, allowing us to speculate that perhaps it really is better to give than to receive, after all! Cialdini speculated in a *USA Today* feature (Elias, 2002) that this "helpers high" may boost the immune system and lower the output of stress hormones. If this is the case it may help account for the increased longevity of the givers. Refer to Chapter 11 for a more in depth discussion of altruism.

Blocks to Empathy

The very human tendency to make what we call "snap judgments" is one inherent stumbling block to the development of empathy. As we discussed in depth in Chapter 1, our perceptions are often automatic, based on ingrained, habitual frames of reference, and are not always accurate. Optical illusions dramatically demonstrate for us that things are not always what they seem to be. In the same way, our first impressions of people are not always right. In fact, because first impressions are often based solely on superficial bits of information and sensory data, without any real knowledge of a person's history or any sense of context of their behavior in a given situation, our initial judgments are often widely off the mark. Recognizing this helps to sensitize us to the danger of relying on snap judgments. You will continue to make snap judgments, of course. To do so is only human nature because the demands and pressures of daily life often force us to make quick assessments. But it is important to be open to new information and to be willing to revise your initial impressions. Oftentimes a prerequisite to empathy is a willingness to resist making such snap judgments.

Why is it that people often rush to judgment so quickly? Psychologist Melvin Lerner (1980) suggests that most people hold a deep seated belief that our world is a just place where people typically get what they deserve. That is, that evil is eventually punished and good is eventually recognized and rewarded; that hard work will be compensated and laziness will ultimately backfire. Furthermore, Lerner holds that people care about justice for themselves and for others and this can motivate them to help others in distress, to some extent in order to validate their worldview that this really is a just world, after all. But conversely, this can also lead people to sometimes find reasons to rationalize injustice, to naively believe that those who are treated well must therefore always be good, and those who are punished must therefore, by definition, always be bad. For example, after World War II, British solders escorted German civilians through a Nazi concentration camp to educate them about the horror. One German remarked that the victims of Nazi atrocities must have been "awful criminals" to have received such abusive treatment at the hands of the Nazi's.

One way to prevent a rush to judgment and foster empathy is to heighten awareness of the similarities between people. Individuals who helped to rescue Jews in Nazi occupied Europe often indicated that it was their perception of common human kinship—a sense of connection to people from diverse backgrounds—that motivated them to take great risks to save the lives of others, some of whom were complete strangers. Those who were rescuers focused on their similarities to others, while non-rescuers trended to focus on how they were different from others. Daloz, Keen, Keen & Parks, (1997), in cataloguing the lives of over 100 humanitarians, found that they shared in common the experience of befriending someone who they had previously thought was very different from them. This experience radically shifted their paradigm about who is and is not one of us.

Cultivating Empathy

How can you learn to become more empathic, to more easily slip your feet into the shoes of others, whether loved ones, friends, or complete strangers in need of help? How do we facilitate the development of social compassion in ourselves and in our children? Research and practice in positive psychology offers the following steps and suggestions:

1. **Practice what is termed *reflective or active listening*.** An in depth discussion of these techniques is presented in the next chapter in the section on listening skills. Learning to really listen will greatly facilitate your ability to be empathic and feel compassion for others.

2. **Utilize reframing to counteract snap judgments about people.** For example, what other factors could account for a person's attitude or behavior, other than your first assumption?

3. **Engage in *random acts of kindness*.** As we have reiterated over and over, *attitude change follows behavior change*. Acting in a compassionate manner will elicit feelings of compassion. To set the stage for this mindset, watch the movie *Play it Forward*.

4. **Pay attention to the similarities** between yourself and people from other backgrounds, nationalities, races, or religious faiths. Too often we focus on the differences; this typically promotes detachment. Empathy and compassion are cultivated by appreciating our kinship with our fellow human beings, by seeing ourselves as fellow travelers on Spaceship Earth. All of us at some point in our lives will deal with illness, with the death of a loved one, or the threat of our own death, with the break-up of a valued relationship, or a loss of prestige in some way. All of us are vulnerable to loss, emotional pain, or to suffering, and we share this in common with all our counterparts on this planet. Awareness of this lifts the walls that divide us, and allows empathy to flow.

5. **Engage in community service.** In your role as a student, involve yourself in service learning programs which will give you an opportunity to provide help or service to those in need, while cultivating your empathic side and challenging your pre-conceived notions. In your role as a private citizen, volunteer in your community. Or provide some pro bono services at your place of business, if that can be arranged.

6. **Open your heart.** Many times we find that we are touched by heart-rending or heart warming stories depicted in films, TV, books, the internet, or even in newspaper or magazine articles. Movies, in particular, often allow us to delve into the experience of another person, to see out

of their eyes and feel what they might feel; to really identify with that character. Such experiences can often lead to dramatic shifts in thinking or in our ability to understand the point of view of another person or group who previously had been alien to us. Likewise, we can be educated about the plight of people who are victimized, marginalized or oppressed.

7. **Try on the shoes of the other.** It isn't always possible to "walk a mile in another person's shoes" as a way of understanding their experience. But sometimes you will have opportunities, if only for a brief time, to assume some responsibilities of another. Doing so will help you to better understand or empathize with that person and their particular struggles in life. For example, a student confided in one of the authors that she was often irritated by her mother's frequent complaints about how much work it was to take care of the numerous, beloved family pets. The student had a hard time comprehending why this was such a big deal to her mother, because everyone in the household just adored all the pooches and pussycats. When her mom went on vacation and the task of doggy and kitty sitting (with all the feeding, cleaning and grooming that accompanied this job) fell to her, she suddenly understood what her mom was talking about. After that, when her mom complained, she commiserated with her and offered to help more with the animals rather than rolling her eyes and tuning her out as she did before.

8. **Raise your children to be helpful.** Martin Bolt (2004) offers these suggestions for raising empathic children.

   ❀ Model empathy for your children. Be an empathic parent to teach your children how to relate to others in a compassionate fashion. Establish a warm and nurturing relationship with your kids. Follow the guidelines for authoritative parenting discussed in Chapter 4.

   ❀ Express your own feelings in an appropriate way and show compassion /empathy towards others in front of your children.

   ❀ Tune into your child's emotions. Ask your kids about their feelings and teach them how to express, describe, and label what they are feeling. Doing this will help them to build their own emotional vocabularies.

   ❀ Explain the reasons for things to your children to deepen their understanding of emotional issues. This fosters emotional, as well as intellectual, insight.

   ❀ Encourage your kids to do volunteer work or community service. Many communities require students to do community service as a high school graduation requirement. If you engage in community service activities, your kids will be more likely to follow your lead.

   ❀ Teach your children to value empathy and compassion as desirable traits to possess, as valuable as honesty, or intelligence, or athletic prowess, or creativity, or any of the other talents or character strengths that we attempt to instill in our children.

THE NATURE OF ANGER

As mentioned previously, one of the biggest barriers to a win-win outlook is your anger. Anger motivates you to want to win, to defeat others whom you view as opponents or adversaries. Effective individuals have learned to cope with anger, to work it through and manage it constructively rather than destructively. This is essential to adopting a win-win framework. But how do you do this? To answer this question, you first need to understand the nature of anger.

Have you experienced times when you were quick to anger, as if your fuse had become significantly shorter? Unless you are a yogi master and have achieved perfect balance and enlightenment, of course you have. All of us have had periods when we were more irritable and less tolerant. Have you noticed that there is a direct relationship between these periods and the level of stress in your life? Undoubtedly, a very common response to stress is anger and irritability. But why? Remember, stress is your body and mind's response to perceived threat. If you consider, that for our ancestors "threat" typically took the form of attacks by animals or other tribes, then anger was an adaptive reaction which mobilized them to take defensive action. Therefore, anger had survival value because typically, for our forebears, the appropriate response was to physically fight for their lives. But in today's world physical confrontations are no longer useful in most situations. Yet, you are left with this holdover emotional baggage of anger. Verbal expression of this anger, particularly if not modulated, is certainly not much more adaptive, either in your personal life or in your work environment.

Violent, unrestrained expression of anger has been at the forefront of national headlines and at the core of many of the most serious problems faced by today's society. The 9/11 attacks on the World Trade Center and the Pentagon focused everyone's attention on the profoundly tragic consequences of violence, while highlighting the need to understand the underpinnings of anger and to develop methods to prevent future bloodshed. Meanwhile, we all struggle to understand why adolescents and college students have engaged in school slaughters over the last few years, and why adults bring firearms to work and shoot co-workers and innocent bystanders. Has our world become more violent, or is it the ever present media coverage which gives this impression? By the same token, is domestic abuse, of both children and spouses, on the rise? Or is domestic violence just more routinely reported and publicized? Either way it is clear that violence is a serious problem with which we must all contend, so as to avoid either becoming a victim or a perpetrator of such. Learning to co-exist is of paramount importance, and the prevention of violence first involves learning to handle anger.

But anger is a basic human emotion that we all experience from time to time, sometimes to the level where we can lose control of our behavior and/or resort to aggression. According to a study by Averill (1983), most people report being angry, at least to the point of getting mildly annoyed, several times weekly. Researcher Diane Tice (1993) found that anger is the emotion that people have the hardest time controlling. Making it even harder is the fact that for some, anger can be energizing or even exhilarating at times, leading to something akin to a rage addiction in certain individuals.

Many theorists have attempted to explain the root causes of anger and aggression. An early theory, the **frustration-aggression hypothesis** (Dollard, Miller, Doob, Mowrer, & Sears, 1939) focused on the role of frustration as a result of being blocked from reaching a goal as a primary factor. Most psychologists readily acknowledge the role of frustration in the development of anger, but agree that other variables are equally important. Freud postulated that humans have an inborn aggressive drive which contributes to personality formation. Furthermore, Freud recommended pursuing an emotional release, which he called **catharsis**, by venting or acting out anger. This, as you will read more about later, is not advisable. There is also some evidence that testosterone levels are related to levels of aggression, but this is based on correlational studies so causation cannot be conclusively inferred.

Currently there is a greater emphasis on the role of learning histories as the primary factor in the etiology of anger. That is, an individual will exhibit anger and hostile behaviors to the extent that anger has been rewarded and modeled (Cantor, 1999). Likewise, to the extent that anger was punished and inhibition of such was modeled, an individual will display the ability to control anger and restrain aggression. Research indicates that merely observing violence can trigger heightened aggression (Bandura, 1965; Lemish, 1998). As a result, there is a lot of controversy today over the role of observational learning or modeling on the expression of anger, particularly in children. Consequently, the debate rages over the extent to which children should be allowed to watch violent movies or TV programs. There is research which suggests that long term viewing of violent TV shows can cause children, particularly boys, to behave more aggressively. One study found that eight year old boys who preferred violent programs were more aggressive at that age, as well as at age eighteen, as compared to a group of boys who preferred less violent entertainment (Lefkowitz, Eron, Walder, & Huesmann, 1977). But because this was correlational research, again it is unclear whether this was a cause or an effect. That is, was their preference a function of a more violent disposition, or did watching violent shows create more violent kids? Bushman & Phillips (2001) concluded that, "the fact that TV violence does not noticeably increase violence in everybody does not mean that TV does not increase violence in anybody." That is, highly aggressive individuals are likely to be drawn to violent media, and after watching violent movies their aggression levels will be heightened (Black & Bevan, 1992).

When is anger likely to lead to violence? There is no foolproof method for predicting who will become aggressive and when violence will occur, but there are factors (Capaldi & Patterson, 1996) which are associated with the likelihood that an individual will engage in violent expression of anger including:

- a previous history of violent behavior
- having been physically abused in childhood
- having witnessed violence in the home as a child
- a history of harming animals as a child
- heavy exposure to violent TV programs or video games
- absence of remorse over hurting others
- family history of mental illness or violence
- brain damage (which can interfere with the brain's inhibitory mechanisms)

Road Rage

One common situation where many individuals experience anger, often to irrational levels, is while they are driving. Does this ever happen to you? This common phenomenon, dubbed road rage, is on the rise, reportedly increasing by 7% yearly since 1990. A leading researcher in this area, Jerry Deffenbacher (1994) surveyed 1500 college drivers and identified the following six situations likely to trigger road rage emotions and behaviors:

- hostile gestures from other drivers
- other drivers breaking traffic laws
- the presence of a police car
- another driver driving too slowly
- driver discourtesy such as being cut off or slow driving in passing lane
- traffic jams or obstructions

Everyone feels aggravation on the road sometimes, but for some individuals, driving to work every day is a never ending exercise in fury. To determine whether you have a problem with road rage, fill out the questionnaire which will compare you with other college students. High scorers are three times more likely to experience road rage than low scorers. High scorers experience road rage because they are likely to personalize the mistakes or behaviors of other drivers, to view these incidents as personal affronts.

Road Rage Scale

This test describes common, potentially anger provoking situations that occur during driving. Imagine that each of the situations described is actually happening to you while driving. Then rate the amount of anger that would be provoked in each situation using the following rating scale:

1 Not at all   **2 A little**   **3 Some**   **4 Much**   **5 Very much**

_____ 1. Someone makes an obscene gesture toward you about your driving.

_____ 2. You pass a radar speed trap.

_____ 3. Someone runs a red light or stop sign.

_____ 4. Someone honks at you about your driving.

_____ 5. Someone is weaving in and out of traffic.

_____ 6. A police officer pulls you over.

_____ 7. You are driving behind a large truck and cannot see around it.

_____ 8. A bicyclist is riding in the middle of the lane and slowing traffic.

_____ 9. Someone is slow in parking and holding up traffic.

_____10. A truck kicks up sand or gravel on the car you are riding in.

_____11. Someone speeds up when you try to pass them.

_____12. A slow vehicle on a mountain road will not pull over and let people by.

Road Rage Scale (cont.)

_____13. Someone backs right out in front of you without looking.

_____14. You are stuck in a traffic jam.

_____ **Total Score**

Interpretation: The higher your score the more likely you are easily provoked and angered while driving. Compare your level of driving anger with that of other college students on the chart below. The percentile tells the percentage of students who scored at or below your level.

Score	Percentile	Score	Percentile	Score	Percentile
21	0	41	25	52	72
26	1	42	28	54	79
30	3	43	32	56	86
32	5	45	40	57	89
35	10	47	50	59	93
38	17	49	60	60	95
40	22	50	64	64+	99

The Physiology of Anger

So what can you do about learning to control your anger and modulate your expression of it? First, it is important that you understand the physiology of anger. Goleman (1995) offers an illuminating explanation of why certain individuals sometimes "go off the deep end" and respond impulsively and explosively with anger. He refers to such outbursts as **emotional hijackings** and explains this in terms of brain circuitry as outlined in the work of LeDoux (1992). Our brains have two basic neural response systems, one governed by a brain structure called the **amygdala**, a center in our primitive brain, and the other controlled by the **prefrontal cortex**, the thinking brain or seat of higher reasoning and planning, responsible for the before mentioned executive functions. By the way, the prefrontal cortex is the last part of the brain to develop. Its axons do not fully complete the process of myelination until age 25 or later. When a myelin layer is completed, the speed at which impulses travel along the myelinated fiber is greatly enhanced. This is also the first part of the brain affected by alcohol. It is especially vulnerable to substances, like alcohol, which dampen its ability to inhibit your behavior. This is why you are more likely to lose your temper under the influence of alcohol. Emotional explosions, particularly anger, occur when the amygdala perceives what it thinks is an emergency and bypasses the prefrontal cortex. In an instant the amygdala triggers the fight/flight response before the cortex has a chance to process any information, let alone determine how to respond appropriately. And if the prefrontal cortex has not yet fully developed (i.e. myelinated), it is even less capable to exercise its restraints.

This capacity to act before you think does have survival value for it gives you the potential to react instantaneously in an emergency so as to avert danger, when taking the time to evaluate the situation might waste precious seconds and endanger your life. The problem is that, for some people, this cortical bypass occurs in many situations where it is not only unnecessary but harmful. Here the brain interprets danger not just from physical threats but also from symbolic threats to our dignity and self esteem, but the failure to activate the prefrontal cortex typically results in behaviors we later regret. This direct amygdala circuit accounts for those instances when our emotions totally overwhelm our rational minds.

The work of psychologist Dolf Zillman (1989) is also relevant here. In a series of studies Zillman demonstrated how rage reactions develop. Typically, once the fight/flight reaction is activated even mildly, the body remains in a state of heightened arousal, or edginess, for awhile. Then, if later stimuli should mobilize the amygdala and trigger an emotional hijacking, the subsequent emotional response, whether it takes the form of anger or anxiety, is of especially great intensity. This cumulative reaction helps explain why people sometimes greatly overreact to what appears to be only mild provocation.

Physiologically, anger is arousal. When you are angry the fight/flight response has been activated, preparing your body to either fight or flee. Clearly, anger helps you if you need to fight. The problem is that when we are stressed we tend to look around to see what is making us angry. That is, we tend to externalize the sources of our anger and/or stress. We assume that something out there is causing our arousal. This is true, not just with humans, but with our animal cousins as well. For example, imagine a lab rat in a box whose floor is covered with an electric grid. If that rat is alone and we shock it, the rat will jump, look for an escape route, and will manifest clear signs of arousal. If we put another lab rat in the box with our first rat, and then shock them both, the rats will attack each other (Weiss, 1971). It's as if the rats are blaming each other for the shock.

The Role of Attribution in Anger

Often, we behave just like our friends the rats. We look around for who is to blame for our uncomfortable feelings and sensations without being consciously aware of what we are doing. Yet even more problematic, paradoxically, those with whom we feel most comfortable are the most likely targets of our direct aggression. The old saying "you always hurt the ones you love" is really true. Don't get us wrong. We also get angry with people with whom we are not close or comfortable, but we are more likely to express our anger towards them indirectly. This is particularly true if they are in a position of authority over you. So instead of telling your boss how angry you feel, you might just complain to your friends at lunch. Then when you go home at the end of the day and your spouse or significant other does something even mildly annoying, you are ready to literally bite his head off.

But physiological arousal, in and of itself, does not produce your emotions. *It is how you label this arousal that determines what you feel.* This point was driven home in a classic experiment (Schacter & Singer, 1962) which changed how psychologists viewed emotions. In this study the researchers injected subjects with adrenalin, which can cause powerful arousal reactions, but told them that they were only getting a vitamin shot. The subjects were then exposed to a confederate (e.g. actor) who supposedly received the same injection, but who then behaved in either an angry or euphoric fashion. Subjects exposed to the angry confederate became angry, and those exposed to the euphoric stooge became happy. However, subjects injected with a placebo and also exposed to the same confederates did not have any strong emotional reactions. Schacter, in formulating his **Attribution theory**, concluded that emotion is much more that a physiological event. If humans are faced with physiological arousal of unknown origin, they will search their environment for an appropriate explanation or label for this arousal.

Thus, emotions are created by your evaluation of your internal and external environment. The subjects in Schacter's study attributed their arousal to either anger or elation depending on what appeared to be the case in the environment. If exposed to an angry confederate they interpreted their own arousal as anger and therefore reported being mad. In a similar vein, Berkowitz & Turner (1974) were able to elicit angry behavior from subjects merely by telling them that they were angry. In this study subjects were exposed to the mildly provoking behavior of two confederates and then given false feedback about their arousal levels. How the subjects subsequently behaved toward the actors was directly tied to the level of feedback they received—to how angry they thought they were based solely on inaccurate feedback.

This tendency to attribute the source of your uncomfortable feelings to an external agent further aggravates the problem because "putting it out there" lowers your control. If you perceive that you are not in control in a particular situation, then you are being reactive. And as we mentioned in Chapter 2, we feel we are in control when we believe we have a choice. Well, the fact is that whether or not you get angry, or stay angry is really *always* your choice. Being able to recognize this gives you control. You see, it is not the event out there that causes you to flare; it is your interpretation of the situation which ultimately leads you to be, or not to be, angry.

The fact that we have choice as to whether we feel anger, or any feeling for that matter, is the reason why two people can be faced with the same situation yet respond in ways that are completely different. For instance, imagine that you are driving in your car and someone cuts you off, almost causing an accident. The common response is to react with immediate anger and to grumble or even scream at the inconsiderate driver who dared to intrude on your sacred vehicular space. You tell yourself, or him, what an idiot he is, perhaps questioning how he ever obtained a drivers license. The incident may even become an indictment of all the drivers in your city, none of which are as skilled as you. Meanwhile you are stewing in your own juices and continuing to aggravate yourself. You are well on the way to experiencing road rage.

Can you see how the meaning you gave this situation led to your angry response? Is it possible that another meaning, that also explains the other driver's behavior, could lead to a different response? What if, instead of assuming incompetence or inconsideration on the part of the other driver, you said to yourself, "poor guy, he must have a lot on his mind. I wonder what is going wrong for him?" Undoubtedly, were you to ask yourself these questions, your response to the same event would be quite different. Once again we are reminded of Covey's motto, "the way you see the problem is the problem." Not surprisingly, the solution invariably lies in changing the way you view the situation.

Anger and the Type A Personality

But you might be sitting there saying, "Why should I change? I have a right to be angry!" The truth is, you are correct. You do have a right to be angry, but are you happy with the results? Persistent or frequent anger has serious deleterious effects on your emotional and physical well being, as well as on your ability to be effective. There is no doubt that anger and resentment damage your health. A convincing example of this comes from what we have learned about the **Type A personality**. In the 1970's cardiologists Meyer Friedman and Ray Rosenman noticed that their patients tended to share certain personality characteristics. They called this cluster of behavioral traits the "Type A personality." Type A individuals tend to be very hard driving, achievement oriented, compulsive, overly concerned with time pressure and easy to anger, as compared to

Type B individuals who are laid back, easygoing, and less concerned with time. A strong relationship was discovered between the Type A orientation and cardiac problems. But, later research revealed that the only aspect of Type A behavior that was really related to heart disease was the "hostility" component. That is, one could be hard driving and compulsive without incurring a greater risk of heart disease if hostility was not present. In one study (Barefoot, Dalhstrom, & Williams, 1983), conducted with physicians who are typically a very Type A group, 250 doctors were administered a hostility scale. Twenty five years later the mortality rate of the high hostility scorers was several times higher. This has led health psychologists to conclude that of all human emotions, hostility is the deadliest. Anger is particularly harmful to your health when it is repressed or when it is turned back onto yourself. But inappropriate expression of anger towards others is also dangerous to your physical well being as well as your interpersonal relationships. Hostility that is characterized by brooding resentment, suspicion and frequent angry outbursts is extremely damaging to your health (Smith, 1992). Take out a moment to fill out the Hostility Scale to help determine if anger and hostility are a problem for you.

The fact that anger is a risk factor for heart attacks is well documented. Anger sets off a physiological mechanism that makes your heart beat faster, your blood pressure rise, your coronary arteries constrict, and your blood get stickier. A study of more than 1,000 patients at Mount Zion Medical Center who had survived heart attacks, found those who had counseling to reduce their anger, aggression and hostility had half the rate of recurring heart attacks as those who received no such help dealing with anger (Friedman, Powell, & Thoresen, 1987).

Hostility Scale

Answer the following questions true or false.

_____ I often get annoyed at checkout cashiers or the people in front of me when I'm waiting in line at the supermarket or other stores.

_____ I usually keep an eye on the people I work or live with to make sure they're doing what they should.

_____ I often wonder how extremely fat people can have so little respect for themselves.

_____ Most people will take advantage of you if you let them.

_____ The habits of friends or family members often annoy me.

_____ When I'm stuck in traffic, I often start breathing faster and my heart pounds.

_____ When I'm annoyed with people, I always let them know about it.

_____ If someone wrongs me, I'll get even.

_____ I usually try to have the last word in an argument.

_____ At least once a week, I feel like yelling or even hitting someone.

If you answered "true" to five or more of these questions, you may qualify as excessively hostile.

Catharsis Is Not Always the Answer

There is a mistaken belief that a good way to release anger is to immediately vent it. George Bach, (1968) in his seminal book *The Intimate Enemy*, describes this as the **Vesuvius effect** when you explode just like a volcano. Often, after such a cathartic expression, you do feel better, as if a load has been lifted off your shoulders. While this might work if you are alone in your room hitting your pillow, can you imagine just letting go with your boss? It is safe to say it probably wouldn't be the most effective strategy. In addition, research indicates that such expressions tend to reinforce the anger, making you quicker to anger in the future. Diane Tice (1993) concluded that giving vent to anger typically failed to dispel it and often only intensified it. She found that it was far more effective for individuals to first cool down and then later, in a constructive, assertive fashion attempt to settle the conflict. Thus, psychologists no longer recommend the catharsis approach espoused by Freud because, in many instances, acting angrily can lead to further anger and perhaps even aggression. The situation in the Middle East between Israel and the Palestinians is the perfect example of this. Both sides justify escalating violence with their "eye for an eye, tooth for a tooth" philosophy. The bloodshed may not end until everyone left alive on both sides is both blind and in need of dentures.

Learning to Control Anger

Is anger always bad for you? Actually, the answer is no. Anger is a normal human reaction. It becomes problematic when it is chronic, persistent and unresolved. There are, in fact, instances when anger can be useful. Anger can be helpful for mobilizing your energy so that you can take appropriate action. If you were never able to get angry you might become so complacent that you would never seek to resolve issues in your life.

The task is not to always prevent anger, but to learn how to move through it efficiently and effectively. We often tell our students that "the only way out is through." You need to be aware of your anger and rather than getting mired in it, recognize it as a signal that something is amiss and must be addressed. Then you can use the energy it creates to mobilize you to take appropriate action. Many other authors and psychologists recommend various systems and methods for avoiding, controlling and redirecting anger. In his book, *The Trusting Heart: Great News about Type A Behavior*, Redford Williams (1989) lists a series of strategies for reducing your hostility level. It is likely that you will find these strategies to be familiar, combining methods outlined in previous as well as upcoming chapters, the only difference being that anger management is the focus. This list represents a good summary of ways to combat hostility.

- ❧ Become self aware. Adopt the witnessing stance and monitor the self talk which fuels your anger.
- ❧ Interrupt angry thoughts. A method called **thought stopping** is very useful here. To use this strategy, wear a rubber band on your wrist and snap it whenever you become aware of engaging in hostile, irrational self talk. The mild pain you experience from the snap should help interrupt your negative thought patterns and provide an opportunity for you to use cognitive restructuring techniques.

- Cultivate empathy by stepping into the shoes of the other.

- Learn to laugh at yourself. Don't take yourself so seriously. Pay careful attention to the upcoming section on reframing.

- Practice the active relaxation techniques you have learned. Counting to ten before you respond and/or practicing diaphragmatic breathing can help you calm yourself and prepare to respond appropriately instead of impulsively to anger.

- Improve your listening skills. The next chapter will help you in this regard.

- Take the risk to trust others.

- Practice the art of forgiving others. The final section in this chapter will assist you in your personal journey of forgiveness.

Zillman (1989) recommends two main strategies for defusing anger. The first method basically involves using cognitive restructuring and reframing techniques to challenge anger provoking thoughts, in order to facilitate a reevaluation of the original interpretation that triggered anger in the first place. However, he points out that timing is absolutely crucial in this process. The earlier in the anger sequence this occurs, the more likely it is to be useful for defusing or reducing anger. He refers to a "window of opportunity" for this to work. If anger has already escalated to the point of rage, efforts to think rationally often will not work because of what he terms a state of "cognitive incapacitation," where individuals literally cannot think straight because they are so blinded by rage. Can you ever recall a situation when you were beyond rational thinking because you were so enraged?

Zillman also advises that you pursue a "cooling off period" to defuse anger, that you allow yourself to cool down physiologically by seeking out a setting devoid of further triggers for anger. There are various ways to promote cooling off. Engaging in physical exercise such as walking, jogging, or lifting weights can be very useful because it works off the physical tension built up in fight/flight arousal, and can provide time for you to reflect on the situation and engage in rational thinking. Likewise, involvement in active relaxation techniques such as breathing exercises or progressive muscle relaxation is an excellent way to facilitate cooling off. Or it could be as simple as getting some space from another person during an argument to prevent an unproductive escalation of hostilities. In general, Zillman stresses that distraction is vital to allow for cool down. Many of these activities allow for distraction as well as direct tension reduction. Zillman further emphasizes that this cooling down period will backfire if that time is used to pursue a train of anger inducing thoughts, for in that case the anger will continue to build rather than dissipate. The power of distraction is that it can derail an angry train of thought. Diane Tice surveyed strategies people use for handling anger, and found most people do find distractions such as watching TV, movies or reading useful in interfering with angry thoughts. But interestingly, she found that common indulgences such as shopping and eating proved to be ineffective distractions as individuals tended to stew in angry thoughts while engaging in these pursuits (Tice & Baumeister, 1993).

Reframing Revisited

To quote Daniel Goleman:

> The train of angry thoughts that stokes anger is also potentially the key to one of the most powerful ways to defuse anger: undermining the convictions that are fueling the anger in the first place. The longer we ruminate about what has made us angry, the more 'good reasons' and self justifications for being angry we can invent. Brooding fuels anger's flames. But seeing things differently douses those flames. Tice found that reframing a situation more positively was one of the most potent ways to put anger to rest. (1995, p. 60)

We totally agree with Goleman's view. The most effective way of beginning to use anger rather than be used up by it, is to remember to consider the frame through which you are viewing the particular situation. Take a couple of deep diaphragmatic breaths and then shift your attention to your muscles, particularly those muscles in your shoulders, neck and jaw. Take a moment to relax these. Then assume the witness/observer stance. Look at the situation from the outside. Ask yourself, "How can I look at this differently?" Reframing is a powerful method for dealing effectively with anger. We would like to offer you a couple of reframes we have found particularly useful for working through anger.

Look for Comedy

One approach involves viewing your life as a sitcom in progress. It asks that you think of yourself as a comedy writer of your own life. In almost all situations an element of humor or absurdity can be found if you look at it from a different perspective. Seeing the humor inherent in a situation effectively defuses much of the anger. Think for a moment, if you were an objective, uninvolved bystander witnessing your situation, is there any aspect of your circumstance that could be seen as humorous? Who is your favorite stand-up comedian? If that comic was observing what was happening to you, what pithy or funny remarks would she make about you or your dilemma? You can probably remember times when you witnessed an event where a friend, colleague, or relative became angry, while you had a hard time keeping a straight face because you could see the absurdity in the situation. You can do this with yourself as well. As a matter of fact, almost any situation will seem funny when you are looking back at it after the passage of time. Realize that you have the choice to imagine that time has already passed when you are involved in your particular dramas.

The "Grand Drama" Viewpoint

Or, yet another useful reframe involves looking at your situation from a frame of reference where you view your life as an unfolding drama for the benefit and entertainment of a higher being. And why not? People who believe in a higher power may consider that their life is a gift from God, and how they live their life is their gift to God. Seligman (2002) notes the relationship between emotional equilibrium and having a spiritual dimension in your life.

A Chapter in Your Life

A related reframe is to consider that your life is a novel in progress, and what is happening to you at any moment can make for a fascinating chapter in the book that is your life. How can you write this chapter taking into account what you will ultimately learn from the experience? We find that any of these perspectives will help to get you unstuck from the anger of the moment. If none of these appeal to you, can you think of others that would serve you better? Take some time to reflect on this now.

Viewing Criticism as Feedback

One of the things that often triggers your anger is criticism. It goes without saying, that no one really likes to be criticized. But, some individuals handle criticism better than others. Why is it that some people seem to take negative feedback in stride and even appear to benefit from it, while others are overwhelmed with anger and self-doubt? Again the answer lies in the meaning attributed to the criticism. One of the main reasons is that often people tend to equate criticism with themselves rather than about their actions. Therefore, negative feedback is viewed as a statement about self worth rather than an observation about behavior. When viewed this way criticism tends to remind you of your inadequacies.

However, if you are able to adopt the reframe that it is not you but your actions that are being critiqued, it becomes easier to consider the possibility that there is validity to the complaint. You no longer need to feel as though there is something wrong with you, that you are a bad or worthless person, rather you need to focus your attention on the appropriateness, effectiveness or worthiness of a particular behavior.

You need to recognize that in any situation where you receive criticism, three possibilities exist: (1) your behavior is definitely out of line and the other person's complaint is valid; (2) your behavior is questionable but the criticism is also a reflection of biases, or difficulties on the part of the critic; or (3) your behavior is fine and it is the critic who has the problem. There is an old saying, "criticism reflects the critic," which is very applicable here. It is important to take a good look at your behavior, but how you respond will depend on which possibility you decide best fits the situation. If you decide that your behavior has been inappropriate, you must be careful not to fall into the trap of taking this as evidence that you have done something wrong and should feel bad about it. This trap is avoided by remembering to look differently at your mistakes. As previously discussed, you can decide to view mistakes as feedback—important feedback—which helps train you how to do things properly. It is when you realize that your mistakes are invaluable teachers that you will cease to repeat them.

Case Study in Anger Control: Road Rage

Sally is a high powered executive who works downtown in a major metropolitan area. She enjoys the excitement and cultural amenities of the big city, but she prefers to live in a more rural atmosphere. To accomplish this aim she purchased a home on the outskirts of the suburbs in an area that still feels like country. The price of this is that she has a very long commute, in rush hour traffic, to and from her job. On a good day it takes her 45 minutes to get to the office, and most days it takes over an hour to reach work. She hates the drive, but she is very satisfied with her job, and has no desire to move closer to work and lose the country environment she cherishes. Lately Sally has found herself frequently engulfed in road rage, getting furious at bad drivers or inconsiderate motorists who cut her off. She found herself often screaming in her car, leaning on the horn unnecessarily long, making obscene hand gestures to other motorists, and then feeling agitated throughout the drive and even after she reached her destination. She was very concerned about her feelings and her behavior. She feared that she might anger strangers with her offensive gestures, who might then attempt to retaliate in some fashion. Mostly she was upset about the holdover agitation she felt even after getting out of the car. Her blood pressure was up and she was getting frequent tension headaches during her drive home which lingered all night.

Assisting Sally to work through road rage to achieve road peace first involved helping her to recognize that she had a choice whether or not to respond with anger to difficult driving situations. Sally was encouraged to identify the underlying assumptions that were fueling her anger. She believed that she had no control in the situation; after all, she couldn't stop lousy drivers from making driving mistakes, going too slow, or cutting her off. But the thought that triggered the bulk of her anger was her assumption that, "they got away with it," while putting her in danger in the process.

Sally was able to overcome her road rage by being willing to shift her thinking. She began to acknowledge that, while she certainly had absolutely no control over the driving behavior or competency of other motorists, she always had control over how she chose to respond to any given driving situation. She then searched for a way to *reframe* the trigger assumption: bad drivers get away with it. She recognized that if a given driver was really that unskilled, then it was just a matter of time before that person was either ticketed by police or hospitalized from a traffic accident. The next time she witnessed a bad driver, she fantasized that driver got a speeding ticket later that day. She further realized that if a person wasn't an incompetent driver but just inconsiderate, then this inconsideration would catch up with him in other areas of life, particularly in interpersonal relationships. A person who always puts her needs above others rarely can sustain lasting relationships. So the next day, when a dapper businessman in a new Mercedes almost ran her off the road to cut into her lane, Sally imagined that he returned home that night and discovered that his wife had left him for being so insensitive.

Sally was amazed at how adopting these alternative perspectives, these reframes, and engaging in these reframed fantasies defused her anger. Remembering to breathe slowly from the diaphragm when the driving got tense, helped her to keep her mind open to new perspectives, rather than engaging in knee jerk reactions of rage. She also began using her time in the car more constructively. She began listening to books on tape, rather than complaining that she didn't have time to read. She also began carrying a tape recorder in the car, and periodically dictating reports that didn't get finished at work. Using her time more productively lowered her stress level, and reduced her feeling that she was wasting two hours a day in the car. The *distraction value* of these activities was such that she stopped spending time searching the landscape for bad drivers or driving errors as she had before. Within two weeks of adopting this change in perspective Sally was free of road rage.

Case Study 2: Workplace Anger

Carlos had been working at his sales job for a mid-sized manufacturing company for two years and had enjoyed phenomenal success. He had quadrupled his earnings in that time due to his high sales figures and the company's commission structure. He was the top salesman in the company. His forte was in developing new accounts and generating increased orders from existing customers. Rather than enjoy his success, Carlos became even more driven and began having inappropriate temper outbursts at work when other workers did not meet his expectations. He became enraged when other workers made minor errors which delayed the processing of orders for his customers. He would often yell at these co-workers and insult them. What upset him the most was what he perceived as the meddling behavior of the sales manager, his immediate boss. When his boss would attempt to assist him on an account to help with paperwork, Carlos took offense. He assumed that his boss was implying that he couldn't handle it by himself. Mostly he was worried about getting fired because of his temper outbursts or because he was disliked. He feared that the bosses wanted to fire him so they could hire someone else at a much lower salary level. He knew he had to deal with the situation when his boss took him aside and told him that he needed to work on his attitude. Carlos was having problems sleeping at night and relaxing on the weekends with his family because he was so caught up in anger and worry.

Carlos was encouraged to use diaphragmatic breathing, and wait ten minutes before responding to any mistakes made by co-workers or perceived slights by his superiors, so he would have time to *cool down*. Using cognitive restructuring he confronted his irrational expectation that people should always be perfect and never make mistakes. He was encouraged to identify the other assumptions that were underlying his anger. The first assumption was that he was soon to be fired despite his success. To find a reframe to combat this, he was encouraged to think of everything his company had to lose by firing him. He quickly realized that the company stood to lose a lot of money and business if he was let go, even if they did hire a lower paid replacement. He had to admit that it would be a very foolish move for his employers to fire him, even if they did find him to be a "pain in the butt." The second assumption involved his belief that his boss' efforts to help him with paperwork implied that he was not competent. When reflecting upon alternate explanations for his boss' behavior, Carlos realized that when his boss helped with paperwork it freed him up to do that which he did best. Therefore, assistance from his boss could help both Carlos and the company increase earnings.

When Carlos returned to work he practiced breathing techniques and taking a ten minute breather to walk around the office if hassles arose. Using the guidelines in Chapter 10 for practicing assertive, as opposed to aggressive behavior, he approached his co-workers diplomatically and calmly. When his boss came to assist with his paperwork, rather than resenting it and glaring at him as he had done previously, he thanked him. Within a week he and his boss were on much better terms. They had a heart to heart talk, and his boss confirmed that he wanted to pitch in so as to enable Carlos to focus solely on selling. Carlos suggested a brainstorming meeting between the sales and shipping departments to foster improved communication and problem solving to expedite timely shipment of orders. At the meeting Carlos practiced empathic listening and began to understand why his co-workers made many of the errors. This meeting was very productive, and as a result numerous suggestions were made to help fix the existing problems. Carlos acknowledged that mistakes would still occur, but he was hopeful that the frequency could be significantly reduced by implementing the ideas offered at the meeting. Lastly, Carlos kept reminding himself that he was a very valuable employee who had control over whether he was fired by how he chose to behave in the workplace. Several weeks later his bosses took him aside and praised his work and the improvement in his attitude. From the discussion it was abundantly clear to him that he was, indeed, a very valuable employee with a secure job. Within two weeks he began to enjoy going to work again. His sleep normalized and he began to relax and have fun on his weekends.

Positive Psychology Self-Exercise: Developing Your Own Plan to Defuse Anger.

Take a moment and think about a situation or a person that often triggers your anger. Notice that we did not say something or someone who makes you angry—no one can make you angry, for whether you respond with anger is always your choice. Now, take a few moments to practice diaphragmatic breathing, and consciously release the tension from your muscles to better prepare you to deal with the stress of these thoughts. If it is a situation that you are thinking about, what alternate perspective or reframe can you create to help you view things differently? Are you harboring any irrational ideas which contribute to your anger and could be challenged? Spend a few minutes pondering the situation from this new frame of reference? What happens to your anger? Do you find it diminishing or perhaps even fading entirely? If you have been thinking about a person who often triggers your anger, make your best attempt to put yourself in the shoes of that individual. What feelings or motivations might that person have that led them to behave in ways that anger you. This does not mean that you have to agree with that person or condone her behavior, the only requirement is that you spend some time viewing the world from her eyes. Do you notice that it is harder to generate anger when you understand where someone else is coming from, even if you don't agree with them? Does that person's point of view have any validity, given that person's experiences or beliefs? Now that you have likely diminished your anger by thinking differently, are there any other alternative behaviors you could adopt that might help you cope? For example, would being more assertive help you to deal better with the person or situation? If your answer is yes, pay special attention to the next chapter.

FORGIVENESS

Since anger and resentment are damaging to your health and can undermine your effectiveness with others, then clearly, the ability to forgive and let go of past hurts and disappointments is a desirable goal. Let's be clear about what forgiveness is and is not. **Forgiveness** is not necessarily forgetting what happened, thereby placing yourself again in a situation where you could be mistreated. It is certainly not about condoning behavior you find offensive or hurtful. It is the process of letting go of the energy invested in past hurts or disappointments so that you can free that energy for more productive, growth oriented activities. The decision to forgive stems from the realization that anger and resentment have a damaging effect on you. There is an old Chinese saying, "Before embarking on a mission of revenge, dig two graves." We wonder if you or anyone you know has ever said, "I don't get mad, I get even!" As cool as that statement might sound, you must realize the eventual toll such an approach will take on you.

Although forgiveness begins with a decision to do so, it is important to remember that it is a process. As such, it takes time and a willingness to go through the particular emotions involved, be it hurt, anger, or even depression. The problem develops when you get stuck in this process because of righteous indignation. Do not get caught in the trap of believing that you can only begin to forgive when an apology is offered or amends made. When and how you forgive is totally up to you, whatever the circumstances.

It is vitally important that you realize that forgiveness is a healing process that takes time, and will ebb and flow. Particularly if you have been hurt in a deep and profound way (either physically or emotionally), it is likely that your journey toward forgiveness will proceed through a series of steps that won't necessarily flow in a linear progression. You may move forward unevenly, and may even temporarily backtrack at times as you ultimately move forward. Sidney and Susan Simon (1990), in their book *Forgiveness: How to Make Peace with Your Past and Get on with Your Life*, describe six stages that provide an excellent description of the path to forgiveness. The stages are summarized as follows:

1. DENIAL

   Shortly after you have been hurt, you may find that you attempt to minimize the impact or importance of what happened to you, and suppress your feelings as part of the denying.

2. SELF-BLAME

   Your early attempts to make sense of what happened to you often involve the assumption that somehow you were to blame. If only you had done something different; perhaps if you had been less trusting, you could have avoided being hurt. Your self-esteem is often negatively affected by such self-recriminations.

3. VICTIM

   After you stop blaming yourself, you realize that you did not deserve the hurt you received, that you were, at best, treated unfairly and, at worst, victimized. But this recognition often leads to self-pity, emotional upset, misdirected anger, and other destructive emotions. While it is certainly necessary to pass through this stage, it is also vital not to become mired in it or you risk getting stuck in the victim role.

4. INDIGNATION

   To mobilize yourself out of the victim role, you will likely need to marshal a sense of righteous indignation about what happened to you, directed towards those responsible for your hurt. Anger towards those who hurt you and even the world at large may prevail, and thoughts of revenge may be prominent.

5. SURVIVOR

   As your anger begins to wane, you will recognize that although you were hurt and did not deserve such, you survived. Your painful past experience may have robbed you in many ways, but may also have bolstered your strength and coping resources. Your compassion, empathy, and sense of humor begin to return as your obsession with your emotional pain begins to subside. You begin to recognize that you did the best that you could do in a difficult situation. As a result, your self concept shifts from one of victim to survivor.

6. INTEGRATION

    In this last stage, when forgiveness has really begun to take hold, you start to acknowledge that those who hurt you may have been playing out patterns of hurt or victimization from their own lives. You realize that just as you are much more than a victim, those who hurt you are more than just perpetrators. You begin to let go of the emotional energy involved in nursing hate, anger, bitterness, grudges, and/or revenge fantasies, which frees up your energy to focus on living your life fully. You are able to put your past in perspective, without forgetting it, recognize lessons learned from your hurt, and ultimately let go of unnecessary emotional baggage.

There have been at least eight studies in the domain of Positive Psychology measuring the effects of forgiveness on the emotional health of the forgivers. In the best designed and most recent study, Thoresen and his colleagues (2001) found that forgiveness fosters lowered stress levels, less anger, increased optimism and improved health. Their results also showed that the greater the extent of forgiveness, the larger the improvements in emotional and physical well-being. The research of Michael McCullough (2001) indicates that the more you develop empathy, the more you are able to forgive. VanOyen Witvliet and her colleagues (2001) examined the physiological responses of college undergraduates as they imagined responding to their real life offenders in forgiving and unforgiving ways. The forgiving imagery emphasized developing empathy for the humanity of the offender. The results were very consistent with the Thoresen study. During forgiveness visualizations the participants experienced less stress, more positive emotions, less negative emotions, and a greater sense of personal control.

One method for freeing yourself up to forgive involves creating a forgiveness journal which puts the emphasis on the development of empathy. Robert Enright (2001), in his book *Forgiveness is a Choice*, reminds us that just about everyone has to live with a painful memory from someone who hurt us, oftentimes someone close to us, someone we trusted. He recommends that you attempt to tell the story of the person who hurt you in order to create an empathic state of mind. He provides suggested questions to address in your journal such as...

1. What was life like for the person who hurt you when that individual was growing up? Describe elements of that person's life that may have set the stage for the hurtful behavior. Be careful not to confuse forgiving with excusing.

2. At the time you were hurt, what was life like for that person?

3. Tell the story of your relationship with this person in a broader sense than the hurtful behavior or incident. What was the rest of your relationship with that person like?

4. How might that person be worse off now as a result of what was done to you?

5. Apart from how that person hurt you, what is this person like in other ways? Remember that you do not have to resume a relationship with this person even if he or she has other admirable qualities.

6. Has there been any change in your view of this person in any way as a result of this exercise?

Keeping a forgiveness journal or answering questions such as those posed above can help you develop empathy. This can allow you to move through the healing stages of forgiveness and reach the integration stage more quickly. While you need to go through the stages, you do not want to be mired in them for decades. If you find yourself stuck in the process and are in a good deal of emotional pain, consider consulting a professional therapist who can assist you in moving through your own process of healing.

Assertiveness

Some situations that anger you certainly call for some type of response beyond letting go of your anger. Many times you will need to respond to individuals who have angered you so as to rectify the situation or prevent future occurrences of whatever is provoking your hostility. This is best accomplished by dealing diplomatically and assertively with the other person or persons rather than passively avoiding conflict, and allowing your resentment to build and take a toll on you, or responding aggressively where you risk alienating others, making the situation worse and later being ashamed of yourself. A comprehensive treatment of effective and responsible assertive behavior is included in the next chapter.

KEY TERMS

Emotional Intelligence	EQ	Interdependence
Co-dependency	Synergy	Win-Win Outcomes
Win-Lose Outcomes	Lose-Lose Outcomes	Win-Win or No Deal
Emotional Bank Account	Empathy	Mirror Neurons
Frustration-Aggression Hypothesis	Catharsis	Road Rage
	Amygdala	Prefrontal Cortex
Emotional Hijacking	Type A Personality	Type B Personality
Attribution Theory	Thought Stopping	Forgiveness
Vesuvius Effect		

CHAPTER 9 QUESTIONS

True or False Questions (T or F)

1. _____ IQ is more important for success in life than EQ.

2. _____ Independence is always superior to interdependence.

3. _____ In order to be interdependent you must be co-dependent.

4. _____ Interpersonal effectiveness is characterized by going for win-lose outcomes.

5. _____ It is not always possible to get a win-win outcome.

6. _____ To be interpersonally effective you need to prove to other people that your way is the right way.

7. _____ Stepping into the shoes of the other serves as a block to empathy.

8. _____ Empathy leads to altruism which helps us to feel happier, the *do good, feel good effect*.

9. _____ Snap judgments often serve as blocks to empathy.

10. _____ Your learning history has no impact on how you express anger or how short your fuse will be.

11. _____ An emotional hijacking occurs when your prefrontal cortex is bypassed by your amygdala.

12. _____ Type A persons are typically very laid back.

13. _____ The best way to deal with anger is to have a catharsis and immediately vent.

14. _____ You always have a choice whether to be angry.

15. _____ Anger is always bad for you.

16. _____ Physical exercise can help defuse anger.

17. _____ Reframing is not useful for defusing anger.

18. _____ Never pay attention to criticism under any circumstances.

19. _____ Forgiveness is as much for you as for the other person.

20. _____ The process of forgiveness is an all or nothing experience and does not follow any particular stages.

Short-Answer Questions

1. Skill in understanding yourself and reading the emotional reactions of others is an important component in _____ _____.

2. _____ refers to the fact that individuals working together can achieve more than the sum of their individual accomplishments.

3. A person who enables or supports the problems of a significant other out of fear of angering that person is said to be _____.

4. According to Covey, in order to go for a win-win outcome you need both _____ and _____.

5. In order to really understand and appreciate another person's point of view you need to _____.

6. _____ _____ in the brain provide the neurological basis for the empathic response.

7. Emotional explosions, particularly anger, occur when the _____ perceives what it thinks is an emergency and bypasses the _____.

8. Unrestrained expression of anger has been termed the _____ effect.

9. _____ individuals tend to be very hard driving, achievement oriented, compulsive, overly concerned with time pressure and easy to anger, as compared to _____ individuals who are laid back, easygoing, and less concerned with time.

10. Cognitive restructuring techniques are more effective if used _____ in the anger sequence.

11. Forgiveness is facilitated through the development of _____.

Essay Questions

1. What are the components of emotional intelligence?

2. Describe the barriers to going for win-win outcomes.

3. What do you need to do to keep a positive balance in the emotional bank account? What behaviors lead to deposits and which to withdrawals?

4. Give an example of a situation where you would be well advised to not try for a win-win outcome.

5. What are some methods to help you cultivate a more empathic attitude towards others?

6. When is anger most likely to lead to violent behavior?

7. What is the relationship between your perception of a situation, the meanings you give to it, and anger?

8. Describe and discuss the theory you think best accounts for the development of anger or rage reactions.

9. Persistent anger and hostility have been linked to which physical problems? How does anger lead to ill health?

10. Describe the initial steps that are helpful for working through anger.

11. List some useful reframing strategies for defusing anger.

12. Describe the process for working towards forgiveness.

10

Building Effective Communication Skills

Communication can be most simply defined as the transfer of information among individuals. What are the means by which human beings communicate? Basically, we share information with each other in one of four ways: (1) speaking, (2) writing, (3) reading, and (4) listening. These are obviously not abilities which are inborn, but skills you learn and develop through experience. However, most of us have not received an equal amount of instruction in all these areas. From infancy you began the process of learning to speak, both in terms of mastering the words and the particular gestures characteristic of your language. As a young child your parents and other care givers would repeat words and sounds and encourage you to mimic them. Later in school, you likely received more formal training in how to speak appropriately. Over the years you expanded your vocabulary and learned proper grammar. In fact, most colleges currently include a speech class as one of the general educational requirements. Similarly, your education in reading may have begun even before you attended school if your parents read to you. By the time you reached your school years you were taught how to translate the symbols on the page into meaningful sounds and words. Throughout your school career you took formal classes in reading, learning to refine your skills in this area. Your training in writing also began at an early age, from first scribbling your own name, to printing simple words, until you finally mastered cursive writing sometime in elementary school. Throughout your educational career you were exposed to numerous courses in writing, often called English classes, including multiple required courses in college.

Yet how many of you have ever received formal instruction in listening? If you are like most people, the answer to this question is that you have spent virtually no time or very minimal time actively learning how to listen. You might remember your parents saying, "shut up and listen," or your teachers admonishing you to stop talking to your classmates and listen to the lecture. But listening involves so much more than just being quiet.

LISTENING VS. HEARING

It is important to realize the difference between listening and hearing. If we were able to emerge from these pages and stand before you clapping loudly, you would surely be able to hear the sound of the palms of two hands forcefully colliding against each other, unless of course you had a severely disturbed hearing apparatus. Hearing, you see, is automatic. It can occur passively. It is very possible to hear what someone says, but not really listen to it. Your auditory membranes process the sound waves, but your brain could be oblivious to the message or meanings being transmitted.

Listening, on the other hand, is much more active. It is something you consciously choose to do. It cannot occur without your effort, your attention, and your concentration. Really listening requires a proactive decision to do so, followed by internal and external behaviors aimed at maximizing the probability of receiving an accurate message. Yet despite our inadequate training in this area, a study conducted with college students found that the majority of their time, up to 53%, was spent in listening activities (Barker, Edwards, & colleagues, 1981). This same study revealed that students spent approximately 14% of their communicating time writing, 16% reading, and 17% speaking. Another study (Wolvin & Coakley, 1991) showed that employees of major Fortune 500 corporations spend about 60% of their workday listening to others. It is very ironic that the communication skill we use the most is the one for which we are least prepared.

The Epidemic of Poor Listening

Communication is very much a two way street. It does not matter how well you speak if no one is there to listen. Studies of the listening ability of thousands of subjects reveal that most people fail to listen well (Atwater, 1986). Some of this is tied to memory. Research indicates that after hearing a ten minute presentation, the average person understands and retains only about half of what was said. After two days another one-half of the information is forgotten. Thus, you can expect to remember approximately one-forth of what you heard someone say two days before.

We have even more disquieting news about how poorly most of us listen. How well do you think college students listen? Not very well according to Paul Cameron, a professor at Wayne State University (cited in Adler & Towne, 1993), who assessed the thoughts of students in his introductory psychology class at random intervals during his lecture. Much to Professor Cameron's dismay the vast majority of his students were not necessarily listening to him. He found that 20% of his students, both male and female, were enjoying erotic thoughts! Another 20% were reminiscing about something. Only 20% were actually paying attention to his lesson, and of those only 12% were really actively listening and thinking about the lecture material. The other students were busy daydreaming, yearning for lunch, worrying, or, surprisingly, thinking about religion. Now perhaps Professor Cameron was a boring lecturer, but it is much more likely that his students' sexual fantasies were just more compelling than anything taught in class.

To add to the problem, when attempting to improve communication skills, many people overlook the importance of strengthening listening ability (Chiasson and Hayes, 1993). Although most of us agree that listening is important, the overemphasis on sending skills and the under emphasis on receiving skills cause many to fail to recognize the vital nature of effective listening. This is not surprising. Our society stresses the value of speaking your mind, of being able to clearly state your position, feelings or needs. Think about it. When you picture an effective individual, don't you imagine someone who is not afraid to say what they think? Yet, as Covey (1991) observes, individuals who are interpersonally effective "seek first to understand, then to be understood." When your first emphasis is on truly comprehending and appreciating the other's paradigm or frame, you are building rapport. When people really feel understood, they are much more likely to develop trust in you. No wonder listening is a skill that is essential to making and keeping relationships. It involves making a commitment to understanding how other people feel, how they see their world, getting a sense of their particular map. It is about making the attempt to see the world through their eyes. Listening is arguably the most important deposit you can make into the emotional bank account you hold with someone. It is a compliment to others because when you truly listen it directly implies that you care about what is happening to them, that their life and experiences are important enough that you will pay attention to them. It is a way in which you can join in their world.

How well do you listen? Fill out the following questionnaire as straightforwardly as possible to assess your listening ability. This inventory lists behaviors involved in good and bad listening. Using the scale, objectively rate how you typically behave by checking the appropriate response. Don't feel bad if your score is not what you want it to be. Most people are not good listeners for reasons explained in the next section. This inventory may help you identify some listening behaviors you can begin working on to improve your listening skills.

Listening Questionnaire

1. Making eye contact with the person who is speaking.

Never	Seldom	Sometimes	Often	Always
1	2	3	4	5

2. Judging the subject as uninteresting.

Never	Seldom	Sometimes	Often	Always
1	2	3	4	5

3. Letting personal feeling and thoughts of prejudice interfere.

Never	Seldom	Sometimes	Often	Always
1	2	3	4	5

4. Keeping an open mind about the speaker's ideas.

Never	Seldom	Sometimes	Often	Always
1	2	3	4	5

5. Faking attention.

Never	Seldom	Sometimes	Often	Always
1	2	3	4	5

Listening Questionnaire (cont.)

6. Listening just for the facts.

Never	Seldom	Sometimes	Often	Always
1	2	3	4	5

7. Resisting internal and external distractions.

Never	Seldom	Sometimes	Often	Always
1	2	3	4	5

8. Judging the speakers delivery.

Never	Seldom	Sometimes	Often	Always
1	2	3	4	5

9. Using your thinking speed to reflect on the message.

Never	Seldom	Sometimes	Often	Always
1	2	3	4	5

10. Interrupting the speaker or jumping to conclusions.

Never	Seldom	Sometimes	Often	Always
1	2	3	4	5

Add up your score from all ten questions. Your score can be interpreted as follows:

25 or below: You need to work on your listening skills. Your difficulties in this area may be causing problems in your interpersonal relationships. Pay careful attention to the guidelines in this chapter and you can improve significantly in this area.

26 to 35: You are an average listener. With more attention to the fundamentals explained in this chapter, you should be able to improve your skills dramatically.

36 to 45: You are a good listener. Follow the suggestions outlined in this chapter and you can become an excellent listener.

46 to 50: You are an excellent listener. Keep it up. This chapter should help you refine your skills even further.

BARRIERS TO EFFECTIVE LISTENING

As mentioned earlier, true listening is more than just being quiet while someone else is talking. In *Messages: The Communication Skills Book* the authors (McKay, Davis, & Fanning, 1983) point out that true listening requires that you have at least one of the four following intentions in mind.

1. To understand someone.

2. To enjoy someone.

3. To learn something.

4. To give help or solace.

So real listening does not occur unless you have at least one of the intentions stated above, and you act on it by paying attention and concentrating on what the other person is saying. According to McKay and his colleagues, pseudo or fake listening occurs when some other intention is being satisfied. There are many reasons why you may fail to listen. You may not feel like putting in the effort required to listen. Or you may avoid listening because someone is saying something you don't want to hear or that threatens you, so you manage to block it out, either by not hearing it in the first place (selective attention) or forgetting it immediately (repression). Or you may listen poorly because you never learned how to listen effectively. Unfortunately, people sometimes pretend to listen when they really are not, and many pseudolisteners are adept at appearing attentive. This may even be true for you, for each of us is guilty of occasionally acting as if we are listening when our attention is elsewhere. We may look at the person, nod our head in encouragement as if we agree with what the person is saying, even murmur "Mm-hmm" occasionally, but if asked to repeat or explain what was being said, we would be at a total loss.

When you are pseudo-listening you are pretending to listen; your intention is not to listen but to meet some other need, such as:

1. Pretending to listen to make people think you're interested in them so you will be liked.

2. Being vigilant to watch for signs of potential rejection.

3. Listening for one specific bit of information and ignoring everything else.

4. Focusing on your rebuttal or the next thing you want to say rather than on anything the person is saying.

5. Pretending to listen so someone will listen to you.

6. Listening to uncover someone's vulnerabilities or weakness in order to gain an advantage.

7. Looking only for the weak points in the speaker's line of reasoning so you can get ammunition for your counterattack, or to try to win an argument.

8. Checking only to see how the speaker is reacting to make sure you produce the desired effect.

9. Half-listening because that is what a nice person would do in the same situation.

10. Feigning listening because you don't know how to get away without hurting someone's feelings or offending them. Or your willingness to listen falters because the other person is boring you, and you are unsure how to make a graceful exit. In other words, you pretend to listen to be polite.

Even when it is our sincere intention to listen there are factors which interfere with our ability to do so. The most common reason is that you may be preoccupied, so caught up in your own thoughts, fantasies or emotions that you cannot give sufficient attention to the other person. Or the other person may overload you with information, or speak so quickly that you cannot process it all at once. Sometimes there are so many distractions in the surrounding environments, such as loud noise, that it is hard to pay careful attention, even when you want to do so. By the same token, you may be behaving in ways that may give the other person the impression that you are not listening. It will be very useful for you to familiarize yourself with the most common barriers to effective listening and communication which are summarized as follows:

1. **Judging**—Our natural tendency to judge, to define things as good or bad, cool or uncool, can be an enormous barrier to effective communication. Prejudging someone in a negative way influences your ability to listen. Negative labels have tremendous power. For example, quickly labeling someone as stupid or crazy makes it highly unlikely that you will pay much attention to what that person has to say. When you are judgmental, other people are put on the defensive and typically turned off.

2. **Mind Reading**—Rather than paying attention to what the person is really saying you are busy operating on the basis of your assumptions about what the person is thinking and saying. Once in a while, if you are very perceptive, your efforts at mind reading may be on target, but for the most part mind reading usually leads to miscommunications and misunderstandings. Remember the old joke, "When you assume you make an ass out of you and me" (ass/u/me).

3. **Stereotyping**—When you operate on the basis of your widespread generalizations about a person based on group membership or some physical characteristic, rather than getting to know that person for who he or she is, you are setting the stage for poor listening and distorted communications.

4. **Interrupting**—Frequent or needless interruptions disrupt communication and interfere with the flow of the conversation. When a speaker is interrupted repeatedly she will often become distracted, lose her train of thought, and feel frustrated. And if you are the one chronically interrupting, you are obviously attending more to what you want to say than to what is being said. Giving the other time and space to talk is more than being polite, it is the essence of true listening. And the other person owes you the same respect. Interruptions are more likely to be made by persons in positions of authority over you like parents, teachers, or bosses. And men tend to interrupt more than women, particularly in male-female conversations.

5. **Comparing**—You are listening for the purpose of seeing how you measure up to the other person, drawing comparisons and contrasts in your head. The end result is that you are so busy feeling either inferior or superior that minimal attention is given to the speaker.

6. **Advising**—You put yourself in the role of the problem-solver and put your attention on searching for the right advice for the speaker. In the meantime, you don't hear what is most important, how the speaker is

feeling and, consequently, you fail to acknowledge these emotions. Of course, there are many times when people will ask for your advice. In this instance we are referring to the tendency to take on that role even when your advice has not been solicited. Sometimes all the speaker wants is an opportunity to vent, to have someone listen sympathetically, and she is not looking to have the problem solved at that moment. This is a common occurrence in male-female conversations. Oftentimes women just want to be listened to, while men feel a compulsion to solve the problem rather than empathize.

7. **Rehearsing**—You are busy concentrating on and reviewing what you want to say next which detracts from your ability to listen to the speaker.

8. **Stage-Hogging**—Stage hogs, also called conversational narcissists, listen with the primary intent of changing the focus of the conversation back onto them. At every opportunity they shift the topic back to what happened to them, and their feelings.

9. **Filtering**—This occurs when you only listen to what you want to hear and ignore or forget the rest.

10. **Dueling**—You are so invested in arguing and debating, perhaps to show off your verbal or intellectual prowess or just to prove you are right, that you fail to listen to any valid points made by the speaker. You argue for the sake of the argument.

11. **Derailing**—You keep changing the subject or making jokes to create detours in the conversation. This prevents the discussion from reaching any closure. The speaker may end up very annoyed with you.

12. **Daydreaming**—This occurs when something the person has said triggers off a chain of private associations, and before you know it you are attending to your fantasy and not the speaker. This is more likely to happen if you are bored or anxious. Be aware that this often ends up communicating that you do not value what the speaker has to say.

13. **Placating**—You are so invested in being "nice" or "polite" that you agree with everything the speaker says, either ignoring your true opinions or feelings, or pretending you feel differently.

14. **Hidden Agendas**—When you enter a conversation with special interests or needs that are not evident on the surface and about which you are not forthcoming, the resulting communication is often distorted. It becomes difficult to really listen because you are looking for openings to further your agenda.

15. **Overreacting**—In this case you allow yourself to get caught up in emotion over a word or words that you find offensive or insulting, and your emotional reaction prevents you from hearing or being open to the main message being conveyed.

THE BUILDING BLOCKS OF EFFECTIVE LISTENING

> We have been given two ears but a single mouth,
> in order that we may hear more and talk less.
>
> Zeno of Citium

Active Listening

Active listening, also called **reflective listening**, is a process of giving the speaker non-judgmental responses as a way of checking the accuracy of what you have heard, and whether you fully understand the message the speaker is attempting to communicate. Psychologists, clinical social workers, and marriage counselors, who are professional listeners, have long practiced this type of listening as a way of truly understanding and helping troubled individuals. It has become apparent that everyone could benefit from learning how to listen in this fashion to facilitate effective communication. Pay careful attention to these elements for active listening. If you make a sincere attempt to practice and incorporate these we guarantee that your listening skills will improve dramatically. Reflective listening has three essential components which are typically used in conjunction with one another, but will be presented separately for purposes of explanation.

1. Paraphrasing

This involves stating in your own words what you think someone has just said. This gives the speaker the opportunity to find out if you have really understood what he was trying to convey. In the event that you have misunderstood, partially misunderstood, or missed an important point, the speaker can then clarify matters so that your understanding more nearly matches the intended message. It is important to paraphrase in your own words so that you do not fall prey to "parroting." **Paraphrasing** involves highlighting the main points of the speaker's message, rather than getting mired in exhaustive repetition or minor details. This technique is ideal for establishing rapport and really making the other person feel like you have heard him or her. Paraphrasing usually begins with phrases such as:

"It sounds like you are saying..."

"As I understand you..."

"What I hear you saying is..."

"You mean..."

"Correct me if I'm wrong, but are you saying..."

"You think..."

"From your point of view..."

If the speakers message is long or complicated it is best to summarize in your own words your understanding of the communication. Summarizing helps you to tie the various parts of the conversation into a meaningful whole. It lets the speaker know that you have heard the overall message and that you haven't just focused on one salient point. The use of summarization is especially useful when you are trying to resolve differences, defuse an argument, or problem solve. Summarizing responses could start with:

"Summing up what you've said..."

"Your main points, as I understand you are..."

"Recapping what you have been saying..."

2. Clarifying

When you **clarify** you are basically asking questions to facilitate your understanding of the speaker's message, to get background information, additional relevant facts, or to fill in gaps in the narrative. This enables you to get the big picture. It is important to ask for clarification in the context of what the speaker thought and felt, from his or her relevant personal history. Of course, there is no right or wrong way to ask a question, as long as it is phrased in a nonjudgmental way, and the tenor of the query will depend on the message being questioned. But some common clarification questions include:

"What do you mean?"

"I'm confused, could you clarify that?"

"Could you repeat that?"

"How did it happen?"

3. Feedback

This involves sharing your reactions to what you have heard the speaker say. There are three rules for giving **feedback**. It should be:

1. Immediate
2. Honest
3. Supportive

For example, if your gut reaction is that the speaker has left something out of the message you could say, "I get the feeling that there's something you are not telling me." This invites the speaker to open up more if this is the case, to disagree if you are in error, and to feel as though you care enough to want to hear the whole story. If you had responded with non-supportive comments such as "You're holding out on me," or, "You're lying," you would likely only elicit defensiveness on the part of the speaker.

Feedback can also involve sharing whether you agree or disagree with the speaker, particularly if the speaker is looking for your opinion. Imagine a scenario where a friend recounts to you a story of a foolish thing he has done, and he is asking you to confirm or deny this. A supportive but honest remark might be, "I think there is a real possibility that you did make a mistake." If you had responded with judgmental comments like, "You've been a total fool," or "You are such an idiot," this would only serve to hurt his feelings and make him think twice about sharing his weaknesses with you ever again.

Empathic Listening

This type of listening goes further than reflective listening because it involves putting yourself in the shoes of the other, as discussed in the previous chapter. Reik (1972) refers to this as "listening with the third ear," where you listen not just to the words but to the meanings behind the words such as to what the speaker is feeling and thinking. When you listen empathically you do your best to literally get inside of the other person's frame of reference, to attempt to see the world through his eyes, to understand his particular paradigm, and to understand how he feels. Perhaps, to go even a step further, to feel his or her pain. One requirement for empathic listening is that you recognize that everyone is trying to survive the best that they can. Here many of your reflective comments are focused on the feeling or emotional tone of the speaker's message, gleaned from the speaker's words and your reading of the speakers body language. That is, you paraphrase and reflect or mirror back the speaker's feelings, attitudes and emotions. Reflective comments that focus on feelings could begin with phrases such as:

"I sense you are feeling..."

"You feel...(angry, sad, frustrated, etc.)"

"Do you feel...?"

"It appears that you feel..."

"You seem really...(sad, hurt, angry, etc.)"

Empathic listening is a powerful tool for enabling you to get accurate data from which to understand another person. Instead of projecting your own assumptions and feelings, based on your personal history and making interpretations, you are getting in touch with the reality inside another person's head and heart. Empathic listening generates deposits in the emotional bank account. That is, because you are taking the time to really listen and understand, by virtue of this process you become supportive. When you listen empathically you are communicating, "I value you," and this, in and of itself, is one of the most important emotional bank account deposits you can possibly make.

When you first practice active or empathic listening it may feel somewhat artificial or phony, like you are talking in a way that is unnatural for you. Remember that the acquisition of any new skill usually feels awkward in the initial learning stages. Do you recall how awkward you felt when you were first learning to drive a car? But over time and with practice, driving became automatic and second nature to you. The same is true with reflective or empathic listening. Over time and with practice, it will become a natural part of you. The rewards of being a good listener will make the effort you put into developing this skill well worth it. It can be very gratifying to be told, "Thank you so much for listening to me."

THE GLOBAL PERSPECTIVE–Recognizing Our Basic Humanity

"At its simplest, empathy means feeling the same thing that another person is feeling; at its most sophisticated, it's understanding his entire life situation" (Glass, 2001). In order to be compassionate, it is often necessary that we question our initial judgmental perspective and look beneath the surface, genuinely seeking to understand what it must be like to be that other person. Too often, we insist on holding on to a paradigm that describes the other as evil, crazy, fanatic, brainwashed, retarded, or otherwise deranged and totally different from us. What if instead, we choose to assume that we are all just struggling humans trying to survive? That underneath our diversity is the fact that we are all human beings, and as Robert C. Roberts (1982) points out, our vulnerability to suffering, weakness, and death are things we have in common with absolutely every human being. These undeniable similarities give us the opportunity for fellowship with anyone who crosses our path. As global citizens, to truly foster compassion we need to believe that kinship extends beyond our immediate family, group, and country, to every member of the human race.

This is not to imply that coming to such awareness is easy, particularly when the other appears to be oblivious to that fact himself. Yet, it is essential to the development of empathy and true understanding. Consider the case of Mohammad Sidique Khan, a 30-year-old Briton of Pakistani ancestry and lifetime resident of the English city of Leeds. Khan was one of the four suicide attackers who bombed London's transit system on July 7, 2005. On that day, 56 people were killed in the attacks on three subway trains and a double-decker bus. There is no question that such waste of human life is wrong. It is hard to imagine the suffering of the victims and their surviving families, as well as the nation itself. Such acts deny our interconnectedness. It would be easy, if justifiable, to dismiss Khan and others like him as madmen or merely brainwashed puppets. But what if instead, we attempt to step into his shoes? What if we, out of a belief in our common humanity, really tried to imagine seeing the world through his eyes? What could have driven Khan to such desperation that he would willingly give up his life to deliver his message? It turns out that in a videotape recorded by Khan an undetermined amount of time prior to the attacks, we have a small chance to do that. Addressing himself to the Westerners, Khan said, "Until we feel security, you will be our targets. Until you will stop the bombing, gassing, imprisonment and torture of my people, we will not stop this fight." He said Westerners had failed to heed previous warnings, and that "therefore we will talk to you in a language that you understand. Our words are dead until we give them life with our blood." He went on to accuse Western civilians for the terror attacks against them (*Miami Herald*, September 3, 2005).

Why does he feel oppressed by us? What is it that we are allegedly doing? How are we attacking them? What bombings, gassing, torturing is he talking about? Do we share some responsibility for aggression in the world? Do they really just want to be left alone, to be separate? Can such disconnectedness be tolerated in a shrinking world or is our interconnectedness unavoidable? Can all of us come to the table to decide how we want the world to be?

Positive Psychology Exercise: Empathic Listening

Consider this story. For years you have been close friends with a woman, Maria, who has a habit of getting involved with men who treat her poorly. She had a rough childhood. Her father abandoned the family when she was a child, and her mother was so busy working to support Maria and her siblings that she had very little time for them while Maria was growing up. Maria has been involved with a man, Donald, who is an alcoholic. Although he treats her adequately when sober, when drunk he becomes verbally abusive and on one occasion he was physically abusive to her. She forgave him. Recently Maria lost her job, and when Donald invited her to live with him she jumped at the chance because she was broke. Late one night Maria knocks on your door, distraught and weeping. Her lower lip is swollen and bloody and her arm is bruised. She explains, "Donald came home drunk and flew into a rage because the apartment wasn't spotless. He said if that if I am at home and not working, the least I could do was clean up. I tried to explain to him that I was feeling sick today so I rested, but he wouldn't listen. He started screaming at me, calling me awful names, and then he grabbed my arm really hard and punched me in the mouth. I'm so afraid to go home, but I'm even more afraid to leave him. I can't make it on my own. It was my fault. I drove him to this. I should have cleaned up today and I didn't. I don't know what to do! But I don't have any choice; I have to go home to Donald."

Think about this event. Now take a few moments and rewrite the episode from the point of view of this woman. Before you give any consideration to how you might advise her to deal with this situation, imagine you are her, seeing the world through her eyes, walking in her shoes, and write down the thoughts, feelings and conscious experiences you have as Maria during the situation described above. In other words, try to experience the incidents just as Maria did. The goal here is not to condone Maria's decision to stay in abusive relationships, but to try to understand and empathize with her from her point of view. If you do want to have an impact on her future decision making, empathizing with her first will help pave the way. If you are unable to put yourself in Maria's shoes you may have written something like this:

> What is wrong with Maria? How can she let herself be abused like that? If she had any sense at all she'd leave him immediately and never speak to him again. But she is obviously too stupid to do that. She's obviously very insecure and she clings to him because she is too cowardly to stand on her own two feet. She was abandoned by her father so she is trying to win the love of another man who is "no good" to compensate.

Here you were not putting yourself in Maria's shoes.

1. You were evaluating—she is stupid.
2. You were analyzing—she is insecure and cowardly.
3. You were explaining—she is trying to compensate for paternal abandonment.

Listening with Openness

It is very difficult to listen, to really hear what another person is telling you, if you are busy finding fault with the speaker or his or her words. When you adopt a judgmental stance you filter information and focus on whatever seems false, silly, or foolish, meanwhile you are ignoring any valid points or expressions of feeling.

Nearly everyone has trouble listening openly at least some of the time, particularly when the speaker is saying something that disagrees with your point of view, or contradicts your beliefs. Why is this? Because all of us, at least to some extent, fear being wrong. Your opinions and beliefs are closely tied to your self-esteem. You may equate being wrong with being stupid, bad or worthless. And it can be very threatening to witness your sacred cows being chopped into bits. How different the world would be if everyone could view their beliefs and opinions as temporary hypotheses, held until disproved or modified. The resulting openness to other paradigms or contradictory information would be a major step forward in interpersonal and international relations.

Adopting an accepting attitude is critical for creating a favorable climate for communication. Acceptance does not mean that you automatically agree with what the speaker is saying, or that you condone improper behavior. Acceptance refers to maintaining a basic attitude of positive regard towards the speaker, regardless of whether you agree with his or her words or behaviors. When people feel accepted it is much easier for them to be honest and open with you, and to put more stock in what you have to say. Adopting a judgmental stance puts others on the defensive and practically insures that they will be very guarded in what they say and reveal to you.

Positive Psychology Self-Exercise

In order to practice listening with openness, deliberately choose to listen to a radio or TV talk personality who espouses a view contrary to your own, be it political, religious, or moral. Take the time to listen with openness and find just one statement you can agree with, or fact that shouldn't be ignored. The point here is not to give up or forsake your whole philosophy on life, but to recognize common ground and the fact that even individuals with views diametrically opposed to yours will, from time to time, make points you consider valid.

THE GLOBAL PERSPECTIVE—The Global Ear

As you learned in Chapter 1, your paradigms about the world influence how you interpret your reality and even what you believe is truth. Most of us learn about past or current events in the world from TV news, the local newspaper, or school. If you are a news junkie then perhaps you read periodicals such as *Time* or *Newsweek*, listen to talk radio, or surf the blogosphere to pick up news items or commentary. We assume that our media reports the truth. And indeed they do, but it is the truth from their perspective. The media plays a vital watchdog role in our society, but it is important to note that most popular media outlets (newspapers, TV channels, periodicals, radio stations) have, over the last twenty years, been increasingly taken over by powerful corporate conglomerates, and as such, they are not nearly as independent as they once were. As a result we are getting increasingly homogenized news accounts with less intensive investigative reporting, as the news has become more ratings driven than concerned with discerning the facts. In addition, to some extent we are all brainwashed by the media who are now increasingly beholden to the corporate interests who own them.

If you take the time to look into news reports from other cultures or countries, you might find that often the same events are presented from very different perspectives. For example, reports from European news outlets, such as the BBC, often differ from U.S. broadcasts. Not surprisingly, the Al Jazeera TV network typically presents a very different take on events in the Middle East than U.S. TV networks. Is anyone lying or is this just a function of how different perspectives affect reporting of supposedly objective "facts"? As a global citizen it is important to listen with openness to the views and perspectives of those in other cultures, even if you disagree. A refusal to even consider the views of others keeps you in the dark. Usually, common ground can be found when you are open minded enough to listen. In our quest to improve world wide relations and establish a lasting peace, a refusal to listen makes you a part of the problem rather than part of the solution. Take the risk and read or watch the news or commentary from other cultures. If you have friends who are recent arrivals from others countries, ask them how various world situations are perceived in their culture of origin. Open your global ears.

Listening with Awareness

This involves listening with your eyes as well as your ears by paying as much attention to **nonverbal behavior** and voice tones as the words themselves. A good listener listens to and watches for more than the speaker's words. Attending to this dimension will give you valuable insights beyond the words and greatly enhance your ability to listen empathically.

In particular, pay attention to whether there is congruence, a match, between the speaker's body language, actions/nonverbal behaviors, and spoken words. Does the person's tone of voice, emphasis, facial expression, posture, and body movements fit the content of his or her communication? For example if a speaker nods his or her head while saying no, or the reverse, subtly shaking the head no when agreeing to something, then obviously the person has ambivalent feelings. Or for a more extreme example, let's say someone tells you that his mother has just died, but meanwhile he is grinning and leaning back comfortably with his legs propped up on his desk. In this case you are receiving mixed signals, also referred to as **double messages**. There is no congruence between his words and his actions thus the message is very confusing.

If the person's body language, facial expression, tone of voice and words don't match, your job as a listener is to clarify and give feedback about the discrepancy so as to deduce what the speaker is really feeling, or what is really going on. If you ignore the incongruity, you are settling for an incomplete or confusing message. It is important for you to realize that incongruity does not necessarily negate the veracity or sincerity of the spoken words. Resist the temptation to over interpret nonverbal behavior. There typically are many potential explanations for incongruent body language. For example, in the case that someone smiles when telling you how sad he is that his mother has died, you should not necessarily assume that the person is secretly thrilled about the death. Sometimes people smile out of embarrassment over intense emotions, or as a way of distancing themselves from strong feelings. Similarly, if someone fails to keep eye contact when telling you she cares about you, does that necessarily mean that she is lying? Can you think of other reasons why she would behave in such a manner? For example, consider cultural differences in maintaining eye contact. Or think about the role of shyness in a person's ability to maintain eye contact. Remember, truly effective communicators always seek to clarify the message, without assuming that they already know the meaning of the message.

UNDERSTANDING NONVERBAL BEHAVIOR

One of the main reasons why we are sometimes confused by what people say is because so much of what is being expressed is nonverbal. It has been estimated that only 7% of the emotional meaning of a face-to-face communication is conveyed by the words alone! That is a staggering figure. Up to 93% of meaning is communicated nonverbally (Mehrabian, 1971). It has been estimated that 38% of the emotional impact of our words is communicated by the vocal aspects of the message. This is referred to as **paralanguage**, which is a term given to how something is said rather that what is said. This includes characteristics such as the tone and pitch of voice, vocal inflections, emphasis on certain words, and the length and frequency of pauses. The other 55% of meaning is conveyed by facial expressions, bodily movements and gestures, duration of eye contact, and posture (Mehrabian, 1989). The reason why it is so important to pay close attention to nonverbal signals is that much of nonverbal behavior is unintentional and unconscious, thereby revealing deep, underlying feelings or attitudes. A good listener attends to paralanguage, to those clues in voice tone, changes in pitch and tempo, and how quickly someone speaks. When anxious or excited people tend to talk faster, but when depressed, grief-stricken, or overtired, speech generally is slower than normal.

Facial expressions are especially revealing, particularly the mouth and the lips. Smirking usually accompanies sarcasm. While in deep thought many people purse their lips, but when tense they may bite their lower lip. Most people recognize how revealing their faces are and may try to mask their emotions by putting on a face, such as smiling to hide anger. To a trained observer such forced expressions seem strained or put on, but an untrained eye could be fooled. The eyes have often been referred to as the "windows to the soul" because of what they can reveal. Our eyes are a good barometer of our level of social comfort. Avoidance of eye contact often reflects shyness, guilt or disinterest. Maintaining good eye contact communicates openness, interest and comfort. In addition, we tend to unconsciously perceive pupil dilation as an indication of sexual attraction or interest. Too much eye contact, like staring, can reflect aggressiveness or erotic interests.

Body postures, bodily movements and gestures also reveal volumes about attitudes. If someone leans toward you it usually indicates interest and involvement in what you are saying, but if that person leans back it may reflect disinterest or a desire to get away. When people feel threatened there is a tendency to cross their arms over their body, a response known as body armoring. We get clues as to whether a person likes us or not by reading nonverbal cues. The kinds of nonverbal behaviors which can denote that someone likes you include smiling, head nodding, touching you, gesturing freely, raising the eyebrows, moving closer to you, and facing you squarely. On the other hand, body language that indicates dislike could include frowning, yawning, moving away, standing obliquely from you, shaking one's head and self grooming actions (Kleinke, 1986).

Another important aspect of nonverbal communication is expressed through touch and the distance with which we choose to stand when interacting with others, referred to as **personal space**. Touching is perhaps the most intimate kind of physical closeness, which communicates different meanings depending on who does the touching and under what circumstances. Touch can reflect affection, sexual interest, dominance, caring, and sometimes aggression. The message that touch conveys will depend on how gentle or rough the touch, the length of the contact, whether it occurs in an appropriate context, whether it is a friend or a stranger doing the touching, and whether it is from the same or opposite sex. In an acceptable context, touch usually is well received. Touching behavior can also an indicator of status and dominance. A higher status individual often feels free to touch a lower status person, but the reverse rarely happens. In addition, cultural factors play an important role because touching is considered more acceptable in some cultures than in others. For example, Latinos are much more comfortable with touching than say, the British. Cultural factors also play a focal role in acceptable distances for personal space. Intimate distance (0 to 18 inches away from the body) is reserved for family members, lovers, and very close friends. Personal distance (1 to 4 feet) is the space we earmark for conversations with friends and coworkers. Social distance (4 to 10 feet) is used for impersonal business and casual conversations. Public distance (10 feet and beyond) is reserved for speaking to a group. Carrying on personal or private business at such a distance would likely be considered very inappropriate, cold and aloof. Significant ethnic differences are apparent in the amount of personal space needed for comfortable interpersonal interactions. Americans, Germans and the English like more distance while Arabs, Greeks, Latin Americans, and the French prefer to interact at closer distances. Touching or standing too close to another person too soon can be perceived as an invasion of personal space.

The distance from which we stand from others when interacting can be very revealing about the nature of the relationship. One study demonstrated that couples in troubled marriages stood or sat significantly farther away from each other during conversations than those who were happily married (Crane, Dollahite, Griffin, & Taylor, 1987). A skilled marital counselor can learn volumes about a new couple presenting for marital therapy just by noting how far they sit from one another in the waiting room prior to their first appointment.

What about when an individual's words and overt behaviors do not match, even when words and nonverbal behaviors appear to be in synch? For example, let's consider a situation where someone appears to sincerely express interest in having a relationship with you, but continually makes excuses why he or she cannot spend any time with you. Or a situation where someone insists that engaging in a certain activity is very important to him, yet when the time comes to follow through he consistently fails to show up or do anything that is required. Oftentimes we are faced with dilemmas such as these, where people are giving very mixed messages between their words and their behaviors. As in the case with non-matching verbal and nonverbal cues, your job is to point out the discrepancy and ask for clarification. Follow the guidelines for the Perception Check explained later in this chapter for a method to get such clarification. If you have already done this and the discrepancy persists despite your best efforts, then the best rule of thumb, in general, is to believe the overt actions over the words.

The Rules for Effective Nonverbal Communication

Learning to accurately read nonverbal signals will greatly improve your ability to be perceptive and responsive to other people. As an added bonus, picking up on nonverbal cues will assist you in knowing when to adjust your own behavior. For example, if you are doing or saying something that offends or hurts another person, you can modify your behavior before the situation gets out of hand, as it might if you are oblivious to your impact on others. To summarize, we have synthesized this information into what we call the five rules for effective nonverbal communication:

Rule 1 Maintain good eye contact but be careful not to stare at others.

Rule 2 Use your body language appropriately to communicate interest in another, if that is your intent. Face the person squarely, lean forward, smile, gesture freely, keep your arms open, and nod your head at the appropriate times.

Rule 3 Speak clearly, fairly rapidly, and modulate your tone of voice and vocal inflections to keep your speech interesting.

Rule 4 Use the power of touch appropriately. Touch can be a potent tool for establishing rapport, but be careful. Strangers typically do not want or expect to be touched. Men often are not comfortable being touched by other men, except for close friends.

Rule 5 Respect the personal space of other people. Be sensitive to the cultural differences in what is perceived as an acceptable amount of personal space.

The subject of body language is fascinating and complicated, but a more in depth discussion of this is beyond the scope of this chapter. If you are interested in learning more about nonverbal cues and how to accurately read them some suggested readings include:

Body Language by Julius Fast

Manwatching by Desmond Morris

Nonverbal Behavior for Effective Listening

Just as you the listener will be attuned to the body language of the speaker to help pick up feelings or underlying attitudes, the speaker will also react to the nonverbal aspects of how you listen. Certain nonverbal behaviors associated with good listening skills include:

1. Maintaining good eye contact

2. Leaning forward slightly

3. Nodding or saying, *"Uh huh,"* to let the speaker know that you are listening and to continue.

4. Keeping your arms open

A Final Note on Effective Listening

The ancient Greeks had an enlightening philosophy which was reflected in three sequentially arranged words: **Ethos**, **Pathos** and **Logos**. The first, **Ethos**, refers to your personal credibility, your trustworthiness, the faith people have in your integrity. It also refers to your balance in the emotional bank account. **Pathos** refers to your empathic side. It means that you are capable of perceiving and attuning yourself with the emotional content of another person's communication. **Logos** is the logical, reasoning aspect of your character and your communication.

The sequence of these is important: First Ethos, then Pathos, then Logos. Your character comes first, then your relationships, and then your logic. This is a paradigm shift for most people who tend to go straight for the Logos, the left brain logic, in communicating. That is, they immediately resort to their logic without first taking the Ethos and the Pathos into consideration. This brings us back to Covey's essential precept regarding the need to "seek first to understand before attempting to be understood."

EFFECTIVE COMMUNICATION—ASSERTIVE SKILLS

Effective communicators are adept at listening, but also skilled at expressing their own needs and desires. As mentioned earlier, effective communication is a two way street. It isn't enough to be a great listener if you cannot express yourself effectively in return. Oftentimes, the type of verbal expression that is hardest to master is the art of being appropriately and effectively **assertive**. Consider the following scenarios which may resemble situations that you or someone you know has had to face. These scenes were derived from stressful work situations presented by participants in our Assertiveness Training workshops.

Scenario 1

You are a full time student and also employed part time to cover your expenses. A close friend of yours lost his job and was broke. Since you had some savings you offered to lend him several hundred dollars to meet his bills until he could find employment. He enthusiastically accepted your offer, and promised to pay you back as soon as he got a new job. A few weeks later he landed a job but made no mention about repaying the loan. You waited a few weeks for him get paid and caught up with bills. A month passed and still no word from him on loan repayment. Then he invited you over to his home to see the brand new flat screen TV he just bought. You are feeling angry and thinking he may have taken advantage of your generosity by buying a luxury item before paying you back. Meanwhile, your car breaks down and without savings you are now in debt for the repair.

Scenario 2

You have developed a reputation at your company for being an excellent worker. As a result of your competence your boss keeps adding to your responsibilities. Although your workload has increased significantly, your boss has not offered you a raise. In order to keep up with your rising workload you have to work overtime several times a week. Since you are a salaried employee you do not get paid for overtime. You are growing increasingly resentful and stressed out. You worry constantly about keeping up with your work, but you are afraid to turn down new assignments and disappoint your boss.

Scenario 3

You have a long standing friendship with someone whom you often get together with on the weekends. However, your friend has a habit of frequently canceling plans with you at the last minute, sometimes with good reason and other times not. You have been very understanding about this, and have not wanted to complain for fear of jeopardizing the relationship. It is Saturday night and you have special plans with this friend. You are all dressed and ready to leave when your phone rings and, once again, your friend cancels out. You feel very angry and disappointed.

Scenario 4

You are a legal secretary working for a high powered attorney in a large law firm. Your boss, Mr. Reynolds, has a habit of strolling into work mid- morning and wasting time until the afternoon when he goes into high gear and is quite productive. But because of his delays in getting down to work, paperwork that needs to be finished and filed that day is often not completed by the end of the workday at 5.00 p.m. You routinely work overtime for up to one full hour on almost a daily basis in order to complete paperwork that must be filed that day. Although this is inconvenient, the extra money you earn from overtime pay comes in handy and makes it worth your while. One day the firm's top managers announce that due to dwindling profits, all overtime work and pay will be indefinitely suspended. Your boss is not in agreement with this new policy, but has no power to change the mandate. You are very worried that you will be put in the uncomfortable position of having to work overtime for free in order to complete necessary tasks.

Assertiveness Defined

The scenarios described above represent the kinds of difficult situations that we all confront periodically. What these situations have in common is that they call for an assertive response. Whether you are a student, employee, employer, friend, or parent, situations will arise where you will need to assert yourself in order to deal with the situation. Assertion involves standing up for your personal rights and expressing ideas, needs, feelings and beliefs in direct, honest and appropriate ways without violating the rights of other people (Lange & Jakubowski, 1976). When you are assertive you can accept compliments and take criticisms. You can negotiate for what you need, disagree with another, and ask for clarification when you don't understand. You can set limits when necessary, and you are able to say, "No."

The basic message you are communicating when you are assertive is: *This is what I think. This is what I feel. This is how I view the situation.* This message expresses who you are and is said without dominating, humiliating or degrading the other person. Assertion involves respect for others, but not deference. Deference is acting in a subservient manner as though the other person is right, or better simply because they are older, more powerful, experienced, knowledgeable or in an authority position over you. When you express yourself in ways that are self-effacing, appeasing, or overly apologetic you are showing deference. Two types of respect are intimately involved in assertion: (1) respect for yourself, that is, expressing your needs and defending your rights and; (2) respect for the rights and needs of the other.

Assertive self-expression is a hallmark of effective communication skills. It is a prerequisite for satisfying interpersonal relationships. Being assertive will not give you an iron clad guarantee of having things go your way, but you maximize your chances of success while minimizing the chance of alienating others. Assertiveness contributes to interpersonal effectiveness, higher self-esteem, lower levels of stress, and more satisfying relationships (Davis, Eshelman, & McKay, 1988). Take a moment to fill out the following inventory (Rathus, 1973) to assess your level of assertiveness. In a nutshell, do you stand up for your rights or do you wimp out?

The Rathus Assertiveness Schedule (RAS): Do You Assert Yourself or Wimp Out?

Indicate how well each item describes you by using the following scale:

3 = **very much like me**	**−1** = **slightly unlike me**
2 = **rather like me**	**−2** = **rather unlike me**
1 = **slightly like me**	**−3** = **very much unlike me**

_____ 1. Most people seem to be more aggressive and assertive than I am.*

_____ 2. I have hesitated to make or accept dates because of "shyness."*

_____ 3. When the food served at a restaurant is not done to my satisfaction, I complain about it to the waiter or waitress.

_____ 4. I am careful to avoid hurting other people's feelings, even when I feel that I have been injured.*

_____ 5. If a salesperson has gone to considerable trouble to show me merchandise that is not quite suitable, I have a difficult time saying, "No."*

_____ 6. When I am asked to do something, I insist upon knowing why.

_____ 7. At times, I look for a good, vigorous argument.

The Rathus Assertiveness Schedule (RAS): Do You Assert Yourself or Wimp Out? (cont.)

Indicate how well each item describes you by using the following scale:

3 = very much like me	**−1 = slightly unlike me**
2 = rather like me	**−2 = rather unlike me**
1 = slightly like me	**−3 = very much unlike me**

_____ 8. I strive to get ahead as well as most people in my position.

_____ 9. To be honest, people often take advantage of me.*

_____ 10. I enjoy starting conversations with new acquaintances and strangers.

_____ 11. I often don't know what to say to people who are sexually attractive to me.*

_____ 12. I will hesitate to make phone calls to business establishments and institutions. *

_____ 13. I would rather apply for a job or admission to a college by writing letters than by going through with a personal interview.*

_____ 14. I find it embarrassing to return merchandise.*

_____ 15. If a close and respected relative were annoying me, I would smother my feelings rather than express my annoyance.*

_____ 16. I have avoided asking questions for fear of sounding stupid.*

_____ 17. During an argument I am sometimes afraid that I will get so upset that I will shake all over.*

_____ 18. If a famed and respected lecturer makes a comment which I think is incorrect, I will have the audience hear my point of view as well.

_____ 19. I avoid arguing over prices with clerks and salespeople.*

_____ 20. When I have done something important or worthwhile, I manage to let others know about it.

_____ 21. I am open and frank about my feelings.

_____ 22. If someone has been spreading false and bad stories about me, I see him or her as soon as possible and "have a talk" about it.

_____ 23. I often have a hard time saying, "No."*

_____ 24. I tend to bottle up my emotions rather than make a scene.*

_____ 25. I complain about poor service in a restaurant and elsewhere.

_____ 26. When I am given a compliment, I sometimes just don't know what to say.*

_____ 27. If a couple near me in a theater or at a lecture were conversing rather loudly, I would ask them to be quiet or take their conversation elsewhere.

_____ 28. Anyone attempting to push ahead of me in a line is in for a good battle.

_____ 29. I am quick to express an opinion.

_____ 30. There are times when I just can't say anything.*

The Rathus Assertiveness Schedule (RAS): Do You Assert Yourself or Wimp Out? (cont.)

Scoring: For those items followed by an asterisk (*), change the signs (plus to minus, minus to plus). For example, if the response to an asterisked item was 2 it would then become −2. Then add up all the scores of the 30 items. Scores on this survey can vary from +90 to −90. The following table will show you how your score compares to those of 764 college women and 637 men from 35 college campuses across the U.S. For example, if you are a woman with a score of 26, your score exceeded 80% of the women in the sample, indicating that you are a very assertive person. If you are a man and you scored a 6, this is in the 40th percentile, a bit below average, which may indicate that you could benefit from becoming more assertive.

Percentiles for Scores on the RAS

Women's Scores	Percentile	Men's Scores	Women's Scores	Percentile	Men's Scores
55	99	65	6	45	8
48	97	54	2	40	6
45	95	48	−1	35	3
37	90	40	−4	30	1
31	85	33	−8	25	−3
26	80	30	−13	20	−7
23	75	26	−17	15	−11
19	70	24	−24	10	−15
17	65	19	−34	5	−24
14	60	17	−39	3	−30
11	55	15	−48	1	−41
8	50	11			

Differentiating Assertiveness from Passivity and Aggression.

Non-assertion, also called **passivity**, involves violating your own rights by failing to express honest feelings, needs, thoughts and beliefs and consequently permitting others to potentially take advantage of you. It also involves expressing your thoughts and feelings in such an apologetic, diffident, or self-effacing manner that others can easily disregard you and/or your message. Nonassertion shows a lack of respect for your own needs. It can also imply a subtle lack of respect for the other person's ability to handle disappointments, to shoulder some responsibility, or to handle his or her own problems. The goal of passivity is to appease others and to avoid conflict at any cost. And often there is a high price to pay for routinely avoiding conflict. Part of the price paid for passivity is that it renders you ineffective.

Aggression involves directly standing up for your personal rights and expressing thoughts, feelings needs and beliefs in ways which can be dishonest, usually inappropriate or intimidating, and always violates the rights of other people. The usual goal of aggression is domination and winning by intimidation, forcing the other person to lose, or at the very least, to lose face. Winning is assured by humiliating, degrading, belittling, or overpowering others so they become weaker and less able to express and defend their needs and rights. You need not get physical in order to be aggressive. Individuals who are aggressive directly compromise their effectiveness by alienating others.

We can think of assertiveness, passivity and aggression as being on a continuum with assertiveness representing the effective middle ground between aggression and nonassertion. It represents a balance of respecting the rights of others while also respecting your own rights. It represents the effective middle ground of diplomacy between the deference and self-effacement characteristic of passivity, and the intimidation and bullying characteristic of aggressiveness. Put simply, when you are assertive you can set up a win-win situation. When passive you create a lose-win scenario and, obviously, when you are aggressive you produce a win-lose situation.

There is another ineffective option to assertiveness, and that is what we refer to as **passive-aggression**, which may sound like a contradiction in terms, but represents a form of behavior which we have all, at one time or another, demonstrated. Passive-aggressiveness is an indirect form of aggressiveness where we literally get back at someone, not by what we directly do or say, but by what we fail to do or say. The classic example is when you give someone the silent treatment when you are angry at him or her. This cold shoulder approach allows you to get back at the person by what you fail to do, that is, talk and be friendly. Or for another example, take the case of a formerly dedicated employee who feels that his boss is too demanding and eventually adopts an "I don't care attitude," deliberately working slowly and finding excuses to take time off work.

Negative Consequences of Non-assertion

Failure to handle situations in an assertive fashion can have very negative consequences for you and your personal and business relationships. In the short run, a passive stance helps you avoid anxiety producing conflicts. However, in the long run, if you are frequently passive you will feel a growing loss of self-esteem and an increasing sense of resentment or anger. This increases your stress level which can lead to anxiety, depression and/or psychosomatic difficulties such as headaches, ulcers, or hypertension. On the other hand, handling situations in an aggressive manner also works in the short run because you may achieve a temporary emotional release and get your needs met through intimidation. But in the long run, the negative consequences of aggressiveness are obvious. Highly aggressive behavior at work may ultimately cost you promotions or even your job. If you are the boss, bullying your employees, supervisees, or co-workers leads to poor interpersonal relationships and literally invites passive-aggressive retaliation on the part of your colleagues. For example, a tyrannical boss may find that his subordinates react to his aggressive, authoritarian stance with work slowdowns, deliberate mistakes, property damage, theft, or backbiting. In your personal life, aggression can lead to failed relationships, high blood pressure, fights and even trouble with the law. People who are frequently aggressive eventually feel deeply misunderstood, unloved and unlovable because they fail to recognize the impact of their behavior on others, and how such alienation is inevitable.

Benefits of Assertion

Being assertive maximizes the likelihood that your needs and the needs of others will be met, therefore increasing your effectiveness. It will definitely lower your personal level of stress and help ward off illness. One of the greatest benefits of assertiveness is that it will definitely increase your self-respect and sense of self-efficacy, as well as garner respect from others. Numerous research studies support these conclusions. Galassi, Galassi, & Fulkerson (1984) reviewed the research on the effectiveness of assertive behavior as compared with either aggressive or passive behaviors for accomplishing the desired results, along with the impact of those differing styles. They concluded that an assertive approach is more likely to elicit compliance, greater respect, and sympathy, along with generating far less resentment or dislike than an aggressive approach. Although a passive approach is generally viewed by others as pleasant and friendly, it is far less likely to achieve compliance. In one study (Linehan, Brown, Neilson, Olney, & McFall, 1980) the effects of assertive responses were compared to the end results of flattery, fibbing, passivity and indirectness. Needless to say, the assertive responses won the day and were by far the most effective.

Why People Fail to Behave Assertively

There are many reasons and not all will apply to you. Ponder those reasons that are relevant for you and be aware of the misconceptions that often underlie your line of reasoning.

- Fear of loss of approval from others or of getting an angry response.
- Failing to distinguish between assertiveness and aggression. That is, mistaking assertiveness for aggression. This is a particular problem for women in our culture who are given so many double messages, who are encouraged to be strong and outspoken and then vilified for being bitchy or masculine.
- Mistaking non-assertion for politeness or consideration. How can you learn to differentiate non-assertion from graciousness or politeness? A good rule of thumb is to listen to your body. Certain body signals will cue you when your response changes from politeness to non-assertion. Tension and discomfort will arise that typically are not present when you are being polite. If you are confused as to whether to assert yourself or whether to keep quiet and "be polite," you need to ask yourself the following questions:

    Am I likely to bring this up later?

    Will my relationship with this person suffer or change if I keep silent?

    Is there a hidden expectation present?

    Will I feel used because I have unexpressed expectations about reciprocity that may go unfulfilled?

- Mistaking passivity for being helpful because agreeing to do things you really don't want to do might help another person. In genuine helping you eventually make yourself obsolete. In rescuing you end up in the victim role with feelings of being used or taken advantage of by someone with an expectation that you will always be there to bail him out.
- Aggression is often an outgrowth of feelings of powerlessness, where a person believes that he will be controlled too easily by others unless he behaves aggressively. Here there is a tendency to behave aggressively as an overreaction to past emotional experiences.

- A maladaptive belief that aggression is justified and the only way to get through to other people.

- Aggression also often results from feelings of anger or hurt that have built up to a boiling point, leading to an explosion. If the situation had been dealt with assertively in the first place, the aggressive episode could have been prevented.

- Failure to accept your personal rights. It is hard to be assertive if you do not believe you have the right to express your reactions, take care of your needs and stand up for yourself. Some people not only feel they shouldn't express their needs, but think they should not even have them in the first place.

The foundation of improving your assertive skills involves understanding and believing that you have certain rights as an individual and that it is not only okay, but healthy and useful to yourself and others to stand up for your rights. Individuals who are appropriately assertive and self confident have internalized the following tenets (Lange & Jakubowski, 1976).

THE ASSERTIVE BILL OF RIGHTS

1. I have the right as a human being to have needs, and my needs are as important as the needs of others. I have the right to ask (not demand) that other people respond to my needs.

2. I have the right as a human being to have feelings and form opinions. Furthermore, I have the right to express these in ways that respect the feelings and opinions of others.

3. I have the right to expect respect from other people. It is incumbent upon me to also display the same respect for others. Respecting others does not mean that I allow them to take advantage of me or disregard my needs.

4. I have the right to choose whether, in a particular situation, I want or can reasonably meet other people's needs or expectations.

5. I have the right to say, "No."

6. If I frequently compromise my needs or sacrifice my rights, I am teaching others to take advantage of me.

7. If I live my life in such a way as to always avoid conflict or the possibility of hurting someone under any circumstances, I will end up hurting myself and others in the long run. It is only through the honest and timely expression of needs, feelings, reactions and thoughts that I can ultimately develop satisfying interpersonal relationships. When I am assertive everyone will benefit in the long run.

8. If I stand up for myself while simultaneously showing respect for others, I will gain self-respect as well as the respect of others.

9. By being assertive with others and explaining how their behavior affects me, I am giving them the opportunity to change their behavior and respecting their right to know where they stand with me.

10. I do not have the right to demean, intimidate, or manipulate other people into meeting my needs. I do have the right to ask, however, and to attempt to persuade while respecting their right to refuse.

A USEFUL FRAMEWORK FOR ASSERTIVE BEHAVIOR

When learning to become more assertive or to polish your assertive skills, it can be very useful to have a framework or steps to follow in order to know how to construct a potentially effective assertive response. This applies on the job or in your personal life. A useful method known as "I Language" assertion, based upon the work of Thomas Gordon, (1970) was developed to provide such a framework. In "I Language" assertion it is important that whenever possible, your language should include **"I statements."** These statements refer to what you have observed, witnessed, or felt, so that you are taking responsibility for your feelings, experience and observations. This is in contrast to **"You Statements"** which typically involve pointing the finger at another person. What follows is a four step framework that you should find helpful, especially at those times when you may not be sure how to proceed, for you can always fall back on these steps. This framework is not the gospel; you don't always have to follow this format, and this is not the only effective way to proceed. But nonetheless, this is still a very useful summary of how to construct an assertive response.

Step One: The Problem Behavior

The first step is to identify the problem behavior. It is important to keep your language to specific discussions of observable behaviors; do not address personality characteristics. For example, it is much more effective to say, "I am aware that you have not completed several reports that were due," rather than, "lately you have been so lazy!" The first sentence is merely a description of behavior or lack of behavior you observed, wherein the second sentence includes value judgments. If you make value judgments or comment on personality characteristics, particularly in a derogatory fashion, you are just likely to anger the other person, even if your description is totally accurate. You stand a greater chance of resolving the issue, and getting the other person to listen to you if you limit your descriptions to observable behavior. If you merely tell someone he is "an idiot," it only demeans him and gives absolutely no information about what he did or did not do behaviorally to have merited that insult. Throughout the assertive steps, remember to use I statements that express your feelings without evaluating or blaming others. Just beginning your sentence with "I" is not enough. The focus of your statements needs to be on your feelings and your reactions, along with a statement connecting this to the specific observable behaviors of the other person. Recognize that there is a big difference between saying, "I feel hurt when you say _____," rather than, "You hurt me." Or contrast the blaming statement, "You are so mean to me," with the clarity of this message, "I feel angry when you fail to keep your promises."

Step Two: Effects

Next you identify what effects the problem behavior has on you. There are two types of effects. The first refers to the difficulties or inconvenience that the problem behavior causes for you, and the second refers to emotions you have about the problem behavior such as anger, confusion, hurt, or disappointment. In some cases only difficulties are involved, in others only feelings, and in some instances both occur. In some cases where both are involved you may opt only to mention the difficulties and keep the feelings to yourself, such as in situations where you are dealing with strangers or peripheral acquaintances. This can also apply in a business situation, where it might be far more appropriate to deal with the problem behavior at hand than to express personal feelings.

Step Three: Alternatives to the Problem Behavior

The third step involves specifying alternatives to the problem behavior. What is it that you would like the other person to do instead of or in addition to the problem behavior? You may think that this should be obvious and you don't need to spell it out, but many times, just because it is obvious to you what the person ought to be doing; it may not be obvious to him or her. Other people are not mind readers. If you are going to give feedback, give it fully and let others know clearly and diplomatically what your expectations are. Once you have elucidated your expectations and have some inclination from the other person that she is receptive, you need to ask for a commitment for change. Do not be afraid to ask a person to commit to behaving differently. If she verbally agrees to change then she is more likely to follow through.

Step Four: Consequences (optional)

It is very important to note that this last step is optional. Here you identify the consequences of the problem behavior if it persists. Basically, you are saying what will happen if the person does not stop the problem behavior. It is not always appropriate or possible to specify consequences, and that is why this step is optional. Sometimes the situation only calls for you to express how you feel about something and specifying consequences would be overkill. At other times it may be more strategic to wait to specify consequences and determine whether there is a need for escalation later on if the person refuses to change or acknowledge that there is a problem. Never specify a consequence that you are not thoroughly willing or able to follow through with, for then you run the risk that the other person will call your bluff and your credibility and clout will be damaged. If there are no consequences you can readily state and follow up on, then skip this step entirely.

Fine-Tuning the Assertive Steps

When asserting yourself, it is often very helpful to incorporate a style known as **empathic assertion**. Here you convey sensitivity to other person over and above expressing your feelings or needs. When it is possible to proceed in this fashion, it is often highly effective because it helps to establish rapport and minimize defensiveness on the part of the other. It involves making a statement, usually in the first step, that conveys recognition of the other person's situation or feelings followed by another statement where you stand up for your rights and suggest other alternatives. It requires that you put yourself in the shoes of the other, and let him know that you have at least some understanding of his situation or feelings, but you still have your own needs to take into consideration.

Likewise, there are times when your initial efforts to be assertive are discounted and you will need to escalate. **Escalating assertiveness** describes a situation where you start with a minimal assertive response and, for whatever reason, it does not work. At this point, you do not back down but rather become increasingly firm and escalate without becoming aggressive. It is here that you may opt to include step four, the "consequences," because the other person has not responded appropriately to less firm statements on your part. Here you can gradually increase from a request to a demand. Or when someone is asking something of you, increase from stating a preference of "no" to an outright refusal. Or it could represent switching from an empathic assertive approach to a more firm, straightforward approach.

In the course of asserting yourself there are a variety of tactics that others will often use to derail you before you get your point across. The most common tactic involves the other person interrupting you to tell their side of the story. Do not allow this. Firmly speak up and say, "Excuse me, I'd like to finish what I am saying." If they persist with interruptions, escalate and say, "Please stop interrupting me. I will give you plenty of time to reply, but now I would appreciate it if you would let me finish." Another side tracking tactic is deflecting. Here a person responds to your assertion by bringing up things from the past, often irrelevant, that you have done to aggravate him. The best way to handle this is not to take the bait. Refuse to let the conversation be drawn in another direction, even if the complaint is valid. If it is valid you should promise to deal with it after your issue is resolved or thoroughly discussed. For example, you could say, "That is not relevant. If you want we can discuss that after we get through this."

Using the Four Step Framework

If we return to the scenarios at the beginning of this chapter we can construct assertive responses using the four step framework and I statements. Study the following examples.

Scenario 1

Step One. "Several months ago, when you were in a financial jam, I lent you $ 300. I was glad to help out. Over a month ago you got a new job but so far you have not paid back anything towards the loan. I recall that you had promised to pay me back as soon as you got a job. It has been over a month since you got hired at your new job."

Step Two. "I am feeling angry and disappointed that you chose to buy a new TV before paying me back. Right now I'm in debt because I had to pay to fix my car."

Step Three. "I would appreciate it if you could pay me back as soon as possible. If you cannot pay it back now, could you pay it in two or three installments? Can I have a commitment from you to pay back at least $ 100, if not the whole amount, by the end of this week?"

Step Four. "I am concerned that if this persists it will hurt our friendship."

Scenario 2

Step One. "I have been with this company for four years now and I'm pleased that you are happy with the quality of my work. Over the last few months, at your request, I have greatly increased my workload. In order to finish I have to work overtime and/or bring work home for which I do not get paid because I am salaried. And I have not gotten a salary raise in two years."

Step Two. "Given all the extra work I have taken on, I am easily doing the work of two employees. Although I have been willing to do the extra work, I do not feel I am being adequately compensated for the work I am doing."

Step Three. "I truly feel I deserve at least a 10% raise. My taking on extra work, over and above my job description, saves you from hiring someone else full or part time. I deserve to get some of that savings to you back in terms of increasing my salary. Can I receive a raise at this time?"

Note: If this should fail and the boss refuses, then escalate and include step four.

Step Four (option 1). "If you can't raise my salary at this time then I have no choice but to refuse to take on any more extra work. My job description does not indicate that I am responsible for those tasks."

Step Four (option 2). *This option is designed to use your leverage as a highly valued worker to persuade your boss to give you a raise.* "If you can't raise my salary at this time, I may have to begin searching for a new job. If I am going to be doing work at this level, then I deserve to be paid for my efforts. I know I can make significantly more money at other companies. My preference would be to stay here, but I may have no choice if you cannot raise my salary. By the way, keep in mind that if I have to leave, you may need to hire two people to handle my workload. So I believe it is in everyone's best interest for you to give me a raise."

Scenario 3

Step One. (Empathic assertion) "We have been friends for many years, and over this time there have been many times when you have canceled your plans with me, often at the last moment. I understand that sometimes things have come up for you that were out of your control, and you had to change our plans. But this has happened so often that I now feel I must speak up."

Step Two. "When you cancel out at the last minute it leaves me stranded because it is usually too late for me to make other plans, like tonight. And I feel irritated and disappointed, like I can't count on you. I fear our friendship will suffer."

Step Three. "I would greatly appreciate it if you could give me more advance notice when you are unable to keep our plans."

Step Four. (optional) "If you cannot commit to this then I may decide not to make plans with you again."

Scenario 4

Step One. "Mr. Reynolds, it is very important that we discuss the new rule about working overtime. (Empathic Assertion) I know that you had nothing to do with the new rules. But this is creating a problem for both of us. You usually don't come to the office until mid-morning and don't really get down to business until the afternoon. As a result, I have to stay overtime almost daily to get all the paperwork finished and filed on time."

Step Two. "If I do not stay late then important papers may not be filed on time. Our clients and your reputation will suffer, and I will feel as though I am not doing a good job. I am concerned that I will be put in the difficult position of having to work over-time for free which I feel is unfair to me. Working overtime takes away from my time with my family and makes it hard for me to keep up with my other responsibilities. I was willing to do it when I could earn a significant amount of extra money."

Step Three. "But I have some ideas about how we can resolve our mutual dilemma. First of all, you could agree to pay me out of your own pocket for overtime work and then I will be glad to continue as before. If that is not acceptable to you then we need to work together on time management. You need to come to the office by 9:00 a.m. and use your morning time more productively. If you are able to get the paperwork to me earlier in the day, then I will have no difficulty completing and filing all necessary papers by 5:00 p.m. I am willing to meet with you early each morning to help you organize your time more efficiently. We have to do something different because clearly we cannot continue functioning the same way. Which of these alternatives would you prefer?" *When assert-ing yourself with individuals in authority over you, it can be very effective to offer several options and ask them to pick one. That way they retain some control because they get to choose, and will often admire your ingenuity in developing solutions.*

Step Four. "I am not willing to work overtime on a regular basis unless I am compen-sated for my time. I may have to leave the office at closing time without completing important papers."

THE PERCEPTION CHECK

Effective individuals are also adept at communicating in many situations, not all of which require an assertive response. There is an offshoot of the assertive response which has been called the Perception Check (Adler & Towne, 1993). This involves situations where there is not a need to assert yourself, per se, but when you are confused about the behavior of another and you want to check out what is really happening. A classic exam-ple, one that all of us have experienced at some point in our lives, is a situation where someone you care about is acting differently towards you, perhaps uncommunicative or standoffish. You don't have a clue as to what is going on. Is the person angry with you? Is the person upset, and if so, is that person just upset for reasons that have absolutely nothing to do with you? The perception check is a useful, caring method for finding out and answering questions like those above.

The perception check is a three step method which has similarities to the four step framework for assertiveness, but with several fundamental differences. Here your aim is to be empathic, to elicit an honest response, and to listen so as to truly understand what is going on with the other person. Of course, you do not always have to follow these steps, but if you are unsure how to proceed then this framework will come in very handy.

Step One: Identify what you have noticed about the other person by referring to observable behaviors. When possible use "I statements."

Step Two: Give two possible alternatives or interpretations of what the person's behav-ior might mean or might be about.

Step Three: Ask for clarification.

Here is an example of how to use the perception check.

Step One: "Katrina, lately I've noticed that you have been very quiet around me, not like your usual talkative self. And you have also seemed so distant. At the party last night you didn't even come over and say, "Hi" to me. And whenever I looked at you, it seemed like you looked away."
Step Two: "I'm worried that perhaps I have done something to hurt you. Or perhaps you are just upset or worried about something else."
Step Three: "Please tell me what is going on. Are you angry with me?"

Now Katrina is free to tell you what she is feeling and why she may be feeling that way. Your job now is to really listen without getting defensive, and to put yourself into her shoes in order to understand her behavior.

NONVERBAL ASPECTS OF ASSERTIVENESS

How you say what you say is just as important as what you say. That is, the body language you display has a profound effect on how your words will be interpreted and on the responses you will get. No matter how well crafted your assertive response may be or how appropriate your words, if your nonverbal behaviors are not congruent with your verbal communication you can totally sabotage your message, and greatly reduce the likelihood of getting the reaction you seek. If your nonverbal behaviors reflect passivity, deference, self-effacement, timidity, or lack of confidence you will undermine your message and invite others to discount your words. On the other hand, if your words are assertive and appropriate, but your demeanor is intimidating or aggressive it will also detract from your message. Other people will respond with fear or resentment rather than accommodation. Effective communicators are congruent in words and body language.

Basically, you want to present a demeanor that is consistent with assertiveness. You want to put forth a bearing that is neither timid nor aggressive, but rather one that is forthright, confident, and matter-of-fact. In western culture one of the most effective ways to present a confident demeanor is to maintain eye contact. When you look directly into someone's eyes while talking to them it conveys confidence, self-assurance, and that you mean what you say. A passive stance usually involves minimal eye contact or looking down which conveys lack of confidence or uncertainty about your position. An aggressive stance often involves staring a person down, which is not what we mean when we suggest making eye contact. Sometimes it is hard to maintain eye contact, particularly if you have trouble with being assertive, because it may make you uncomfortable. Despite this, we encourage you to force yourself to do so for several reasons: (1) it will make your assertive responses more effective, and (2) keeping eye contact gets a lot easier once you practice doing it.

Posture is also important when delivering an assertive response. You can maximize your effectiveness if you stand up straight, face the person squarely, and lean forward slightly. This conveys a sense of confidence. Likewise, if you are sitting down it is useful to lean forward slightly. Leaning back conveys fear or lack of confidence. People tend to lean back and look down when they are unsure of themselves or afraid. Obviously, getting too close to someone or getting in their face is an aggressive posture that you would want to avoid. It is always wise to respect the personal space of other people.

What you do with your arms reveals a lot about your internal state. For example, have you ever seen two people sitting across from each other in a restaurant, both with their arms folded across their body? Even though you might not overhear the content of their conversation, you can usually tell, just from their arm postures, that they are either arguing or annoyed with each other. How do you know this? Recall from the section on nonverbal communication earlier in this chapter that arms crossed over the body is a "body armoring" response, an unconscious way to protect or hug yourself when feeling threatened. When threatened, most people will immediately adopt this posture unconsciously. Thus, it is very important not to cross your arms over your body or you will convey that you feel intimidated by the encounter. Rather, make a point to leave your arms open. Open arms communicates that you are confident, comfortable and that you mean what you say. Incidentally, when on the receiving end of feedback, continue to maintain the open arm posture. In this way you will come across as non-defensive and open to feedback, qualities that are respected by others.

Also, allow yourself to gesture freely while asserting yourself. People tend to gesture and use their arms when they are comfortable. When you gesture you communicate comfort and confidence, therefore people are much more likely to take you seriously. But, there is one gesture we recommend that you definitely avoid: pointing at someone. People hate it when you point at them like a scolding parent or an angry schoolteacher. They will tune you out and resist you if you resort to finger pointing.

Perhaps the most important nonverbal aspect of assertiveness is your tone of voice. So much is conveyed by the volume, pitch and rhythm of your voice. Avoid shouting which is perceived as aggressive. Also avoid being so soft-spoken that you come off as timid. It is best to speak in a firm, consistent voice tone where you pause for emphasis, and also emphasize key words by slowing down your voice tempo and increasing your volume slightly. Do not talk fast or swallow your words when asserting yourself. It may be useful to talk a little slower, particularly if you are a fast talker, and a little louder than usual for emphasis. Table 10.1 summarizes the differences between assertive vs. passive or aggressive communication styles.

Asserting Yourself with Aggressive People

It can be difficult and stressful to have to deal with aggressive, unreasonable, or nasty individuals, whether in your personal life or at your workplace. When dealing with such people it is common to feel as if you have no control, and to become angry and aggressive yourself. The following pointers should prove useful for handling encounters with aggressive people.

* Make ample use of empathic assertion. Try paraphrasing what you have heard the person say or commenting on the feelings expressed in their demeanor. For example, simple comments such as: "You sound like you are feeling very angry," or, "This is obviously very upsetting for you," can help an angry person to feel understood, and in some cases can help defuse their anger. It is also helpful to ask questions to get the person to clarify the problem and work towards a solution.

* Keep your focus. Aggressive interactions, particularly with people you know well, often get sidetracked from the original issue with laundry

TABLE 10.1 Differentiating Communication Styles

	PASSIVE	ASSERTIVE	AGGRESSIVE
Verbal Behaviors	Apologetic Indirect statements Rambling Not saying what you really mean Giving up easily	Direct statements Honest expression of feelings Describing objective behavior "I" statements Straightforward Good listener Talking slowly Emphasize key words	Accusations, threats Insults, put-downs Blaming "You" statements Sarcasm Failure to listen Manipulative comments
Nonverbal Behaviors	Incongruencies Poor eye contact Soft, timid voice Looking down Fidgeting Leaning back Slumped posture	Actions congruent with words Good eye contact Firm, calm voice Assured manner Gesturing Leaning forward Erect posture Open arms Face person squarely	Staring Yelling, shouting Loud, hostile voice tone Arms crossed over body Finger pointing Getting too close Clenched fists Breaking things
You Are	Scared, anxious Helpless Manipulated Ignored Resentful	Confident Effective Respectful Valued Relieved	Angry, full of rage Indignant Misunderstood Controlling Guilty
Others Feel	Frustrated Puzzled Unsure of your needs	Respected Valued	Intimidated Alienated Angry, resentful Humiliated, hurt Defensive
End Results	Stress Depression Low self-esteem Helplessness Failure to solve problem Resentment Lost opportunities Health problems	Problem solving Healthy self-esteem Self-respect Respect of others Satisfaction Good relationships Less stress Improved health	Interpersonal stress Guilt, remorse Low self-esteem Loss of self-respect Loss of respect from others Passive-Aggressive responses Frustration Failure to solve problems Broken relationships Loneliness Hostility from others Potential legal problems

THE GLOBAL PERSPECTIVE—Cross Cultural Body Language

As you have learned, nonverbal communication is extremely important in any interaction with others. We tend to attribute more meaning to nonverbal aspects of communication and rely on nonverbal cues, especially when verbal messages are unclear or ambiguous. Since nonverbal behavior arises from our "cultural common sense," that is, our ideas about what is appropriate, normal, and effective (LeBaron, 2003), we interpret gestures, posture, silence, spatial relations, emotional expression, touch, physical appearance, and other nonverbal cues differently, depending on the part of the world in which we live. No wonder the importance of nonverbal communication becomes greatly multiplied when dealing with the varied cultures of our globe!

There are elements of nonverbal communication that are consistent across various cultures. Research has demonstrated that the emotions of enjoyment, anger, fear, sadness, and surprise are expressed in a very similar manner around the world. However, there are dramatic differences with regard to which emotions are appropriate to display in various cultures and by whom. For example, in many parts of the United States, it is more socially acceptable for women to display fear, but not anger, and for men to show anger, but not fear (Okun, Fried, and Okun, 1999).

Facial expressions can also lead to differing interpretations depending on the part of the world in which you live and the culture that predominates. In China and Japan, for instance, a facial expression that would signify happiness in other places may actually express anger or masked sadness, both of which would be inappropriate to express overtly. It is not difficult to see how these differences in interpretation may lead to confusion or conflict. Imagine a Japanese woman is attempting to explain that the reason she had to cancel the previous meeting was due to a death in the family. She would likely do so with a smile on her face, based on her cultural belief that it is not appropriate to inflict the pain of grieving upon others. Her Western listeners, who understand smiles to mean friendliness and happiness, might interpret her behavior as cold or heartless. In addition, different norms regarding the appropriate degree of assertiveness in communicating can add to cultural misunderstandings. For example, most white Americans typically consider raised voices to be a sign that a fight has begun. In contrast, many African-American, Jewish, Italian, and Cuban Americans often feel that an increase in volume is a sign of an exciting conversation among friends.

Another nonverbal behavior, which varies greatly across cultures, is what is called proxemics, or the ways of relating to space. Very different ideas exist in different parts of the world about what constitutes polite space for conversations and negotiations. North Americans tend to prefer a large amount of personal space. This is likely because they are surrounded by it in their homes and countryside. Europeans, on the other hand, tend to stand closer to each other when talking, perhaps because they are accustomed to smaller personal spaces. An interesting study comparing North American and French children on a beach revealed that the French children tended to stay in a relatively small space near their parents, while U.S. children roamed up and down a large area of the beach (Okun, Fried, and Okun, 1999). The problem with our different ways of relating to space is the interpretations and judgments that we make regarding them. If Europeans are used to sitting or standing very close when they are talking to each other, they are likely to interpret the Americans' attempt to create more space as clear evidence of their coldness, condescension, or lack of interest. Conversely, an American who is accustomed to more personal space may perceive attempts to get closer as pushy, disrespectful, or aggressive.

Anthropologists Avruch and Black (1993) have noted that, when faced by an interaction that we don't understand, people tend to interpret the others involved as "abnormal," "weird," or "wrong." As global citizens, it is vital that we learn to control the human tendency to translate "different from me" into "less than me." Such a paradigm does not engender trust or communication. It is important to remember the insight of a Maricopa Community College student in response to his participation in a collaborative project with a student in China: "I am happy to have met someone just like me, and yet nothing like me."

The key to effective cross-cultural communication is to begin with the assumption that there is a significant possibility that cultural differences are causing communication problems. Then, be willing to be patient and forgiving, rather than hostile and aggressive, should problems develop. You should always respond slowly and carefully in cross-cultural exchanges, not jumping to the conclusion that you know what is being thought and said. If things seem to be going badly, stop or slow down and think: What could be going on here? Is it possible I misinterpreted what they said, or they misunderstood me? Am I misreading their nonverbal behavior or vice versa?

lists of everything else that is a problem. Work to bring the focus back to the issue at hand. Use phrases such as, "We've gotten off the subject. You were talking to me about..."

- Postpone the discussion until cooler heads prevail. If you and/or the other person are enraged, and neither of you will cool off soon, it may be wise to suggest discussing the matter later when both of you have calmed down. If the other person refuses to delay, explain that you need time to think about the issue and make a definite appointment to discuss it as soon as possible.

- Try the **broken record technique**. In an ordinary situation calling for an assertive response, the broken record technique could come off as obnoxious. But when dealing with an aggressive person who refuses to listen to your assertive response, and who fails to respond to your efforts at escalation, this technique can come in handy to reinforce your request. Basically it involves repeating your request over and over, like a broken record, even if the other person is arguing, or ranting and raving. You just calmly continue to state your request, even during their protestations. It often involves being willing to interrupt. All parents have had to rely on this method at times when dealing with resistance or disobedience from children.

In summary, we urge you to practice using the four step framework the next time you find yourself in a situation that calls for an assertive response, whether this happens in your personal life or on the job. These principles apply to all situations calling for effective assertiveness. Pay careful attention to how you feel after you assert yourself. Although you might experience some fight/flight activation as you initially engage in assertive behavior, the resulting relief and surge in self confidence you are likely to experience afterwards will go a long way towards enhancing your perceived self-efficacy, boosting your self-esteem, and lowering your stress level.

POSITIVE PSYCHOLOGY SELF-EXERCISE:

We can virtually guarantee you that sometime in the next few weeks a situation will arise where you will feel the need to assert yourself, to express your needs, to say "No," or to check out a discrepancy you observe in the behavior of a friend or significant other. The situation may be as mundane as asking for a refund on damaged merchandise, or asking the noisy people behind you in the movie theater to be quiet. Whatever the situation may be, practice using the four step framework and see the difference it will make. Some people find it useful to rehearse the four steps in their mind prior to beginning the assertion, provided of course that you have the time to do so.

KEY TERMS

Pseudo Listening	Nonverbal Behavior	Aggression
Active Listening	Paralanguage	Passive-Aggression
Reflective Listening	Ethos	Empathic Assertion
Paraphrasing	Pathos	Escalating Assertiveness
Clarifying	Logos	Broken Record
Feedback	Assertion	Perception Check
Empathic Listening	Passivity	Double Messages

CHAPTER 10 QUESTIONS

True or False Questions (T or F)

1. _____ Listening happens automatically without any conscious effort on your part.

2. _____ It is important to be judgmental so people know where you stand.

3. _____ Good listeners are careful not to interrupt needlessly.

4. _____ Good listeners don't ask questions, they just keep quiet.

5. _____ 93% of the meaning of a face-to-face communication is conveyed by nonverbal behaviors.

6. _____ Words are a much more valid and true expression of a person's feelings than nonverbal behaviors.

7. _____ If someone has their arms crossed over his/her body it may indicate that he/she feels threatened or angry.

8. _____ In effective communication logos should precede ethos and pathos.

9. _____ When you are assertive you are respectful of your own rights and needs as well as the rights and needs of the other person.

10. _____ Assertiveness and aggressiveness are the same.

11. _____ When asserting yourself it is recommended that you make "You statements" instead of "I statements" whenever possible.

12. _____ When asserting yourself it is important to inhibit all gestures.

13. ____ The broken record technique should be used as often as possible, preferably any time you need to assert yourself.

Short–Answer Questions

1. The communication skill we use the most is _____.
2. After two days the average person remembers _____ % of a conversation.
3. Reflective listening involves _____ what you have heard the speaker say so he/she can let you know if you have understood.
4. _____ listening focuses on reflecting back feelings and attempting to truly understand the other person's frame of reference.
5. We give _____ when our verbal behavior is not congruent with our _____ behavior.
6. _____ refers to your integrity, _____ to your empathy, and _____ to your logic.
7. Expressing your anger towards someone indirectly, by what you fail to do, is called _____.
8. When dealing with highly verbally aggressive individuals the _____ technique may prove useful.

Essay Questions

1. Name and describe the important elements in being a good listener.
2. Describe several blocks to good listening.
3. How does being judgmental influence the communication process?
4. Describe the three elements of reflective listening.
5. How does empathic listening differ from reflective listening?
6. How does assertiveness differ from passivity and aggression?
7. What benefits are possible as a result of assertive behavior?
8. Identify the four steps for assertive communication. Why is step four optional?
9. Explain empathic assertion.
10. Why is your nonverbal behavior so important when delivering an assertive response?
11. What are three important nonverbal behaviors that should accompany your assertive responses to maximize your effectiveness?
12. When would you use the perception check?

11

Establishing Positive Relationships

In its totality, positive psychology is about all that makes for optimal human flourishing, and it goes without saying that what is of paramount importance to this is good relationships. In this context, we want to refer you back to the section in Chapter 7 which discusses the two questions of utmost importance at the end of anyone's life. To reiterate, those questions are:

WAS I LOVED?

DID I LOVE WELL?

According to two current leading love researchers, Harry Reis and Shelly Gable (2003), even across different cultures and age groups, it is likely that having good relationships with other people is the single most important source of life satisfaction and emotional well-being for most individuals. In the same vein, positive psychology was characterized by one its founders, Christopher Peterson, as about "other people." For this reason Seligman (2011) included positive relationships as one of the core elements of PERMA. He asserts that "other people are the best antidote to the downs of life and the single most reliable up." This just underscores the lessons from Chapter 3 that good friends, harmonious relations with family, and healthy marriages promote happiness in ways that wealth, possessions, beauty and fame consistently fail to provide. Veroff, Douvan, & Kukla (1981) report that people, when asked to describe a very negative life event, invariably tell of the loss of an important relationship, either through death or break-up. Indeed, relationship problems are one of the most common reasons that individuals begin psychotherapy (Pinsker, Nepps, Redfield, & Winston, 1985).

HOW TO BE A GOOD CONVERSATIONALIST

In order for relationships to develop and thrive, whether these ties are friendships, romances, or acquaintanceships, you need to utilize and fine tune your social skills. In the previous chapter we discussed the art of listening along with the importance of learning to read and understand nonverbal behaviors, and we also offered a framework for allowing you to express your needs and concerns in an assertive fashion. Recognize that initiating and growing relationships involve knowing how to engage in conversation and establish rapport with other people. Ultimately, effective communication is a two way street. It requires good listening skills *and* good conversational skills. The foundation of successful interpersonal relationships, whether in your personal life or the workplace, depends on your ability to communicate your thoughts, feelings, concerns and needs. But just as hearing and listening are not necessarily the same thing, talking and communicating are not always the same. True communication only occurs if the speaker clearly expresses and the listener attends to and understands the message being conveyed.

People who are popular and well liked tend to be good at making conversation. But being a good conversationalist is much more than just talking a lot. We have all had the experience of being in the presence of someone who talked on and on, but bored us to death or made us uncomfortable with sustained self-absorption. Fontana (1990) offers these tips for expressing yourself effectively in conversations:

1. **Keep your message interesting.** Avoid rattling on incessantly about minor details, unless you know for sure that the listener sincerely wants to hear this trivia. Pay attention to nonverbal cues to discern whether the listener is getting bored and adjust your speech accordingly. If the listener starts to fidget, change the subject or ask a question.

2. **Show your sense of humor.** This doesn't mean you have to tell jokes or be a stand-up comedian. Allow yourself to make humorous or witty remarks when appropriate, and by all means, demonstrate that you have the capacity to poke fun or laugh at yourself. This puts others at ease by demonstrating that you don't take yourself too seriously.

3. **Show an interest in the other person.** Refrain from being nosy, but do ask questions to draw the other person out. Most people will enjoy talking about themselves if given a chance, so you will make a good impression if you show a genuine interest in another person. Open ended questions, rather than yes or no questions, make for better conversation.

4. **Avoid monopolizing the conversation.** Avoid interrupting the other person.

5. **Stay focused on the topic at hand.** While everyone occasionally goes off on tangents, and sometimes this helps keep the conversation interesting, resist the urge to ramble on without completing your main point.

6. **Offer sincere compliments when appropriate.** Everyone loves positive feedback.

7. **Refrain from engaging in annoying mannerisms** such as fidgeting or using irritating expressions, such as punctuating your statements with "you know" or "whatever."

8. **Engage in open, confident, non-verbal behaviors.** Face the person squarely, lean forward, stand upright, maintain good eye contact, keep

your arms open and avoid shifting your weight from leg to leg which might appear as if you want to get away as soon as possible.

9. **Talk fairly rapidly, but not too rapidly.** A quick speech rate conveys enthusiasm, intelligence, confidence or expertise. If you notice signs of impatience in your listener, or if people are often finishing your sentences for you, this is a good tip-off that you are talking too slowly and need to pick up the tempo.

10. **Avoid controversy.** If this is an initial encounter and your goal is to make a good first impression then, according to Mary Mitchell (1998), refrain from discussing controversial topics such as religion or politics. Jokes are fine but avoid those that are vulgar or possibly could be perceived as prejudicial. Also, no one wants to hear about your health problems at a first meeting. Save the constipation stories for your loved ones!

Lastly, don't be afraid of small talk. While small talk is often dismissed as superficial or unimportant, nothing could be further from the truth. This idle chitchat or, "how's the weather" banter often serves as the ice breaker or lead-in to more meaningful encounters. Bernardo Carducci (1999) reminds us that just about every romance, or friendship or business deal begins with small talk when people first meet each other.

Building Rapport

There is yet another more sophisticated aspect of being a good conversationalist which has to do with being able to develop **rapport** with another person. Two people are said to have a good rapport when they are comfortable with one another and can get on the same wavelength, either emotionally, intellectually or both. To the extent that you can develop a good rapport with someone, you will increase the probability that you can put that person at ease and/or develop a friendship. Rapport building is affected by many variables. For example, it is often easier to establish a connection with someone if you share similar interests, backgrounds, values, or ways of thinking or expressing yourselves. Then rapport builds naturally. Likewise, if you are engaged in an activity together, like working on a project for a class or at work, this can help lay the groundwork for rapport. Psychologists have long known this **propinquity**, that is, having frequent contact with a person because you live close by or work nearby at the same workplace, is a big factor in who we develop as friends. But just being around a person a lot is no guarantee of friendship; propinquity only provides ample opportunity to develop rapport.

So how do you go about trying to establish rapport with another, be it a stranger or an acquaintance you would like to know better? To a great extent, developing rapport is about putting someone at ease by mirroring their nonverbal and verbal behavior. What does this mean? It requires that you be willing to be flexible in your presentation of self. This does not mean you need to be phony, but rather you need to mirror back those aspects of that person's behavior that you feel comfortable with. For example, if the person is very down to earth, feel free to let your hair down, but if the person is rather formal and uses a lot of big words, trot out your best vocabulary. If the person talks very fast, speed up your rate of speech. Likewise, if the person talks slowly, speak in a more languid way to mirror him or her. If the person gestures frequently, do the same, but if she is rather stiff, hold back on your gestures. Why does this work? Because most of us are most comfortable with people we perceive as being like us. Mirroring is one way of accomplishing this. Used in conjunction with empathic listening you will have the skills necessary to establish relationships. Charismatic and well liked individuals do this unconsciously.

Overcoming Shyness

Some of you might react to these suggestions by saying, "I can't do this; I'm just too shy." Indeed, shyness is a fairly common problem reported by many people. Some people are shy in general, even with people they know well, while for others shyness is an issue mostly with strangers or in unfamiliar situations with new people. According to experts on shyness, Phillip Zimbardo and Lyn Henderson (2008), up to 40% of adults in the U.S. experience shyness during their lifetimes, from mild to severe. In addition, they claim that up to 13% of the U.S. population may have severe shyness, referred to as social anxiety disorder. There is clear evidence of a genetic component to shyness. Research has demonstrated that some infants show higher levels of stranger anxiety than others (Kagan, 1994). However, if you recall from previous discussions of the genetic loading on personality variables, at best only 40–50% of shyness can be attributed to genetic factors. The other 50% depends on your learning history and the choices you make. In other words, you can learn how to overcome shyness.

According to Bernardo Carducci, founder of the Shyness Research Institute and author of *Shyness: A Bold New Approach* (1999), there are three primary aspects of shyness:

1. **Excessive Self-Consciousness**—being overly aware of yourself in social situations, which leads to social anxiety.
2. **Excessive Negative Self-Evaluation**—having low self-esteem, viewing yourself in a negative light.
3. **Excessive Negative Self Preoccupation**—paying way too much attention to all of the things you imagine you are doing wrong around other people.

In general, overcoming shyness is about slowly desensitizing yourself to talking with people. This is accomplished by learning to relax, gradually exposing yourself to progressively more challenging social situations, and practicing social skills such as those previously discussed. The good news is that the more you practice, the better you get. On the other hand, being a loner, talking only to a select few people you know well, or avoiding situations with new people prevents you from having opportunities for growth and practicing social skills, and could ultimately serve to reinforce your shyness. The following tips and suggestions are invaluable for overcoming social anxiety. You are now already familiar with many of these steps which have been discussed in previous chapters.

Steps to Overcoming Shyness

- **Understand your shyness** by recognizing the three factors previously mentioned and convert your self-consciousness into self-awareness.

- **Utilize cognitive restructuring** to challenge the negative thoughts or negative self-statements that reinforce your anxiety in social situations. Recognize that the world is not focusing primarily on you, as most people are too busy worrying about themselves.

- **Learn to accept yourself.** Remember that the most important relationship you have is with yourself.

- **Find and enhance your signature strengths and virtues.** How do your strengths give you an advantage? For example, being a quiet person allows you to be a better listener which gives you a natural advantage for making and keeping friends.

- **Embrace your differences.** Be okay with being different. Trying to conform and be just like everyone else is exhausting.

- **Remember to remember to breathe** slowly from your diaphragm to calm yourself if you feel anxious in a social situation.

- **Release stress and tension though the practice of regular physical exercise.** Regular aerobic exercise will improve your mood, self-confidence, and self-esteem.

- **Use Visualization.** Imagine yourself conversing freely and confidently with others.

- **Practice thinking optimistically.** This will enhance your self-confidence.

- **Practice Social Skills.** Like any other skill, social skills can be cultivated through practice and real life experience. Practice in your head using visualization, or you can role play with a trusted friend.

- **Put the focus on other people instead of on yourself.** Ask open ended questions of others.

- **Practice being in uncomfortable situations.** Desensitize yourself by placing yourself in situations and gradually building up your tolerance. Start by going into social situations that are less intimidating and work your way up to more challenging encounters over time.

- **Know what settings bring out the best in you and begin there.** Going to bars and clubs is not the ideal setting for everyone.

- **Focus on the present moment.** Remember that when you are anxious you are either thinking about the past or the future. Bring yourself back to the here and now.

- **Do not leave an uncomfortable situation.** Turn the anxiety provoking situation into an opportunity for personal growth and introspection. Ask yourself, "What caused me to feel this way?" And more importantly, "Is there an alternate explanation for what is happening?" Although the desire to "escape" may be strong, it would be counterproductive because, even though it decreases your anxiety in the short term, leaving the scene rewards and increases your shyness in the long term. It is very important to break this cycle of avoidance. Keep in mind that even the most popular individuals feel insecure and awkward at times.

❖ **Give up being perfect.** Do you tend to set unrealistic expectations for yourself by comparing yourself to TV celebrities, or people you idolize? If so, knock it off! Those "perfect" people you use for comparison are human as well. They make mistakes, do stupid things, say foolish things, and have bad breath in the morning just like you. You just don't hear about it or see it. Focus on excellence instead of perfection.

❖ **Accept rejection.** Into every life some rejection will flow. Accept that you will experience some rejection in your life, and so will everyone else. It will not kill you. In fact, learning to cope with it is an important part of learning to deal effectively with life. To help you handle rejection consider the following tips:

   ❖ Don't take it personally. It just wasn't meant to be. Not only was it not the best fit for you, it might even be a blessing in disguise.

   ❖ Find the lesson. In every disappointment there is an important lesson to be learned and the potential for you to improve and gain insight into yourself. Nothing is lost if knowledge is gained.

   ❖ Move on. When you throw a pity party, you are staying stuck. Self pity never changed anything. Pick yourself up, dust yourself off, and try again and again and again. It will pay off.

❖ **Record your successes.** Keep a record or journal of your success. Visualize and remember those breakthroughs to help build your confidence prior to facing a social situation. Pull out your journal and read it when you need to remind yourself of your progress.

FRIENDSHIP

All other relationships and connections in this life are empty if friendship is not at the back of them to strengthen them. The relationship between mother and daughter, father and son, brother and sister, husband and wife, teacher and pupil, all these connections need a spirit behind them; and this spirit is the spirit of friendship.

Hazrat Inayat Khan from *In An Eastern Rose Garden*

In chapter 7 we noted that when people reach the end of their lives they seldom wish that they had spent more time at the office. But when they look back at what gave their lives meaning, they invariably rate their close relationships as most important to that pursuit even if they have had remarkable career achievements (Bolt, 2004). Relationships are what make life worth living. Our happiness depends upon them. According to Peterson's (2006) summary of the research on friendship, feelings of well-being and life satisfaction are strongly associated with having high quality friendships.

As we look more carefully at friendships and the social support they provide, we realize that friendships do a lot more than keep us from being lonely on a Saturday night. It is literally a matter of life and death. Study after study links friendship and social support with health. For instance, a summary by David Myers (2004) noted the following:

- Leukemia patients who reported having strong social support had almost triple the two year survival rate of patients who were more isolated.

- Heart attack recurrence was practically doubled in the six months after an initial attack when people were living alone. Over a five year period, 50% of heart disease patients who lived alone died. Those who were married or had a close friend had an 84% survival rate.

- Studies consistently confirm a reduction in stress hormones, lowered blood pressure, and improvement in cardiovascular functioning when patients have a network of social support.

No one is entirely sure exactly how friends help us stay healthy. It may simply be that their presence is relaxing and reassuring and helps reduce the fight or flight response thereby promoting relaxation. We know that this boosts immune functioning. For many people, and especially for women, talking with a friend about a problem is a primary strategy for reducing stress. However, it may also be that friends encourage us to maintain healthier habits around eating, drinking, and smoking. Of course, this assumes that your friends have healthy habits. It is fairly common knowledge that some friends need to be left behind when people are attempting to cope with issues surrounding addiction.

It is also worth noting that being socially rejected by others not only impacts that individual but also affects those around him or her. One may literally become a less productive member of society and in the extreme may go on a murderous rampage as we witness periodically on the evening news. Bolt (2004) quotes Roy Baumeister at the 2002 APA convention summarizing this notion:

> A great deal of psychological functioning is predicated on belonging to the group and enjoying the benefits, both direct and indirect, of that belongingness. Social exclusion undermines the basis for these sacrifices- it ceases to be worth it. The whole purpose of controlling yourself, behaving appropriately and making sacrifices is defeated. And so behavior may become impulsive, chaotic, selfish, disorganized and even destructive. (p.184)

What Constitutes Friendship?

Beverly Fehr (1996) defined friendship as a "voluntary, personal relationship, typically providing intimacy and assistance, in which two parties like one another and seek out each other's company." Bolt (2004) notes that this definition highlights what seem to be the two critical dimensions of friendship, sharing and caring. Sharing and caring move us past liking and acquaintance, toward the deeper realm of friendship. Bolt noted that individuals who lack the opportunity to share their problems with a confidante experience more anxiety, depression, and physical symptoms. True caring between friends goes beyond exchanging support and favors. While a relationship is probably doomed to failure when there is no mutual give and take, true friends give their support and assistance without worrying about being repaid as soon as possible.

Creating Friendships

Friendships don't just happen. Like most other things of value they require committed effort. To a great extent we have already detailed the skill groups that are needed to form friendships. We would suggest that you revisit the section on creating win-win relationships in Chapter 9 with particular attention paid to the emotional bank account. Friendship is built upon trust and making regular deposits in the emotional bank account is the surest way to build that foundation. We would like to finish this section by noting what Bolt (2004) referred to as the "universal rules of friendship." The research reviewed suggests that the following thirteen rules provide excellent guidelines if you wish to have the joy of true friendship in your life.

1. Volunteer help in a time of need.
2. Respect the friend's privacy.
3. Keep confidences.
4. Trust and confide in each other.
5. Stand up for the person in their absence.
6. Don't criticize each other in public.
7. Show emotional support
8. Strive to make him/her happy while in each other's company.
9. Don't be jealous or critical of a friend's other relationships.
10. Be tolerant of each other's friends.
11. Share news of success with the other.
12. Don't nag.
13. Seek to repay debts and favors and compliments.

ATTACHMENT

The concept of **attachment** has become important to understanding close emotional bonds, particularly those between family members and romantic partners. It would be fair to say that attachment begins at the moment of birth and represents the emotional linkage that forms between a child and its caregivers, typically mom and dad, and allows for bonding over time (Ainsworth, Bell, & Stayton, 1992). A helpless newborn will only survive if an adult is willing, ready and able to meet its basic needs. So at birth a newborn's first and vital first questions concern whether he or she can count on his or her caregivers to be available, responsive, and responsible.

If caregivers fail to be appropriately available it can have a lasting impact on later behavior, as was initially documented by the British psychiatrist John Bowlby (1951), who introduced **attachment theory**. In 1950 Bolwby was assigned by the World Health Organization (WHO) to check on the mental health of children orphaned by WWII. What Bowlby discovered was that children raised in orphanages, even if clean and well fed, often developed pathological behaviors such as depression or head banging because they were profoundly emotionally neglected. That is, they had no opportunities to form warm, continuous relationships with a caring, adult caregiver. These children were basically just warehoused. Many of these orphans failed to thrive physically, and some even died from a lack of love. Bowlby's 1951 report revolutionized how children were treated at orphanages from that point forward. Bowlby spent the next twenty years studying how children form emotional bonds, and over the course of three volumes (1969, 1973, 1980) he elucidated his theory of attachment whereby he posited that humans are born with an innate predisposition to bond with an adult caregiver. Attachment evolved to ensure the survival of the species and operates via behaviors designed to regulate and indulge an infant's desire to be in close proximity to its primary caregiver. That is, an infant will continually monitor the whereabouts of the primary caregiver. If that caregiver is close by, the infant will be content and will play comfortably. If the caregiver moves away the child will become upset and all attention will be redirected towards regaining close proximity with the primary caregiver. And, according to Bowlby (1979) this attachment system does not disappear after diapers are shed; it operates throughout the lifespan of all individuals, but is manifested in different ways.

Since that time Bowlby's theory has been refined and updated and several variations on the theme exist. The most elegant variation was introduced by Hazan and Shaver (1994) who explained that the question of whether a caregiver could be counted on to be available and responsive had three potential answers: yes, no, and maybe. They described three types of caregivers depending on which of the three answers they would give:

1. **Warm/Responsive**—Warm, loving, knows when to be supportive and when to back off, can be counted on to be there, reliable, trustworthy

2. **Cold/Rejecting**—Cold, distant, rejecting, not very responsive, very self-centered, child not a very high priority-often gives off message that child is a burden or a bother

3. **Ambivalent/Inconsistent**—Warm one minute and cold the next—loving and rejecting, unpredictable, has own agenda, does not always put child's needs first, loves child but does not always show it in the best possible way

Attachment Styles

All children are born with an inherent tendency or desire to bond. All children also have their own individual temperament, which combines with the level of responsiveness of the caregiver. This creates an interaction which leads to three distinct attachment styles as demonstrated by the behavior of young children in the Strange Situation Test (Ainsworth, 1973). In this experimental situation the behavior of one year old children is observed in a playroom that is unfamiliar to them while in the presence of their mother, after their mother leaves the room, and when a stranger enters the room prior to the return of their mother. This laboratory situation is designed to provide a wealth of information on how young children handle different separation situations. These three distinct patterns of attachment are observed:

1. **SECURE**—Young children with warm, responsive caregivers typically display secure attachments. While in the lab playroom with their moms they are comfortable exploring the unfamiliar environment. If mom leaves, the child becomes upset but then upon mom's return the child

runs to her, is comforted, then calms down and resumes playing. Approximately 60% of North American infants displayed this pattern according to Hazan and Shaver (1994).

2. **AVOIDANT**—Young children with cold, rejecting caregivers display avoidant attachment. These kids don't cry when mom leaves the room nor do they seek her out when she returns. They ignore her as she may have ignored the child. They do not cling to mom like the securely attached young child. These children are just as unresponsive to strangers as to their mothers, preferring to focus on their toys. Approximately 25% of North American infants show this attachment pattern.

3. **ANXIOUS**—Young children who have experienced inconsistent and ambivalent parenting display anxious attachment. In the strange environment they are fearful and cling to mom and cry when she leaves the room, but at her return they are either indifferent or angry. Their inconsistent approach to mom mirrors her own inconsistency in parenting. These children are reluctant to explore their environments. They are hard to comfort and often cry even after being picked up. This style is displayed by approximately 15% of North American infants and is the rarest of the three patterns.

Benefits of Secure Attachment

Children with a secure attachment history seem to fare better in a wide variety of social situations (Peterson, 2006) such as:

- Having more friends—being more popular (Sroufe, 1983)
- Less likely to be bullies or victims (Troy & Sroufe, 1987)
- More socially skilled (Pierrehumbert, Iannotti, Cumming, & Zahn-Waxler, 1989)
- Adapt better to school (Sroufe, Fox, & Pancake, 1983)
- More assertive with parents (Lyons-Ruth, 1991)
- Greater likelihood of good relationships (Peterson, 2006)
- Become more appealing to their caregivers and other people (Snyder & Lopez, 2007)

Attachment Styles in Romantic Relationships

What is really interesting about all of this is that attachment style isn't something that just describes how you interacted with your mom, or dad, or whoever was your primary caretaker when you were a baby or a teenager. It isn't a phenomenon that only affects the tenor of your relationships as a young child. The fact is that adult love relationships tend to mirror early infant attachments (Myers, 2002).

Your early care-giving experiences affect your expectations and view of the social world around you, whether you realize it or not. Our expectations revolve around questions such as, "Are people to be trusted?" Or, "Am I lovable or worthy of being loved?" The answers to these questions are rooted more in your early, not consciously remembered experiences than in any middle school trauma you may recall. And those answers will shape how you approach your close relationships, as it will affect two important components of your ability to relate: (1) your level of comfort with closeness (intimacy); and (2) your degree of anxiety or expectation of abandonment.

Think of your childhood attachment style as a paradigm you hold about what to expect from the world regarding relationships with a significant other. If you were fortunate to be raised by warm and responsive parents/caregivers, you likely have a secure mindset and view the world as typically safe, and others as reliable and trustworthy until proven otherwise. If you were raised by cold/rejecting parents, you likely hold negative and insecure schemas, and may expect rejection from others. You may feel uncomfortable with closeness as you probably experienced minimal intimacy with caregivers when young. You may feel more comfortable avoiding intimacy. If you experienced inconsistent parenting, then it is likely that you expect the world to be a very unpredictable place, and you anticipate rejection at every turn.

So it is not at all surprising that attachment styles established in infancy spill over in how adults conduct themselves in the context of romantic relationships with significant others. Cindy Hazan and Phillip Shaver (1987) had the insight that the three attachment types associated with children towards their caregivers could be utilized to describe how adults approached their intimate relationships. The three distinct styles can be described as follows:

1. **SECURE** adults are comfortable with getting close to others and are not overly concerned about either being abandoned or becoming too dependent on their significant other. Intimacy comes easily for secure adults whose relationships are characterized by trust, friendship, and the happiness that often flows as a result. Secure adults turn to others for comfort and support and are willing to be supportive to others. In marriage, secure adults are better able to accept their partners in spite of their faults and their relationships tend to be healthier and more long lasting.

2. **AVOIDANT** adults consistently find ways to keep emotional distance in their relationships with significant others. They tend to put less energy into maintaining relationships and are more likely to leave them. Some are fearful of or uncomfortable with closeness and intimacy while others are just dismissive of closeness and value independence and self sufficiency over all else. Avoidant adults tend to withdraw when distressed rather than reaching out for comfort from loved ones. Their relationships often have emotional highs and lows, and they are prone to brief sexual encounters without emotional involvement.

3. **ANXIOUS** adults become obsessive when in love. Due to problems with trust and insecurity due their unpredictable upbringing, these individuals are constantly expecting to be rejected. These adults are often jealous, overly possessive, demand constant reassurance and reciprocity, and typically want more closeness than their partners are willing or able to give. Their relationships are often marked with instability, fraught with multiple break-ups and emotional angry outbursts. Such individuals can

sometimes elicit self-fulfilling prophecies, that is, they are so afraid of abandonment that they literally drive their partners to leave them.

Benefits of Secure Attachment in Adult Relationships:

- Less likely to divorce (Hazan & Shaver, 1987)
- Higher levels of compromise (Pistole, 1989)
- Lower rates of domestic violence and abuse (Dutton, Saunders, Starzomski, & Bartholomew, 1994)
- Better able to handle stress (Mikulincer, Florian, & Weller, 1993)
- More supportive of each other in joint problem solving tasks (Kobak & Hazen, 1991)
- More likely to practice safe sex practices (Brennan & Shaver, 1995)

Can Attachment Style Change?

By now you have probably figured out which attachment style best describes you both in terms of your relationship with your parents and in your current love life. If you have a secure attachment, then this bodes well for the future of your relationships. But if you fall into one of the other two categories, are you forever stuck in relationship hell? Fortunately, the answer is no. Avoidant or anxious attachment styles can shift to a more secure attachment (Bolt, 2004). Understanding your attachment style and how it affects your behavior and expectations in relationships is the place to start. Using the cognitive restructuring techniques you have learned, you can begin to challenge any irrational thoughts that lead to maladaptive behaviors on your part, such as irrational jealousy or refusing to communicate with your partner by withdrawing.

Attachment patterns do not have to remain fixed. The ability to change an attachment pattern through awareness is a testament to the power of the interaction of nature and nurture to shape the course of your life. Bowlby (1988) argued that corrective relationship experiences foster more secure attachments. He postulated that since the purpose of attachment in the first place is to attain security, then change is more likely to occur in the direction of secure rather than insecure attachment. That is, we are more likely to pursue relationships that offer more as opposed to less security, than that to which we have become accustomed. Secure relationships are typically much more stable than either avoidant or anxious attachments.

Other Factors Affecting Attachment

There are three other components that strongly affect the strength and quality of attachment: closeness, care and commitment. Close physical proximity is a necessary component that allows both healthy infant and adult attachments to develop. These attachments have different primal motives, of course; for infants it is security, while for adults typically sexual attraction is at the core of an unfolding romantic attachment. But in both types of relationships the importance of physical touch is vital to emotional bonding, and close physical contact allows for this to occur.

The second important component for attachment to occur is a sense of safety that is mediated by care. Attachment grows best when there is easily accessed comfort and emotional support, whether from parent to child or between consenting adults. In this vein, it is interesting to note that research indicates that sensitivity and caring towards a significant other is a much better predictor of the strength of a relationship over the long term than passionate sexual attraction (Kotler, 1985).

Security is derived from an environment of care, but that is only half of the story. The other half has to do with commitment. Children need to know that they can rely on caregivers who are consistently available, supportive, and committed to them in order to go forward into the world and meet the inevitable challenges of growing up. An adult in a stable, committed relationship is often better prepared to face the world of work and responsibility in a confident fashion. According to Hazan & Shaver (1994), commitment is the glue that ultimately holds relationships together over the long haul, ensuring security. But while commitment to children comes naturally for most parents, commitment in adult relationships is a much trickier, requiring decisions and proactive behavior. Ultimately, closeness, care and commitment create an environment conducive to the development of attachment and even for love to grow.

EXPLORING THE MEANING OF LOVE

We think of love, sing of love, and say love makes the world go "round." Certainly for many people, love is the most important thing in their lives. We use the term "love" to describe everything from the food we eat ("I love pizza") to objects ("I love that chair!") to deep enduring feelings we have for a cherished other human. We talk about love as if it is a single, uniform phenomenon, yet there are differing types of love. Robert Sternberg (1987) describes eight types of love as part of his triangular theory of love. They include:

1. Non-love
2. Liking
3. Infatuated love (both strong emotional and sexual attraction)
4. Empty love (devoid of emotional involvement and physical attraction)
5. Romantic love (physically and emotionally bonded)
6. Companionate love
7. Fatuous love (instant attraction, passion and early short lived commitment)
8. Consummate love (passionate, intimate, and committed relationship)

Acknowledging these many types of love helps you realize that not all love is the same. The motives, thoughts, feelings, and behaviors attached to specific types of relationships can help you be aware of what type of "love" you may be seeking and/or experiencing. This can enhance your self-awareness and thoughtfulness about your caring connections with other people.

The Triangle Theory of Love

Sternberg (1987) describes the recipe for love as having three main ingredients: **intimacy**, **passion**, and **commitment**. Intimacy includes those feelings and behaviors that promote a sense of closeness, bondedness, and connectedness. Sternberg writes that **intimacy** includes at least ten elements:

1. Desiring to promote the welfare of the loved one.
2. Experiencing happiness with the loved one.
3. Holding the loved one in high regard.
4. Being able to count on the loved one in times of need.
5. Having mutual understanding with the loved one.
6. Sharing oneself and one's possessions with the loved one.
7. Receiving emotional support from the loved one.
8. Giving emotional support to the loved one.
9. Communicating intimately with the loved one.
10. Valuing the loved one.

Passion is primarily an expression of desires and needs such as self-esteem, nurturance, affiliation, dominance, submission, and sexual fulfillment. How strongly and which needs emerge depends on the person, situations and the kind of loving relationship. Passion and intimacy often interact with each other and fuel one another. Most people associate passion with sexual experiences, but it can be a part of any of the various needs one is feeling such as those listed above.

Commitment has two parts. The first part is a decision to love that person and the second is a commitment to maintain that love. This ingredient in a love relationship is especially important when (notice we didn't say "if") the couple gets into conflict. What the commitment means to each partner is important to be understood, although it can change within the relationship. In a marriage, does it mean commitment for life or commitment until the marriage isn't working?

Reexamining Sternberg's eight types of love, look at the connection between the type of love and the three ingredients of intimacy, passion and commitment in the table below.

TABLE 11.1 Taxonomy of Kinds of Love

Kinds of Love	Intimacy	Passion	Commitment
Nonlove	−	−	−
Liking	+	−	−
Infatuated Love	−	+	−
Empty Love	−	−	+
Romantic Love	+	+	−
Companionate Love	+	−	+
Fatuous Love	−	+	+
Consummate Love	+	+	+

Note: + = component present; − = component absent. These kinds of love represent idealized cases based on the triangular theory. Most loving relationships will fit between categories, because the components of love occur in varying degrees, rather than being simply present or absent. (Sternberg, 1987, p.51)

From this table you will note that Liking involves intimacy alone, Infatuated Love has passion alone, Empty Love has only commitment, Romantic Love integrates intimacy and passion, Companionate Love includes intimacy and commitment, Fatuous Love blends passion and commitment, but the ideal kind of loving relationship, Consummate Love includes all three ingredients, intimacy, passion, and commitment. It is this latter type of love that most of us aspire to and some achieve. It is important, however, to remember that even if you accomplish consummate love, relationships are dynamic entities. Therefore, to make that ideal love last, it is important that you and your partner build a strong emotional bank account, and that both of you nurture in a proactive way the positive relationship you enjoy.

Nonlove lacks any of the three components. There is no passion, no intimacy, no commitment. For example, suppose you have a neighbor, Mrs. Ventura, who lives a few houses down the block. You know her name, you recognize her, and sometimes you exchange a wave in passing or even have some brief spoken exchanges. There really is no relationship. This type of impersonal interaction is generally what we experience with people we see infrequently at work, in public, and with our other acquaintances.

Liking includes feelings we might have for our friends that we have known for years. For example, consider Jose and Tanika, a married couple. Tanika was constantly feeling jealous because Jose had a female friend, Aida, with whom he spent quite a lot of time. Tanika brought this up with Jose who explained to her that he and Aida had been close friends since middle school, and that is all it was. He assured Tanika that she was the one he loved.

When one experiences intimacy alone, we have liking, the type of platonic love that involves our friends. This is not, as Sternberg cautions, a casual non-important relationship, but rather a true friendship that does include a sense of connection, closeness and caring for the person. Liking, however does not include passion or commitment.

Infatuated Love involves only passion. Jamal first saw Maria at the gym and was smitten! He couldn't stop thinking about her and began getting up a half hour early to get to the gym just to be near her. He was overcome by his emotions toward her, and finally got up the nerve to talk to her. He asked her out for coffee after the workout, but she informed him that she was married. He had to back off, and in a short while he got over her. He no longer caught himself staring at her, and one day he realized that she had stopped coming to the gym.

This "love at first sight" is sudden, and can turn into an obsession about the other person. Being infatuated with someone results in a high state of passionate arousal but does not include either intimacy or commitment. In the case of Jamal, he did not even know Maria when he became fixated on her. As is usually the case in this type of love, it came upon him very suddenly, and was dispelled rather quickly when it did not lead to anything more. In infatuated love, the person loved becomes idealized rather than viewed realistically. Actually getting to know the person often leads to unpleasant surprises when he or she turns out not to be that prince or princess the obsessed person has imagined. This often leads to a swift termination. Likewise, the realization that there is no hope for this relationship to occur often leads to an abrupt end. Another concern with this type of love is that a person's obsession can become very awkward for the recipient of such fixation. Infatuated love often comes across as a self-centered love, where personal needs rather than a true feeling of love are behind the pursuit of the beloved.

Empty Love is just as the term suggests—vacant. Many long-term marriages exist in such a barren environment. Take for example, the story of Rebecca and Stephen. They are an older couple who married years ago and raised their children who moved to other cities. Theirs was a traditional marriage where Stephen was the bread-winner and Rebecca, who never worked, was the homemaker and nurturer to the children. They had fallen into a predictable routine with minimal one-on-one interaction. But each person did their part of the unwritten bargain to keep their lives going. Empty love has commitment as its only component. There is no passion; there is no intimacy. Why do they stay together? They stay because they find the arrangement convenient for survival, and they may have insecurities about "making it" in the world on their own.

In many cases this is the state of long lasting marriages that began with a spark of passion, and had intimacy early on, which later faded. The couples seem resigned to this emotional emptiness. Sternberg points out that empty love, as in any type of love, can be one-sided where one partner still feels closeness and bonded to the other, but such is not reciprocated. Arnold Lazarus (1985) notes that when a long-term marriage devolves into empty love, it is difficult if not impossible to resurrect the old feelings of passion or intimacy that once existed.

Romantic Love combines intimacy with passion. Take into account the situation with Latoya and Dwayne. They met at a university summer program for advanced juniors in high school that introduced them to college course work. Their relationship started off friendly, but quickly advanced to a deep sense of love. They were inseparable during the six week program. But they lived across town and attended different high schools. They also had ambitious study and career plans for their lives. They recognized they were young with exciting futures ahead, and were both reluctant to commit to a permanent relationship, although they professed love for each other. Each got accepted to excellent colleges, but hers was on the east coast and he went to a university in California. Neither partner felt much certainty that their relationship would last through such separation. During their freshman year they saw each other occasionally, but eventually the relationship ended.

This is the typical pattern of romantic love where commitment is not included in the mix of intimacy and passion that provides the strong emotional attraction and friendship during the relationship. Although often the couple realizes they are not into commitment, this does not seem to deter the relationship, often seeing commitment as something to think about down the road. A summer romance, like the one described here is often highly exciting for the short term with no real chance for continuing when the summer ends. Romantic love is found in classic literary works about couples that feel strongly passionate about each other and become true soul mates, only to have the relationship end such as in Romeo and Juliet. Such a theme has been the plot of many popular movie scripts. Although Elaine Hatfield and G. William Walster (1981) believe that there is no difference between romantic love and infatuation, Sternberg (1988) views the two as dissimilar, noting that although some infatuations never progress beyond that stage, others do as the physical attraction leads to a realization that they have many aspects in common beyond emotional chemistry. Furthermore, romantic love may not start off as infatuation, but evolve from a strong friendship that eventually grows into a fervent passion.

Companionate Love is a type that can endure throughout long term relationships and marriages, but is lacking passion. It is comprised of intimacy which enables the partners to know each other extremely well, along with commitment which leads to sticking together through good times and bad as best friends. Millie and Miguel were married for more than two decades. They were certain that they were each other's best friend and were there for each other through major life crises. They were comfortable with each other and felt trust, security, and confidence in the strength of their commitment. Although they both realized that they were not now or maybe never were wildly passionate lovers, they were happy together and enjoyed each other's company.

Most romantic relationships, if they last long enough, do eventually shift into a companionate bond. Passion that may have existed in the early stage transitions into a strong commitment that keeps the relationship intact. However, sometimes one of the partners may long for romance. This can lead to affairs outside the marriage which the roaming partner may rationalize is actually helping to keep the marriage in place. Or that partner may eventually leave the marriage to seek romance in a new love cycle.

Fatuous Love is similar to infatuation, but it has one difference. The couple not only feels a sudden intense passion, but they move rapidly to commitment. Take for example, Emily and Carlos. They both attended the same convention when they met in Las Vegas. Instantly they were mutually attracted. Emily had broken her engagement a few months before, and Carlos' former girlfriend had recently called off their relationship. Certain they were meant for each other, they had a passionate fling that led to an elopement within a month. Shortly thereafter they began discovering aspects about each other that they were unaware of prior to the wedding. Needless to say, they ended up turning heartache into more heartbreak when their new marriage collapsed.

Typically those in fatuous love are those who are on the rebound from a failed relationship and have a strong need to be loved. They marry after knowing their partner for only a brief time. When they begin finding out about each other, imagine the surprises that emerge! Such marriages are usually a disaster and short lived. This is the type of romance and marriage often written about in tabloids from the Hollywood scene. Fatuous love is missing the intimacy that, over time, enables each person to learn about the other. Also, since the commitment is not there long enough to be well established, many fatuous love stories end in an early break-up.

Consummate Love is that glorious love for which most people yearn. This delightful type of love has it all—passion, intimacy and commitment. This composition is illustrated in the case of Jolinda and Juan. They were admired as a model couple by their friends and family. They felt close and connected to each other and had great sex together even after twelve years of marriage. They seemed to read each other's minds and know each other so well they could predict each other's thoughts and behaviors. They had their ups and downs, as all couples do, but both remained enchanted with the relationship and had an extremely high regard for the other.

Consummate love is a complete love that results when all three components of Sternberg's triangular theory are present. Consummate love is not easy to attain, but even more difficult to maintain. We don't look for or expect to find consummate love in all our relationships. In fact, this type of love is often reserved only for that special love of one's life, a love that means the most to us and one we want to be as complete, complimentary, and as close to perfect as possible.

Think about the relationships you have with others in your life. Upon which of the ingredients of love are those connections built? Are you satisfied with that? If not, what changes could you make to achieve the kind of relationship you want?

Stages of Relationships

Continuing our focus on relationship development, the work of George Levinger (1976) enumerates the pattern of progression in a relationship as a whole. This would hold true for any type of connection whether it is a friendship, a significant other, or a family member. Levinger pointed out that remembering the stages of relationships is as easy as learning your A-B-C's. The stages he describes are:

A **Attraction**—When we meet other people and feel an initial appeal, often based on physical attributes and similarity. Something catches your interest and you want to know more about that person.

B **Building**—We reciprocate by revealing ourselves to one another. With the passage of time we may get annoyed with one another, but the preponderance of positive aspects fosters continuation of the relationship. We have established a relationship.

C **Continuation**—We make longer term commitments. We continue to grow together in our stable relationship.

D **Decline**—Over time as we may take each other and the relationship for granted, stop consciously nurturing the bond, have alternatives emerge, and/or experience unresolved conflicts. The relationship begins to deteriorate.

This is the time when it is crucial that the partners become aware of the situation and address the problems by cycling back to the B stage and begin re-**B**uilding the relationship. This is where each partner needs to examine how he or she has contributed to the decline and these issues are discussed together. Professional counseling may be called for if needed. If the decline of the relationship is not addressed, it will move to the final stage.

E **End**—The relationship ends when partners agree to separate or one leaves.

Where are you in your various love relationships? Are you in the stage you want to be at this time? If you want to sustain your relationships, you must act to prevent deterioration. Relationships are not static; they are dynamic changing entities. If you want to terminate them, it is wise to make your way to the decline stage as quickly as possible.

THE CHEMISTRY OF LOVE

Remember falling in love? When we ask our students in class to recollect, they invariably offer descriptions such as "beyond exciting," "lost my appetite," "couldn't sleep," "had butterflies in my stomach," "was obsessed," "thought about the person 24/7," "everything they did was wonderful," "wanted to be with them all the time." In contrast, when we ask them what it was like staying in love, the responses change to less dramatic adjectives such as "felt really comfortable," "felt secure," "thought of my lover as a best friend," "could share things easily," "saw my partner's faults, but it was okay." Most of us recognize that enduring love does inevitably change to an attachment phase that is deeper, yet much less exciting than the initial infatuation.

According to Helen Fisher (2004), an evolutionary anthropologist and research professor at Rutgers University, the experience of love can be best understood as a biological drive that is orchestrated by neurotransmitters and hormones. These **biochemicals** have evolved as a means of assuring the continuation of the species. The bliss we feel when we first fall in love is the result of significantly elevated levels of **dopamine** and **norepinephrine**, which cause, among other things, sleeplessness, lack of appetite, exhilaration, and single-mindedness. Add to this a decrease in serotonin, and no wonder you become so obsessed with the object of your affection! Fischer likens the effects when we are in the throes of passion to an addiction. And, indeed, as it turns out, these are the same brain chemicals released when you use cocaine. So whether from cocaine or Maria in apartment 3, the elevated levels of norepinephrine and dopamine electrify the reward system in the brain.

Using *f* MRI technology, on both American and Japanese subjects of all ages, Fisher discovered that when someone falls in love, the parts of the brain that light up and become active are part of the reward system of the brain. One of them is the ventral tegmental area, a tiny part in the midbrain that makes dopamine and pumps it around the brain. This dopamine leads your prefrontal cortex (the thinking part of your brain) to feel more intense ecstasy, and increased motivation to make sure that your lover, or the drug, is there to give you more reward. That is probably responsible for the well documented Romeo and Juliet effect, the fact that when there are external barriers to a relationship, you try harder and you love harder.

Yet this "awe" brought about by norepinephrine and dopamine must eventually subside, as the levels of the neurochemicals themselves decrease. Truth be told, regardless of the generating source, you could not survive the elevated levels of the neourohormones. As the relationship becomes less novel, other neurochemicals begin to replace them, namely, **vasopressin** in men, and **oxytocin** in women. These are hormones that lead to long lasting attachment. They are called satisfaction hormones, because they do give a sense of calm and peace and security and often a cosmic sense of union. These "cuddle chemicals," released primarily during sex, facilitate the bond needed to raise children together.

So why is knowing this important? What practical application does it have? It turns out that the chemicals that give you the "high" get released in novel situations. It is the newness of an experience, which prompts dopamine, with its intoxicating properties, to flood our synapses. In other words, new and varied stimuli can be sufficiently arousing to recapture what was initially so exciting about your mate. Not surprisingly, several studies have shown that couples who share exciting experiences report more relationship satisfaction, as well as romance, than do couples with more mundane habits. Endless routine, while perhaps comforting and stress reducing, can be the death of a relationship.

> *When two people are under the influence of the most violent, most insane, most delusive, and most transient of passions, they are required to swear that they will remain in that excited, abnormal and exhausting condition until death do them part.*

> George Bernard Shaw

The lessons here are that in any long term relationship, infatuation and sexual passion will eventually wear off because so much of it is based on novelty. After you have known someone and spent a lot of time with that person over several years (or in some cases several months), the novelty will eventually dissipate and the faults in your beloved's character will inevitably surface. In good relationships the infatuation is replaced with a deeper attachment not based solely on novelty. Intense passion can sometimes be stretched out for longer time periods in cases of long distance relationships, where you see your beloved infrequently, so novelty takes longer to wear off, or in affairs where there is a danger and naughtiness factor that adds to the excitement and limits how much time a couple can spend with one another. But the bottom line is that the initial infatuation is always time limited even in the best of relationships. Understanding this and knowing that it is normal helps foster realistic expectations for relationships. Couples can help to keep excitement alive in long term relationships by avoiding endless routine and making an effort to engage in interesting and stimulating activities together whenever possible, to bring novelty back into the relationship.

COHABITATION

More than ever before couples are choosing to live together in loving and sexual relationships without getting married. This pattern is referred to as cohabitation, and data from Census 2000 revealed a 71% increase in the number of unmarried partners who lived together between 1990 and 2000 (U.S. Bureau of the Census, 2001). At present more than 5 million people in the United States are cohabitating. With over half of all women aged 25 to 39 having cohabitated at some point in their lives, living together in such an arrangement appears to have become the norm, rather than the exception. A generation or two ago, people who lived together were referred to as "living in sin." Be assured this was meant not in humor, but as a criticism. Witness the fact that until around 1970, cohabitation was illegal in all 50 states (Economist, 1999)! In contrast today, more than half of the Fortune 500 companies provide "domestic partner benefits" to both homosexual and heterosexual cohabiters (Miller & Solot, 1999).

Why do people cohabitate rather than marry? There are obviously multiple reasons, which include really getting to know a partner and their habits and character, wanting to see if they are compatible, saving money by living together, and feeling like they are not ready to marry yet (Poponoe & Whitehead, 2001). Interestingly, the cohabitation rate in the United States, which is about 5%, is low compared to the rate in other countries, such as Sweden and Norway, where 12% of heterosexual couples cohabit (Renzetti & Curren, 1998).

But are cohabitations successful? Do cohabitating couples have a higher rate of success if they marry later than do married couples who did not live together first? A study of 3,300 adults found that couples who live together before marriage are 46% more likely to divorce than those who did not (Labi, 1999). At first glance, this data might seem to indicate that cohabitating is, indeed, harmful to the longevity of the marriage and some conservative groups have alleged just that, calling it the "cohabitation effect." However, if you apply critical thinking you become aware that reaching such a conclusion about causality is definitely premature. Remember the difference between causation and correlation we discussed in earlier chapters. There seem to be other factors that contribute to the difference, rather that the fact that the couple is cohabitating. For instance, couples who cohabitate tend to be less traditionally religious and more likely to believe in divorce when a marriage is not working. Whereas, couples who do not live together prior to marriage are likely to be more religious and less accepting of divorce (Miller & Solot, 1999). Thus, the causal factors are just as likely to be religion and the couple's attitude towards divorce, rather than whether or not they cohabitated. Another factor is that, on average, married couples have higher incomes than couples who live together outside of marriage. Given that financial problems are the most common factor associated with divorce, it might be that what we are actually seeing is the effect of wealth and not cohabitation. Yet another possible factor is the age difference between cohabitating couples and married couples, since couples who choose to live together tend to be younger and the older the couple the less likely the divorce (Popenoe & Whitehead (2001).

So the answer to the question initially posed regarding the effectiveness of cohabitation is that we really don't know. Perhaps more importantly, the emphasis should be on the commitment between two people and the quality of the relationship, rather than whether or not they signed a marriage license.

MARRIAGE

By far, more adults marry than never marry, and the vast majority of individuals spend most of their lives within a marital relationship. Even today, the majority of young people say they are planning to marry at some point in their lives (Thornton & Young-DeMarco, 2001). In Western culture, romantic love and sexual attraction have become the basis for marriage. This has not always been the case, and it still is not in other cultures around the globe where marriages are arranged by the parents on the basis of age and social status. The partners in these couplings are expected to build their union and learn to love each other after marriage. It is surprising to most of us to note that a study comparing the levels of marital satisfaction between arranged marriages and those who married by choice demonstrated no significant difference between the two (Myers, Madathil, & Tingle, 2005)!

Regardless of how the original pairing took place, maintaining satisfaction in the relationship over a long period of time takes attention, work, and commitment. Commitment in a relationship is often demonstrated by the decision to marry. Yet it is important to mention that many couples have long-term committed relationships, either heterosexual or homosexual, that do not involve marriage. Nonetheless, 93% of Americans say that a happy marriage is one of their most important life goals (Gallagher & Waite, 2000).

Factors Contributing to Long Term Marital Satisfaction

So what are some of the factors that contribute to enduring satisfaction in relationships? One of these appears to be a sense of equality between the partners, particularly about decision making. Another is a genuine appreciation for one another and an attempt to understand the other's point of view. Also important is the ability to face conflict and disagreement early on, along with a willingness to work on the relationship by using effective communication (Byers, 2005).

John Gottman (1994), a renowned marital therapist, described four factors that were associated with long-term loving relationships. The first of these were positive memories about the beginning of the relationship. One of the authors, a practicing psychologist with a specialty in marital therapy, became aware of this fact early in his career. As part of the initial interview with couples, he asked each member of the pair if they remembered when they first fell in love. He noticed a better prognosis for resolving the issues they brought to psychotherapy when both partners were able to recall the loving feeling. A second factor involved similar levels of emotional expression between the partners. That is, it was okay when both partners were either very demonstrative or, conversely, more inhibited. Problems arose when there were very strong differences in styles of emotional expression. The third factor outlined by Gottman and already previously mentioned was early confrontation of complaints and differences. When couples confronted each other constructively about disagreements early in their relationship, rather than sweeping them under the rug, the likelihood of continued satisfaction in the long run increased. Interestingly, Gottman did not find an absence of conflicts as predictive of marital happiness and fulfillment; rather it was how they handled such conflicts. Lastly, and perhaps most controversial in the field at the time, was Gottman's report that for marriages to be happy and fulfilling, there needed to exist a 5 to 1 ratio between positive and negative interactions. This ratio, referred to as the **"Losada ratio"** was discovered by Marcel Losada, who originally studied flourishing in business environments (Losada, 1999; Losada & Heaphy, 2004). His research determined that when there was better than a 2.9 : 1 ratio of positive to negative statements among employees within an organization, that business flourished economically. Gottman (1993) derived the same results when analyzing the weekend conversations of married couples. Below the 2.9 : 1 ratio couples were on the road to divorce, with the average Losada ratio at the time of divorce down to 1.5 : 1. A 5 : 1 Losada ratio, that is, five positive statements to every negative statement, between spouses predicts a healthy and loving marriage.

The fact is that maintaining frequent positive interactions is crucial to continued satisfaction in a relationship. It does appear that it is the little things that count. When a partner tells another, "You don't love me anymore," what it most likely means is "You are not doing the many little things you used to do that I interpreted as meaning you loved me." Once again, continuing to make deposits into the emotional bank account emerges as critical to the success of a marriage or any other relationship. And it appears that not allowing the account to go into deficit is not enough. Instead, for a relationship to flourish there needs to be a reserve of funds. In a latter study, Gottman found that the quality of the friendship with one's spouse is the most important factor in marital satisfaction for both men and women (Gottman & Silver, 2000).

An earlier study where 351 married couples were asked why their marriages have lasted found that marriages seem to last longest when both partners have a positive attitude toward the marriage, view their partner as a best friend, and like their partner as a person. Qualities that individuals particularly liked in their partner were being caring and giving, having integrity, and having a sense of humor. It was not that these couples were not aware of flaws in their partners; it was that they felt that the positive qualities far exceeded the negative ones. They preferred shared activities as opposed to separate ones and they also believed marriage to be a long-term commitment (Lauer, Lauer, & Kerr, 1990).

A review of the literature on marital satisfaction by Karney & Bradbury (1995) concluded that successful marriages that remain strong over the long haul often exhibit certain other characteristics. These included parents of both spouses having had successful, happy marriages, spouses with similar attitudes, interests, and personality styles, an adequate and steady income for the couple, satisfaction for both the partners regarding their sexual sharing (the quality was much more important than the frequency), and the woman having not been pregnant when the couple married.

In yet another study in which the investigators asked a sample of 560 women and men to judge the relative importance of a number of varying ingredients to the continued success of a relationship, the following elements were judged as most important to high-quality relationships (Sprecher, Metts, Burleson, Hatfield, & Thompson, 1995):

- Companionship: Sharing mutual interests and enjoying many activities together.
- Sexual expression: Spontaneity and variety in sexual sharing and feeling sexually attractive to one's partner.
- Supportive communication: Open and honest communication and a willingness to talk about difficult issues and concerns.

But why worry so much about making relationships last? With the divorce rate hovering around 50%, why not just accept that maybe, as some argue, we are not meant to be together "until death do us part?" One reason, as we have discussed earlier, is that researchers have consistently found that marriage positively affects a person's health and general level of happiness. People who are married tend to be healthier, happier, and enjoy longer lives than either single, widowed, or divorced individuals of similar ages (Zheng & Hart, 2002). Marriage, it seems, makes us more resistant and resilient to the impact of a number of possible traumatic events, such as losing our job, retiring, or becoming significantly ill. Suicide rates in single men are twice as high as those of married men. Similarly, single men experience more psychological problems, such as depression and nightmares (Faludi, 1991). While initially, these benefits seemed to apply more to men, the last few years have evidenced a trend in the physical and mental health benefits of marriage applying equally to both men and women (Simon, 2002).

Improving Marital Communication—Active and Constructive Responding

One of the goals of positive psychology is to teach individuals how to improve the quality of their relationships. The following discussion, while geared towards improving marital communication, is applicable to any relationship with a significant other or friend. Learning to engage in **active, constructive responding** will enhance your Losada ratio with others, thereby enabling you to improve troubled relationships and turn good relationships into great ones.

Our significant others often come to us to share news about their accomplishments, successes, as well as a myriad of other positive or interesting things that happen to them. According to Shelly Gable, how we respond to these communications can either build the relationship or undermine it. In general, there are four basic ways of responding (Gable & colleagues, 2004; 2006), summarized as follows:

Active & Constructive: Acknowledging what the speaker has said, asking questions, offering praise, excitement and optimistic expectations, sharing the good feelings and supporting the positive emotions of the other.

Passive & Constructive: An unemotional reaction, giving polite but subdued acknowledgement to the speaker with minimal enthusiasm or follow-up questions.

Passive & Destructive: Ignoring what the speaker is telling you, shrugging it off as if it has no importance and/or changing the subject quickly.

Active & Destructive: Immediately pointing out all the potential pitfalls about what the speaker has told you, complaining about the effects of the news on you, expressions of pessimism or negative emotions about the news, failure to express congratulations or offer any enthusiasm.

To flesh this out, review the example of these four possible responses to the following scenario: Your significant other comes home from work and informs you he just got a "terrific performance review" which should positively impact the size of his yearly bonus.

Active & Constructive: "That's wonderful! I'm so glad your boss is finally appreciating how hard you work and the quality of your work. I am so proud of you! You deserve a big bonus and I'm sure you will get it. Tell me all about your review. What compliments did you get and from whom?" *Nonverbal behavior:* Displays of positive emotion, good eye contact, smiles, laughs, hugs if appropriate.

Passive & Constructive: "That's nice. It's about time." *Nonverbal behavior:* No follow up questions, minimal emotions like it is no big deal or unimportant, a demeanor equivalent to being told some neutral information about the weather.

Passive & Destructive: "OK, now what we need to think about is what to cook for dinner." *Nonverbal behavior:* Disinterest, minimal eye contact, no questions or comments, changing the subject to a neutral, unrelated topic.

Active & Destructive: "I'll bet you use that as an excuse to work longer hours than you are now, and then what happens to me? I'll be stuck doing even more stuff at home alone while you are busy getting your ego propped up at work. I hope you are happy. By the way, don't get your hopes up. Your boss is way too cheap to give you a bonus." *Nonverbal behavior:* Anger, sarcasm, glaring, passive-aggressive looking away or walking away. No questions or praise.

Which one of these attitudes would you like to come home to? That's a no brainer! If you put yourself in the shoes of the person coming home with good news, it is very easy to see how the active and constructive response would build good feelings and rapport in your relationship. The other three options would either lead to disappointment on your part or even anger and resentment if your significant other chose an active, destructive reply. Using active and constructive responding allows you to make deposits in the emotional bank account you hold with your significant others.

Remember that positive emotions are contagious. Allow yourself to be infused with the joyous emotions of the other and then give the gift of returning it. The more you do this with a spouse or significant other, the better your Losada ratio, and the better the relationship. In addition, engaging in active and constructive responding will draw people to you. They will like you more and want to talk to you. Everyone likes someone who shows a sincere interest in them combined with a willingness to acknowledge and celebrate their successes.

Positive Psychology Exercise: Practice Active and Constructive Responding

The next time a friend, relative, co-worker or especially your spouse tells you about something good that happened to them, go out of your way to reply in an active and constructive fashion. Ask them all about it and show enthusiasm. Pay attention to their response and to how you feel.

The Importance of Providing Emotional Support

What about when your partner comes home with negative news, particularly involving work related complaints or stressors? Providing emotional support to a spouse or significant other is just as important as responding constructively to good news. Emotionally supportive partners improve the quality of their relationships with an extra added benefit: this helps your partner cope better with workplace stress. Consider the following unpublished study conducted in 2011 by Wayne Hochwarter, professor at the Florida International University college of Business (as reported in the Miami Herald on 2/15/2012). In this study 400 working couples in both blue and white collar professions were surveyed to determine how couples handle it when both experience daily workplace stress. Partners who did not feel that they received adequate emotional support at home returned to work even more distressed. When mutual positive spousal support was present, these couples reported the following as compared to the non-supportive couples:

- 33% more positive relationships with co-workers
- 33% more satisfaction with time spent with spouse
- 20% higher level of career satisfaction
- 25% less fatigue
- 25% higher ability to concentrate at work

Clearly, it is important to be there for your partner, to be available as a sounding board, a shoulder to cry on, or just to be willing to listen to the other vent. Partners can also help their significant other to problem solve or reframe workplace issues. In Hochwarter's study, there were differences between men and women in the type of supportive behaviors they desired. Both genders wanted their partner to understand the unique demands and stressors of their particular job or work environment. However, the women wanted empathic responses from their men, and to be cut slack on household chores when they were overworked. In general, what men wanted from their significant others was affection, expressions of appreciation and opportunities to have some time alone. This brings us to the very interesting topic of how gender influences communication styles and patterns between men and women.

COMMUNICATION STYLES—DO MEN AND WOMEN SPEAK A DIFFERENT LANGUAGE?

Most of us have a wealth of experience from our own history of relationships to recognize that one of the most important factors affecting the longevity and quality of relationships is communication. Have you ever experienced difficulties communicating with the opposite sex? Did it ever feel like you were speaking a different language? Most of us have had the experience of looking back at an argument with a heterosexual partner and wondering what we were actually fighting about. Research supports the fact that conversations among men and women are, indeed, more difficult than same-sex groups (Athenstaedt, Haas, & Schwab, 2004; Edwards & Hamilton, 2004). Deborah Tannen (1990, 1994), a professor of linguistics at Georgetown University has done extensive research on the different communication patterns between men and women. She contends that while not necessarily speaking a different language, it is as if we are speaking different dialects of the language. She refers to these conflicting dialects as **genderlects**. A word of caution here, please be aware that the patterns we will discuss are generalizations and do not necessarily apply to every individual man or woman. Remember that at our core, we are far more similar than we are different (Hyde, 2005).

Men's and women's genderlects stem from different paradigms each appears to hold about the world. Men tend to perceive the world and their relationship with others as hierarchical. A hierarchy is much like a ladder, with each man posed on one of its rungs. They must struggle to either move up the ladder or at least maintain their position. Women, on the other hand, are more likely to view the world as a series of interactions and interconnections. Their goal is to remain connected and avoid isolation. Studies have revealed that women tend to use more rapport-talk, aimed at establishing connections and relationships, while men favor report-talk, which imparts knowledge (Eckstein & Goldman, 2001).

Tannen (1990) studied videotapes of individuals from a variety of age groups talking to members of their own gender. As she watched children communicate and interact with each other in same-sex playgroups, she became aware that girls habitually faced each other squarely when talking, maintained good eye contact, and seemed to enjoy conversing with one another. Girls were also more likely to play in small groups, or even in pairs. Winning or losing in their play was not as important as maintaining intimacy and a sense of community. This is clearly demonstrated when girls play house. They wanted to get along with their friends so that everyone could have a turn. On the other hand, boys appeared to use speech as a way to express dominance in groups which were hierarchically organized and everyone knew their place in the hierarchy. Their main focus seemed to be on directing and winning. Their play groups tended to have a leader who would tell everyone what to do. Interactions among the boys reflected attempts to vie for attention and deflect the challenges of other boys in order to remain the center of attention. They often jockeyed for position by telling jokes, showing off, or claiming they were the best at things. When boys and girls encountered conflict, both wanted to get their own way, but their methods were starkly different. Boys tended to rely on insistence and threats of physical violence, while girls usually tried to avoid confrontation and arrive at a compromise.

Differences in communication style between adult men and women are rooted in this apparent fact that they have grown up in different sociolinguistic subcultures and have learned different communication rules and assumptions (Maccoby, 1998; Maltz & Borker, 1982). These rules follow them through life and become problematic when as adolescents, they begin to communicate in mixed-sex groups with the same rules they used to communicate with their same-sexed peers.

Status vs. Support

For men, conversation is often about getting and maintaining the upper hand and preventing others from pushing them around. For women, talking is frequently a way to exchange confirmation and support. Tannen offers an example from her own life which amply demonstrates this difference. Tannen and her husband are both following academic careers, doing research and teaching in higher education. Because such vocations most often require a job setting at a university, for a period of their lives they lived a few hours away from each other. Tannen noticed that whenever she and her husband were at a gathering and someone would comment on how difficult it must have been to live apart, her husband's typical retort was something like, "Oh, it's not so bad. We see each other every weekend and because we are academics, we have summers off. With transportation as easy at it is these days, it's not really a big burden." He would interpret the comment as an attack on the quality of their marriage, and thereby his status, and seek to defend it. She on the other hand, would respond more with something like, "It is really difficult. I miss him so much at nights during the week. And the packing and unpacking can get really old quickly." For her the communication was about support, about empathizing with how hard it must be for Tannen and her husband. Given these different paradigms, no wonder we often hear women tell their opposite sex partners, "Why do you have to be so aggressive?" and men respond with, "Why do you have to be so talkative?"

Independence vs. Intimacy

Because women think in terms of being close and giving and receiving support, very often, their goal is to achieve and preserve intimacy. In contrast, men, given their concern with status, instead value being perceived as independent. A personal example that occurred to one of the male authors provides a perfect illustration. The couple had been married about a year when an old graduate school friend of the husband called him to tell him he would be visiting Miami for the weekend to help his father move to an assisted living facility. He would be done with his responsibilities by Friday evening and rather than return to New York, wondered if he could come and spend a couple of nights at the couple's home. The husband had not seen his friend for years so his natural response was, "Sure, it will be great! That way you can also meet my new wife." Imagine his surprise when he got home and announced the good news.

"Why didn't you call me?" his wife hurtfully inquired.

"Why, do you have a problem with it? Are we doing something this weekend?" he asked.

"Well no, but we should make these decisions together," she tried explaining.

"But that would seem like I have to ask your permission! I would have had no problems calling him back and canceling if we had something else planned," he pleaded.

Clearly the man was concerned about checking in with his wife, because in his mind it would imply a lack of independence. His wife, on the other hand, placed in a similar situation would love to call her husband and check in because it would signify the level of closeness that they possessed. "See how close we are, we check with each other for everything!"

Advice vs. Understanding

One of the hallmarks of independence is the ability to come up with solutions to problems with which we are presented. Typically, when someone approaches a man to talk about a problem, his general tendency is to provide advice, to offer a solution. In contrast, for intimacy to be achieved it is important to really understand the other person's experience. It follows that more often than not, when a woman complains about something, she is not necessarily looking for an answer to a problem, but rather to feel understood. Tannen (1990) provides a wonderful example in her book *You Just Don't Understand* about a woman who had a benign lump removed from her breast. She hesitantly shared with her husband her discomfort with the scar and the change in her breast's shape. He quickly responded with the solution. "You can always have plastic surgery." His wife was hurt and accused him of being insensitive for feeling that she should again go under the knife just because he didn't like the scar. Her husband was hurt and puzzled. "I don't care about the scar," he retorted. "It doesn't bother me at all." To which his wife replied, "Then why are you telling me to have plastic surgery?" She was not looking for solutions; she was looking for emotional support.

Information vs. Feelings

Generally for men, conversations are vehicles with which to impart information. Not surprisingly, research shows that, in opposition to popular belief, men tend to talk more than women in public situations. They are likely to ask the first question, ask more questions, and engage in monologues for a longer time than women do. They are also much more prone to interrupt others (Moore & Davidson, 2000). In contrast, women speak much more at home than their heterosexual partners. They talk about their feelings and problems and see the discussion as a way to work on them. Men often perceive the communication as just wallowing in complaints. For women, not being told about something such as personal feelings or troubles seems like a rejection from their partner. They value the intimacy involved in sharing secrets and worries, whereas men are more likely to feel vulnerable doing so. Consider how this is manifested in the different ways men and women manage stress. In response to stress, men tend to isolate, to withdraw; they are likely to want to unplug and perhaps just watch TV. Women are more prone to lean towards what has been called the "tend and befriend" response. The tendency towards making sure the environment is in order and then talk. For women, conversing will lead to a decrease in the fight/flight response, yet for men it will likely cause an increase. No wonder women often complain that their husbands never share what goes on at work! When her husband responds with "nothing" to his wife's request about what happened that day, he is thinking there is no new information to report and besides he wants to get away from it, not relive it. To his wife he is not sharing his feelings and his day, which will decrease her understanding of her partner and thereby lead to less intimacy between them.

Orders vs. Proposals

Women often begin statements with words such as "Let's" or "Why don't we," as in statements like "Let's park over here" or "Why don't we stop for coffee?" Such statements are meant as suggestions, not demands, intended to begin a negotiation about what the couple will do next. This style of speaking is aimed at getting others to do what they want, but by first winning agreement. Men, because of the hierarchical nature of their world do not want to feel dominated or like they are in a one-down position. Not surprisingly, they frequently resist being told what to do. They are likely to interpret the woman's communication as a veiled command and become resentful of it. It is interesting to note that when stating an opinion, women, but not men, often end their statements with tag questions, such as "It's really dreary today, isn't it?" or "That's a great suggestion, isn't it?" These tag questions appear aimed at initiating discussion and decreasing the chances of disagreement. For similar reasons, women tend to use disclaimers, as in "Maybe I'm wrong, but..." and question statements, such as "Am I wrong? as well as hedge words like "kind of" or "sort of" (Carroll, 2007).

Conflict vs. Compromise

Because of their goal of preserving harmony and remaining connected, women often attempt to prevent confrontation by refusing to openly oppose what others want. While a win/win attitude is clearly helpful, sometimes it's a lot more useful for a woman to assert herself, even if doing so might lead to conflict. In fact, one of the factors associated with successful long term relationships according to John Gottman (2000) is early confrontation of complaints and differences. This is not to suggest that habitually opposing others is a recipe for success. Clearly, a balance between seeking to compromise with a willingness to face conflict when necessary would have the greatest chance of success.

Okay, so there are differences in the way men and women communicate. Now that you know this, what good is it? Tannen asserts that the first step in improving communication between the sexes is being aware of and accepting that there are gender differences in communication styles. It is not a question of one style being better or worse or more right or wrong than the other. When we understand the differences and the dissimilar paradigms from which they stem, we can question our own interpretation of an interaction and arrive at solutions to difficult or seemingly irresolvable problems or predicaments. So when a man says, "I'm tired; I don't want to talk; I just want to watch TV or something," rather than taking that as a personal rejection, his female partner might realize he is just stressed and wants get away from anything that reminds him of it. Or when a woman says she wants to talk, her mate might remember that she is not asking for her problem to be solved, just for him to listen. He might then let go of being Mr. Fix it, and practice some of the skills and principles discussed in Chapter 10 on empathic listening.

There have been some criticisms of Tannen's genderlect theory. For one, Tannen believes gender differences are based on biological sex. A different model argues that the stylistic differences are found more on the basis of gender roles than biological sex (Edwards & Hamilton, 2004). According to this theory, men who are higher in nurturance exhibit more cooperative speech, while women low in nurturance evidence more dominance speech. Additionally, most studies on gender differences in communication have used primarily young subjects who were middle-class and well educated Americans. It is questionable whether these differences are true of other cultures. For example, none of these differences in communication were found when Chinese men and women were studied (Mortenson, 2002). Perhaps this again reflects the different goals between individualistic societies and collectivist cultures.

ALTRUISM

The early Greeks described three types of love: Eros, Philo, and Agape. **Eros**, from which the word "erotic" come, is the "love at first sight" experience that sparks quickly with intense feelings but is not long lasting, often vanishing as quickly as it began. That is what was referred to as Infatuation by Sternberg and discussed earlier in this chapter. **Philo** is the reciprocal type of mutual brotherly love. It is based on friendship between two people and has an "I'll love you as long as you love me" connection. It is based on give and take where two people benefit from each other. This equates to Sternberg's conception of Companionate Love. **Agape** love is that which is given without any expectation of return. It is selfless love like the love a mother has for her child or that we show for those in need. It may be given with, but often given without any returned benefit to the giver. This is the type of love that leads to the self-sacrificing caring for others we call **altruism**.

So let us return to a theme we have been exploring from the very first pages of this book, the value of stepping into another's shoes and feeling as if you are that person. The best relationships are built around our capacity for empathy, as well as our willingness to give freely and forgive gracefully. The data is clear. When you give help or service, you get something in return even if you don't expect it. Adults involved in giving service experience improvements on all measures of happiness and well-being. The elderly experience improved health and longer life from their participation in volunteer work (Brown, Nesse, Vinokur, & Smith, 2003). Seligman (2002) found that college students discovered service to be more gratifying than pleasurable activities, the so-called "do good, feel good" effect. It is obviously good for those who receive the kindness and if the recipient of the kindness is happier as a result then they will tend to be kinder and more helpful themselves (Isen, 1972). Most interestingly, it is even good for those who observe an act of kindness, like seeing someone helping a lost child find their parents. As you witness an act of kindness or a loving gesture, neurochemicals, such as oxytocin in women, are released and literally give you that heartwarming feeling in your chest that makes you feel more open, loving and trusting (Haidt, 2006).

An evolutionary argument can also be made for altruism. Darwin theorized that if a group of unrelated individuals out survives or out propagates a competing group, its' gene pool will multiply. Therefore, it follows that cooperation within that group would enhance survival. Cooperation is possible because of human hive emotions such as love, forgiveness, gratitude and empathy – the foundation of altruism. Cacioppo & Patrick (2008) remind us that we humans are not an impressive physical species in terms of strength, speed or natural weapons. Our competitive advantage comes from our ability to work together, plan, reason and problem solve to achieve goals. A group that displays such cooperation and altruism is more likely to survive to pass on its genes.

But altruism is the willingness to act in another's interest even if there is no apparent reward or benefit for doing so. The truly altruistic person is motivated by the prospect of improving someone else's situation. Considering the paragraph above, it has been suggested that this type of motivation for behavior is non-existent. In other words, no one does anything without some sort of benefit, however subtle, flowing back to them. But as we noted in Chapter 9 in our discussion of empathy, people seem to be willing to sacrifice for others for no other reason than reducing another's suffering. This has been confirmed in over 25 studies (Batson, Ahmad, Lishner, and Tsang, 2005).

Ultimately, is this really so surprising? Perhaps it is only to scientists who need experimental data to be convinced. In the annals of human history we have always been captivated by the capacity of the sage or saint to sacrifice for the benefit of another completely unknown to them. For example, in the Christian tradition we see Jesus speaking up to prevent a woman from being stoned to death. In this incident, he even educates the murderous crowd giving them a lesson in empathy. He points out that those who wish to punish this woman are no different than her when he says, "Let he who is without sin cast the first stone." Indeed, the central premise of Christianity itself is that Christians are saved because Jesus died for their sins. Matthieu Ricard (2006) in *Happiness* shares this story from the Buddhist tradition.

> Dola Jigme Kalsang was a Tibetan sage of the nineteenth century. One day while on pilgrimage to China, he came to the central square of a small town where a crowd had gathered. As he approached, he found that a thief was about to be put to death in a particularly cruel fashion: he was to be made to straddle an iron horse that had been heated to red-hot. Dola Jigme pushed his way through the crowd and proclaimed, "I am the thief!" A great silence fell; the presiding mandarin turned impassively to the newcomer and asked, "Are you ready to assume the consequences of what you have just told us?" Dola Jigme nodded. He died on the horse and the thief was spared. (p. 207)

We are equally fascinated by the hero or parent who willingly gives their life so that another life or lives can be saved. What is happening when this happens? More importantly, what questions does it pose for all of us who seek to lead a life worth living, and want to experience a sense of well-being, what the Greeks called eudemonia. In other words, how does this knowledge inform our most deeply held values?

The essential insight of the mystic is the realization that all of life is unified. There is no real distinction between us and the objects of our perception. Through various practices, mystics work to see through the illusion or perspective that we are separate from the people and things around us. This is how it is written in the Upanishads, the earliest recorded sacred writings.

> *Who sees all beings in his own Self, and his own Self in all beings, loses all fear... When a sage sees this great Unity and his Self has become all beings, what delusion and what sorrow can ever be near him?*

> Isa Upanishad, verses 6-7

All religions have capitalized on this notion of all the members being part of a single body. Thus, when we are exhorted to follow the Golden Rule and treat others as we would like to be treated, what we are actually doing is recognizing ourselves in the other and helping us because we really are not separate at all.

Science can give us insight into how this mystical consciousness arises in the body. Jonathan Haidt (2006) in his book, *The Happiness Hypothesis*, summarizes some of the most fascinating data in psychology in regard to various religious practices. The method most common among the various religious traditions for accessing the state of unitive or cosmic consciousness is meditation. Modern technology allows us to look into the brain and see exactly what happens when meditators report being in this mystical state. As it turns out, two areas in the parietal lobes of the brain experience a drastic reduction in activity. These areas are responsible for your orientation in space. In other words, they keep track of the boundaries of your body and where you perceive your body to be in space. When these areas are deprived of this information regarding the edges of your body and where you are in space, they continue to try to locate you. As a result of this you begin to feel expanded out into space with no boundaries. You lose the limited sense of yourself and, in Haidt's own words, "feel(s) merged with something vast, something larger than the self." You have in Buddhist terms become empty of the sense of the self but full of everything else, experiencing unitive or mystical consciousness. The emotional state which accompanies this is usually a feeling of unconditional love for all things.

These states can also be accessed by groups who participate in meditative or rhythmic activities such as drumming, chanting, or even marching. The result is an extraordinary bonding among the members of the group. This identification with the group can be so intense that group members are willing to do anything including sacrificing their lives to protect the group. In a real sense, at this moment of ultimate sacrifice, the individual may have the sense that they are not really dying because the group they are so identified with goes on. There is a part of being human that is very much like being part of a hive.

Sadly, while this breeds tremendous cohesion within groups, it also can lead to branding anyone outside the group as evil. We need look no further than national and international politics, hostilities between religious factions all claiming to serve God, or the tragic lessons of Nazi Germany where an entire country was brought together for what were ultimately evil ends. Can we begin to take seriously the notion of global citizenship; where we do our best to affirm life for ever greater numbers of people and animals and the plants that support them?

So, science shows us what happens in the brain and body when we perceive unitive consciousness. But, is this just an illusion or is it something real upon which you should base your relationships? Perhaps that is the wrong question. Remember, since this is a book about optimal functioning, the better question would be to ask, "Does it help to enhance the quality of your life and relationships?" We feel secure in saying that your world and our world will be a better place if you seek to fulfill your capacity to be altruistic. Consider this final word on happiness and relationships from Jonathan Haidt:

> *Happiness is not something that you can find, acquire, or achieve directly. You have to get the conditions right and then wait. Some of those conditions are within you…..Other conditions require relationships to things beyond you. Just as plants need sun, water, and good soil to thrive, people need love, work, and a connection to something larger. It is worth striving to get the right relationships between yourself and others, between yourself and your work, and between yourself and something larger than yourself. If you get these relationships right, a sense of purpose and meaning will emerge.*

> *The Happiness Hypothesis* (p. 283–9)

POSITIVE PSYCHOLOGY EXERCISE: PAY IT FORWARD

Think of an unexpected kind thing to do for someone, be it a stranger, friend or significant other, and go do it! Pay attention to what happens to your mood.

KEY TERMS

Rapport

Attachment Theory

Commitment

Infatuated Love

Companionate Love

Biochemicals

Vasopressin

Genderlects

Agape

Active and Constructive
   Responding

Propinquity

Intimacy

Nonlove

Empty Love

Fatuous Love

Dopamine

Oxytocin

Eros

Altruism

Attachment

Passion

Liking

Romantic Love

Consummate Love

Norepinephrine

Cohabitation

Philo

Losada Ratio

CHAPTER 11 QUESTIONS

True or False Questions (T or F)

1. ____ Talking and communicating are the same thing.

2. ____ In conversation you can avoid boring another person by going into minute details.

3. ____ Small talk is always a waste of time.

4. ____ People are more likely to feel at ease with you if you establish rapport.

5. ____ It is easier to develop rapport with someone who is similar to you.

6. ____ During conversation, refrain from asking questions of other people because they might find it annoying.

7. ____ Shyness is a very rare problem.

8. ____ It is impossible to overcome shyness.

9. ____ Having friends and a strong social support network helps you to stay physically and emotionally healthy.

10. ____ With true friends you can ignore the emotional bank account.

11. ____ Cold, rejecting parents tend to produce children with secure attachment styles.

12. ____ Adult love relationships tend to mirror early infant attachments.

13. _____ It is possible to change your attachment style, to grow into a secure attachment.

14. _____ Romantic love includes the three primary ingredients of intimacy, passion and commitment.

15. _____ In Fatuous love one party merely pretends to love the other, perhaps to inherit money.

16. _____ The bliss we feel when we first fall in love is due to elevated levels of brain chemicals such as dopamine and norepinephrine.

17. _____ Novelty is the primary factor in infatuation.

18. _____ Cohabitation typically causes couples to divorce later on if they marry.

19. _____ The level of marital satisfaction between arranged marriages and those who married by choice are not significantly different.

20. _____ For marriages to be happy and fulfilling the ratio of positive to negative interactions must exceed 25 to 1.

21. _____ Dealing with conflicts constructively is a big predictor of marital success.

22. _____ If you are emotionally supportive to your spouse it will increase his stress level.

23. _____ Men favor rapport-talk while women favor report-talk.

24. _____ For men conversation is often about getting the upper hand and achieving dominance.

25. _____ It is a myth that there are gender differences in communication styles between men and women.

26. _____ Altruistic acts can benefit the giver as well as the recipient.

Short-Answer Questions

1. _____ exists when you have frequent contact with someone by virtue of living or working close by.

2. _____ begins at birth and represents the emotional linkage between an infant and its caregivers and allows for bonding to take place over time.

3. Children who have experienced inconsistent and ambivalent parenting display an _____ attachment style.

4. According to Sternberg, the full recipe of Consummate Love includes the three ingredients of _____, _____ and _____.

5. _____ Love involves only passion.

6. When we first fall in love we experience elevated levels of brain chemicals such as _____ and _____.

7. When couples chose to live together prior to marriage this is referred to as _____.

8. The best way to reply to your significant other when he tells you something positive that has happened to him is to use _____ and _____ responding.

9. The conflicting dialects used by men and women are called _____ by Tannen.

10. _____ refers to an altruistic love given without any expectation of return.

Essay Questions

1. Describe what you need to do to carry on a conversation in an effective fashion.

2. What causes shyness and what are some methods for overcoming it?

3. Discuss the important aspects of maintaining friendships.

4. What is the association between childhood attachment style and how adults approach romantic relationships later in life?

5. What makes Consummate Love superior to the other seven types of love described by Sternberg?

6. Describe the typical stages of relationships.

7. What insights about the biochemistry of love can be gleaned to foster realistic expectations for romantic relationships?

8. What are the important factors in sustaining a healthy, satisfying, long term marriage?

9. Describe some of the differences in the way men and women typically communicate.

10. What is the value of altruism for the individual and for society as a whole?

Occupational Effectiveness

Knowing the Workplace

Designing Your Own Career

Applying Positive Psychology at Work

12

Knowing the Workplace

Do you remember when you started college? You had to get yourself registered for classes. The campus was full of buildings that housed, among other things, classrooms...and you had to find the rooms where your classes would be held. You had to figure out where the bookstore and cafeteria were. You were probably not able to function comfortably or effectively until you knew your way around. It also helped to learn specific terms used by other students to describe things related to college life. Understanding what "credits" are and how they relate to completing a degree was also useful information. Once you became familiar with the college environment, things made more sense. You could move around, make choices and decisions and figure things out a lot easier.

Likewise, when you first enter your work life, you could find yourself in a similar situation. To function better in the career world, you need to know some of the basics. Consider what is going on around you, what you will be experiencing, and why there is an expected conformity in the way you behave professionally and personally. Knowing these basics helps you anticipate things, adapt more easily and in general be more effective in your career behavior. This sophistication makes you more confident in your decision-making processes and work habits, making the quality of your work more rewarding. Even if you are a more seasoned worker with years of experience returning to college, you still have to orient to a new college experience and/or the possibility of a new work environment as your professional career changes.

The average worker has typically worked eight hours a day, five days a week, 50 of the 52 weeks in a year. That's most of your year right there! Add to that the trend with technology to expect workers to be available 24/7 and it is even more consuming. When you consider that you may work thirty or more years of your adult life, it becomes clear that the most of your life is spent in your career. Get the picture? And what if your career is not rewarding? How many people do you know or hear about who hate their work? You don't want to be one of them, right? It is probably not a coincidence that most heart attacks occur at 9:00 a.m. on Monday mornings! Could this be related to work? So there's something to be said about getting some basic information about the dynamic environment in which we fulfill our career aspirations. So let's find out what's happening in the world of work.

OCCUPATIONAL TRENDS

One trend that is obvious to everyone is that the workplace is constantly evolving. Alvin Toffler (1971), a sociologist, pointed out decades ago that change was changing. It is speeding up like a boulder coming down the mountainside. Unlike the lives our parents or grandparents lived, things now are changing so fast it is mind-boggling! We have moved from an agriculture-based economy to a manufacturing economy to a service economy. Now we are in an information economy. Add to all of that the influence of portable computers, electronic notebooks, smart phones, social networking sites and WOW what profound changes.

It may be difficult for you to imagine that there was life without computers. Computers have changed the way things happen in so many arenas. To name a few, consider business, government, education, communications, and automobile operations. We depend on computers to operate practically everything in life. What would happen if the computers suddenly stopped? At the turn of the century in 2000, there was great concern about computers and Y2K. Experts pondered the potential chaos and disaster that could result from failed computers. Now, since 9/11, there is concern that chaos could be caused by terrorists' attacks on computer systems which could greatly damage our economy. Since computers are so important to keeping things running there is a new term for these experts in information and communications technology. We call them **gold collar workers**.

It is estimated that well over 80% of the world's technological advances have occurred in the last hundred years. Technology feeds on itself—one breakthrough leads to a host of other advances which then spur on even more developments. This cycle is never ending and will keep accelerating. Additionally the Internet is changing the way we do everything from shopping to research to communicating. This is related to the information explosion that we are experiencing. There was more information produced in the 30 years from 1965 to 1995 than had accumulated in the entire previous history of civilization, in the roughly 5000 year period spanning 3000 B.C. through 1965! A study conducted at the University of California at Berkeley found that five exabytes of information was produced in 2002. An exabyte is equal to a billion gigabytes or approximately 500,000 times the amount of data in the Library of Congress' print collection. These researchers estimate that the amount of available information is doubling every three years (Lyman and Varian, 2003). This information is available to us instantaneously, not only from the Internet, but TV, and satellites or we may read about it on our handheld communication device. The more we learn and discover, the more we must change or risk falling more and more behind.

Other changes are happening today. These include such things as increased diversity in the workforce, global competition and interdependence, and new organizational patterns in the workplace. Other factors influencing change are uncertainty following the terrorist attacks of 9/11, unemployment and major instability in the economy, the blending of work and non-work in employees' lifestyles, and how one views work security.

Increased Diversity

One of the changes we see in society is the increasing diversity in the workforce. Unlike previous decades where white males dominated the work force, the Bureau of Labor Statistics projects that those entering the workforce will include greater representation of diverse groups and older workers. Minorities, which comprise about one third of the U.S. population in 2008 are projected to become the majority in the workforce in 2039. By 2023, minorities will comprise more than half of all children. (U.S. Census Bureau News, August 14, 2008). Minority representation in major counties shows that one in every ten of the nation's counties has more than 50 percent minority population, with Miami Dade County, Florida having the highest proportion at 82 percent.

Hispanics have become the largest minority group in the United States at 15 percent in 2008 and are projected to be 30 percent by 2050. Although there are high concentrations of Hispanics in several states, this population is dispersed throughout the nation. More than half of all immigrants coming here in 2000 were from Latin America. Within the Hispanic population are subgroups with cultural and socioeconomic differences. Asian Americans, with their many subgroups, are a smaller total number, but comprise a fast growing ethnic group in the U.S. African American and Native American growth rates are higher than the growth rate for Caucasians which are expected to drop from 74 percent in 2008 to 46 percent by 2050. The portion of our population made up of persons born outside the United States is 12.9% (U.S. Census Bureau, 2010).

We see the rising numbers and influence of women who comprised 47.9% of our civilian labor force in 2010. This is an increase of 15 percentage points in the decade from 2000. In 2008 there was a drop in the number of women for the first time in 48 years. This was attributed to job losses of one million women since 2001 from meager earnings, outsourcing, and layoffs. Such diversity means a variety of ethnic, social, and cultural customs and attitudes among workers who co-exist in the same workplace. Additionally, more disabled workers, who comprise the fastest growing minority group in the workforce, are broadening the scope of workplace differences. The potential for misunderstandings and conflict is obvious. Learning to interact positively with people of varied backgrounds, cultures and characteristics brings a growing challenge.

Often we are unaware of our prejudicial attitudes or behaviors. When describing a group of people involved in an activity, how many times do we hear someone refer to a particular person in the group as "this Black guy" when no one else's skin color is mentioned. It is irrelevant in any case; is it not? Why is this person's skin color singled out? Why isn't he just referred to as "a guy" as the others were? And what goes on in the minds of those who heard that man so described. What stereotypes do we carry around relating to African Americans? Hispanics? Women? Asians? Persons with disabilities? To work well with a variety of people whose personalities and attitudes are formed from environments different from the one we know, suggests we have an open mind. We must be willing to respect differences and to learn about and appreciate a broad array of perceptions and behaviors in the workplace. Remember empathic listening? The extent to which we can understand what it is like to be in that person's shoes impacts our sensitivity and level of respect. Further, if we learn to value and appreciate diversity as a richness that surpasses homogeneity, it increases our chances for success in our careers. Remember, not only the workforce, but the clients, customers, patients, or students you count on for your work are also diverse. Relating effectively with a mix of people is necessary for success.

In addition to the diverse groups mentioned above, another source of diversity in the workplace is the growing age gap found among present day workers. Workers are living longer and working longer. Life expectancy for the U.S. population reached 77.8 in 2005 (Kung, H, Hoyert, D, Xu, J and Murphy, S. April 24, 2008). Eighty percent of baby boomers say they plan to work at least part-time during their retirement (MarksJarvis, November 13, 2007). DeCenzo (1997) breaks age groups into three separate eras: (1) those born pre-1946; (2) those born between 1946-1964; and (3) those born after 1964. He labels these groups and summarizes some of the differences in the following chart:

	Mature Workers Born pre-1946	Baby Boomers born 1946-1964	Baby Busters/Generation X Born after 1964
Value Most	Family	Careers/Money	Personal Gratification
Want from Job	Security	Advancement	Control own destiny
Ideal Vacation	Trip to town of ancestors	Disneyland	Deserted Caribbean island

The differences in these generations' values and attitudes are obvious. The **mature workers** lived during or close to the time of the Great Depression. In that era resources were scarce, unemployment abounded, and people learned to be exceedingly frugal to survive. It makes sense that this group desires security from their jobs. This group likes to watch news magazine types of TV shows as they do not want to be caught unaware as in the stock market crash of 1929 or the Pearl Harbor of 1941.

The **baby boomers** evolved in a great era of building. The space program, the rapid advancement of technological innovation such as TV and other communications networks evolved. These post-World War II babies had a more plentiful life than their parents. They came to see careers as central to their lives and value advancement and the money it brings. Many workers of this era are "workaholics."

The **baby busters** or **Generation X** group born after 1964 are seeking personal gratification and want work to allow them the freedom to pursue their own interests. They are looked upon as selfish and intolerant by the older two age groups.

More recent studies have reported on the group following the Generation Xers. This group is referred to as **Generation Y**, representing individuals born between about 1977 to 2000. There are about 70 million who comprise 26% of the U.S. population. These group members grew up in an era of prosperity, expanding technology, and are more ethnically diverse than any previous generations. They are expected to outnumber the large number of baby boomers that made up that generation. Gen Y individuals, also referred to as "Millennials" or "Net Generation," have grown up with computers and are astute in computer use; the majority have computers and internet access. They are less cynical, more optimistic, self-confident, and expect to be better off financially than their parents. They are the most educationally oriented generation in history, recognizing that education is the key to their success. "They are more open and tolerant as products of biracial and multicultural marriages, and rail against sexism and homophobia. They are the best hope we've had so far for a more open, tolerant society" (Tulgan and Martin, 2001). They are socially conscious and are spurring a trend of volunteerism with a concern for the environment, poverty, health status, the elderly and other community problems or issues. They want their careers to offer them meaningful roles at work where they feel they are making a contribution. They want to be a part of a very motivated work team and develop an open-minded workplace. They have high monetary and personal goals. Their self-confidence has prepared them to make the moves necessary from one job to another to fulfill their goals.

So what is the generation after Generation Y? You guessed it, **Generation Z**. This group was born from the 1990's to 2011. They are also called Generation M for multi-tasking, or the Net Generation or Generation 9/11. They are highly connected as they have been exposed throughout to technologies such as the World Wide Web, smart phones and texting, tablet computers, YouTube and other social media. They are therefore called "digital natives" and, unlike their predecessors, they have never known a world without these technologies. Generation Z are known for quickly gathering, organizing, and storing information on-line leading to the term *digital curation*. They are also very open in sharing their ideas and perspectives on an assortment of media, topics, and products.

How do you imagine these diverse groups might interact together in the same workplace? What types of conflicts can you envision? Have you had any experiences with this issue in your work history?

Changes in Organizational Structure

In addition to working in a global economy, another continuing trend is businesses seeking more economical practices to improve profits. We see changes occurring both among and within organizations. In the corporate world, we see businesses grouping together, merging with each other, buying out others and otherwise combining forces. We see companies going bankrupt or being swallowed up in takeovers, resulting in long standing firms going out of business. Another business issue is that of the gap in earnings between corporate executives and workers, as well as concerns regarding ethical practices within corporations causing losses to shareholders of stocks.

The national and international economic downturn beginning in 2007 brought major layoffs in all types of businesses. Real estate sales came to a standstill, banks were struggling to survive, retail sales dropped, and automobile manufacturers reduced production and staffing. In 2008 health care was eventually the only industry hiring workers. Companies in the U. S. and in Europe closed down for extended periods during the holiday season in December.

One continuing trend is **downsizing**, which was used extensively in the economic downturn of the late 2000's. This of course brings major organizational change within a company. The process of downsizing means doing more with less as positions are cut from the payroll to reduce costs. Once the workforce within the company is leaner, companies begin to expect workers to cross-train, meaning learning the work of another employee. For instance, we see respiratory therapists and nurses cross-training in hospitals; we see financial aid and registration clerks cross-training on a college campus.

Further, technology is being implemented to increase efficiency and minimize the need for personnel. Personnel costs, by the way, are the most expensive items in the budget. Robots or computers are also being used to replace humans in doing tasks.

This "reduction in the workforce" has led to two categories of workers...(1) full time or **core workers** and (2) part-time or **contingent workers** (DeCenzo, 1997). Historically we have expected that most people would be "core" workers. However, since change is so common in organizations, the best way to be prepared for changing personnel needs is to hire people for projects or short-term temporary work. Then when there are seasonal changes, changing needs for expertise, or different priorities and projects, there is no need to retain them. Tourism companies, hospitals, colleges, and a host of other businesses use these hiring practices. Full-time workers usually have benefits not offered to part timers and full-time employees have more job stability. Part-time workers may receive higher salaries, but generally do not receive health insurance, retirement packages, and other benefits.

The advantages to working full time includes the security of a paycheck, job stability, position or rank, and benefits, such as paid vacations, retirement packages, sick leave and others. The advantages of being a contingent worker include flexibility in work schedule, extended time off, possibly higher salary and opportunity to change work environments frequently. With the increased use of technology, workers are "connected" electronically to their work through cell phones, cyber cafes, and the like. This is having implications for the nature of the work day or work week. As mentioned earlier, there is an increasing expectation among managers that their employees will be available 24/7 to solve problems that could impact profits. This is causing a blurring between work and non-work time. The portability of technology has a growing number of workers working at home, telecommuting, and trouble-shooting from remote locales.

The self-confidence, technological expertise, interest in continued learning, and optimism of the Generation Y and Z groups has produced self-reliant, competent, flexible individuals who are better able to deal with the changes in organizational structure than their older counterparts. Continuing change has been a greater part of their lives and they not only cope, but *seek* new challenges and opportunities for career fulfillment.

GLOBAL INTERDEPENDENCE

People say we live in a shrinking world. Yet, we know the earth hasn't actually shrunk (except, perhaps for melting ice caps!). Today, interacting with people around the world has become so easy and accessible. The marketplace is no longer just *our* community, *our* state, or even *our* country. We are intermixed in many ways. Not only is travel easier and more accessible, but people are more mobile, living and working in different parts of the world. Communicating with someone on the other side of the globe is only a computer and e-dress away. It is even being said that we have moved from an information economy to a global information economy. More and more countries are finding new groups of people in their presence, and diversity is an issue on every continent. So called "American" cars today are built from car parts made all over the world. Businesses begun in one country now operate everywhere. If we made a note of it, we would probably discover that we have an "international" day most every day, using household items, tools, medicines and foods from other countries as part of our routine. Some countries earn more than half their income from exports. In fact, what began hundreds of years ago as trading between countries has evolved into the workplace becoming the whole earth.

To succeed in this global community, it is imperative that one has a respect for diversity and appreciation of culture. Consideration for political values, moral patterns, as well as social and economic conditions is also necessary. To get a sense of the increasing worldwide influence on our lives, it is useful to examine what is happening with **outsourcing**.

When you dial your technical support number with a computer problem, and a representative residing in India and speaking with a British accent answers to help you, you have just experienced "outsourcing." Outsourcing refers to the *source* of the production being *outside*. The "outside" may be out of the company, the city, the state, the nation or the continent.

Outsourcing is not a new idea. In fact, in many ways outsourcing is an extension of the contingent workers discussed above. These workers are not employees of the company, but work for a separate company who contracts to do the work from another place, perhaps from anywhere around the globe. Historically in the United States, lower-paid laborers from other countries have been used to build railroads, to cut sugar cane, and to harvest other crops. More recently nurses have been recruited from abroad to fill the gap of labor shortages in that field. For years manufacturing has been using inexpensive labor from overseas to make clothing and other items. Increasingly, lesser-paid workers are still being used, but no longer do they have to leave their homes and take up residence in a new culture. We all wear articles with labels that read "Made in China," or Russia, Indonesia, Poland, to name a few countries. Business services, however, do not have "made in" labels. Therefore, we may be unaware that as a customer in the U.S., we are being served by someone on the other side of the earth. American companies are increasingly contracting with businesses located elsewhere to provide the work from there.

However, outsourcing is a two way street. Many American companies are the vendors for other national or international businesses outsourcing manufacturing, computer technology, and other services. There is increasing competition to American providers as other companies around the world are getting into outsourcing. The complementary term **insourcing** refers to workers in one country locally providing labor for companies owned outside of their country. For example, American workers are employed here for a European or Asian company. A report by the U.S. Chamber of Commerce (2004) found that direct foreign investment now exceeds $487 billion and supports 6.4 million jobs in the U.S. Consider, for instance, the automobile industry where large numbers of Americans are working here at home for Honda, Toyota, and Nissan, all foreign owned companies. It is estimated that some 150,000 jobs have been insourced from Mexico to the U.S. (Fraser, 2004).

What *is* new is the growth of outsourcing to include not only manufacturing labor, but information technology and services of all kinds. Thomas Friedman, *New York Times* columnist and author who visited Bangalore, India (the Silicon Valley of India) in 2004, points out that all sorts of U.S. jobs can be outsourced. He notes that "we visited …everything from radiological labs that are reading the x-rays done by big American hospitals to accounting firms that are now using Indian CPA's to do your taxes, to cartoons and game companies that now have Indian artists drawing for American games…" (News Hour with Jim Lehrer, 2004). In addition to manufacturing being outsourced and technical support teams for computer companies, we have workers on outsourcing contracts for all sorts of services. These include selling credit cards; making airline reservations and tracing lost luggage; handling purchasing, human resources tasks, customer relations, and on-line ordering; processing banking operations; transcribing medical records and radiologists reading x-rays; as well as a variety of call centers in many fields. One begins to wonder what job could not be outsourced and therefore done at a lesser cost to a company or organization?

In the case of **off-shoring** (i.e., outsourcing to another country), comparing salary differences requires a look at the economics of outsourcing for both countries involved. It is rather obvious why companies in America are seeking to outsource all sorts of work to lower labor costs. Traditionally in America not only salaries, but benefits such as vacation time, sick leave, insurances, employment taxes and the like contribute to the high cost of labor. Total costs for personnel are the major expense of nearly all service companies and organizations, often running well over 90% of the total budget. Imagine the increased earnings of businesses that can greatly reduce their personnel costs by contracting for outsourced labor. This leads to lowering the costs for consumers and improving their own companies. Catherine Mann (2004) reports that, based on price reductions from global sourcing, the U.S. Gross Domestic Product (GDP) in 2004 was $230 billion more than it would have been, or the equivalent of each working person in the U.S. making $2000 more that year.

Although the cost of labor in India and other countries is much less than in the United States, these same salaries are an increase for the workers in these countries. For example as Friedman notes, previously many young college graduates in India who were not engineers could never get jobs there paying $200 to $300 a month, which is the beginning pay for a call center employee. Obviously such low starting salaries would be impossible in the United States, thus the cost savings for the businesses that outsource. At the same time, the salaries and ultimately the standard of living increases for the workers and their country's economy is increased accordingly.

Outsourcing is not only expanding to all sorts of work categories, but is also spreading all over the globe. India has been the major nation to take in outsourced American work, and interestingly enough is now outsourcing some of their contract work to other countries. The *New York Times* (September 25, 2007) reported that Infosys, an Indian Company of 75,000 employees is opening offices in numerous countries around the world such as Mexico, the Czech Republic, Thailand and China, and in low-cost regions of the U.S. The global interdependence that outsourcing has forged is seen in the example of an American bank needing a computer system to handle loans for Hispanic customers using Infosys, an Indian vendor (7000 miles away), to supply it with Mexican engineers working 150 miles south of the U.S. border.. Although India has been the prime country involved in outsourcing, many other countries are scrambling to get into the act. Ireland has been active for several years in contracting commitments. Russia, who has had a surplus of scientists and engineers from the Cold War, is engaging these professionals for contracted scientific and computer systems work. Hungary and Mexico are vying for contracts with U.S. companies. Growth has been seen not just in countries seeking contracted work, but in the number of countries who are now also outsourcing their labor. Friedman described accent classes he visited in India where not only the American accent was being taught, but also British and Canadian accents to accommodate call center clients from the United Kingdom and Canada.

This increased interconnection in trading work within and among countries of the world reflects a growing global interdependence which has contributed to the global economic issues of recent years. The impact of outsourcing raises implications for the level of education or re-education needed for 21st century workers. When your job disappears, it's not just a matter of finding similar work at another firm…it has broader implications for change. The questions for you to keep in mind are: "How will this influence my career experience as I enter or continue in the labor market? What does it mean for my educational requirements and employment patterns? How can I be most effective in my career where the workplace has become the whole world?"

THE GLOBAL PERSPECTIVE–Is Outsourcing a Blessing or a Curse?

Since outsourcing now involves countries all over the world interacting in the trade of goods and services, what are the economic, political, and social impacts of this global interdependence? Is outsourcing a blessing for enhancing and sustaining our world, or is it a curse? The debate has been intense in the United States.

Those who are against outsourcing include many labor unions, industry associations, and of course displaced workers who are infuriated. Researchers estimate the total number of American jobs outsourced will reach 3.3 million or more by 2015 (McCarthy, 2002). Brainard and Litan (2004) report that up to 14 million Americans work in occupations that could reasonably be considered "at risk."

A most outspoken critic of outsourcing is Lou Dobbs, former anchor and managing editor of CNN's Lou Dobbs Tonight. He contends that U.S. corporations are sending American jobs overseas so rapidly that this country's economy is facing a crisis of historic proportions (NOW, 2004). Dobbs (2004) believes that corporate America controls the politicians through campaign funding and lobbying, and controls the media through which most of us get our information, including Congress. This is why, he suggests, that trade laws and agreements, as well as government reports and agencies support outsourcing as good for our economy, when in reality it is seriously hurting the middle class. Is outsourcing *increasing* the gap between the "haves" and the "have nots" within America? Are we now a government "by the corporations" rather than "by the people"?

Finance Professor Rory L. Terry (2004) also argues against outsourcing, stating that we are not inherently superior to our foreign competitors in creativity and innovation as some suggest. He points to the many international students enrolled in our most difficult degree programs at prestigious universities, and our low rank in mathematics and science education. He also notes that many of our highest paying jobs can be exported such as doctors, accountants, engineers, computer programmers, architects, and scientists.

There are other advantages to companies from outsourcing beyond the low cost of labor such as no labor unions, no Social Security or Medicare benefit payments, no unemployment taxes, no health benefits for workers, no child labor laws, no safety or environmental protection costs or restrictions, no worker retirement benefits or pension costs. But what does this means for off shore workers doing the jobs? In addition to working conditions, what is the impact on the environment if there are no safety nor environmental protection measures? Is off shoring negatively impacting the health and safety of workers *and* the environment?

Terry (2004) and others enumerate social costs in the U.S. from outsourcing that are paid for by the people . . . *not* by the corporations. Beyond the loss of jobs, he points out the costs of a reduced tax base, high unemployment costs, pricey government retraining programs, loss of national sovereignty, more expensive raw materials, not to mention the social problems of higher rates of child abuse, spousal abuse, alcoholism, bankruptcy, divorce and the like as unemployment climbs. What does this do to our standard of living? Are we allowing corporate profits to diminish our quality of life?

Although there are many against outsourcing, there are those who see it very positively. As many point out, all socio-economic changes cause a shift in the jobs available. Indeed, the advent of the automobile put those who worked making saddles, horseshoes, and tackle for horses out of work. Likewise, the coming of the computer put typewriter companies out of business. Changes always create temporary losses, but lead to increased gains in new jobs being created. In fact, each year there are thousands of jobs lost and new ones created as processes and technology change. This is known as "churning" of jobs as they shift and has been going on for centuries. Proponents of outsourcing point out such patterns of replacement are natural in an economy and not any different today than in past history.

THE GLOBAL PERSPECTIVE—Is Outsourcing a Blessing or a Curse? (cont.)

Fraser (2004) sees outsourcing as a win-win opportunity, giving us more goods and services at a lower cost. It raises the standard of living for everyone with huge benefits to low-income people and seniors living on fixed incomes. Equally positive is "in sourcing" and the estimated total of 6.4 million insourced jobs brought to the U.S. Fraser also points out that "this global synergy improves freedom and opportunity across the world by helping to eradicate poverty in the poorest countries" (2004).

An IT industry study reports that outsourcing in fact creates jobs (CNN/Money, 2004). This study indicates that off shoring lowers costs, inflation, and interest rates while it increases productivity. This in turn boosts business and consumer spending and increases our economy. These benefits are projected to produce a total of 317,000 net new jobs through 2008.

The increase in the U.S. economy as well as in the receiving countries implies outsourcing is reducing the gap between the "haves" in the U.S. and the "have nots" in less developed countries. Though the wages paid are low by American standards, they are an increase for the workers there. Does this not help those workers and the global economy? A government official in India reported their economy increasing at a remarkable 8% per year. He also touted their educational preparedness with more than 18 million graduates a year, more than a million of them in engineering. His area now has 15 universities, 1500 IT companies, and 180,000 workers in IT that are expected to rise to 500,000 (Gowda, 2005). Isn't what outsourcing has done for India possible elsewhere? These are some of the arguments for and against outsourcing. What would a global citizen think, feel and do about outsourcing? How might outsourcing affect your decisions about your career? Looking at the broader picture, how can we ensure that outsourcing is a plus for our globe?

OCCUPATIONS IN DEMAND

With an ever expanding, aging and more and more diverse population we will have a changing mix of goods and services being demanded. Workers' skills will have to change to meet these changing requirements. Employers will continue increasing the use of technological developments and revised business practices to enhance their production at lower costs. Data from the Bureau of Labor Statistics indicates that total employment is expected to increase 15% in the 2002-2012 period. The fastest growing occupations will be those that require more education and training. However, there is also an increase in the number of occupations that involve short-term training. It is an important issue to be aware of what "hot" new jobs or steady old ones are in demand. For example, suppose you wanted to be a blacksmith. These workers make the metal shoes that horses wear. That dream would have been easy to fulfill a hundred years ago, when horses were used for transportation, but today you will find very limited opportunities.

What careers are projected to have the fastest growth in the decade from 2008-2018? The ten fastest growing occupations are listed here in descending order:

- Biomedical engineers
- Network systems and data communications analysts
- Home health aides
- Financial examiners
- Medical scientists, except epidemiologists
- Physician assistants
- Skin care specialists

- Biochemists and biophysicists
- Athletic trainers
- Physical therapist aides

What occupations are projected to have the largest in employment by category of education and training over the 2008 to 2018 period? For each education category, the increase is calculated by adding the expansion across all occupations in the category. The ten highest growing categories are listed below in descending order:

- Associate degree
- Master's degree
- First professional degree (i.e. lawyer, architect)
- Bachelor's degree
- Doctoral degree
- Postsecondary vocational award
- Bachelor's degree, plus work experience
- Moderate-term on-the-job training
- Work experience in a related occupation
- Short-term on-the-job training

Although this information is current for the latest report from the Bureau of Labor Statistics, at the time of this printing, it is important to note that unanticipated events such as terrorist attacks, widespread hurricane disaster, collapse of mortgage businesses, failures of banks and investment companies, and major stock market losses can greatly impact the economy and therefore the resultant employment and unemployment patterns. For example, costs to industries for increased security, insurance, shipping and delays at borders were estimated to be as high as $150 billion just for the year following the September 11 attack on the World Trade Center (Bernasek, 2002). Therefore you as the reader are encouraged to secure the most recent data and projections that can be found on the Bureau of Labor Statistics web site at http://stats.bls.gov. This site has a large volume of information, employment related topics, recent news releases and monthly updates.

LEADERSHIP IN THE WORKPLACE

In small businesses or offices as well as large organizations, there is a "climate" that reflects the personalities of the people there, especially the person or persons in charge. This may vary from place to place depending on such things as the nature of the work, the type of organization, but especially important is the style of leadership provided by those with administrative responsibility. The setting may be very structured and formal, or it may be loose and casual, depending on the type of work and the size of the organization. For example, if you work in a small automotive repair shop with a single owner/operator, you may have few employees and a casual climate. If you work for the county court system, you may have hundreds of employees in specialized jobs. There may be strict job expectations, highly structured procedures, policies, and a great deal of formal documentation.

In every work setting, the type of organization is summed up in the basic mission or purpose that the organization exists to achieve. The more the members of the organization understand and agree with the mission, the more likely people will work as a team to accomplish the purpose. However, there are other things besides the purpose that affects how employees work together.

A major consideration is the type of leadership that is demonstrated in the work environment. Think of the leaders you have known in organizations or jobs. What differences in behavior styles have you noticed in the people who are in charge? Obviously, in any work setting you are going to be affected by the leadership operating in the environment. So let's take a look at leadership. Let's consider what it means. Then, let's examine variations in style that produce differing results. Finally, let's ask about the possibility of leadership in your future.

What is Leadership?

There are endless definitions, but they all seem to come down to the idea that **leadership** means influencing people to think and/or act a certain way. Leadership implies there is a goal or desired outcome, and that communication is used to guide members of a group to accomplish that goal or achieve that outcome.

Many people use the words "leader" and "manager" to mean the same thing, but many researchers and writers distinguish between these terms. In general, the main difference between a leader and a manager is that the leader is concerned with people. The leader focuses on the attitudes, reactions, motivations and the behaviors people exhibit toward accomplishing the mission of the organization. Leaders also usually have a broad long-range vision of where the company is headed. Managers, on the other hand, are more concerned with the details of the tasks to be accomplished in a work group. They keep the operations going smoothly. Their focus is directed on day-to-day processes. Some distinctions between **leadership** and **management** are summarized below:

Management	Leadership
Appointed to role	Emerge from group
Formal authority	May have no formal authority
Efficiency	Effectiveness
Systems	Innovation
Controls	Creativity
Policies	Adaptability
Procedures	Flexibility
Structure	Vision
Look to bottom line	Look to horizon
Reward and punish	Inspire

Warren Bennis (1989) illustrates the difference in function between a manager and a leader as follows:

Manager	Leader
Is a copy	Is an original
Asks how and when?	Asks what and why?
Accepts the status quo	Challenges the status quo
Is the good classic soldier	Is his or her own person
Does things right	Does the right thing

The role of a manager and leader may exist in the same person in an organization but often do not. Managers may or may not be leaders; leaders may or may not have management skills. Some people consider leadership a part of management; others see leadership and management as very different functions. What do you think?

Variations and Outcomes

Early on we talked about how reality is all in your head, and how perceptions influence how you think, react, and behave. Douglas McGregor (1960) stated that leader behavior is a function of how a leader perceives workers. McGregor determined two general ways leaders might see reality. In what he called **Theory X**, the leader views workers as people who dislike work, have to be closely supervised or pushed because they are basically lazy, irresponsible, or self-centered with little concern for the organization. However, McGregor's **Theory Y** leaders see workers as people who consider work as a pleasurable, natural part of life. They are internally motivated to be productive, accomplish goals, and are willing to learn and accept responsibility. These people are looked upon as creative and capable of contributing ideas to the organization.

Leadership styles can be categorized in three major categories (1) autocratic, (2) democratic, and (3) laissez faire. They fall on the continuum from the *power* being concentrated in a single person (**autocratic**), concentrated on the group and its leader (**democratic**), or to the group operating rather independently from the leader (**laissez faire**). The relationship of the leader to the group is visually depicted in the figure below:

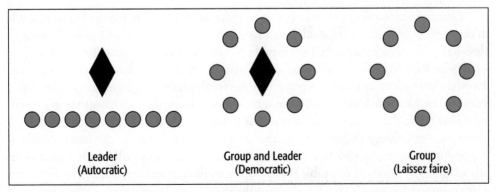

Figure 12.1

In the **autocratic** style, the information flows from the leader to the group in a one-way direction. The leader is like a dictator who makes the decisions and maintains control. Workers are told what to do and they do it. Workers are in a submissive relationship to the leader. Some autocratic leaders are "benevolent dictators" who make decisions with the interests of employees in mind and are supportive of employees. But there is no gathering of information from employees in determining decisions.

In the **democratic** style, also called participative style, the leader embraces employee involvement in decision-making and gathers opinions, information, suggestions and preferences from employees. The participative leader may or may not actually implement the employee's recommendations, but at least considers the employee input in arriving at a decision. If the decision of the leader were different from the group, the democratic leader usually explains his or her rationale for the decision made and indicates how the employee opinions played into the outcome. Valuing employee input is believed by the leader to make the workers feel more a part of the process and therefore keeping them more committed. This typically is the case. For the best results with the democratic style, the group needs to have an appropriate amount of interest in common with the leader, and the necessary knowledge and skills to contribute significantly to the decision making process.

The **laissez faire** style of leadership places the power for decision making within the group. The leader is more of a liaison between the work group and outsiders and secures needed resources for the group to meet its goals. **Empowerment** is a term heard frequently in discussions of work settings; this means providing the group with the authority to make decisions as a group. Of the three leadership styles, the laissez faire approach imparts the most power to the group.

Is there one best style of leadership? Not really. It all depends on the context in which the leadership occurs. There are times when an autocratic approach is most definitely the best way. Consider this…What if a fire broke out in your classroom? You would not want your professor to say, (while the room is filling up with smoke!) "Now students…let's brainstorm ideas together and discuss how we should respond to this fire alarm that's sounding." Clearly autocratic orders given to vacate the room are the most efficient and appropriate response.

Laissez faire leadership works best when the work group is highly knowledgeable about their work and highly motivated toward the goals of the organization. Physicians doing research in a laboratory, for example, probably need very little direction to do a good job. Professors in a college are rarely told by their deans how to teach a course. Having the freedom to work independently has traditionally been reserved for the highly educated and knowledgeable professions. Now in the workplace we have a trend for self-managed teams that have no traditional boss or supervisor. Rather, the responsibility for planning, organizing, and overseeing their work is carried out by the team members. Large American companies with fifty or more employees have half of their employees working in self-managed or problem-solving teams (Boyett and Snyder, 1998). Goleman (1995) quotes Soshona Zuboff, a Harvard Business School psychologist who noted that

> Corporations have gone through a radical revolution within this century, and with this has come a corresponding transformation of the emotional landscape. There was a long period of managerial domination of the corporate hierarchy when the manipulative, jungle-fighter boss was rewarded. But that rigid hierarchy started breaking

down in the 1980's under the twin pressures of globalization and information technology. The jungle fighter symbolizes where the corporation has been; the virtuoso in interpersonal skills is the corporate future. (p.149)

Although democratic leadership is the best balance of power by involving more people in the decision making process, there are times when a more autocratic or laissez faire approach may be the most appropriate. Leadership doesn't occur in a vacuum and the context of the leadership determines which is the best method to follow.

Numerous researchers have referred to this "it depends on the situation" idea as contingency leadership, situational leadership, or contextual leadership. In fact, it is suggested that the truly effective leader can vary his or her style to match the needs of the situation at hand. In this case the leader should consider not only the situation, but also the type of followers and the leader's own preferred style. These are qualities embedded in what Daniel Goldman calls *emotional intelligence* (1995). When people are anxious or upset, they cannot focus, remember, or make good decisions. As Goleman states, "leadership is not domination, but the art of persuading people to work toward a common goal." For our own careers, recognition of our core feelings about what we do and what changes might make us more satisfied is basic to our own emotional intelligence and therefore our success. Goleman suggested in 1995 that three applications of emotional intelligence in the workplace are (1) being able to air grievances as helpful critiques, (2) creating an atmosphere in which diversity is valued rather than a source of friction, and (3) networking effectively. As discussed earlier, these skills are reflected in the characteristics of Generation Y individuals now entering the workplace in huge numbers.

Leadership from a Positive Psychology Perspective

Transformational Leadership, a style of leading first introduced by James MacGregor Burns (1978) in his dealing with political leadership provides a complementary fit with a Positive Psychology approach to organization in the workplace. According to Burns, transformational leadership involves engagement with others in such a way that leaders and followers elevate each other to higher levels of motivation and morality. They share the same purpose. Transformational leaders offer a purpose that transcends short-term goals and focuses on higher level intrinsic needs. This results in followers identifying with the leader. Bass (1985, 1998) enumerates four components of transformational leadership. These are:

1. **Idealized influence.** This is similar in some ways to charisma. It involves behaviors that leaders exhibit because they *choose* to do the right thing. They do this because of their commitment to their own character strengths, integrity and actions as well as commitment to their followers. Employees respect leaders that make such choices in their behavior. Seeing this makes them likely to trust their leader and have positive perceptions of interpersonal fairness. Such leadership is also referred to as "authentic leadership" (Avolio, Griffith, Wernsing and Walumbwa, 2010).

2. **Inspirational motivation.** Leaders convey a vision that is appealing to the employees regarding their workplace and working patterns, leading

to optimism toward future goals, and the meaning of their work. Meaning is, of course, one of the five PERMA components. This is shown when leaders inspire their followers to be their very best and to achieve greater levels than the followers themselves ever thought possible. Such leaders convince employees that they can break through perceived barriers to high accomplishments. Leaders instill in their employees a sense of self-efficacy and confidence.

3. **Intellectual stimulation.** Leaders do not offer all the answers. Rather they encourage their employees to challenge assumptions, respect their ability to think for themselves, and to question long held perspectives and practices. This leads employees to become more confident and ultimately strengthens their perceived effectiveness.

4. **Individualized consideration.** Leaders exhibit this by showing caring for their employees' development, and physical and psychological safety. By behaviors such as mentoring, listening empathically, showing concern, being compassionate in dealing individually with employees, they are expressing their individualized consideration. They are particularly sensitive when employees are having a difficult time. Such behavior fosters a positive interpersonal relationship with each employee (Bass, 1985, 1998; Sivanathan, Arnold, Turner and Barling, 2004).

Transformational leadership is positive in its approach, focused on what can go right in an organization as a workgroup. Seligman (2011) would refer to such institutions as positive institutions where leaders and employees share a common vision and goals for the group. In their mutual teamwork and synergy in carrying out the work of the organization, they stimulate and elevate each other to achieve at higher levels of optimal functioning and well-being. All employees and the leader work hard to produce high levels of accomplishments (another of the PERMA components) and celebrate together their mutual success. When all members of the work group are on the same page, working as a team to accomplish mutual goals, the environment leads to individual well being, high productivity, high job satisfaction and positive institutions. It is a win-win for all involved! Colonel Mark A. Homrig, U.S.Airforce, (2001, December 21), writing about transformational leadership, closes his discussion with an excerpt from an Army officer in Afghanistan on whose body a diary was found that compared the U.S. with fighting the Russians.

> He noted that when you take out the Russian leader, the units stop and mill about, not sure of what to do next. But he added that when you take out a U.S. leader, somebody always and quickly takes his place and with no loss of momentum. A squad leader goes down, it may be a private that steps up to the plate before they can iron out the new chain of command. And the ...thing is that the private knows what...he is doing. (p. 7)

Colonel Homrig closes, "When leader and led values are in sync, followers don't have to be supervised—they will know what to do when the time comes, and isn't that the goal of good leadership?"

Is Leadership in My Future?

Are you already a leader? Are leaders born or made? There are ideas and research for both sides. Perhaps you can develop leadership skills just like any other skills you acquire with work and practice, like how to drive a car, how to write a paragraph, or how to play a musical instrument. Some research has suggested that there may be some inborn traits that characterize an effective leader such as emotional stability, dominance, enthusiasm, conscientiousness, social boldness, being somewhat emotionally detached, self-assured and compulsive. Whether evolving from nature or nurture, to be effective as a leader, people need to have skills in several areas. Specifically, there is a need for (1) technical knowledge related to the area of work, (2) interpersonal effectiveness and (3) critical thinking skills.

Management consultants Frigon and Jackson (1996) suggest that successful leaders should be able to do the following:

1. Share power and authority
2. Build mutual trust and respect
3. Use team building, problem solving and process analysis
4. View all tasks as cooperative undertakings
5. Decentralize decision making
6. Stop finger pointing
7. Believe that everyone has good ideas
8. Chase fear out of the workplace
9. Cooperate with organized labor
10. Recognize that this is a long-term commitment

Dubrin (1999) lists the following behaviors and skills as those of an effective leader:

1. Develop appropriate self-confidence (not too weak; not too confident)
2. Practice strong ethics
3. Develop partnerships with people (emphasize power sharing)
4. Help group members reach goals and achieve satisfaction
5. Make expectations known
6. Set high expectations
7. Give frequent feedback on performance
8. Manage a crisis effectively
9. Cultivate a strong customer orientation
10. Ask the right questions

Gardner (2002) notes that the advantages of leadership include financial and status rewards as well as a sense of satisfaction from successfully leading a group to a common goal. On the down side, leaders must invest a huge amount of time and energy and may be the brunt of criticism from others such as questioning the motives and integrity of the leader. He notes that leaders typically have a strong desire to use power over others or a strong need to accomplish great things. Other characteristics of a leader are ambition and the ability and willingness to work extremely hard.

Kirkpatrick and Locke (1991) enumerate the following leadership traits:

1. Drive
2. Honesty and Integrity
3. Self-confidence
4. Creativity
5. Expertise
6. Cognitive ability
7. Leadership motivation
8. Flexibility

Flexibility may well be the single most important one of these traits which enables leaders to recognize the most appropriate approach or actions to take in a given situation.

Gender differences continue to be seen regarding leadership. Few women hold leadership positions in government; only 12 of the Fortune 500 major corporations have a woman heading the company. The idea of a woman, the nurturer, as a corporate head has not been the traditional thinking in American society. However, as Jean Lipman-Blumen (1992) points out, the concept of female leadership is no longer an oxymoron. Considering global interdependence, the trends toward team driven work patterns in corporations, and the technologically networked world, the traditional leadership of the past based on competitive, controlling, aggressive, self-reliant individualists is not well suited for the world ahead. What she calls "connective leadership," an integrative model of leadership that creatively revitalizes individualism with the female perspective, sees the world as a system of interconnected uniquely important parts, rather than as independent, competitive, isolated and unequal entities.

The leaders of the 21st Century must have the essential elements for optimal functioning we have been learning throughout this text. These include knowing how to reframe and be flexible, being proactive, self-confident, able to master stress in the midst of constant change, maintain a high level of wellness, think ahead as a visionary, and managing oneself for accomplishment. Further, leaders for this century must be emotionally intelligent, be good at listening to and expressing thoughts and feelings, and be knowledgeable about workplace trends and how to thrive in career endeavors.

As you prepare for your future and your contributions as a leader in the workplace, keep this in mind. A good place to continue developing your skills in the areas listed above is in your role right now as a student in your college career. You are a potential leader in your classes, in your peer groups, on your campus, in your jobs at this moment.

As a Chinese philosopher stated in the 6th century B.C.:

> To lead people, walk beside them...
> As for the best leaders, the people do not
> Notice their existence.
> The next best, the people honor and praise.
> The next, the people fear;

And the next, the people hate...
When the best leader's work is done the
People say,
"We did it ourselves!"

—Lao-tsu

PERFORMANCE EVALUATIONS

Many of us have a reaction when the term "performance rating" comes up. It certainly gets our attention...like when a teacher says, "This is going to be on a test"...and we start writing down this now *important* information! We may have been taught that we should not be judgmental about other people and most of us get a little anxious about someone officially "judging" us. Of course our reaction to the idea of having our work performance evaluated in writing depends on many things. First, our level of self-esteem comes into play. Secondly, our reaction is based on how we perceive we are doing in the job. Additionally, the level of trust we have for the evaluator and the process also impacts our reaction.

In our careers, we can count on there being a formal evaluation process that documents our work performance. **Performance reviews** in a large organization may be more formal than in a small business. The process is usually done at least once annually, with shorter periods involved during a probationary period. Performance appraisal is used in all kinds of organizations to make decisions about employees. These decisions could include getting a raise or promotion, identifying a need for training or development, or even being terminated. Performance evaluations are something you need to be aware of when you first start a new position. In fact, keep in mind the ideas, discussed earlier, to create a vision of yourself as you want to be in this new position. This provides the basis for setting your goals to achieve that vision.

Why Are Performance Reviews Important?

Basically, performance reviews are formal methods for giving you written feedback about how you are doing your job, and identifying your strengths and weaknesses. If you need to improve or need more training in some aspect of your work, identifying this is the first step to enhancing your performance. The "documenting" part of the process is important to the organization and to you. This begins a permanent part of your personnel file and "follows" you throughout your work history at this organization, and perhaps beyond! It is important, not only to the organization, but to you as a record of your work. Suppose you perform years of excellent work. Then you encounter a supervisor who may have inappropriate or capricious reasons for wanting to terminate you. Your *documented* excellence becomes your basis for raising questions in this situation.

The Review Process

Ideally, the performance evaluation process is a joint activity that involves your supervisor and you. The expectations for the work that is being evaluated should have been established in the beginning. Goal setting with your supervisor is the first step. If formal goal setting is not a part of the review process, then a set of standards, job description, or written expectations should be the *a priori* (or before the fact) basis for rating your work behavior. It's pretty hard to know if you are performing well if it's not clear what you're supposed to be doing. Some specific expectations communicated before you begin the evaluation period should become the basis for comparison or rating of your work.

DeCenzo (1997) describes the performance appraisal process as including the following steps:

1. Performance standards for your job are established by the organization.
2. You and your supervisor set measurable goals.
3. Your performance is evaluated using some type of evaluation form.
4. Your performance is compared to the pre-established measurable goals. You may be asked to evaluate yourself.
5. You and your supervisor discuss the formal appraisal.
6. Your performance is "rewarded" or corrective action taken.

You wouldn't be satisfied if you sat in a class for a whole semester and didn't get any feedback on your progress until you got your final grade. Likewise, you wouldn't want to work for a whole year without any feedback on your progress. There's a saying that "no news is good news" meaning if something were wrong, you'd hear about it. That is not a good rule to apply in your work evaluation. If you have not received any indications from your supervisor regarding the level of your performance, remember that you are in charge of your success....ASK! You might say to your manager, "I've been working here for about two months now, and I wanted to ask you about how you think I am doing. If you have a few minutes to share your feedback, I would really appreciate it." Feedback should be a continuous yearlong process that gets documented in the annual performance review. There really shouldn't be any surprises for you or your supervisor if there has been communication throughout the year.

What your performance is judged by may be individual goals that you and your supervisor have set. If not, there may be a list of expectations that appear on the standard company evaluation form. The format for the written document may also vary. It could be essay, or short answer, or checking a rating form. The categories of description of your performance may vary. Some have only two ratings, satisfactory and unsatisfactory. Others may have a broader range of ratings such as Outstanding, Above Expectations, Met Expectations, Below Expectations, Unsatisfactory (this sounds like an A,B,C...situation, doesn't it!)

Although ideally, the final judgment of your performance will involve input from both your supervisor and you, the supervisor has the final word in rating your performance. Many appraisal systems allow for the employee to register differing opinions in writing. This does not change the supervisor's official rating of you as an employee or the copy of that in your file. However, the employee's rebuttal may become a part of the documentation for that evaluation.

The annual evaluation should be a quiet, private, un-rushed meeting between the supervisor and the employee. This may be one of the few times or even the only time that you and your supervisor have a one-on-one discussion of this significance. It is an opportunity to confirm mutually known information and discuss information about work that is new to either the supervisor or the employee. For example, an employee may share that he is taking a college course related to work of which the supervisor was not aware. Likewise, the supervisor may know of resources to help an employee that was previously unknown. It may also be a time to discuss goals for the next evaluation period. Some people report that their formal work appraisal is just a quick going over of a checklist. This may leave the impression that such sessions and the documents are not really that important. Don't be misled. It still goes in your personnel file as a formal record of your year's work. Look over the document carefully and discuss any points you think are inaccurate or incomplete. Use all the skills learned earlier in this book to assertively communicate any areas of concern with your supervisor.

How Can I Use the Performance Review?

You should keep a file of your performance reviews for several reasons. First, they comprise a record of your work performance over time from which you can find patterns in your behavior. This is extremely significant information for your career development. You may note that more than one supervisor has commented upon an area of strength. You may also see a pattern of observations about areas in which you need to improve. This can be useful in helping you identify your strengths as well as those areas that need development.

Secondly, your compilation of performance reviews serves as a reality check regarding your own self awareness and self assessment. It is helpful to receive feedback from others about what you excel in, even if you already feel you are skilled in the area. It confirms for you aspects that increase or affirm your strengths. Although it may "sting" momentarily, it is also an opportunity to discover places where you need improvement.

A third reason for hanging on to your performance reviews is that it provides you with information that you may want to use to update your resume every year. Even though you do not expect to be "job hunting" every year, the process of updating your resume when the information is fresh will keep you ready should the need or the opportunity present itself. Performance rating forms are found in many and varied forms. Some are open ended for supervisor comments; some have specific topics and ratings. Items taken from an actual performance rating form are shown below. These are only sample items and not a complete employee evaluation form.

Purpose:	To assist in accurately appraising employees, to improve performance, to enhance the supervisor/employee relationship, to improve the motivational climate, and to serve as a useful tool in the growth and development of employees.
Instructions:	1. Evaluate employee's work performance for the evaluation period under your supervision (refrain from basing judgments on recent events or isolated incidents). Do not allow personal feelings or personalities to govern your evaluation.
	2. Check the appropriate rating that best describes the employee's performance; Check ALL categories.
	3. After the employee signs this evaluation, no changes may be made without the employee's knowledge.

QUALITY OF WORK Consider standard of workmanship, accuracy, neatness, skill and thoroughness of work accomplished

Makes frequent errors. Needs improvement.	Makes recurrent errors. Needs improvement.	Usually accurate.	Is almost always accurate.	Is exact and precise.

QUANTITY OF WORK Consider use of time, ability to meet schedules, and productivity levels expected of this position

Does not meet minimum requirements.	Does just enough to get by.	Volume of work is satisfactory.	Very industrious, more than required.	Superior work and production.

JOB KNOWLEDGE Knowledge concerning work duties which an individual should have to accomplish a satisfactory job performance rating

Poorly informed, lacks work experience.	Lacks knowledge of some phases of work.	Moderately informed. Good potential.	Understands all phases of work.	Has complete mastery of all phases of assigned work.

ATTITUDE Consider cooperation with supervisor, co-workers and other groups with whom this employee associates in accomplishing his/her work

Problems in working with others in office/ outside contacts.	Occasionally has problems in working with others.	No problem working with others.	Cooperative, tolerant, able to work with others to accomplish tasks.	Exceptional; effective in personal relations at all levels.

If you were designing a performance rating form, what descriptors or strengths of character do you think you would want to include? From the items on the form above, which, if any, do you think are not clear, or not appropriate?

Policies and Procedures—The Rules of the Game

Another area that matters in knowing the workplace is being familiar with policies and procedures. Imagine that you are driving in city traffic and there are no traffic signs, no traffic lights, and no stop signs. Everyone is driving however and wherever he or she wants. Some people are on the left side of the street; some are driving on the right side. What a mess...total chaos! It's pretty obvious, we need some "rules of the game" to bring direction and order to driving (in fact, it's hard enough *with* rules!).

Suppose you enroll in a college course and there is no course syllabus. This leaves the student with no explanation of what the course is about, requirements and expectations, or the grading policy. How secure would you feel? How would you be able to predict what is going to happen? See the point? We really DO want rules! It helps us know what to expect and how to succeed.

When we look at it this way, it is easy to see that we need some level of conformity. It helps groups of people accomplish their mission. There is a need for structure and organization. We really do need to know the "rules of the game."

In order to bring consistency and order to the workplace, companies have rules that are usually called "Policies and Procedures." These explain how things are supposed to work. The **policies** describe the general guidelines or rules for governing activity; the **procedures** tied to them indicate how these guidelines are to be carried out in actual task activities. Jeannette Lannon (2007) distinguishes the differences between policies and procedures as:

Policies

- ❖ Global in nature
- ❖ Does not change often
- ❖ Broad terms and requirement
- ❖ Explains what and why
- ❖ Approved by the board

Procedures

- ❖ Specific actions are identified
- ❖ Continually improved upon
- ❖ Detailed description of activities
- ❖ Explains how, when, and who
- ❖ Enforced by management

Policies and Procedures—Written and Unwritten

Policies and procedures are documented in some written volume and/or available through an on-line network. The length, detail and formal presentation of the rules can be voluminous or brief.

At the College where three of the authors are employed, there was traditionally two huge volumes, one for policies and a second for procedures. Fortunately, all these policies and procedures are now accessible to employees on-line for ready reference.

Usually a handbook and/or a formal orientation session will serve to highlight the policies and procedures that are relevant for specific employees. These explain such policies as work hours, benefits, safety issues, absenteeism, and disciplinary procedures. It is important to read your employee handbook and keep it for future referral. If you violate a policy or procedure you weren't aware of, but you've been given the information in writing…well, you can see how this could affect you at the workplace.

In addition to the formal written company or organization policies and procedures, there are endless "unwritten" practices, norms, ways of doing things that are not written down anywhere, but like so many social conventions in life, that are known and followed by the majority of workers. In society, for example, if we walk into a restaurant and all the tables are empty except for only one person sitting at one of the tables, we would not walk over to that table and sit next to that person. In fact, we would probably select a seat that is some distance from that one other customer. This is an example of a social convention regarding selecting seating in a public place. This "rule" of behavior is probably not written down in an etiquette book anywhere, but it is one that most people learn with experience. So how do you, as a new employee get the scoop on these workplace practices that are not recorded anywhere? The answer is to find a mentor.

A **mentor** is a senior or experienced employee who serves to assist a new employee through advising, role modeling, explaining normative behavior, introducing contacts, and generally being available to answer questions and give support. Several studies have examined the effect of having a mentor and found that employees with mentors tended to make more money at a younger age and were more likely to follow a career plan than those employees without a mentor (Gomez-Majia, Balkin, and Cardy, 1995). Many companies and organizations have formalized mentoring programs where a new employee is assigned a mentor to help him or her integrate into the workplace. Such mentoring programs should have specific goals, clear role definition of the mentor and the protégé, training for mentors, and should encourage the new employee's independence and self-reliance (Newby and Heide, 1992). If you are not assigned a mentor when joining an organization, it is important to seek out as a mentor an experienced employee who appears to be successful. Professional and trade associations are another area where mentoring from experts in the field is available. Not only educational aspects are valuable from such associations, but the social connections and networking opportunities are important to members (Dansky, 1996). The Social Security Administration (SSA) of the U. S. which is a huge bureaucracy instituted a mentoring system to shepherd new employees through entry-level training. It has been a plus for both the new and the seasoned employees doing the mentoring. The SSA jumped from number 21 into the top 10 in 2007, ranking number 7 in the "Best Places to Work in the Federal Government" study. They attribute the jump and improved service to the implementation of a mentoring program (Walker, April 30, 2007).

Advantages of Policies and Procedures

Since we like to be in charge of our lives, sometimes rules and regulations seem confining or controlling and even something to be ignored. But, in the workplace we need to recognize there are some advantages to having clearly spelled out rules. Some of the advantages include:

1. Clear understanding of expectations and responsibilities
2. Understanding of consequences of behavior
3. Predictability of the work environment
4. Security of knowing how to succeed
5. Fairness and equity in rules applying to all employees
6. Continuity and consistency of services throughout your organization
7. Enabling employees to direct themselves rather than management micro-managing staff

If we are unfamiliar with the "rules of the game" and have not received any information as a new employee, we should find out information by asking and by seeking a mentor. Develop your own "employee handbook" as you collect information if you receive little or no orientation to a new position.

STRESS IN THE WORKPLACE

We have addressed stress earlier in this text in order to understand what it is. Further, we learned methods for keeping stress at levels that allow us to remain in charge of ourselves. Since recognizing the potential for stress is important to knowing the workplace, a few more words on the topic are in order.

There are some things that are a given. One is that the stimulation from events in most any workplace today sets the stage for a stress epidemic. The potential is there. A second given is that one of two things will happen. You will either:

1. Succumb to stress at work and suffer the consequences of physical, psychological, and spiritual drain, or

2. Master stress at work and keep your body, mind, and spirit balanced and productive in meeting your goals and enjoying the rewards.

To help you in the process of discovering how you are experiencing your workplace, the following Workplace Stress Test may provide insight and stir your thoughts on the matter. Take a moment to complete this exercise. Perhaps ask a co-worker or friend to complete it, too. Then talk it over and be sure to include ideas for bringing things into physical and psychological equilibrium.

WORKPLACE STRESS TEST

If your score is 35 to 55 you are moderately stressed.
If your score is 55 or more you are definitely stressed.

1 = Never   2 = Rarely   3 = Some of the time   4 = All of the time

1. I feel tired at work even with adequate sleep.	1	2	3	4
2. I feel frustrated in carrying out my responsibilities at work.	1	2	3	4
3. I am moody, irritable, or impatient over small problems.	1	2	3	4
4. I want to withdraw from the constant demands on my time and energy.	1	2	3	4
5. I feel negative, futile, or depressed about work.	1	2	3	4
6. My decision-making ability is less than usual because of work.	1	2	3	4
7. I think that I am not as efficient at work as I should be.	1	2	3	4
8. I feel physically, emotionally, or spiritually depleted.	1	2	3	4
9. The quality of my work is less than it should be.	1	2	3	4
10. My resistance to illness is lowered because of my work.	1	2	3	4
11. My interest in doing fun activities is lowered because of work.	1	2	3	4

12. I feel uncaring about the problems and needs of my
    co-workers, customers, clients, patients, etc., at work.   1   2   3   4

13. Communication with my co-workers, friends, or family
    seems strained.   1   2   3   4

14. I am forgetful.   1   2   3   4

15. I have difficulty concentrating on my job.   1   2   3   4

16. I am easily bored with my job.   1   2   3   4

17. I feel a sense of dissatisfaction with my job—that there's
    something wrong or missing.   1   2   3   4

18. When I ask myself why I get up and go to work, the only
    answer that occurs to me is "I have to."   1   2   3   4

A second point on stress is the issue of **pacing**. Work environments may be super busy, or slow and laid back. You may not be able to control the pace of the atmosphere at work, but you surely can control yourself, right? The whole notion of "pacing yourself" on the job to lower stress is a good idea, but only if you pace yourself in the right way. Pacing yourself properly can enhance productivity and lower stress. Pacing yourself wisely is not a matter of slowing down, but rather using strategic planning for structuring your time. Here are some pacing tips that will enable you to recharge your batteries, revitalize yourself and ultimately be more productive and creative.

Tips for Pacing Yourself

* Pay attention to your natural body rhythms to determine at what times you function at your best. Are you a morning or a night person? When possible, schedule your most difficult tasks for your peak performance hours. Try to avoid tackling difficult or exhausting projects during that part of the day when your energy is at its lowest.

* Shift between pleasant and unpleasant tasks. After finishing a difficult piece of work, shift to something mindless, easy and/or pleasant.

* Allow some time each day, even when you are swamped with work, for pleasurable work tasks, even if they are not highly productive.

* Use your breaks and lunches to relax. Do not work over lunch unless it is absolutely essential.

* Take mini-breaks for three to five minutes throughout the day to de-stress and balance yourself. Talk to a co-worker, have a refreshing drink.

* Choose leisure activities that balance the unique stresses in your line of work. For example, if you deal with people's complaints all day long then choose solitary, peaceful pursuits, or if you are cooped up in a windowless office all day then choose outdoor activities. If you work alone make sure your leisure time includes social activities with friends.

❀ Take vacations. Carefully consider the length and type of vacation you plan in order to balance work stresses. If your work is very sedentary, plan an active vacation. If your work is physically exhausting, plan a vacation where you allow a good amount of time for just kicking back and relaxing. If you work alone and feel lonely, visit friends or family or vacation with others.

❀ If possible take a break during your workday to exercise, do relaxation practices, or run an errand. We have discussed the importance of stretching your muscles for decreasing stress and physical strain. Take a moment several times during the day to stretch one or more of those muscle groups when you feel tense or fatigued.

SUMMARY

In this chapter we have been examining aspects of the work environment that are important for you to recognize, anticipate, and confront. We have prepared you with strategies to enable you to "move around" with ease. We have looked at trends in the world of work such as change, new organizational patterns, global interdependence, diversity, and leadership styles. We have reviewed some of the administrative realities of the workplace such as policies, procedures and performance evaluations. These topics were presented to give an overview of what to expect in today's workplace. We have closed with added suggestions on how to master the stress that looms in the work environment. Having looked at the workplace, you are now ready to move on to examining your role in this milieu as you create it for yourself.

POSITIVE PSYCHOLOGY SELF EXERCISES:

1. Pick three people in your life (present or past) that represent each of these three major styles of leadership: autocratic, democratic and laissez faire. How did you respond to each of these leaders? If you are or were a leader, which type would you aspire to be most of the time?

2. Design a performance appraisal form for a job you have done or are now doing. Consider the main areas of work. Imagine that you are the owner of the company or the chief operating officer (CEO) of the organization. What would be most important to the organization?

3. If you were a transformational leader, list six things you would be sure to do to make your workplace a positive one that promotes optimal productivity and optimal functioning for you and each employee.

4. Visualize a work environment that takes place in a positive institution. List the elements or events that reflect positivity and support wellbeing.

KEY TERMS

Gold Collar Worker	Theory Y	Generation X
Baby Boomers	Autocratic	Generation Y
Baby Busters	Democratic	Generation Z
Laissez Faire	Management	Downsizing
Core Workers	Empowerment	Emotional Intelligence
Contingent Workers	Mentor	Performance Appraisal
Manager	Policy	Outsourcing
Leader	Procedure	Insourcing
Theory X	SAW	Idealized Influence
Intellectual Stimulation	Off Shoring	Inspirational Motivation
Individualized Consideration	Transformational Leadership	

CHAPTER 12 QUESTIONS

Short-Answer Questions

1. Alvin Toffler wrote that change is _____.
2. It is estimated that well over 80% of the world's technological advances have occurred in _____ years.
3. The workforce of the future will no longer be dominated by what group of employees? _____
4. Who are the largest minority group in the U.S.? _____.
5. The age group referred to as mature workers (born before 1946) want _____ from their job.
6. Persons born between 1977 and 2000 are a group called _____.
7. Reducing personnel in organizations to cut costs and increase profits is called _____.
8. Workers who work part-time or temporarily on a given project are called _____ workers.
9. Businesses are saving labor costs by _____ the work elsewhere.
10. The most job openings found in the fastest growing industries are in the _____ field.
11. If your boss sees you as lazy, not liking work and irresponsible, he/she is following Theory _____.
12. If a leader behaves like a dictator, we would say the leadership style is _____.

13. Being sensitive to the impact a decision may have on employees is what Daniel Goleman would call _____ _____.

14. A formal written evaluation of our work performance is called a _____ _____.

15. The "rules of the game" in work settings are called _____ and _____.

16. One way to pace yourself is to _____.

Essay Questions

1. What is the historical progression of technological change?
2. How is the workforce composition changing to become more diverse?
3. How have corporations changed the way they are organized to cut costs?
4. Compare and contrast the core worker to a contingent worker.
5. What would you do if your line of work is being outsourced?
6. Compare the role of manager to the role of leader.
7. Compare and contrast autocratic, democratic, and laissez faire leadership styles.
8. Describe the advantages of performance reviews.
9. Outline the ideal process for a performance review.
10. What are the advantages to policies and procedures?
11. Describe three strategies you could use to reduce stress in the workplace.

13

Designing Your Own Career

Suppose you were going to build a house. You would have a lot invested in your home, right? And you wouldn't want a house just "put together" on a whim. No, you'd want an architectural drawing carefully planned showing the details of the whole project. The house plan would be based on information about your needs, limits, and preferences. Houses are a lot like careers...a lot is invested and you may live in them a long time. Yet, in your educational experience we'll bet that you have not (in a decade or more of schooling) had a meaningful experience of learning about occupations, how to choose one, how to plan your work life, or how to achieve career success. Career education is just not a priority for our K–12 school curriculum. For a decision and an area of our lives that we spend so much time in, and that has such an impact on our lives, it is extremely important to select a career as an informed choice rather than in a casual way or by default.

THEORIES ABOUT CAREER CHOICES

Many psychologists have studied and developed theories about career choice. Some wrote about stage theories saying we move from childhood fantasies of career toward more realistic ideas. There are some people who determined as a child they wanted to be in a certain profession and remained committed to that goal through their life career. In contrast, there are many students who know they want a college degree, but they're not sure in what area or how this relates to their career life after college. Some students have decided on a career, but may actually know very little about what is required to enter that profession, or what life in that career means in terms of day to day activities or demands, salary, availability, work locations or the like.

Psychologist John Holland (1985) developed a theory regarding vocational behavior that considers six basic personality orientations. He described the six types as:

1. **Realistic**—These people apply scientific principles in things that they do. They may have mechanical abilities; they like doing or making

things. Examples of occupations in this category would be pilot, electrician, engineer, or construction worker.

2. **Investigative**—People in this group like abstract thinking, discovering new knowledge, testing hypotheses, solving problems. Examples of workers in this category would be a research scientist such as a physicist, chemist, medical researcher, college or university professor.

3. **Conventional**—People in this category enjoy working in structured situations. They are usually very self-disciplined, orderly, like organizing and can work comfortably at routine, repetitive tasks. Occupations in this area include clerical worker, accountant, bank teller, data entry or billing clerk.

4. **Enterprising**—This group includes people who are persuasive, like to influence other people, are risk-takers, and enjoy business ventures. Sales managers, real estate brokers, and business owners would fall in this category.

5. **Social**—Individuals with this orientation like to work with people especially in helping relationships. Occupations in this area would include social worker, counselor, teacher, and health care worker.

6. **Artistic**—This group includes people who are creative, imaginative, emotional, and who hold unconventional perspectives which they like to express in artistic forms such as painting, sculpting, music, writing, and dance.

Holland noted that everyone has some of all these inclinations, but we could rank order them in terms of preferences for ourselves. Review these six types and place them in order from the most to least preferred orientation as you see yourself. Completing an interest inventory such as the Strong Interest Inventory can help you in determining the order of these orientations. Occupations that combine your top two or three of Holland's orientations may be the ones that fit your personality best.

Anne Roe (1972), another psychologist and occupational theorist, identified an array of variables that relate to vocational behavior. She sees these components interacting for each of us changing in importance as we move through our career development. The elements she discusses include the following:

State of the economy—the general state of things…war, peace, inflation, recession, labor markets and employment rates, trends for specific businesses, expansion or failures of specific business areas.

Family Background—Family origin, culture, socio-economic circumstances, values, educational levels, aspirations and expectations.

Chance—Unexpected events such as running into someone who knows of a position that just became open, being "in the right place at the right time." One's reaction to the chance event, however, is not a matter of chance! Also, many so called "chance" events are not really random…they are influenced by the person's behavior.

Marital Situation—If not married, nor aspiring to be, the effect of this variable will be different than for someone married. Particularly with two partners having careers in today's world, the degree of willingness to re-locate to accommodate a partner's promotion, the concern for care of children, and the amount of time available for family life all affect careers.

Physical—Refers to physical capacities, not only appearance and strength, but additionally sensory and perceptual capacities

Intellectual—Cognitive abilities of a general nature as well as special abilities of all sorts. The more recent ideas of multiple intelligences relates here.

Temperament and Personality—Natural or acquired patterns of behaviors, preferences, styles, ways of taking in and responding to stimuli in the environment.

Interests and Values—What activities, environments, and events capture our attention and liking? What values are basic to our lives? What is most important to us?

Learning and Education—What we know from general education and experience.

Acquired Skills—Special skills and techniques learned through organized training.

Roe suggested that the further from the average that any of these variables may be at any given time, the more significance that element will have in influencing career behavior. For example, in time of economic extremes—war, depression—the *economy* becomes a large factor; if a physical handicap develops then *physical* becomes a looming factor. The advantage of Roe's theory is that it goes beyond the individual in looking at career decisions and planning to family issues and other environmental realities. Since none of us operates in isolation, this is a reminder that our careers occur in the social context of which we are a part. Consider the variables from Roe's theory of vocational behavior. What insights can you gain about yourself in relation to the factors listed above?

Focusing on Strengths—Applying Positive Psychology in Your Career

A relevant philosophy about personal satisfaction and professional development has been inspired by Buckingham and Clifton, both from the Gallup Organization, based on hundreds of thousands of case studies and careful analysis. In their book, *Now, Discover Your Strengths* (2001), these authors say most organizations are built on two flawed assumptions: (1) that each person can learn to be competent in almost anything, and (2) that each person's greatest room for growth is in his or her areas of greatest weakness. Instead, they contend, the best managers in corporations and organizations assume that (1) each person's talents are enduring and unique, and (2) the greatest room for growth is in areas of greatest strength. They note that training and development in companies that focus on "improving weaknesses" are doing damage control…not development. A *strength* is defined as "a consistent, near perfect performance in an activity." From over two million interviews, these authors extracted 34 themes that in combination help capture the unique themes in each person's life. Questions they would ask a person include: "What are your strengths?" How can you capitalize on them?" "What are your most powerful combinations?" "Where do they take you?" "What one, two or three things can you do better than 10,000 other people? These writers affirm the notion that instead our **talents** are what we must develop and let shine, instead of focusing on our weaknesses. They provide numerous case examples from anonymous individuals in the world of work as well as some famous people like Tiger Woods and Bill Gates. Tiger Woods has learned to maximize his strengths in driving his golf ball, rather than focusing on his weakness in getting out of sand traps. Gates was not talented in running a business, so he had a partner who is. This allowed Gates to focus on his talent and strengths in software development and to excel. In this new philosophy of career decisions and development, some of Buckingham and Clifton's 34 specific themes will become apparent in a combination that helps capture the unique themes in each person. Among these, the five most dominate themes form a cluster they would call one's "signature theme." This signature theme is then related to career areas. Three principles of living a life of strength include (1) being able to do consistently, over and over the same work happily and successfully; (2) not needing strength in every aspect of a role to excel; and (3) that you will excel only by maximizing your strengths, never by "fixing" your weaknesses. These authors have developed an inventory called the *StrengthsFinder*, an on-line questionnaire that yields your five dominant themes. To use this resource, one must purchase their book to obtain an identification number for access to this inventory. Talents are considered to be any recurring pattern of thought, feeling or behavior that can be productively applied. Reviewing the physiology of the brain in early development, these writers note that recurring patterns evolve from early years. Since the brain retains connections that are related to these evolving talents and discards neural connections not being used, it is not possible to switch to a new design of talents after a certain age. Therefore, our talents are enduring qualities that must be developed if we are to excel in the workplace.

Seligman (2002) also writes about strengths and the importance of capitalizing on them. We have discussed his six core virtues that comprise good character which are acted out through what Seligman terms *signature strengths*. We have reviewed the 24 of them as they relate specifically to the six virtues. He makes a point of differentiating between a "talent" and a "strength," considering a talent an innate, non-moral, and relatively fixed phenomenon that you either have or you don't. Strengths, on the other hand, are acquired, moral, and open to further development. You can develop a strength by your own will by first deciding to acquire it and then working to develop it. Seligman states that building strengths and virtues and using them on a day to day basis is about making proactive choices. He suggests beginning by determining which strengths you own and can use, and that this process of discovery can inspire your creativity and desire to lead the good life. To help you determine your strengths, you can use the results of the Signature Strengths Survey in Chapter 4 or complete the full version of Seligman's Values-In-Action Strengths Survey, on-line at *www.authentichappiness.org*. You are encouraged to do this to gather important information about yourself that will help you in determining your own career area. Keep in mind, however, that Seligman believes that to be a virtuous person, one displays, by acts of will, all or most of the six core virtues by exhibiting at least one of the related strengths to each.

The positive tone of these philosophies are similar to the work of researchers who have studied professional reward and satisfaction in the workplace, discovering a connection between (1) people who are passionate about their work and find it fulfilling and (2) the success of the companies for whom they work. As more and more workers become passionately engaged, (remember the "E" in PERMA) the company's productivity increases. It is important to discover your natural talents and strengths and develop them to be used in your career life. Centering on building our strengths rather than worrying about "weaknesses" is a relieving thought for many of us!

THE GLOBAL PERSPECTIVE—Strengths and Virtues Embraced Worldwide

In his research on the nature of happiness, Martin Seligman resurrected the idea of *character* into the field of psychology. He considered the development of character an important aspect of leading a happier, more effective life. He and his colleagues began a search through the literature of all major religions and philosophical traditions. These included Aristotle and Plato, Aquinas and Augustine, the Old Testament and the Talmud, Confucius, Buddha, Lao-Tze, the Koran and many others. They were amazed to find the same six core virtues emerging over centuries, from all over the earth, and from all of the over two hundred volumes they reviewed. The virtues that these diverse cultures and religions agreed upon were (1) wisdom and knowledge, (2) courage, (3) love and humanity, (4) justice, (5) temperance, and (6) spirituality and transcendence.

Since it is difficult to scientifically measure such abstract characteristics, Seligman studied observable behaviors reflecting these traits. He calls these behavior clusters "strengths." For example, the core virtue of justice includes duty, acting in accordance with requirements of one's position, social custom, law or religion. But how *duty* might be shown behaviorally may differ from one culture to another. For instance, consider Joe, a manager in a U.S. restaurant, whose boss assigns him the task of implementing a new procedure on order taking. He thinks about how he might carry out this task using his individual skills and talents to meet his needs and do the job well. He generates some ideas and then asks for some time with the boss to discuss his ideas. Joe is exhibiting the individualistic tradition of problem solving in American culture. Across the globe, in a restaurant in Japan, Tanaka is a manager whose boss gives her the same assignment to implement a new procedure on order taking. She nods when receiving the task assignment and proceeds, without questioning her boss, to complete the job. She is concerned about the best way to complete the task to everyone's satisfaction. In Japan, there is strong collectivist tradition which focuses on the group as a whole and workers are motivated to maintain *wa* (harmony). She is representing that tradition in her approach. Both Tanaka and Joe are serious about being responsible for their assignment; they are each demonstrating the strength of *duty*, but the approach is slightly different, following cultural traditions. Seligman (2002) and his researchers purposely sought to identify traits that were consistent across the globe. As Seligman stated, "…I want my formulation of the good life to apply just as well to Japanese and to Iranians as to Americans."

Another illustration of the overlap of these virtues is seen in an exhibit in the Smithsonian National Museum of the American Indian. Although this group was not among those studied by Seligman, the key values of this culture are very similar to those same six core virtues. The museum display describes the story of the "Seven Grandfathers" from Native American folklore portraying seven specific virtues that together represent good character. These include (1) honesty, (2) love, (3) courage, (4) trust, (5) wisdom, (6) humility and (7) respect. Through storytelling of a legend about a young brave who confronted the grandfathers in a dream, this oral tradition taught character development in the tribes.

Why were Seligman's virtues found nearly everywhere? Because they represent traits that are basic and universal to a world that is fit for human habitation. Proof of this comes from considering the kind of world we would have without these virtues. Imagine the opposites of the six virtues: (1) stupidity and ignorance, (2) fear and withdrawal, (3) hate and egoism, (4) unfairness and inequality, (5) volatility, and (6) isolation and self-centeredness. Think of how such core patterns of behavior would play out in a world with a fragile environment and scarce resources such as water and energy.

Since a large part of how we all function in the world is in terms of our career, it is important to consider the link between your strengths and your life's work. Seligman makes a clear connection between tapping into your personal strengths and virtues for choosing a career. The research shows that above a certain basic standard of living, money does not buy happiness. It is more effective to choose a career that capitalizes on your personal strengths, as this leads not only to your own happiness, but to the ideals of global citizenship.

Self-Assessment

Whether it is deciding on a specific career, deciding where to complete your studies for that line of work, or determining your goals and long-range objectives for your professional life, the place to begin is looking at yourself. Self-awareness is the first step. How well do you know yourself? How can you find out about yourself? Where do you begin?

Looking inward at ourselves is referred to as **introspection**—the process of discovering what is going on inside ourselves and noticing patterns in our behaviors, feelings, and attitudes. It is an interesting journey, one we are often too busy and too caught up in the day to day demands to do. Introspection takes time, quietness, reflection.

You might be wondering, "So how do I 'introspect' myself?" Well, you could stand before a mirror and have a conversation with yourself. Ask yourself questions about what you think is important in life, your personality characteristics, your interests, dislikes, and on and on. We discussed earlier in the text the *witnessing stance* where you psychologically step outside yourself and view yourself as a witness, attempting, as much as anyone can, to be objective. Some other approaches to self-awareness include writing, getting feedback, completing assessment instruments, and portfolio development.

Writing

Whenever we are trying to figure out what we do think about things, writing can be a helpful tool. Having to write down your thoughts often allows you to crystallize your thoughts and discover your own ideas. Writing diaries or journals of various types can help you to expose patterns in your life. Keeping a career related journal where you capture information about yourself related to your work life might be a useful way to enhance your self-awareness.

Nancy Anderson (2004), a professional career counselor and author, uses writing as a major part of her work with clients. She suggests you write an autobiography starting with your grandparents and describe the beliefs of each grandparent about money, work, sex, gender, religion and love. If you don't know, ask your parents or a relative. Pay attention especially to the grandparent of the same gender as you. Next describe how your parents were brought up by their parents. Anderson urges journaling how your parents met, their marriage, children, then focus on you—your birth, early care-taking, preschool, socialization, elementary and secondary schooling, and so forth to your life today. Anderson recognizes that such a writing project may take a long while and may produce fears for you. She discusses six basic fears—fear of poverty, criticism, illness, losing love, old age, and death and encourages you to examine them, determining which of them affects you most. The purpose of writing this autobiography is to understand your past—then let it go. This and other writing projects such as your personal mission statement can lead to a greater awareness of who you are and how you got there. Writing helps you sort out your thinking, find insights, as well as helping you discover your feelings and values.

Feedback

Gathering feedback from other people is another way to learn about yourself. What kinds of impressions, personality quirks, strengths, hang-ups, habits others see in you is useful...and sometimes surprising. You can gather information from others informally and verbally by asking them what they see you doing, how they would characterize your personality, what they see as your strengths and weak areas. Many times getting unsolicited feedback is a part of our interaction with others. Our bosses, teachers, co-workers, friends give us feedback regularly by their comments to us, their requests of us, the referrals they make to us, suggestions they give us, questions they ask us. Sometimes their relationship with us requires written feedback of a more formal nature. Work supervisors and teachers evaluate us regularly and their feedback of our behavior is documented in our personnel file or the grade roll. Reviewing such feedback may expand your awareness of self.

Assessment Instruments

Many inventories, surveys, and rating scales exist for helping people to assess themselves. Many of these assessment tools are available through campus career counseling centers, testing centers or through faculty. Popular inventories include the Strong Interest Inventory, COPS-P and the Myers-Briggs Type Indicator. The Strong inventory asks questions about your preferences and provides a profile of your interest patterns. This inventory has integrated the Holland theory of six orientations into the interpretation of the interest information.

The COPS-P Interest Inventory provides interest scores referencing the COPSystem Career Clusters. With a focus on professional occupations, the COPS-P can be used to explore college majors, help college students conquer career indecision and assist adult professionals with career issues. The inventory heightens self-awareness while providing access to the most current occupational information available. The Myers-Briggs Type Indicator (MBTI) is a personality instrument built on Jungian theory of human behavior. It is one of the most researched instruments in existence. This inventory yields a personality type (one of 16 possibilities) which helps you see the way you take in and process information and your style of decision-making. The MBTI yields your *type* based on your preference for (1) focusing more on the world of people or of ideas, (2) perceiving through intuition or sensing, (3) making decisions based on thinking or feeling, and (4) structuring tasks for completion or seeking new possibilities. Although we all use both options in each of the four dimensions, we lean toward using our preference. Each of the possible 16 MBTI *types* offers equal strengths for ways of functioning optimally.

The National Career Development Association maintains a web site (*http:ncda.org*) that lists and sells books for career planning. Readers are encouraged to visit this site and others to explore ways to gain assistance in self-assessment.

Other written information is available by reviewing your performance on aptitude or achievement testing. In high school, what was your profile of scores on the achievement tests you took? Did you take the SAT or ACT examinations? Are there other tests you have taken such as course placement tests? Your patterns of scores on these tests are another piece of information to plug into the "Who am I?" equation.

On-line Assessment Opportunities

In addition to published inventories and surveys, as mentioned above, there are numerous websites that contain self-assessment inventories or surveys that can be answered on line. Many of these ask that you complete questions which are then analyzed and feed-back given you as to the "fit" for certain career groups. Robert Reardon, Program Director of the Career Center at Florida State University as a test author and researcher considers test validity, reliability, standardization procedures, theory base and quality of work as areas to be concerned about in using on-line assessments (Hansen, 2002). Richard Bolles (2001, 2002) author of a career classic book, *What Color is Your Parachute* lists seven rules about taking career tests as follows:

1. There is no test that everyone loves.
2. There is no one test that always gives better results than others.
3. No test should necessarily be assumed to be accurate.
4. You should take several tests, rather than just one.
5. Always let your intuition be your guide.
6. Don't let tests make you forget that you are absolutely unique on the face of the earth—as your fingerprints attest.
7. You are never finished with a test until you've done some good hard thinking about yourself.

The Florida Academic Counseling and Tracking for Students organization and the Florida Department of Education have partnered to provide students with the internet version of Florida eChoices, a career exploration and information system from Careerware. This program allows students and adults to assess and identify interests and match those interests with occupations within Florida. The site *http://facts.org* also has extensive databases of occupations, colleges, universities and graduate schools. This site includes career planning assistance, helps individuals assess their work related values, interests, and skills as well as help in searching for related occupations and college majors. This highly researched and comprehensive program is updated regularly and provides students and adults with a realistic view of the best educational and career options for future success.

Portfolio Development

Artists have used portfolios—examples of their achievement—for years to apply for positions, to seek entrance into educational programs, to sell their work and ideas to others. A portfolio is a collection of representative samples of what you have done. Some school programs have expanded portfolios to English classes and other subjects where the portfolio becomes a collection of papers written and work completed to document learning. Keeping a job or career portfolio wherein you collect evidence of your accomplishments can help you write an annual self-assessment of your work, and can help document reasons you might make requests for such things as a promotion or a raise. Such a notebook of information is most useful when you begin writing or updating your resume. The Florida eChoices site *http://facts.org* can help you in preparing your portfolio.

You may decide to use Holland's theory to rank personality orientations for yourself. You can use Roe's ideas to determine what you know about physical characteristics, personality patterns, family background, values, intellectual skills, interests, and the like. You may try writing or gathering feedback from people and assessment instruments. Through on-line assessments you can determine patterns in your values, interests, and skills. By whatever means you employ, it is important in self-assessment to determine the answers to questions like: "What do I *value* in life?" "What's more important—money or family—or something else?" "What are my *personality* characteristics? Am I an introvert or extrovert, organized or unstructured, quiet or talkative, dominant or submissive, emotional or not, rely on thinking or feelings to make decisions, a leader or a follower, assertive, creative, modest, tenacious, versatile, efficient, conservative, humorous, ambitious?" "What are my *skills* and talents? What are my *strengths*? Am I best at thinking, talking, creating, fixing, analyzing, learning, organizing, explaining, helping, writing, problem solving, or leading? Who Am I?" The more I can understand myself, the better prepared I am to determine the career path I plan to take.

Occupational Information

After completing your self-assessment, the next step is to gather information about careers that relate to your own personality, interests, values and aspirations. Instead of focusing on one specific career, it is helpful to look at information about **career families** such as technology, health and human services, research, business, marketing, or categories of work environments such as corporations, government, educational institutions, and hospitals. The *Dictionary of Occupational Titles* (DOT) classifies jobs by the focus on concern for people, for data, or for things. This is an example of a broad grouping of tasks and interest. Which of these three categories interests you most?

FINDING INFORMATION ABOUT CAREERS

There are several sources you may want to tap to find information about careers. One place you do *not* want to get your information is from television programs that portray stories of people in specific fields. The real world may not be nearly as exciting as a T.V. series in the field of police work, law, hospitals, crime scene investigation or other work settings. Furthermore, a TV show probably will not portray the profession realistically. Consider the difference between the activities of policemen shown on a particular TV series and some of the actual footage of police work in real localities.

Using Books

There are several ways of finding information about occupations such as the nature of the work, the necessary preparation, work environments, employment outlook, and salaries. In addition to the DOT mentioned above, the *Occupational Outlook Handbook* is an excellent source of information about careers. *Careers Encyclopedia* is another book resource. There are also many books on specific career areas. Most major book stores have a career section which contains books for specific careers and occupational areas. Many sources for information are found on-line such as the Occupational Outlook Handbook.

Using On Line Resources

There are several ways the computer can be an excellent resource for finding information. One advantage to computer sources is that they can be updated more quickly than book sources and therefore may be more current. On-line searches can enable you to find statistics and information especially through the Bureau of Labor Statistics (web site: stats.bls.gov). Many other career related sites can be found by searching on specific key words. Popular sites for students seeking career help include the following:

> Monster Board—*www.monster.com*
>
> CareerBuilder—*www.careerbuilder.com*
>
> Quintessential Careers—*http://quintcareers.com*
>
> Jobhunters—*www.jobhuntersbible.com*
>
> JobWeb—*www.jobweb.org*

Readers are encouraged to explore search engines with key words such as *career planning, career decisions, career development* and the like to find other on-line sources.

Campus Career Centers

One of the best and most helpful things you could do for yourself is to visit the Career Center or Career Advisors at your Campus Advisement Office. These resource centers have tons of information from the books we mentioned and others. Further they usually have an array of software programs designed to help you gather information. You can get help in how to use on-line programs to assist you in career planning. Career counselors are available to guide you in sorting out the information you have gathered about yourself and occupations. They will help you in making a career decision and evaluating your decision.

Professional Associations and Organizations

Another good source of information can be found by tapping into websites for professional organizations and associations. Search engines can lead you to a variety of occupational groups that have information about their own professions designed for prospective students in those fields. If you go to www.quintcareers.com/professional_organizations and scroll down, you can find several sites for finding numerous associations. For example, the American Society of Information Science and Technology lists conferences, displays news articles about the field, and has an on-line journal of the organization as well as other career resources. The National Education Association, at *www.nea.org* has a variety of resources in the teaching field. It contains news articles, information for teachers, and special information for students. Likewise the American Psychological Association at *www.apa.org* lists scholarships available in psychology, articles regarding careers in the field, and links to related APA sites such as *www.psyccareers.com*. APA offers a 40 page printable brochure about the field of psychology for prospective students in the field.

Interview

An excellent way to find out about the real picture of the day-to-day activities of an occupation is to interview a person in the career. Determine questions you want that person to answer before you arrange a meeting. Be sure to ask them at the beginning of the interview how they feel about their work. Remember if they are negative about their employment, they will probably give more negative answers to your questions. Try to sort out how much of their information is filtered through a generally pessimistic lens. Conversely, if they enjoy their work, you can find out why they say this…again remember that an optimistic person will enjoy anything more. So be sure to ask questions about facts, hours, details…not just opinions.

Gaining First Hand Experience—Intern or Volunteer

Some type of opportunity to spend time at a work site is even better than an interview. Not only can you actually see the work of a person or many persons in that occupation, but you can get a broader picture of the work environment. You can get a feel for the skills required to do the tasks, the pace of operations, organizational patterns, team versus individual work, and generalization versus specialization in activities.

If you are unable to find a formal "internship" program, you may be able to arrange to be an observer, shadow a worker for a period of time, or be a volunteer in the organization. Another role for finding placement in a work setting to learn the environment is through Service Learning assignments in college classes whereby students put in volunteer hours in businesses and community organizations. Another opportunity for learning about careers while earning college credit is through cooperative education courses. In cooperative education courses, students are placed in a business or organization with the opportunity to learn and gain college credits while volunteering their time. All of these methods for first hand experience not only add to your knowledge, but could be added to a resume when you seek your first position in your chosen profession.

No matter what sources of information you investigate, it is necessary to gather information about any careers you may be considering. If you have acquired a lot of information about yourself in your Self-Assessment, it is equally important to find out as much as possible about careers. These two areas of information prepare you for deciding or confirming a career choice or a career change and preparing you for designing your career life.

Making the Decision

Psychologists have studied the "decision making" processes people use to determine choices. It seems safe to say that day-to-day decisions like what to eat for breakfast, what to wear, where to study on campus are easily made in routine ways. However, when a more significant and complex decision like where to attend college, whether to get married, *and what career to choose* has to be made, more sophisticated methods may be called for. Researchers have identified different patterns for making complex decisions that include several variables. Most suggest that a better decision is made by use of a systematic method of comparing important factors against the alternate choices.

A planned method of making a decision requires committing thoughts on paper. It could be a simple plus or negative column for given alternatives. Or it could involve a more elaborate process such as making a table on a page listing one or several factors involved in a decision. For example suppose Maria has completed her self-assessment and determined her areas of strength, interests, personality patterns, and these results point to possibilities in three careers she is considering. Suppose now she considers her values regarding what is most or least important to her. She determines that salary is less important than considerations such as growth opportunities, work schedule, "fit" with personality. To accommodate this she decides to give each factor a weighted value from 1 (lowest) to 3 (highest). She then gives a rating to each choice from one to three (low to high) regarding how she rates this career on that criterion. So she makes a matrix comparing factors with the three choices as follows:

Factors	Factor Value	Career A Law	Career B Nursing	Career C Teaching
Opportunity for professional growth	(3)	2	2	2
Work schedule	(3)	1	2	3
Location	(2)	1	2	3
Size of organization	(2)	2	2	3
Benefits	(3)	2	1	3
"Fit" with personality	(3)	3	1	3
Core position availability	(2)	2	3	2
Flexibility for horizontal moves	(2)	2	3	3
Advancement	(2)	3	2	2
Salary	(1)	3	2	2

Because the factors are not equal in her value system, Maria decides to multiply the factor value times the rating for each career choice. Then by adding the products for each career, a total is found for each of the three choices. In this case, the teaching career option clearly has the most weight and stands out as the best choice.

Factors	Factor Value	Career A Law	Career B Nursing	Career C Teaching
Opportunity for professional growth	(3)	2 = 6	2 = 6	2 = 6
Work schedule	(3)	1 = 3	2 = 6	3 = 9
Location	(2)	1 = 2	2 = 4	3 = 6
Size of organization	(2)	2 = 4	2 = 4	3 = 6
Benefits	(3)	2 = 6	1 = 3	3 = 9
"Fit" with personality	(3)	3 = 9	1 = 3	3 = 9
Core position availability	(2)	2 = 4	3 = 6	2 = 4
Flexibility for horizontal moves	(2)	2 = 4	3 = 6	3 = 6
Advancement	(2)	3 = 6	2 = 4	2 = 4
Salary	(1)	3 = 3	2 = 2	2 = 2
		47	44	61

This may seem like an involved way of trying to make a decision, but considering the importance and the consequences of a career choice, it is worth the effort. If you use the Florida CHOICES on-line program, it will automatically integrate your work values as a factor into the decision-making process and determine the outstanding choice.

Whether you determined your decision the "long way" per above or through a software program, a final step in decision-making is to reflect upon, review, and as time goes on re-affirm the decision that is made. It is always a good idea after you make a major decision to look inside, what psychologists call **introspection**, and ask yourself how you feel about the decision. In this age of rapid change and with new experiences, it may be that your decisions will have to be revised or changed as you move along. Coming back to re-evaluate the decision is, in any case, a helpful last step.

Setting Goals

After deciding on a career to pursue, the next step is to set specific *goals* to get you from where you are now to entering that field and planning your career path. Again, this is the time to put to work the ideas we discussed about creating a vision. Your career development vision embodies the goals for your career path. As you now envision yourself in the career you have chosen, What do you see yourself doing? What is your role? What added responsibilities have you taken on? How have you grown in the profession? What you see in your vision is the basis for your long term goals.

Since it is difficult to nail down every detail of what you want your life to be at the other end of your career, you may want to be more specific with goals to get yourself from here to entering the profession. Where are you right now in your educational process? What short-range goals do you want to achieve in the next two years? In the next five years? What is the next step for your educational process? And bringing your goal setting even closer, what are the implications for your goals right now and your plans for next semester? Or this semester, for that matter!

Again, this means getting information. You may need to collect information from colleges and universities where you will possibly complete your education to enter your chosen profession. It is a good idea to review the course requirements for the completion of your degree and your reaction to taking these courses. Hopefully, you will feel eager to study the requirements of your chosen career. If you review the curriculum and discover that the list of courses really turns you off, maybe you need to revisit your decision. This doesn't mean that the advanced study will be easy, but the topics should be areas you are at least interested in learning about.

When you have determined your goals, you are ready to begin a written career plan. Huge numbers of small businesses fail every year. In looking at why this occurs, one of the variables that seem to make a difference is the business plan. Most failed businesses have a poorly thought out business plan, or none at all. If you are more or less a spontaneous person and "planning" makes you uncomfortable, then you need work harder than others to develop your plan in writing. In a sense, isn't your career the "business" of your life? The better you plan based on information, the more likely it is that you will succeed.

A **career plan** should include your basic mission or goal, your long range requirements, your current skills, interests and experiences, and your short term goals. A sample career plan is as follows:

Career Goal

To become a licensed registered nurse. To provide assessment, care planning, implementation of nursing intervention, and evaluation of results with hospitalized patients.

Long-range, general abilities and requirements:

- At least a bachelor's degree in nursing
- Ability to work as part of a health care team
- Knowledge of the scientific method
- Critical thinking skills
- Capacity for record keeping
- Teaching skills
- Skills in writing care plans
- Knowledge of chemistry, anatomy and physiology, and microbiology
- License from state Board of Professional Regulations

Current skills, interests, and experiences:

- Summer employment with home health company
- High school science courses
- Experience working within a team
  (summer employment, school organizations, course projects)
- High school writing courses (four years of English, technical writing)
- Top 10% in high school class
- Problem solving ability and organizational skills
- Interest in helping others

Short term, specific goals to make your dreams a reality:

- Complete current college semester
- Good test scores
- Acceptance to a university with a good nursing program
- Keep grades up to meet requirements for nursing school
- Continue work experience or part-time employment in local hospital
- Participate in campus organizations for nursing students
- Earn a bachelor's degree
- Consider graduate school
- Improve assessment and planning skills through courses to enhance these skills
- Determine areas of content for preparing for board examination

(Adapted from Adventures in Education, Planning a Career, Texas Guaranteed Student Loan Corporation, 1998)

GETTING THE JOB

There are many important sources you can turn to for assistance in seeking employment. The campus career center has materials that will help you. Your college may have recruitment days/weeks, job fairs and special programs for job seekers. Additionally, there is an abundance of help on the Internet for open positions and tips on resume writing, search ideas, and such. Some of these are listed above. Your career service center staff will help you find these and other sites if you need help.

Also a number of business and industry directories are found in your campus library. The librarian will help you locate and use career related directories. Contacting the human resources department of these companies will provide information on job postings. Another library resource that is helpful is the collection of professional journals. These are published by organizations for the profession and often contain employment advertising. Writing or calling the headquarters office of the organization may yield additional resources for listings of employment opportunities.

Other methods to use include:

1. Newspaper advertising—want ads

2. Developing a network of contacts—professional, family, work associates, faculty members, friends, former employers, religious or other community groups

3. Using the internet—*http://jobhuntersbible.com* and many other sites have invaluable information on where to find job openings, how to make contacts, and website information for professional organizations.

Preparing Your Resume

Again, there are many publications that can be helpful in your campus career center, in the campus or public library and in large bookstores. Further, going on-line is an excellent way to find tips for developing your **resume** and viewing sample resumes. The best plan regarding your resume is to customize your resume for each specific position opening for which you are applying. In today's world of technology, among large companies the first "screener" of your resume may very well be a scanner, not a person. Scanners can be programmed to read and sort out specific key words in a resume that relate to the specific position. Resumes not containing those key words are never read by a person. If however, you are copying quantities of general information resumes to circulate, keep in mind that these are usually organized by (1) most recent first chronological order or (2) function or task accomplishments. A third way to organize is by targeted information for a specific position and would be a customized single resume.

The chronological order format is the one most employers prefer even though it is rather traditional. The second style, function or task accomplishments, usually identifies a general area under which examples of achievements are listed. For example:

PROGRAM DEVELOPMENT
  – Developed new employee orientation program
  – Implemented weekly seminars for improvement ideas
  – Wrote materials for personal finance program for employees

The third, and preferred, way of organizing is the targeted format which tailors the resume to fit a specific position or job opening. Here the information presented about you is not of a general nature. Instead it includes only those items about you that are related to the job opening. This type of resume focuses on the match between you and the requirements of the position.

Resumes are to be brief, usually only one page. Items to be included are:

1. *Who You Are*—Full name (highlighted or large type), address, zip codes, and phone area code and number(s). Be sure you can be contacted through the information given in this section.

2. *Job Objective or Goal*—This is optimal here, but could be in cover letter instead.

3. *Education*—Other educational activities such as organizations, offices held, internship or co-op experiences, scholarships, and the like may be included here.

4. *Experience and Achievements*—List in reverse chronological sequence. Don't just list title; explain responsibilities of the job in brief.

5. *References*—Three or four actual references may be given (be sure to check with the person first), or you can say "References are available upon request."

6. As a guideline, use action verbs in writing such as "managed, coordinated, developed, wrote, designed, evaluated, organized and prepared."

Following is a sample resume:

Maria Student
245 College Street
Anywhere, Virginia 24609
(480) 394-5575
mstudent@compugo.com

OBJECTIVE
A challenging position in marketing and sales management

EDUCATION
Bachelor of Business Administration, Marketing Major
Wilson University, Atlanta, Georgia
Co-op Student in Sales Director's Office
Mainstream Manufacturing Company, Atlanta, Georgia

RELATED EXPERIENCE
Sales Representative
- Full-time temporary in summers; part-time during academic year, General Warehouse Products, Atlanta, Georgia
- Handled general sales and specialized in computer-related products
- Learned sales protocol, account follow-up, and packaging
- Served as back-up to sales manager in his absence

Co-op Intern
- Assigned to assist sales director, Mainstream Manufacturing Company, Atlanta, Georgia
- Coordinated sales representatives schedules
- Monitored sales records
- Developed and presented in-service training sessions
- Received award from sales representatives for contributions as an intern

Service in University Student Business Leaders Association
- Member for three years
- Chairperson, Charity Drive Project, raised $5,000 through projects
- Recording Secretary, maintained minutes, records, agendas
- President, senior year. Developed orientation program for high school students, computerized financial and historical records systems, led development of a video program for business students

Professional Characteristics
- Highly motivated, organized
- Excellent writing, oral and presentation skills
- Positive attitude, broad perspective in planning and problem solving
- Enthusiastic and energetic
- Eager to learn, grow and develop professionally

Writing Your Cover Letter

Your **cover letter** is an original business letter that complements your resume. The purpose of this letter is to get the employer to read the resume. You may want to obtain extra plain paper of the same type your resume is copied on to match the pair for a professional look. In your cover letter you want to introduce yourself to an employer and let them know why you are sending your resume. If there is a specific opening, this letter serves as your **letter of application**; if there is not a specific job posting, this then becomes your **letter of inquiry**. The letter should be brief—one page—and to the point. It should be addressed to a specific person. If you do not know the name of the person at the company accepting applications or inquiries, call the receptionist and indicate that you are sending correspondence to the person accepting such letters and wish to know the correct spelling of the name and exact address.

1. Your first paragraph is to stimulate interest…to indicate why you are writing, how you found out about this company, and what position you are seeking.

2. Your second paragraph (and third, if there is one) should make clear what you have to offer the company. You should point out how your skills and knowledge and experience match those listed in the job posting and/or how your skills fit with the company.

3. Your last paragraph is designed to get a response from the employer. Indicate in this closing paragraph when and how you will contact the employer to follow up.

Following is a sample cover letter:

Maria Student
245 College Street
Anywhere, Virginia 24609

Today's date

Joshua Barker, Manager
Sales Division
BCD Corporation
2420 N. W. Major Boulevard
Atlanta, Georgia 30319

Dear Mr. Barker:

I am writing to apply for the sales manager position that you advertised in the *Atlanta Daily News*. I see in this position an opportunity to use my knowledge and skills in salesmanship and my organizational skills in management.

The enclosed resume details my education and related experience. I will receive my degree in marketing with an emphasis in management from Wilson University in April. I have worked during summers and part-time in the academic year at General Warehouse Products as a sales representative. At the University I was a co-op student in the sales director's office at the Mainstream Manufacturing Company in Atlanta. As president of the Student Business Leaders Association on campus, I enhanced my leadership and organizational skills through several service projects we achieved. I am highly motivated, energetic and hard working.

I would appreciate an opportunity to meet with you personally to discuss my qualifications and your organization's needs. I will call your office next week to inquire regarding an appointment.

Sincerely,

Your full name

Enclosure

When your cover letter is successful, the employer will read your resume. When your resume is successful, you will be selected for an interview. Now let's think of some pointers for the actual meeting with a prospective employer.

Preparing for the Job Interview

How you write your application letter, fill out an application, present your qualifications in your resume, handle yourself on the telephone are all important, but the *single most* significant factor in the selection process is how you conduct yourself in your employment interview. One survey (Byham, 1997) revealed that 80% of respondents in a national study didn't consider interview preparation as important as having a positive attitude. Yet, recruiters and interviewers for companies report that such preparation is one of the most important factors in persuading an employer to consider an applicant for a position. You can be a happy, smiling, easy-going, perfectly positive person in the interview, but corporate interviewers indicate that if it is apparent you have not prepared for this event, you can *positively* count yourself out of the running!

The goal of your interview, that you must have firmly tattooed in your brain, is to get an offer for a position. The interview is the prime opportunity for you to communicate what you can do for the company or organization. Your job is to make clear to the employer how your skills, knowledge, experience, motivation, and work habits match what is needed in the desired position. As the saying goes, remember, "You never get a second chance to make a first impression!"

Preparation for your interview means doing your homework—gathering information, anticipating your response to questions, devising your own questions, rehearsing your introductions. Think through and practice giving an overview of who you are and your qualifications. You should prep for an interview with just as much enthusiasm, intensity and interest as you would for a final exam.

It is necessary to gather information about the organization or company and the position. What you should know:

  a. What is the nature and purpose of the organization?

  b. Who are the key leaders in the company?

  c. How small or large is the organization? Number of employees? Amount of sales? Number of clients served?

  d. In what other locations do branches exist?

  e. What is the organizational pattern for the company?

  f. Who are the major competitors for this product or service?

  g. What is the organization's reputation?

  h. What information about this company has been in the news?

  i. What are the requirements of the position you are seeking?

  j. What does the job description include as responsibilities of the job?

  k. Why is the position you are seeking available?

Where you can find the information:

Corporate Directories, Annual Reports, publications circulated within and publicly by the organization, the company's home webpage, Chambers of Commerce, newspaper articles, and magazine and trade journal articles and advertisements. You can also call the company as ask questions, request brochures, and inquire about other publications or video presentations designed to provide information about the organization. Try to obtain a copy of the job description if you are seeking a specific job that is posted for applications. In learning about the company, determine the vocabulary used to describe customers, products, services and processes; in other words, learn the "lingo" of the culture.

The Five C's to Keep in Mind

There are several reminders that need to be stored in your head as you prepare for your interview. Five specific pointers to remember are the five C's. These are as follows:

1. **Challenged**—Feel the spirit of challenge as you face the task of selling yourself to an employer. Recognize that this is important, but that you can do this…and do it well!

2. **Communicative**—This is the time to put all you skills learned in this text on interpersonal effectiveness. Be sure you are listening to understand, that you clearly know what is being asked. Don't answer before you have a moment to gather your thoughts and organize your answer. Then when you have thought it out, answer clearly and concisely.

3. **Candid**—BE honest and direct and you will come across as the trustful, genuine person that you are.

4. **Comfortable**—Be relaxed and at ease. If you are tense and anxious, you make interviewers tense (a situation you don't want!). Be yourself. Don't try to put on a show or be something you are not. Imagine if you were hired yet someone other than you got the job??? That is, imagine what a mess you create if you project yourself as someone you are not and they hire that impersonator! Your troubles would just be beginning!!

5. **Confident**—Never make a clear negative statement about yourself. Even if someone asks you directly "What do you see as your weakness?" do *not* put yourself down. Find a way to respond that doesn't make you look compromised. For example, you might say, "Some people consider me overly concerned with facts, but others will tell you I am extremely thorough and that if I report something, you can count on it being on the money!" Your phraseology is extremely important. Consider the difference between how these two responses sound…"I am out of work" compared to "I am in transition in my career." When asked about your academic career contrast "My G.P.A. was 2.0" to "I experienced a variety of opportunities in college from which I learned. In addition to my coursework, I learned about teamwork, persistence and leadership as part of the baseball team, and I organized the Career Forum sponsored by the student government association."

The Actual Interview Process

1. Introductions—Introduce yourself in a friendly and courteous way. Pay close attention and remember information given as you meet your interviewer, both verbal and non-verbal information.

2. Wait to be invited to be seated.

3. Listen, respond, and ask your questions in the exchange of the interview.

4. Mentally note any follow-up requests such as supplying references or transcripts.

5. Sense when the interview is drawing to a close.

6. Clarify with the interviewer the next steps in the process.

7. Summarize your pleasure at the interview experience, what you will do as the next step, and state succinctly your enthusiasm and qualifications for the job.

8. Thank the interviewer as you prepare to leave.

9. Follow up with a written (handwritten or typed) letter of thank you.

Tips to Keep in Mind

DOs	DON'Ts
Your homework . . . gather information	Appear uninformed regarding the organization
Rehearse . . . practice orally	
Prepare questions you might ask	Talk too much
Dress a level above the job you are seeking	Pretend to be listening
Arrive on time	Interrupt the interviewer
Have a firm handshake	Put yourself down
LISTEN	Be arrogant
Show interest	Be rude
Be nice	Question about salary early
Be yourself	in the interview—do it
Think what it's like to be	at the end, if at all
in the interviewer's shoes	Be an extremist . . . moderation
Ask your questions	is the key . . . in dress and
Think before responding	ideas or attitudes
Maintain eye contact most of the time	Have a telephone interview if
Thank the interviewer when you leave	you can avoid it
Send a written follow-up expressing your	Be vague or indirect
appreciation and interest in the position	Be negative

After Leaving the Interview

Although you may feel a sense of relief and accomplishment after the interview; before you call a friend to get together to celebrate; force yourself to sit with a pad and pencil and review and jot notes about the interview. What did the interviewer ask you? Where were you more uncertain about your responses? Where did you shine? What did the interviewer say or do that gave you clues as to how you were doing in the interview? Were there areas of knowledge where you wish you had had more information?

Capture in writing as much as you can about the experience before you even leave the area. You will remember the most about the experience right after it happened. Even an hour later, your recollection will be less complete. This is hard to make yourself do, but can be very significant to preparation for a second interview...either at this company or at another. You have proven your ability to write a cover letter, resume and secure an interview! After you have rendered your experience to writing, pat yourself on the back!

Keeping Your Job

In preparing your resume, in your conduct during your interview and especially in the process of maintaining your position, it is important to think through and have clearly in your mind the ways that you add value to the establishment for which you are working. When you actually get the job…you think, "Whew! I did it, I got the job." But the needed energy for the task is not over, it is just starting. You have conveyed your *potential* value added to this organization, now you have to prove it. This is where the rubber hits the road, so to speak. Especially in times of downsizing and higher unemployment rates, what you can contribute to the bottom line of your company or organization is paramount. You did a lot of work to understand your assets, your skills, your strengths of character that you bring to this workgroup. You prepared for and made your career decision, wrote your resume, and interviewed successfully. All this effort will help build your skills in assuring that you are contributing considerably to your workplace entity. A valued employee is more likely to be a continuing and positively progressing employee. Loza (2009) offers the following tips for keeping your job:

- Show value—if you are not adding value, there is little reason to keep you
- Stay current—staying up to date in your field increases your employer's options
- Network internally—you can find out about opportunities in other departments
- Sell your organization or department—be an advocate for your place of work
- Sell yourself—adding value is good; having others *know* you add value is better
- Show a good attitude—nobody wants a whiner or complainer around
- Assess your role—determine your strengths that can help your company
- Show flexibility—show willingness to be used in ways that benefit your company
- Build respect—for your abilities and for yourself as a person; do the right things
- Have a plan—apply these tips; have a plan for the worst case scenario

SUMMARY

In this chapter we have reviewed the process of planning your own career and making it happen. We examined the six personality orientations of Holland and how these relate to career fit. We considered the variables that Roe believes influence our career success. We investigated the power to excel by discovering and enhancing our strengths. We noted the importance of discovering and building your strengths. We described ways you can gain information about your interests, personality characteristics, values, and skills. We explored the ways to find information about careers in order to analyze the connection between the nature of the work and your own "human nature." We reviewed methods for decision making that allowed for value differences for specific factors. We discussed goal setting and development of a career plan. We looked at the steps in getting the job, preparing your resume, cover letter and the interview process. We emphasized the importance of adding value to your company, and shared other ways to help you keep your job. Whether you are preparing to enter a profession for the first time, or if you have years of experience in the professional world, the real value of all of this is you putting it to work in designing your own career!

KEY TERMS

Realistic	Values	Talent
Investigative	Personality	Added Value
Conventional	Career Plan	Career Families
Enterprising	Introspection	
Social	Resume	
Artistic	Cover Letter	
Letter of Application	Letter of Inquiry	

POSITIVE PSYCHOLOGY SELF EXERCISES:

1. Take Seligman's Positive Psychology Values-in-Action survey to identify your signature strengths.
2. Complete the *Self Directed Search* or *Strong Interest Inventory* and list three occupations that fit your orientation and that appeal to you.
3. Discuss your career goal or tentative goal with a friend using the factors in Anne Roe's vocational theory.
4. Develop a career plan using the sample in the chapter as a guide.
5. Keep a self-assessment journal, recording new insights and information as you gather it.
6. Visit your campus career center with a group of fellow students. After your visit, design a brochure for the center.

CHAPTER 13 QUESTIONS

Short-Answer Questions

1. The psychologist who developed six basic personality orientations was _____.
2. One of these orientations is _____.
3. The psychologist who looks at marital situation as a factor in career decision is _____.
4. In assessing myself, I should focus on my _____ (areas of consistent, near perfect performance)

5. The process of discovering what is going on inside ourselves including behaviors, feelings, and attitudes is _____.

6. The popular personality inventory that includes 16 possible types is the _____ _____ _____ _____.

7. The Positive Psychology on-line inventory by Seligman helps you determine your _____.

8. The "OOH" as a source of career information stands for the _____ _____ _____ published by the government.

9. In addition to interviews, and internships, an excellent first place to look for career information and job listings is on the _____.

10. After making a career choice, the next step is to develop a _____.

11. A resume should be _____ page(s).

12. A letter that responds to a specific position open is referred to as a letter of _____.

13. The goal of your interview is to _____.

14. What are the 5 C's to remember in an interview?

_____

_____.

15. After leaving the interview, you should follow up with a _____ letter to the interviewer.

16. One of the most important behaviors for keeping your job is adding _____ to your company.

Essay Questions

1. Describe a position that requires three of Holland's personality orientations.

2. Discuss how family background is an influential factor in career choice.

3. Describe three ways that you can get information about yourself.

4. Discuss the advantages of visiting your campus career center to determine or explore your career choice.

5. Discuss your signature strengths and link them to career areas where they would be assets.

6. Explain to a friend in writing how to make a decision that considers various factors of different importance. Give a written example.

7. Distinguish between a cover letter and a resume.

8. Describe to a friend how to prepare for a job interview.

9. What do the 5C's for interviewing mean?

10. What do you plan to do in a job interview? Describe the process.

11. Explain the contents of a career plan and why each part is important.

12. Contrast the behaviors between an employee who is likely to be kept on the job with an employee who is likely to be terminated.

14

Applying Positive Psychology at Work

Positive Psychology, the science and study of psychological strengths and positive emotions, brings great promise for achieving pleasure and fulfillment in the workplace. Through the development and use of strengths, such as creativity, open-mindedness, integrity, interpersonal skills, leadership, hope, and enthusiasm, we are able to enhance production, fulfillment and the satisfaction that we enjoy in our work life (Seligman, 2002, 2011). Strengths that are vital to a positive work life are emotional and social intelligence (Goleman, 1998, 2006), which are related to our ability to work effectively with others. When you have these skills, you are known as being **people smart**.

In the 1600's John Donne wrote, "no man is an island...." He was right. We all have to deal with people. No matter what type of career you may be in, whether you are a computer programmer, sales manager, engineer, artist, physical therapist, teacher, or other, you will be doing your work in the company of other people. Some occupations have a great deal of contact with other people; some involve minimal interaction, but *all* jobs involve working in a social context of some sort. Aristotle said centuries ago that humans are social animals. So it makes sense that to be successful and excel on the job, you will also have to be people smart. Research shows that the reason most people are fired from their jobs is not because they lack the technical skills and knowledge to do the job, but because they cannot get along with other people, their bosses, co-workers, clients, customers, patients, students, whomever their position requires they serve. The increasing use of work teams to complete projects in the workplace further emphasizes this skill.

Is there someone you know who is really "smart" when it comes to taking a test, spewing out dates and knowledge, answering questions with the most obscure facts? They might win a million with their final answers, *but* how do they do on the job, working in a populated environment? Do they have a working knowledge of how to interact effectively with people?

414 / Section Three: Occupational Effectiveness

WHAT DOES IT MEAN TO BE PEOPLE SMART?

When we think of being "smart" we think of having a high IQ, supposedly being very intelligent when is comes to cognitive skills. However, what we have traditionally referred to and tested with IQ tests are skills in language and analytic/mathematics problem solving. Thus, our concept of "intelligence" centers around thinking skills involving memory, logic, organizing ideas and the like. In 1983, Howard Gardner challenged this traditional concept of intelligence when he proposed his theory of multiple intelligences. He described eight different types of intelligence that exist in humans. The two of import here are the personal ones, **intrapersonal** and **interpersonal intelligences**. These speak to our ability to be aware of our inner selves and to connect effectively in working with other people.

Daniel Goleman (1995), discussed earlier, notes the significance of knowing yourself as a part of emotional intelligence. For him, self awareness is an ongoing attention to one's internal states that can be at best a non-judgmental consciousness of feelings or at a minimum recognition of what is happening emotionally rather than "being immersed and lost in it." Goleman discusses the anatomy of our brain and cerebral emotional centers that are involved in normal functioning. He relates a story of a man who, because of brain surgery for a tumor, lost the normal neural connections in his brain between his cognitive and emotional centers, which left his thinking devoid of emotional connections. This disability in his emotional functioning caused the man severe problems. He lost his job as a corporate lawyer; his wife left him; he couldn't handle his financial affairs; and he was even unable to make simple decisions. This illustrates how important our emotions are to normal functioning. Goleman points out that even in usual day-to-day activity, a person who is annoyed by a rude encounter in the early part of the day, but unaware of his feelings, is likely to continue for hours afterward snapping at other people and making curt responses for no good reason. As Goleman explains, once this person brings the feelings from the initial morning rude encounter into his awareness, he can then evaluate things anew. This allows him to change his frame and his behavior positively toward others. Thus, Goleman illustrates the importance of our being able to feel emotions and to be aware of them as a basis for behaving with emotional intelligence.

Silberman and Hansburg (2000) state that those who are people smart exhibit the following competencies:

1. **Understanding People**—listening actively, empathically, clarifying, interpreting beyond words to non-verbal messages, and able to read other people's styles and motives in order to work with them effectively.

2. **Expressing Yourself Clearly**—knowing how to get your message across by reading the verbal and non-verbal responses of those with whom you are communicating.

3. **Asserting Your Needs**—being your own person, having and establishing limits, and being straightforward with your wishes.

4. **Exchanging Feedback**—giving feedback easily and without being offensive as well as seeking feedback from others.

5. **Influencing Others**—being able to motivate others to action, able to connect with others, discover their needs, knowing how to reduce resistance and to make persuasive appeals.

6. **Resolving Conflict**—able to use the above mentioned skills to get the subject on the table, able to figure out what's bothering you and the other person and to suggest creative solutions.

7. **Being a Team Player**—accepting the challenge to work with others through complementing their styles, coordinating the efforts of team members without being bossy, and building consensus.

8. **Shifting Gears**—Understanding differences in people, able to make changes in one's own behavior, willing to try things new and different, able to reframe, and knowing how to handle the risk of change.

There are meaningful rewards for developing these skills. When you understand someone else, you are appreciated; when you explain yourself clearly, you are understood; when you assert yourself, you are respected; when you exchange feedback, you are enlightened; when you influence others positively, you are valued; when you resolve conflict effectively, you are trusted; when you collaborate with teammates, you are prized; when you shift gears, your relationships are renewed. (Silberman and Hansburg, 2000).

These competencies described by Silberman and Hansburg echo the ideas of Goleman regarding emotional intelligence. Do these eight competencies ring any bells related to the steps you've been learning throughout this text about being a more effective person? Hopefully, you are mentally connecting reframing, being proactive, listening and expressive skills and thinking about how these all play out in the workplace.

UNDERSTANDING YOURSELF

The aged admonitions from Socrates and Shakespeare to know and be true to yourself are filled with wisdom. Just as you probably can't really love someone fully if you don't love yourself first, you obviously need to understand yourself before you can become astute in knowing others. So let's start with some questions to think about.

What Do You Want the Outcome to Be?

Whether you are talking about your career, your marriage or family, your grades for this semester, or your tennis swing, you have to have a vision of the desired result. As we discussed previously, athletes training for Olympic feats work with psychologists to visualize their success. The more specific and clear the image in your mind, the more likely you are to achieve it. If you don't have a goal in mind, it's like going on a trip with no destination. How do you know if you're getting closer? How do you know when you're there? How *can* you know, if you don't even know where you're going? Have you ever tried to do a class project when you didn't understand the assignment? How can you know if you're doing a good job, if you don't have a clue what you are trying to accomplish? Or why you're doing this thing in the first place?

Goal setting is the answer to the mysteries here. If you have a clear goal you are trying to achieve, it gives you direction and focus. This helps you know if you are staying on track, moving in the right direction, and how well you are doing.

Imagine yourself ten years down the road. What do you see for your life? For your career life? Family life? If you said you wanted to be a successful lawyer, for example, and you wanted to be a parent who is involved with your two children, how is that going to work? Lawyers spend an incredible amount of time at their jobs, especially in the first decade or so of their work. How are you going to do this and still manage to spend time with your children? Suppose you want to make a lot of money in a career in demand. So you decide to be a computer engineer. But, you really enjoy outdoor sports and participating in mountain bike races with your significant other. How are you going to work those long hours and be on call at all hours when systems problems occur, yet spend a long vacation biking in France or finding time to travel for races out of town? Is there a way to reconcile competing goals?

As you can see, setting a goal leads you to the next steps of planning how you are going to accomplish this. In companies and organizations employers report that the best performing employees are those that consistently set goals for themselves. Research over the years has confirmed that college students who complete their degrees, compared to those who drop out, are more likely to have begun their studies with a specific major and career goal in mind. It makes it a lot easier to do your assignments, prepare for tests, get yourself to those early classes and such when you know why you are doing these things.

Goals are usually classified into two categories…long-term and short-term. We have many short-term goals everyday. Sometimes, just getting through the day is one of your short-term goals! Turning your thoughts toward what you want the outcome to be is an important first step. Daily goals might be in the form of a *To Do* list. For important matters related to career, family, or health issues the goals will be longer term goals. Clarifying your goals helps provide the direction, like a lighthouse blinking a steady reminder regarding your course ahead. Keep a file, folder, a notebook or journal in which you discuss and record your goals, both long and short term. We all talk to ourselves anyway, so begin a written dialogue with yourself about what you want the outcome to be. Also, refer back to your mission statement for guidance.

What Is Your Personality Like?

This second question will also help you be smarter about who you are. We use the word "personality" in everyday speaking. We might say, "Oh, she has such an out-going personality." What do we mean when we use that term? **Personality** refers to our characteristic patterns of behavior including our thoughts and emotions. In other words, even though we have lots of thoughts and feelings, and behave in all kinds of ways, we have consistency in certain ways of behaving. It is like a theme or refrain in a musical piece that comes back to repeat itself.

Each individual has his own collection of unique behavioral quirks. You and your brothers and sisters (if you have any) may have some behavior characteristics that are alike, but the whole package of how you and your brother behave is different for each one. So we each have our own personality scheme. Most researchers agree that this pattern of behaviors is formed in our early years and we probably cannot make major changes in our behavior patterns. Even though we may not be able to move from being a perfectionist to becoming a person who is the opposite and tolerates or even likes disorder, we can learn how our perfectionist pattern helps and hinders us. It is unlikely that an extrovert would change and become an introvert. But again, an extrovert can recognize how his outgoing nature is an asset or a liability and change his behavior accordingly.

In trying to develop an awareness and understanding of your personality, there are many sources or methods you could use. Numerous personality assessment instruments have been developed by theorists to determine personality patterns. One of the most popular instruments is the Myers-Briggs Type Indicator.

Without visiting a psychologist for psychological assessment, you already have a handle on some of your patterns of behavior. You sense whether or not you are decisive, bright, shy, disorganized, out-going, competitive, calm, sad, suspicious, or quiet, for example. So besides formal psychological evaluation, introspection, looking inside yourself, is one way of discerning your personality patterns.

How Can You Get and Use Feedback?

You can determine information about your personality by gathering feedback from others who know you well and have seen you behave over time. Ask them to describe you. Another place where written and verbal feedback is available is in learning settings. You have been getting teachers' comments on your behavior and work patterns for years in the form of anecdotal comments and in formal grading or rating systems. Think back over your report cards, and other school experiences to see what patterns in behavior are evident. Think of your interactions with your friends. How did they describe you or react to you when you were in school?

How Can You Keep a Balance?

Sometimes, the very thing at which you are best, if taken to extreme, becomes your downfall. For example, if you are really good at persuasion, that can lead to a successful career in law, sales, business, or politics, but if you over-do your capacity for influencing others, it can begin to create the opposite affect. You might be self-destructive if you carry your strength too far by behaving in ways that are seen as dominant, insensitive, pushy, or overbearing. So the secret is to know your personality and find a healthy balance. This means recognizing how your personality patterns help and hinder you. Learning to use your personality traits to maximize your effectiveness and monitor and manage them when they become ineffective is a key to success.

Positive Psychology Exercise

Through thinking about yourself, reviewing and gathering feedback, and perhaps completing a personality survey, determine five adjectives that describe your personality. Decide how they are strengths and how they could be weaknesses. Keep them in mind, and use them well!

HOW PERSONAL NEEDS DRIVE BEHAVIOR

Understanding your needs is another important key to behaving in ways that move you closer to achieving your goals. You might have heard people commenting about someone's behavior by saying, "Oh, she just needs to be with people" or "he needs to always be at the top of the class," or "they always want to be in charge." These three comments reflect the work of David McClelland (1961) who pioneered research, which described and explained what drives people to behave in certain patterns. He called the first need alluded to above, the need for **affiliation**, to be in social settings, connected to other people. The second comment above describes someone McClelland would say has a need for achievement, always striving to be at the top, to accomplish a lot, to exhibit high levels of performance. The third description portrays what McClelland called the need for power. We all have some of these needs, but if you were to rank order these three from the most to middle to least in your behavior, how would you order them? Do you see examples of this ranking in your behavior? In any of your role models? What about your parents?

Another psychologist who studied needs and developed a theory was Abraham Maslow (1970). Maslow spent much of his life examining what was right with people instead of what is wrong. He was interested in determining the characteristics of extremely psychologically healthy people, extraordinary people who made a difference in this world. From his research he developed a **hierarchy of needs** that are depicted in pyramid form, since each level presumes the lower level(s) of needs is/are already met. His hierarchy is as follows:

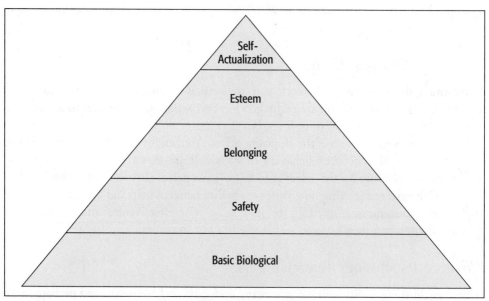

Figure 14.1 Maslow's Hierarchy of Needs

Maslow explained that our initial requirements were biological for sustaining life, such as air, water, food, and sex. When these are satisfied, the next level of need that emerges is safety which causes us to behave in ways to feel secure and safe. This would include shelter from the elements, and in today's world might include locks, alarms systems and bars on our windows! When safety concerns are met, Maslow said we then experience desires for connecting to other people, a craving for affiliation, belonging, and social interaction. Then esteem necessities would emerge and we would behave in ways to meet those. The highest level in Maslow's hierarchy is self-actualization needs. These are of the highest order and include concern for things like *the good, the true, and the beautiful*. People who are aspiring to be self-actualizing are experiencing a high level of fulfillment in their lives. As Maslow said, they are actualizing, or bringing to reality, the potential we all have as humans for the good life. However, Maslow said that most people never reach functioning at this highest level. He described the characteristics of **self-actualized** people as:

Being practical and realistic in problem solving
Accepting of themselves and other people
Being genuine, natural and spontaneous
Having a need for privacy
Being independent, self-reliant
Having **peak experiences**, moments of exhilaration and ecstasy
Identifying with and respecting all humankind
Following strongly held values and ethics
Maintaining deep, close relationships with a small number of people
Demonstrating a broad, non-hostile sense of humor
Being innovative and creative
Being individualistic and resisting conformity
Appreciating the natural and social environment

The extent to which you can identify with your needs, be they for achievement, social connections, for power, for safety, and so forth, the more you can understand why you may be behaving in a certain way. Needs can be conscious or unconscious. The idea of needs explains what motivates our behavior. This is why public schools have instituted breakfast programs for students. Administrators have recognized that if kids are hungry, they aren't going to care much about learning that one-plus-one makes two.

A good way to get in touch with what needs *are* operating in your life is to take an inventory of where you spend your time. What are you investing your efforts and energies doing? The theory suggests *there* is the answer to your **motivation**. It's not a question of are you motivated or not motivated. It is a question of what needs are you motivated (and therefore behaving) to meet? What is the focus of your motivation?

We can learn a huge lesson from the advertisement industry in our country. Massive amounts of money are spent on advertising, and for what purpose? No, it's not to make us buy a product or service. It is for us to be convinced that we need it; then *we* take care of the buying part, sometimes even if we can't afford it! And look what a great success the advertisement industry has had. Think of all the things we are convinced we need to live such as cell phones, flat screen TV's, IPads, laptops, and faster wireless service.

If we are rationally convinced that a specific degree, occupation, or lifestyle, is what we need, we will behave in ways to make it happen. So this brings us back to our goals. If we set goals and then find ourselves not motivated to do the things we must to achieve those goals...perhaps we *need* to work on our needs! If we can convince ourselves, like the advertisers, that we need what those goals will bring, then we will behave to achieve those goals. This cycle of behavior starts with awareness of our need pattern that is presently operating and convincing ourselves to make changes in our priorities, to see our goals as *necessary*. This will bring us to the power of commitment. Can you think of something in your life, perhaps not necessarily easy to achieve, that you decided you *were* going to do? You didn't say, "Maybe I'll do this," " I'll try to do this." Instead, you said, "I *am* going to do this." Notice that whatever obstacle you had to overcome to do this thing, you figured a way to handle it? And remember how good it felt when you could say, "Yessssss…I did it!"

If you convince yourself you **need** to meet that goal, you are lighting the flame of commitment which fires you into action. The intensity of this kind of energy is amazing. And you are on your way to achieving your goal, meeting your new need!

The first step to reaching success is awareness…then commitment…then comes change. Become aware of what needs are driving your behavior. Think of how can you work with those needs, using them to maximize your success, override them with newly determined needs, or stop and satisfy them, then move on.

Triggers for Positive and Negative Behaviors

One of the smartest things you can do in learning about yourself, is to become aware of **triggers**. Triggers set you off, either in a positive way—energized to behave in ways to be effective, or in a negative way—aroused to act out your emotions and attitudes in ways that are destructive, to others and/or yourself. In the medical world they speak of "triggers" that set off physical problems, like allergies or migraine headaches and admonish patients to become aware of trigger situations and avoid them. On the positive side, health care givers encourage the presence of trigger situations like aromatherapy, massage, meditation, deep breathing and the like that activate calming behaviors and reduce stress.

The triggers we have come from somewhere. Are we born with them? No way. The specific events or incidents or words or situations that initiate predictable responses from us are learned associations. And we probably learned them early in our lives, perhaps long before we really remember the original incidents. These incidents involved pleasant or unpleasant consequences in our earlier times and those same feelings get generated today, even though the circumstances are different. Triggers can stir feelings that are happy, delightful, and positive as well as feelings that are sad, uncomfortable, and negative. The key is to identify the triggers that set off negative responses, avoid and monitor them, and seek out those triggers that spark our joyous feelings.

Positive Psychology Exercise: Identifying Triggers

If you think about common feelings, you can identify behavioral responses, that is, how you react when feeling this emotion. You can also identify what happened just before the feeling became evident. This probably triggered the emotion. For example if you think of a time when you felt *anger*, you can identify the behavioral response that occurred. You can also identify what triggered the emotion and determine if this is a common antecedent to angry feelings, and complete the form that lists numerous common feelings, filling in your responses. This will give you insight about specific triggers and behaviors that you may want to revisit and alter. Now consider the following set of emotions and fill in the blanks for examples of patterns in your behavior:

FEELING	BEHAVIORAL RESPONSE	TRIGGERED BY
Anger		
Sadness		
Anxiety		
Power		
Compulsion		
Joy		
Calm		
Amused		
Alive		
Happy		
Warmth		
Love		
Exhilaration		

The steps for managing negative trigger situations in your life are:

1. Be aware of what sets off the reaction.
2. Monitor the situation.
3. Use your cognitive self to explore the logic of the situation.
4. Determine alternative responses that you can employ to minimize or avoid self-destructive consequences.

In the case of positive emotions, become aware of the triggers that initiate them. Then deliberately gravitate to situations that expose you to those triggers that enhance your happiness.

Handling your personality patterns is important in moving toward achieving your goals and meeting your needs. The extent to which you become proficient in using triggers to your advantage, the more personally effective you will be. You will be people smart about yourself. You will also be better prepared to engage in understanding the behaviors of others.

UNDERSTANDING OTHERS

In addition to understanding yourself, your career success also hinges on your being able to understand and interact effectively with other people. Hiring and firing data shows the importance of working effectively with others. Research on ratings of top performers consistently ranks interpersonal skills, emotional intelligence, and political skills as being more important than mental ability or intelligence (Goleman, 1998, Ferris, 1999, Kaplan and Kaiser, 2010).

In other words, no matter how traditionally *smart* you may be, it is your *people smarts* that carry the most weight in achieving *excellence* in your performance ratings. Such ratings are the bases for decisions about retention, promotion, advancement and growth opportunities in employment settings. There are many parallels between managing yourself and working well with others in sensing, analyzing, and behaving effectively in your work setting. These can be seen in the following model that is called the *People Smart Pagoda*. In building any structure, you have to start from the ground up. The same is true in building your skills in working with people.

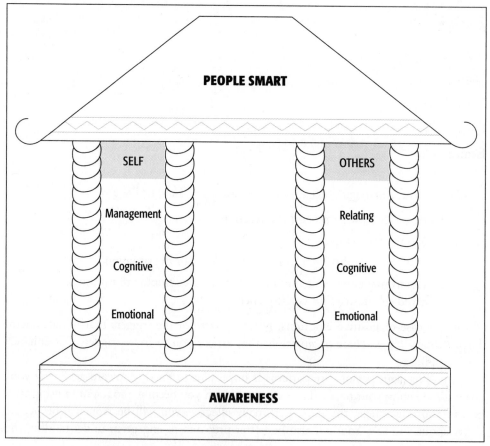

Figure 14.2

Awareness—of yourself and of others—stands as a foundation upon which to build skills for self-management and skills for connecting effectively with the other people in your work environment. We've discussed methods for becoming more aware of yourself. We looked at how introspection and feedback help you gather information to better understand your goals, needs, personality and situational triggers. In the same way we can develop a sharper awareness of others in our environment by examining these same factors in the people at work.

To begin, you can carefully observe those around you. This means tuning in all your senses to gather information about them. Not only do you need to look at and listen as intently as you can at the behavior, but you must look at the non-verbal messages being sent. In listening empathically, you attempt to understand what it is like to be in another person's skin. This enables you to gain insights into why that person is behaving as she does. In other words, the best way to understand the personalities, needs, goals, and behavioral triggers of others is to be a keen observer of cues and a sensitive and empathic listener.

Group Goals

Just as understanding how your goals direct your behavior, you can gain a sense of how the goals of group members at work influence their behavior. This will help you understand the dynamics of the group. Ask yourself, "What appear to be the goals of the group as a whole? Does a common group goal exist? Is it written down anywhere? Does everyone understand and agree on what the group is trying to achieve?" Likewise, ask yourself, "What goals have individual members articulated for themselves as members of this group?" What is each individual person trying to achieve in addition to the common group goal? Such goals could be an opportunity to learn new things, a promotion, a chance to do something different, or a chance to make more money.

Personality of Others in the Workplace

Obviously, you are not going to administer a personality assessment inventory to anyone, but through actual careful observation of the behaviors of others, you can learn something about their personality patterns. Remember, we all have some of these behaviors going on from time to time. What consistency or patterns do we see in the actions of others? Are they:

Extroverted or Introverted?
Rigid or Flexible?
Organized or Free Flowing?
Happy or Sad?
Stable or Moody?
Secure or Insecure?
Decisive or Wishy-Washy?
Conservative or Liberal?
Confident or Uncertain?
Energetic or Laid Back?
Positive or Negative?

You become more competent in "reading" other's behavior from a process that simulates the method scientists use to find out new information. It begins with experience in being a detective of sorts in a work group. First you observe carefully, trying to gather evidence of actions, comments, and body language that give you a hunch about that person. Then "test out" your hunch or hypothesis about that person's personality by future observations, even predicting what that person will do and discovering you are either (1) right (maybe this **is** a pattern), or (2) you're wrong (mistaken impression, start over). We do this sort of thing at some level each time we meet a new person and form impressions. Usually we are not aware we are doing this. But if we work consciously at being a better observer of behavior, both verbal and non-verbal, this can help us develop expertise in "psyching" out people in our work environment.

When we get a better sense of the personality patterns of those we work with, we are better able to understand their behavior. This allows us to think and choose approaches that are more effective in dealing with that specific person. For example, in working with a person who has "dominance" as part of their personality, when making suggestions for change at work, you might make a special effort to express your suggestion in a way that doesn't threaten that person's perceived authority. Compare the two approaches here:

Scene 1

Roger: "Hi Steve, how's it going?"

Steve: "Pretty busy. Hey Roger, I thought I told you to be here at 7:30. It's almost 7:45. We're going to be slammed with customers today."

Roger: "Well, instead of you always making up the schedule like we are just robots, why don't you let us pick when we want to come in. I'm not a morning person. If we did the scheduling a different way, maybe things would go better."

Steve: "I am the manager, and don't *you* forget it! I know how we need to staff this place! Now get busy!"

Scene 2

Roger: "Hi Steve, how's it going?

Steve: "Pretty busy. Hey Roger, I thought I told you to be here at 7:30. It's almost 7:45. We're going to be slammed with customers today."

Roger: "Sorry I got here late. Listen, I was thinking about my being late sometimes, and I know you have a handle on what would work and what wouldn't. I was wondering what you might think of this thought I had about scheduling. When things are less busy, maybe we could talk and I could share my ideas to see what you think about them. Okay?"

Steve: "That sounds okay for later. Right now we have to get going."

Roger: "Right, we'll talk later. Thanks for listening. I'd better hustle."

In the first scene, Roger does two things that tick Steve off. First he tries to put the blame on Steve, his manager, for his being late. This means he is not being **proactive**. Secondly, he is attacking Steve's competence and authority in how he does the staff scheduling. Especially if he knows that Steve has a dominant personality, can you see what a mistake this is? The first scene will probably continue to go "down hill" from there.

In the second scene, Roger takes responsibility for his lateness. He recognizes that Steve has a need to be in control, and acknowledges his "competence" in knowing what will work or not before Roger indicates he has an idea about scheduling. He asks, doesn't tell, Steve about sharing his idea. He is also sensitive to the reality that there is a lot of work to do as the place is busy and he has contributed to the stress with his lateness. He doesn't expect that things will stop here and now so he can discuss his idea. He does, however, plant a seed…that he wants to share an idea, and he solicits some agreement from

Steve to listen later. Wisely, he doesn't press for a specific time at the moment as he needs to address the need to pitch in and get to work. He can come back to Steve's agreement to talk at another less busy time and try to set up a specific time for discussion.

Roger achieves his goals in this situation by being aware of Steve's personality, as well as being proactive. With practice, you get better and better at observing and analyzing how the exchange between people moves back and forth. You can pinpoint the specific comments and emotional expressions that shift the content and the tone of the interaction. Knowing something about how the parties involved "tick" can help you anticipate their behavior.

Needs of Others in the Workplace

Closely related to "personality," the needs that are operating at a given time will motivate a person to act one way or another. Just as you gain an understanding of your own needs and how that causes you to behave to meet those needs, the same is going on for others with whom you work. Using Maslow's hierarchy or McClelland's theory of needs, you can gain an awareness of patterns of behavior that reflect the needs of those around you.

To the extent that you can sense needs others may have, you can be a part of meeting those while also meeting your own needs. In the example above with Roger and Steve, the need for power was operating in both parties. Steve, being very dominant, needed to maintain control. Roger, desiring to have some power in giving input to decision making, wanted to share his idea. In scene 2 we could see both of these needs being met. It would appear that Roger also had a need for affiliation operating that was stronger than his need for power, as he addressed the issue in a different way in scene 2, one designed to avoid being alienated by Steve. Roger's behavior in scene 2 paved the way for a possible win-win outcome, but in scene 1, Roger was obviously pushing for a win-lose outcome that could only further hamper their working relationship.

Social and Cultural Conventions

If we are to understand behavior exchanges we must be aware of the influences of culture, ethnicity, age, gender and other social or cultural aspects that shape our behavior and that of others. The increasing diversity of the workplace and global interdependence challenges us to expand our knowledge in this area. To the extent that we can recognize the context from which a person comes, we can appreciate their differences from ourselves rather than being threatened by them. These skills and attitudes are also part of what makes us a global citizen, and promotes awareness of and empathy for others.

An awareness of social conventions regarding **idioms**, expressions or sayings, in a culture is important to our understanding of others. If we take everything said in its literal meaning we may be confused and uninformed. If someone refers to a person as "a nut" someone unfamiliar with the idiom might be confused, wondering "a walnut, an almond? I don't get it!"

Further, the general rules of courtesy and custom, sometimes called etiquette, are important to understand lest we unknowingly offend someone by behavior that is considered by that person to be rude, as we discussed earlier. Discomfort might be caused when different customs are practiced in the workplace.

THE GLOBAL PERSPECTIVE—How Are Global Citizens "People Smart"?

Global citizens are "people smart" in effectively extending their connections to others way beyond those in their inner circles. They operate within a frame of openness and a willingness to identify with all of humanity. If we observe global citizens as they relate to others, we will see the following attitudes and behaviors exhibited:

- Accepting responsibility for global citizenship
- Being comfortable with differences
- Relating with empathy to those within cultures different than their own
- Reading about international events
- Listening effectively
- Believing they are empowered to make a difference
- Communicating with non-English speakers
- Recognizing that today's challenges cannot be solved by the same kind of thinking and actions that created them
- Understanding the impact of culture on our lives, and its effect on attitudes and behaviors
- Acknowledging that one's own culture, religion, and values are not universally shared
- Speaking at least one language other than their native tongue
- Appreciating different groupings in America's own multicultural structure
- Volunteering in service programs (local, national, and international)
- Working effectively in diverse teams
- Motivated by love rather than fear
- Regarding all people of the world as important
- Tolerating ambiguity
- Articulating human differences and similarities
- Exercising moral leadership
- Having respect for human dignity
- Behaving ethically
- Conserving environmental resources

Which of the above attitudes and behaviors relate to your strengths? Which ones might you work on in your quest to be a global citizen? Which one do you want to work on first? How can developing these competencies enhance your being "people smart" in the workplace?

Triggers for Positive and Negative Behaviors in Others

Just as we discussed emotional intelligence as helping us recognize triggers that set off emotions and behaviors in yourself, it is helpful to be able to identify triggers that can set off, or annoy, other people. Being aware of what makes others *tick* can not only help you avoid *ticking them off*, but can assist in contributing to their positive thoughts, feelings and behaviors. Behaviorist theories hold that all behavior is conditioned by what happens in the environment. This would suggest that we *can* influence those around us to behave positively. Gaining an understanding of what events initiate what responses, perhaps we can help our bosses, co-workers, and customers act positively. This, in turn, becomes a reward for us.

USING YOUR STRENGTHS AS YOU DEVELOP IN THE WORKPLACE

One of the aspects of Positive Psychology is the focus on strengths rather than weaknesses. Some managers, administrators, educators, and others in leadership roles around the world are leading with their employee's talents in mind. However they are in the minority in the United States, United Kingdom, Canada, France, Japan, and China, all countries where a Gallup study was conducted (Hodges and Clifton, 2004).

Clifton and Hodges distinguish between the terms strength, talent and theme, pointing out that a strength is the ability to provide consistent, near-perfect performance in a given activity. The process of building a strength involves three steps: (1) identifying dominant themes of talent, (2) discovering specific talents, and (3) refining them with knowledge and skills. Talent naturally exists within you, while skills and knowledge must be acquired.

Individuals who go through identifying talents and integrating them into their frames, then change their behavior to match their talents, report increased satisfaction and production, in other words, optimal functioning, as a result of focusing on what they do best. The StrengthsFinder web-based assessment (at http://www.strengthsfinder.com) can assist individuals in working through these stages and has more than three decades of study of success in more than 30 countries.

Neuroscience explains that between the ages of 3 and 15, the human brain organizes itself by strengthening the synaptic connections used often, while seldom used connections diminish over time. Harry Chugani, professor of pediatrics, neurology and radiology notes that regarding synaptic connections in the brain "Roads with the most traffic get widened. The ones rarely used fall into disrepair" (Coffman & Gonzalez-Molina, 2002, p. 21). After age 15, the pattern of synaptic connections does not have major change. This is scientific support for the idea that synaptic connections become predominately stable. Therefore, the greatest payoff in development is to focus on your talents, where the synaptic connections are already robust.

Positive Outcomes of Strength-Based Development

Data from follow-up surveys of people who completed strengths assessment shows that strength-based development is related to positive outcomes. In a study on this issue, respondents reported that learning about strengths helped them make better life choices, resulted in greater productivity, and increased their self-confidence (Hodges and Clifton, 2004).

In the workplace, strengths-based development was incorporated into the Toyota North American Parts Center California with 400 employees on 54 work teams Workers were assessed and given results on their strengths and managers were trained in the use of strengths. A session was held to move employees from focusing on their own strengths to exploring the strengths of their team members in order to optimize their team relationships and performance. This effort resulted in a per-person increase in productivity of 6%. In this project two teams received a more intensive strengths-based development program and achieved a productivity increase of 9% in only six months (Connelly, 2002).

Employee engagement is tied to such performance outcomes as customer satisfaction, productivity, and employee turnover (Harter, Schmidt, and Hayes, 2002). A survey item that has strong conceptual relationship to a focus on strengths is "opportunity to do what I do best." This same item is strongly linked to success, and is defined as above median workplace performance. A meta-analysis of more than 300,000 employees in 51 companies indicates that when employees had an above average response of having the opportunity to do what they do best, there was a 38% higher probability of success on productivity and 44% higher probability of success on customer loyalty and employee retention (Harter and Schmidt, 2002).

A study of 65 organizations using employee engagement interventions was compared to a control group of 61 companies who were not. The study group registered higher employee engagement from year one to two and even more when followed for three years (Clifton and Harter, 2003). Following a strengths-based and employee engagement intervention program at St. Lucie Medical Center in Florida, employee turnover dropped 50% and engagement scores rose to the top quarter in the study's database. Patient satisfaction jumped by 160%.

These findings show that focusing on strengths is a powerful way to increase your positive feelings, thoughts and behaviors in the workplace. It also has implications for the development of positive psychological and organizational behavior, in other words, positive institutions, in which to carry out your work. Focusing on strengths can also increase hope, subjective well-being, and confidence. As noted above, strength-based organizations and companies yield rich returns in **P**ositive emotions, **E**ngagement, and **M**eaning for workers as they enhance their **A**ccomplishments—all PERMA components of an optimally functioning individual. Workers in a high state of well-being thus increase the bottom lines in production toward meeting the organization's goals. Again, a win-win for all.

Positive Institutions

Building *positive institutions* has been a pillar of positive psychology since its inception, and refers to studying strengths that foster better communities. Creating family and school environments that help children flourish, identifying and building workplaces that support satisfaction and high productivity and generating communities that promote civic engagement are goals of positive psychology. Characteristics of positive institutions have been identified by numerous researchers to include:

- Exhibiting transparency, authenticity, open honesty
- Having, knowing, and achieving the mission
- Working constructively to deal with conflict and adversity
- Performing in a growth mode
- Modeling a positive role by the CEO
- Considering the whole as greater than the sum of the parts
- Empowering people to have greater decision latitude

- ❀ Having a strong sense of purpose that is shared across the organization
- ❀ Looking forward
- ❀ Emphasizing getting better
- ❀ Focusing on strengths-based approach
- ❀ Treating people as individuals with individual strengths

Greenberg (2007) considers two additional characteristics that are central to positive institutions: *meaning* and *recognition*. Pratt and Ashford (2003) analyzed the distinctions between meaning *at work* and meaning *in work*. Meaning that comes from one's work involves identifying and applying strengths and re-crafting one's job. Meaning *at* work includes contributing to the greater good in some way. The growing implementation of positive organizational programs and applied research to determine results is being referred to as *positive organizational scholarship (POS)*. Examples include Seligman's (2011) description of the Comprehensive Soldier Fitness program, a strength-based positive approach the U.S. Army has employed to the training of troops. Results showed more resilience and less post-tramatic-stress-disorder (PTSD) and depression related to combat experiences. Positive institutional programs have been developed for use in schools. One example is School-Wide Positive Behavior Support (SWPBS) with the goal of facilitating the academic achievement and healthy, prosocial development of children and youth in environments that are safe and conducive to learning (Sprague and Horner, 2006). Studies examining the effectiveness of SWPBS in schools have shown reduced discipline office visits, vandalism, aggression, delinquency, and alcohol and drug use. Praise is an important component of the program for reinforcing positive behavior. Likewise, in the workplace, Greenberg (2007) found, using internal performance measures, that managers who give frequent recognition and encouragement had employees who were more optimistic and engaged, and produced better results.

Positive institutions have potential for improving the well being of their participants, whether it is a family, a school, an army, or a workplace. Finding positive functioning at any stage, age or setting is exciting, considering as Seligman does (2011) that positivity could spread beyond the community to the nation and the world. This does not mean living in "happiology" all the time, but being stronger and more able to elicit the resilience needed to cope successfully.

THE GLOBAL PERSPECTIVE—Bright Green, Deep Green, or Green Yet Unseen

In his latest book, *1493*, Charles Mann discusses the impact of the "discovery" of the new world by Christopher Columbus. Most of us know it as a tale of genocide and devastation of indigenous populations. However, it is a much more complex story of the impact of introducing new plants and animals into an existing ecosystem, and the unintended and unforeseen consequences that followed around the entire planet. For example, with the exception of llamas and alpacas in the Andes mountains, the Americas had no grazing animals such as cows, horses, goats and sheep. Pigs, chickens, ducks and the parasite that causes malaria were also absent. The genocide of the native peoples of the Americas was enabled by the diseases brought by these explorers, who for millennia had been living in close quarters with these animals. Smallpox, measles, influenzas, and malaria were unknown in the Americas. Up to 90% of native peoples were killed by these diseases. In many respects the European explorers didn't destroy the wilderness; they created it with the loss of the peoples who had been tending the land.

THE GLOBAL PERSPECTIVE—Bright Green, Deep Green, or Green Yet Unseen (cont.)

As we have noted earlier, there is little quarrel with the notion that with seven billion people on the planet, we are in the middle of another major disruption of Earth's systems with no certainty whatsoever what the outcome will be in terms of the survival of our own or other species. We are, however, perhaps the only species that knows consciously that something is happening and that are able to take action. Consider two schools of thought that suggest what we might do.

The *deep green movement* generally believes that humans must return to a simpler way of life that involves voluntarily reducing population and decentralizing food and energy production and distribution. They maintain that large cities, factory farming, and huge centralized power production as seen in the most developed countries in the world are altering the climate and poisoning Earth and the life on it. On the extreme ends of this movement some envision the destruction of dams and returning to life without electricity. While many may envy and aspire to gain the material advantages of modernity, they are ultimately unsustainable. Further, they add that these technological developments have separated us from a meaningful connection with Earth and the life on it. In fact, they come from a misunderstanding of our place in the story of the universe. On the body of Gaia, humans have become the moral equivalent of a cancer interested only in its own growth while unaware of destroying the body, the source of its life.

The *bright green movement* responds that we cannot turn back the hands of the clock and return to a time of small family farms. They agree that our technological reach has left no place on the planet unpolluted and that our numbers are too large; but they also would maintain that what we need is a kind of forward escape using technology to create a better designed future. The problems we face are problems we have created. We have been driven solely by profit and a false economy that did not take into account the cost of the consequences of poorly designed manufacturing, farming, and energy production. Well-designed cities, farms, and production processes would account for the inevitable waste that they generate. Prior to production they would determine how every single by-product could be recycled. Their mantra is *waste equals food*. If a material cannot be safely discarded and reabsorbed into the environment, it must be captured and reused in industrial cycles. Anything that does not fit these criteria must be phased out of use as soon as possible (McDonough and Braungart, 2002).

Both of these movements believe the other is naïve. Deep green for instance states that cities are inherently unsustainable and have always had to plunder the countryside around them to survive. "Where do you get the food, the energy, the water? Where does the shit go?...we can[not] have an industrial culture and also wild nature" (Jensen, 2011). Bright green would argue that kind of thinking is a failure of imagination. Properly designed cities can in fact provide food, energy, and recycling of waste without polluting their surroundings. They also note that women who move to cities begin to have fewer children and that this may be an approach to helping reduce population.

We have no choice but to choose and choose again. Where do you stand? How can you find out more about both positions? Can you choose even knowing that all decisions are made on the basis of insufficient information and there, indeed, may be unintended consequences?

OVERCOMING PROBLEMS IN THE WORKPLACE

As you think about enjoying your work and functioning on a motivated high, it is important to come back to the reality that problems are inevitable in the workplace if you are there long enough. Being informed about some of these potential problems and ways to cope with them can help you proactively prevent or lessen the intensity of these situations. Let us examine some of the more common problems found in most work settings.

Beware of Polarization

Being people smart as you interact with co-workers, clients, supervisors, or others, it is important that you remember the lessons of reframing to avoid falling into the trap of

polarization. Deborah Tannen in her book *The Argument Culture* (1998) makes the case that many aspects of life in Western culture including the U.S. are couched in a debate of two opposing views. This is seen in the political arena in our country where there is a war of sorts between those on the *left* and those on the *right*. Both groups refuse to listen to each other or to consider that there are other points of view beside just those two. Sometimes in employment settings it can be viewed as *us* against *them*. Tannen believes that framing information into an argument between two sides focuses on the contention, which in the process fails to integrate ideas and information of the broader picture. Most issues have more than just two alternatives; yet, journalism, the media, politics and even education have conditioned us to be more interested when there is a fight, a conflict, a debate. This results in many Americans embracing the frame that a debate always produces better information when in many cases it may limit being fully informed. She suggests that to move from debate to dialogue, it is important to remember that those in our work setting who disagree are still members of the same community. She lists rules of engagement to remember, which are:

- Don't demonize colleagues with whom you disagree
- Don't affront their deepest moral commitments
- Talk less of rights, which are nonnegotiable, and more of needs, wants, and interests
- Leave some issues out
- Engage in a dialogue of convictions. Don't be *so* reasonable and conciliatory that you lose touch with a core of belief you feel passionately about

Tannen notes that Asian cultures emphasize harmony and seek methods of inquiry that focus more on assimilating ideas and exploring relations among them than on opposing ideas and fighting over them. The Chinese approach to **yin** and **yang** depicts integration where each is dynamic and changing. Rather than the dualism of debate, yin is always present in yang and changing into yang and vice versa.

Engaging in empathy with a co-worker who holds a different view provides the opportunity to "try on" the perspective of holding that view. This, in turn, may broaden your own thinking and help you discover commonalities with your colleague, rather than just completely shutting out the other's view. Remember that war is a lose-lose situation, even in a war of ideas or words.

How to Resolve Conflict—A Model for Conflict Resolution

Many authors have put forth useful guidelines for conflict resolution. What follows is our synthesis of several systems which we have broken down into seven major steps. In theory, this format is designed to be used in more formalized situations, but can be applied for any need to resolve conflict.

In reality the steps may not flow as smoothly as presented here. You may find it necessary to jockey back and forth between steps as snags develop in the process, or if you encounter resistance on the part of the other side. But in any event, it is important not to skip any of the steps. They all build upon one another. You can't have a building without a foundation, and you can't have a fourth floor without a third floor.

STEP ONE: Acknowledge/Identify the Problem or Conflict to Yourself.

Don't run away from the conflict or attempt to avoid it with a premature resolution like immediately giving in, or insisting on your way. Admit that there is a problem, and recognize that some conflict is an unavoidable part of life, particularly among people who live or work together. What is important is how it is handled. But you also need to recognize that the problem that is causing the conflict belongs to you. Why? Because you are the one who is dissatisfied; you are the one who therefore needs to "own" the problem as yours. This is not the same as saying that it is all your fault, or that you are to blame, but rather that it is your problem because it causes discontent for you. Recognizing this important fact will make a difference when the time comes to approach the other party involved. Instead of ranting or raving or being judgmental, it can help you state your concerns in a descriptive fashion, which will likely be more accurate and objective, and will minimize the possibility of eliciting a defensive reaction on the part of the other party. Part of acknowledging what the problem is for you is to identify to yourself what needs you have that are not being met as a result of this problem or conflict.

STEP TWO: Agree on a Date and a Procedure.

It may be pointless to try to resolve a conflict unless all parties are prepared to do so and have set aside the time to do so. Fights often ensue because one party confronts another who isn't ready at that moment to deal with the issue at hand. It is very useful to set aside a time beforehand to deal with the issues. Request that a meeting time be set up at a mutually agreeable time and date with adequate time allotted. Decide the appropriate place where the meeting should take place. Where negotiations may take place over several meetings, it may be wise to alternate locations since most people feel more comfortable on their home turf, or to have the meeting in a neutral location. Another important procedural issue involves who will attend the meeting. If more than two parties are involved in the dispute, agree beforehand on who can and should be included in the meeting.

STEP THREE: Describe Your Problem and Your Needs.

Even though your position may be different or in conflict with that of the other party, that does not mean that you do not have some shared or compatible interests. If you didn't have some shared interests you probably would not be sitting at the bargaining table to begin with.

Describing your position has several aspects to it. The first aspect involves stating your position and your needs clearly and forthrightly. Follow the guidelines for assertive responses, which will allow you to present your side effectively. To present your position effectively, it is important to do your homework. By this we mean plan what you intend to say. Feel free to use prepared statements, even charts or tables of figures if appropriate to highlight the salient points of your position.

After stating your wants and needs it is then often strategically useful to define the conflict in terms of a mutual problem to be solved, building on the notion of shared interests. This "we are in this together" approach helps to tap the motivation of all involved parties to cooperate in reaching a win-win outcome. Endeavor to consider the situation or the conflict separately from the personalities involved. It helps if you are willing to be at least somewhat flexible in your position, and that you enter the negotiations with the mind set that both you and the other party are basically reasonable people who want to reach a fair resolution to a problem in which you both have legitimate interests. Notice that we never refer to the other person or persons as your "opponent" or "adversary," but rather simply as the other party. This helps to foster a climate where a win-win outcome has a chance.

Recognize that you begin creating a climate for either cooperation or contention from the moment the negotiations begin. To create a cooperative atmosphere, begin the meeting with ice-breaker conversation. In prolonged negotiations, it can be useful to have meals together so as to promote an opportunity to view each other as people, apart from the conflict, and build rapport.

It is also very important that you manage your emotions appropriately. If you did not have strong emotions regarding the issue at hand, it is unlikely that you would be going through a complicated process like conflict resolution. It is important to control your anger for it will not serve you well in this process. Direct expression or indulgence of anger will likely lead to defensiveness on the part of the other party and may cause them to dig in their heels. Anger will cloud your ability to think rationally and be flexible in your own best interest. Avoid giving ultimatums. We advise you to exert your positive power by being assertive. Positive power thrives on a willingness to believe that the problem can be solved and a commitment to remain with the process.

Once you have presented your position you need to check whether the other party has understood what you said and what you meant. Given that this may be an emotionally charged situation, it is certainly possible that there have been some miscommunications or misunderstandings. Before proceeding, make sure that the other party has fully understood your point of view, not that they need to necessarily agree with you at this point in the process, but at least that they comprehend your message, what you want, what you need, and why this is so for you. Ask the other party to tell you their understanding of your position. If they have misunderstood some aspect of it, then take this opportunity to correct their misconceptions.

STEP FOUR: *Seriously Consider the Other Party's Point of View.*

Give the other party their say on the issues and afford their point of view serious consideration. Do your best to step into the shoes of the other party, to see the situation or conflict from their eyes. Remember the value of being willing to give up being right. Just as you asked the other party to feed back to you their understanding and interpretation of your position, do the same for them and share your understanding of their point of view. Give them the opportunity to clarify their position on issues or correct any misunderstandings you may have developed about where they stand and why.

Equalize the amount of time that both parties get to present their sides. The other party has just as much right as you to get their needs met and find satisfaction. First, if you expect them to cooperate in meeting your needs, it is reasonable to expect that you will behave in a fair fashion. Secondly, it is essential if you want to achieve a win-win outcome, or any solutions for that matter. If the other side has difficulty expressing themselves, then ask questions to draw them out and help them to clarify their position. In some situations, it may be appropriate to ask about the feelings and experiences that led to their current position. The more you understand about them and the more they understand about you, the more likely you can arrive at a win-win solution.

STEP FIVE: *Explore Possible Solutions.*

Generate as many potential solutions as possible and later evaluate them to decide which one best meets everyone's needs. Adopt the attitude that there are may be more than one solution that is mutually satisfying. The advice of McKay, Davis and Fanning (1983), from their book *Messages: The Communication Skills Book*, is especially relevant here. They enjoin you to...

> Get rid of the notion that there is only one best way to divide up the pie, that the pie is only so big, and that you absolutely must get the biggest piece. These are all self-defeating ideas. There are actually several good ways to cut up a pie. You may even find a way to make the pie bigger. And ending up with the biggest piece isn't always ideal, especially if you antagonize people and end up getting your pie in the face. (p.152)

It may be very important to do homework beforehand to determine what is fair, especially in a business negotiation or some type of deal involving merchandise and/or money. Tracking down precedents or benchmarks will help you generate proposals that are reasonable.

Brainstorming involves the uninhibited offering of ideas and suggestion by all members of a group. All interested parties should be encouraged to participate. All suggestions, no matter how outlandish or unrealistic, should be listed on a blackboard or large writing pad without judgment. Do not, at this stage, criticize, praise, or in any other way evaluate the suggestions. Just list them all, no matter how ridiculous or unworkable any might be. Generate as many ideas as possible for further exploration. Remember that even a seemingly crazy idea may lead to another great idea. Try to come up with as long a list as possible, the more and the wilder the better. Approach the problem from every angle. Try to go beyond the 9 dots. To facilitate this process try looking at the problem through the eyes of imaginary experts. How would a judge solve the problem, or a cop, or a psychologist or a school principal? What about your mother, or your brother? How would a banker, or a priest, minister or rabbi attempt to resolve this issue? Oftentimes shifting to the mind set of another can free you of your blinders and help you see possibilities that had eluded you beforehand. This last suggestion is especially helpful if you are stuck brainstorming all by yourself.

While brainstorming, also consider time honored methods for resolving issues or forging compromises. The classic way of dividing disputed assets or property is splitting it down the middle, if possible. In buying or selling the equivalent solution is to split the difference. Consider the ways you could soften aspects of your position that are not critical to you in order to make your proposal more palatable to the other party. Permanent changes can be proposed as temporary ones to see how they will work out. Major changes can be done in steps. Unconditional demands can be made contingent upon something important to the other party.

STEP SIX: *Evaluate and Negotiate.*

Set a reasonable deadline that is agreeable to all parties involved, otherwise negotiations could go on forever. Many people become willing to budge when they see the deadline approaching. Of course you can always extend the deadline if necessary, but having one in place helps to move things along.

Begin to evaluate each option. Some will be easily identified as unworkable or unrealistic and quickly discarded. At first glance, some will be acceptable to one side but totally unacceptable to the other side. Discuss these using the guidelines for clear communication and effective listening, and eliminate those that will never, under any circumstances, be considered by one side or other. At this point the list should be whittled down to those solutions which are potentially acceptable to each side.

At this point, if you have communicated your position effectively and been a good listener, you should have developed an improved working relationship with the other side. State the options that you favor as proposals. Approach the proposal slowly and describe your favored solution in detail. Then move on to your second or third choice, if such exist. Listen to what option or options are favored by the other side. This creates a cycle of proposal/counter proposal that may be repeated several times, including discussions and time-outs to consider various propositions. Discuss the difficulties that you each have with the proposals. As the proposals and counter proposals evolve, it is likely that their terms will keep moving ever closer together. Look for the overlap between your proposal and that of the other party. What adjustments can be made to make the proposals more aligned with one another? Keep in mind what needs to happen to generate a win-win solution, based on your needs and your knowledge of the needs of the other party. By offering choices, being flexible, and open to new information, you create a cooperative climate that makes this type of back and forth negotiation possible. Do not offer your proposal as an ultimatum for that is guaranteed to fail.

While this negotiation is ongoing, if you sense that the other party is in an agreeable frame of mind, this is the time to present a "**yesable proposal.**" A "yesable proposal" is an aspect of your position that, if stated as a direct question, it would be easy for the other side to answer yes. For example, if you are negotiating for a pay raise, you could ask whether such a raise would be forthcoming if you agreed to increased productivity on your part. If you know that improved productivity is important to your boss, then you are offering to meet his/her needs in exchange for what you want (a win-win solution).

If a win-win solution is just not possible despite all your best efforts, then you need to begin to negotiate a compromise. Even in this case the process of working toward win-win has not been in vain. You likely have, as a result of this process, forged a better working relationship with the other party. The resulting atmosphere of goodwill may prevent future conflicts or may help in solving further dilemmas down the road.

To reach an agreement, of course, there must be consensus. It is usually quite clear when this has been achieved when only two people are negotiating, but if there are more than two participants, especially if the issues at hand are important, it may be best to take a more formal vote. Usually a hand vote will suffice, but in a business negotiation involving many individuals it may be useful to do a confidential written vote to minimize group pressures and allow each party to vote freely.

Herb Cohen, in his book *You Can Negotiate Anything* (1980), recommends that you write what he terms a memorandum of agreement, intent, or understanding, detailing all aspects of the agreement. This written record is there to remind all parties of the exact nature of the agreement you have reached. All parties should sign it. It can prevent misunderstandings later on if one party insists that the agreement was different from your memory of such. It also builds on the fact that people are more likely to follow through after they have entered into a more formalized, signed arrangement. This memorandum should be written in straightforward, common-sense language. In a more formal negotiating situation such as collective bargaining, such agreements need to be written in legal language and may need to be composed by an attorney.

STEP SEVEN: *Enact the Solution and Follow-Up.*

Develop a plan regarding what is to be done, when, where, and who is responsible for what. It helps to include this information in the written agreement. It is also useful to begin implementing the plan as soon as possible to avoid the resistance or suspicions that delays could arouse.

Until you have enacted the plan and given it some time to see how it is working, you cannot reasonably evaluate whether the solution has worked. As you close your negotiations decide when and how to evaluate the plan. How long to wait and how to conduct the evaluation process depends on the nature of the plan and how complicated it is. After a reasonable amount of time has passed to test the viability of the solution, have another meeting and discuss the results of the follow-up evaluation. If there are difficulties with implementation, then brainstorm how to adjust or modify the plan. If it is a total disaster, you may need to scrap it and start from scratch.

Substance Abuse

Millions of people on this earth are dependent on alcohol and other drugs. The cost of this in the workplace is seen in behaviors such as shoddy quality of work, low productivity, inconsistent performance, bizarre behaviors, absenteeism, and problems relating to others. In addition, there is often a lack of interest in work as well as a lack of concentration that adds to carelessness. This, in turn, adds to health hazards in the workplace such as the 40% of on-the-job injuries and about half of all work-related deaths that occur because of alcohol or drug abuse (Dubrin, 1999, DeCenzo, 1997).

Many larger companies maintain employee assistance programs where help with substance abuse and other personal problems is provided. In the case of alcohol or drug abuse there are hospital based rehabilitation programs that help with overcoming addiction. Also there are self-help twelve step groups such as Alcoholics Anonymous and Narcotics Anonymous that are available to people who want to overcome their addictions. Twelve step programs help individuals with substance abuse problems to develop a support network of people to aid in recovery and maintenance of sobriety.

Lack of Advancement

Another problem that may be experienced in the workplace is not being considered for promotions for which you have aspirations. Studies have shown that having a **mentor** in the work setting is significant for success. A mentor is an experienced worker who takes a new worker "under his or her wing" to help one understand such realities as (1) how things work in the environment, (2) the accepted norms for behavior, (3) who key people are in the organization, and (3) how one can get ahead. One problem for female workers is that, especially in certain business and professional settings, there are few if any mentors available. It is important to seek out experienced workers that might serve as mentors when you begin your career.

Another strategy for moving up in the organization is to discuss your aspirations with your supervisor, especially when you meet for your annual performance appraisal. Obviously, this assumes you have rapport with your supervisor and that your evaluations of your work have been positive. Your supervisor has the information or can point you in the right direction to find it regarding position postings, availability, and educational/experience requirements for these positions. The human resource or personnel office is another source of information and guidance for exploring ways to move ahead in your organization.

Demonstrating your commitment and motivation for meeting the organization's goals is of paramount importance if you have aspirations for advancement. In your career, if you wish to make a move, you need information about the positions in which you are interested. You need to know what is required for that job and then demonstrate that you have the desired skills and knowledge. In today's terms, what we bring to an organization is referred to as our "added value." We need to know that what we do, in fact, adds value to a company or organization, and be thoughtful in making this known effectively as we seek advancement. Companies are beginning to recognize that employees who truly add the most value to the organization are those who are engaged in their work and enjoying what they do. These companies are seeking to increase opportunities for intrinsic rather than extrinsic rewards (Hay Group, 2001).

Your people smarts and leadership skills are important since these assets are especially crucial for positions that involve managing others. Inquire with the training department (if there is one in your company) for ways to secure assistance in enhancing your skills in this area if needed.

Be aware that moving up in your own department or area may be more difficult than seeking a position in a new section or division of the organization. Sometimes, making a move up means making a move out...not only out of the department, but out of the company or organization to another employer.

Remember the power of persistence. Gather as much information and feedback as you can if you have been passed over for promotions. Try to identify your goals for preparing yourself for the position you want, and don't give up.

Burnout

Another potential problem in the workplace is **burnout**. This is a collection of physical, emotional and mental reactions that reflect exhaustion. Burnout is the result of constant and re-occurring emotional pressures with people in the workplace and/or at home. It can also be caused by poor management of yourself in time, feeling unable or unequal to do a job, an overwhelming workload, inability to adapt to change, lack of supervision from a manager, and an inability to meet deadlines. Burnout sufferers tend to disengage from their work and possibly the people around them. Production suffers. The person begins to have a negative self-concept and negative attitudes toward work and the workplace. The person is drained and may appear apathetic, angry, withdrawn, or lazy. Physical symptoms such as headaches, chest pains, gastrointestinal problems and back pains may occur.

Burnout can happen to anyone who is experiencing too many pressures with too little support, but it is especially found among the helping professions such as health care, social work, law enforcement, and education. Persons feeling burnout may see themselves as a failure and may be in positions where they give and give to others but lack a source of support for their own needs. Burnout can result in people behaving as if they are powerless to turn things around. They may behave like victims and begin blaming others, further compromising their relationships with co-workers.

Burnout is often found among persons who are perfectionists, idealists, or workaholics. They may start their work with great enthusiasm, very intense energy and highly positive attitudes. They are usually high achievers. Eventually they push themselves beyond their own limits and things begin to break down, leading to burnout.

Difficult People

If you work long enough, undoubtedly you will find yourself dealing with some difficult people. Learning to be effective in conflict resolution, in being assertive, and in listening with empathy can help you immensely in finding ways to work effectively with such people. Maintaining your own calm in these cases is half the battle and enables you to think through your plan for confronting the situation as early as possible. If you are unsuccessful in your efforts, consider seeking a third party who might act as a mediator to assist you and the person you find so difficult. Be alert; don't allow yourself to slip into denial. The problem doesn't go away, and could get worse.

Sexual Harassment

Sexual harassment has been around for years. Business law professors Roberts and Mann (1996) examined the extent of sexual harassment in the workplace. They report that a 1976 poll found 9 out of 10 women said they had been subjected to unwanted sexual advances at work. A Federal Government survey found that 42 percent of women and 15 percent of men reported some sexual harassment at work. A Federal Government study for the years 1985-87 estimated government costs from the effects of sexual harassment at $267 million.

In 1992, Anita Hill (1997) accused Supreme Court nominee Clarence Thomas of sexual harassment. This case was highly publicized and the following year, the number of sexual harassment cases increased dramatically.

Sexual harassment is defined by the U. S. Equal Employment Opportunity Commission (March 4, 2008) as "unwelcome sexual advances, requests for sexual favors, and other verbal or physical conduct of a sexual nature constitute sexual harassment when this conduct explicitly or implicitly affects an individual's employment, unreasonably interferes with an individual's work performance, or creates an intimidating, hostile, or offensive work environment." In 2007, the EEOC resolved 11,592 charges of sexual harassment and recovered $49.9 million in monetary benefits (not including monetary benefits from litigation). There are two conditions under which sexual harassment may fall. One is referred to as (1) **quid pro quo**, which involves getting something for giving something, such as a person in authority demanding sexual favors to keep a job benefit. A second condition referred to as (2) **hostile environment** involves a situation where (a) a co-worker or supervisor engages in unwanted sex based behavior which renders the workplace intimidating, or hostile, or (b) the purpose is to unreasonably interfere with work performance. Hostile environment cases are more controversial since there may be so many perceptions of "intimidating" or "offensive." A company is liable if they are informed of sexual harassment and ignore it. However, a company may be held liable even if they did not know about the sexual harassment. The safest bet for a company is to have a clear policy and to be sure all employees are aware of the rules.

DeCenzo (1997) summarizes ideas for protecting yourself from sexual harassment as follows:

1. Know the organizations policy on sexual harassment.
2. Let the offending individual know you're irritated by his or her behavior.
3. Document such events.
4. If the offensive behavior is repeated, complain to someone in authority.
5. Keep records of your work.
6. Seek help from an attorney if you're not satisfied with what the organization is doing or has done.
7. Keep your spirits high.

Discrimination

Since the Civil Rights movement began over thirty years ago we have become more sensitive to the need to treat all people equally. We are aware of concern for discrimination based on race or gender, but there is a broader range of areas that fall under the Equal Employment Opportunity (EEO) guidelines. The following factors are the official bases for EEO **discrimination**:

Race	Age
Color	National Origin
Religion	Sex
Disability	Reprisal

Color discrimination occurs in situations where members of the same race are treated differently because of the color of their skin or because of the shades of brown skinned persons. National origin refers to ancestors or country of origin. **Reprisal** refers to disciplinary action for raising an allegation of discrimination.

Age discrimination involves decisions being made about employees based on their age, usually affecting older workers. Steinhauser (1998, 1999) notes that in 1994 the median age of workers was 38 years. In 2005 the median age was 41. According to AARP, nearly one-in-three U.S. workers will be over 50 by the year 2012 (Career-Builder.com, February 7, 2008). Between 1996 and 1998 American companies paid out over $200 million in fines for age discrimination. This amount does not include legal fees. First Union Corporation, a large bank, agreed to pay $58.5 million to 239 of its former employees who sued for age discrimination. Steinhauser says this is just the "tip of the iceberg," and notes that jury verdicts are historically higher in age discrimination than those based on race, gender or disability.

In the work situation if you are experiencing discrimination in any of the above categories, it is important to seek the guidance of the human resources representative at your place of employment in charge of EEO compliance.

Being aware of these many problems and issues in the workplace and having strategies to prevent or deal with them increases the probability that our workplace experience can be positive. Especially since we spend so much of our adult life at work, it is critical that our workweek include positive emotions and fulfillment. In fact, we should have enjoyment.

MAKING WORK FUN

Once upon a time there were two people sleeping in their own houses. At 6:30 a.m. alarm clocks sounded in both homes. In both bedrooms an arm stretched over to the alarm clock to find the button. And that was the end of the similarity.

GEORGE hit the snooze alarm and dozed off for a few more minutes. When the alarm sounded again, he thought, "Oh, darn, it's Monday morning already." George dragged himself out of bed and stumbled toward the kitchen to find the coffee pot. "Why does it have to be Monday?" he moaned. Eventually he grabbed a donut with his coffee, got himself dressed and dashed out thinking, "I'm going to be late again...oh well, who cares?"

At work, George frowned as he entered the office. "Man, it is too hot in here. Why do they keep this office so hot?" He passed a couple of co-workers who greeted him smiling. "What's with them?" he thought. "What's there to be so happy about?" He sat at his desk and stared blankly at the pile of papers on his desk. "I'll never get this all done. This is too much." For a moment he put his head down on his desk, but lifted it up and started taking the papers off the pile, to begin work.

At noontime, George decided he had to stay in and work. So he ordered a quick sandwich and brought it back to the office to eat while working over lunch. "I'm so far behind, I'll never catch up," he mumbled as the clock struck one.

In the afternoon, George kept looking at the clock. "It's moving so slowly," he muttered. "When will this day end?"

HARRY turned off the alarm and hopped out of bed to stretch. "What a sleep; boy, I slept like a rock," he thought. He dressed eagerly and ate breakfast while reading the newspaper. Then he rose slowly and eagerly headed for the door. "What a nice day," he thought as he headed out into the morning sun. "Not a cloud in that blue sky...nice way to start."

At work, Harry smiled and greeted his co-workers. "How was your weekend?" he asked the fellow at the next desk, remembering that this guy was meeting his girlfriend's parents over the weekend. He settled in at his desk and reviewed his calendar. Next, he began organizing his day by making a "To Do" list. Then he launched into reviewing a report for the scheduled afternoon meeting. He mused, "This is a well done report."

At noontime, Harry left the office to meet his friend from college for lunch. He strolled down the block to the sidewalk café they agreed on. "Couldn't have picked a better day to enjoy eating outside," he thought.

In the afternoon, Harry, report and notes in hand, entered the meeting thinking, "This'll be a challenge!"

Which of these two would you rather be? If these guys worked for Snow White, we might have Grumpy George and Happy Harry. How are their attitudes different? How are they approaching their work? Which one is making work fun?

Given how much of our lives is invested in our work, and how closely the quality of our lives is linked to our work gratification, it's something to think about. Earlier we discussed how important your career choice is to your happiness. The greatest occupational arrangement is when your work reflects your passion, that which you love to do. This is usually something that you do very well. It is like a positive cycle. Those things we like, we prefer to do. Since we prefer them, we do them more often. Doing them more often makes us more proficient and so we like them even more. Think of your history. What subjects did you like the best in elementary school? Did that continue into high school? Is there some connection between that subject and the career choice you've considered or decided upon? A study by British behavioral scientists (Lonier, 1994) found a connection between desires in youth and success in adult life. In this longitudinal study, fifty people were followed from age 7 to age 35 (a total of 28 years). The findings showed that nearly all of the subjects wound up in a professional area related to their interests during ages 7 to 14. Most strayed from these interests after childhood, but those adults who were successful returned to their childhood dreams by the age of 35. For some it was as a hobby or leisure time activity. This suggests that we re-visit our early years and look for patterns in our interests. If you have years of working experience, what have been your likes and dislikes in these experiences? Terri Levine (2002), marketing expert, author, and professional coach for people exploring work issues, suggests a "looking back exercise" where you find a quiet place to think and ask yourself questions and write down your answers. Ask questions such as "What were the activities that gave you pleasure? What jobs or volunteer activities did you really like in your teen years. How did you feel about doing the job or activity?" She relates case studies where by doing this "looking back exercise," adults seeking a career change discovered their real enthusiasm. Do you know what really engages your excitement? Are you following your passion?

Additional factors that matter for work enjoyment include autonomy, opportunities for growth and learning, and positive triggers that keep you feeling good. Also significant is the ability to cope with problems in the workplace and resolve them in a way that doesn't compromise your values and ethics. Being informed regarding potential issues can help you prevent problems or minimize their impact.

Taking Charge

When you think about going to work, who are you really working for? Are you working for a company or organization? A boss? Your landlord? The auto insurance company? Or are you working for yourself? By this we don't necessarily mean that you are self-employed but that you are an employed self. Confusing? Well, look at it this way. Your whole being is involved in your career. If you change jobs, *you* are the thing that stays intact that is moving to a new position. You need to see yourself as somewhat of an entrepreneur in the workplace. More and more today, workers in all types of fields are recognizing that the stability of a life long position or even several years in the same company isn't going to happen. As one study points out, before 1990 an unspoken contract existed between employer and employee. That was, "You commit to working here for the long term and we will offer you job security, good pay and promotions." However, economic recession, re-engineering, and downsizing caused a breach in that contract. Now there is a new mindset among young people beginning their careers since 1990. They do not expect life-time employment with a single employer. They consider personal fulfillment in their work a birthright, and to find it they will take different options. They work as free agents or even become self-employed to find fulfillment (Hay Group, 2000). In reality, we are all self-employed. You need to sense that you are in charge of you, and that the skills and talents you possess are valuable to the organization.

Being proactive and taking responsibility for yourself is an important step to personal effectiveness. Likewise, applying this habit in your work life will contribute to your autonomy, your being in control. Remember the discussion of stress hardiness attitudes. Control was the first one. If problems occur, you are the one to do something about the impact these problems have on you. If there is something you want or desire to achieve, you are the one to make that happen. Remember we referred to this as having an internal locus of control. If you are not in control of your life then who is? Do you want others controlling you or do you want to take charge of your life?

Being at the helm in your life leads to a sense of hope. This is an emotion that is tied to optimism. If not this, what is the alternative? Hopelessness, helplessness and despair. Who wants that in life? A German study (Lundberg, 1980) examined subjects faced with a task of increasing pressure. Subjects with the highest hope of success produced brain chemicals that enabled them to keep functioning at a high level of effectiveness. Further, they did not produce levels of cortisol, a chemical which is harmful to our bodies and is typically released during stress. In contrast, subjects in this study who were motivated by fear of failure had very high cortisol levels. This finding reinforces the old self-fulfilling prophecy idea that "what I believe will happen, will happen." In this study, those with an "I can do this" attitude of self efficacy stayed more calm, focused and productive. This is where the ideas and strategies for mastering stress come in handy. Keep in mind the old adage: "Can't never did anything."

Optimism is also related to persistence. This is an important key to career success. You may know about former basketball star, Michael Jordan, who holds numerous records in the National Basketball Association (NBA) including 6 times as most valuable player in the finals. He was told by his school coach one year that he wasn't good enough to play on his high school team. Now think about it. He could have given up, given away his basketball, and quit. But he was using the other two C's of stress hardiness attitudes. He had commitment to his goal and he saw this as a challenge, not a defeat. Do you suppose Michael Jordan has made or missed most of the basketball shots he's tried? Of course, he has missed more. Look at the lesson in persistence he exemplifies.

When things don't go our way, when difficult things happen, when we make mistakes, we have the opportunity to learn. Mistakes are a blessing in disguise. Think about it. When you leave a test you have taken, which questions are you pondering in your mind? Probably not the ones you got right, but the one's you missed. This spurs you to figure things out. A workshop speaker once shared an expression that has relevance here:

Winners lose more than losers,
but they're winners because they stay in the game.

Remember this and choose to be a winner, to be the master of your life, and take charge!

INTRINSIC AND EXTRINSIC MOTIVATION

The source of your motivation can be **intrinsic** (internal) or **extrinsic** (external). We have experience with both throughout our lives in interactions with our parents, friends, teachers, and bosses.

The two types of motivation are contrasted as follows:

Intrinsic	Extrinsic
Comes from within	Comes from external world
Incites passion	Helps set goals
Makes you feel good	Heightens expectation
Rewards you while you work	Rewards you outside of work, afterward

Examples of intrinsic motivation would include mastery, self-esteem, the joy from accomplishment, pleasure while doing the task, and intensive engagement in the work. Examples of extrinsic motivation would include money, grades, candy, and praise. A family trying to promote learning in their child might give him money for each "A" he brings home on his report card. The child makes the connection between "A's" and money. As he gets older, he may avoid subjects in which he thinks he might not get an "A." What's happened? Perhaps, getting grades has become more important than learning. Hopefully, some learning occurred in the classes in which he got the "A's", but what about the subjects he avoided in high school? When grades become the extrinsic reward we are seeking, it influences our behavior. For example, you might put off studying a subject, then cram for an exam just to get a high grade. You may pass the course but not retain much information. In contrast, what about a situation when a person wants the knowledge? She may not even take a course. She may get a book, a video, attend a demonstration, or ask someone to learn what she wants to know. There is no grade because the knowledge is the thing! And she feels the reward *while* she is learning.

How does this show up in the workplace? Managers and supervisors try to "motivate" people to work hard and do a good job. Often they use rewards such as money, time off, or public recognition to manipulate workers into working hard. In many places we have seen an "Employee of the Month" plaque hanging on the wall with the name and picture of a worker being displayed.

Flow

Mihalyi Csikzentmihalyi, former chair of the University of Chicago Department of Psychology, now at Claremont Graduate University and Director of the Quality of Life Research Center has for over 30 years been studying the lives of thousands of people seeking to find what makes people satisfied, fulfilled, and happy. He has described the concept of **flow**, a state in which people find their work exhilarating and in which they perform at their best no matter what type of work they do. Flow occurs when our skills are fully engaged and we feel ourselves stretching to meet challenges. We become lost in our work and so fully engaged that we lose all concept of time. In this state our work seems to run smoothly, effortlessly, with adaptability. The flow itself is a pleasure. In studying flow this researcher discovered that workers, on average, were in this state about half the time while on the job, and about 20 percent of time during leisure time. In contrast, workers reported the most common emotional state during leisure was apathy (Goleman, 1998). Csikzentmihalyi (pronounced chick-sent-me-high-ee) found that most people live at two extremes. They are (1) stressed by work or obligations or (2) they are bored by spending their leisure time on activities that were passive. He states that people can live enhanced, happier lives by learning new skills and increasing the challenges they face each day (Chamberlain, 1998). He has found that a typical day is full of anxiety and boredom; however "flow experiences provide the flashes of intense living against this dull background" (Csikszentmihalyi, 1990). Flow as an optimal experience is characterized by:

- a sense of playfulness
- a feeling of being in control
- concentration and highly focused attention
- mental enjoyment of activity for its own sake
- a distorted sense of time
- a match between the challenge at hand and one's skills

People experience more flow from what they do on their jobs than from leisure activities such as watching television. It seems that TV's main virtue is that is occupies the mind without demands. Flow is hard to achieve without effort. Flow is not "wasting time." Those who learn to control inner experience will be able to determine the quality of their lives, which Csikszentmihalyi (1993) says is as close as any of us can get to being happy. He outlines the pathway to flow as follows:

1. **Make it a Game**—Consider tasks as games, with rules, objectives, challenges to be overcome and with rewards.

2. **Have a Powerful Goal**—As you play the game, think often of the overriding social, intellectual or spiritual purpose that drives your efforts.

3. **Focus**—Let all distractions, those within or without, go. Center all your attention on the game.

4. **Surrender to the Process**—Just let go. Don't try or strain to achieve your objective. Let it happen and enjoy the process of work.

5. **Experience Ecstasy**—(the feeling, not the drug!) This is the natural results of the previous four steps. It will hit you suddenly, by surprise. There is no mistaking it. This is a "natural high."

6. **Create Peak Productivity**—Your ecstatic state opens reservoirs of resourcefulness, creativity and energy. Productivity and quality of work shoot through the roof (1990).

What this researcher determined after many years of examining this concept of flow is that happiness is not something that just happens. It isn't from being lucky or random chance. It is not something that money can buy or power command. It doesn't depend on external events, but instead, how we interpret them. Happiness, Csikszentmihalyi writes, is a condition that must be prepared for, cultivated, and defended privately by each individual. It is in learning to control our inner selves that we create the merit of life's experience. Indeed our happiness comes not from the outer world around us, but from what we experience within. It comes from intrinsic, not extrinsic payoffs.

Although all work settings have extrinsic rewards such as positive performance reviews, promotions, and bonuses, Goleman (1998) also considers the most powerful motivators as those that are internal, not external. He points out that both *motivation* and *emotion* come from the same Latin root meaning "to move." The internal feelings we experience while working on a task are more intense than rewards being offered by others. Holahan and Sears (1995) surveyed 1,528 men and women at the end of their business or professional careers who were asked what were the greatest sources of satisfaction. Results showed that the first three were: (1) creative challenge of the work, (2) stimulation of the work, and (3) the chance to keep learning. The next three in order were: (1) pride in accomplishments, (2) friendships at work and (3) assisting or teaching other workers. Further down the list came status and even lower than that came the financial rewards. The indications from research are that what we are feeling about our work is much more significant than the external "carrots" that may be held out to us. Knowing this, it makes lots of sense to tune in once more to our self-awareness and discover our feelings. We know how high-spirited our mood is when we are doing what we love to do.

Your Frame Determines Your Work Orientation

Writers describe three different frames about work: a job, a career, and a calling. We do a **job** to pay bills. Collecting a paycheck on a regular basis is the prime motivator for you to show up and do your work. When you no longer need the paycheck or your wages get lowered or stopped, you leave the job. A **career** is something into which you invest much more of yourself. It usually requires more educational preparation than a job. It is something you stay with over an extended period of your life. You have more of your identity tied up with your career. A career offers more than just a paycheck. There are opportunities for advancement that mean more money, status and power. However, when you reach your highest position, you may not be able to advance further and begin to lose interest. You no longer feel so invested in this career. You may start looking elsewhere for satisfaction and reward. Seligman (2002) contrasts these levels of work with a third level—a **calling**, which he describes as a passionate commitment to work for its own sake. We often think of people in helping professions as having a "calling," especially those in religious work. People with a calling view their work as contributing to the greater good, to something larger than they are and find their work fulfilling in its own right, without concern for money or advancement. They may accept a position without even knowing what the salary pays.

Historically, positions with a calling included prestigious workers such as rabbis, priests, or other clergy, Supreme Court Justices, physicians, and scientific researchers. Seligman points out that new research now shows that any job can become a calling, and any calling can become a job. For example, a physician who only cares about money and not about his patients has a job. Conversely, a garbage collector who sees his work as making the environment cleaner has a calling. It is possible to reframe any job into a calling by identifying the far-reaching impacts that your work has on others and the environment. In this way you are shifting from being extrinsically motivated to intrinsically motivated in your work.

Think of how a telephone operator can have a calling. What about a grocery store cashier? What type of frame would elevate this work to a calling? How does reframing these positions impact the motivation for the person doing the work? If you are employed, how do you frame your own work?

THE GLOBAL PERSPECTIVE–Happiness and Meaning in Work

Do global citizens have more fun? Are they happier? Do they experience a deeper sense of meaning in their work? As we examine the link between the behaviors of global citizens and the essence of fun, satisfaction and meaning, we will see that the answer to these questions is a resounding "Yes!"

Let's explore "fun" first. Most of us have a clear sense of what it feels like to have fun and we know it involves positive feelings. Having "fun" at work, however, doesn't mean that we walk around giggling all day, being frivolous about our work. Rather, it means we are feeling optimistic and positive a lot more than we feel pessimistic and negative. So how is fun connected to global citizenship? Global citizens relate comfortably to all kinds of people, far beyond the circle of those from their own culture. They relate to people with respect and regard them as important, and work effectively with diverse teams. Basically, they are motivated by love not fear. These behaviors mean that they experience other people in a positive, joyous way rather than in a suspicious or frightened way. In the final analysis, we can see that global citizens are able to positively engage with a wide variety of people, increasing their opportunities for fun.

When we look at "happiness," it is important to distinguish between a transient burst of joy that can come from things like a funny movie, a good grade on a quiz, recognition at work, in contrast to what Seligman (2002) calls *enduring* happiness, a lasting and general sense which impacts your life. In studying happiness nationally and internationally, he found that once the standard of living gets above meeting basic needs, the correlation between wealth and satisfaction with life disappears. In other words, you cannot buy happiness. Seligman states that "by activating an expansive, tolerant, and creative mindset, positive feelings maximize the social, intellectual and physical benefits that will accrue" (2002). If we look at the behaviors of a global citizen, we note they do have an expansive mindset shown by relating with empathy to those of differing cultures, acknowledging that their views and values are not universally shared, and that they are able to tolerate ambiguity. Using these traits, global citizens will accrue the benefits of enduring happiness, not only in the workplace, but additionally, in their lives.

Examining the broader aspect of *meaning* in our work life, remember our discussion of *flow* wherein a person is fully engaged in an activity. Csikszentmihaly (1990) calls these experiences "the enjoyments" and they are *not* momentary pleasures. They can be of the mind, or social, or from a physical activity but include the following aspects: a challenging task, requiring skill; concentration; clear goals; getting immediate feedback; deep, effortless involvement; a sense of control; lack of a sense of self; and the stopping of time. Unlike engaging in pleasures which lead to biological satiation, when we are in flow, we are being proactive–investing–growing psychologically for our future. People who use their signature strengths are more likely to experience flow in their day-to-day lives. People who are good listeners, who read about international events, who are bilingual, who recognize that a new mode of thinking is necessary to solve today's challenges (all characteristics of a global citizen), are less likely to spend their lives passively. Instead, they are more likely to engage in activities that facilitate growth leading to lasting gratification and a deeper sense of meaning.

Is it possible that human lives can have a noble purpose? Is it possible that our lives have meaning that goes beyond the meaning we create for ourselves? These are questions Seligman pondered when considering that biological evolution in humans has perhaps powered our species to grow from being savage, to barbarian, to civilized. Seligman says a meaningful life is "one that joins with something larger than we are–and the larger that something is, the more meaning our lives have" (2002). We have choices and the possibility to contribute not only to our own, but to all of humankind's continuing growth. Seligman describes the good life as one where deriving happiness is the result of using your signature strengths every day to forward knowledge, power, or goodness. A life that does this is filled with meaning. Those who accept responsibility for global citizenship believe they are empowered to make a difference, behave ethically, and exercise moral leadership and will undoubtedly find increased satisfaction and meaning in their careers.

SUMMARY

In this chapter we have examined the Positive Psychology concepts of being people smart. We have emphasized the importance of being an astute observer and developing your strengths related to people skills. We began recognizing how important it is to know yourself, your goals, personality, needs and behavioral triggers. This means having a sense of awareness about your own emotions, thoughts and behaviors. It also means using your cognitive self in concert with your emotional self to manage yourself for success.

When you turned to knowing about others, you discovered that the process is parallel to that for yourself. You also need to know about the goals, personality, needs and triggers that guide not only your behavior but also the behavior of others. The social conventions of courtesy and etiquette and other social and cultural norms are important, too. If you seek to achieve career success, knowing your job and having the required work training and skills is a necessary, but not sufficient condition. To really reach excellence in your work performance, you must also be people smart!

We also looked at issues related to experiencing your work as pleasurable. We reviewed those aspects that reside primarily in your power, like taking charge and seeking intrinsic motivation. We described exciting new findings regarding the personally rewarding feelings of "flow." We also discussed potential problems you may encounter in the workplace including substance abuse, conflict resolution, lack of advancement, burnout, sexual harassment and discrimination.

Bearing in mind your work and career effectiveness, it is important that you know the workplace, spend time designing or re-designing your career, and sharpen your people skills. Start with an "I can" attitude. Stay aware of what's happening to you...not only your work and your thoughts, but your feelings. Work with the strength of social intelligence. If you realize things are not right, take charge and work to change the things you can. Determine goals to revitalize your self in your current position, or determine a goal for changing positions. Remember, you are in charge of your life and your happiness in the workplace.

KEY TERMS

Hierarchy of Needs	Affiliation	Interpersonal
Motivation	Self-Actualization	Intrapersonal
Triggers	Idioms	Yesable Proposal
People Smart	Personality	Peak Experiences
Needs	Polarization	Yin/Yang
Burnout	Job	Calling
Intrinsic Motivation	Sexual Harassment	Career
Extrinsic Motivation	Quid Pro Quo	Reprisal
Flow	Hostile Environment	Conflict Resolution
Brainstorming	Substance Abuse	Discrimination
Positive Institution(s)		

POSITIVE PSYCHOLOGY SELF EXERCISES:

1. Grab a piece of paper and let's do some free writing. Jot down the things that come to mind regarding your career. What do you want to accomplish in your career? How long will this take? Who are the other people who figure into the equation such as spouse, children, co-workers, clients, or boss? After you have listed about five different things you want to achieve through your career, ask yourself what these successes look like. Imagine yourself ten years from now…what will your life be like?

2. In your self-discovery journaling, write down three to five areas where you invest most of your time. This will reveal to you something about your motivations and the needs that are operating in your life.

3. Identify someone you consider to be "people smart." Observe their behavior carefully and how their interactions are effective. Do you see any patterns?

4. Interview a friend to determine if they have more of an internal or external locus of control.

5. List three intrinsic and three extrinsic motivators operating in your life right now.

6. Think of three separate times you were in "flow" while doing a task. What were you doing in each situation?

7. Describe the frames and behavior of someone in a job, a career, and a calling.

8. Write three possible questions you might ask your supervisor to determine the degree to which she values positivity in her management role.

CHAPTER 14 QUESTIONS

Short-Answer Questions

1. If I am able to understand myself and appreciate my feelings, Gardner would say this is _____ intelligence.

2. To determine direction and focus, it is helpful to set _____.

3. Characteristic patterns of behavior including thoughts and feelings is a definition of _____.

4. Three sources of feedback to learn about yourself are

   _____.

5. What three types of needs did McClelland identify?

   _____.

6. List the five levels of Maslow's hierarchy of needs.

   _____.

7. If a person realizes his or her potential and has peak experiences, is realistic, self-reliant, centered in values and ethics, and identifies with all human beings. We would say that this person is _____.

8. A way to understand our needs is to take an inventory of _____.

9. Environmental stimuli that cause us to have an intense emotional reaction are referred to as _____.

10. Who should be in charge of you in the workplace? _____

11. If you decide to change something in you that causes you problems at work, you would be exhibiting an _____ locus of control.

12. If I believe something will happen, it _____.

13. If I cram all night to pass a test, I am being motivated _____trinsically.

14. In _____ motivation, the reward comes at the end of the task.

15. When people are fully engaged in their work, finding their work exhilarating and performing at their best, we would say that they are experiencing _____.

16. Surveys of workers at the end of their careers showed that financial rewards rank _____ in importance and source of satisfaction.

17. Someone who works for the fulfillment it offers has not a *job*, but a _____.

18. An experienced worker that shows "the ropes" to a newcomer is called a _____.

Essay Questions

1. Compare and contrast the behavior of someone you know who is "people smart" and someone who is not.

2. Describe the behavior of someone with a need for power.

3. Discuss a "trigger" that sets you off in a positive mood.

4. Why are "people skills" so important in the workplace?

5. Discuss the difference between group goals and individual goals. Give examples.

6. Describe a "trigger" either positive or negative you have identified for a person in your family.

7. Describe how you might avoid "polarization" in a workplace discussion.

8. Compare internal and external locus of control.

9. Describe extrinsic motivators you experience in your life, at home, school, or work.

10. Describe a time when you were in "flow" on a task.
11. Describe three examples of your frames if you are happy in your work.
12. Discuss *quid pro quo* in sexual harassment and give examples.
13. Discuss what you would do if someone made you feel sexually harassed.
14. How does the deep green movement differ from the bright green perspective?

References

Aaron, A., Norman, C., Aaron E., McKenna, C., & Heyman, R. (2000). Couples shared participation in novel and arousing activities and experienced relationship quality. *Journal of Personality and Social Psychology*, 78, 273–283.

Abascal, J. R., Brucato, L., & Brucato, D. (2001). *Stress Mastery: The Art of Coping Gracefully.* Upper Saddle River, N.J.: Prentice Hall Press.

Abel, E. & Kruger, M. (2010). Smile intensity in photographs predicts longevity. *Psychological Science*, 20, 1–3.

Abramson, L., Alloy, L., Hankin, B., Clements, C., Zhu, L., & Hogan, M. (2000). Optimistic cognitive style and invulnerability to depression. In J. Gillham (Ed.), *The Science of Optimism and Hope* (pp. 75–98). Philadelphia, PA: Templeton Foundation Press.

Abramson, M., Seligman, M., & Teasdale, J. (1978). Learned Helplessness in Humans: Critique and Reformulation. *Journal of Abnormal Psychology*, 87, 49–74.

Achtenberg, J. (1985). *Imagery in Healing*. Boston: New Science Library.

Ader, R. & Cohen, N. (1975). Behaviorally conditioned immunosuppression. *Psychosomatic Medicine*, 37 (4), 333–340.

Ader, R. & Cohen, N. (1982). Behaviorally conditioned immunosuppression and murine systemic lupus erythematosus. *Science*, 2315 (4539), 1534–1536.

Adler, A. (1928). *Understanding Human Nature*. London: Allen & Unwin.

Adler, R. & Towne, N. (1993). *Looking Out/Looking In*. San Diego, CA.: Harcourt Brace Jovanovich.

Ainsworth, M. (1973). The development of infant-mother attachment. In B. M. Caldwell & H.N. Ricciuti (Eds.), *Review of Child Development Research* (Vol. 3, pp. 1–94). Chicago, IL: University of Chicago Press.

Ainsworth, M., Bell, S., & Stayton, D. (1992). Infant-mother attachment and social development: "Socialization" as a product of reciprocal responsiveness to signals. In M. Woodhead, R. Carr, & P. Light (Eds.), *Becoming a Person* (pp. 30–55). London: Routledge.

Alberti, R. & Emmons, M. (1974). *Your Perfect Right.* California: Impact Press.

Alexander, C., Swanson, G., Rainforth, M., Carlilse, T., Todd, C., & Oates, R. (1993). Effects of the Transcendental Meditation Program on Stress Reduction, Health, and Employee Development: A Prospective Study in two Occupational Settings. *Anxiety, Stress and Coping,* 6, 245–262.

Allred, K.D., & Smith, T.W. (1989). The Hardy Personality: Cognitive and Physiological Responses to Evaluative Threat. *Journal of Personality and Social Psychology,* 56, 257–266.

American Institute of Stress (AIS). *http.//www.stress.org/job.htm.*

American Psychological Association (APA). (2007) Stress in America Survey. *http.//www.apa.org/release/stressproblem.html*

Anderson, N. (2004). *Work with Passion: How to Do What You Love for a Living.* Novato, CA.: New World Library.

Anderson, S. M. (1998). *Service Learning: A National Strategy for Youth Development.* Position paper issued by the Task Force on Education Policy. Washington, D.C. Institute for Communitarian Policy Studies, George Washington University.

Andreas, C., & Andreas, S. (1989). *Heart of Mind: Engaging your Inner Power to Change with Neuro-Linguistic Programming.* Moab, Utah: Real People Press.

Andreas, G., Tennat, C., Hewsen, D., & Schonell, M. (1979). The Relation of Social Factors to Physical and Psychiatric Illness. *American Journal of Epidemiology,* 109, 186–204.

Antonucci, T., & Jackson, J. (1983). Physical health and self-esteem. *Family Community Health,* 6 (2), 1–9.

Ardell, D. (1975, April). Meet John Travis, Doctor of Well-Being. *Prevention Magazine.*

Ardell, D. (1986). *High Level Wellness.* Berkeley: Ten Speed Press.

Argyle, M. (1987). *The Psychology of Happiness.* London: Methuen.

Argyle, M. (1987). *The Psychology of Happiness (2nd Ed.).* East Sussex, England: Routledge.

Ariely, D. (2008). *Predictably Irrational.* New York: Harper Collins

Aspinwall, L. C., Taylor, S. E. (1992). Modeling Cognitive Adaptation: A Longitudinal Investigation of the Impact of Individual Differences and Coping on College Adjustment and Performance. *Journal of Personality and Social Psychology,* 63, 989–1063.

Astin, A. W., & Sax, L. J. (1998). How Undergraduates are Affected by Service Participation. *Journal of College Student Development.* 39(3), 251–263.

Astin, A. W., Vogelgesang, L. J., Ikeda, E. K., & Yee, J. A. (2000). How Service Learning affects Students. Los Angeles: UCLA Higher Education Research Institute. *ERIC Ed.* No. 445, 577.

Athenstaedt, U., Haas, E., & Schwab, S. (2004). *Gender Role Self-Concept and Gender-Typed Communication-Behavior in Mixed Sex and Same Sex Dyads.* Netherlands: Springer.

Atwater, E. (1986). *Human Relations.* New York: Prentice Hall.

Auerbach, S. M., & Grambling, S. E. (1998). *Stress Management: Psychological Foundations.* Upper Saddle River, N.J.: Prentice Hall.

Auerbach, S. M., Martelli, M., & Mercuri, L. G. (1983). Anxiety Information, Interpersonal Impacts and Adjustment to a Stressful Health Care Situation. *Journal of Personality and Social Psychology,* 44, 1284–1296.

Averill, J. R. (1983). Studies on Anger and Aggression: Implications for Theories of Emotion. *American Psychologist,* 38, 1145–1160.

Avolio, B., Jakari, G., Wensing, T. & Walumbwa, F. (2010). What is Authentic Leadership Development? In Linley, P.A., Harrington, S. & Garcea, N. (Eds.), *Oxford Handbook of Positive Psychology and Work.* (pp 39–51). New York: Oxford University Press, Inc.

Avruch, K. & Black, P. W. (1993). Conflict Resolution in Inter-cultural settings. In Sandole, D. & Van der Merwe, H. (Eds.). *Conflict Resolution Theory and Practice: Integration and Application.* (pp. 131–145). Manchester: Manchester University Press.

Bach, G., & Wyden, P. (1968). *The Intimate Enemy.* New York: Avon.

Bandler, R., & Grinder, J. (1975). *The Structure of Magic I.* Palo Alto, California: Science and Behavior Books.

Bandura, A. (1965). Influence of model's reinforcement contingencies on the acquisition of imitative behaviors. *Journal of Personality and Social Psychology,* 1, 589–595.

Bandura, A. (1977). Self-Efficacy: Toward a theory of behavioral change. *Psychological Review,* 84, 191–215.

Bandura, A. (1986). *Social Foundations of Thought and Action.* New York: Prentice Hall.

Bandura, A. (1997). *Self-Efficacy: The Exercise of Control.* New York: Freeman.

Banks, P., Present, D. & Steiner, P. (1983). *The Chrohn's Disease and Ulcerative Colitis Fact Book.* New York, New York: Simon & Schuster.

Banyon Partners. (2011). 2011 in Review: The Market. *Quarterly Outlook.*

Barefoot, J. R., Dahlstrom, W. G., & Williams, R. B. (1983). Hostility, CHD Incidence and Total Mortality: A 25 Year Follow-up Study of 255 Physicians. *Psychosomatic Medicine*, 45, 559–563.

Barker, L., Edwards, R., Gaines, C., Gladney, K., & Holley, F. (1981). An Investigation of Proportional Time Spent in Various Activities by College Students. *Journal of Applied Communication Research*, 8, 101–109.

Barkow, J. (1997). Happiness in evolutionary perspective. In N.L. Segal, G.E. Weisfeld, & C.C. Weisfeld (Eds.), *Uniting Psychology and Biology: Integrating Perspectives on Human Development* (pp. 397–418). Washington, D.C.: American Psychological Association.

Barnett T. P. (March, 2003). The Pentagon's New Map-War and Peace in the 21st Century. *Esquire*, Vol. 139, Issue 3.

Bass, B.M. (1998). *Transformational Leadership: Industrial, Military and Educational Impact.* Mahwah, New Jersey: Lawrence Erlbaum.

Batson, C. D. (1991). *The Altruism Question: Toward a Social-Psychological Answer.* Hillsdale, New Jersey: Lawrence Erlbaum Publishers.

Batson, C., Ahmed, N., Lishner, D., & Tsang, J. (2005). Empathy and altruism. In C.R. Snyder & S.J. Lopez (Eds.) *Handbook of Positive Psychology.* (pp.485–498). New York: Oxford University Press.

Batson, C., Duncan, B., Ackerman, P., Buckley, T., & Birch, K. (1981). Is empathic emotion a source of altruistic motivation? *Journal of Personality and Social Psychology*, 40, 290–302.

Baumeister, R. F. (1996). Should Schools Try to Boost Self-Esteem? Beware the Dark Side. *American Educator*, 20, 14–19.

Baumeister, R. F. (August, 2000). Psychology of evil and violence. *Paper presented at the 110th Annual Convention of the American Psychological Association*, Chicago, IL.

Baumeister, R., Gailliot, M., DeWall, C., & Oaten, M. (2006). Self Regulation and Personality: How interventions increase regulatory success, and how depletion moderates the effects of traits on behavior. *Journal of Personality*, 74, 1773–1801.

Baumeister, R., Vohs, K., & Tice, D. (2007). The strength model of self-control. *Current Directions in Psychological Science*, 16, 351–355.

Baumrind, D. (1991). Effective Parenting during the Early Adolescent Transition. In Cowen, P. & Hetherington, E. (Eds.). *Advances in Family Research.* (pp. 28–31), Vol. 2, Hillsdale, N.J.: Lawrence Erlbaum Associates.

Beck, A. (1970). Cognitive Therapy: Nature and Relation to Behavior Therapy. *Behavior Therapy*, 1, 84–200.

Beck, A. (1979). *Cognitive Therapy and Emotional Disorders.* New York: New American Library.

Becklen, R. & Cervone, D. (1983). Selective looking and the noticing of unexpected events. *Memory and Cognition*, 11, 601–608.

Benjamin, L.T., Cavell, T.A., & Shallenberger, W.R. (1987). Staying with Initial Answers on Objective Tests: Is It a Myth? In M.E. Ware & R. J. Millard (Eds.). *Handbook on Student Development: Advising, Career Development and Field Placement*. (pp. 45–52), Hillsdale, N. J.: Lawrence Erlbaum Associates.

Bennis, W. G. (1989). *On Becoming a Leader*. Reading, PA.: Addison Wesley.

Benson, H. (1976). *The Relaxation Response*. New York: Avon Books.

Benson, H. (1979). *The Mind-Body Effect*. New York: Simon & Schuster.

Benson, H. (1985). *Beyond the Relaxation Response*. Berkeley, California: Berkeley Books.

Benson, H. (1997). *Timeless Healing: The Power and Biology of Belief*. New York: Simon & Schuster.

Bergeman, C., Chipuer, H., Plomin, R., Pederson, N., McClearn, G., & Nessel-roade, J. (1993). Genetic and environmental effects on openness to experience, agreeableness, and conscientiousness.: An adoption/twin study. *Journal of Personality*, 61, 159–179.

Berk, I. S., Tan, S. A., Nehlsen-Cannarella, S. L, Napier, B. J., Lee, J. W., Hubbard, R. W. Lewis, J. E., Eby, W. C., & Fry, W. F. (1988). Humor Associated Laughter Decreases Cortisol and Increases Spontaneous Lymphocyte Blastogenesis. *Clinical Research*, 36, 435A.

Bernasek, A. (Feb., 2002). The Friction Economy. American Business Just Got the Bill for the Terrorist Attacks: $ 151 Billion a Year. *Fortune*, 145, 104.

Bernstein, R. & Edwards, T. (2008, August, 14th). An older and more diverse nation by Midcentury. U.S Census Bureau News. *http://www.census.gov/Press-lease/www/eleaes/aschides/population/012496.html*

Berns, G., Chappelow, J., Zink, C., Pagnoni, G., Martin-Skurski, M. & Richards, J. (2005). Neurobiological correlates of social conformity and independence during mental rotation. *Biological Psychiatry*, 58, No. 3.

Berns, G. (2010). *Iconoclast*. Boston, MA: Harvard Business Press.

Black, S. & Bevan, S. (1992). At the movies with Buss and Durkee: A natural experiment on film violence. *Aggressive Behavior*, 18, 37–45.

Bolt, M. (2004). *Pursuing Human Strengths: A Positive Psychology Guide*. New York: Worth Publishers.

Bourne, E. J. (1990). *The Anxiety and Phobia Workbook*. Oakland, CA.: New Harbinger Publications.

Bolles, R. (2002). Free On-line Tests Dealing with Careers. *http://www.JobHuntersBible.com*.

Bolles, R. (2006). *What Color is Your Parachute?* Berkeley, CA.: Ten Speed Press.

Bonner, R. L., & Rich, A. R. (1991). Predicting Vulnerability to Hopelessness: A Longitudinal Analysis. *The Journal of Nervous and Mental Disease*, 179, 129–32.

Bowlby, J. (1951). *Maternal Care and Mental Health.* Geneva, Switzerland: World Health Organization.

Bowlby, J. (1969). *Attachment and Loss: Vol I. Attachment.* New York: Basic Books.

Bowlby, J. (1973). *Attachment and Loss: Vol. 2. Separation: Anxiety and Anger.* New York: Basic Books.

Bowlby, J. (1980). *Attachment and Loss: Vol. 3. Loss, Sadness and Depression.* New York: Basic Books.

Bowlby, J. (1988). *A Secure Base: Parent-Child Attachment and Healthy Human Development.* New York: Basic Books.

Boyett, J. H., & Snyder, D. P. (1998). Twenty-First Century Workplace Trends. *On the Horizon.* 6 (2), 4–9.

Boyke, J., Driemeyer, J., Gaser, C., Buchel, C. & May, A. (2008). Induced brain structure changes in the elderly. *The Journal of Neuroscience*, 28(28), 7031–7035.

Brainard, L., & Litan, R. E. (April, 2004). *"Offshoring" Service Jobs: Bane or Boom and What to Do?* Brookings Institution Policy Brief, No. 132.

Breathnach, S. B. (1995). *Simple Abundance: A Daybook of Comfort and Joy.* New York: Warner Books.

Brehm, B. (1998). *Stress Management. Increasing Your Stress Resistance.* New York: Longman.

Brennan, K. & Shaver, P. (1995). Dimensions of adult attachment, affect regulation, and romantic relationship functioning. *Personality and Social Psychology Bulletin*, 23, 23–31.

Breslow, L. (1983). The Potential of Health Promotion. In D. Mechanic (Ed.). *Handbook of Health, Health Care and the Health Professions.* New York: Free Press.

Brickman, P. & Campbell, D. (1971). Hedonic relativism and planning the good society. In M.H. Appley (Ed.), *Adaptation-level Theory* (pp. 287–305). New York: Academic Press.

Brickman, P., Coates, D., & Janoff-Bulman, J. R. (1978). Lottery Winners and Accident Victims: Is Happiness Relative? *Journal of Personality and Social Psychology*, 36, 917–927.

Brockner, J., & Guare, J. (1983). Improving the Performance of Low Self-Esteem Individuals: An Attributional Approach. *Academy of Managerial Psychology*, 26, 642–656.

Brosnan, S. & deWaal, F. (2003). Monkeys reject unequal pay, *Nature*, 425, 297–299.

Brown, J. D. (1998). *The Self.* New York: McGraw-Hill.

Brown, J. D. (2007). *The Self.* New York: Psychology Press.

Brown, J. P. (1991). Staying Fit and Staying Well: Physical Fitness as a Moderator of Life Stress. *Journal of Personality and Social Psychology,* 60, 555–561.

Brown, S. L., Nesse, R. M., Vinokur, A. D., & Smith, D. M. (2003). Providing Social Support May be more Beneficial than Receiving it: Results from a Prospective Study of Mortality. *Psychological Science,* 14, 320–327.

Bruhn, J. & Wolf, S. (1979). *The Roseta Story.* Norman, OK: University of Oklahoma Press.

Bruhn, J. & Wolf, S. (1993). *The Power of Clan: The Influence of Human Relationships in Heart Disease.* New Brunswick, N.J.: Transaction Publishers.

Bruner, J., & Postman, L. (1949). On the Perception of Incongruity: A Problem. *Journal of Personality,* 18, 206–233.

Brunwasser, S. & Gillham, J. (2008). *A Meta-Analytic Review of the Penn Resiliency Programme* (paper presented at the Society for Prevention Research), San Francisco, CA. May, 2008.

Bryant, F. (2003). Savoring Beliefs Inventory (SBI): A Scale for measuring beliefs about savoring. *Journal of Mental Health,* 12, 175–196.

Bryant, F. (2006). *The Process of Savoring: A New Model of Positive Experience.* Mahwah, N.J.: Erlbaum.

Bryant, F. B., Veroff, J. *Savoring: A Process Model for Positive Psychology.* Unpublished manuscript.

Brydon, L, Magid, K., & Steptoe, A. (2006). Platelets, coronary heart disease, and stress. *Brain, Behavior and Immunity,* 20, 113–119.

Buchanan, G., Gardenswartz, C., & Seligman, M. (1999). Physical health following a cognitive behavioral intervention. *Prevention and Treatment,* 2.

Buckingham, M., & Clifton, D. (2001). *Now, Discover Your Strengths.* New York: The Free Press.

Burger, J. M. (2004). *Personality* (6th Ed.). Belmont, CA.: Wadsworth/Thomson Publishers.

Buscaglia, L. (1982). *Love.* New York: Ballantine Books.

Bushman, B. & Phillips, C. (2001). If the television program bleeds, memory for the advertisement recedes. *Current Directions in Psychological Science,* 2, 43–47.

Byham, W. (1999). *Landing the Job You Want.* New York: Crown Publishing Group.

Byers, E. S. (2005). Relationship satisfaction and sexual satisfaction: A longitudinal study of individuals in long-term relationships. *Journal of Sex Research,* 42(2), 113–118.

Cacioppo, J., Hawkley, L., Crawford, L., Ernst, J., Burleson, R., Kowalewski, W., Kowalewski, E., Van Cauter, E., & Berntson, G. (2002). Loneliness and Health: Potential Mechanisms. *Psychosomatic Medicine*, 64, 407–417.

Cacioppo, J. & Patrick, W. (2008). *Loneliness: Human Nature and the Need for Social Connection*. New York: W.W. Norton.

Callahan, C., Mchorney, C., & Murrow, C., Eds. (2003). Determinants of Successful Aging: Developing an Integrated Research Agenda for the 21st Century. *Annals of Internal Medicine*, 139(8).

Campbell, J. (1959). *Masks of God: Creative Mythology*. New York: The Viking Press.

Campbell, J. (1988). Joseph Campbell and The Power of Myth with Bill Moyers. *A production of Apostrophe S. Productions in association with Public Affairs Television Inc. and Alvin H. Perlmutter, Inc.* Audio CD version, (2001) St. Paul, Minnesota: HighBridge Co.

Canfield, J., & Hansen, M. (1995). *The Aladdin Factor*. New York: The Berkeley Publishing Group.

Cannon, T., Kaprio, J., Lonnquist, J., Huttunen, M., & Koskenvuo, M. (1998). The Genetic Epidemiology of Schizophrenia in a Finnish Twin Cohort. *Archives of General Psychiatry*, 55, 67–754.

Cantor, J. (1999). Review of the book Children and media violence. *Journal of International Communication*, 6(1). *http://www.mnstate.edu/gunarat/jicreviews6-1.htm*

Cantor, J. (2009). *Conquer CyberOverload: Get more Done, Boost your Creativity and Reduce Stress*. Cyber Outlook Press.

Capaldi, D. & Patterson, G. (1996). Can violent offenders be distinguished from frequent offenders? Predictions from childhood to adolescence. *Journal of Research in Crime and Delinquency*, 33, 206–231.

Carducci, B. (1999). *The Pocket Guide to Making Successful Small Talk*. New York: Mass Market Publishing.

Carducci, B. (1999). *Shyness; A Bold New Approach*. New York: Harper Collins.

Carpi, J. (Jan./Feb., 1996). Stress...Its Worse Than You Think. *Psychology Today*, 34–76.

Carter, R. (1974). *The Sixteenth Round*. New York: Viking Press.

Carvalha, A., Del Bel Cury, A., & Garcia, R. (2008). Prevalence of bruxism and emotional stress and the association between them in Brazilian police officers. *Brazilian Oral Research*. Vol. 22., No. 1.

Carver, C. S., & Gaines, J. G. (1987). Optimism, Pessimism and Postpartum Depression. *Cognitive Therapy and Research*, 11, 449–462.

Carver, C. S., Pozo, C., Harris, S.D., Noriega, V., Scheier, M. E., & Robinson, D. S. (1993). How Coping Mediates the Effect of Optimism on Distress: A Study of Women with Early Stage Breast Cancer. *Journal of Personality and Social Psychology*, 65, 375–390.

Carver, C. S., & Scheier, M. E. (1999). Optimism. In C. R. Snyder (Ed.). *Coping: The Psychology of What Works.* (pp. 182–204). New York: Oxford University Press.

Castenada, C. (1998). *The Teachings of Don Juan: A Yaqui Way of Knowledge.* California: University of California Press.

Castenada, C. (1991). *Journey to Ixtlan: The Lessons of Don Juan.* New York: Simon & Schuster.

Chamber of Commerce of the U. S. (2004, April). *Special Report: Jobs, Trade, Sourcing and the Future of the American Workforce.* http//www.uschamber.com/media/pdfs/outsourcing/pdf.

Chamberlain, J. (July, 1998). Reaching Flow to Optimize Work and Play, *APA Monitor Online www.apa.org/monitor.* Washington, D.C.: American Psychological Association, Vol 29, No. 7.

Chang, E. (1996a). Evidence for the cultural specificity of pessimism in Asians vs. Caucasians: A test of a general negativity hypothesis. *Personality and Individual Differences*, 21, 819–822.

Chang, E. (2001a). A look at the coping strategies and styles of Asian Americans: Similar and different? In C.R. Snyder (Ed.). *Coping with Stress: Effective People and Processes* (pp. 222–239). New York: Oxford University Press.

Chiasson, C., & Hayes, L. (1993). The Effects of Subtle Differences between Listeners and Speakers on the Referential Speech of College Freshmen. *The Psychological Record*, 43, 13–24.

Chiu, A., Chon, S., & Kimball, A. (2003). Changes in the severity of acne vulgaris as affected by examination stress. *Archives of Dermatology*, Vol. 139, No. 7, 897–900.

Christakis, M. & Fowler, J. (2008). Dynamic spread of happiness in a large social network: Longitudinal analysis over 20 years in the Framington Heart Study. *British Medical Journal online.*

Chopra, D. (1993). *Ageless Body, Timeless Mind: The Quantamal Alternative to Growing Old.* New York: Harmony Books.

Clark, D. & Watson, D. (1999). Temperament: A new paradigm for trait psychology. In L.A. Perwin & O.P. John (Eds.) *Handbook of Personality* (2nd Ed., pp. 399–423). New York: Guilford Press.

Clifton, D., & Harter, J. (2003). Strengths investment. In K.S. Cameron, J. E. Dalton, & R. E. Quinn (Eds.). *Positive Organizational Scholarship* (pp. 111–121). San Francisco, CA.: Barrett-Koehler.

Cohen, H. (1980). *You Can Negotiate Anything.* New York: Bantam Books.

Cohen, S., Alper, C., Doyle, W., Treanor, J., & Turner, R. (2006). Positive emotional style predicts resistance to illness after experimental exposure to rhinovirus or influenza A virus. *Psychosomatic Medicine*, 68, 809–815.

Cohen, S., Doyle, W., Turner, R., Alper, C., & Skoner, D. (2003). Emotional style and susceptibility to the common cold. *Psychosomatic Medicine*, 65, 652–657.

Cohen, S., & Edwards, J. (1989). Personality Characteristics as Moderators of the Relationship Between Stress and Disorder. In Neufeld, R. (Ed.). *Advances in the Investigation of Psychological Stress.* New York: Wiley and Sons.

Cohen, S., Frank, E., Doyle, W., Skoner, D., Rubin, B., & Gualtney, J. (1998). Types of stressors that increase susceptibility to the common cold in adults. *Health Psychology*, 17, 214–223.

Cohen, S., Tyrell, D., & Smith, A. (1991). Psychological stress and susceptibility to the common cold. *New England Journal of Medicine*, 325, 606–612.

Cohen, S., Tyrell, D., & Smith, A. (1993). Life events, perceived stress, negative affect and susceptibility to the common cold. *Journal of Personality and Social Psychology*, 64, 131–140.

Cohen, S., & Wills, T. A. (1985). Stress, Social Support and the Buffering Hypothesis. *Psychological Bulletin*, 98, 310–357.

Connelly, J. (2002). All together now. *Gallup Managerial Journal*, 2(1), 13–18.

Contrada, R. (1989). Type A behaviors, Personality Hardiness and Cardiovascular Responses to Stress. *Journal of Personality and Social Psychology*, 57, 895–903.

Coopersmith, S. (1967). *Antecedents of Self-Esteem.* San Francisco, CA.: Freeman Press.

Coue', E. (1922). *Self-Mastery Through Conscious Auto-Suggestion.* London: Allen & Unwin.

Covey, S. (1991). *The Seven Habits of Highly Effective People.* New York: Simon & Schuster.

Covey, S., Merrill, A., & Merrill, R. (1994). *First Things First.* New York: Simon & Schuster.

Cousins, N. (1981). *Anatomy of An Illness as Perceived by the Patient.* New York: Bantam Books.

Cousins, N. (1983) *The Healing Heart.* New York: Norton Books.

Crane, D. R., Dollahit, D. C., Griffin, W., & Taylor, V. L. (1987). Diagnosing Relationships with Spatial Distance: An Empirical Test of a Clinical Principle. *Journal of Marital and Family Therapy*, 13, 307–318.

Crocker, J., Luhtanen, R. & Bouvrette, S. (2001). *Contingencies of Self Worth in College Students: Predicting Freshman Year Activities.* Unpublished manuscript, University of Michigan, Ann Arbor, Michigan.

Crocker, J. & Wolfe, C. T. (2001). Contingencies of Self-Worth. *Psychological Review*, 108, 593–623.

Csikszentmihalyi, M. (1990). *Flow: The Psychology of Optimal Experience*. New York: Harper & Row.

Csikszentmihalyi, M. (1993). *The Evolving Self: A Psychology for the Third Millennium*. New York: Harper Collins Publishers.

Cutuli, J., Chaplin, T., Gillham, J., Reivich, K. & Seligman, M. (2006). Preventing co-occuring depression symptoms in adolescents with conduct problems: The Penn Resiliency Program. *New York Academy of Science*, 1094, 282–286.

Daloz, L., Keen, C., Keen, J., & Parks, S. (1997). *Common Fire: Lives of Commitment in a Complex World*. New York: Beacon Press.

Danner, D., Snowden, D., & Friesen, W. (2001). Positive Emotions in Early Life and Longevity: Findings from the Nun Study. *Journal of Personality and Social Psychology*, 80, 804–813.

Dansky, K. H. (1996). The Effect of Group Mentoring on Career Outcomes. *Group and Organizational Management*. 21, 5–21.

David, C., & Kistner, J. (2006). Do positive self-perceptions have a dark side? *Journal of Abnormal Child Psychology*.

Davidson, R., & Kabat-Zinn, J. (2003). Alterations in brain and mind function produced by mindfulness meditation. *Psychosomatic Medicine*, 65, 564–570.

Davis, M. (1980). A multidimensional approach to individual differences in empathy. *Catalog of Selected Documents in Psychology*, 10, 85.

Davis, M., Eshelman, E.R., & McKay, M. (1988). *The Relaxation and Stress Reduction Workbook*. Oakland, California: New Harbinger Publications.

Dawes, R. M. (1994). *House of Cards: Psychology and Psychotherapy Built on Myth*. New York: Free Press.

DeCenzo, D. (1997). *Human Relations: Personal and Professional Development*. Upper Saddle River, N.J.: Prentice Hall.

Deci, E. L. (1995). *Why We Do What We Do: The Dynamics of Personal Autonomy*. New York: Putnam Books.

Deci, E. L. & Ryan, R. M. (1995). Human Autonomy: The Basis for True Self Esteem. In M. H. Kemis (Ed.), *Efficacy, Agency and Self Esteem* (pp 31–49). New York: Plenum.

Deffenbacher, J. L., Oeting, E. R., & Lynch, R. S. (1994). Development of a Driving Anger Scale. *Psychological Reports*, 74, 83–91.

Dekoven, B. (2001). *Discover the Fun of Work*. Washington, D. C.: Greater Washington Society of Association Executives. *http//www.gwsae.org*.

Deinzer, R., Kleineidam, C., Stiller-Winkler, R., Idel, H., & Bachg, D. (2000). Prolonged reduction of salivary immunoglobulin A (slgA) after a major academic exam. *International Journal of Psychophysiology*, Vol. 37, No. 3, 219–232.

Diener, E. (1984). Subjective well-being. *Psychological Bulletin*, 95(3), 542–575.

Dement, W., & Vaughan, C. (1999). *The Promise of Sleep: A Pioneer in Sleep Medicine Explores the Vital Connection Between Health, Happiness and a Good Night's Sleep.* California: Harcourt Press.

Diamond, J. (2005). *Collapse: How Societies Choose to Fail or Succeed.* New York, N. Y.: Penguin Group.

DiClemente, C., Fairhurst, S., & Piotrowski, N. (1995). Self-Efficacy and addictive behaviors. In J.E. Maddux (Ed.) *Self-Efficacy, Adaptation and Adjustment: Theory, Research and Application* (pp. 109–142). New York: Plenum.

Dillon, K., Baker, K., & Minchoff, B. (1985). Positive Emotional States and the Enhancement of the Immune System. *International Journal of Psychiatry.* Med 15: 13–18.

DiMarco, C. (1997). *Career Transitions: A Journey of Survival and Growth.* Scottsdale, Arizona: Gorsuch Scarisbrick Publishers.

Dobbs, L. (2004). *Exporting America: 'Why Corporate Greed is Shipping American Jobs Overseas.* New York, N. Y.: Warner Books.

Dollard, J., Miller, N. E., Doob, L. W., Mowrer, O. H., & Sears, R. R. (1939). *Frustration and Aggression.* New Haven, CT: Yale University Press.

Donne, J. (1995). *Poems and Prose.* New York: A.A. Knopf: Distributed by Random House.

Dossey, L. (1989). *Recovering the Soul.* New York: Random House.

Doyle, W., Gentile, D. & Cohen, S. (2006). Emotional style, nasal cytokines and illness expression after experimental rhinovirus exposure. *Brain, Behavior and Immunity*, 20, 175–181.

Draganski, B., Gaser, C., Kempermann, G., Kuhn, H., Winkler, J., Buchel, C., & May, A. (2006). Temporal and spatial dynamics of brain structure changes during extensive learning. *The Journal of Neuroscience*, 26 (23), 6314–6317.

Dubrin, A. (1999). *Human Relations: Personal and Professional Development*, 5th Ed. Upper Saddle River, N.J.: Prentice Hall.

Dunn, H. L. (1961). *High Level Wellness.* Arlington, Virginia: R.W. Beatty.

Dutton, D., Saunders, K., Starzomski, A., & Bartholomew, K. (1994). Intimacy-anger and insecure attachment as precursors of abuse in intimate relationships. *Journal of Applied Social Psychology*, 24, 1367–1386.

Dutton, J. & Glynn, M. (2009). Positive Organizational Scholarship. In Barling, J. & Cooper, C. (Eds.). *The Sage Handook of Organizational Behavior* (pp. 693–712). Vol. 1, Micro Approaches. Los Angeles, CA: Sage.

Dweck, C. S. (1999). *Self-Theories: Their Role in Motivation, Personality and Development.* Philadelphia: Psychology Press.

Easterbrook, G. (2003). *The Progress Paradox: How Life Gets Better while People Feel Worse.* New York: Random House.

Eckstein, D., & Goldman, A. (2001). The couple's gender-based communication questionnaire (CGCQ). *The Family Journal: Counseling and Therapy for Couples and Families*, 10, 1, 101–108.

Edwards, R., & Hamilton, M. (2004). You need to understand my gender role: An emprirical test of Tannen's model of gender and communication. *Sex Roles*, 50 (7–8), 491–504.

Ehrenreich, B. (2009). *Bright Sided: How the Relentless Promotion of Positive Thinking has Undermined America.* New York: Holt.

Elias, M. (November, 11, 2002). A generous spirit may yield generous life span. *USA Today*. p. 4A.

Elkind, M. (2004). Diagnosis and classification of primary headache disorders. In: *Standards of Care for Headache Diagnosis and Treatment* (pp. 4–18). Chicago, IL: National Headache Foundation.

Elliot, W. (2001). Cyclic and circadian variations in cardiovascular events. *American Journal of Hypertension*, 14, 291–295.

Ellis, A. (1975). *A New Guide to Rational Living.* California: Wilshire Books.

Ellis, A., & Harper, R. (1961). *A Guide to Rational Living.* California: Wilshire Books.

Ellis, A., & Knaus, W. J. (1977). *Overcoming Procrastination.* New York: Signet, New American Library.

Emler, N. (2001). *Self-Esteem: The costs and causes of low self worth.* York, PA: York Publishing Services.

Emmons, R. A., & McCullough, M. E. (2003). Counting Blessings vs. Burdens: An Experimental Investigation of Gratitude and Subjective Well-Being in Daily Life. *Journal of Personality and Social Psychology*, 84, 377–389.

Enright, R. D. (2001). *Forgiveness is a Choice: A Step by Step Process for Resolving Anger and Restoring Hope.* Washington, D. C.: American Psychological Association.

Epstein, S. (1992). Coping Ability, Negative Self-Evaluation, and Overgeneralization: Experiment and Theory. *Journal of Personality and Social Psychology*, 62, 826–836.

Ericsson, K. & Ward, P. (2007). Capturing the naturally occurring superior performance of experts in the laboratory. *Current Directions in Psychological Science*, 16, 346–350.

Estrada, C., Isen, A., & Young, M. (1997). Positive affect facilitates integration of information and decreases anchoring in reasoning among physicians. *Organizational Behavior and Human Decision Processes*, 72, 117–135.

Eyler, J., Giles, D., & Braxton, J. (1997). The Impact of Service Learning on College Students. *Michigan Journal of Community Service Learning*, 4, 5–15.

Faludi, S. (1991). *Backlash: The undeclared war against American women*. New York: Crown.

Fanning, P. (1988). *Visualization for Change*. Oakland, CA.: New Harbinger Publications.

Farah, M. J. (2000). The neural bases of mental imagery. In M.S. Gazzaniga (Ed.), *The Cognitive Neurosciences* (2nd. Ed., pp. 965–974). Cambridge, MA: MIT Press.

Fast, J. (1970). *Body Language*. New York: M. Evans & Co.

Feather, D. T. (1991). Human values, global self-esteem and belief in a just world. *Journal of Personality*, 59, 83–107.

Fehr, B. (1996). *Friendship Processes*. Thousand Oaks, CA: Sage Publications.

Felsman, J. K., & Vaillant, G. E. (1987). Resilient Children as Adults: A 40 Year Study. In Anderson, F. J. & Cohler, B. J. (Eds.) *The Invulnerable Child*. New York: Guilford Press.

Fensterheim, H., & Baer, J. (1975). *Don't Say Yes When You Want to Say No*. New York: David McKay.

Ferris, G. (June, 1999). *Political Skill at Work*. Champaign, IL.: University of Illinois News Bureau.

Fibel, B., & Hale, W. (1978). The generalized expectancy for success scale—A new measure. *Journal of Consulting and Clinical Psychology*, 46, 924–931.

Fincham, F. (2000). Optimism and the family. In J. Gillham (Ed.), *The Science of Optimism and Hope* (pp. 271–298). Philadelphia, PA: Templeton Foundation Press.

Finkel, D., & McGue, M. (1997). Sex differences in nonadditivity of the multidimensional personality questionnaire scales. *Journal of Personality and Social Psychology*, 72, 929–938.

Fisher, H. (2004). *Why we Love: The Nature and Chemistry of Romantic Love*. New York: Henry Holt.

Fitzgerald, T. E., Tennen, H., Affleck, G., & Pransky, G. S. (1993). The Relative Importance of Dispositional Optimism and Control Appraisals in Quality of Life after Coronary Artery Bypass Surgery. *Journal of Behavioral Medicine*, 16, 375–390.

Fleming, J., & Courtney, B. (1984). The Dimensionality of Self-Esteem: II Hierarchical Facet Model for Revised Measurement Scales. *Journal of Personality and Social Psychology*, 46, 404–421.

Flett, T. K., Blankstein, K. R., Hewitt, P. L., & Koledin, S. (1992). Components of Perfectionism and Procrastination in College Students. *Social Behavior and Personality*, 20, 85–94.

Fontana, D. (1990). *Social Skills at Work*. Leicester, England: British Psychological Society.

Fordyce, M. (1977). Development of a program to increase personal happiness. *Journal of Counseling Psychology*, 24, 511–520.

Fordyce, M. (1983). A program to increase happiness: Further studies. *Journal of Counseling Psychology*, 30, 483–498.

Frankl, V. (1959). *Man's Search for Meaning*. New York: Pocket Books.

Fraser, A. A. (2004, March 10). *What's Really Happening with Jobs and Outsourcing?* Heritage Foundation Lecture # 827 (delivered to Employers Association in Peoria, Illinois.) *www.heritage.org/Research/Labor/h/827.cfm.*

Fredrickson, B. (1998). What good are positive emotions? *Review of General Psychology*, 2, 300–319.

Fredrickson, B. (2000). Cultivating positive emotions to optimize health and well-being. *Prevention and Treatment*, 3. *http//journals.apa.org/prevention.*

Fredrickson, B., & Branigan, C. (2005). Positive emotions broaden the scope of attention and thought-action repertoires. *Cognition and Emotion*, 19, 313–332.

Fredrickson, B. & Losada, M. (2005). Positive affect and the complex dynamics of human flourishing. *American Psychologist*, 60, 678–681.

Fredrickson, B., Mancuso, R, Branigan, C., & Tugade, M. (2000). The undoing effects of positive emotions. *Motivation and Emotion*, 24, 237–258.

Freedberg, S. (Nov, 17th, 1996). Mounting Cost of White Collar Stress. *Miami Herald*, 1B.

Freidman, M. & Rosenman, R. H. (1974). *Type A Behavior and Your Heart*. New York: Knopf.

Freud, S. (1924). *A General Introduction to Psychoanalysis*. London: Boni & Liveright.

Friedman, M., Powell, L., & Thoresen, C. (1987). Effect of discontinuing Type A behavior counseling on Type A behavior and cardiac recurrence rate of post myocardiac infarction. *American Heart Journal*, 114, 483–490.

Frigon, N., & Jackson, H. (1996). *The Leader: Developing the Skills and Qualities You Need to Lead Effectively*. New York: Amacom Books.

Frijda, N. (1994). Emotions are functional, most of the time. In. P. Ekman & R. Davidson (Eds.) *The Nature of Emotion: Fundamental Questions* (pp. 112–122). New York: Oxford University Press.

Fuller, B. (1970). *Operating Manual for Spaceship Earth*. New York: Pocket Books.

Gable, S., Gonzaga, G. & Strachman, A. (2006). Will you be there for me when things go right? Supportive responses to positive events disclosures. *Journal of Personality and Social Psychology*, 89, 904–917.

Gable, S., Reis, H., Impett, E., & Asher, E. (2004). What do you do when things go right? The intrapersonal and interpersonal benefits of sharing good events. *Journal of Personality and Social Psychology*, 87, 228–245.

Galassi, J. P., Galassi, M. D., & Fulkerson, K. (1984). Assertion Training in Theory and Practice: An Update. In C. M. Franks (Ed.). *New Developments in Behavior Therapy: From Research to Clinical Application.* (pp. 319–376). New York: Haworth Press.

Gallagher, M., & Waite, L. (2000). *The Case for Marriage*. New York: Doubleday.

Gardiner, J., Gawlik, B. & Richardson-Klavehn, A. (1994). Maintenance rehearsal affects knowing, not remembering; Elaborative rehearsal affects remembering, not knowing. *Psychonomic Bulletin and Review*, 1, 107–110.

Gardner, H. (1983). *Frames of Mind: The Theory of Multiple Intelligences*. New York: Basic Books.

Gardner, H. (1993). *Multiple Intelligences: The Theory in Practice*. New York: Basic Books.

Gardner, H. (1999). *Intelligence Reframed: Multiple Intelligences for the 21st Century*. New York: Basic Books.

Gardner, H., & Hatch, T. (1989). Multiple Intelligences Go To School. *Educational Researcher*, 18, 8–9.

Gardner, R. (2002). *Psychology Applied to Everyday Life*. U. S. A.: Wadsworth/Thomson Learning, Inc.

Garfield, C. (1984). *Peak Performance*. Los Angeles, CA.: Houghton Mifflin & Co.

Gaser, C., & Schlang, G. (2003). Brain structures differ between musicians and non-musicians. *Journal of Neuroscience*, 23(27), 9240–9245.

Gawain, S. (1978). *Creative Visualization*. California: Whatever Publishing.

Gilbert, D., Pinel, E., Wilson, T., Blumberg, S., & Wheatley, T. (1998). Immune neglect: A source of durability bias in affective forecasting. *Journal of Personality and Social Psychology*, 75, 617–638.

Gillham, J., Hamilton, J. Freres, D., Patton, K. & Gallop, R. (2006). Preventing depression among early adolescents in the primary care setting: A randomized controlled study of the Penn Resiliency Program. *Journal of Abnormal Child Psychology*, 34, 203–219.

Gillham, J., Reivich, K., Jaycox, L & Seligman, M. (1993). Prevention of depressive symptoms in schoolchildren: Two year follow-up. *Psychological Science*, 6, 343–351.

Giltay, E, Gelenijnse, J, Zitman, F., Hoekstra, T. & Schouten, E. (2004). Dispositional optimism, and all- cause and cardiovascular mortality in a prospective cohort of elderly Dutch men and women. *Archives of General Psychiatry*, 61, 1126–1135.

Giridharadas, A. (2007, September, 25th). Outsourcing Work, So India is Exporting Jobs. *New York Times*. *http://www.nytimes.com/2007/09/25/business/worldbusiness/25outsource.html?-r=1*

Gladwell, M. (2008). *Outliers: The Story of Success*. New York: Little, Brown & Co.

Glass, P. (June-July, 2001). Nurturing Empathy. *Parenting Magazine*. p. 72.

Gleick, J. (1987). *Chaos—Making a New Science*. New York: Penguin Books.

Goleman, D. (1977). *The Varieties of the Meditative Experience*. New York: E. P. Dutton.

Goleman, D. (1988). *The Meditative Mind*. New York. Penguin Books.

Goleman, D. (1995). *Emotional Intelligence*. New York, N. Y.: Bantam Books.

Goleman, D. (1998). *Working with Emotional Intelligence*. New York, N.Y.: Bantam Books.

Goleman, D. (2006). *Social Intelligence: The New Science of Human Relationships*. New York, New York: Bantam Dell.

Gollwitzer, P. M. (1999). Implementation Intentions. *American Psychologist*, 54, 493–503.

Gomez-Mejia, L. R., Balkin, D, & Cardy, R. (1995). *Managing Human Resources*. Upper Saddle River, N.J.: Prentice Hall.

Goodman, C. (2012). Support at Home Good for Career. *The Miami Herald*. (2/15/2012), 5–6.

Goodman, D. (1974). *Emotional Well-Being Through Rational Behavior Training*. Springfield, IL.: Charles C. Thomas.

Gordan, T. (1970). *Parent Effectiveness Training*. New York: Peter H. Wyden.

Gore, S. (1978). The Effect of Social Support in Moderating the Health Consequences of Unemployment. *Journal of Health and Social Behavior*, 19, 157–165.

Gottesmann, I. (1991). *Schizophrenia Genesis: The Origins of Madness*. New York: W. H. Freeman.

Gottlieb, K., & Robinson, G. (2002). *A Practical Guide for Integrating Civic Responsibility into the Curriculum*. Washington, D. C.: Community College Press.

Gottman, J.M. (1993). The roles of conflict engagement, escalation and avoidance in marital interaction: A longitudinal view of five types of couples. *Journal of Consulting and Clinical Psychology*, 61, 6–15.

Gottman, J. M. (1994). *Why Marriages Succeed or Fail*. New York: Simon & Schuster.

Gottman, J. M. (2000). *Seven Principles for Making Marriages Work*, New York: Three Rivers Press.

Gottman, J., & Silver, N. (2000). *The Seven Principles for Making Marriages Work*. New York: Crown Publishers.

Gowda, S. (2005). Offshoring in India. *Offshoring-Process, Pain or Profit*. Report of a workshop held at the London School of Business.

Gradanski, B., Gaser, C., Busch, V., Schuierer, G., Bogdahn, U. & May, A. (2004). Neuroplasticity: Changes in grey matter induced by training. *Nature*, 427, 311–312.

Gramling, S. E., & Auerbach, S. M. (1998). *Stress Management Workbook: Techniques and Self-Assessment Procedures*. Englewood Cliffs, N. J.: Prentice Hall.

Greenberg, M. (2007). Positive Psychology and Institutions: Highlights from a Panel Discussion. *Positive Psychology News Daily. http://positivepsychologynews.com*

Grof, S. (1985). *Beyond the Brain*. Albany, New York: State University of New York Press.

Grof, S. (1988). *The Adventure of Self Discovery*. Albany, New York: State University of New York Press.

Gura, T. (December, 2008). I'll Do It Tomorrow. *Scientific American Mind*, 27–33.

Haidt, J. (2006). *The Happiness Hypothesis*. Cambridge, MA: Basic Books.

Hamburg, D. (1994). *Today's Children: Creating a Future for a Generation in Crisis*. New York: Time Books.

Hammond, S. A. (1998). *The Thin Book of Appreciative Inquiry*. Thin Book Publishing.

Hansen, K. (2002). *Online Career Assessments: Helpful Tools of Self-Discovery*. Deland, FL.: Quintessential Careers. *http//www.quintcareers.com*.

Harker, L., & Keltner, D. (2001). Expressions of positive emotion in women's college yearbook pictures and their relationships to personality and life outcomes across adulthood. *Journal of Personality and Social Psychology*, 80, 112–124.

Harris, T. (1967). *I'm OK, You're OK: A Practical Guide to Transactional Analysis*. New York: Avon Books.

Harter, J., & Schmidt, F. (2002). *Employee engagement, satisfaction and business-unit level outcomes: Meta-analysis*. Princeton, N.J.: The Gallup Organization.

Harter, J., Schmidt, F., & Hayes, T. (2002). Business-unit level relationship between employee satisfaction, employee engagement, and business outcomes: A meta-analysis. *Journal of Applied Psychology*, 877, 268–279.

Hartmann, T. (1998). *The Last Hours of Ancient Sunlight.* New York, N. Y.: Three Rivers Press.

Haskins, R. & Sawhill, I. (2009). *Creating an Opportunity Society.* Washington, D.C.: Brookings Institution Press.

Harvard Medical School. (April, 2002). The Mind and the Immune System–Part I. *The Harvard Mental Health Letter*, Vol. 18, No. 10, 1–3.

Harvard University. *Check Out Policy.* Harvard Botanical Library. Cambridge, Mass.: Harvard University.

Hazan, C., & Shaver, P. (1987). Romantic love conceptualized as an attachment process. *Journal of Personality and Social Psychology*, 52, 511–524.

Hazan, C., & Shaver, P. (1994). Attachment as an organizational framework for research on close relationships. *Psychological Inquiry*, 5, 1–22.

Heine, S., Lehman, D., Markus, H., & Kitayama, S. (1999). Is there a universal need for positive self-regard? *Psychological Review*, 106, 766–794.

Hellman, C., Budd, M., Borysenko, J., McClelland, D, & Benson, H. (1990). The study of the effectiveness of two group behavior medicine interventions for patients with psychosomatic complaints. *Behavioral Medicine*, 16, 165–173.

Helson, R. (1967). Personality characteristics and developmental history of creative college women. *Genetic Psychology Monographs*, 76, 205–256.

Hewitt, J. R., (2005). The social construction of self-esteem. In C. R. Snyder & S. J. Lopez (Eds.) *Handbook of Positive Psychology* (pp. 135–147). New York: Oxford University Press.

Higbee, K. L. (1988). *Your Memory: How It Works and How to Improve It.* (2nd Ed.). New York: Prentice Hall Press.

Hill, A. (1997). *Speaking Truth to Power.* New York: Doubleday.

Hinder, S. (1998). Time for a New Role. *Mail Tribune.* Medford, Oregon.

Holahan, C., & Sears, R., (1995). *The Gifted Group in Later Maturity.* Palo Alto, CA: Stanford University Press.

Holland, J. (1985). *Making Vocational Choices: A Theory of Vocational Personalities and Work Environment*, 2nd. Ed., Upper Saddle River, N.J.: Prentice-Hall.

Holmes, D. S., & Roth, D. L. (1988). Effects of Aerobic Exercise Training and Relaxation Training on Cardiovascular Activity during Psychological Stress. *Journal of Psychosomatic Research*, 32, 469–474.

Holmes, T. H., & Rahe, R. H. (1967). The Social Readjustment Rating Scale. *Journal of Psychosomatic Research*, 11, 213–218.

Holt, P., Fine, M. J., & Tollefson, N. (1987). Mediating Stress: Survival of the Hardy. *Psychology in the Schools*, 24, 51–58.

Horney, K. (1956). The Search for Glory. In Moustakas, C. (Ed.) *Self-Exploration and Personal Growth*. (pp. 86–91). New York: Harper Colophan Books.

Horrigan, M. W. (2004, February). Employment projections to 2012: Concepts and Context. *Monthly Labor Review*, Bureau of Labor Statistics.

Houston, J. (1987). *The Search for the Beloved*. New York: Tarcher/Putnam Books.

Huppert, F. & So, T. (2009). What percentage of people in Europe are flourishing and what characterizes them. *www.isgols2009.institutodeglinnocenti.it/Content_en/Huppert.pdf.*

Huta, V., Park, N., Peterson, C., & Seligman, M. (2005). Pursuing pleasure versus eudemonia: Links with different aspects of well-being. *Unpublished manuscript*, McGill University, Montreal, Canada.

Hyde, J. S. (2005). The gender similarities hypothesis. *American Psychologist*, 60(6), 581–592.

Inglehart, R., Foa, R., Peterson, C., & Wetzel, C. (2008). Development, Freedom and Rising Happiness: A Global Perspective (1981–2007). *Perspectives in Psychological Science*, Vol. 3, No. 4, 264–285.

Isen, A. (1991). The Influence of Positive Affect on Clinical Problem Solving. *Medical Decision Making*. (July–Sept.).

Iyengar, S. (2010). *The Art of Choosing*. New York, New York: Grand Central Publishing.

IT World.com. (2005). *Study: Europe Overtakes U.S. in Big Outsourcing Deals. ITWorld.com/Man/2701/050114outsourcing/*

Jacobson, E. (1929, 1974). *Progressive Relaxation*. Chicago: The University of Chicago Press, Midway Reprint.

Janes, L., & Olson, J. (2000). Jeer pressures: The behavioral effects of observing ridicule of others. *Personality and Social Psychology Bulletin*, 26(4), 474–485.

Jensen, D. (2011). Bright Green Reality Check. *Orion*, Nov-Dec., 12–13.

Johnson, L. (2008). *Handouts from the Brief Therapy Center*. Salt Lake City, UT: Head Acre Books.

Jorason, D., & Lietman, R. (1994). *The McNeil National Pain Study*. New York: Louis Harris & Associates.

Jung, C. (1972). *Synchronicity – An Acausal Connecting Principle*. London: Routledge.

Jung, C. (1981). *The Archetypes and the Collective Unconscious*. Princeton, N.J.: Princeton University Press.

Kabat-Zinn, J. (1990). *Full Catastrophe Living*. New York: Dell Publishing.

Kabat-Zinn, J. (1994). *Wherever You Go There You Are*. New York: Hyperion.

Kagen, J. (1994). *Galen's prophecy. Temperament in Human Nature*. New York: Basic Books.

Kahneman, D. (1999). Objective happiness. In D. Kahneman, E. Diener & N. Schwarz (Eds.) *Well-being: The Foundations of Hedonic Psychology* (pp. 3–25). New York: Russell Sage.

Kahneman, D. (2011). *Thinking, Fast and Slow.* New York: Farrar, Strauss & Giroux.

Kalanit, G., Henson, R. & Martin, A. (2006). Repetition and the brain: Neural models of stimulus-specific effects. *Trends in Cognitive Sciences* Vol 10, No. 1, 14–23.

Kamen-Siegel, L., Rodin, J., Seligman, M. & Dwyer, J. (1991). Explanatory style and cell-mediated immunity in elderly men and women. *Health Psychology,* 10, 229–235.

Kanar, C. (1991). *The Confident Student.* Boston, Mass.: Houghton Mifflin Co.

Kaniel, R., Massey, C. & Robinson, D. (2010). The importance of being an optimist: Evidence from labor markets. *The National Bureau of Economic Research.* NBER Working Paper #16328. *www.nber.org/papers/w16328.pdf*

Kaplan, R. & Kaiser, R. (2010). Toward a Positive Psychology for Leaders. In Linley, P., Harrington, S. & Garcea, N. (Eds.). *Oxford Handbook of Positive Psychology and Work.* (pp. 107–117). New York: Oxford University Press.

Karney, B., & Bradbury, T. (1995). The longitudinal course of marital quality and stability: A review of theory, method and research. *Psychological Review,* 118, 3–34.

Kasser, T., & Ryan, R. M. (1993). A Dark Side of the American Dream: Correlates of Financial Success as a Central Life Aspiration. *Journal of Personality and Social Psychology,* 65, 410–422.

Kasser, T., & Ryan, R. M. (1996). Further Examining the American Dream: Differential Correlates of Intrinsic and Extrinsic Goals. *Personality and Social Psychology Bulletin,* 22, 280–286.

Keita, G., & Hurrell, J. (1994). *Job Stress in a Changing Workforce: Investigating Gender, Diversity and Family Issues.* Washington, D.C.: APA Books.

Kemeny, M. E., Gruenewald, T. L. (2000). Affect, Cognition, the Immune System and Health. In Mayer, E. A. & Saper, J. (Eds.). *The Biological Basis for Mind Body Interactions: Progress in Brain Research Series.* (pp. 291–308). Amsterdam: Elsevier Science B.V.

Khan, H. I. In an Eastern Rose Garden. In *The Message Volumes Of Hazrat Inayat Khan. Vol. VII.*

Kirkpatrick, S., & Locke, E. (1991). Leadership: Do Traits Matter? *Academy of Management Executive.* 5 (2), 48–60.

Kleinke, C. L. (1986). *Meeting and Understanding People.* New York: W. H. Freeman & Co.

Kobak, R., & Hazan, C. (1991). Attachment in marriage: The effects of security and accuracy of working models. *Journal of Personality and Social Psychology*, 60, 861–869.

Koch, H. (1986). The management of chronic pain in office-based ambulatory care: *National Ambulatory Medical Care Survey*, No. 123, (DHHS Publication No. PHS 86-1250). Hyattsville, MO: U.S. Public Health Service.

Kobasa, S. C. (1979). Stressful Life Events, Personality and Health: An Inquiry into Hardiness. *Journal of Personality and Social Psychology*, 37, 1–11.

Kobasa, S. C. (1982). Commitment and Coping in Stress Resistance among Lawyers. *Journal of Personality and Social Psychology*, 42, 707–717.

Kobasa, S. C. (Sept., 1984). How much Stress Can You Survive? *American Health*, 64–71.

Kobasa, S. C., Maddi, S. R., & Puccetti, M. C. (1982). Personality and Exercise as Buffers in the Stress-Illness Relationship. *Journal of Behavioral Medicine*, 5, 391–404.

Kopp, S. (1972). *If You Meet the Buddha on the Road, Kill Him!* Palo Alto, CA.: Bantam Books/Science & Behavior Books.

Kosslyn, S., Thompson, W., Kim, I, & Alpert, N. (1995). Topographical representations of mental images in primary visual cortex. *Nature*, 6565, 496–498.

Kotler, T. (1985). Security and autonomy within marriage. *Human Relations*, 38, 299–321.

Kuhn, T. (1962). *The Structure of Scientific Revolutions.* Chicago, IL.: University of Chicago Press.

Kumano, H. (2005). Osteoporosis and stress. *Clinical Calcium*, 15(9), 1544–1547.

Kung, H., Hoyert, D., Xu, J., & Murphy, S. (2008, April, 24th). Deaths: Final Data for 2005. *National Vital Statistics Reports.* 56:ID.

Kuwayama, T. (1992). The reference other orientation. In N. R. Rosenberger (Ed.), *Japanese Sense of Self* (pp. 121–149). Cambridge: Cambridge University Press.

Labi, N. (1999, February, 15th). A bad start? *Time Magazine*, 153, 6.

Lamont, K. (1975). *Escape from Stress.* New York: G. P. Putnam & Sons.

Lange, A., & Jakubowski, P. (1976). *Responsible Assertive Behavior.* U.S.A.: Research Press.

Lannon, J. (2007, December, 5th). *Policies and Procedure—Not Just for Large Corporations. http://ezinearticles.com/?Policies-and-Procedures—Not-Just-for-Large-Organizations&id=867371*

Lappe, Frances Moore. (1991). *Diet for a Small Planet.* New York: Ballantine Books.

Larson, R. J., & Buss, D. M. (2002). *Personality Psychology: Domains of Knowledge about Human Nature.* New York: McGraw–Hill.

Lauer, R., Lauer, J., & Kerr, S. (1990). The long-term marriage: Perceptions of stability and satisfaction. *International Journal of Aging and Human Development,* 31(3), 189–195.

Lawler, K.A., & Smied, L.A. (1987). The Relationship of Stress, Type A behavior and Powerlessness to Physiological Responses in Female Clerical Workers. *Journal of Psychosomatic Research,* 31, 555–563.

Lazarus, R. (1966). *Psychological Stress and the Coping Process.* New York: McGraw-Hill.

Lazarus, R. (1991). *Emotions and Adaptation.* New York: Oxford University Press.

Lazarus, R., & Folkman, S. (1984). *Stress Appraisal and Coping.* New York: Springer Publishing Co.

Leach, G. (2008). Stress Statistics. *www.hardcore.stressmanagement.com*

LeBaron, J. (July, 2003). *Beyond Intractibility: A Free Knowledge Base on More Constructive Approaches to Destructive Conflict.* www/beyondintractibility.org.

LeDoux, J. (1993). Emotional Memory Systems in the Brain. *Behavioral Brain Research,* 58.

Lee, D., Sui, X. & Blair, S. (2009). Does physical activity ameliorate the health hazards of obesity? *British Journal of Sports Medicine,* 43, 49–51.

Lee, Y., & Seligman, M. (1997). Are Americans more optimistic than the Chinese? *Personality and Social Psychology Bulletin,* 23, 32–40.

Lefcourt, H. (2005). Humor. In C. R. Snyder & S. J. Lopez (Eds.) *Handbook of Positive Psychology* (pp. 619–631). New York: Oxford University Press.

Lefkowitz, M. M., Eron, L. D., Walder, L. O., & Huesmann, L. R. (1977). *Growing Up to be Violent: A Longitudinal Study of the Development of Aggression.* New York: Pergamon Press.

Lemish, D. (1998). Fighting against television violence: An Israeli case study. In U. Carlsson & C. von Feilitzen (Eds.) *Children and Media Violence.* Goteborg, Sweden: The UNESCO Int. Clearinghouse on Children and Media Violence.

Lerner, M. (1980). *The Belief in a Just World.* New York: Plenum.

Levenson, H. (1981). Differentiating among Internality, Powerful Others and Change. In H. M. Lefcourt (Ed.). *Research with the Locus of Control Construct* (Vol. I, pp. 1–63). New York: Academic Press.

Levine, T. (2000). *Work Yourself Happy: A Step-by-Step Guide to Creating Joy in Your Life and Work.* Buckingham, Pa: Lahaska Press.

Linehan, M. D., Brown, S. H., Nielson, S. L., Olney, K. G., & McFall, R. M. (Nov., 1980). *The Effectiveness of Seven Styles of Assertion.* Paper presented at the Annual Convention of the Association for the Advancement of Behavior Therapy, New York.

Linley, P., Harrington, S. & Garcea, N. (2010). *Oxford Handbook of Positive Psychology and Work.* New York: Oxford University Press, Inc.

Lipman-Blumen, J. (1992). Connective Leadership: Female Leadership Styles in the 21st Century Workplace. *Sociological Perspectives.* Berkeley, CA.: University of California Press.

Loehr, J.E., & Migdow, J.A. (1986). *Take a Deep Breath.* New York: Villard Books.

Long, B. C. (1984). Aerobic Conditioning and Stress Inoculation: A Comparison of Stress Management Interventions. *Cognitive Therapy and Research*, 8, 517–542.

Lonier, T. (1994). *Working Solo.* New York: Portico Press.

Lovelock, J. (1979). *Gaia: A New Look at Life.* Oxford: Oxford University Press.

Losada, M. (1999). The complex dynamics of high performance teams. *Mathematical and Computer Modeling*, 30, 179–192.

Losada, M. & Heaphy, E. (2004). The role of positivity and connectivity in the performance of business teams: A nonlinear dynamics model. *American Behavioral Scientist*, 47, 740–765.

Loza, J. (2009). *10 Ways to Keep your Job despite the tough economy. www.techrepurblic.com.*

Lundbergk U. (1980). Catecholamine and cortisol excretion under psychologically different laboratory conditions. In J. Usdin, T. Kvetnanski, & D. Kopin (Eds.), *Catecholamines and Stress: Recent Advances*, North Holland: Elsesvier.

Lykken, D., McGue, M., Tellegen, A., & Bouchard, T. (1992). Emergenesis: Genetic traits that may not run in families. *American Psychologist*, 47, 1565–1577.

Lyman, P. & Varian, H. (2003). How much Information? *http://www.sims.berkeley.edu/how-much.info-2003*

Lyons-Ruth, K. (1991). Rapprochement or approchement: Mahler's theory reconsidered from the vantage point of recent research on early attachment relationships. *Psychoanalytic Psychology*, 8, 1–23.

Lyubormirsky, S., King, L., & Diener, E. (2005). The benefits of frequent positive affect: Does happiness lead to success? *Psychological Bulletin*, 131, 803–855.

Lyubormirsky, S., Sheldon, K., & Schkade, D. (2005). Pursuing happiness: The architecture of sustainable change. *Review of General Psychology*, 9, 111–131.

Maccoby, E. (1998). *The Two Sexes: Growing up Apart, Coming Together.* Cambridge, Mass: Harvard Press.

Maccoby, E. & Martin, J. (1983). Socialization in the Context of the Family. In Munsen, P. (Ed.). *Handbook of Child Psychology*. (pp. 28–41), 4th Ed., Vol. 4. Hillsdale, N. J.: Erlbaum.

Maddi, S., & Kobasa, S., (1984). *The Hardy Executive: Health Under Stress*. Homewood, IL: Dow Jones-Irwin.

Maddux, J. (1995). Self-efficacy Theory: An Introduction. In J.E. Maddux (Ed.). *Self-Efficacy, Adaptation and Adjustment: Theory, Research and Application* (pp. 3–36). New York: Plenum.

Maddux, J. (2005). Self-Efficacy: The power of believing that you can. In C. Snyder & S. Lopez (Eds.) *Handbook of Positive Psychology* (pp. 277–287). New York: Oxford University Press.

Maguire, E., Woollett, K., & Spiers, H. (2006). London taxi drivers and bus drivers: A structural MRI and neuropsychological analysis. *Hippocampus*, 16(12), 1091–1101.

Maier, S. F., & Watkins, L. R. (1998). Cytokines for Psychologists: Implications of Bi- directional Immune-to-Brain Communication for Understanding Behavior, Mood and Cognition. *Psychological Review*, 105(1), 83–107.

Maier, S. F. & Seligman, M. E. (1976). Learned Helplessness: Theory and Evidence. *Journal of Experimental Psychology: General*, 105, 3–46.

Maltz, D., & Borker, R. (1982). A cultural approach to male-female miscommunication. In J. Gumperz (Ed.) *Language and Social Identity* (pp. 281–312). New York: Oxford University Press.

Mann, C. L. (2004). What outsourcing means for the U.S. IT workers and for the U.S. economy. *Communications of the ACM*, Vol 47, No. 7. *http//www.acmqueue.com.*

Manning, M. R., Williams, R.F., & Wolfe, D.M. (1988). Hardiness and the Relationship between Stressors and Outcomes. *Work and Stress*, 2, 205–216.

MarksJarvis, G. (2007, November 13th). Baby boomers and retirement happiness. *Chicago Tribune.com. http://newsblog.chicagoTribune.com/marksjarvis-on-money/*

Maslow, A. (1968). *Toward a Psychology of Being*. 2nd Ed. New York: Van Nostrand Reinhold.

Maslow, A. (1970). *Motivation and Personality*, 2nd. Ed., New York: Harper & Row.

Matheny, K., Aycock, D., Pugh, J., Curlette, W., & Cannella, K. (1986). Stress coping: A qualitative and quantitative synthesis with implications for treatment. *The Counseling Psychologist*, 14, 499–549.

Matthews, K., Owens, J., Edmundowicz, D., Lee, L. & Kuller, L. (2006). Positive and negative attributes and risk for coronary and aortic calcification in healthy women. *Psychosomatic Medicine*, 68, 355–361.

Mattiasson, I., Lindgarde, F., Nilsson, J., & Theorell, T. (1990). Threat of unemployment and cardiovascular risk factors: Longitudinal study of quality of sleep and serum cholesterol concentrations in men threatened with redundancy. *British Medical Journal*, 301, 461–466.

McCann, I. L., & Holmes, D. S. (1984). Influence of Aerobic Exercise on Depression. *Journal of Personality and Social Psychology*, 46, 1142–1147.

McCarthy, J. (2002). *"3.3 Million Jobs go Offshore"*. Cambridge: MA: Forrester Research, Inc.

McClain, L. (1987). Behavior During Examinations: A Comparison of "A", "C" and "F" Students. In M. E. Ware & R. J. Millard (Eds.). *Handbook on Student Development: Advising, Career Development and Field Placement*. (pp. 40–42). Hillsdale, N.J.: Lawrence Erlbaum Associates.

McClelland, D. (1961). *The Achieving Society*. New York: Van Nostrand.

McCraty, R. (2003). Influence of cardiac afferent input on heart-brain synchronization and cognitive performance. *International Journal of Psychophysiology*, 45, 72–73.

McCraty, R., & Atkinson, M. (2003). Psychophysiological coherence. Boulder Creek, CA: HeartMath Research Center, *Institute of HeartMath Publication No. 03-016*.

McCullough, M. E. (2001). Forgiving. In C. R. Snyder (Ed.). *Coping with Stress: Effective People and Processes*. (pp. 93–113). New York: Oxford University Press.

McDonough, W. & Braungart, M. (2002). *Cradle to Cradle*. New York: North Point Press.

McGilley, B. M., & Holmes, D. S. (1989). Aerobic Fitness Response to Psychological Stress. *Journal of Research on Personality*, 22, 129–139.

McGuigan, F.L. (1984). Progressive Relaxation: Origins, Principles and Clinical Applications. In Woolfolk, R.L., & Lehrer, P.M. (Eds.). *Principles and Practices of Stress Management*. New York: Guilford Press.

McGregor, D. (1960). *The Human Side of Enterprise*. New York: McGraw-Hill.

McKay, M., Davis, M., & Fanning, P. (1981). *Thoughts and Feelings: The Art of Cognitive Stress Intervention*. Oakland, California: New Harbinger Publications.

McKay, M., Davis, M., & Fanning, P. (1983). *Messages: The Communication Skills Book*. Oakland, CA: New Harbinger Publications.

McKay, M., & Fanning, P. (1987). *Self Esteem*. Oakland, CA: New Harbinger Publications.

Mechelli, A., Crinion, J., Noppeney, V, O'Doherty, J., & Ashburner, J. (2004). Structural plasticity in the bilingual brain. *Nature*, 431.

Medina, J. (2008). *Brain Rules*. Seattle, WA: Pear Press.

Meehl, P. (1975). Hedonic capacity: Some conjectures. *Bulletin of the Menninger Clinic*, 39, 295–307.

Mehrabian, A. (1971). *Silent Messages*. Belmont, CA: Wadsworth.

Mehrabian, A. (Sept., 1989). Communication Without Words. *Psychology Today*, 53–55.

Miami-Dade College. *Classified Staff Evaluation Form*. Miami, FL: Department of Human Relations.

Miami-Dade College. *Policy Manual*. Miami, FL.

Miami-Dade College. *Procedures Manual*. Miami, FL.

Mikulincer, M., Florian, V., & Weller, A. (1993). Attachment styles, coping strategies, and posttraumatic psychological distress: The impact of the Gulf War in Israel. *Journal of Personality and Social Psychology*, 64, 817–826.

Miller, A. (April, 1988). Stress on the Job. *Newsweek Magazine*, 40–45.

Miller, M., & Soldt, D. (1999). Organization for unmarried people condemns cohabitation report.

Millman, D. (1991). *Sacred Journey of the Peaceful Warrior*. Tiburn, CA: H. J. Kramer, Inc.

Mirsky, A., & Quinn, O. (1988). The Genain Quadruplets. *Schizophrenia Bulletin*, 14, 595–612.

Mischel., W., Ebbesen, E., $ Zeiss, A. (1972). Cognitive and attentional mechanisms in delay of gratification. *Journal of Personality and Social Psychology*, 21, 204–218.

Mischel, W. & Peake, P. K. (1990). Predicting Adolescent Cognitive and Self Regulatory Competencies from Preschool Delay of Gratification. *Developmental Psychology*, 6, 978–986.

Moneta, G., & Csikszentmihalyi, M. (1991). The effect of perceived challenges and skills on the quality of subjective experience. *Journal of Personality*, 64, 275–310.

Moore, N., & Davidson, J. (2000). Communicating with new sex partners: College women and questions that make a difference. *Journal of Sex and Marital Therapy*, Vol 26., (3), 215–230.

Morris, T., Spittle, M., & Watt, A. (2005). *Imagery in Sport*. Human Kinetics Publishers, Inc.

Mortenson, S. T. (2002). Sex, communication, values, and cultural values. *Communication Reports*, 15(1), 57–71.

Murphy, L. R. (1987). A Review of Organizational Stress Management Research: Methodological Considerations. In J. M. Ivancevich & D.C. Ganster (Eds.). *Job Stress: From Theory to Suggestions*. (pp. 215–227), New York: Haworth Press.

Myers, D. G. (1992). *The Pursuit of Happiness: Who is Happy and Why*. New York: William Morrow.

Myers, D. G. (1993). *The Pursuit of Happiness*. New York: Avon.

Myers, D. G. (2002). *Social Psychology* (7th Ed.). New York: McGraw Hill.

Myers, D. G. (2004). *Psychology* (7th Ed.). New York: Worth Publishers.

Myers, D., & Diener, E. (1995). Who is happy? *Psychological Science*, 6, 10–19.

Myers, J., Madathil, J., & Tingle, L. (2005). Marriage satisfaction and wellness in India and the United States: A preliminary comparison of arranged marriages and marriages of choice. *Journal of Counseling and Development*, 83, 183–190.

Myers-Briggs, I. (1993). *Introduction to Type: A Guide to Understanding your Results on the Myers-Briggs Type Indicator*. Palo Alto, CA.: Consulting Psychologists Press.

Nakazawa, D. (2008). *The AutoImmune Epidemic*. New York: Simon & Schuster.

Neisser, V. (1979). The control of information pickup in selective looking. In A. D. Pick, (Ed.) *Perception and its Development: A Tribute to Eleanor J. Gibson* (pp. 201–219). New Jersey: Lawrence Erlbaum Associates.

Newby, T., & Ashlyn, H. (1992). The Value of Mentoring. *Performance Improvement Quarterly*. Tallahassee, Fl.: The Learning Systems Institute, Florida State University, 54, 2–15.

National Ambulatory Medical Care Survey (2006). National Center for Health Statistics. *http://www.cdc.gov/nationalcenterforhealthstatistics*

National Institute on Alcohol Abuse an Alcoholism (NIAAA). *www.niaaa.nih.gov.*

National Institute of Mental Health (NIMH). *http//nimh.nih.gov/index.shtml.*

Newshour with Jim Lehrer. (March 9, 2004). *Terence Smith interviewing Thomas Friedman. http//www.pbs.org/newshour/bb/asia/jan-june04/friedman/03-09.html.*

Niven, D. (2002). *100 Simple Secrets of Successful People*. San Francisco, CA.: Harper Collins Publishers.

Nolen-Hoeksema, S. (2000). Growth and resilience among bereaved people. In J. Gillham (Ed.) *The Science of Optimism and Hope* (pp. 107–127). Philadelphia, PA: Templeton Foundation Press.

Norem, J. (2001). *The Positive Power of Negative Thinking: Using Defensive Pessimism to Harness Anxiety and Perform at Your Peak*. New York: Basic Books.

Norem, J., & Cantor, N. (1986). Defensive pessimism: "Harnessing" anxiety as motivation. *Journal of Personality and Social Psychology*, 51, 1208–1217.

NOW with Bill Moyers. (August 4, 2004). Interview with Lou Dobbs. *www.pbs.org/now/transcript/transcript334.*

Nowck, K. M. (1989). Coping Style, Cognitive Hardiness and Health Status. *Journal of Behavioral Medicine*, 12, 145–158.

Nuernberger, P. (1981). *Freedom from Stress: A Holistic Approach*. Pennsylvania: Himalayan Intl. Inst. of Yoga Science and Philosophy Publishers.

Oberman, L., Hubbard, E., McCleery, J., Altschuler, I., Ramachandran, V., & Pineda, J. (2006). EEG evidence for mirror neuron dysfunction in autism spectral disorders. *Cognitive Brain Research*, 24(2), 190–198.

Ochsner, K. (2002). Rethinking feelings: An fMRI study of the cognitive regulation of emotion. *Journal of Cognitive Neuroscience*, 14, 1215–1229.

Okun, B. F., Fried, J., & Okun M. L. (1999). *Understanding Diversity: A Learning as Practice Primer*. Pacific Grove, CA.: Brooks/Cole Publishing.

O'Leary, A., & Brown, S. (1995). Self-efficacy and the physiological stress response. In J.E. Maddux (Ed.). *Self-Efficacy, Adaptation and Adjustment: Theory, research and Application* (pp 227–248). New York: Plenum.

Orman, S. (2007). *Women and Money*. New York: Spielgel & Grau.

Orman, S. (2010). *Suze Orman's Action Plan: New Rules for New Times*. New York: Spiegel & Grau.

Ornish, D. (1972). *Dr. Dean Ornish's Program for Reversing Coronary Heart Disease without Drugs or Surgery*. New York: Ballantine Books.

Ornish, D. (1990). *Dr. Dean Ornish's Program for Reversing Heart Disease*. New York: Ballantine Books.

Ornish, D. (Oct. 3, 2005). *Love is Real Medicine*. Newsweek Magazine, p. 56.

Osterkamp, L., & Press, A. (1988). *Stress? Find Your Balance*. Lawrence, Kansas: Preventive Measures, Inc.

Otto, M., Pollack, M., & Burlow, D. (2004). *Stopping Anxiety Medication (SAM): Pain Control therapy for Benzodiazepine Discontinuation*. New York: Oxford University Press.

Ozner, M. (2006). *Miami Mediterranean Diet*. Cambridge, MA.: Cambridge House.

Patel, C. (1984). Yogic therapy. In R.L. Woolfolk & P. M. Lehrer (Eds.). *Principles and Practice of Stress Management*. New York: Guilford Press.

Patel, D. (2002). *Workplace Forecast: A Strategic Outlook*. Alexandria, Va.: Society for Human Resource Management.

Pauk, W. (1997). *How to Study in College*. Boston: Houghton Mifflin.

Paul, A. (2011). The Uses and Abuses of Optimism and Pessimism. *Psychology Today*, (December), 56–63.

Pavlov, I. (1927/1960). *Conditioned Reflexes: An Investigation of the Physiological Activity of the Cerebral Cortex*. (G.V. Anvey, Translator). New York: Dover (Original translation published 1927).

Peavey, B. (1982). Biofeedback assisted relaxation: Effects on phagocytic immune function. *Doctoral dissertation*, North Texas State University, Denton, Texas.

Pelham, B., & Swann, W. (1989). From Self-Conceptions to Self Worth: On the Sources and Structure of Global Self-Esteem. *Journal of Personality and Social Psychology*, 57, 672–680.

Pelletier, K. (1984). *Healthy People in Unhealthy Places: Stress and Fitness at Work*. New York: Delacorte Press/Seymour Lawrence.

Peterson, C. (2000). The Future of Optimism. *American Psychologist*, 55(1), 44–55.

Peterson, C. (2006). *A Primer In Positive Psychology*. New York: Oxford University Press.

Peterson, C., & Barrett, L. (1987). Explanatory style and academic performance among university freshmen. *Journal of Personality and Social Psychology*, 53, 603–607.

Peterson, C., & deAvila, M. (1995). Optimistic explanatory style and the perception of health problems. *Journal of Clinical Psychology*, 51, 128–132.

Peterson, C., Maier, S., & Seligman, M. (1993). *Learned Helplessness: A Theory for the Age of Personal Control*. New York: Oxford University Press.

Peterson, C., & Park, C. (1998). Learned helplessness and explanatory style. In D. G. F.Barone, V. B. Van Hasselt & M. Herson (Eds.) *Advanced Personality* (pp. 287–310). New York: Plenum.

Peterson, C., Park, N., & Seligman, M. (2005b). Orientations to happiness and life satisfaction: The full life versus the empty life. *Journal of Happiness Studies*, 6, 25–41.

Peterson, C., Seligman, M., & Valliant, G. (1988). Pessimistic explanatory style is a risk factor for physical illness: A 35 year longitudinal study. *Journal of Personality and Social Psychology*, 55, 23–27.

Peterson, C., Seligman, M., Yurko, K., Martin, L., & Friedman, N. (1998). Catastrophizing and untimely death. *Psychological Science*, 9, 49–52.

Peterson, D. (1984). *Human Error Reduction and Safety Management*. Deer Park, New York: Alovey.

Phelps, S., & Austin, N. (1987). *The Assertive Woman*. California: Impact Publishers.

Pierrehumbert, B., Iannotti, R., Cummings, E., & Zahn-Waxler, C. (1989). Social functioning with mother and peers at 2 and 5 years: The influence of attachment. *International Journal of Behavioral Development*, 12, 85–100.

Pistole, M. (1989). Attachment in adult romantic relationships: Style of conflict resolution and relationship satisfaction. *Journal of Social and Personal Relationships*, 6, 505–510.

Plomin, R., Owen, M., & McGuffin, P. (1994). The genetic basis of complex human behaviors. *Science*, 264, 1733–1739.

Popenol, D., & Whitehead, B. (2001). *The State of our Unions 2000: The Social Health of Marriage in America, The National Marriage Project*. Rutgers, the State University of New Jersey.

Powell, K. E., Spain, K. G., Christenson, G. M., & Mollenkamp, M. P. (1986). The Status of the 1990 Objective for Physical Illness and Exercise. *Public Health Reports*, 101, 15–21.

Pratt, M. & Ashford, B. (2003). Fostering meaningfulness in working and at work. In Cameron, K., Dutton, J. & Quinn, R. (Eds.) *Positive Organizational Scholarship: Foundations of a New Discipline* (pp. 309–327). San Francisco, CA: Berrett-Kohler Publishers.

Premack, D. (1959). Toward Empirical Behavior Laws I. Positive Reinforcement. *Psychological Review*, 66(4), 219–233.

Putnam, R. (2000). *Bowling Alone*. New York: Simon & Schuster.

Pychel, T. (2000). Don't delay. *http://blogs.psychologytoday.com/blog/don't-delay*

Radin, D. (1997). *The Conscious Universe*. New York, New York: Harper Collins.

Rajendran, R., & Kaliappan, K. (1990). Efficacy of behavioral programme in managing the academic stress and improving academic performance. *Journal of Personality and Clinical Studies*, 6, 193–196.

Ramachandran, V. (2000). Mirror neurons and imitation learning as the driving force behind the "great leap forward" in human evolution. *Edge*, the third culture, No. 69. *http://www.edge.org/3rd_culture/ramachandran/ramachandran_index.html*.

Ram Dass. (1990). *Journey Of Awakening-A Meditators Guidebook*. New York: Bantam Books.

Rasmussen, H., Scheier, M. & Greenhouse, J. (2009). Optimism and Physical Health: A Meta-Analytic Review. *Annals of Behavioral Medicine*, 37, 239–256.

Rathus, S. A. (1973). A 30-item schedule for assessing assertive behavior. *Behavior Therapy*, 4, 398–406.

Rathus, S., & Nevid, J. (1995). *Adjustment and Growth: The Challenges of Life* (6th Ed.) New York: Harcourt Brace.

Raymond, M., & Moser, R. (1995). Aviators at Risk. *Aviation, Space and Environmental Medicine*, 66, 35–39.

Reckmeyer, W. J. (July, 2005). *Developing Global Citizenship–Leadership for the 21st Century*. Salzburg, Austria Seminar: Community Colleges as Sites for Global Citizenship.

Reik, T. (1972). *Listening with the Third Ear*. New York: Pyramid Press.

Renzetti, C., & Curren, D. (1998). *Living Sociology*. Needham Heights, MA: Allyn & Bacon.

Reuben, D. R. (1981). *Save-Your-Life-Diet: High Fiber Protection from Six of the Most Serious Diseases of Civilization*. New York: Ballantine Books.

Rhodewalt, F., & Zone, J.B. (1989). Appraisal of Life Change, Depression and Illness in Hardy and Non-Hardy Women. *Journal of Personality and Social Psychology*, 56: 81–88.

Ricard, M. (2006). *Happiness.* New York, New York: Little, Brown & Co.

Richardson, A. (1969). *Mental Imagery.* New York: Springer-Verlag.

Rimland, B. (1982). The altruism paradox. *The Southern Psychologist*, 2(1), 8–9.

Rizzolatti, G., & Craighero, L. (2004). The mirror-neuron system. *Annual Review of Neuroscience*, 27, 169–192.

Robbins, A. (1986). *Unlimited Power.* New York: Ballantine Books.

Roberts, B., & Mann, R. (Winter, 1996). Sexual Harassment in the Workplace: A Primer. *Akron Law Review*, 29, 269.

Roberts, R. C. (1982). *Spirituality and Human Emotion.* Grand Rapids, MI: Eerdmans.

Robinson, F.R. (1970). *Effective Study* (4th Ed.). New York: Harper & Row Publishers.

Robinson, J., & Martin, S. (2008, December). Channeling unhappiness: In Good and Bad Economic times. *Social Indicators Research online.* University of Maryland. *http://www.newsdesk.umd.edu/mar/send.cfm?articleID+1798*

Roe, A. (1972). Perspectives on Vocational Development. Whiteley, J. & Resnikoff, A. (Eds.) *Perspectives on Vocational Development.* Washington, D.C.: American Personnel and Guidance Association.

Rogers, C. (1951). *Client-Centered Therapy: Its Current Practice, Implications and Theory.* Boston: Houghton Mifflin.

Rogers, C. (1959). A Theory of Therapy, Personality and Interpersonal Relationships as Developed in the Client-Centered Framework. In Koch, S. (Ed.). *Psychology: A Study of a Science.* (pp. 33–51), Vol 3. New York: McGraw Hill.

Roper Starch Worldwide, Inc. (1999). *Baby Boomers Envision their Retirement.* Washington, D. C.: American Association of Retired Persons.

Roseman, M., Milette, K., Zhao, Y. & Thombs, B. (2010). Is optimism associated with physical health? A commentary on Rasmussen et. al. *Annals of Behavioral Medicine*, 39, 204–206.

Rosengren, A., Tibblin, G. & Wilhelmsen, L. (1991). Self perceived psychological stress and incidence of coronary artery disease in middle-aged men. *American Journal of Cardiology*, 68, 1171–1175.

Rossi, E. (1986). *The PsychoBiology of Mind-Body Healing.* New York: W. W. Norton & Co.

Roth, D. L., & Holmes, D. S. (1987). Influences of Aerobic Exercise Training and Relaxation Training on Physical and Psychological Health Following Stressful Life Events. *Psychosomatic Medicine*, 49, 355–365.

Roth, D., Weibe, D., Fillingian, R., & Shay, K. (1989). Life Events, Fitness, Hardiness and Health: A Simultaneous Analysis of Proposed Stress-Resistance Effects. *Journal of Personality and Social Psychology*, 57, 136–142.

Rotter, J. (1966). Generalized Expectancies for Internal vs. External Locus of Control of Reinforcement. *Psychological Monographs: General and Applied*, 80, (Whole No. 609).

Ryan, R. M., & Deci, E. L. (2000). Self Determination Theory and the Facilitation of Intrinsic Motivation, Social Development, and Well Being. *American Psychologist*, 55, 68–78.

Ryff, C., & Singer, B. (1996). Psychological well-being: Meaning, measurement, and implications for psychotherapy research. *Psychotherapy and Psychosomatics*, 65, 14–23.

Sachs, B. (1991). Coping with stress. *Stress Medicine*, 7, 61–63.

Salovey, P., Mayer, J. D., & Caruso, D. (2002). The Positive Psychology of Emotional Intelligence. In C. R. Snyder & S. J. Lopez (Eds.). *Handbook of Positive Psychology*. (pp. 159–171). New York: Oxford University Press.

Sanfey, A. (2003). The neural basis of economic decision-making in the ultimatum game. *Science*, 300, 1755–1758.

Sanorajski, RT., Delaney, C., Durham, L., Ordy, J. M., Johnson, J. A., & Dunlop, W. P. (1985). Effect of Exercise on Longevity, Body Weight, Locomotor Performance and Passive Aggressive Memory of Mice. *Neurobiology of Aging*, 6, 17–24.

Sarason, B. R., Sarason, I. G., & Pierce, G. R. (Eds.). (1990). *Social Support: An Interactional View.* pp. 9–25. New York: Wiley.

Sawka-Miller, K. & Miller, D. (2007). The Third Pillar: Linking positive psychology and school-wide positive behavior support. *School Psychology Forum: Research in Practice*, Vol. 2, Issue 1, 26–38.

Schacter, S., & Singer, J. (1962). Cognitive, Social and Physiological Determinants of Emotional State. *Psychological Review*, 69, 379–399.

Scheier, M. F., & Carver, C. S. (1993). On the Power of Positive Thinking: The Benefits of Being Optimistic. *Current Directions in Psychological Science*, 2, 26–30.

Scheier, M. F., Carver, C. S., & Bridges, M. W. (1994). Distinguishing Optimism from Neuroticism (and Trait Anxiety, Self Mastery, and Self-Esteem): A Reevaluation of the Life Orientation Test. *Journal of Personality and Social Psychology*, 57, 1024–1040.

Schiraldi, G. (1993). *Building Self-esteem: A 125 day program.* Dubuque, IO: Kendall/Hunt.

Schneider, I., Smith, W., & Witcher, S. (1984). The relationship of mental imagery to white blood cell (neutrophil) function: Experimental studies of normal subjects. *Paper presented at the 36th Annual Scientific Meeting of the International Society for Clinical and Experimental Hypnosis*, San Antonio, Texas (10/25/84).

Schneider, S. L. (2001). In Search of Realistic Optimism: Meaning, Knowledge, and Warm Fuzziness. *American Psychologist*, 56, 250–263.

Scholz, J., Klein, M., Behrens, T. & Johansen-Berg, H. (2009). Training induces changing in white matter architercture. *Natural Neuroscience*, Vol. 12 (11), 1370–1371.

Scott, D. (1980). *How to Put More Time in Your Life*. New York: Rawson, Wade Publishers.

Schroeder, D., Penner, L., Dovidio, J., & Piliavin, J. (1995). *The Psychology of Helping and Altruism*. New York: McGraw Hill.

Seaward, B. L. (1997). *Managing Stress*. Boston: Jones & Bartlett.

Segerstrom, F., & Miller, G. (2004) Psychological stress and the human immune system: A meta-analytic study of 30 years of inquiry. *Psychological Bulletin*, 104, 601–630.

Seligman, M. (1991). *Learned Optimism*. New York: Knopf.

Seligman, M. (1995). The effectiveness of psychotherapy: The consumer report study. *American Psychologist*, 50, 965–974.

Seligman, M. (1998b). *Learned Optimism: How to Change Your Mind and Your Life* 2nd Ed. New York: Pocket Books.

Seligman, M. (2002). *Authentic Happiness*. New York: Free Press.

Seligman, M. (2011). *Flourish*. New York: Free Press.

Seligman, M., Nolen-Hoeksema, S., Thornton, N., & Thornton, K. (1990). Explanatory style as a mechanism of disappointing athletic performance. *Psychological Science*, 1, 143–146.

Seligman, M., & Shulman, P. (1986). Explanatory Styles as a Predictor of Productivity and Quitting among Life Insurance Sales Agents. *Journal of Personality and Social Psychology*, 50, 832–838.

Seligman, M., Steen, T., Park, N., & Peterson, C. (2005). Positive Psychology progress. Empirical validation of interventions. *American Psychologist*, 60, 410–421.

Seligman, M., Reivich, K., Jaycox, L., & Gillham, J. (1995). *The Optimistic Child*. New York: Houghton Mifflin.

Selye, H. (1956). *The Stress of Life*. New York: McGraw Hill.

Selye, H. (1974). *Stress Without Distress*. New York: Dutton.

Selye, H. (1982). History and Present Status of the Stress Concept. In Goldberg, L. & Breznitz, S. (Eds.). *Handbook of Stress; Theoretical and Clinical Aspects*. New York: Free Press.

Sheppard, J.A., & Kashani, J.H. (1991). The Relationship of Hardiness, Gender and Stress to Health Outcomes in Adolescents. *Journal of Personality*, 59, 747–768.

Sheldrake, R. (1981). *A New Science of Life: The Hypothesis of Formative Causation.* London: Blond & Briggs.

Sheikh, A. (Ed.) (2005). *Healing Images: The Role of Imagination in Health.* Amityville, New York: Baywood Publishing Company.

Sherwood, B. (2009, February 2nd). What it takes to survive. *Newsweek Magazine*, 50–53.

Siebert, A. (1996). *The Survivor Personality*. Perigree Books, Berkley Publishing Group.

Siegel, B. (1986). *Love, Medicine and Miracles*. New York: Harper & Row.

Silberman, M, & Hansburg, F. (2000). *People Smart: Developing your Intepersonal Intelligence*. San Francisco, CA.: Berrett-Kochler Publishers.

Simon, S. B., & Simon, S. (1990). *Forgiveness: How to Make Peace with Your Past and Get on with Your Life*. New York, N. Y.: Warner Books.

Simon, R. W. (2002). Revisiting the relationships among gender, martial status, and mental health. *American Journal of Sociology*, 107(4), 1065–1097.

Simonton, O., Matthews-Simonton, S., & Creighton, J. (1978). *Getting Well Again*. New York: Bantam Books.

Skinner, B. F. (1953). *Science and Human Behavior*. New York: MacMillan.

Smith, M. (1975). *When I Say No, I Feel Guilty*. New York: The Dial Press.

Smith, T. W. (1992). Hostility and Health: Current Status of a Psychosomatic Hypothesis. *Health Psychology*, 11, 139–150.

Snyder, C. R., & Feldman, D. B. (2000). Hope for the Many: An Empowering Social Agenda. In C. R. Snyder (Ed.). *Handbook of Hope: Theory, Measures and Applications*. (pp.389–412). San Diego, CA.: Academic Press.

Snyder, C., & Lopez, S. (Eds.), (2005). *Handbook of Positive Psychology*. New York: Oxford University Press.

Snyder, C., & Lopez, S. (2007). *Positive Psychology*. California: Sage Publications.

Solnick, S., & Hemenway, D. (1998). Is more always better?: A survey on positional concerns. *Journal of Economic Behavior and Organization*, 37(3), 373–383.

Sone, T., Nakaya, N., Ohmori, K., Shimozu, T., Higashiguchi, M. & Kakizaki, M. (2008). Sense of life worth living (ikigai) and mortality in Japan: Ohsaski study. *Psychosomatic Medicine*, 70, 709–715.

Sorbi, M., & Tellegen, B. (1986). Differential effects of training in relaxation and stress-coping in patients with migraine. *Headache*, 26, 473–481.

Spence, J. T. (1985). Achievement American style: The rewards and costs of individualism. *American Psychologist*, 40, 1287–1288.

Sprague, J. & Horner, R. (2006). School wide positive behavior supports. In Jamerson, S. & Furlong, M. (Eds.). *Handbook of School Violence and School Safety: From Research to Practice* (pp. 413–427). Mahwah, N. J.: Erlbaum.

Sprecher, S., Metts, S., Burleson, B., Hatfield, E., & Thompson, A. (1995). Domains of excessive interaction in intimate relationships: Associations with satisfaction and commitment. *Family Relations*, 44, 203–210.

Sroufe, L. (1983). Infant-caregiver attachment and patterns of adaptation in preschool: The roots of maladaptation and competence. In M. Perlmutter (Ed.) *Minnesota Symposium in Child Psychology* (Vol. 16, pp. 41–81). Hillsdale, N.J.: Erlbaum.

Sroufe, L., Fox, N., & Pancake, V. (1983). Attachment and dependency in developmental perspective. *Child Development*, 54, 1615–1627.

State University System Board of Regents. *Policy Manual.* Atlanta: State of Georgia.

Steel, P. (2007). The nature of procrastination: A meta-analytic and theoretical review of quintessential self-regulatory failure. *Psychological Bulletin*, Vol. 133, No. 1, 65–94.

Steele, C. M. (1997). A Threat in the Air: How Stereotypes Shape Intellectual Identity and Performance. *American Psychologist*, 52, 613–629.

Steinhauser, S. (July, 1998). Age Bias: Is Your Corporate Culture in Need of an Overhaul? *H.R. Magazine*, 87–91.

Steinhauser, S. (Sept./Oct., 1999). Beyond Age Bias: Successfully Managing an Older Workforce. *Aging Today*.

Steptoe, A., Wardle, J. & Marmot, M. (2005). Positive affect and health related neuroendocrine, cardiovascular and inflammatory processes. *Proceedings of the National Academy of Sciences*, 102, 6508-6512.

Stewart, S. (October, 2002). The Worst of All Possible Worlds. *The University of Chicago Magazine*, Vol. 95, Issue 1.

Stotland, E. (1969). Exploratory investigations of empathy. In L. Berkowitz (Ed.) *Advances in Experimental Social Psychology* (Vol. 4, pp. 271–314). New York: Academic Press.

Sui, X., Laditka, J., Hardin, J. & Blair, S. (2007). Estimated functional capacity predicts mortality in older adults. *Journal of the American Geriatric Society*, 55, 1940–1947.

Sullivan, H.S. (1953). *The Interpersonal Theory of Psychiatry.* New York: Norton.

Talbot, M. (1991). *The Holographic Universe*. New York, New York: HarperCollins Publishers.

Tafardi, R., & Swann, Jr., W. (1995). Self-liking and self-competence as dimensions of global self-esteem: Initial validation of a measure. *Journal of Personality Assessment*, 65(2), 332–342.

Tafardi, R., & Swann, Jr., W. (1996). Individualism-collectivism and global self-esteem. *Journal of Cross-Cultural Psychology*, 27(6), 651–672.

Tangney, J. P., & Baumeister, R. F. (2000). *High Self Control Predicts Good Adjustment, Less Pathology, Better Grades and Interpersonal Success*. Unpublished Manuscript. George Mason University, Fairfax, Va.

Tannen, D. (1990). *You Just Don't Understand: Women and Men in Conversation*. New York: Ballantine Books.

Tannen, D. (1994). *Talking from 9 to 5*. New York: William Morrow.

Tannen, D. (1998). *The Argument Culture*. New York, N.Y.: Random House.

Tart, C. (1986). *Waking Up*. Boston: Shambhala.

Taylor, S. E. (2000). Biobehavioral Responses to Stress in Females: Tend and Befriend, not Fight or Flight. *Psychological Review*, 107 (3), 411–429.

Taylor, S., & Brown, J. (1988). Illusion and well-being- a social psychological perspective on mental health. *Psychological Bulletin*, 103(2), 193–210.

Tellegen, A., Lykken, D., Bouchard, T., Wilcox, K., Segal, N., & Rich, S. (1988). Personality similarity in twins reared apart and together. *Journal of Personality and Social Psychology*, 54, 1031–1039.

Terry, R. L. (2004, March 12). Answers on Outsourcing. *CNN Money*. *www.money.cnn/2004/03/11/commentary*

Thoresen, C., Luskin F., & Harris, A. (1998). Science and Forgiveness Interventions: Reflections and Recommendations. In E. L. Worthington (Ed.). *Dimensions of Forgiveness: Psychological Research and Theological Perspectives*. Philadelphia, PA.: Templeton Foundation Press.

Thornton, A., & Young-DeMarco, L. (2001). Four decades in attitudes toward family issues in the U.S. The 1960's to the 1990's. *Journal of Marriage and Family*, 63(4), 1009.

Tice, D., & Baumeister, R. (1993). *Handbook of Mental Control*. Vol. 5. In Wegner, D, & Pennebaker, J. (Eds.). Englewood Cliffs, N. J.: Prentice Hall Press.

Tice, D. & Baumeister, R. (1997). Longitudinal Study of Procrastination, Performance, Stress and Health: The Costs and Benefits of Dawdling. *Psychological Science*, 8, 454–458.

Tindle, H., Chang, Y., Kuller, L., Manson, J., Robinson, J., Rosal, M., Siegle, G. & Matthews, K. (2009). Optimism, clinical hostility and incident coronary heart disease and mortality in the Women's Health Initiative. *Circulation*, 118, 1145–1146.

Titchener, E. (1909). *Elementary Psychology of the Thought Processes*. New York: Macmillan.

Toffler, A. (1971). *Future Shock*. New York, N, Y.: Bantam Books.

Toffler, A. (1981). *The Third Wave*. New York, N. Y.: Bantam Books.

Tolle, E. (2005). *A New Earth: Awakening to Your Life's Purpose*. New York, N. Y.: Penguin Group.

Travis, J. (1981). *Wellness Workbook*. Berkeley, CA: Ten Speed Press.

Troy, M., & Sroufe, L. (1987). Victimization among preschoolers: Role of attachment relationship history. *Journal of American Academy of Child and Adolescent Psychiatry*, 26, 166–172.

Tugade, M., & Fredrickson, B. (2004). Resilient individuals use positive emotions to bounce back from negative emotional experiences. *Journal of Personality and Social Psychology*, 86, 320–333.

Uhl, C. (2004). *Developing Ecological Consciousness: Path to a Sustainable World*. Boulder, Col.: Rowman & Littlefield Publishers.

Underwood. A., & Kalb, C. (June, 1999). STRESS. *Newsweek Magazine*, 56–63.

Unger, L., & Thumuluri, L. (1997). Trait empathy and continuous helping. *Journal of Social Behavior and Personality*, 12, 785–800.

U.S. Census Bureau. (2001). Unmarried Couples Increase. *Intel/Health*. *http://www.intel.health.com*

U.S. Census Bureau. (2010). Selected Social Characteristics in the United States. *American Fact Finder*. *http://factfinder2.census.gov/faces/tableservices/jsf/pages*.

U.S. Dept. of Labor. Bureau of Labor Statistics. (2000). Washington, D.C.: U.S. Government Printing Office. *www.state.bls.gov.com*.

U.S. Dept. of Labor. Bureau of Labor Statistics (2011). Overview of the 2008–2009 projections. *Occupational Outlook Handbook*. *http://www.bls.gov/oco/oco2003.htm*

U.S. Dept. Of Labor, Employment and Training Administration. (1991). *Dictionary of Occupational Titles*. Lanham, MD.: Bernan Press.

U.S. Dept. Of Labor. *Occupational Outlook Handbook*. Washington, D. C.: U.S. Government Printing Office.

U.S. Equal Employment Opportunity Commission. (April, 1997). *Technical Assistance Manual*. Washington D.C.: USEEOC Technical Assistance Program.

U.S. Surgeon General. (1979). Healthy People: The Surgeon General's Report on Health Promotion and Disease Prevention. *U.S. Dept. of Health, Education and Welfare (PHS) Publication No. 79-55071*, Washington, D. C.: U.S. Government Printing Office.

U.S. Surgeon General. (2008). *www.cdc.gov/nccdphp/sgr/index.htm* (1999).

Vaillant, G. E. (1977). *Adaptation to Life*. Boston, Mass.: Little, Brown Publishers.

Vaillant, G. E. (2003). *Aging Well: Surprising Guideposts to a Happier Life from the landmark Harvard Study of Adult Development*. New York: Little, Brown & Co.

Veenhoven, R. (Oct., 2006). *How do we Assess how Happy we are? Tenets, Implications and Tenability of Three Theories*. Paper presented at New Directions in the Study of Happiness conference. University of Notre Dame, South Bend, Indiana.

Walker, R. (2008). Mentoring helps SSA become a better workplace. *http://www.fcw.com/print/13-131news/102557-1.html*

Wallace, R. & Benson, H. (1972). The Physiology of Meditation. *Scientific American*, 226, 85–90.

Watson, D. (2000). *Mood and Termperament*. New York: Guilford Press.

Watson, D. (2005). Positive affectivity: The disposition to experience pleasurable emotional states. In C.R. Snyder & S.J. Lopez (Eds.) *Handbook of Positive Psychology* (pp. 106–119). New York: Oxford University Press.

Weinstein, N. (1989). Optimistic biases about personal risks. *Science*, 246, 1232–1233.

Weiss, J. (1971). Effects of coping behavior in different warning signal conditions on stress pathology in rats. *Journal of Comparative and Physiological Psychology*, 77, 113.

White, A. (2007). A Global Projection of Subjective Well-Being: A Challenge to Positive Psychology? *Psychtalk*, 56, 17–20.

Wilber, K. (1979). *No Boundary*. Los Angeles: Center Publications.

Williams, J., Hogan, T., & Anderson, M. (1993). Positive states of mind and athletic injury risk. *Psychosomatic Medicine*, 55, 468–472.

Williams, R. (1989). *The Trusting Heart: Great News about Type A Behavior*. New York: Random House.

Wilson, T., Wheatley, T., Myers, J., Gilbert, D., & Assom., D. (2000). Focalism: A source of durability bias in affective forecasting. *Journal of Personality and Social Psychology*, 78, 821–836.

Winner, E. (2000). The origins and ends of giftedness. *American Psychologist*, 55(1), 159–169.

Wiseman, R. (2003). *The Luck Factor*. London, UK: Random House.

Witvliet, C. V., Ludwig, T., & Vander-Laan, K. (2001). Granting Forgiveness or Harboring Grudges: Implications for Emotion, Physiology and Health. *Psychological Science*, 121, 117–123.

Wolvin, A. & Coakley, C. (1991). A Survey of the Status of Listening Training in some Fortune 500 Corporations. *Communication Education*, 40, 152–164.

Yerkes, R. M., & Dodson, J. D. (1908). The Relation of Strength of Stimulus to Rapidity of Habit Formation. *Journal of Comparative and Neurological Psychology*, 18, 459–482.

Zillman, D. (1989). Mental Control of Angry Aggression. In Wegner, D., & Pennebaker, J. (Eds.). *Handbook of Mental Control.* Englewood Cliffs, N.J.: Prentice Hall Press.

Zimbardo, P., & Henderson, L. (2008). Shyness. *Encyclopedia of Mental Health.* San Diego, CA: Academic Press.

Zheng, W., & Hart, R. (2002). The effects of martial and nonmarital union transition on health. *Journal of Marriage and Family*, 64(2), 420–433.

Zullow, H., Oettingen, G., Peterson, C., & Seligman, M. (1988). Explanatory style and pessimism in the historical record: CAVing, LBJ, presidential candidates and east vs. west Berlin. *American Psychologist*, 673–682.

Zyfowsky, D. G. (1970). Fifteen needs and values. *Vocational Guidance Quarterly*, 18, 182.

_____ *Basis of EEO Discrimination.* Washington, D. C.: Equal Employment Opportunity Commission. *www.eeoc.gov.com.*

_____ (2001). Engage Employees and Boost Performance. *Working Paper.* Philadelphia, PA.: Hay Group.

_____ (1998). Planning a Career. *Adventures in Education*, Texas Guaranteed Loan Corporation.

_____ (1998). *Self-Directed Search.* Odessa, FL.: Psychological Assessment Resources, Inc. Website (@www.sdstest3.com).

_____ (1994). *Strong Vocational Interest Inventory.* Palo Alto, CA.: Consulting Psychologists Press.

_____ (2004, August). The Foreign Born Population in the United States: 2003. *Population Statistics*, U.S. Census Bureau.

_____ (2006, January 30th). The Future of Outsourcing. *http://www.businessweek.com/print/magaizine/content/06_05/b3969401.htm?chang=gl*

_____ (2003, March). *Current Population Survey. U.S. Census Bureau http://census.gov/populaton/www/socdemo/foreign/cps2003.html*

_____ (2009). 12 Step Guide to Financial Success. *MappingyourFuture.org.*

Index